Bike Cult

The Ultimate Guide to
Human-Powered Vehicles

ex LIBRIS.

Bike Cult

The Ultimate Guide to
Human-Powered Vehicles

David B. Perry

Four Walls Eight Windows

New York / London

Published in the United States by:
Four Walls Eight Windows
39 West 14th Street, room 503
New York, N.Y., 10011

U.K. offices:
Four Walls Eight Windows/Turnaround
27 Horsell Road
London, N51 XL, England

First printing July 1995.

Library of Congress Cataloging-in-Publication Data:
Perry, David Brunn, 1955–
          Bike Cult: The Ultimate Guide to Human-Powered Vehicles/
by David Brunn Perry
p. cm.
Includes bibliographical references and indexes.
ISBN 1-56 858-027-4
1. Cycling—History. 2. Bicycles—History. I. Title.
GV1040.5.P47 1995
796.6—dc20
95-5128
CIP

Printed in the United States

10 9 8 7 6 5 4 3

Contents

Acknowledgments

For major support of this project, special thanks are due to Transportation Alternatives, including Paul Harrison, Charles Komanoff, and Jon Orcutt; to Bill Stark and Susan Davis of the 13th St. Recyclery; and especially to Steve Stollman of Lightwheels. I also give special thanks to George Bliss, Pryor Dodge, John Dowlin (Bicycle Network), Mary Frances Dunham, Carl Hultberg, John and Vera Kraus, James Rosar, and Ted White.

Thank you to those who got me into cycling: Larry Walpole (Belmont Bicycle Club) and Keith Vierra (Palo Alto Cycling Club). Thanks to those mentioned herein whose contribution to the world of cycling inspired me to do this project: Jobst Brandt, Gary Fisher, John Forester, Anne Hansen, Eric and Jon Hjertberg, Bud Hoffacker, Greg LeMond, Paul MacCready, Owen Mulholland, Tom Ritchey, Andrew Ritchie, Robert Rodale, Bob Silverman, and Jack Simes. Thanks for special contributions: Kevin Bryne, George Carty, Cheryl Daitch, Charles Fraser, Adam Fuss, Diana Graham, Rick Hyman, Monroe Litman, Susan Richter, Melora Walters, and Jim Westby.

I am grateful to John Oakes of Four Walls Eight Windows for publishing this book, and I appreciate the editorial work of Tom Downs and JillEllyn Riley. Thanks to Cary Rosmarin for production assitance. Thank you Zoe Waldron for asking the correct questions. This is dedicated to my loving parents, Allan and Hallie Perry.

.

Part One

Human-Powered Vehicles

1 Beginnings

Bike, mythical Goddess of Cycling, c.100 B.C., from *Bicycling!,* 1969.

A few people have insinuated falsely that Jesus' machine was a draisienne, *an unlikely mount for an uphill race. According to the old cyclophile hagiographers, St. Briget, St. Gregory of Tours, and St. Irene, the cross was equipped with a device which they named* suppedaneum. *There is no need to be a great scholar to translate this as "pedal."*

    —Alfred Jarry, "The Passion Considered as an Uphill Bicycle Race" (1900)

Circles and Wheels

At the heart of the bicycle is a circle. Numerous components, the shape and function of which consist of circles, come together to form the bicycle. Riding a bike is a cyclical exercise that activates the body's circulatory systems. Even the journey of a cyclist is circuitous.

Circles have many symbolic shapes and meanings in the ancient mythologies. The perfect circle is considered a divine creation, being eternal, impossible, and encompassing all manifestations of the world in one. The open circle, or the snake that chases its tail, has been used since the beginning of recorded time to symbolize birth, death, and regeneration. The spiraling circle is an image of the universe and the golden number. When the spiral expands we see a galaxy, when it contracts a whirlpool forms, when fixed in time we find a nautilus shell. Spirals are perhaps the most ubiquitous design in nature and the works of humanity.

Circles contain the transcendental number *pi* (3.1415926...) which describes the ratio of a circle's perimeter to its diameter. With decimal digits that extend infinitely according to some unknown random order, *pi* appears as a symbol of Mother Nature or God. Physicists have said that all processes are cycles or cyclical, from the micro to the macro, and cosmologists have the idea of a circular unified field theory for all creation.

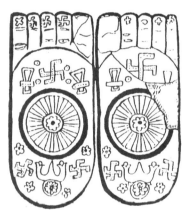

Buddha's footprint carved on the Amaravâti Tope.

The wheel came rolling into existence as a circle that revolves around a central point, perhaps originating in the culture of Sumer, in Lower Mesopotamia, around 3,500 B.C.[1] The early wheel myths serve as a prophecy of the bicycle idea with its eventual embodiment and impact in modern life. For many ancient philosophers, the wheel held the power of the sun, life, the stars and destiny. The wheel's spokes, of which "none is the last," delineate time and space. Among Aryans and Semites, the daily passage of the sun followed by the moon was thought to be a two-wheeled chariot. To his followers, Buddha (c.563–483 B.C.) was the Wheel King who rolled over the whole world with his footprints showing two bicycle-like lotus wheels, and created the Wheel of Law, Truth and Life, with the Round of Existence. The Wheels of Fate and Fortune revolve relentlessly and irreversibly, like the Astrological Wheel.[2]

Eventually the wonder of the wheel was balanced by its practical nature. Wheeled devices were developed for agriculture and craft-work, for quantifying time, space, and number. Two wheels combined with an axle became the hub of humanity's emerging transportation technology, with wheeled chariots powered by animals for thousands of years. The bicycle idea appears to fall from the skies into the minds of prophetic artists of the Renaissance. For three hundred years inventors working for the royalty of Europe experimented with cumbersome human-powered chariots, until some aristocrats discovered the hobby horse. With the Industrial Revolution and the Machine Age, wheels came to symbolize modern civilization, and the bicycle came to represent the most civilized form of human progress.

Bicycle Archaeology

The "Pre-Historic Bicycle Age" begins with the evolution and conception of the bicycle idea and spans thousands of years before the construction of the bicycle's actual ancestors, the swift-walkers of the nineteenth century. What we are looking for is the seemingly simple idea or image of a human-powered wheeled vehicle, like two wheels mounted in line along a beam for people to straddle or balance upon and propel themselves forward.

Two wheels mounted in-line.

There are several manifestations of pre-industrial bicycles. Early bicycle myths are speculative visions found in archeological rubble or myths. Many ideas are manifest as legends, part fact and part fiction. Closer to reality are actual examples of the earliest bicycle ideas, preludes of bicycle development, recognized only after the bicycle was invented.

Among ancient civilizations, the hint of a bicycle can be found in few places. The earliest mode of transport is considered the boat, powered by wind and oar. On land, it was the sledge of rolled logs, followed by the wheel. Although most civilizations had working variations of the wheel, there is no definitive evidence of the bicycle idea entering the mind of humanity until the Renaissance of 1500 A.D.[3] Ancient civilizations that supposedly used or depicted a pre-industrial bicycle include China (c.2300 B.C.), Babylonia (c.1775 B.C.), Egypt (c.1600 B.C.), and Pompeii (c.100 B.C.).

The legend from China describes a kind of bicycle invented during the Jau Dynasty. It was called the "Happy Dragon," perhaps named after the *Lung Meis*, or Dragon's Paths, the routes linking sacred places in the countryside. It was supposedly favored by women of the court until the Emperor banned it because of its unfavorable influence on the birth rate.[4] This "her-story" sounds like a fable, but many take it seriously because significant inventions came from China, including paper-making, pasta, printing, gunpowder, and the compass.

A huge amount of time, some 3,000 years from 1500 B.C. to 1500 A.D., spanned the development of the first spoked wheels and the first bicycle images. The Bronze Age (c.3500 B.C. to 800 A.D.) saw many wheeled vehicles powered by draft animals, or slaves, used for agriculture and transport, with more grandiose chariots for military battles and funeral rituals. Logically, one might think that the first people to put two wheels on an axle and combine it with an animal to make a chariot could just as easily put

Roman-powered snail, 308 B.C., attributed to Demetrius of Phaleron, from *De Fiets*.

them in line to make a set of walking wheels. Yet perhaps human-powered two-wheelers had no place in ancient history because public works were more important than personal mobility, and perhaps using a pair of wheels for balancing and locomotion was considered taboo or outside the realm of possibility.

If ancient human-powered two-wheelers cannot be found in fact, there seems to be a tendency to invent them in fiction. In "The Bicycle-Realization of a Myth," (*Bicycling!*, 1969) by Jay Ruckel, we find "The Mythical Goddess of Cycling," called *Bike* (rhymes with Nike), as a bas-relief of a Trojan wheeled woman warrior with a Greek name from an invented place called Mervinius.

Reverse reincarnation can be found in the work of the French poet Alfred Jarry, who introduced a bicycle into the Bible's New Testament in his short story "The Passion Considered as an Uphill Bicycle Race." It revolves around Jesus Christ, a cyclist in the "Passion Race," whose well-known punctures—in his tires, not his hands—force him to carry his "cross-frame" bicycle to the finish.

Renaissance Prophecy

With the Renaissance, humanity rediscovered the physical phenomena of nature and human anatomy. The laws of mechanics and causality began to replace mysticism and alchemy in the sciences, and the wheel came to embody the forces of technology. In Renaissance art we see the first known drawings of pre-industrial cycles in works by Hieronymus Bosch and Leonardo da Vinci. Their images are quite different, yet both form visions of the bicycle idea characteristic of their personal style.

A unicycle appears in a drawing by Hieronymus Bosch (c.1450–1516). "Witches," shows a woman perched on a primitive wooden four-part disk apparently mounted with pedal-cranks strapped to her feet. The "bi" in this "cycle" may be her companion, who provides guidance in their balancing duet. Whether Bosch saw or imagined this wheeled witch, it seems logical that a unicycle would be among the creations of the painter of *The Garden of Earthly Delights*.

Bosch's unicycling witch has special symbolism for bicycle history. While witchcraft is considered a primal ritual of magic and fertility, during the Inquisitions, witches were tortured as pagans while strapped to wheels. It is suggested that this wheel, like the witch's broomstick, served to enhance journeys into the sexual and psychic realms.[5]

The most interesting pre-industrial bicycle drawing, one that may be evidence of the earliest true bicycle idea, was recently uncovered in one of Leonardo da Vinci's notebooks, called the *Codex Atlanticus*. The drawing is a revelation, and historians have evaluated many details in search of its origin. A few suggest it is a fake, while many attribute the idea to Leonardo, but think the drawing was done by an assistant in his studio around 1493.

"Witches" c.1500, by Hieronymus Bosch, from Musée du Louvre.

Leonardo da Vinci (1452–1519) was the archetypal Renaissance person: he was an artist, inventor, engineer, architect, scientist, geologist, physicist, and musician. He had the talent to comprehend and advance the realms of science and art, and his strange genius is found in his unique mirror-image left-handed script that was his own code language.

The *Codex Atlanticus* is a volume of Leonardo's drawings and notations assembled after Leonardo's death by the sculptor Pompeo Leoni sometime in the sixteenth century. It has been kept in the archives of the Biblioteca Ambrosiana, in Milan, since about 1637. The folio was originally compiled by mounting Leonardo's papers onto large mat-boards of an album. Where his notations appeared on both sides of the pages, they were mounted in a mat with a window. When the papers underwent restoration by Roman monks of Grottoferrata in 1966, every sheet was examined and several drawings were discovered that had been mounted beneath the album pages without a window. The bicycle drawing was found on the back of a paper with Leonardo's architectural plans for circular forts.

The bicycle is drawn with pencil and colored brown to look like wood. The wheels were obviously drawn with a compass and each have eight symmetrical spokes. The frame appears incomplete or erased, as does the steering or tiller bar. The pedals, chain drive mechanism, and saddle supports are crude but complete. The bicycle is compared to the early safety bicycle that began to appear around 1885, some 400 years later. Because of its mythic nature, the drawing has been reproduced as scale models, life-size bikes, and computer-animated images. David Davenport, writing in *Da Vinci's Bicycles* (1979), describes the essence of the drawing as "light with extravagence and precision, mirror of itself *atomo per atomo* from its dash against the abruptness of matter to the jelly of the eye."

Most historians of Leonardo believe he did not make this drawing because it lacks his notations and refined style. It is not known whose idea it was, but most likely the drawing was made by an assistant in Leonardo's studio, around 1493, when Leonardo was employed by Duke Ludovico Svorza in Milan and he designed chain and cog wheel mechanisms that appear in this *Codex* and the *Codex Madrid I*. It is assumed that Leonardo or his protégé understood the idea of balancing upon two wheels in line using a chain-drive mechanism for pedaling.

Like the chain, the ball bearing is another design by Leonardo that was not realized with the tools and materials of his time. His notebook technology includes many inventions, such as a self-propelled four-wheel wagon with a clock-like engine and a differential on the drive wheels, a geared treadle-drive boat, and various flying contraptions. According to some, this bicycle may have been designed for the military, to which a soldier of the Duke Svorza could attach other battlefield inventions by Leonardo, such as his machine gun, projectiles, giant crossbows, and horse-drawn scythe carriage. Although Leonardo was a vegetarian and spoke against warfare, he worked on the hardware and strategies for the battles of his patrons in Italy.[6]

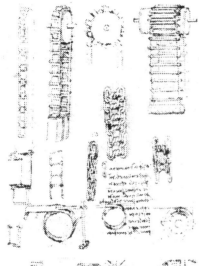

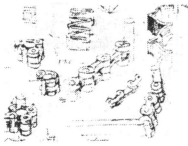

Chains and cogs, from Da Vinci's *Codex Madrid.*

Those who believe the drawing is a fake claim it was drawn while the *Codex* was in the archives of the Biblioteca Ambrosiana, sometime after the development of the safety bicycle. The motives for such a hoax would be to link the bicycle's invention to Leonardo, and to Milan, which has a tradition of fine design. Because the forger could hardly duplicate Leonardo's hand, the bicycle idea was introduced as a student drawing.

The bicycle shares the page with "various youthful scribblings," made before the paper was cut in two and the blank backsides were used by Leonardo in 1502 for his architectural studies.[7] Leonardo's notebooks contain many sketches by others in his workshop and he often used the blank sides of others' doodlings. The scribblings include a portrait of Leonardo's companion Salai and the caricature of a pair of male genitals. Salai entered Leonardo's studio around 1490, at the age of ten, and he became Leonardo's favorite pupil, model, and companion. A rivalry developed between Salai and the older apprentices Marco d'Oggiono and Gian Antonio Boltraffio, and Salai gained a reputation as the "stubborn one, thief, liar, and glutton," thus being the likely butt of resentment. From this evidence, scholars believe the bicycle was drawn by Salai, and made fun of by Marco or Gian Antonio around 1493.

Axonometric projections of the *Codex Atlanticus Bicycle* by Antonio Calegari, from *The Unknown Leonardo*.

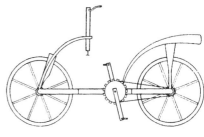

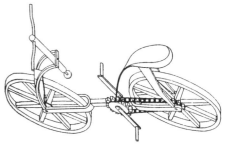

Codex Atlanticus Bicycle, c.1493, by an apprentice of Leonardo Da Vinci, from Biblioteca Ambrosiana.

The Bicycle Window

Before the bicycle was uncovered in the *Codex Atlanticus*, the earliest known vision of the bicycle idea appeared in a stained-glass window at the Church of St. Giles at Stoke Poges in Buckinghamshire, England. Known as the "Bicycle Window" or "Cycle Window," it shows a cherub astride a wheel that could be an early hobby horse. It was crafted in Italy around 1580 and installed at Stoke Poges in 1642.

The story of the Bicycle Window has been embellished with much myth-making in its time. Like many artifacts found in the United Kingdom, its origin and meaning has been studied and retold in fabulous ways. A Buckinghamshire County archivist wrote that the window appeared to be made of Flemish or German glass, and that other churches in Coventry and Cirenchester had stained-glass depictions of cherubim standing on wheels of fire.[8]

Since historians believe the glass was crafted in Italy, some have taken it, along with the findings of the *Codex Atlanticus*, as evidence that Italian craftsmen of the sixteenth century may have developed a kind of wheeled walking vehicle. Many scholars see the wheel in the Bicycle Window as a fanciful perambulator, an instrument used to survey the land, or to divinate sacred areas, such as the Stoke Poges churchyard. The string, which leads to the sun and sky, may have been for making measurements, or for guidance from heaven.

The Bicycle Window existed throughout the bicycle's development, and was reportedly first brought to public attention by the writer and member of the English Society of Cyclists, T.B. Marsh in the 1890s.[9] History provides no evidence of anything akin to a hobby horse existing in Great Britain until 1665, when the diarist John Evelyn described a visit with friends living near Epsom, England, who were making a "wheele for one to run races in."[10] Eventually, the image was enhanced from the original stained glass to a full-fledged bicycle myth. Herbert O. Duncan's *World on Wheels* (1926) shows a redrawn Bicycle Window, an image that became widely known in bicycle history. The writer Robert Benchley claimed a personal link to the Bicycle Window rider, in an article called "The Return of the Bicycle" for *Liberty* magazine (1930):

> The man looks quite a lot like me, except for a full beard and a more nervous expression around the eyes. The name underneath the figure is in Gothic letters and very difficult to make out, but it certainly begins with "Ben" and the rest seems to be something of a compromise between "wgalle" and "chhaalle."
>
> Now my people originally came from Wales (which, in itself, would account for the spelling), and, for a man with a contraption like the one in the picture, a spin from Wales to Buckinghamshire would have been mere child's play. As I figure it out, this man Benwgaalle or Benchhaalle built his bicycle, took along some lunch, and pushed him-

Detail of *Bicycle Window*, 1642.

Enhanced drawing of Bicycle Window, from *World on Wheels*.

self along to Stoke Poges, at which place he became a sort of local hero, like Lindbergh at Le Bourget, and a stained-glass window was made in his honor. I rather imagine that he stayed in Stoke Poges all the rest of his life, as he probably was pretty lame.

Human-Powered Ancestors

Human-powered wheeled vehicles, as an idea, date back thousands of years, but the technology needed to produce a bicycle-like device was lacking until the 19th century. In the prelude to the Industrial Revolution, imaginative designs existing only on paper gradually evolved into a succession of experimental self-propelled carriages, prototypes of future railroad locomotives, tricycles, and automobiles. These large human-powered vehicles were cumbersome multi-wheel carriages of wood and iron, with four big wheels and one or more people supplying power by hand (manumotive) or foot (pedomotive) with cranked axles, treadles and ratchets, and hand-pulley devices. The machines were often regally decorated and their unloaded weight was several hundred pounds, about equal to their cost in sterling silver. They were royal works on wheels, as rare as a king's crown.

These vehicles first appeared in the Renaissance with designs by Giovanni Fontana of Padova, Italy, c.1418, Leonardo da Vinci, c.1490, and Albrecht Dürer of Germany, c.1520. For two hundred years, from 1600 to 1800, several inventors designed and occasionally built them for royalty and aristocracy, whom inventive coach builders or blacksmiths relied on for the patronage needed to execute their ideas. A description of the King of Denmark's machine built by Johann Hautsch appeared in M. de Monconys' *Journal de Voyages* (1665): "It goes backwards and forwards and turns around and goes 3,000 paces in an hour, propelled only by handles which are turned by two children who are inside the carriage."

This was the first wave of ingenuity applied to mechanically driven wheeled vehicles. Powering these hefty machines were children, servants, royal families, and the inventors themselves. With crude drive technology, they tried to make the hard work more efficient. The peak of ingenuity came around 1770, as the trend began to get mentioned in various rare books, magazines, and newspapers that constituted the growing industrial age press.

In Paris, Blanchard and Masurier, the makers of carriages and balloons, demonstrated their mechanical carriage in the Versailles gardens for King Louis XVI, Marie Antoinette, and their court, as reported in the *Journal de Paris* in 1779. François Blanchard visited America in 1783, giving demonstrations in Philadelphia. He later wrote: "I once drove Doctor (Benjamin) Franklin from Paris to Versailles in 1 hour 45 minutes."[11] Long rides were rare: these carriages were most often used in parks, gardens, or on smooth paths around estates. Most attempts at cross-country voyaging, facing inevitable obstacles like steep hills, mud holes, horse-ruts, or out-of-control downhill runs, were too much for machines

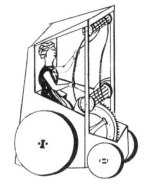

Manumotive carriage
by Giovanni Fontana, 1420.

Invalid carriage
by Stephan Farffler, 1680.

possessing an impossible man-power to weight ratio. In *Rational Recreations*, a British book of 1774, William Hooper described many inventions, but saw very little progress since 1696. He suggested that "it would be more efficient to have only one passenger to do the driving and steering at the same time."

With this thinking applied, inventors of wheeled vehicles were faced with a dilemma. On the one hand, they could try to increase the power of these great machines with steam engines, or they could reduce the vehicle's size and weight to a basic individual form, like the horse. Around this time, children were using several kinds of horse-shaped toys, called hobby horses, like the rocking horse or the horse's head attached to a pole. At some point, someone must have set wheels on the legs of a wooden horse, sat upon it, and given it a little push.

"*Voiture à pèdales essayée en France vers 1770*," by Blanchard and Masurier, from *Journal de Paris* 1779, New York Public Library.

The King of Denmark's human-powered carriage, by Johann Hautsch, 1665.

2 Velo Development

Wheeled Horse
De Sivrac's Célérifère

Swift Walker
Drais's Laufmaschine

Missing Link
Macmillan's Treadler

Boneshaker
Michaux's Vélocipède

Tricycle
Starley's Coventry Lever

High Wheeler
Pope's Standard Ordinary

Early Safety
Rudge's Cross-Frame Safety

Modern Safety
Golden Sunbeam Two-Speed Roadster

Post-Modern Roadster
Bowden's Spacelander

Mountain Bike
Fisher's Mt. Tam

Recumbent Bike
Brummer's Lightning P-38

Aero Bike
Burrows' Lotus Sport

Whoever invented the bicycle deserves the thanks of humanity.
—Lord Charles Beresford

The Bicycle's Birth

Depending on how you define the bicycle, the search for its birthplace and inventor is a long tale that travels through the nineteenth century in France, England, Germany, Scotland, and the United States. According to legend, the bicycle was born as a walking hobby horse, an amusement for aristocratic "Dandies" in England, and the so-called *Incroyables* in Paris, around 1790. Although there is little evidence of the use of a walking horse before 1800, an elaborate—though largely false—history of its use continues to be told and untold. Seamus McGonagle symbolized the bicycle's origins in *The Bicycle in Life, Love, War and Literature* (1969):

> Fathered by the remnant of a dying feudal system, mothered by the still young Industrial Revolution, the bicycle—with the horny-handed, ever present human curiosity and inventiveness as mid-wife—was born around about the tail end of the eighteenth century.

Cycle historians of the 1890s believed these zoomorphic wheelers were the first vehicles with two wheels mounted in line for human propulsion. The rider moved by walking or running. Made of wood, with small carriage wheels, they had no steering or brakes. Carved into various animal shapes, they have names such as *accélérateur*, *accélérifère*, *célérifère*, *céléripède*, *vélocifère,* and wheele.

Zoomorphic wheelers, serpent and lion.

An eccentric Parisian Marquis, the Comte de Sivrac, is supposed to have demonstrated his hobby horse for Marie Antoinette at Versailles before the fall of the Bastille. Later, he frequented the gardens of the Palais Royale around 1791. The tales of his time sound quite convincing, as shown in this recent history by Robert Wilkinson-Latham's *Cycles in Colour* (Blandford Press, 1978):

> It is doubtful if Sivrac was the inventor of this machine as smaller horses similar to this had for some years been children's toys. The machine was named the 'Célérifère'. The new machine immediately caught on and soon numbers of Incroyables were to be seen scudding around the gardens of the Palais Royale to catch the eyes of the prostitutes who sat there or paraded in the arcades. In 1793, the machine was renamed the Vélocifère and enjoyed immense popularity but rather than a machine of practical use, they were purely of a fashionable one. The bodywork was by no means exclusively horses and some were fitted with carved lion's heads. The popularity of the machine led rise to a number of satirical cartoons as well as a comedy produced at the Vaudeville Theater in 1804 entitled 'Les Vélocifères.'[1]

Comte de Sivrac.

This legend originated in L. Baudry de Saunier's *Histoire Générale de la Vélocipèdie* (1891), which shows animal-shaped wheelers, and introduces the Marquis de Sivrac. It had been told for nearly a century, until researchers found evidence disputing its truth. Lexicographers of the French language say that before about 1870 a vélocifère was defined as "a fast lightweight stagecoach." Then it gradually began to be defined as "a primitive kind of hobby horse going back to the Directoire." A researcher at the Sorbonne, Richard Jeanes, wrote: "I have been unable to find a single example of a vehicle with two wheels in tandem before the year 1817, nor have I seen the names célérifère and vélocifère applied to such a vehicle in the writings of the period."[2]

In the mid-1970s, bicycle historian Jacques Seray discovered further inconsistencies with de Saunier's *Histoire*—namely, that the célérifère's inventor was invented. The name Comte de Sivrac probably came from a French patent of 1817 for a "fast coach" called a vélocifère, which was imported from Britain by Jean-Henri Sievrac. Seray also noted that a sketch showing a group of "agile gentlemen of the Directoire" in Baudry's book are actually dressed in the styles of 1818, and that the Vaudeville Theatre act, "Les Vélocifères," was a musical comedy about a stagecoach journey.[3]

Vélocifère coach of 1800.

That it is possible to ride a two-wheeler without a steering mechanism was recently confirmed by Roger Street of the Christchurch Tricycle Museum in England, when he built a hobby horse and was able to turn it by a combination of shifting sideways in the saddle while skidding the rear wheel, and wobbling the crude axle of the front wheel.

Swift-Walking Machines

The title "father of the bicycle" is given to Karl von Drais (1775–1851) of Karlsruhe, in Baden, Germany, because he was the first to patent and popularize his invention, the Laufmaschine, a swift-walking two-wheeler. Drais was named after his father, and his many names and titles cause confusion for historians: Freiherr Karl Friedrich Wilhelm Ludwig Christian von Drais, von Sauerbrunn, Master of the Woods and Forests, Professor of Mechanics of the Grand Duke of Badenia and Father of the Bicycle.

Drais studied forestry, mathematics, physics, and architecture at Heidelberg University, while his father became the "most eminent judge of the country." In 1810, Drais became Master of the Woods and Forests of Badenia. He proposed a method of renewing agricultural soil from forests, and the common use of a binary number system.

In 1813, Drais built a lightweight manumotive four-wheeler, able to drive two to four people and easily adaptable for horse power. Drais demonstrated this machine at the Vienna Congress of 1814–15, and in other European cities for such notables as Russia's Czar Alexander I. Then he applied his talents to a single-track two-wheel vehicle. No one is

Karl von Drais, 1775–1851.

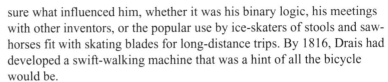

sure what influenced him, whether it was his binary logic, his meetings with other inventors, or the popular use by ice-skaters of stools and saw-horses fit with skating blades for long-distance trips. By 1816, Drais had developed a swift-walking machine that was a hint of all the bicycle would be.

Drais' swift-walker was called a Laufmaschine, or Draisine. It had a wooden beam with triangulated legs, wooden wheels with leather-covered tires and iron rims, a steering tiller with arm rest, an upholstered seat, a spoon brake operated by hand, a kickstand, and luggage rack. Drais' was a practical and efficient vehicle for touring the woods and forests, tending his projects.

Drais Laufmaschine,
from Museum für Verkehr und Technik,
Berlin.

The Laufmaschine was first reported in the *Karlsruher Zeitung* on August 1, 1817. The story describes how Drais rode from Mannheim to Schwetzinger in one hour, while the postwagon took four hours, that his machine weighed 40 kilograms and cost 35 gulden.

In 1817, the Laufmaschine was introduced in Paris at the Luxembourg Gardens, the first of Drais' many public demonstrations around Paris with crowds of paying spectators. He and his assitants held more the following year, and eventually Drais obtained permits and patents for Badenia, Bavaria, Prussia and France. His first patent states his machine's capabilities:

1. That on a well-maintained post-road, it will travel uphill as fast as a man can walk.
2. On a plain, even after heavy rain, it will go 6 to 7 miles an hour, which is as swift as a courier.
3. When the roads are dry and firm, it runs on the plain at the rate of 8 to 9 miles an hour, which is equal to a horse's gallop.
4. On a descent, it equals a horse at full speed.

Drais marketed his idea using a system of construction plans and license marks, leaving its manufacture to others. His French patent of February 17, 1818, was good for ten years.

One early swift-walking enthusiast was also an inventor of photography. Joseph Nicéphore Niépce (1765–1833) lived at Grâs, near Chalon-sur-Saône, in Dijon, France. In 1813, Niépce and his son Isodore began experimenting with lithography. By 1816, he was using a *camera obscura* to make reproductions. This is supposedly when Niépce restored an old célérifère, added steering, and named it the Céléripède. He displayed it in Paris at the Luxembourg Gardens in 1817, the same year the Draisine was demonstrated. Three letters from Niépce's brother Claude mention the machine, such as this one sent from Hammersmith, England, in November 1818:

Drais' patent.

Dear Brother, thank you very much for the information which was in your letter about the new machine, the velocipede, which you have already been using, and which I didn't know anything about at all. It seems to me, after what you've told me, that it could be really useful, in this country especially, where there are so many well maintained roads. It seems that with effort and a good road, you could go very fast, although you would look rather funny on it. I should think that someone with long legs like Isodore might go very fast, since you make use of your legs to propel you forward and the longer your paces, the better you would get along without tiring yourself. I'm anxious to hear some other details about this new machine; I'm sure if you wanted to, you could succeed in perfecting it.[4]

Karl von Drais astride his swift-walker.

In England, Denis Johnson, a coach-maker and entrepreneur from Long Acre, in Covent Garden, London, received the British patent on June 21, 1818. The design of his "Pedestrian Curricle" may have been still incubating as his patent reads: "The dimensions of this machine must depend upon the height and weight of the person who is to use it, as well as the materials of which it is formed, consequently no specific directions can be given about them."[5]

The new machines made a big impact in England by 1819. More refined than the Draisine, English models had the rider sitting more upright, with arm rests, and padded or suspended saddles. Curved wooden backbones allowed larger wheels, with iron bindings as tires. The steering bar, front forks, and rear stays were made of light metal.

Swift-walkers enjoyed a couple of seasons of public attention in England, France, Prussia, Italy, and America. In England they were called hobby horses, dandy horses, swift-walkers, and numerous other names. Perceived as a major innovation and a frightful threat, their effect on society was shown in caricatures making fun of the fashionable people, the hazards of roads, and the extinction of horses. Aristocrats and dandies were usually the first able to afford the machines. By 1820 swift-walkers were used by doctors, clergymen, postmen, merchants, children, and the elderly. As their novelty waned, prices came down, and used models became available. Around London and Paris, races were held with betting.

Denis Johnson.

Johnson opened a riding school in Soho offering rentals for those unable to buy. He and Drais introduced women's models with side-saddles and three-wheelers. *London Magazine* reported that Johnson was making a good profit in 1819: "The first cost of the machine to the patentee [Johnson] is not more than forty or fifty shillings; but the price to the public is from eight to ten pounds." In the United States, velocipedes first appeared in Boston and Troy, New York. In New York City, where W.K. Clarkson received the first U.S. swift-walker patent in 1819, "the swains frequented the hill from Chatham Street to City Hall Park," and a law was passed prohibiting hobby horses from public places and sidewalks.

Karl von Drais continued using his invention for some twenty-five years after its debut. In 1819, because of political troubles involving Drais' father, the King of Prussia banned outdoor athletics thought to be subversive, including use of the Laufmaschine, and the Duke of Badenia urged Drais to stop using his vehicle for official duties. But Drais was stubborn and he strode onward. In 1832, *Mechanics Magazine* featured a drawing of "Drais' Improved Velocipede" and spoke of his mission: "Since his arrival in England, he has been endeavoring to revive the use of the velocipede, and insists that it must have been owing to some error in the construction of our English edition of the invention, or great inexpertness in the management of it, that it fell into such general discredit among us."

Drais himself fell into discredit in 1837, when a reporter claimed he was an alcoholic and a lunatic, "who once tried to revive a dead girl, already cold, by resuscitation and he had consequently been sent to prison."[6] In 1842, Drais invented a human-powered railcar, which he claimed was faster than the Mannheim-Heidelberg locomotive. Drais died in 1851, but his name lives on as the bicycle's father.

Mechanical Drive

The next pivotal step for swift-walkers was the arrival of a drive mechanism that utilized human power to make riding faster and easier. The first of this kind was constructed in 1821 by Louis Gompertz of Surrey, England, who later co-founded the Society for the Prevention of Cruelty to Animals. He designed a ratchet bar for the front fork, connected to a cog on the front hub. When the rider pulled the handlebar ratchet, the cog turned the wheel forward. Hands could assist feet, an option with great potential, but using arms for leverage were not as effective as legs for applying human power. Gompertz saw more than a fashionable hobby in the machine. In the *Repertory of Arts, Manufactures and Agriculture* (1821), he claimed that:

> Being converted from one of the slowest animals in creation, to one of great continued speed from his own salubrious exertions; the ridicule then with which they have been assailed by some of the idle caricaturists must yield to the advantages which they will bestow on the world.

By 1825, swift-walkers and hobby horses declined in popularity. Still a crude and cumbersome means of locomotion, there would be only isolated developments towards the bicycle in the following 40 years. There were problems of weight, materials, and tooling, along with the basic question of balancing while driving a mechanical contraption with two wheels on rough roads. Yet many inventive carriage-makers, blacksmiths, carpenters, and wheelwrights in England, Europe, and America were experimenting with multi-wheel vehicles that were also called velocipedes.

As the Industrial Revolution and the Machine Age blossomed, an

Gompertz's velocipede, 1821, with arm-powered sector gear.

inventive spirit took hold of Western society. All kinds of contraptions and manufacturing processes developed from a growing population of technical workers. Ideas for transport, communication, materials, and manufacturing were exchanged in a collective fervor for ingenuity, progress, and material perfection. Many talented hands were engaged in large-scale engineering projects, such as railroads and bridge construction, and the velocipede emerged as a golden opportunity for entrepreneurs and independent tinkerers.

Willard Sawyer's velocipede carriage, 1855.

Various human-powered carriages appeared that were powered by hand (manumotive) or foot (pedomotive). Rural postmen around Paris attempted their practical use when a M. Dreuze developed vehicles in 1830. In summer, service was reportedly excellent. The velocipede had "conquered the prejudice of the country." However, when winter turned severe, "their wheels rotated rapidly on the slippery surface, but not a yard would they progress."[7]

Willard Sawyer was a carpenter who developed a business of building and selling velocipede carriages that continued for many seasons. He began making treadle-crank driven manumotives around 1840 in Dover, England, calling them Direct-Action Self-Locomotives. By 1860, he was a prospering craftsman and engineer, with a factory in Kent, and his machines were owned by royalty throughout the world. He offered several machines, including the Sociable, Racer, Tourist and Traveller, Promenade and Visiting, Lady's and Invalid's Carriages.

MISSING LINKS

Treadle-cranks were the first kind of foot-powered mechanical drive to be applied to two-wheelers, and two Scotsmen, Kirkpatrick Macmillan (1813–1878) and Gavin Dalzell (1811–1865), are credited as the inventors of the first mechanical bicycles. Macmillan's treadler was considered the first, but recent research and photographic evidence suggests his was a three-wheeler, so the original two-wheel treadler made by Dalzell is possibly the world's first mechanical bicycle.

Macmillan was a blacksmith from the village of Courthill in Dumfriesshire, Scotland, and an apprentice engineer in the city of Glasgow. In the early 1840s he probably worked at the Vulcan Foundry in Glasgow while attending night school, and by the 1850s he took over his father's blacksmith business. According to legend, while working at the Drumlanrig Estate of the Duke of Bacchleuch around 1840, a man from Dumfries named Mr. Charteris brought a swift-walker to the workshop for repair, and copies were made by both Macmillan and his assistant John Findlater. They rode on the estate and around Dumfries county, where Macmillan had a reputation as a jack-of-all-trades. He was known locally as "Daft Pate," always willing to try any task. He worked on all kinds of farm machinery, making improvements to the horse-drawn plow, and he was a talented veterinarian. His son John said he could "make wooden pumps, play the harmonium, pull out teeth, and was well known at parties in the district for his grand whistling and fiddling."[8]

Kirkpatrick Macmillan, 1813–1878.

Macmillan's two-wheel treadler,
from the Science Museum, London.

Gavin Dalzell's treadler.

The myth of Macmillan was his supposed isolation; according to one historian, he was "separated in time and space from predecessors and successors, almost unaffected by the crudities of the past and without influence upon the future."[9] Rooted in the age of the traditional rural craftsman, he was more experimenter than entrepreneur, and did not go into business with his design, nor publish articles or advertise. Macmillan's last remaining machine was destroyed by fire in Liverpool, and copies of his two-wheeler were built by historians based on machines made by Macmillan's contemporaries.

A report of an accident in the *Glasgow Argus* on June 9th, 1842 is the most famous evidence of Macmillan's machine—even though he isn't named in the article. Supposedly, on the evening of June 6, 1842, Macmillan set out to test his machine by riding to his sister's home in Glasgow, a round-trip journey of 140 miles. Stopping at Old Cumnock the first night, he went on to Glasgow the next day, and in the outskirts of the city, in the Gorbals, he had an accident involving a child and was summoned to the Gorbals South Side Police Court the following day.

> Yesterday, a gentleman, belonging to Dumfries-shire, was placed at the Gorbals public bar, charged with riding along the pavement on a velocipede, to the obstruction of the passage, and with having, by so doing, thrown over a child. It appeared from his statement that he had on the day previous come all the way from Old Cumnock, a distance of 40 miles, bestriding the velocipede, and that he performed the journey in the space of five hours. On reaching the Barony of Gorbals he had gone upon the pavement, and was soon surrounded by a large crowd, attracted by the novelty of the machine. The child who was thrown down had not sustained any injury, and under the circumstances the offender was fined only 5 shillings. The velocipede employed in this instance was very ingeniously constructed. It moved on wheels turned with the hand by means of a crank; but to make it 'progress' appeared to require more labour than will be compensated for by the increase of speed. This invention will not supersede the railways.

One account of the sentencing claims the judge was so intrigued by the machine that he offered to pay the fine himself if Macmillan would let him ride it. Another version suggests a skeptical magistrate believed "it's no possible for flesh and bluid tae sit on tap o'a wheel without coupin." Regarding the "gentleman" rider and who it was, Alistair Dodds, a transport historian at the Scottish Museum, believes it was not Kirkpatrick Macmillan the artisan, but one of his schoolmaster brothers. The description of the machine, which "turned with the hand, by means of a crank," was thought to be the reporter's error, until a recently discovered photograph suggests that the reporter was correct. The photograph, possibly the world's first of a human-powered vehicle, depicts a tricycle with hand-cranks driven by a man believed to be Macmillan.

Tricycle attributed to Macmillan, from Glasgow Transport Museum.

Gavin Dalzell was a tea merchant from Lesmahgow, a village on the route between Dumfries and Glasgow. In 1847, he commissioned a blacksmith to add a treadle-drive mechanism to a swift-walker as a way to deliver goods to his customers through the region. According to his nephew, Dalzell had it built after seeing someone on a similar machine pass by his house. His velocipede had a long wheelbase with treadles placed to allow easier steering of the front wheel. The restored original is in Glasgow's Museum of Transport.

Thomas McCall, from Kilmarnock, Scotland, built several copies of the Macmillan–Dalzell velocipede some twenty years later, when pedal-crank velocipedes became popular. As a schoolboy, McCall ran alongside Macmillan riding his velocipede, and as a wheelwright and joiner he probably had commercial ambitions with the vehicle. In 1869, McCall's machine was reported on twice in *English Mechanic* magazine, by the correspondent "Mechanical Hawk:"

> It has, as my brother readers will perceive, a far better steering handle, being fitted with brake and gun-metal bearings; the connecting rods are also made alterable to a long or short leg. It is a remarkably safe velocipede, being so low and easily mounted. The speed is from 8 to 12 miles an hour, though I have gone downhill at what I should think a much greater speed. The price, through improved fittings, has risen to seven pounds. The machine weighs about 58 pounds.

Thomas McCall's treadler, 1869.

Velocipedomania

At last we come to the launch of the true bicycle, the two-wheel velocipede with pedal-cranks attached to the hub for turning the drive wheel forward and backward. Simple as it seems, this was a revolution in motion. The invention of the pedal velocipede or "boneshaker" created a new industry, a new sport, a new mode of transport, and a new craze, called velocipedomania.

The origins of the pedal velocipede—who first put pedals on a bicycle, and when—is a complicated story that continues to evolve with new claims and evidence. As some historians search for a single eureka event, it appears to others that the bicycle was invented by more than one person.

Pierre and Ernest Michaux, father and son, take credit for inventing and popularizing the pedal velocipede. Pierre Michaux (1813–83; his birth record said Michaut) was an ironworker from Bar-le-Duc who came to Paris in the mid-1850s and opened a shop making carriage parts, with assistance from his young sons, Ernest (1842–1882), Henry (1854–1901), Edmond (1848–1880), and Francisque (1859–1938). According to legend, a hat maker named M. Brunel from rue de Verneuil brought a broken *velocifer* (a swift-walker) for repair to Michaux's shop at 5-7 Cité Godot-de Mauroy, an alleyway at 29 Avenue Montaigne. Depending on whose history you read, between 1855 and 1866, either Pierre or Ernest got the idea of putting pedal-cranks on the front wheel, and they built two machines.

Baudry de Saunier cites 1855 in his *Histoire Générale*, but that appears to be the year when Pierre Michaux patented a pair of iron garden shears. In 1893, Henry Michaux recollected in the Paris newspaper *L'Eclair* that it was in March 1861, when he was seven years old, that his father told Ernest to fit a cranked axle to the wheel "as you would a grindstone," and Ernest did. In 1864 the Englishman J. Townsend Trench saw a velocipedist and met the maker, Pierre Michaux:

> I went and found a fine, burly, busy blacksmith, very clever and most amusing, working in an enormous forge, with his carriage building irons and all sorts of things making. He told me that he had just invented those machines, and sold five and had one left.[10]

Henry Michaux said that in about 1865, his father hired Pierre Lallement (1843–91), an apprentice carriage builder from Nancy, not far from Bar-le-Duc, "to assist in perfecting the bicycle." Lallement claims he first got the idea of a pedal-driven velocipede in Nancy around 1862, not long after seeing a child's hand-cranked mechanical horse in a toy shop, and a man riding a swift-walker. As the idea "stuck and grew in his mind," Lallement moved to Paris and in July or August, 1863, he built his first pedal velocipede at Stromaier's carriage shop where he was employed, and shortly thereafter rode his machine on the Boulevard St. Martin,

Ernest Michaux, 1842–1882.

Pierre Lallement in Paris, 1869.

where "all the people saw it."[11]

In 1865, Lallement began building his second velocipede at the shop of another employer, Jacquier, and without much money and knowing little English, Lallement went with his invention to America, to Ansonia, Connecticut, near New Haven. With the support of local businessman James Carroll, Lallement obtained the world's first known pedal velocipede patent on November 20, 1866. Lallement was, according to Charles Pratt, "incapable in every way of promoting his invention," and in 1867 or 1868 Lallement returned to Paris where he opened a bike shop called the Ancienne Compagnie Vélocipèdienne. In 1868 or 1869, Carroll and Lallement sold their patent to Calvin Witty, a businessman and carriage-maker from Brooklyn, New York. Witty paid Lallement about $1,000 (10,000 francs) for the patent, and with attorney fees Witty said it cost him $10,000.

The velocipede was gradually refined, from the wooden "Serpentine" frame of 1866 to the "Diagonal" frame of 1868, from the use of hand-made malleable iron (attributed to Pierre Michaux) to factory produced drop forged iron (attributed to René Olivier). Its features included a sprung saddle rail, adjustable crank arms, counter-weight pedals (attributed to Pierre Lallement), twist-grip brake handle, and the popular curlicue headpiece with foot rests. More commonly, pedals were round shafts and velocipedists pedaled with the arch of their feet, using the heel of their shoes as a cleat. The wooden wheels with rubber-shod iron rims came in various sizes to fit the rider's legs. Front-drive wheels were 32 to 48 inches in diameter, rear wheels were 28 to 32 inches. The machines weighed about 55 pounds and cost 350 to 500 francs. Fancy models were painted bright red and yellow with pin-stripes.

Velocipede designs: Serpentine (Lallement), Diagonal (Michaux).

Michaux et Cie. became known for their craftsmanship, production management, and promotion of riding and racing. The company's legendary growth reflects the velocipede's success: they produced 142 machines in 1862, 400 in 1863, 1,100 by early 1867, and in 1868 they had 300 workers making three to five velos per day. Even then, they could not keep up with demand in France. In May 1868, Michaux et Cie. moved into a larger shop at 19-27 Rue Jean-Goujon, with capital provided by René and Aimé Olivier de Sanderval. In April 1869, the Olivier brothers bought all Michaux's shares and the use of his name for 150,000 francs, and then formed the big Compagnie Parisienne des Vélocipèdes with a 8,200 square meter factory at 12 Avenue Bugeaud and a cycling school at the Rue Jean-Goujon premises.

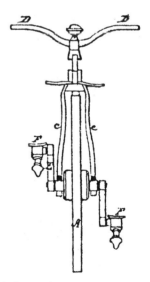

Lallement's patent, 1866.

Compagnie Parisienne, 1869, with workshop, showroom and riding halls.

Velocipede with spring suspension, 1869.

Tandem velocipede. The woman is riding sidesaddle.

In June 1869, Pierre Michaux regretted his early retirement and went back to making velocipedes (bearing his name) at Cité Godot-de Mauroy and Avenue Montaigne. Because he broke his contract, the Oliviers' Compagnie Parisienne sued Michaux. Michaux had to cease making velocipedes and pay the Oliviers 25,000 francs plus legal costs, although they still owed him 50,000 francs. He was ruined and died in 1883 in the Hospice de Bicêtre in Paris, "wearing the hospital uniform for the poor and insane." In 1894, a monument in Bar-le-Duc was dedicated to Pierre and Ernest as "inventeurs et propagateurs du vélocipède à pédale" ("inventors and propagators of the pedal velocipede").

Michaux Monument, in Bar-le-Duc, France.

By 1869, velocipede manufacturers were spreading through Europe and England, with growing trans-Atlantic trade and world-wide shipments. Makers such as Vellani in Modena, Starley and Spencer in Coventry, and Pickering and Hanlon in New York set the bicycle industry in motion. There was intense competition in the manufacture and marketing of the machine, with fierce rivalries for its growing profits. With the Franco-Prussian war of 1870–71, the French velocipede makers converted to making military arms, thus allowing the cycle industry to grow elsewhere, especially in England.

In the United States, several velocipede makers opened shop on the East Coast, while patent owner Calvin Witty forced manufacturers to pay him a royalty fee of $10 to $27 per velocipede. This stifled the industry, as velocipedes sold for about $160 in the U.S., but inspired inventors, who swamped the U.S. patent office with "improvements to velocipedes." Eighty velocipede applications were filed in one week in 1869.

In 1878, with the arrival of high-wheel bicycles in the U.S., the valuable Lallement-Witty patent was bought by retired Colonel Albert A. Pope of Boston (1843–1909), known as "the father of American bicycling," who controlled the industry by hoarding patents. Both Witty and Pope commissioned investigations into Lallement and his patent, and their demands were upheld in court. In 1883, when his patent finally expired, Lallement moved to Boston and worked as a machinist for the Pope Manufacturing Co. Lallement's interview with Charles Pratt, the first president of the League of American Wheelmen, in *Wheelmen Illustrated* (1883), forms much of his claim as inventor of the pedal-driven velocipede. Today, Lallement's star is rising, as roads are named in his honor, in Pont-à-Mousson where he was born, and in Boston where he died. The Lallement Memorial Committee was formed in Boston by historian David Herlihy in 1990, and the Fourth International Cycle History Conference was held there in 1993.

Wiseman Velocipede, 1870.

In England, some people were skeptical of Parisian fads, and more than in France or America the English velocipede developed as a tool rather than a toy. Rowley Turner was an English student and entrepreneur living in Paris who became charmed by the velocipede in 1868 and started a business with workshops and a riding school. As velocipedomania grew in Paris, he brought a velocipede to Coventry to show his uncle Josiah Turner, who owned the Coventry Sewing Machine Company and

Needham Safety Tricycle, 1869.

employed James Starley as foreman. The firm was in a recession, so a new venture was begun, with the name changed to Coventry Machinist's Company. A first batch of about 400 velocipedes was built to sell in France. In January 1869, John Mayall witnessed Rowley Turner introduce his French velocipede in London, and he recounted the event in *Ixion—A Journal of Velocipeding* (1875):

> Mr. Turner took off his coat, grasped the handles of the machine, and with a short run, to my intense surprise, vaulted on to it, and putting his feet on the treadles, made a circuit of the room. We were some half-dozen spectators, and I shall never forget our astonishment at the sight of Mr. Turner whirling himself round the room, sitting on a pair of wheels in a line, that ought, as we innocently supposed, to fall down immediately he jumped off the ground. Judge then of our greater surprise, when instead of stopping by tilting over sideways on one foot, he slowly halted and turning the front wheel diagonally, remained quite still, balancing on the wheels.

Rowley Turner persuaded Charles Spencer of the Snoxell & Spencer Company, makers of gymnasium apparatus in London, to market his machine in England, where the velocipede sold for about £10 to £15. In 1869, over 30 manufacturers sprouted throughout England. Various riding schools, races, books, and magazines were devoted to this revolutionary new vehicle, which fed an ever-increasing desire for speed, practicality, comfort, and safety.

Velocipedomania was a magical phenomenon around 1869. It was the beginning of bicycle ingenuity, when the components of bike technology were developed and the family of cycling machines branched out, eventually evolving into three forms: high-wheel bicycles, multi-wheel cycles, and safety bicycles. The velocipede offered a new means of personal mobility, but as a practical machine there was much to improve. As the mechanical means of production gradually caught up with ideas and innovations, inventors began developing the first modern cycling machines during the 1870s.

Velocipedes took many new shapes, including the innovative Phantom Veloce by Reynolds and Mays (1869) with central steering and metal-spoked suspension wheels, and Thomas Wiseman's front-drive rear-steer semi-recumbent velocipede (1870). Celebrating the power of human-sized wheels, many kinds of big-wheeled contraptions appeared. Monocycles were huge single-wheel vehicles which riders can sit or stand inside while pedaling. They developed in America, England, Italy, and France, where big-wheel unicycles appeared on the market. Dicycles were an intriguing design, with riders sitting between two big wheels, but these were unstable without weights, or three or four supporting wheels.

Multi-wheel cycles developed from human-powered carriages to become sociables and tricycles. These were important links in bicycle evolution, providing techincal innovations such as hollow steel tubing, spoked wheels, and differential gears. Multi-wheel cycles became popular alternatives to two-wheelers because many riders preferred the added stability and carrying capacity. Riders of the Jackson Sociable velocipede (1870) sat side-by-side between a pair of five-foot carriage wheels, steering with two tiny front wheels. Boneshaker makers offered three-wheelers and trailers, including the sturdy Needham Safety tricycle, the sociable Bath Chair velocipede, the practical Dublin tricycle, and the Celermane, a five-person rowing vehicle that weighed around 280 pounds.

Chain-drive transmissions were first developed during the period of velocipedomania, but these were prototypes that took about twenty years of refinements to evolve into modern safety bicycles. In Paris, the German engineer Ernest Meyer and the watch-maker André Guilmet began building a chain and cog rear-wheel-drive velocipede in 1868. Their invention was not known until the 1890s, after Guilmet died in the Franco-Prussian war. In England, Frederick Shearing published a sketch in 1869 of his Norfolk bicycle with a belt-drive transmission, which he later built and rode. Similar machines include the Flying Dutchman by H.L. Bate, and a home-made chain-drive safety bicycle constructed by the amateur mechanic Thomas Shergold of Glochester in 1876.

Unicycle and monocycles, 1869.

Guilmet and Meyer bicycle, 1868.
Shearing's Norfolk bicycle, 1869.

High-Wheelers

The high-wheel bicycle was the next logical way for velocipedes to go faster, inspiring another cycling craze. Taking the novelty of balance and wheel-power one step higher, they became the first modern cycling machines. Simply increasing the wheel size, to make it roll further with each revolution of the pedals, caused every aspect of cycling to grow. Bicycle production, speeds and distances, cyclists' rights, club events, road construction, anything to do with bicycles seems to have increased with wheel size.

High-wheelers were the first machines to be commonly called "bicycles." English names included "wheel" and "balance." When high-wheelers became the most common variety, they were called "ordinary" bicycles to distinguish them from all the other ingenious cycles becoming available. At the peak of the high-wheel craze, names like "dwarf ordinary" and "Xtraordinary" appeared. By the 1900s, when the "big wheel" was an old curio, it became known as a "penny farthing," because the wheels resemble the two British coins.

High-wheelers were in use for nearly twenty years. When they peaked around 1880, they were the most popular kind of bicycle before the modern safety. During the high-wheel's rise, basic elements of modern bicycles were developed, including ball bearings, tangent spoked wheels, and hollow steel tubing. The book *Bicycling: Its Rise and Development* (1874) stated that:

> The arrangements of springs, brakes and rubber tyres, have removed half the terrors of ruts and steep gradients, and the testimony of hundreds of experienced bicyclists is that the bicycle is more useful than the cleverest nag man ever bestrode, with additional advantage that a bicycle consumes nothing but a little oil.

The Ariel Bicycle (1871), with a 48-inch lever-tension front wheel, was one of the first all-metal mass-produced high-wheelers. Patented by James Starley and William Hillman, formerly of the Coventry Machinists' Co., and manfactured by Smith, Starley and Co., it weighed about 50 pounds and sold for £8. Smith, Starley and Co. offered a speedier model with a 2:1 gear ratio (about 96-inch gear) for £12, and a Ladies Ariel with a side-saddle riding position with treadles and an off-set rudder wheel on the left side. The Ariel was advertised as "the lightest, strongest, safest, swiftest, easiest, cheapest, best finished and most elegant of modern velocipedes."

High-wheel bicycles for racing weighed about 25 pounds—the lightest was just over eleven pounds—and touring models weighed 50 to 70 pounds. Front wheels usually ranged from 50 to 60 inches in diameter, almost "twice the rider's inseam length," with about 60 radial or tangent spokes, and hollow steel rims with red Pará rubber tires. Hubs and axles had adjustable ball bearings, and crank lengths were adjustable from four to six inches by moving the pedals. Forks were usually straight tapered

By Her Majesty's Royal Letters Patent

THE "ARIEL" BICYCLE.

Fitted with Lever Tension Wheels, India Rubber Tyres, Improved Rudder, Registered Cliptail Sliding Spring, &c.

SMITH, STARLEY, & CO.,
PATENTEES & MANUFACTURERS,
ST. AGNES WORKS, COVENTRY.

Ariel bicycle, 1871.

tubes, fit with bearings at the steering headset. Frames of round or oval steel tubing curved and tapered as a spine around the back of the high-wheel to the rear wheel forks. Mounting steps were located along the spine almost as high as the pedals. Rear wheels were about eighteen inches in diameter and the wheelbase about 30 inches. Straight handlebars, with vulcanite pear-shaped grips, evolved into curving "cow-horn" bars, with "spade" or "shovel" handgrip shapes. Whatton bars curved under the legs from behind so the rider could jump forward to land feet first, instead of being catapulted over the bars head first. Saddles were covered in leather, and suspended on leaf or coil-mounted springs, or fixed solidly to the "perch." The typical "spoon brake" was applied by a lever to create friction on the front tire. Racing models usually did not have brakes, since the rider could slow and stop by back-pedaling with the fixed-gear. Caliper brakes were developed but not yet in common use.

High-wheelers were built by more and more cycle manufacturers. In 1875, there were about 30 makers in Britain, with some fourteen firms in Coventry, and an estimated 50,000 bicycles in the country, costing about £15 each. By 1885, there were about 22 makers in Coventry and over 400,000 bicycles that cost around £7. High-wheelers were built in Paris by Ernest Meyer, in Italy by the firm Turri & Porri, and in Japan by Teikoku in Tokyo and Kajino in Yokohama.

In America, several high-wheelers from England were shown at the 1876 Centennial Exposition in Philadelphia. Those machines reportedly found their way to San Francisco, St. Louis, Baltimore, Hartford, and Boston. In 1878, Albert A. Pope of Boston proceeded to import, manufacture, and promote the Columbia high-wheel bicycle. The first Columbia was a 70-pound ordinary costing $313; by 1887 the Pope Manufacturing Co. catalog offered several models, such as the 22½-pound $140 Racer. Massachusetts was the center of activity for cycling, with club rides, races, magazines, and cycle makers such as the Overman Wheel Company, whose Victor bicycle was known for its high quality and race victories. In 1879, there were less than 10,000 high-wheelers made in the U.S., but in 1889 an estimated 200,000 safeties, ordinaries, and tricycles were produced.

There were many variations to the high-wheel design. Rear-driving machines had the big wheel placed behind the rider. The first of this type was Harry John Lawson's Lever Safety bicycle (1876), which had a 50-inch lever-driven rear wheel and weighed 60 pounds. Another popular and race-worthy rear-driver was the Star-type bicycle. Patented by George Pressey, it was first built in 1881 by the Smith Machine Company of Smithville, New Jersey, and known as the Smith Star, or American Star when exported. It had a triangulated frame and an early two-speed gear clutch made with leather. Stability was proven by a ride down the Capitol steps in Washington, D.C.

Bayliss-Thomas Ordinary, 1879, with 55-inch wheel.

Columbia bicycle poster, 1880.

Singer Xtraordinary, 1878.

Kangaroo bicycle, 1884, by Hillman, Herbert & Cooper, with chain drive.

Testing the Smith Star bicycle, at the U.S. Capitol Building, Washington, D.C., about 1884 from Library of Congress.

Assembly room, Columbia factory, Hartford, Connecticut, 1884.

Most ingenuity went into changing the ratio between gear and wheel size, to give better control and more speed. Early geared "dwarf" high-wheel bicycles used lever-driven gears with an oscillating up and down foot stroke, such as on the Smith Star, the Xtraordinary (1878) by George Singer & Company, and the Facile (1879) by Ellis and Company, which was used to set a 24-hour record of 266.5 miles in England. The popular Kangaroo bicycle (1884) by Hillman, Herbert & Cooper Ltd. was one of the first to use double chain sets on both sides of the 36-inch front wheel.

Some designs straddled the gap between the high-wheeler and the safety bicycle, such as the long wheelbase front-driving Sphinx by Truffault, and the rear-driving Bicyclette built in 1873–79 by H.J. Lawson, who became manager of the Tangent and Coventry Tricycle Company. Nicknamed the Crocodile, the Bicyclette was a 60-pound machine with a 40-inch front wheel. It had indirect steering and a 24-inch rear wheel for a 60-inch wheelbase. Production began in the early 1880s, and it brought a new form of cycling machine to the scene, the rear-driving dwarf ordinary, also known as a safety bicycle.

The high-wheeler had a cult-like following of daring men who felt they were the fastest beings on earth. Wheelmen were perched as high as horsemen, yet they were a strange new presence on the roads. Cyclists often ran into frightened horses, mad carriage drivers, and restrictive toll-road gate keepers. Riding schools and booklets discussed the art of mounting the high-wheel and ways to avoid the most severe problem, falling head first, called "taking a header." The high center of gravity and narrow rubber tires, which could roll off, made potential hazards of ordinary obstructions like small rocks, animals, and children.

Thomas Stevens, the first round-the-world cyclist.

The high-wheel bicycle inspired intense competition for racers and tourists. The first big ride to gather attention was the 800-mile, fourteen-day trip from London to John O'Groats, the northernmost point in Scotland, made by Charles Spencer and members of the Middlesex Bicycle Club in 1873. An early benchmark for cycling performance was the famous trans-Britain ride from Land's End, the southernmost point in Cornwall, to John O'Groats, roughly 924 miles. On high-wheel bicycles, the ride took thirteen days in 1882, and ten days in 1883. The following year, J.H. Adams used a Facile bicycle and the ride took 6 days 23 hours 45 minutes. A decade later in 1893, a cyclist on a safety bicycle with pneumatic tires, lowered the record to 3 days 5 hours 49 minutes. In 1990, on a road time trial bike, Andrew Wilkinson set the current record of 1 day 21 hours 2 minutes 18 seconds. More high-wheeler milestones came with the hour record by Herbert Lydell Cortis of 20 miles 300 yards, and the 13,500 mile trans-world trek by Thomas Stevens in 1884 to 1887. He journeyed from San Francisco to Boston in 125 days, and then from Europe across Asia to Japan.

Multi-Cycles and Sociables

In the years 1880 to 1900, tricycles and multi-wheel cycles enjoyed a hey-day of ingenuity and popularity. These machines combined the development of high-wheelers, safety bicycles, and horseless carriages, when the craze for cycling was reaching its Golden Age. Multi-cycles shared the pace of technical developments with their cousins the bicycles, sometimes following and sometimes leading the race for the ideal cycling machine. Multi-cycles evolved in two or three stages with many styles, uses, and riding configurations. They were made for those excluded from handling a high-wheeler, for carrying passengers, for transporting goods, and for racing. Multi-cycles are categorized by the number of wheels (tricycles, quadricycles, etc.), by function (tandem, sociable, carrier, utility, etc.), and by the position of the drive wheel(s) (front [FWD], center [CWD], or rear [RWD]).

When the high-wheeler still held its influence on cycle makers in the early 1880s, the typical first-generation multi-cycles had a pair of large driving wheels with small steering wheels, placed in front or behind the rider, such as Starley's Salvos, Singer's Omnicycle and the Demon Hill Climber. Some were equipped with seats for two or more riders, either side-by-side, as in the Coventry Cheylesmore sociable, or in line, one behind the other, as in the racy Humber Ordinary Tandem. The machines weighed from about 60 to 150 pounds and cost £25 to £50. Henry Sturmey described their evolution in the *Indispensable Tricyclist's Handbook* (1881):

Coventry Lever tricycle, 1876.

The heavy lumbering vehicle of yesterday has given place to dozens of varieties of light, airy, handsome structures, the outcome of the best mechanical skill in the country.... It is but a year or two since that rattling, creaking, clumsy contrivance, mounted on three or four wheels, and propelled laboriously in a tortuous and erratic fashion by some mechanic or labouring man, was the *tout ensemble* of tricycling.

Rudge Quad Triplet, 1888.

Bad road conditions gave thought to reducing the number of wheels in line, or tracks, in multi-cycles, because fewer tracks run into fewer obstacles. A common design was the side-steering two-track single-drive tricycle, such as the Coventry Club, with the front steering wheel in line with the non-driving rear wheel. Other designs include rear-drive machines with double front steering wheels, including the Facile Rear-Driver, the Phantom tricycle, and the Rudge Quad Triplet with four equal-sized wheels and seating for three.

The Bayliss and Thomas Folding Tricycle was made to collapse for easy storage. Convertible cycles offered further possibilities, with the addition of seats, or extra wheels, or the joining of two cycles. For example, the Regent cycle combined the front of a Kangaroo with the rear of a Cripper, and the Rucker Tandem connected two high-wheelers in line.

Most manufacturers offered cargo cycles. Some were based on their sociables with storage instead of seats, such as the Singer Carrier, used to deliver the *London Standard*, or the Horsham Pentacycle, a high-wheeler surrounded by four small wheels, used to deliver the Royal Mail and nicknamed Hen and Chickens.

In theory, tricycles should be more stable than bicycles, especially high-wheelers. Neophyte tricyclists believed they could ride without learning the art of balancing, or that there was no problem dismounting passengers from machines that were stopped. Yet newspaper records of 1883 show the number of tricycle accidents about equal to bicycle accidents. The pros and cons of front and rear steering caused considerable debate, as front steering with small wheels created a skittish vehicle on the road, and rear steering required turning in the opposite direction the vehicle goes. In the 1890s, the principles for geometrically-correct steering in three- and four-wheel vehicles were developed by Ackermann, and tricycle design united with the development of the safety bicycle, as machines began to appear with direct front steering, in line with the chain-drive and centered between the rear driving wheels.

Facile Rear-Driver.

Cycle makers in Coventry worked amidst a whirl of activity. In 1879 there were about twenty types of tricycles and multi-cycles manufactured in Coventry. By 1884, there were over 120 different models, with twenty makers employing thousands of workers. New machines were exported all over the world, and tricycling had the approval of the Imperial Crown. A class struggle developed between the sedate, civilized tricyclists, and the athletic, high-wheeling bicyclists. Fighting also erupted on the road, as tricycles took more space.

James Starley, 1830–1881.
"Father of the Bicycle Industry."

Starley's Coventry Royal Salvo, 1881.

STARLEY'S WHEELS

James Starley (1830–1881) is known as the "father of the bicycle indus-try" for his inventive genius in developing spoked wheels, differential gears, and hollow frame tubes. Starley was a central figure among cycle makers in Coventry, which was the hub of the world's cycle industry from 1870 to 1900. He worked with many pioneers of the bicycle, motorcycle, and automobile industry, and he managed to remain independent, building his own line of cycles, while offering his patents in partnership with other manufacturers. Despite intense rivalries in the bicycle industry, when Starley died of cancer at 51 years he was admired by all, with no personal enemies.[12] His sons carried on the family business, Starley Brothers Ltd. at St. John's Works in Coventry, where a complete line of bicycles, tricycles and sociable cycles were produced, and where James' nephew, John Kemp Starley, developed the famed Rover safety bicycles in the 1880s.

As foreman of the Coventry Machinist's Company, James Starley began building velocipedes with Josiah and Rowley Turner and George Singer. In 1871, he and William Hillman built the Ariel bicycle with "lever tension" metal-spoked wheels. The "Battle of the Wheel" began, and W.H.J. Grout introduced his "tension" wheels, with radial spokes tightened by nipples along the rim. Starley followed with his "tangent" wheels, the cross-spoke design still in common use. These wheels appeared on his Coventry Lever Tricycle (1876), the first lightweight mass-produced tricycle. It had rack-and-pinion steering, with a 50-inch drive-wheel offset by a pair of 24-inch wheels placed in front and behind five feet apart. The Coventry Lever tricycle was converted to the Coventry Rotary in 1877, when Starley constructed a chainset consisting of chainwheel, cogs, and a block chain. Chains were already available for other machines, including those used in cycle factories, and Starley helped refine them for cycling machines.

High-wheelers were popular, but exclusive, so Starley concentrated on tricycles and multi-wheel cycles. Somewhat more stable than bicycles, multi-track cycles have their own problems, such as the clumsiness of turning corners with double-drive wheels. When Starley tried making a tandem machine with two fixed-gear high-wheel bikes coupled side-by-side—the so-called Honeymoon Sociable—in a demonstration with his son William, James couldn't keep pace and the machine veered off-road into a patch of nettles. Starley realized that with his machine, the average bride and groom would end up riding in circles. He built a system of bevel gears and pinions, allowing the two drive wheels to turn independently at the appropriate speed, thereby inventing a differential gear for cycles.

Called the balance gear or double-drive gear, Starley's device was the first application of a differential to a horseless carriage, and it appeared on one of Starley's finest machines, the Salvo Quadricycle (1877). When he sold two models to Queen Victoria in 1881 and was invited to meet her, the "Quad" was renamed Royal Salvo. When James Starley died, he had inspired cycle makers in Coventry to further develop tricycles and sociables.

MODERN TRICYCLES

The Humber Cripper (1885) was typical of the second-generation tricycle, and was perhaps the first cycle named after a professional racer, Robert Cripps. Thomas Humber was known for his block chain design and refined frame geometry. He built several versions of the Cripper as it evolved along with his first safety bicycles. One model had a cross-frame design, while another resembled a diamond frame. Wheels were 18 to 24 inches on the front, and 40 inches on the rear, with an average 32-inch measure for both the wheelbase and track-width. The roadster models weighed about 75 pounds and the racing model was about 40 pounds.

Humber Cripper tricycle, 1885.

As the safety bicycle developed between 1885 and 1888, most manufacturers produced a Cripper-style safety tricycle. These include the Psycho cycles by Starley Bros., the Premier Racer by Hillman, Herbert & Cooper, the Singer Straight Steering Tandem, the Invincible by Raleigh, and the American Lever by Smith. Wheels became more equal in size, but they still had solid, or at best, hollow rubber tires, which offered a hard, shaky ride and limited speed. By the 1890s, with the conversion to pneumatic tires, both bicycles and the tricycles evolved to a higher level of efficiency.

Representing the third generation tricycle is Starley's Psycho (1895), which had 28-inch wheels and a seamless diamond frame that melded into a central, fully enclosed gear casing for chain-drive or chainless bevel-gear drive. For some, the stability provided by tricycles was found in pneumatic-tire safety bicycles. As motors powered by steam, electricity and gasoline came into use, many bicycle and tricycle makers fit engines to their machines, thus becoming pioneering names in the automobile industry. The use of tricycles for carrying passengers and cargo continues throughout the twentieth century.

Starley Psycho tricycle, 1892.

Safety Bicycles

The safety bicycle is the most common kind of cycling machine. With the cyclist upright, pedaling between two same-sized wheels, the front for steering and the rear for traction, the safety evolved in a series of inventive leaps amidst a growing understanding of cycling dynamics. Fully developed at the turn of the twentieth century, this modern machine revolutionized cycling, and is widely considered the optimum design. Technical refinements in frame design, gearing, and tires, along with trend setting mass-production and marketing techniques, made it the most influential and efficient traveling vehicle of all time.

The first step toward the safety was the development of a chain-drive mechanism. As shown above, these had been applied in various configurations for high-wheelers and tricycles since the mid-1870s. The famous series of Rover safety bicycles, produced between 1884 and 1894 by John Kemp Starley, founder of the Rover Company, illustrates the evolution of refinements in the modern bicycle. The Rover of 1886 had a fixed-gear

Humber bicycle, 1885, with diamond frame.

J.K. Starley's Rover bicycles:
with indirect steering, 1884–85,
with direct steering, 1885,
Rover Cob 1887–88.

driving a 30-inch rear wheel, with a tubular steel open-diamond frame and direct steering on the 32-inch front wheel. Tangent spoked wheels had ball-bearings in the hubs, and straight-rake forks had foot-rest pins for coasting. By 1890, the Rover catalog had eight different models for women, touring, and racing, along with trikes and tandems.

During the mid-1880s, inventors sensed that the perfection of the bicycle was close at hand, and many innovative frame and tire designs appeared. Lightweight structures, such as the cross-frame, the diamond frame, the racquet frame, and other peculiar frame designs were developed as equal size wheels began to appear. Frames with tension wires and curving wheel-shaped tubing supported seats, handlebars and pedal cranks that seem to be mounted as an afterthought. The common diamond frame design first appeared on Humber's safety of 1888.

As long as safety bicycles had solid rubber tires their popularity was elusive. High-wheelers and dwarf ordinaries offered more shock absorption than early safety bikes because their large wheels were more flexible. Various accessories were developed to remedy the vibrations of the road, such as hollow rubber "cushion" tires, and studded tires with replaceable rubber knobs. The Whippet bicycle, issued by Linely and Biggs in 1885, utilized springs and frame joints that suspended both the handlebars and saddle over the wheels of the bike. Dan Rudge developed a four-blade front fork with spring suspension in 1887, and the design gained popularity on the luxurious Overman Victor and Victoria bicycles.

Probably the most important innovation for the bicycle was the invention of pneumatic tires by John Boyd Dunlop around 1888. His early tires were crude, costly, and successful. By the early 1890s detachable tires with inflatable tubes made by Dunlop, Michelin, Hutchinson, U.S. Rubber, and many others became the standard for virtually all wheeled vehicles. Air-filled tires brought speed, stability, and comfort to the bicycle, making it available for more people. The tire and rubber industry expanded and merged interests with the powerful bicycle industry.

Until 1898, most bicycles had foot-rests and a fixed-gear. They had no neutral freewheeling gear because pedals, cranks, chain, and rear wheel were fixed and turned as one system. Whenever the fixed-gear bike is in motion the pedals go round and back-pedaling slows or stops the cycle. On faster downhill runs, the rider's feet usually could not follow the spinning pedals, a situation referred to as "losing the pedals." When this happened on a crowded road, the voice became louder and the words were shortened to "Loose pedals!" As higher speeds were possible with "pneu" tires, better ways of braking and coasting were needed. The first modern freewheel appeared around 1897, allowing coasting with a clutch bearing separating the rear hub and sprocket. By 1899, *Bicycling World* reported that "with a coaster and brake device, the rider pedals a distance considerably less than that covered by the machine."

Most bikes had a roller or spoon brake, which could damage air-filled tires, so alternatives like Humber's pneumatic pressure brakes evolved into lever-actuated caliper rim brakes and the Bowden brake system. With the New Departure coaster hub brake of 1898, riders could both freewheel and brake securely by back-pedaling. This had a clutch brake inside the hub, with a lever attached to the frame. Eventually two, three, four and five-speed hub gears were developed by Sturmey-Archer, and multi-speed derailleur mechanisms appeared on the market around 1900, but took years to catch on.

John Boyd Dunlop in 1888.

RALEIGH

ROADSTERS are equally **FAMOUS** for **LIGHT-
NESS, ELEGANCE, EASY RUNNING** and
DURABILITY.

E" Pattern with DUNLOP DETACHABLE TIRES. weight 55-lbs.

☞ **PRICES TO SUIT ALL, EXCEPT BUYERS
OF RUBBISH.**

MACHINES FITTED WITH CARTER'S OR OUR OWN GEAR CASE.
ILLUSTRATED CATALOGUES,
and quotations for style of bicycle desired, **post free.**
SOLE AGENCIES IN ALL PARTS OF THE WORLD.

THE RALEIGH CYCLE CO., LTD., NOTTINGHAM, ENG.
American Factory and Offices:
Bank and Greenwich Streets, NEW YORK.

Ignaz Schwinn.

THE GOLDEN AGE OF INDUSTRY

In 1887, an Englishman named Frank Bowden retired from his insurance business in Hong Kong with "only a few months to live," and took up cycling. In six months he was perfectly fit again, and acquired a substantial interest in the cycle makers Woodhead and Angois on Raleigh Street in Nottingham, England. This was a small workshop of about a dozen mechanics making three high-wheelers a week. Bowden re-named it the Raleigh Cycle Company. In 1895, the British stockbroker Terah Hooley bought controlling shares of Raleigh for £180,000 and quickly sold them for £200,000. He did likewise with the Dunlop Tire Company, buying it for £3 million and selling for £5 million. In 1896, Raleigh had the world's largest factory, occupying 7½ acres with 850 employees making about 30,000 bikes per year.[13]

Subsequently, Raleigh expanded by buying out and consolidating other cycle makers throughout the twentieth century. The company bought Sturmey-Archer in 1902, Humber Cycles in 1932, Rudge-Whitworth in 1943, Triumph Cycle Co. in 1953, and BSA (Birmingham Small Arms) in 1957. In 1960, Raleigh was bought out by its subsidiary, the Tube Investments Group, which held most of Raleigh's international subsidiaries. In 1982, Raleigh USA was bought by the Huffy Corporation, and by 1988, the Raleigh name was bought by Derby International Corporation, a conglomerate with headquarters in Luxembourg, which also owns the West Coast Cycle Company, makers of Nishiki bicycles. Raleigh has the distinction of having bicycles in more countries of the world than any other.[14]

Ignaz Schwinn began building high-wheelers and safety bicycles with several makers in northern Germany such as Adler, and after immigrating to America, in 1895, he joined with the the meat-packing businessman Adolf Arnold to form the Arnold Schwinn Company in Chicago. Schwinn bought out Arnold in 1907, and his innovative son, Frank W. Schwinn, led the company from 1933 to 1963 as it became one of the leading American brands of the twentieth century.

The modern safety launched cycle makers into the realm of industrial and financial power. From an era of inventive factory shops run by cycle enthusiasts and mechanics with individual investors, the industry grew into automated assembly line factories managed by corporate capitalists. A look inside the Overman Wheel Works in Chicopee, Massachusetts, by *Scientific American* (1891) showed "nothing but a huge machine," with the whole bicycle made entirely within. The Works had electric lighting, its own steam-powered generating system, and separate buildings for drop-forging, nickel-plating, and rubber tire fabrication. They tested pedal torque with a dynamometer and durability on a test track with various road surfaces.

During the Golden Age of cycling in the 1890s, bicycles were a driving force in the U.S. economy. It was a time when politicians swarmed around cyclists for votes, when bicycles affected virtually every business or trade, when the burgeoning and consolidated bicycle industry shocked the stock market. People were spending more of their money on bicycling than on many other goods, and according to the *New York Journal of Commerce*, the bicycle brought an annual loss of $112 million to other businesses.[15] One historian said there were 1,200 makers of bicycles and parts in New York City with 83 bicycle shops within a one mile radius around lower Broadway.[16] The history of the U.S. Playing Card Company describes the bicycle's Golden Age socio-economic impact as part of the reason the bicycle became a popular image on their playing cards:

> People were spending so much money on bicycles that other business-es suffered a sharp recession. Shoemakers sat idle. They said it was because hardly anyone walks anymore. By 1896 the piano business was off 50 percent, jewelry stores were empty, and a prominent hat manufacturer, in desperation, demanded that Congress pass a law requiring every cyclist to buy two felt hats a year, whether he wore them or not.[17]

Bicycling Joker,
U.S. Playing Card Company.

The bicycle was a popular scapegoat in the 1890s, noted *Bicycle World* (1898):

> Nowadays, if there is an elopement, a stagnation in the peanut market, a glut in smoking tobacco, or a small attendance at the theaters, every-one who is a loser points to the bicycle and says, "You did it."[18]

In the mid-1890s there were two patent offices in the U.S.—one for bicy-cles and one for everything else. In 1896, there were some 500 companies in the U.S. making 1.2 million bicycles which sold for about $125. New bicycle sales totaled over $300 million, with bicycle accessories adding another $200 million. Then, Albert Pope began the troublesome price wars by lowering his Columbia bicycle's retail cost to $75, and others fol-lowed by dumping their machines into the department store market selling as low as $16. Lower priced bicycles made them available for more peo-ple, and two million bikes were sold in 1897. Soon the market was satu-rated, and inventories bulged for 1898. This brought what was known as the "Bust," which inspired the "Trust," a monopolistic corporation formed in New York in 1899 called the American Bicycle Company (ABC).

The ABC controlled most of the major U.S. cycle manufacturers, sup-pliers, and patents, and was itself controlled by financially powerful men including A.G. Spaulding, Albert Pope, John D. Rockefeller, and Albert Coleman. After various buy-outs, trade-offs, stock manipulations, bank-ruptcies, and the loss of some 400 small cycle makers, the Trust went bust in 1903. When the Trust was liquidated, about a hundred cycle makers remained. As large sums of capital were siphoned out of the bicycle industry, its public image was tarnished. Independent cycle makers suf-fered a recession while the major manufacturers branched off into the development of motorcycles, automobiles, and military machines. The

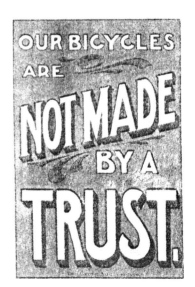

Advertising against the
American Bicycle Company, 1900.

bicycle became an outsider in the plans of corporate interests—some have even described the bicycle as a martyred saint of the machine age.

TWENTIETH CENTURY BIKES

For most of the twentieth century, safety bicycles remained the most popular design, even as the family of cycling machines branched into many special kinds of vehicles for land, air, and water (liquid or frozen). Bikes were made as toys for children, weapons for military, engines for flight, and vehicles for business. Racing bikes adapted lighter, stronger, more refined materials and components, and became standardized by the sport's world governing body, the Union Cycliste Internationale (UCI), to favor the performance of athletes instead of machines. Human-powered vehicles with aerodynamic and recumbent designs were the next step in bicycle evolution, but they were not fully exploited for standard racing and rarely mass-marketed by the bicycle industry. Significant innovations for safety-style bikes include the balloon-tire roadsters of the 1930s and 40s, the small-wheel folding bikes and ten-speed racers of the 1960s and 70s, and the mountain bikes and aero-bikes of the 1980s and 90s.

Safety bicycles changed during the pedal-pushing revival of the late 1930s, with the development of the classic balloon-tire roadster, when U.S. bicycle sales returned to Golden Age levels and again reached over one million per year. While most bicycles of the world kept the diamond-shape frame, in America, "Square was out, teardrops and curves were in." The 26-inch balloon-tire was introduced by Schwinn in 1933, and bikes came equipped with streamlined fenders, chainguards, fake gas tanks, electric battery-powered lights and horns. By 1939, the Murray Ohio Manufacturing Company advertised that the "prevailing lines of motor car design have been engineered into a bicycle."[19]

In the early 1970s the bicycle boom grew with the availability of affordable bikes. The world market grew with standardization of parts, and the global spread of diverse international designs. In the U.S., fifteen million bikes were sold in 1973, more than any year before or after. Bicycles were stereotyped as Italian "racers," French "tourists," Dutch "clunkers," British "lightweights," American "department store lemons," and Japanese "clones." Others had mixed nationality—for example, an American touring bike could have been equipped with English tubing (Reynolds), Japanese derailleurs (SunTour), a French saddle (Idéale), Swiss brakes (Weinmann), Italian handlebars (TTT), a German carrier rack (Pletscher), and Taiwanese tires (IRC). Components sold in one country were manufactured in another country, under the patents of third, with the threadings and fittings of a fourth. Still, some components were not interchangeable, even with the same intended sizes. In 1971, the International Organization for Standardization (ISO) formed its Technical Committee TC/149 Cycles to develop voluntary world standards for bicycle manufacturing. Technical Subcommittee SC/2 was charged with setting dimensional, testing, and performance standards for bicycle components. Much progress has been made in the twenty years since, though there are

20th century bikes:
Murray balloon tire roadster, 1933.
Moulton bike, 1965, with suspension.

occasional problems as components continue to evolve. Today, very few bicycles are made from raw materials at one factory, or even from one country, except bad examples from Bangladesh and Tanzania, where the government-sponsored NABISCO bike factory lost some $10 million.[20]

The mountain bike (MTB) is a further refinement of the safety design, developed around 1978 in northern California and Colorado by Joe Breeze, Gary Fisher, Tom Ritchey, and many others who were searching for new thrills and new ways to get more people on bikes. They combined the stability and durability of the classic balloon-tire roadsters with light-weight racing and touring components, plus the off-road features of moto-cross bikes. The Specialized Stump Jumper (1981) was the first mass-produced MTB, and its components were a global assemblage of specialty parts. The frame was specified for production in Taiwan, it had TA triple-chainring alloy cranksets, Mafac cantilever brakes from France, Tomaselli moto-cross brake levers from Italy, and SunTour derailleurs and thumb-shifters from Japan.

Mountain bikes were originally designed for off-road use, but their wide knobby tires, upright handlebar controls, and relaxed frame angles became popular for on-road touring and urban commuting, especially with the development of the hybrid design around 1987, a cross between mountain and road bikes. By 1990, the "fat tire" cult had reached around the world as MTBs were made in Europe, India, China, and Brazil, with a flourishing specialty parts market, the sport's first official UCI world championship, and a Hall of Fame museum in Colorado. In the U.S., mountain bike sales outnumbered all other types of adult bikes, and they became one of the few popular American manufactured exports.[21]

Crested Butte town bike, 1978.

Specialized StumpJumper, 1982.

Fisher's Mt. Tam.

Recumbents and HPVs

The next advancement in speed and comfort for the bicycle came with the development of recumbent cycles and human-powered vehicles (HPVs), the kinds of cycling machines that are driven in a seated position. As high performance vehicles, recumbents and HPVs have surpassed most of the speed and endurance records set on standard road racing bikes. As practical vehicles, recumbents and HPVs are dubbed as the next revolution in personal and public transport, with the most potential to replicate the protection and privacy of automobiles.

Recumbents and HPVs come in various designs that combine aspects of bikes, trikes and cars. They have two, three, or four wheels, often with aerodynamic, weatherproof enclosures, called fairings, with seats for one or more pedalers or passengers, sitting in recumbent positions, supine (belly-up), or prone (belly-down). While riding high-wheel and safety bikes in the upright position modeled after horseback riding, the rider's center of gravity is on top of the pedals, allowing a cyclist to apply body weight and handlebar leverage to assist the pedal force. Most recumbent cycles, however, seat the rider in a chair, in the position of driving a car, with the pedals in front and a backrest and handlebars for assisting the pedal force.

Recumbents branched out from the safety bicycle in the late 1890s, with the semi-recumbent "Bicyclette Normale" (1895) by Charles Challand of Geneva, Switzerland, the supine recumbent of 1896 by I.F. Wales in the U.S., and the prone position Darling recumbent of 1897. In 1901, an American named Brown built a 30-pound $100 recumbent with a long wheelbase. It was brought to England and reviewed in *The Cyclist*: "The machine runs light and is a good hill climber, and it is only fair to say that the general action of this queerest of all attempts at cycle improvements is easy and good—far better than its appearance indicates."[22]

Recumbent cycles became more popular in Europe around World War I. In 1914, the Union Cycliste Internationale (UCI) revised its racing rules, with Article 31 limiting bicycle dimensions (2 meters long, 75 centimeters wide) and prohibiting use of any "apparatus or device intended to reduce air resistance." That same year, Peugeot Cycles marketed a semi-recumbent bicycle, the Chaise or Arm-Chair cycle. Around 1920, the Swiss zeppelin maker Paul Jaray built the popular semi-recumbent J-Cycle in Stuttgart, using a foot-powered 3-speed swing-lever and cable-drive transmission. Soon, a variety of pedal cars and rowmobiles emerged with a new sport called cycle-car racing. In Germany, Manfred Curry built a streamlined sliding seat four-wheeler, called the Landskiff (land boat), used for racing, touring, and transport around town. Around 1930, Alexander Metz of Munich built single and tandem rowmobiles weighing 35 and 45 kilograms.

The bicycle revival of the 1930s saw more recumbent bicycles marketed,

Normal Bicyclette, 1895, by Charles Challand.

Peugeot Chaise, 1914.

J-Cycle, 1920, by Paul Jaray.

such as the short wheelbase Cycloratio (1934), the long wheelbase F.W. Grubb, the Triumph Moller with an automobile steering wheel, and the Kingston recumbent with handlebars under the seat. Charles Mochet of Puteaux, France, was a manufacturer of small motor cars who turned to making pedal cars after he built a single-seat four-wheeler for his son Georges. Around 1930, he made the affordable Velocar, an adult-sized two-seat three-speed four-wheeled pedal car with luggage space. Then, Mochet got the idea of cutting his vehicle in half, making a long wheelbase, laid-back recumbent bicycle, which he also called Velocar.

After tests showed the Velocar's potential, in October 1932 Mochet asked the UCI if his bike fit their rules. They referred him to Article 31 from the 1914 race rules, but made no judgment. Mochet figured it was allowed, so in the spring of 1933, riding the open Velocar recumbent, Paul Morand won the Paris-Limoges pro road race, and in July, François Faure broke the prestigious world hour record, riding 45.055 kilometers. The UCI formed a special technical commission to decide the legality of Mochet's Velocar, and on April 1, 1934, the commission set limits on the bicycle's dimensions to fit the safety design, and rejected Faure's record. These rules passed in the spirit of safety and fairness so racing would be a competition for riders rather than bicycle makers.[23]

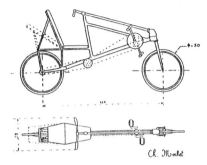

Mochet's Velocar bicycle patent, 1933.

UCI ARTICLE 49

—The distance between the axis of the crank and the ground shall be 24 cm minimum and 30 cm maximum.

—The distance between the vertical from the nose of the saddle and the axis of the crank must be less than 12 cm.

—The distance from the vertical passing through the center of the front wheel and the axis of the crank shall be 58 cm minimum and 75 cm maximum.

—The distance from the vertical passing through the center of the back wheel and the axis of the crank shall be equal to or less than 55 cm.

—Any propulsion using circular, alternating, or any other motion which utilizes the hands is forbidden. The use of protective shields, wind screens, fairings, and all other means of reducing air resistance is forbidden.

After Charles Mochet's death, his son Georges continued the pedal car business, selling about 1,000 vehicles per year. In 1938, Georges Mochet and Faure began testing a streamlined Velocar, and in March 1939 Faure covered 50.375 kilometers, a new human-powered vehicle hour record. When World War II broke out, Faure took a Velocar to Australia where streamlined races were happening. After the war, Mochet made motorized Velocars until 1960. Thirty years later a few original bicycle Velocars were still in use, rented by the hour at a park in Marseilles, and renovated for the Swiss Tour de Sol. Meanwhile, Georges Mochet made an appearance with his grandson, Sebastian, at an HPV event in Thamesmead, England.

Streamlined Velocar, 1939, powered by François Faure.

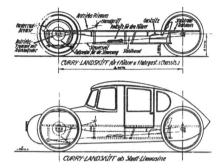

Curry Landskiff, 1930

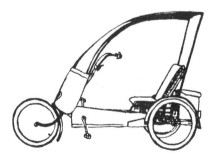

Easy Muscar, 1974,
by Paul Schondorf.

After World War II, bicycle ingenuity advanced in Europe, South Africa, Asia, and the U.S. In the 1960s, pedal car racing for youngsters flourished in Britain, Japan, and Hong Kong. In 1968, an international contest for human-powered land transport was organized by *Engineering Magazine* and David Gordon Wilson, a professor at the Massachusetts Institute of Technology (MIT) who co-designed the Avatar 2000 recumbent with Fred Willkie. The contest drew 74 entries from several countries, with first prize going to the Bicar, a fully faired short-wheelbase recumbent bicycle with sixteen-inch wheels, one of three vehicles built by W.G. Lydiard, a British aircraft engineer. Wilson wrote that "A problem identified by Mr. Lydiard with two-wheel reclining-rider bicycles is that either the wheelbase and overall length becomes excessive, or the legs must be positioned to pedal over the front wheel."[24]

THE HPV MOVEMENT

The human-powered vehicle movement came in the 1970s as bicycles sales were booming and concerns about energy use reached crisis proportions. As data showed bicycles to be the world's most energy-efficient way of moving a body, various scientific studies were applied to cycling, such as coast-down and wind tunnel tests that measure the mechanical and wind resistance of bicycles, known as the coefficient of drag or Cd. Using materials and methods of construction from the auto, aircraft, and aerospace industry, a group of engineers, professors, and "future-bike" enthusiasts from California and Europe began to revolutionize the human-powered vehicle.[25]

In 1974, Dr. Paul Schondorf of Cologne introduced a pair of all-weather recumbent tricycles called the Easy Muscar and the Muscabrio, which set the pattern for practical design. In Southern California, the first race was organized with fourteen entrants, who eventually founded the International Human-Powered Vehicle Association (IHPVA) in 1975. The rules were mostly open: recumbents, fairings, and hand-drives were allowed, but there could be no energy storage or generating device other than the human body. Top speed was the primary goal and the record went from 45 to 65 miles per hour in about ten years.

When three vehicles with seven riders (two tandems and a triplet) exceeded the 55 mph U.S. speed limit they were given honorary summons by the California Highway Patrol. These streamliners were built for multiple riders, such as the White Lightning, a 75-pound tandem recumbent tricycle built by Northrop University students, and the series of Vector cycles, developed by Al Voigt and engineers from General Dynamics and Versatron Corporation. Many experts believe these vehicles found the peak of human-powered possibilities.

The first Vector was a streamlined prone position triplet quadricycle with arm and foot drive. It was 22 feet long, weighed 100 pounds (600 pounds with riders) and had a drag coefficient of 0.14. Unlike bicycles, which can accelerate and peak out in about 200 meters, some HPVs take up to 1,000 meters to reach top speed. They were suitable mainly for the race track or open highway, since energy storage was not allowed by the IHPVA. By 1979, the next generation of Vectors were shorter supine tricycles, either single or in tandem with the riders back-to-back.

The single prone two-wheeler has the smallest frontal area and wind drag for an HPV, with an estimated 0.06 Cd. These were popular at first, with designs by Allan Abbott, Paul Van Valkenberg, and Gardner Martin, whose bicycle "Jaws" was the first to break the 50 mph barrier. With shark's teeth painted on the fairing, its uncomfortable, unstable design "ate" riders who crashed head first at full speed.

The supine recumbent position is recognized as the most comfortable and practical design, and numerous speed and endurance records prove its efficiency. These come in various formats, as bikes, trikes, and quadricycles, as tandems and triplets, with short and long wheelbases (SWB and LWB), with semi-recumbent and low-rider positions, and with front and rear wheel drives (FWD and RWD). Many practical recumbents evolved from HPV racing, such as the Easy Racer Tour Easy (1984) by Gardner Martin of Freedom, California, the Lightning P-38 and F-40 by Tim Brummer of Lompoc, California, and the Kingcycle Bean by Miles and John Kingsbury of Buckinghamshire, England. The Windcheetah Speedy by Mike Burrows of Norfolk, England is considered by many to be the most stable and ergonomically correct HPV tricycle. The trike costs about $5,700, plus $1,500 for the optional fairing.

There are about 1,000 cycle makers throughout the world offering recumbents and HPVs in 1995, with Germany, Britain, Holland, Denmark, and Switzerland as the hot seats in Europe. North American recumbent and HPV makers have been innovative and are having steady growth, though only about one percent of tourists use recumbents. Rounding out the global trend, there are HPV enthusiasts in Russia, Australia, and South Africa.

Easy Racer Tour Easy, 1985,
by Gardner Martin.

Kingcycle, 1990,
by Miles and John Kingsbury.

Windcheetah Speedy, 1994,
by Mike Burrows.

3 Bicycle Ingenuity

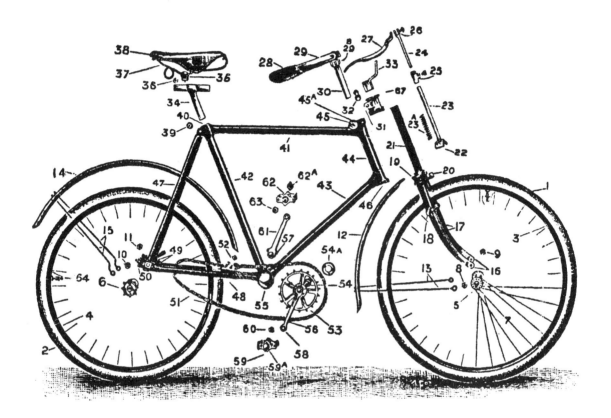

Exploded safety bicycle, 1900.

1, tire. 2, pneumatic tube. 3, spoke nipple. 4, rim. 5, front hub. 6, rear hub and gear cog (8 teeth). 7, spoke. 8–11, front and rear axle nuts. 12, front mudguard. 13, mudguard stays. 14, rear fender. 15, fender stays. 16, fork tips. 17, fork blades. 18, footrest. 19, fork crown. 20, brake mount. 21, steering tube. 22, plunger brake shoe. 23a, brake spring. 23, lower brake rod. 24, upper brake rod. 25, brake spring stop. 26, brake lever pivot. 27, brake lever. 28, handle-bar grip. 29, handlebar. 29b, handlebar-brake fitting. 30, stem tube. 31, headset assembly. 32, headset bearings. 33, head piece. 34, seatpost. 35, seat rail assembly. 36, seat rail nut. 37, saddle springs. 38, leather saddle. 39, seatpin bolt. 40, seat tube lug. 41, top tube. 42, seat tube. 43, down tube. 44, head tube. 45–45a. 46, lower head lug and headset assembly. 47, seat stays. 48, chain stays. 49, rear dropouts. 50, rear axle mounts. 51, inch-pitch chain. 52, miss-ing link. 53, chainwheel (18 teeth). 54, spindle, bottom bracket axle. 54a, bottom bracket. 55, bottom bracket lug. 56, chainwheel crank arm. 57, cotter pin crank assembly. 58, right pedal threading. 59, pedal. 59a, pedal bearing assembly. 60, right pedal axle nut. 61, left crank arm. 62, left pedal. 62a, pedal bearing nut. 63, left pedal axle nut. 64, tire valve.

The most beautiful things in the world are those from which all excess weight has been eliminated.
— Henry Ford (1893)

Human-Powered Technology

A continuing theme in the evolution of cycling machines is the ingenious spirit of humanity. Human-powered vehicles inspire a kind of inventiveness called "bicycle ingenuity," which is a special blend of resourcefulness, practicality, and "can do" optimism. Bicycles embody a human-scaled, mechanically contrived, self-sufficient way of doing things.

Many parts make the bicycle and many things make cycling machines special. Basic components of the Machine Age were created in the course of the bicycle's development, such as ball bearings, tangent spoked wheels, tubular steel frames, chain drive transmissions, air-filled tires, and differential axles. There is a continuous flow of ingenious new refinements in bicycle components, as many ideas are recycled from earlier generations, and new becomes old and new again. Most experts see three epic periods of bicycle ingenuity: the rush towards the Golden Age (1870 to 1900), the Bicycle Revival (1930 to 1950) and the ongoing Bike Boom (1970 to present).

Bicycle technology has a powerfully human aspect—in shape, use, form and function. Because cycling is such an efficient means of propulsion, bicycle technology inspires a unity of design, combining body, mind and machine. According to novelist Jerome K. Jerome in *Three Men on the Bummel* (1900), there are two ways to get exercise from a bicycle: you can overhaul it, or you can ride it. Jobst Brandt, an engineer for Porsche and Hewlett Packard, once said that he took to the bicycle so he could "have as much time using the machine as fixing it." Jobst spends much of his time designing components and teaching cycling. In his book *The Bicycle Wheel,* he says: "The bicycle enables us to escape many other machines; we use it for transportation, sport, recreation, and make it a way of life."[1]

Bicycle ingenuity inspires the idea of recycling, as used and throw-away bikes are often repaired in cooperative workshops by people learning a new trade, or who otherwise do not have access to new bikes. The bicycle is an essential technology for humanity, transporting people and cargo at minimal cost, offering people the closest thing to flight by their own power. Many philosophers of technology and society believe the bicycle is one of the highest forms of technology. At the Tech Museum of Innovation in San Jose, interactive displays show the six major "new" technologies of Silicon Valley, including bicycles, microchips, biotechnology, robotics, space sciences, and materials fabrication.[2]

Jobst Brandt cornering,
photo by Ted Mock for Avocet.

Materials and Components

There are about 1,275 individual parts that comprise the 25 functioning components on a 22-pound road bicycle.[3] About one-fourth of the 92 natural elements found on the Periodic Chart are used to make bicycles, and cycle makers have utilized nearly every natural material and many synthetic substances for production, including wood, metal, non-ferrous alloys, platings, plastics, rubbers, hides, fiber, oils, glues, and pigments used in frames, bearings, seats, wheels, tires, transmissions, tools, and accessories.

Today, more refined materials such as synthetic polymers, ceramics, and carbon composites are used in the bicycle. E.I. du Pont de Nemours & Company, known as DuPont, is probably the best-known marketer of man-made materials for cycling, with their "12 Key Cycling Products" including Nylon plastic, Kevlar fiber, Imron enamel, Teflon lubricant, Lycra fiber, Zytel plastic, Delrin coating, Hytrel elastomer, and Rynite polyester. In 1990, DuPont was the single largest industrial polluter in the United States, according to the Environmental Protection Agency, so there is a trade-off as material advances may negate the bicycle's environmental advantages.[4]

Bicycle components are made in various ways, depending on the material. The highest-quality aluminum parts are usually cold forged- or hot-forged, while average quality aluminum parts are gravity cast or melt-forged. CNC machining, in which parts are cut into shape by automation, is widely used for finishing parts and specialty components.

Cycling machines are compatible with the human dimension and their components require a particular mix of lightness and durability, rigidity and flexibility. Parts are designed around the size, strength, and endurance of variously equipped human bodies. They are usually constructed to exceed structural tolerances, known as the "factor of safety." Perhaps more than most machines, bicycles come close to approaching their breaking point. In most situations, the normal bicycle can serve its intended use for many years, while requiring only a handful of replacement parts. Abnormal bikes include the department store lemons, such as the "Huffy Puffy," that is an accident waiting to happen, and the "trick" racing bikes which have lightness at the expense of durability. For people of special size, like Jobst Brandt, who is two meters (6'7") tall and weighs 220 pounds, the tolerances of the bicycle must balance the heavy loads made. In much of the world, cycles are used to carry extra passengers or cargo, weighing up to a half ton, placing strains on racks, frames, wheels.

Terrain and weather conditions subject bicycles to stress. Notable trouble areas on roads include cobblestones, potholes and buckled pavement, high curbs, glass, debris, heavy rain, mud, sand, and salts. When bikes are left outdoors throughout the year, rust and corrosion weaken the steel and rubber parts. One story tells of a bicycle that survived Hurricane Hugo in 1989. In preparations for the storm, Charles Hunter Moss of St. Croix in

CRUSH THE ROCKS

CULL THE GOOD GRAINS

POWDERIZE THE CONCENTRATE

COOK THE PELLETS

MAKE MOLTEN IRON

PURIFY, THEN MAKE THE ALLOY IN AN ELECTRICAL FURNACE.

MAKE THE "BILLET"

Steel-making process, drawn by George Retseck, 1994 Bridgestone catalog.

the Virgin Islands secured his bike in a closet. When he returned three days later, the roof was blown off, and most of his house was devastated. Fortunately, the closet was still standing, his bike was intact, and the front wheel was spinning. His computer-cyclometer had recorded the storm, showing a maximum speed of 91 mph and a total trip distance of 2,800 miles.[5]

BICYCLE TESTING

There have been many attempts to test the strength of the materials used in bicycles. In the early years of bicycle development, mechanics combined the scientific theories of tension, compression, and torsion with trial and error methods carried out by practical use, as the breaking point of early components were discovered along the road. To explain the bicycle's relative strength, a variety of controlled experiments were made, such as crushing bearings, stretching chains, and the weight of dozens of men loaded on a saddle. By the 1890s there was a better understanding of materials and metallurgy, and a cyclograph, or dynamometer, was developed to measure pedal forces. Bicycle manufacturers employed automatic cycling machines to test strength and durability. Testing machines used weights to stress the structure of the frame and the components, with notched rollers simulating road bumps for the wheels, and twisting rotating masses to imitate human-powered pedal torque.

Today, a wider variety of materials are used in bicycles and there is more data on what constitutes materials failure. The factor of safety is generally based on the "ultimate tensile strength" (UTS) of a material, and the determining factor in a bicycle's durability is "fatigue." Many factors cause fatigue in bicycles, including low-cycle high-impact stress (crashing into a parked car), and high-cycle low-impact stress (riding on cobblestones). There is also the "stress concentration factor" where certain parts are joined, clamped, or threaded together with little relationship to the material's UTS. Most materials are rated by their density (weight in lbs./cubic inch), their stiffness (modulus of elasticity in millions of psi), and their strength (UTS in psi).

Today's high-tech fatigue-testing machines use electronic diodes which generate frequencies that simulate the stresses components are subjected to. Mountain bikes have inspired more testing, as rough trail riding can produce momentary jolts of up to ten G-forces at the handlebars. The bike testers at *Bicycling* magazine have several tools, including the Mobile On-Bike Suspension Tester (nicknamed MONSTER), a set of quartz accelerometers connected to circuit boards and a portable laptop computer.

Bicycle testing at Panasonic, 1980s.

Tullio Campagnolo,
on the Croce d'Aune, 1927.

Campagnolo Record
chainwheel and crank.

PARTS MAKERS

The world's best-known bicycle parts makers are Campagnolo and Shimano: Campagnolo supplies some of the highest quality road bike equipment, and Shimano dominates the mass market, especially mountain bikes. Tullio Campagnolo (1902–1983), maker of the most revered bicycle components for over 50 years, is credited with inventing and perfecting the quick-release mechanism for wheels, and the parallelogram derailleur. Born in the Italian *campagna*, he started bike racing around 1922 and was known as a good climber who entered such classics as Milan-San Remo and the Giro della Lombardia. In November 1927, while leading a race through the Dolomite mountains with freezing temperatures and falling snow, he punctured on the descent. As he tried to loosen the frozen wing nuts on his wheel, dozens of riders passed him by. Because of this experience, he designed a hollow axle quick-release hub which he made on a drill press in his father's hardware store and metal shop and sold to his fellow cyclists. Quick-release hubs soon came into wide use on road racing bikes.

Campagnolo's company, S.P.A. Brevetti Internazionali Campagnolo, eventually produced thousands of bicycle parts and tools, and diversified into components for motorcycles, autos, aircraft, and satellites. Bicycle components come in *gruppos*, which usually include headsets, hubs, cranksets, pedals, seat posts, brakes, and derailleurs. Campagnolo's top lines are called Record, Nuovo Record, Super Record, and C-Record. Other products include a magnificent wood-case tool set, including spanners, wrenches, and frame facing and cutting tools for English and Italian threading, a gold-plated bottle opener, and a rather sweet-smelling bicycle grease. Campagnolo also makes its own production and testing machines. Widely used by racers and aficionados of the finest, the C-Record Ergopower group cost over $1,500 in 1994, and the complete tool set cost $3,500.

In Campagnolo's glory days, people often wondered if the company's equipment was really worth the price, but almost any experienced cyclist needed no convincing. The fact that their components worked correctly was one of the few things in life that could be relied on. The name Campagnolo took on a mythic nature in cycledom. People spoke of a bicycle as being "100 percent Campagnolo," or "all Campy," which was impossible because the firm did not market frames, tires, seats (until 1992), and many other accessories. For one pundit, the thought of a Campagnolo frame "has an almost incestuous tone." Some Frenchmen described beautiful women as "*tout Campagnolo.*" The writer Arlene Plevin named her pet cat "Campy," calling it her "eight-pound component." Riders using inferior products would *Cramp-and-go-slow* rather than *Campagnolo*. Those brands were described by enthusiasts as "Campy replicas," "virtually identical to Campy at a two-foot distance," or "performs like Campy at half the price."

By the 1980s, Campagnolo's hold on high quality was becoming equalled by the world's largest bicycle component maker, the family-run Shimano Industrial Corporation of Osaka, Japan. Begun by his father Shozaburo Shimano who made casting reels for flyrod fishing, Keizo Shimano inspired the Shimano Iron Works to produce freewheels in 1921, its first bicycle component, followed by one-speed hubs in 1945, derailleurs in 1956, and three-speed hubs in 1957. After their father's death in 1958, the company passed to the Shimano brothers, Shozo, Keizo, and Yoshizo, who headed Shimano America. Instead of a lower-priced underdog, Shimano produced the Dura-Ace group which cost slightly less and functioned similarly to Campy. Breaking into the upper end of the American market, which was a bit less tradition-bound, was easier than making European cyclists change.

With the rise of mountain bikes, Shimano's Deore and XTR groups set the pace, followed by SunTour's XC-Pro. Campagnolo, run by Tullio's son Valentino, responded later with the Euclid, Centaur, and Record OR groups. As Campagnolo's reputation declined along with sales of road bikes, Valentino personally reinvested in his company with new manufacturing and service innovations, and by 1994 Campagnolo had reclaimed its top spot on the podium, albeit in the smaller road bike market. Meanwhile, Shimano had gobbled up an estimated 70 to 80 percent of the world's high-quality component market in 1993, with sales of 168.5 billion yen ($1.492 billion), and pretax earnings of 23.57 billion yen ($209.4 million).

Yoshizo Shimano.

Frames

The frame is "the skeleton, the heart, and the soul of the bicycle," and bikes are usually named by the frame makers, who often give it a model name and number, whether they are an individual builder or a corporate brand name. Bicycle frames come in a variety of shapes, materials, and methods of construction reflecting each bike's use, cost, and level of technology. In the early nineteenth century, the frames of swift-walkers and velocipedes were usually built as a single beam of carved wood or forged iron, with forks front and rear to support the wheels. In the 1870s, a major advancement in frames came with the development of hollow steel tubing. High-wheel bicycles had a simple structure: a single backbone tube joined at its top and tail with forks for the wheels. Multi-wheel cycles improved with hollow tubing, which reduced weight.

Safety bicycles required more structural complexity, as pedals were placed between the wheels. Straight-gauge hollow steel tubes were welded together in various patterns using lugs, pin-joints, tension wires, and tie-rods. Eventually the steel diamond frame, typified by the Humber safety bicycle of 1888, became the most common design. Recumbent bicycles, with their long and short wheelbases, required different steering angles and seating positions. Yet many more ingenious designs and mate-

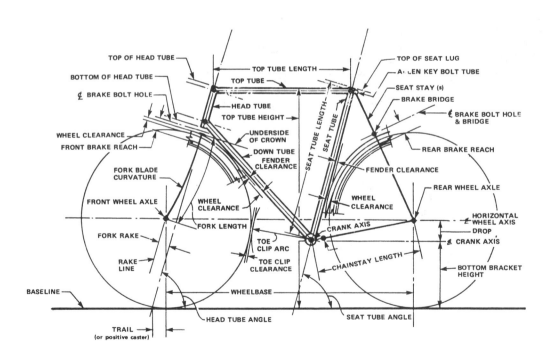

Frameset Geometry and Principle Design Elements by Richard Talbot,
from *Designing and Building Your Own Frameset.*

rials appeared in the frames of cycling machines in subsequent years.

BUTTED STEEL TUBING

In 1887, after several attempts to strengthen seamless tubing joints with smaller gauge reinforced linings, Alfred Milward Reynolds of Birmingham, England, invented the process known as tube butting. He formed the Patented Butted Tube Company, which made tubing exclusively for bicycles. During the 1890s, when manufacturing bicycles was the fastest growing industry in the world, nearly all tubing used in the world's quality bicycles came from Britain. Tubing developed in the U.S. in 1896, after annual bicycle sales passed a million. With the advent of automobiles, flying machines, and the first World War, the demand for high-quality steel tubing was huge.

In 1919, Angelo Luigi Colombo of Italy began making and selling steel tubing for a variety of products, including bicycles, motorcycles, ski poles, aircraft, and furniture. He supplied tubing for Marcel Breuer, designer of the tubular chair, who got his ideas from riding bicycles at the Bauhaus. By 1930, he began making butted tubing with the Columbus trademark. At the same time, the Patent Butted Tube Company renamed itself the Reynolds Tube Company, Ltd. Their best cycle tubing was named "HM" (some called it "Her Majesty") because the steel had a high manganese and low molybdenum content. Columbus and Reynolds are the best-known makers of quality double-butted tubing used on European touring and racing bicycles. For Columbus this was a chrome-molybdenum steel tubing with a large oval shaped fork blade. Reynolds became known for its 531 tubing, which ("five-three-one") refers to the ratio of its manganese and molybdenum steel alloy. Reynolds celebrated 531's Golden (50th) anniversary in 1985 with a commemorative decal, having by then made an estimated twenty million framesets. Here is a description of the butted tube making process as supplied by TI (Tube Investments) Reynolds:

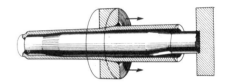

> For lightweight machines, whether for touring or racing, a "cold drawn seamless" tube is required—one which starts life as a solid ingot which is pierced hot, either in a hydraulic press, or by running it between inclined rollers which force it over a pointed mandrel, thus "pushing the hole through the bar." Further hot-rolling results in a "hollow" or "bloom," already looking like a tube, which goes to the seamless tube manufacturer to be cold drawn down to the diameter and gauge required.
>
> At every stage, each bloom is annealed (i.e., softened by heating), and pickled in acid to remove scale. Then one end is reduced to a smaller diameter, known as the "tag," to enable it to pass through the drawing die. After lubricating with a special compound of oil, soft soap, and other ingredients, it is ready for drawing. Drawbenches come in a variety of sizes, some being mighty monsters over a hundred feet long, with the die-plate nearly halfway along.
>
> The bloom is slipped over a shaped plug on a long mandrel bar, fixed to the end of the drawbench, the tag is pushed through the die and

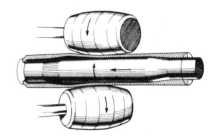

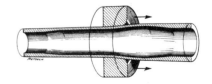

How tubes are butted,
from Bridgestone catalog, 1994.

Fork crown and bottom bracket shell.

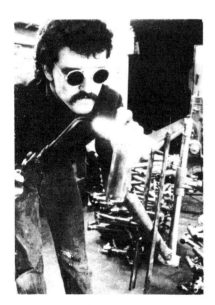

Tom Ritchey, master framebuilder.

gripped relentlessly by serrated steel jaws, known in the tube trade as "dogs." These are mounted on a "wagon," running on a track containing a large continuous multiple-roller chain, to which the wagon is automatically locked when the dogs have gripped the tag, thus drawing the tube through the die, and over the plug on the end of its mandrel. As this has moved to a position within the die, the metal is in effect squeezed between the die and the plug, thus reducing both diameter and thickness, and at the same time increasing the length. Several such "passes" [known as "Pilgrim's Progress"—two movements forward, one movement back], interspersed with annealing and pickling operations, are necessary before the tube is the right diameter and gauge, accurate to within three-thousands of an inch, for the manufacturer of the frame tubes, forks, and stays for your new bicycle.[6]

Other tubing makers include Ateliers de la Rive (Rubis, Durifort, Vitus, and Super-Vitus), and Gautier Trousell (AHR) from France; Falk from Italy; Tange (Mangaloy 2001), Ishiwata (Alpha), and Day and Day from Japan; Mansmann from Germany; and Ritchey (Logic), Easton (ProGram, TaperWall), and True Temper (RC, AVR,) from the U.S.

FRAME BUILDING

In the art of frame building there are two basic methods of assembling steel tubes: welding or brazing with or without lugs. The sources of heat include an open hearth, a molten bath, an oxygen-gas torch, an electric arc welder, or an inert gas welder. Temperatures range from 850°F to 2,600°F, depending on the methods and materials used. The frame lug is a cast or pressed metal sleeve which joins tubes and provides a bonding area for the melted silver, brass, or bronze alloy brazing material which comes in rod, ring, powder or paste form. Tubes are cut or mitered to fit each other and set into position with the desired angles on a frame jig. The lug area is heated, usually to about 1,300°F, and the brazing material flows or "sucks" into the lug joint (called fluction). In both brazing and welding, the temperature and rate of cooling are critical, since re-heated tubes lose strength. After cooling, lugs can be cleaned, filed, and tapered. Some lugs are pre-cut with artistic shapes bearing the maker's trademark such as stars, spades, clubs, hearts, diamonds, clovers, *fleurs de lis*, and other fancy filigree.

Frames without lugs are found at the top and the bottom of the market in cost and quality. Tubes are welded or fillet brazed (pronounced "fill-it"), with the brazing alloy melted around the joined tubes. Sometimes internal liners are used. Achieving a strong and clean lugless fillet braze with little or no filing is considered the peak of the framebuilder's art. Steel alloys continue to be the choice for both mass-production and custom frame building. Tube makers have developed tubes with ridges, grooves, splines, and in oval, square, diamond, and cube-shaped cross-sections.

Beyond Steel

Just as there was a growth of bicycle ingenuity in the 1880s and 1890s, when safety bicycles found their optimal form, a similar growth of ingenuity has been taking place today, with new frame materials and bike designs derived primarily from motorcycle, automobile, aircraft and aerospace technology. Materials such as aluminum, titanium, and carbon composites are appearing increasingly in high-quality and mass-market frames. The whole family of cycling machines, including aero-bikes, mountain bikes, portable bikes, and recumbents are incorporating these "post-modern" materials for frames, suspension systems, fairings, and folding features.

Aluminum frames first appeared on the market in the 1890s with the Beeston Humber and Cycles Aluminum models with aluminum tubes and steel lugs, and the Lu-Mi-Num bicycle with a one-piece cast frame. The use of aluminum tubing continued through the 1930s, but because brazing was impractical, lugs were used with internal plugs, threadings, clamping pins, and bonding glues. Some tubes were octagonal-shaped, as on the French Caminargent, and others followed the curving lines of the classic streamliner bicycle, like the American Silver King.

Since the 1970s, millions of aluminum alloy frames have been produced. Some makers use over-size tubes welded and heat-treated, such as Klein and Cannondale frames from the U.S. Other makers use standard-sized tubes, threaded and bonded to lugs, as on the Italian Alan or French Vitus frames. Some call this process "screwed and glued." Aluminum is comparably priced, non-corrosive, and lightweight, but in bicycle frames it is not easy to repair and it is said to lack the flexible feeling of a steel frame.

Titanium is another non-ferrous metal used in the highest quality bicycle frames. It combines high strength and cost, light weight, resilience, and anti-corrosion, but it is a relatively rare material and requires an oxygen-free welding environment such as tungsten inert gas (TIG) welding. Frames of pure titanium first appeared around 1956 with the Speedwell bicycle. The Teledyne Titan was developed in 1974 by Barry Harvey with the Teledyne-Linair aerospace company. Eventually, titanium alloys such as 3/2.5 (three percent aluminum and 2.5 percent vanadium) became the most common tube material used in bike frames. By 1994, dozens of titanium frames were available, with the some of finest made in the U.S. by Merlin from Massachusetts, and Lightspeed from Tennessee.

Composite materials have the most promise for the future of cycling machines, since they offer "unlimited design applications" and can be molded into various shapes depending on the structure and components of the bike. Carbon fiber composites can be made light, strong, shock absorbent, aerodynamic, and functional. The technologies of their design and manufacture are growing and still relatively expensive for cycle frames. The price of composite materials is falling ($500 per pound in 1970, $100 in 1975, $15 in 1990). Most quality bike makers have marketed

composites, including Giant (Cadex), Schwinn (Cycle Composites), Miyata, Peugeot, Look, Trek, Specialized, Cinetica, Kestrel, Vitus, and TVT.

Carbon fiber composites are assembled by combining layers of synthetic petroleum-based graphite, carbon, or boron fibers with a matrix material, epoxy resin, which is chemically cured and hardened. Carbon fibers used for frames are made in long continuous uni-directional layers. DuPont's Kevlar aramid fiber (1976) is a kind of polyphenylene terephthalamide. More kinds of fibers are becoming available, such as Spectra by Allied Fibers, as advanced military materials trickle onto Main Street. Fiber structure can be modeled with computer-aided-design (CAD) and computer-aided-manufacturing (CAM), allowing the proper choice of fiber density and strand direction before construction. High modulus fibers have nearly double the stiffness per weight as steel. Thermoplastic composites combine the fiber and matrix in a way that allows a stronger, more versatile material. Some composite frames are built with standard size tubes and bonded into steel or aluminum lug joints, such as the Exxon Graftek aluminum-graphite frame (1978). Others, like the Kestrel 500 EMS, have a one-piece monocoque or unibody frame, offering improved aerodynamics. This brings a new way of looking at bicycle design, by incorporating modular components and accessories into the monocoque frame unit.

Many kinds of non-metal materials have been used in cycle frames. Bicycle makers used woods, such as ash, hickory, oak, bamboo, and mixed laminates, continuously through the 1930s. During World War II, steel tubing was in great demand for the military, so the use of wood became a patriotic duty until higher production costs and the need for more wood in the war brought back steel frames in rationed quantities. These days, wood appears on bikes mainly as a luxury or a novelty. One of the finest wooden bikes is the "Campagnolo equipped" 12-speed racing bicycle made entirely of wood by Jean-Claude Palazzo of Cavaillon, France. It took about 600 hours of work to make the replica, which includes wooden spokes, brake cables, and chain links.

Various molded plastics and polymers, such as glass-reinforced nylon, have been used for portable folding bikes and children's models, and home-made frames sometimes have polyvinyl chloride (PVC) tubing. Yoshifumi Kato of the Japan Bicycle Technical Center recently built a prototype composite frame using washi handmade paper and epoxy resin. Advances in metallurgy have produced blends called metal matrix composite, with metallic materials stiffened and strengthened by fibers or non-metal particles, such as aluminum and aluminum oxide. Boralyn, a bulletproof ceramic composite made for the U.S. military and Univega mountain bikes, consists of boron carbon, aluminum, nickel and titanium. In advertising this declassified top-secret material, the company claimed: "We can tell you how we made it, but then we'd have to kill you."

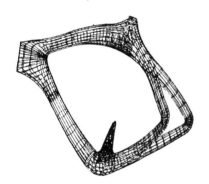

CAD (computer-aided design) drawing of Cinetica composite frame.

SUSPENSION

Suspension systems have been built on all kinds of bikes and cycles since the 1860s. They are designed to absorb ground shocks by suspending either the bike or the rider, as part of the forks, frame, wheels, and cargo platforms, or in the load-carrying components that support the rider, such as seats, seat posts, and handlebar stems. Suspension provides the practical benefits of better traction, less fatigue, and more comfort, especially on rough terrain. Yet many suspension systems have drawbacks, such as less torque, more bounce, and extra weight. Suspension has been a popular feature on luxury bikes and a new craze on mountain bikes, with ongoing improvements in fork and frame suspension systems that allow faster and smoother riding, especially for downhill racing.

One measure of a suspension is the distance it can travel before it stops, or "bottoms out." Pre-load is the amount of spring tension in an unloaded bike, usually set according to the rider's weight. On rigid bikes without suspension (or suspension bikes "locked out" in fixed positions) cyclists generally use their arms and legs as a "live suspension" with several inches of travel, especially when standing on the pedals. Mechanical suspension systems, which average three inches of maximum travel, help reduce body fatigue on long rides by absorbing small bumps, dissipating the shock of deep ruts, and keeping the tires more firmly planted on the ground. On pavement, suspension tends to make a bike safer to handle, but slower to accelerate and often bouncier pedaling uphill.

Various suspension systems developed as offspring of the diamond-frame safety bikes of the 1880s, when tires were hard and roads mostly unpaved. Coil and lever springs were the most common means of absorbing bumps in the road. Other inventions include double-blade rocker-arm forks, hydraulic seat tubes, swing-mounted rear triangles cushioned by coil springs or rubber dampers, and spring-load wheel fittings. Bicycle makers adopted some designs from motorcycles around 1910, later applying them to the classic balloon-tire bicycles of the 1930s. Shock absorbers became a deluxe accessory on front forks, with spring-loaded, rubber damped rocker arms, or coiled steel damped by air/oil chambers.

The 1960s brought advances with Alex Moulton's small-wheel bicycles, which used a front shock and a damping rubber on the rear chainstay, offering mushy acceleration but a smooth, stable-tracking ride. Various bronco-style bicycles, such as the Schwinn Apple Krate, used spring-loaded rubber-damped shocks on the front forks and on "sissy bars" holding up banana seats. The Swing Bike had a spring-loaded parallelogram frame for two-track curbside riding. BMX bikes have appeared with rear triangle suspension systems, such as the Gobby Moto-Cross bike with rocker-arm stays that swing on a steel spring mounted behind the seat tube.

Bicycle ingenuity is in full swing as mountain bikes have inspired considerable progress in suspension systems, making them popular high-end products for the bike industry. The pioneers began by recycling some of

Whippet bicycle with spring frame.

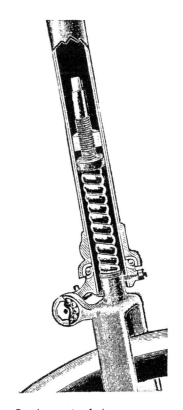

Peerless spring fork.

the old features from balloon-tire cruisers, such as the Knee-Action spring fork of the 1949 Schwinn Autocycle. Suspension hit the mass market in the late 1980s, as more and more designers of motorcycle suspension entered the mountain bike realm. Front fork shock systems include steel coils, air/oil chambers, plastic elastomer cartridges, and elastomer/oil tubes. These are usually located in the forks, between the stanchion tubes fixed to the crown and the sliding tubes fixed to the wheel. Makers of fork shocks include Rock Shox, Manitou, Marzocchi, RST, and ATP. On the Cannondale Headshok, the elastomer spring is above the fork crown inside the steering tube.

Rear suspension systems are more complex because they are part of the frame and the transmission system. To separate shock absorption from pedaling action—so the suspension helps, not hinders the cyclist—is considered the Holy Grail of a full suspension bike. Rear suspension comes in various formats, characterized by the positions of the pivot points relative to the chain line. In high pivot systems, the pedal force extends the suspension components, and the chain force swings the chainstay downward for better traction. This usually shortens the chain line, producing a power-absorbing, rhythmic fore-aft motion known as pedal surge or "biopacing" (after Shimano's Biopace oval chainwheels). On low pivot systems, the pedal force compresses the suspension, with forward pivots more in line with the chain to remedy pedal surge, or with pivots placed near the bottom bracket providing limited travel. Multiple pivot systems combine several linkages instead of a single swingarm in various configurations. Unified rear triangle systems are considered the best format, with the chain line in a rigid frame that pivots at a carefully-measured point in the middle of the frame.

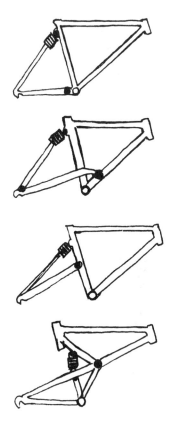

Rear suspension (top to bottom): low pivot behind bottom bracket; low pivot along chain line; high pivot; central pivot with unified rear triangle.

Trek dual suspension mountain bike.

Bearings

Ball bearings—the atoms of the machine age—were first developed for the bicycle. Ball bearings reduce the coefficient of friction to such an extent that with the bicycle they brought about what philosopher Ivan Illich called a "fourth revolution in transport," the first three being the wheel, the horseshoe and stirrup, and the ocean-going vessel.[7] Before ball bearings appeared, plain sleeve bearings made of wood, leather, iron, brass or steel were common with swift-walkers and velocipedes. The first roller and ball bearings, called anti-friction roller bearings, were patented by E.A. Cowper. The majority of patents for fixed and adjustable bearings were applied to bicycles during the 1870s and 1880s. As wheels, pedals, crank axles, and headsets were developed, the cup and cone ball bearing design was likewise refined.

By the 1890s, the first mass-production of ball bearings was begun by Friedrich Fischer of Germany, whose father Philip built an early velocipede. A later innovation was the bearing ring which holds the balls in their separate positions and prevents their loss when repacking. Other designs include cartridge bearings with fixed settings (1890s), made for easy removal; sealed bearings with nylon bushings (1940s), to keep them weatherproof; hardened plastic balls (1970s), for planned obsolescence; and needle bearings (1990s), for greater loads.

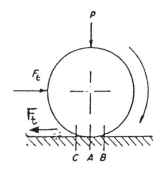

When a set of wheel bearings are properly adjusted so that the load is in equilibrium between tight and loose, their rolling resistance is small compared to other factors in cycling, such as friction in the chain transmission, rolling resistance of tires, wind resistance, the gradients of terrain, and the cyclist's fitness. One ingenious trick to reduce hub friction, known as "track slack," involves removing one ball bearing from the hub and replacing the grease with a lightweight oil. It is suitable only for short cycling events because the bearings quickly wear out.

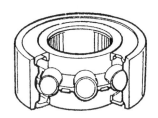

LUBRICANTS

In the early days, bicycle lubricants were derived from natural products. In the 1860s, Sawyer's Velocipede Manufactory recommended using "the best Salad Oil for the bearings," and in 1880 one of the "Golden Rules for Bicycle Riders" was "Never use any oil but the best sperm." After the whales were driven to near-extinction, petroleum became the most common ingredient in bicycle lubricants, with additives such as graphite, lithium, aluminum, silicon, and citrus oils. Du Pont's 100% Teflon bike lubricant reduces friction, displaces oil, bonds to metal components, and won't decompose. At $12.95 for eighteen grams, or $300 per pound, it is one of the most expensive materials in the bike industry.

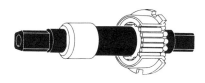

Bearings (top to bottom): loose balls; pressure points; sealed cartridge bearing; needle bearing.

Steering

The balancing act that enables the art of cycling has caused many people to stop and ponder on the gravity of the phenomenon. This is because there is such a big difference between theory and practice. More than any other aspect of cycling, the idea of balancing and steering is related to complex physics, mathematics, and even metaphysics. "So perfect is the safety bicycle," reported *Scientific American* in 1896, "that, if the rider has sufficient skill not to interfere with its action, it will travel straight ahead and keep its own balance."

In a way, learning to ride a bike comes fairly easily for people of all ages since it is one of those things that becomes intuitive. In another way, understanding how it happens is a scientific mystery, a subject involving fourth-order, non-linear, partial differential equations with variable coefficients that have yet to be completely solved.[8] So it seems that scientific theory cannot keep up with the "sixth sense" of steering a bicycle. Most explanations use the metaphor of balancing a broomstick, as shown in the following examples, over one hundred years apart.

From *Popular Science* (April 1891):

> There is something uncanny in the noiseless rush of the cyclist, as he comes into view, passes by, and disappears. The apparent ease and security of his movement excites our wonder. Most of us have tried to walk on the top rail of a fence and have a vivid recollection of the tossing of arms and legs to keep our balance and the assistance we got from a long stick or a stone held in our hands. But the cyclist gets no help. We must ask them, how is it possible for one supported on so narrow a base to keep his seat so securely and, seemingly, so without effort? Gyration has nothing to do with it; centrifugal force has no application to it, except when turning corners, or otherwise changing abruptly the direction of the movement; balancing is a detriment rather than an assistance; and rapid motion alone accounts for nothing. Some other explanation is needed.
>
> The stability of the bicycle is due to turning the wheel to the right or left, whichever way the leaning is, thus keeping the point of support under the rider, just as a boy keeps upright on his finger a broomstick standing on the smallest end.

From Mike Burrows' article, "Riding High, Riding Low," *Bike Culture Quarterly* (December 1993):

> Some things need to be drawn before they can be designed and understood. Others need to be "made," and the bicycle, I would argue, is the classic exmple of the latter. This is because it is inconceivable that the principles involved in the riding of a bicycle could ever be theorized

first. It is far more likely that the principles of balance as related to the bicycle, were discovered by someone playing around with things with wheels on. These principles are by now quite well understood, although apparently still a problem for computers to analyse. Put simply, a cyclist proceeds in a series of "falls" that are compensated for by steering the bicycle back under the centre of gravity. This is all done quite automatically by us clever apes, and, we are told, it is a skill once learned never forgotten.

The best way to visualize this is to try to balance a stick vertically on your finger tip: long sticks are easy, short ones are not. This disparity is especially noticeable when cycling at low speeds, where the safety has a definite advantage. At higher speeds the problem of a low centre of gravity diminishes as the required lateral movement is correspondingly faster, whereas the "fall" occurs at the same rate.

When you steer a safety bicycle it is very largely a matter of leaning or moving your weight: handlebar movement seems almost secondary, at least when gentle manoeuvring is required. If it were not for the need to be able to stop occasionally we could ride safety bicycles most places no hands. Not on a recumbent! Recumbents do not lean-steer in the usual way, and require much more positive use of the handlebars.

The problem in making suitable equations to define bicycle steering is that there are too many interrelated parameters and ridable configurations. In researching the subject of bicycle stability, Jim Papadopoulos, an engineering professor and bicycle-HPV designer, found 25 equations that attempted to define the phenomenon. Only in five of these were the mathematics considered to approach accuracy, and none fully described the subtle interactions of the body and mind, the geometry of bicycles, the conditions of terrain and weather, and the relativity of gravity.

David E.H. Jones, a British research scientist, went about the problem backwards. He wanted to understand the physics of riding a bicycle and why it is so stable, so he decided to build a bicycle that was "completely devoid of stability." Jones called the project Urb (for Unridable bicycle). He built four "Urbs," and one was more stable than a standard bicycle. Urb I was to test the gyroscopic forces generated by the front steering wheel, which Jones thought might keep the bike stable in the same way a spinning top keeps itself upright as long as it revolves fast enough. Jones mounted an additional front wheel to the forks which would spin freely just above the ground, but no matter which way the extra wheel was spinning—backward or forward—the bike still rolled merrily along.

Urb II explored the possibility that the size of the wheel had some effect on stability, so Jones mounted a small furniture caster wheel on a long straight fork. This test was inconclusive because the caster got red hot and could not negotiate bumps on the road larger than half an inch.

Urb III found the correct hypothesis, that the bicycle's stability depends on the relative positions of the steering column and the front wheel axle, defined as an amount of trail. He built Urb III with standard

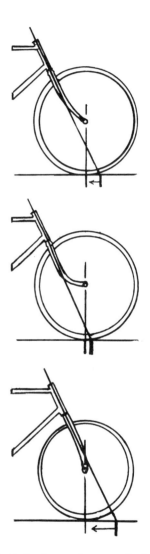

Trail: the distance between the front wheel axle and the steering axis where they intersect the ground.
Safety bikes have 50 mm trail; trikes and long recumbents almost zero; stunt bikes about 100 mm.

raked front forks reversed, so the wheel axle was behind the imaginary line projecting down from the steering column. Jones' Urb III was even more stable than a typical bike, because Jones searched for the bicycle's stability in its instability, requiring fewer balancing adjustments to maintain equilibrium. In fact, Urb III was similar to stunt bikes used by circus performers and cycle ball players, and demi-fond bikes used by motor-paced racers.

Jones finally turned to a computer and in accordance with the computer's instructions, Urb IV had an extra long curving front fork rake, with the wheel axle mounted four inches forward of its standard position. The bicycle toppled over every time he tried to ride it. Jones is aware of the irony in his work as he said, "It seems a lot of tortuous effort to produce in the end a machine of absolutely no utility whatsoever, but that sets me firmly in the mainstream of modern technology." He went on to make a self-balancing bike that can go forever, given a straight, gently descending road.

The steering of tricycles and quadricycles have different variables, depending on which wheels do the turning. In the 1890s, Ackermann developed principles of geometrically correct steering based on the theory that the front wheels of a vehicle must turn along peripheries of two different-sized circles, which have a common center point that must be in line with the rear axle. Independently of Ackermann's patent, the Swedish brothers Birger and Fredrik Ljungström constructed a similar system in their 1894 Svea rickshaw.

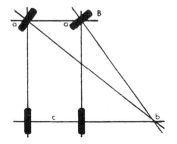

Ackermann's steering principle for tricycles and quadricycles: the axis of front steering wheels should intersect the rear axle at the same point.

Unridable bikes by David Jones.

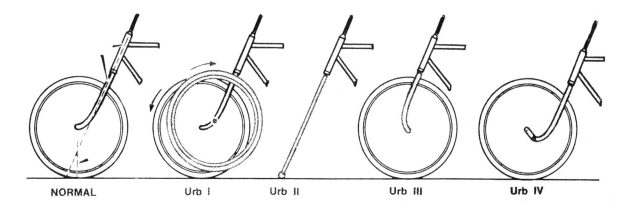

NORMAL Urb I Urb II Urb III Urb IV

HANDLEBARS

Like the curves in the roads, the bends and twists in handlebars take many turns. The high-wheel craze brought the first wave of ingenuity for handlebars. Straight bars were replaced by horn-shaped bars that offered more positions and shock absorption, and came equipped with a lever and link to the brake. When a high-wheeler hit a rut in the road, the rider tended to flip head first over the handlebars, and bars like the Whatton were designed to keep the rider's feet first when falling. The Lillibridge Safety Bar had a lever and spring release allowing it to detach from the stem as the rider's legs fell forward in an accident. Gormully and Jeffery offered the Perfect-Fit Grip, which was formed for "the horny hand of every cyclist."

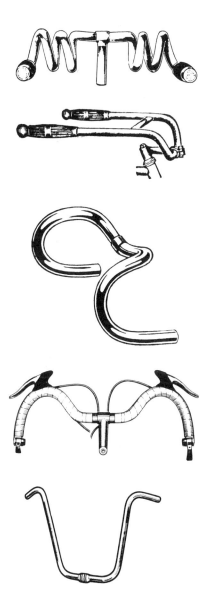

In early safety bicycles, handlebars of chrome steel began to take on their typical swept-back shape, curved down for scorchers and racers. Alternatives included the steam-bent hickory wood bars, the spring-loaded ratchet Ridgeway Instantaneous Adjustable bars, spiraled Ram's Horn bars, and the Duplex combining the upright and racing shaped bars with four handle-grips. The Chapman Automatic-Steering safety let the hips do the turning, with the seat tube attached to the front fork. Regular handlebars were fixed to a "direct stem" which evolved into forward extensions that were sometimes of adjustable length. Grips were made of leather, ivory, vulcanite, rubber, natural cork, and molded "Corkaline," and end caps came in decorative colors and patterns, with attachments like bells, turning flags, or "secret" compartments. In 1901, a handlebar gas generator was developed to fuel an acetylene lamp, with two chambers on each grip for water and carbide.

Handlebars have come in many shapes through the years, some whose form followed function, and others with function following fashion. Some handlebars projected a particular style, and cyclists occasionally positioned them according to their own individual bent. On standard adult bikes, the *guidons* took on a sort of winged human form, inspiring some men to wear their moustaches shaped like their handlebars, known as the handlebar moustache. About a hundred years later, moustache handlebars were a retro feature on bikes by Bridgestone and Ibis. Sport bikes acquired their hook shaped bars with a variety of subtle bends for sprinting (pista), road racing (maes), and touring (randonneur). These allowed the rider to take the bike by the horns, and face any situation.

American youngsters used stylized bike handlebars, often emulating those on motor vehicles, like the popular longhorn-style Motorbike bars with the additional cross-brace as on motorcycles. Steering Wheel handlebars, with a battery-powered horn, mimicked an automobile, and hi-rise, chopper-style Butterfly bars, with plastic grips and multi-colored glittered streamers, were popular in the 1960s. These evolved into BMX bars with "knee-saver" foam or polystyrene pads, moto-cross brace, and race number placard.

Most modern bars are made of aluminum. Others use steel tubing,

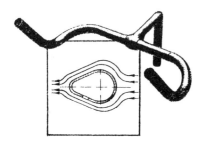

titanium, or composite materials. The current wave of innovation in handlebar design includes a return to straight bars for mountain bikes, with a variety of L-bends, adjustable ratchet-joint grips, and curving "outbcard" designs with aero-bar positions. Recumbent bikes use both chopper-style bars and under-the-seat bars.

Aero-bars and tri-bars are a major innovation for bikes used in time trials, triathlons, and touring. They come in various shapes, such as the simple, curved-up wing shape, with two hand positions, on the grips and near the stem. These are anatomically designed, such as the Profile Airwing, or home-made from standard racing bars turned downside-up with half the hook cut out. Scott-style aero-bars are forward-extending, narrow, U-shaped bars with padded armrests that come as a single unit or clip-on to standard bars. These offer cyclists greater leverage and less wind resistance, and a riding position likened to a praying mantis. Platforms allow riders to comfortably rest the upper body on forearms, to save energy and reduce fatigue. Because the hands are in a narrow, forward position there is less control and stability on rough roads.

Scott's chief designer, Boone Lennon, has extended handlebar design with the drop-in (1989) and drop-on (1993) bars which provide a second position below the tops. One hybrid design is the Profile Airstryke which combines the wing shape with an adjustable forward platform position. Other innovations include the Girvin Flexstem, a stem suspension system that softens the bumps with a pivoting stem using elastomer dampers, and the Modolo Twin 777, a handlebar and stem system with adjustable width and length.

Handlebars also provide a mounting platform for many components and accessories, such as brake levers, gear shifters, bells, horns, water bottles, pannier bags, map clips, and radios. Instrument panels appear on kids bikes, exercycles, aero-bikes, and others. Cycle computers calculate speed (maximum and average), distance (trip and total), time, pedal cadence (rpms), heart rate (beats per minute), and altitude (measured by air pressure). Yet there is no device to measure a cyclist's attitude.

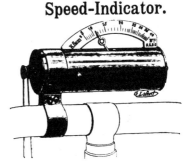

Speed-Indicator.

Seats

Being the bicycle's counterpart to the body's fundamental contact point, the bicycle seat is one of those parts that has been the butt of a good laugh, and the brunt of much suffering. Bicycle seats offer new ways of sitting as inventors have attempted to make a perfect ergonomic, hygienic, and anatomic saddle.

The bicycle seat evolved from the horse's saddle to become an active component of a cyclist's suspension system. The variety of forms include suspended hammocks, spring-loaded saddles, side-saddles, hygienic and anatomic shapes, two-piece seats, cushions filled with air, water, or gels, bucket seats, and chaises. Leather hammock saddles made of cowhide, pigskin, or sealskin were the most popular, until plastics and foam took over after World War II. Leather is cut out of tanned butt hides, according to its grain and thickness, then soaked in warm water and pressed into the familiar shape. After evaporation and dyeing, the "blank" is brass-riveted to the cantle or heel bar and stretched across the rail to the nose.

Brooks saddles, such as the B-33, have been considered the epitome of the leather hammock. With its prominent coils at the nose and braided wire springs under the rear, the B-33 was a status symbol in many countries. J.B. Brooks was a leather goods manufacturer who began making bicycle saddles in 1866 when his horse died, and a neighbor loaned him a bike on which he suffered the most uncomfortable ride he'd ever had.[9]

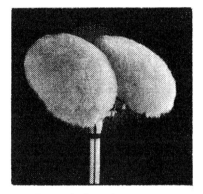

Easy Seat with sheepskin cover.

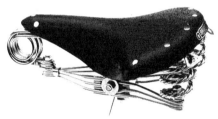

Brooks B-33 saddle, with braided wire rear springs and large front coil.

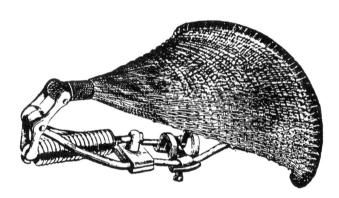

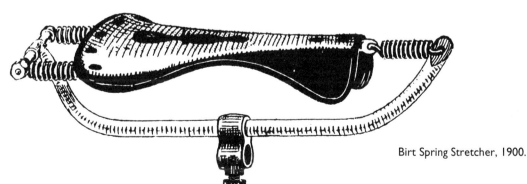

Birt Spring Stretcher, 1900.

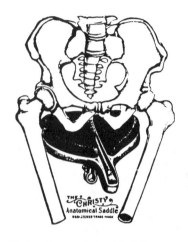

Christy Anatomical, with sit bones.

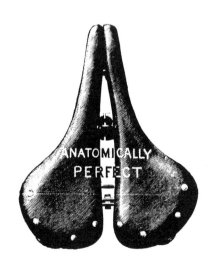

Other ingenious seats include such classics as the side-saddle on velocipedes for chaste Victorian women, and the wide-load heavy-duty mattress-covered spring saddle, which is probably the most comfortable and least efficient. The Lever Hammock saddle had woven-cords stretched by a spring-loaded nose. The Safety Poise, a large doughnut-shaped saddle with a hole in the middle like a toilet seat, claimed to "bring the pressure where it belongs."

The narrow Stretcher saddle with exposed springs was popular for "scorchers," who perhaps needed a pinch to be sure they were not in heaven or hell. For those not inclined to speed, the platform seat, made of steel or aluminum plate, was mounted on rubber dampers and had a form-fit shape with ventilation holes. The appearance of pneumatic seats in the 1890s came with problems of heat build-up, and the tendency of the rider to bounce around without the proper amount of inflation. Pneumatic tires absorbed some road shocks, so seats could be harder, but there was still room for perfection. A general rule was formulated whereby "your seat should be as hard as your tires." In *Three Men on the Bummel*, Jerome K. Jerome offers a bit of wisdom: "There may be a better land where bicycle saddles are made of rainbow, stuffed with cloud; in this world the simplest thing is to get used to something hard."

Physician-cyclists began to develop anatomically-correct saddles around 1890, based on the contact points of the cyclist's pelvic region. A $25 "plaster-cast self-adjusting nature-fitting saddle" was designed for Lillian Russell and was used by other ladies of the Golden Age. The typical anatomic saddle had a pair of "kidney shaped" padded areas on the seat for both the male and female pelvic structure. Anatomic seats are popular today, with saddle padding made of molded foam and sacs of viscous gel, such as the Avocet Touring Gel seat. Various patented chemical concoctions have appeared for padding, such as Florite and Biosoft.

An offspring of the anatomic shape is the two-piece seat, with contraptions such as Oyler's Anatomic with toothed hinges down the middle, or Bray's Moveable Saddle with swiveling pear-shaped halves. Almost a hundred years later, a sheepskin-covered variation appears with the Easy Seat and optional Shock Post, a rubber-damped seatpost. Other kinds of cycling machines such as sociables, tricycle rickshaws, and supine recumbent cycles require seats with backs. Options include upholstered bucket seats, and chairs with hard foam pads, or stretched canvas, as on director chairs. In prone-position HPVs, the rider's front hip bones are supported on small padded benches.

Bicycle seats have a character unlike any other bicycle component. This personality is found in various parodies, such as the inventor of "the first unicycle with an edible seat," the Bidet-Saddle with hot and cold running water pumped by the saddle springs, and the Ejector Seat inspired by those used in airplanes.[10]

Playful ingenuity reflects the reality and possibilities of the consumer market. The Banana seat backed by a "sissy bar" became popular in the 1960s. The Bummer saddle has a suede naugahyde pad slung between an aluminum frame mounted on roller bearings. The Harpoon saddle was booby-trapped with a spring-loaded knife to sabotage bicycle thieves. On the Psychiatrist's Couch, a side-car pedicab built by George Bliss from 100% recycled New York City trash, the shrink cycles as the patient reclines on a soft chaise. Bicycle seat covers come from various species (some endangered), including alligator, leopard, elephant hide, snakeskin, and kid glove. A Wild West motif appears on a saddle by Mountain Goat, with genuine cowhide, chrome buttons, and foot-long leather fringe. Comfy-Buns covers have crushed-velvet with foam, and a Hydro-Chamber cover has water-filled cushions.

Seat posts also have an ingenious character, as several kinds of adjustable seatposts developed, for shifting the seat up-and-down, or back-and-forward. The Hi-Rite spring was developed by Joe Breeze for mountain bikes, for quickly raising and lowering the seat position. The Seat Shifter for aero-bikes shifts forward (sprint position) and backward (hill climb) controlled by a handlebar lever, and the Power Post for mountain bikes shifts in a 135° arc with four positions, including recline, power, climb, and stowaway.

Special-purpose saddles (top to bottom): hi-back saddle for better leverage; mini-saddle for bunny hops; Power Post seat shifter; Kinetic seatpost with suspension.

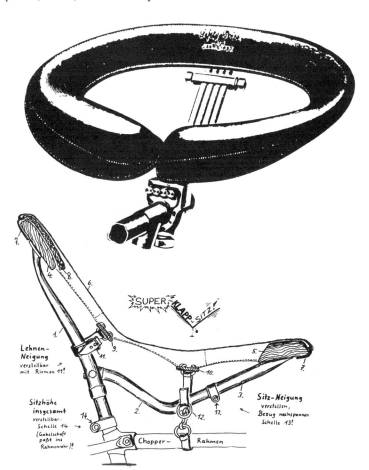

Wheels

Modern bicycle wheels are fascinating and elegant structures because they are so lightweight compared to the loads they carry. With a load to weight ratio of about 400 to one, they are a marvel of engineering, requiring the construction of a complex structure with hand-crafted sensitivity. There is a mystique about the art of wheel building, with its secret knowledge handed down from wheelsmith to apprentice. This mystique has been carried forth and revived, despite the common use of automated wheel building machines and the evolution of the art into an accurate science of physical dynamics with new materials and designs. Bicycle wheels have a symbolic, hypnotic allure that has intrigued and attracted a wide range of people, including preachers, artists, and metaphysicians, as well as various roadside creatures.

Early cycle wheels developed along the lines of carriage wheels, made of hardwood and iron with solid fixed spokes. With the introduction of metal rims and wire spokes around 1869, the "Battle of the Wheel" began with a variety of inventions. The Phantom suspension wheel had long steel rods looping around hooks on the rim which suspended the hub in a double-dish. Starley's lever tension wheel had a radial spoke pattern with an adjustable lever connected by tangential wires to the rim which transmitted the pedal torque. Grout's tension wheel had a radial design with spokes that were tightened by sockets in the rim. Eventually the modern wheel, made of a rim, tangent crossed spokes, nipples, and a hub became the most common form of cycle wheel. Spokes are laced through holes in the flanges of the hub and stretched between the hub and the rim by tightening the threaded nipples set into holes around the rim.

Rims made of hardwoods such as hickory, elm, ash, maple, ebony, amaranth, makrussa, and lemon-tree were widely used until shortly after World War II. They were especially favored for track racing with wooden-soled shoes on wooden velodromes. They are made either as one piece, by steaming and bending the wood into a hoop and connecting it with a finger joint, or by the stronger method, with several circular laminations glued under pressure. Compared to modern steel and aluminum alloy rims, wood tends to be more "alive" and flexible but cannot withstand the higher spoke tensions common today. Wood rims are a popular collectors item and as of 1990 there were still a few makers of wood rims.

Bicycle wheels have been laced in several patterns. Radial spokes project in straight lines from the hub to the rim. They are nice to look at, but are not usually used as driving wheels because they do not transmit torque efficiently. Tangent or crossed spokes are strongest, by working as a lever to transmit torque. When crossed spokes are interlaced, they react together to reduce the shocks of loaded spokes. The "star" and "crow's feet" patterns are decorative combinations of crossed and radial spokes.

Spokes are laced in patterns called cross-one, cross-two, cross-three, or cross-four, in which each spoke crosses a number of other spokes on its

Wooden rim.

way from the hub to the rim, with the limit being the overlapping of spokes on the hub's flange. Because there are two sides to a wheel, they can be laced in either identical or mirror-image patterns, with the spoke heads facing in or out. Both sides can also be "dished" in varying degrees. Wheels are strongest when the rim is centered over the hub, but with the use of multi-cog freewheels and derailleurs, the driving hub is dished off-center. Of all possible patterns the best appears to be the tangent wheel with spokes cross-three, mirror-image, heads facing in.

For most wheels, the greater the spoke tension, the stronger the wheel. Wheelbuilders tighten spokes with a variety of techniques and tools, including plucking the spokes and listening to their tone, and using spoke tensiometers. For $50, the Mako spoke length software (1993) plays a computer-generated tone indicating the correct pitch for each spoke.

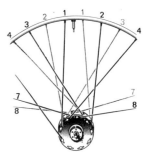

Tangential spokes cross 1, cross 2, cross 3, and cross 4.

HOW WHEELS WORK

There has been considerable discussion as to how the spoked wheel supports its load. The idea that a rigid bicycle wheel can support the weight of the rider while the spokes are pulling the rim toward the hub is confusing, because it seems that the spokes falling below the hub should compress and collapse the wheel. Until recently, the accepted theory held that the load on the hub's axle was taken up primarily by the tension of the spokes at the top of the wheel, while the other spokes took up the slack. It was thought that the wheel's hub "hung from the top spokes." Closer analysis shows that the load on the hub is supported by standing on the spokes at the bottom of the wheel, that "the wheel stands on its spokes."[11]

The bicycle wheel supports various loads, described as static and dynamic loads. Static loads represent the wheel's structure and spoke tension while at rest. Dynamic loads include the cyclist's weight, the effects of the road surface, and the forces of pedaling and braking while the wheel is in motion. Dynamic loads are divided into three important loads: radial (up and down), lateral (side to side), and torsional (twisting), which cause the corresponding forces of compression (pushing), tension (pulling), and torsion (twisting).

Radial loads are caused by the rider's weight, the bumps in the road, and the actions of rim braking. They cause a deflection in the rim by compressing or shortening the spokes and reducing their tension. Lateral loads are caused by the rider's side-to-side movements while standing on the pedals (for example, during hill-climbing), and by rough road conditions which deflect the wheel sideways as it hits the ground, especially while cornering.

Usually there are fewer lateral loads because the bicycle is ridden by balancing. Since wheels are relatively narrow, the lateral strength of a wheel is less than one tenth its radial strength. This makes wheels more vulnerable to lateral collapse when combined with the other loads, resulting in the wave-like saddle-shaped "potato chip" collapsed form. Torsional loads are caused by the torque from pedaling or the use of hub brakes. Torque is transmitted to the rim, the tire, and the ground by all the spokes, with some acting as levers by pulling, and others "pushing" by

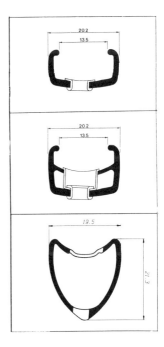

Rim types (top to bottom): single wall clincher rim; double wall clincher rim; deep section tubular rim.

Hide's Disc Wheel, 1891.

pulling less. Pedaling tends to produce varying levels of torque with each stroke, while hub brakes tend to produce more uniform torque. Most of the pedal torque absorbed in wheels is caused by tire pressure rather than spoke tension.

REINVENTING THE WHEEL

There have been various attempts to re-invent bicycle wheels. Since they are already considered one of the strongest man-made structures relative to their weight, much innovation is oriented towards improving aerodynamics, construction techniques, or just for the sake of ingenuity. One innovation is the use of steel, aluminum, and plastic cast wheels for BMX bikes and carrier cycles. The Cinelli Bivalent hub (1961) was a unique system designed to offer quicker wheel changes with a wheel that was interchangeable for the front or the rear while the freewheel cluster remained attached to the frame. Higher weight and production costs, along with incompatibility with the bike market, caused its demise.

Several kinds of spokeless wheels have appeared. In the late 1970s, Arthur Lidov of New York developed a Spokeless Wheel with the idea of making a puncture-proof solid rubber tire with a suspension system. The result was a hollow wheel made of a crescent-shaped fork assembly with two fenders with spring-loaded bearings that encircled a rotating rim with a solid tire tread. The bearings fit into tracks on the inner ring of the wheel which was made of an acetyl resin (ABS) plastic hoop. A removable spherical storage compartment was designed to fit inside the hollow wheel. While most reviewers were reasonably satisfied with the reduced rolling resistance of the wheel, the inventor expressed doubts that it would ever be marketed, because it required major changes in the bike industry. Lidov also envisioned spokeless wheelchairs, and he patented a big wheel spokeless bicycle, based on monocycle designs, in which the rider could pedal while sitting inside the wheel. In 1994, a high-performance carbon composite spokeless wheel was introduced by Wear & Tear, called the Black Hole.

Cinelli Bivalent hub, designed for interchangeable front and rear wheels.

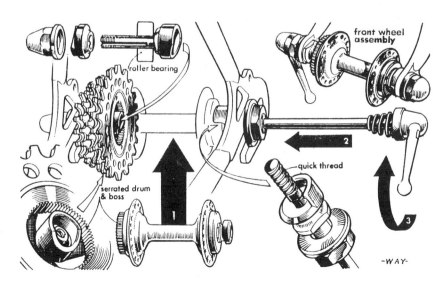

In pursuit of wheels that produce less wind drag and turbulence while spinning, inventors have developed three kinds of aero wheels. Deep-section spoked wheels, such as the Campagnolo Shamal, have v-shaped rims made of aluminum alloys and ceramics, with 16 to 24 adjustable tension spokes made of aero-shaped steel or composites. Composite wheels appear as either full lenticular discs or with two, three or four solid aero-shaped spokes. The "lenses" of the discs are shaped flat (Campagnolo Ghibli) or curved (Fir Jumbo 2). Since the mid-1980s, disc wheels have been used in racing events on the road and track, mostly as a rear wheel, and front wheel discs are also used, but these can be dangerously unstable in severe crosswinds. With colorful logos and stripes, disc wheels in motion create fascinating visual effects, such as the mysterious colors of Benham's Disk. The Tension Disc by Sugino (1989), used mainly for mountain biking, combines a composite disc with a web of spokes fastened to the rim by sixteen adjustable tension bolts.

The three-blade disc wheel developed by Specialized and Du Pont uses carbon, Kevlar, and glass fibers molded over a foam core with an aluminum rim. The designers claim to have spent $1 million on research and development, using NASA airfoil data, a Cray supercomputer, and a wind tunnel. In 1990, the Specialized wheels cost $750 each. By 1994 they became lighter and cost under $400. These wheels refute the old saying that "An ounce of weight in the wheel is like a pound in the frame," since they usually weigh more than spoked alloy wheels. While this makes acceleration slower, their makers are quick to point out that aerodynamic benefits take effect at about 17 mph. Over a distance of 100 miles (four to five hours), they can be ten to fifteen minutes faster.[12]

Traditional spokes have some fascinating uses. Kids imitate the noise of motorcycles by attaching playing cards or inflated balloons to the seat stays of bikes where they rub against the spokes of spinning wheels. To relieve hunger and thirst on the road, clean spokes can be used to slice apples, and spare spokes can be used as chop sticks or to lift corks from wine bottles. T.B. Pawlicki, author of *How To Build A Flying Saucer* (1981), describes how centrifugal force generated by the spokes of a bicycle wheel can be used to construct a prototype UFO.[13]

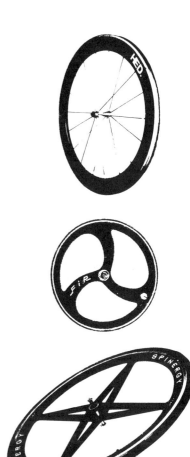

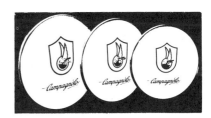

Aero-wheels (top to bottom): Hed deep-section; Fir tri-spoke; Spinergy eight-spoke; Campagnolo disc.

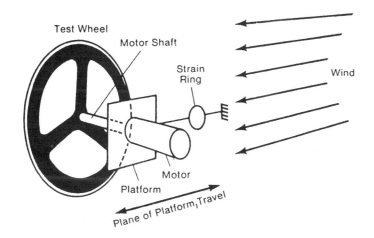

Test rig for aerodynamic wheels.

Tires

The ability to hold air under pressure inside a tire, known as the pneumatic principle, was a breakthrough for speed and comfort that most everyone has experienced. Before pneumatics burst onto the roads in the 1890s, the first tires for swift-walkers were made of iron rims or padded leather. India rubber became available around 1860 and was used on velocipede wheels as a solid strip around the wood or metal rim. Pará rubber (named for Paraguay), with its red color, became popular on high-wheelers and early safeties. Tires were nailed, cemented, glued, crimped or melted with spirit lamps to the rims. Then came the hollow cushion tire, a briefly popular advancement appearing before the arrival of pneumatic tires, when there were already about two million bicycles and only a few automobiles in existence.

PNEUMATIC TIRES

John Boyd Dunlop (1840–1921) born in Dreghorn, Ayrshire, Scotland, was working as a veterinary surgeon in Belfast in 1887, when he began experimenting with the solid tires on his nine year-old son's tricycle. To soften the ride, Dunlop substituted a water-filled hosepipe for the rubber stripping and progressed to making canvas-wrapped inflated India rubber tubes covered with a rubber solution which attached to the wheel rims. On his legendary secret night trials, Dunlop found his invention to be "mush" better. After adding rubber tread, canvas reinforcements, and a one-way valve that could only inflate the tire, he patented his invention in 1888.

Dunlop set up business in Dublin with £25,000 invested by the du Cros family and began selling tires at the costly price of £5 per pair. All fittings and repairs were done at the factory, partly because of the elaborate mounting process and partly to keep an eye on the product. As it happened, this system helped create a monopoly. After a bit of mockery when they were called "sausage," "pudding," "windbag," or "bladder" tires, their advantage was proved by racers and eventually for gentler riders, becoming known as "solution" tires. The business expanded to Coventry, the center of England's cycle trade, where tires were fitted for manufacturers. By 1892, solid and hollow cushion tires were mostly obsolete, and John Dunlop eventually became a millionaire and a household name.

A number of patent disputes were fought over the right to make bicycle tires. In 1890, Dunlop was notified that his patent was invalid because in 1845 a civil engineer from Scotland, R.W. Thompson, had patented a leather-covered pneumatic tube for horse-drawn carriage wheels. Dunlop won the suit, arguing that his was only one application of the pneumatic principle and that anyone could make another. In America in the 1890s, Albert Pope, B.F. Goodrich, the Boston Woven Hose and Rubber Company, the Hartford Rubber Works, and the Hadgman Company merged interests to license their single-tube tires and monopolize the market. One advertisement for their products in *Harper's Weekly* stated: "No honest cyclist will ride infringing tires." Hiram Hutchinson,

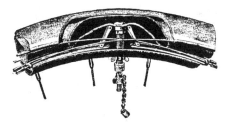

Dunlop detachable tire.

Adjustable wire-on tires.

an American who came to France with a rubber vulcanization process, began making galoshes at his factory in Langlee and entered the bicycle market in the 1880s. The successor company of Charles Goodyear, who had invented a vulcanization process in 1839, entered the bicycle market around 1890. Eventually Goodyear Tire and Rubber quit making bicycle tires and tubes in the U.S. in 1976, when 85 percent of bicycle tires and tubes sold in America were imported.

The pneumatic tire was refined with the detachable wire and bead clincher tire patented by the Michelin Brothers, André and Edouard, of Clermont-Ferrand, France, in 1892. The detachable, clincher or clip-on tire is the most common type, having an inner tube covered by the tire casing which has beaded edges to wedge into the lip on a rim when the tube is inflated. Before clinchers became standardized, there were various other methods of mounting and detaching tires. These included the "Tire of the Future," one of many bolt-on style tires which did not need glue; the Blue Grass clip-on with riveted eyelets in the tire that fit to screws in the rim; the wrap-around Rush detachable with slotted eyelets; and the external beaded tire which seated itself on the outer lip of the rim.

Early inner tubes were straight and could fit a variety of wheel and tire sizes. In a smaller wheel, there was a slight bulge where the inflated part overlapped the extra length; and in large wheels, there was a soft spot if the end of the tubes did not meet. Eventually, these were superseded by various sized "endless" hoop-shaped tubes. Tire casings have been made of rubberized hemp, cotton, silk, nylon, metal mesh, and Kevlar fibers. The Palmer tire was the first to use cross-woven cords. Tire makers have used distinctively colored rubber with white, pink, red, blue, green, yellow, and some marbleized pigments.

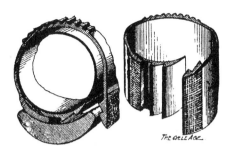

Rush Detachable tire.

Diamond straight tube.

Dunlop advertisment, 1902.

Tubular tires are constructed as a single unit, with the casing sewn around the inner tube, which is cemented to the wheel rim. They are popular for racing because they are lighter than clinchers, they can be inflated to higher pressure, and have less rolling resistance. Tubeless pneumatic tires, with rubber seals in the rim and beading in the casing, were tried on bicycles and became standard for automobiles by the 1940s. Semi-pneumatic tires include those sealed with low pressure and other blends of hollow and foam rubber construction.

Air valves for bicycle tires come in two or three basic formats. The Schraeder valve is the easiest to use since it conforms with auto tire valves. The Presta valve is used for high-pressure tires and has a lock screw to prevent leakage from road shock. The outdated Dunlop valve was shaped like the Schraeder and worked more like the Presta. Valve covers come in various shapes. Some offer prongs for adjusting Schraeder valve cores, some are adapters for Schraeder pumps on Presta valves, and others are for decoration, such as rolling dice.

Tire treads appear in a variety of styles for various uses. The ribbed and herringbone patterns are suitable for most purposes. Knobbies and studs offer extra traction on soft ground but are slower and often make a humming sound on smooth pavement. Slicks or bald tires have the least resistance and are used on smooth roads and in track racing but are more vulnerable to punctures. Some tire makers used their trademark on the tire tread to make an impression with their name on soft ground. Fancy tread patterns have their own social history: for example, during the rise of National Socialism in Germany, bicycle tires bore the imprint of Nazi swastikas.

Sherlock Holmes, the detective invented by avid cyclist Sir Arthur Conan Doyle, used clues from tire tracks to solve a murder in "The Adventure of the Priory School." The story raised a long-standing discussion, one that ranks as one of Doyle's biggest controversies, about whether it is possible to determine a cycle's direction of travel from its tire tracks. In discussing the evidence on a sodden path, Holmes tells Watson "I am familiar with forty-two different impressions left by tyres. This, as you perceive, is a Dunlop, with a patch upon the outer cover.... This track was made by a rider who was going from the direction of the school.... The more deeply sunk impression is, of course, the hind wheel, upon which the weight rests. You perceive several places where it has passed across and obliterated the more shallow mark of the front one."[14]

Holmes could have distinguished 42 different impressions made by tires, as there were over 50 tire makers in England, France and America, and tread patterns were a distinguishing feature. Arthur Conan Doyle knew John Boyd Dunlop, and when this adventure appeared in May 1901, Dunlop introduced the tread with its name in raised letters. Regarding the direction of travel, even the most experienced cyclists are skeptical. James E. Starrs, a cyclist and forensic scientist, outlined the hypotheses in *The Noiseless Tenor* (1982) and concluded that in rough turf a cyclist would likely put a foot down and the shoe would make "an arrow pointing the direction." Doyle was obliged to explain his thinking in his autobiography *Memories and Adventures* (1924):

> I had so many remonstrances upon this point, varying from pity to anger, that I took out my bicycle and tried. I had imagined that the observations of the way in which the track of the hind wheel overlaid the track of the front one when the machine was not running dead straight would show the direction. I found that my correspondents were right and I was wrong, for this would be the same whichever way the cycle was moving. On the other hand the real solution was much simpler, for on an undulating moor the wheels make a much deeper impression uphill and a more shallow one downhill, so Holmes was justified of his wisdom after all.[15]

The tire's imprint is the main factor in its adhesion to the ground, and tire pressure has a major effect on the imprint. High-pressure offers a harder, smaller imprint with less resistance, and low-pressure offers a broader print with more resistance. Recent tests with mountain bikes showed that a slick tire has a larger imprint with a better grip on smooth roads than a knobby tire with the same pressure. The question of proper tire pressure has inspired some rather curious rules, such as, "Tire pressure should be half the rider's weight," "Tire pressure should be equal to the rider's average gear inches," and that a race bike held chest high, should, when dropped, bounce back into one's hands.

Tire tread patterns.

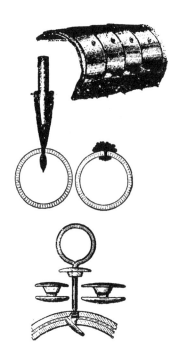

Flat tire remedies (top to bottom):
Non-Puncturable, with flexible metal
plates, 1900; rubber band repair kit,
1904; Glidden Metallic Plug, 1900.

FLAT TIRES

The most common bicycle problem is probably the flat tire. The invention of a truly puncture-proof tire is one of those long-sought breakthroughs in technology that should be worthy of a Nobel Prize or sainthood. As with physical illnesses, there are different ways to deal with flat tires: by prevention, treatment, and surgery. Original designs for the elusive puncture-proof tire began with typical bicycle ingenuity. There were steel-plated boots to go between the tire and tube, cork balls were used to fill tubes, metal plugs sealed holes, and tools were designed for injecting solutions and rubber bands into the tube.

Other notable inventions attempted to create a tire that holds its pressure no matter what may lie in the rider's path, be it wet glass, thorns, tacks, sharp rocks, or potholes. These remedies include the use of liquid inner tube coagulants (Never Leak, 1930s), foam injections (Byk-fil), spring-loaded rims, rubberized sponges (No-Mor Flat), super elastic latex tubes (Avocet), and tire liners (Mr. Tuffy). Natural sealants include condensed milk, molasses and maple syrup. Two of the wildest ideas were the Ball tires made up of 45 walnut-sized individually inflated rubber balls, and the Skinner Automatic Pump which was located inside the wheel and connected to the tire valve. This used an eccentric cam on the hub to produce one pump stroke per wheel turn. The Aerator seatpost pump of 1990 was a pressurized air canister that fit inside the hollow seatpost.

Since few of these contraptions have been 100% effective, a cottage industry of roadside flat fixers emerged, first for cyclists then for motorists. Racers used to carry spare tires looped in a figure eight around their shoulders, and clincher tires were designed to be folded into a small coil. Various patch kits containing tire irons, vulcanized patches, glues and solutions, abrasive materials, a needle and thread, tire boots, and talc have proven useful. Repairing a tube on the road usually takes less than ten minutes, and the world record time for fixing a flat is 1 minute 24 seconds, set by Christopher Wilson of the Bike Surgeon bike shop in Carbondale, Illinois. The art of patching silk and latex tubular tires is an elaborate craft similar to surgery. These days, when mountain bikers have to change a flat tube during a race, they use CO_2 cartridges to pump the tires. There is plenty of business in flat tires, as U.S. cyclists annually spend $200 million fixing punctured tires. It would be a pleasant surprise if someone invented a trouble-free tire for bikes, with all the necessary characteristics of a pneumatic, such as its imprint, its distribution of loads, and its adjustable pressure.

Transmissions

With the popular proverb "a chain is as strong as its weakest link," the bicycle enters the realm of Confucius. It matches perfectly the evolution of the bicycle, since the use of a chain drive became an essential link in the development of modern cycles and a symbol of the machine age and modern civilization. The proverb suggests multiple links in an endless series of strong and weak components, a chain of events similar to the way bicycle transmissions progressed from treadles to pedals and chains to derailleurs. Although a chain drive has its weaknesses, the alternatives are not much better.

The discovery of the ability to drive a wheeled vehicle mechanically with human power has led to numerous inventions. The earliest mechanical drives adapted to swift-walkers were of a linear motion—one invented by Gompertz (1820s) had a supplementary hand-drive sector gear, and one by Macmillan-Dalzell (1840s) used a low-gear treadle-drive with a shoe cleat. A major development for cycling came with the rotary pedal-crank fixed to a wheel's axle, as in the Michaux-Lallement velocipede. By the 1870s, the refinement of the fixed wheel pedal-crank led to the high-wheel bicycle with a typical wheel diameter and gear size of 56 inches, which traveled 176 inches in one revolution of the pedals. Because of varying road conditions, there was a need for gears that didn't rely entirely on the wheel's size. While chains were still in their prototype stage, innovations were applied to the gears of high-wheelers and dwarf ordinary bicycles, including the Sun and Planet Gear, Perry's Front-Driving Gear, the Star two-speed with coaster, the geared-up chain drive of the Kangaroo bicycle, and the epicyclic Crypto gear on the Bantam bike.

THE FLYING BOUDARD GEAR
MADE BY THE
CYCLE COMPONENTS M'F'G C° L'D

Perpetual pedal, 1899.

Pedals and Cranks

Pedals were fit to cranks with adjustable lengths, and some velocipedes had a counter-balance weight to keep the shoe slot upright for easy insertion. On high-wheelers and tricycles, pedals came in many styles. Some had foot platforms on both sides with rubber treads or toothed rails. To improve efficiency in the pedal stroke, inventors of the 1880s came up with stirrup bars, twist-lock pedal cleats, and toe clips. Rat-trap pedals became popular at that time because they grip the shoe and make barefoot or soft shoe pedaling rather stimulating, but with extensive use they can eventually bend or cut the shoe sole in two. For this reason, cycling shoes have a hard sole to distribute the foot pressure over a broader area.

More designs came in the 1890s, like the Perpetual pedal, which offered only a bearing rod with minimal support. The Indispensable pedal had a folding kickstand, and the Aeolus Butterfly was a lightweight rat-trap. Toe clips with straps and shoes with cleats became common in racing at this time. Few changes appeared with pedals until 1970, when Cino Cinelli offered a fixed slotted pedal and cleat with a safety release lever that was used without toe clips mostly by track racers. This was a prelude to the latest innovation, the clipless pedal, invented by Lilian Christol in 1982 and first marketed by the Look Company in 1984.

Clipless pedals (I'd rather call them clip-in pedals) are designed like ski bindings, with a shoe cleat fitting or snapping into an adjustable spring-tensioned platform, without toe clips and straps. By the 1990s, the clipless pedal adopted more flexible, free-floating systems with rotation movement up to about ten degrees, because the knees are such complex and fragile joints. Three or four non-compatible formats dominate the market, including Look, Time, Shimano's SPD, and Speedplay.

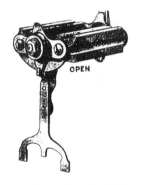

Indispensible pedal with fold-down stand, 1891.

Toe clips with cat's head.

Cinelli M71 clipless pedal.

Shimano SPD clipless pedal.

CHAINS AND COGS

The idea of the chain and cog dates back to Leonardo Da Vinci (c.1493) and was first used by Vaucasson (c.1740). Materials and tools were still relatively crude, and it took many years to construct something applicable to cycling machines. The first Morgan chains of the 1870s were used with tricycles and made of steel wire linked with rollers. Around 1880, the pin-and-stud, or block chain, was already being used with other machinery and was refined for cycling by Thomas Humber. These have a block and a link with a long pitch, usually one or two inches, and require a larger rear sprocket to bend around. Block chains run well when lubricated and clean, but on a bicycle, where the chainwheel lies in the path of road grit spinning off the front wheel, an oil bath chain case was a practical necessity. *Bicycling World* reported that when road grit meshed with a bare chain, it made an "almost unbearable grinding, growling and shrieking, as the protesting chain was forced over the sprocket teeth."[16]

Chains were scaled down in size with the development of the roller chain, which had half as many rivet pins. These came in various tooth and link shapes, but stretching was a major problem until Hans Renold added a bush bearing to the pins, producing the bush-and-roller type common today. The optimal tooth-and-link form for chainsets was developed by Renold and eventually standardized. Chainsets were scaled down again in the early 1900s to half-inch pitch, with a width of 1/8-inch for single-cog gears, and 3/32-inch for derailleur gears. Smaller chains have appeared, at first in 1909 with the Chainette, by Renold's Coventry Chain Company, which had an eight-millimeter pitch, and in 1979 Shimano introduced another eight-millimeter chainset to which only a few people converted. The lightweight Berg SpeeD chains made with stranded steel cables and nylon rollers were used on various human-powered aircraft which required flexibility because they linked cogs at right angles to each other. With cassette freewheels holding up to eight cogs, the latest chains, such as Shimano's Uniglide, feature more narrow and flexible links. To keep chains lubricated, mechanics use light oil, teflon, and the classic "hot wax" method of boiling chains in paraffin.

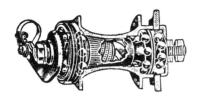

New Departure Coaster Brake hub.

Chainless drive with bevel gears.

GEAR CHANGERS

Freewheels, chainless drives, and multiple-speed gears developed at more or less the same time. A freewheel was first made by Witherbourne in 1866, but freewheels were not widely used until they became part of a brake. When the "brake and coaster" was introduced by the Eclipse Bicycle Company, its president said: "We even had to fight our own agents. Some of them refused to sell our goods with the device affixed."[17] People were still fond of the fixed-gear because they had more control and the rider felt as one with the wheel. The art of pedaling a fixed-gear has been considered the "true" form of cycling, with the cyclist always doing some combination of pushing, pulling, following, and resisting.

Various freewheel designs, such as the New Departure and the Doolittle, came with the "Boom of the Coaster-Brake" of 1898. Chainless, or shaft-drive bicycles became a popular item in the mid-1890s, with three varieties: the spur gear, bevel gear, and roller gear. Despite the advantage of a stylish appearance and sealed gear casings, there were several practical problems with shaft-driven bicycles, including the higher cost of gear cutting, the misalignment and breaking of gear teeth due to a lack of flexibility (especially on steep hills), and the greater weight as opposed to a chain-drive system. The first bevel gear was made in 1894 by the League Cycle Co. of Hartford, Connecticut, followed by the French-made Acetane in 1896, used by racers to set various records. An improvement came with Overman's Victor Chainless bicycle with the spin-roller gear, which replaced cut teeth with roller bearings. Chainless shaft-drive bikes have appeared throughout the twentieth century, and a 1990s model, the Dynamic direct drive, claimed 97% efficiency, compared to 87% for the Pierce and Columbia chainless bikes of the 1890s.

In the 1890s, there were various types of gear changing mechanisms, such as compound driving gears mounted to the bottom-bracket, Sun and Planet hub gears, expanding chainwheel or protean gears, and forerunners of derailleur gear changers, which derail the chain from one rear sprocket to another. Linley and Biggs of England first developed the four-speed Protean gear which was an expanding chainwheel changer with a freewheel around 1894. By stopping the pedal stroke at certain points in the revolution of the crank arm, the chainwheel could be set in four positions or sizes and a jockey or idler wheel near the rear sprocket took up the chain slack. The three-speed Gradient gear of 1899 by E.H. Hodgkinson was one of the first to resemble a modern derailleur. When the rider backpedaled, a spring plate lifted the chain off the rear sprocket. The chain was then lined up with the desired cog and forward pedaling dropped the chain into place.

In 1902, Henry Sturmey and James Archer patented the first of a long line of three-speed geared hubs. The Sturmey-Archer hub uses an epicyclic planetary system of spring-lever clutches and roller bearings, which shift laterally inside the hub by a rod linked to a cable. The shifting controller was located at first on the top tube, and a handlebar-mounted thumbshifter followed in 1903. While the "normal" or middle gear was determined by the number of teeth on the chainwheel and rear cog, the "high" gear was 33 percent larger, and "low" was 25 percent smaller. The hub was made by Raleigh and eventually offered four- and five-speed gear ratios, with freewheeling and neutral. The geared hub is best known for its familiar clickety-click rhythm along the road, and as an initiation ritual for a would-be bike mechanic, the object is to disassemble and rebuild one.

The Frenchman Paul de Vivie (1853–1930), known as Velocio, was the most famous pioneer of the derailleur. After learning to ride a high-wheeler at the age of twenty-eight, he sold his lucrative silk business and opened a bike shop in Saint-Etienne, soon to be the center of the French bicycle industry. There he founded the magazine *Le Cycliste* in 1887. Velocio made his first single-speed bike two years later and then developed a two-speed double chainwheel bike which required the rider to stop and shift the chain from one ring to the other by hand. By the turn of the century, other forms of gear changers had appeared, and he was busy promoting not only the use of gears but also the various health aspects of cycletouring, which became known as Velocio's Commandments. In one gear testing race held by Velocio in 1902, Marthe Hesse (a woman on a three-speed) beat Edouard Fischer (a man on a one-speed) over a 150-mile course with 12,000 feet of climbing.

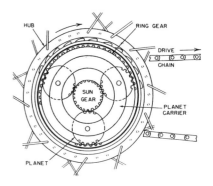

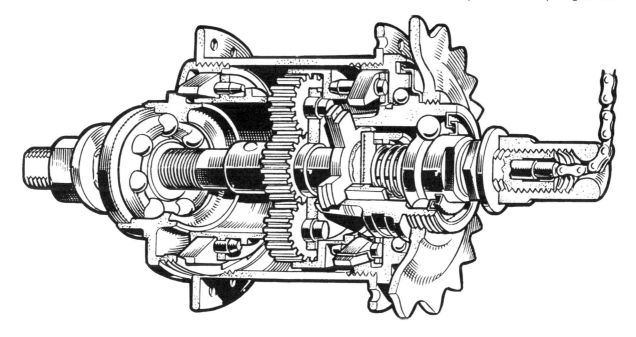

Sturmey-Archer three-speed gear hub.

Modern derailleur systems were the last major component to develop on high quality bicycles, partly because their use was not encouraged in the Tour de France until the 1930s. In 1905, Velocio experimented with a two-speed derailleur called the Cyclist, and in 1911 the first reliable derailleur, the Chemineau, was invented by Joanny Panel. In 1925, Albert Raimond (1885–1953) developed Le Cyclo front derailleur. By the 1930s, many forms of derailleurs were developed for touring. The Osgear, developed by Oscar Egg, had a bottom bracket mounted idler wheel and swinging fork which guided the chain over the rear cluster. The Tri-Velox gear changer held the chain in line and shifted the rear cluster back and forth. Racers contended with gear changes in which they had to stop to remove and rotate the rear wheel, which had a large and small sprocket on either side of the hub.

Two forms of derailleurs developed for multiple rear cogs: the sliding plunger and the parallelogram. The French Cyclo Twinwire, a sliding plunger type, used two cables to rotate a spiral shaft which moved the two jockey wheels in line with two or three rear cluster cogs. The additional spring cable slid the jockey wheels fore and aft to allow large and small cogs. This was superseded by the Simplex Tour de France derailleur, invented by Lucien Juy, which was mounted to the dropout on a swinging arm, bringing it closer (and sometimes too close) to the cluster which had grown to four cogs. It used a single cable connected to an internal chain, which moved the spring-loaded plunger with double jockey wheels. The main problem with sliding plunger derailleurs was their tendency to stick and bend, making a crooked chain alignment.

Cyclo Twinwire derailleur.

Simplex Tour de France derailleur.

Gino Bartali (right), shifting a Campagnolo derailleur in the 1938 Tour de France.

Tullio Campagnolo's derailleur was introduced in 1933, and the first models, such as the Paris-Roubaix, were complicated mechanisms requiring backpedaling to disengage the chain from the cog and the use of a hand lever located along the seat stay for shifting. In 1951, Campagnolo invented a parallelogram derailleur, the Gran Sport, in which the cable shifted two spring loaded plates in an adjustable arc while keeping the chain in proper alignment with the cogs via spring-tensioned double jockey wheels. Parallelogram derailleurs were quickly reproduced first by Simplex, Huret, and Altenbruger, and eventually by Sachs, Shimano, SunTour, Sugino, Triplex, and Zeus (a Campagnolo clone from Spain). Jockey wheels were lengthened to accommodate the larger rear cogs (up to 40 teeth) used in cycletouring, and front derailleurs got a cable and shift lever of their own placed next to the rear derailleur lever.

Among the innovations of the 1990s is the eight-speed freehub, in which the freewheel is part of the hub, making easier cog changes, and the Shimano Hyperglide chain, with bulging links to improve the efficiency of twisted chain lines caused by seven- and eight-speed clusters. By 1991, smaller chainrings and cogs were introduced on mountain bikes with Shimano's Micro Drive and Campagnolo's Compact Drive systems. These save weight and prevent chainrings from scraping over irregular terrain, but small cogs with fewer teeth for the chain have less efficient load distribution. Another innovation is the electronic Mavic Zap derailleur, with a solenoid motor and handlebar mounted push-button controls. The PB derailleur, an invention of Pierre Blanchard of Canada, features 30 percent greater chain wrap around the cogs for more efficiency, a horizontal-moving chain tensioner for more ground clearance and less chain slap, with less weight and less cost to make than a standard parallelogram derailleur.

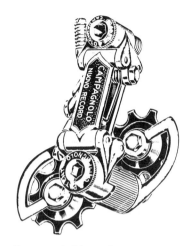

Campagnolo Nuovo Record derailleur.

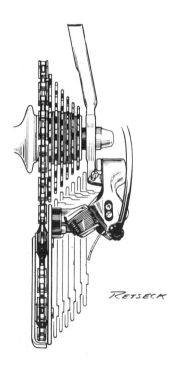

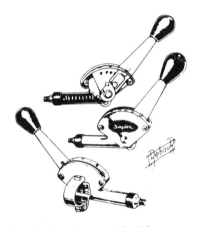

Campagnolo down tube shifters.

Simplex Preselector stick shifter.

Shimano dual brake/shift levers.

GEAR SHIFTING

Shifting a derailleur requires a subtle technique, in which the rider must be pedaling forward with the chain in motion but without using full pedal torque. Only the best systems allow full pedal torque while shifting. Also, the chain should be engaged and aligned with the cogs and chainwheel as much as possible. Usually, with two chainwheels (for road racing) or three chainwheels (for touring) on the front, and five to eight cogs on the rear cluster, a few gear combinations do not line up well, and some multi-gear ratios may have redundant sizes. Shimano and others have introduced small step notches on chainwheels, to help the chain shift across large spaces and to allow more pedal torque while shifting.

Shifters are located in various positions depending on the position of the bike rider. For upright bike riders, shifters are located on the handlebar stem, near the brake levers, or as part of the handgrip with twist-grip controls, such as the popular Grip Shift by Sram. On touring and road racing bikes they usually fit on the down tube of the frame, and on the handlebar ends for cyclo-cross and time trials. An innovation of the 1990s is the dual control brake/shift lever made by Shimano, Campagnolo, and Sachs. Their early lack of capacity for triple chainrings inspired the parasitic Third Dimension shift lever.

One of the biggest innovations is index shifting, which allows positive click-stop gear changing. Various systems were introduced in the 1960s and 1970s, mainly for hi-riser and BMX bikes, with the Simplex Preselector, the Shimano Positron (with derailleur indexing and a freewheel crankset), and SunTour's Mighty Click and Tri-Mec systems. Some kid's bikes had simulated index shifters, such as Schwinn's Goof-Proof gear changer, and their Stik Shifter, similar to that on a car. The popular Shimano Index Shifting system (SIS), introduced in 1985, has a pressure sensitive mechanism as part of the shift lever.

GEAR RATIOS

In the last hundred years the number of available gears on a quality bike has multiplied from one to twenty-four. Some bikes have over a hundred speeds, by combining geared hubs and multiple sets of derailleurs, while various automatic gears claim an infinite range between 27 and 118 inches. The Saint Gass Supertandem, built by Gaston Saint-Pierre in Quebec, is supposedly the world's most complex bicycle, with six chains, seven internal and external cog systems, twelve derailleurs, thirteen shifters, and some 1,458,000 gear ratios.

Gear ratios are measured two ways, by inches (the clumsy way) and meters (the logical way). Gear inches are calculated by dividing the number of teeth on the chainring by the number of teeth on the rear cog, and then multiplying this sum by the diameter of the rear wheel in inches (e.g., 45 ÷ 15 × 26 inches = 78 gear inches). To calculate how far the rear wheel travels in one revolution of the pedals, the number of gear inches is multiplied by *pi* (e.g., 78 × 3.14 = 245 inches). With the metric system, the gear size is called development (from the French), and it represents the meters traveled per pedal revolution. Development is calculated by dividing the number of teeth on the chainring by the number of teeth on the rear cog, and then multiplying this sum by the circumference of the rear wheel in meters, which is about 2.035 meters for a 26-inch wheel (e.g., 45 ÷ 15 × 2.035 = 6.10 meters).

The ideal gear size for an average cyclist ranges between 65 and 75 inches, or about 5.5 meters. This applies to a healthy person pedaling on a flat or rolling road at a cadence of one to two revolutions per second. Cyclists can easily estimate their speed by multiplying their cadence times their development (e.g., 1.5 rps × 6.10 m = 915 m/s or 32.9 kph). The ideal gear can vary considerably, from 20 to 130 inches, depending on the cyclist's purpose, power, weight, position, cadence, musclar fitness, rolling efficiency, surface condition, wind direction, and gradient. Extra low gears, known as "granny gears," usually have a ratio less than one to one. One setup, called the "Limbo Spider," uses 18 to 23 tooth chainrings for gearing below 15 inches.

THE DEAD CENTER

There is a weak link in the cyclist's circular pedal stroke called the "dead center." There are certain "power" points around the circle which generate the majority of the muscular torque, while at "weak" points, when one foot is at the top of the stroke and the other is at the bottom, they are merely following the pedals, generating little or no power. Subtle pedaling techniques, such as the flywheel effect and "ankling" the feet with cleats, can help to minimize the problem, but there is still room for improvement.

A partial remedy for the dead center may be the use of elliptical chainwheels, which were first developed in the 1890s. The Belgian Thetic chainwheel appeared in the 1930s, the Bridgestone Cycle Company introduced a double set in the 1970s, and the Shimano Biopace was a mass-marketed fad from 1986. These give an eccentric gear ratio that is lower at the dead center and higher at the point of maximum thrust, offering more efficient use of muscle power for easy-going cycling. According to theory and scientific testing they can make an eight percent improvement in efficiency with an eight percent eccentricity. The Durham chainwheel had an eccentricity of 25 percent but without a comparable increase in efficiency. While Shimano's oval chainrings became less eccentric, they were rarely used for racing or record-breaking because of the uncomfortable, "warped" feeling in the pedal stroke.[18]

AUTOMATICS

The recognition of this dead center problem, along with an understanding of the muscular action of pedaling, has inspired the search for the ultimate cycling transmission that is mechanically in-synch with the human body. The creation of an automatic pressure-sensitive infinite-ratio drive system is full of bicycle ingenuity, and in the words of John Tetz, a Bell Laboratory inventor and HPV enthusiast, "It's worth a billion dollars." Automatic drive systems can be broken down into two or three types: manually controlled variable-ratio drives, automatic torque-sensitive variable-ratio drives, and automatic continuous-ratio drives. The majority of these systems have used expanding chainrings or cogs mounted to either the cranks or the rear wheel. As their diameter changes so does the gear ratio.

Variable-ratio gears include the Hagen all-speed variable diameter chainwheel drive, the Octo slit-sprocket chainwheel drive, the Tokheim five-speed transmission, the Excel 16-speed Cambiogear drive, the Ferrari-Colnago eight-speed drive with a sealed oil bath alloy gearbox, and the IPD infinitely variable cam-actuated bellcrank drive. Lawrence Brown from Hawaii has developed several models, such as the Facet BioCam drive which uses eccentric cams and pivoted linkage rods which transmits "pulses" that turn the hub. Another model is the Selectocam drive in which the chainwheel can revolve faster or slower than the cranks, depending upon the torque load. Scott Dickson used this system in the 1980 Paris-Brest-Paris 750-mile ride and finished second.

There have been only a few truly automatic variable-ratio transmission systems available. The Deal Drive, introduced by French-Canadian

Michel Deal in 1982, has sixteen speeds which are determined by pedal torque. The Ride-A-Matic transmission, patented by James Reswick in the late-1980s, is a variable-ratio torque-sensitive drive using dual pulleys, one which measures the pedal force, the other determining the speed-ratio. An eleven-speed automatic drive under development in 1991 by Keith Chilcote uses a computer-controlled motor and magnetic sensor to change gears according to the cyclist's pedal revolutions. The Dugil Automatic Derailleur, invented by Canadians Robert Dutil and Raymond Gilbert, uses centrifugal force in the rear wheel to shift gears. Three weights mounted on two spokes each slide in and out with changes in speed, while connecting rods acuate levers that move the derailleur. The unit weighs two pounds more than a standard derailleur, and is featured on the Autobike from Quebec.

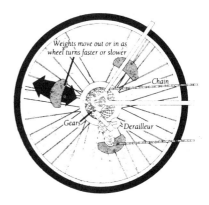

Automatic transmissions promise many advantages, such as low gear start-ups at stop signs or steep hills when a derailleur bike would still be in a big gear, the safety of no fumbling with gear shifters, and continuous power while shifting. However, James Reswick makes an interesting observation about his device: "My young neighbors report that it was 'fun' but they obviously found it much too limiting on their freedom of choice to race ahead or climb a hill while standing on the pedals."[19] Having tried many of these contraptions, I've had a similar feeling: the transmission is so automatic, it fails to acknowledge that some people like to pedal with their own cadence.

Other kinds of human-powered transmissions include linear drive tracks, dual-action lever drives, hand-crank manupeds, and freewheeling chainring derailleurs. A backward pedaling direction is claimed to produce twenty percent more power.[20] Two-wheel drive (2WD) bicycles include the 2 Bi 2 (1991), a mountain bike with a steel cable linking the rear wheel to the front, offering extra stability on slippery surfaces, and a bit more friction. Energy storage devices are another intriguing idea for bicycles, for collecting the energy of momentum from coasting and braking to be used intermittently through an added motor-drive device. Flywheels accumulate energy from the high-speed spin of a heavy wheel. Bicycle wheels do this in a small way, but not enough to climb hills. Flywheels have been used on various cycling machines without much success, because the extra weight and high rpms necessary to convert, store, and reconvert energy do not match the low weight high efficiency of the bicycle. For adding power, gas-powered engines or electric motors perform better.

Alternative drive systems (top to bottom): Legacy two-wheel-drive bike; CVA 1000 cable-drive; linear-drive Avatar recumbent.

The complexity of the subject of transmissions can be summed up by the various meanings of the word "gear." It can be anything attached to your bike, a sprocket, a toothed spur, a cluster, a derailleur, the number of inches the wheel turns in one pedal stroke divided by *pi*, and the Great Eastern Annual Rally (GEAR) of the League of American Bicyclists.

Brakes

Most bicycle ingenuity seeks to make cyclists more comfortable, efficient, and faster by reducing friction. Good brakes help by increasing friction and allowing the rider to slow, stop, and maintain balance in all kinds of situations. Brakes are a touchy and intimate component for cyclists. They like them firm or soft, quick or slow, and they speak of "pumping," "feathering," and "letting it all hang out" on high-speed Alpine descents. A familiar truism is that good brakes make you go dangerously faster, and bad brakes make you go carefully slower. When you suffer from "brake squeal," some say the best remedy is a new pair of leather shoes.

Brake shoes by Kool Stop, 1989.

Several kinds of brake systems have been used on cycles, working on the front or rear wheels, whether steering or driving. Fixed-gear and coaster brakes are foot-operated by backpedaling on the drive wheel hub. Plunger brakes, rim brakes, internal-expanding drum brakes, and disc brakes can work on either wheel, and are usually hand-operated by levers on the handlebar.

Most brake systems function by force, applied by leverage or pressure, times the coefficient of friction in the levers, cables, rods, pulleys, pads, and shoes that resist the wheel's rotation. While a brake's shoes should provide maximum friction, its leverage system should have minimal friction. Brake shoes are considered the most important part of the brake. They are made of soft metals, rubber compounds, graphite composites, and the all-time favorite, porous leather. Average brake levers provide about three times the force applied by the hand, and a variety of mechanisms have developed to increase leverage, including force multipliers and doublers. Shimano's Servo-Wave lever, rated the most powerful, has an extra linkage to make pulling quick and soft at the start of the lever stroke, and slow and strong at the end, allowing more brake pad clearance from mud and for removing fat tires.

PLUNGER

Plunger brakes, now mostly extinct, create friction on the outer surface of the tire by the pressure of a spoon-like lever. Road grit can often enhance their effectiveness, but in wet weather they perform poorly because the water moves to the outer surface by centrifugal force, acting as a slippery lubricant. Plunger brakes were the earliest kind of brake employed on swift-walkers, most often used on the back wheel for fast downhill runs, with handlebar mounted twist-grip pulley systems. Plungers became the most common type of brake on cycling machines even after the appearance of pneumatic tires.

High-wheeler bikes were the first to use plunger brakes operated by a geared rack and pinion system. Another form of high-wheeler plunger was the Harrow brake. This had a spring-mounted rocker-arm surrounding the rear wheel. When a pull cord released it, a foot on the rear end dug into the road. If the cord failed, the spring pulled the front end down to lock up the wheel. Some safety bikes with plunger brakes were activated by foot or saddle, using the rearward movement of the rider's weight to plunge the rear tire. By 1897 the plunger reached its peak of ingenuity with the front- or rear-mounted pneumatic brake developed by Humber. The idea was to equalize the pressure in order to prevent punctures caused by severe tire plunging. The brake was set into action by squeezing on an air-filled bulb, and a nearby button valve released the air and the brake.

FIXED-GEAR

The fixed-gear backpedaling method of braking came into use when pedal-cranks were placed on velocipedes. This method works by backward pedaling or resisting the forward motion of the pedal-cranks when they are fixed to the wheel axle directly, or through a fixed-gear chain-drive system. The fixed-gear brake is very effective because backpedaling legs use some of the strongest muscles in the body, yet it is so simple that it is not often considered to be a brake. The drawbacks are that it will not work with the feet off the pedals, or if the chain falls off. Fixed-gear brakes are often combined with another form of brake, and were a standard feature on most cycling machines until the introduction of freewheels around 1898. They remain standard equipment for track racing, cycling purists, and elite cycle messengers.

COASTER CLUTCH

When the first hub brakes were installed they were part of a freewheel hub called the "coaster and brake," with the reverse motion on the pedals emulating the fixed-gear brake, known as a "backpedal brake." Brakes such as the Eclipse (which became Bendix) and the Doolittle fit inside the rear hub with a lever attached to the frame at the chain stay. While backpedaling, various disks or cones slide together to clutch the hub, which makes the wheel stop. They are relatively impervious to weather since they operate inside the hub. They are rarely used with standard rear derailleurs and will not work if the chain breaks or falls off. The coaster-brake or backpedal brake is probably the most common type of brake used throughout the twentieth century, appearing on children's bikes, balloon-tire bikes, middle-weight cruisers, and utility cycles. Another popular type is the two-speed coasterbrake hub by Bendix, Sachs, and others, in which soft backpedaling shifts the internal gear and hard backpedaling engages the clutch brake.

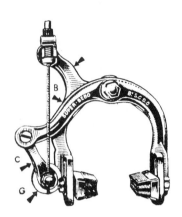

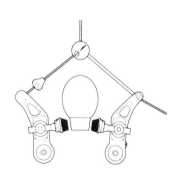

CALIPER

Caliper rim brakes are the most popular lightweight brake. They come in various configurations, including stirrup, side-pull, center-pull, cantilever, U-mount, roller cam, self-energizing, and hydraulic. They operate through the action of levers, cables, or fluids which force pads or shoes against the side or inner rim of front or rear wheels. Because friction is applied to the wheel rim, heat can build up, causing tire problems in extreme situations such as long downhill runs in the summer. In wet weather, rim brakes operate at about 40 to 60 percent less power because water lubricates the rim. "Pumping" the brakes can partially displace the water. Although rims have been serrated or dimpled for various reasons, because friction increases in proportion to the contact area of the braking surface, serrated rims are slightly counterproductive. Recently, rims have been coated with a ceramic material for improved wet weather braking. The Golden Rule for cycling in wet weather with caliper brakes is to always allow twice the stopping distance.

Around 1879, James Starley patented the first center-pull type caliper brake for the small rear wheel of an ordinary bicycle. It was called the Grip brake and had replaceable brass shoes. By the turn of the century, safety bikes began to use the stirrup type brake, activated by levers and rods fixed to the handlebar which pushed a leather or rubber shoe against a flat or V-shaped inner groove along the rim on both sides of the spokes. They became the brake of choice on the classic 28-inch wheel roadster bikes made popular by Raleigh.

Before 1950, side-pull brakes were common on racing bikes because they offered a quick-release mechanism for wheel changes. In the 1950s, the Mafac Racer, Universal, and Weinmann center-pull brakes were widely used. The Campagnolo side-pull was standard racing equipment from the 1960s until the 1980s, when greater diversity came from Mavic, Modolo, Shimano, and SunTour. Campagnolo's stylish Delta brake has a parallelogram linkage.

Cantilever brakes first appeared in the 1890s, and have been used for touring bikes, tandems, cyclo-cross bikes, and mountain bikes. They offer the greater leverage necessary for stopping heavily laden and muddy wheels, with more space for fenders and larger tires. Calipers and shoes are attached to two spring-loaded pivot bolts fit to brazed mounts on the frame, with pulley cables and a harness that make the center pull system. A recent development with mountain bikes is the roller cam caliper. An aluminum roller cam developed by Charles Cunningham in the mid-1980s is perhaps the smoothest, surest brake of all time.

Hydraulic brakes use oil (brake fluid) in the cables, or control lines, thus offering less friction and greater pressure. Since 1970, Mathauser has been the leading maker of hydraulic bike brakes in the U.S., with a bellowphram sealed system, and Mangura from France offers a system with O-ring seals that can be disassembled.

DRUM AND DISC

Drum brakes, or internal-expanding brakes, apply friction from a pad against an enclosed drum that is part of the hub. The balloon-tire stream-liner bicycles of the 1930s made use of them, and they are used on work bikes, tandems, and heavily laden touring bikes. The drawbacks to drum brakes are they are fairly heavy and not always waterproof. Most drum brakes are made by Sturmey-Archer (England), Sachs (Germany), Araya (Japan), or MaxiCar (France), and a few are custom-built by specialty bike makers.

Disc brakes have an additional smaller wheel attached to the hub flange which serves as the friction plate for a pressure pad operated by rod, fluid, or cable. Located away from the perimeter of the wheel, discs are more effective in wet weather than are rim brakes. Because of the added braking torque, spokes must have high tension, and forks should be made of stronger material. In the 1890s, the Chainwheel brake used a disc located on the inner ring of a fixed-gear chainwheel and was operated by a "thumb latch" on the handlebar. The Shimano Self-Energizing disc brake of the 1970s was operated either by cable or hydraulics. Phil Wood designed a front or rear wheel disc brake and hub which offered greater stopping power for touring, tandem, and load-carrying bikes. Pedicabs and cargo cycles often have hydraulic disc brakes, such as those made by Dia-Compe (Japan), Innovative Bicycle Products (U.S.A.), Mangura (France), and Sachs (Germany).

TOUR DE FRANCE EQUIPMENT

Bicycle equipment for a professional team of nine riders during the three-week Tour de France:[21]

20 road bikes
(2 per rider, plus 2 spares)
10 time trial bikes
(1 per rider, plus 1 spare)
4 spare frames
200 tires
200 tubes (for clinchers)
20 cans tire glue (for tubulars)
130 wheels
40 rims
1,000 spokes
500 gear cogs (12 to 26 teeth)
10 freewheels
6 complete component groups
50 chains (one per week)
15 handlebars
80 rolls handlebar tape
4 tool kits
1 gallon of lubricant
5 gallons de-greaser
1 air compressor
1 foot pump
100 meters of air and water hose
3 gallons soap

Accessories

Hey diddle, diddle
The bicycle riddle—
The strangest part of deal.
Just keep your accounts
And add the amounts
The "sundries" cost more than the wheel.
　　—From *Riverside Daily Enterprise*, New York (1896)

The bicycle's accessories comprise another realm of bicycle ingenuity, known as the "after market" in the bike industry. Depending on a cyclist's needs and desires, these sundries include pumps, lights, bells, horns, locks, handles, bags, racks, bottles, spare parts, and tool kits. Here are two shopping lists of cycle accessories, one from the 1890s and the other from the 1990s:

1890s

Jiffy Repair Outfit
Hawthorne Wood Rim Cement
Hurry-Up Lightweight Pump
Banner Foot Pump
Gamages Clean-All Outfit
Heath Combination Tool-Case Pump
Closed Parcel Carrier
St. Nicolaas Handlebar Briefcase
Handlebar Coat Holder
Folding Fork Carrier
Springfield Baby Carriage Seat
Platform Carrier and Cushion
Rosenblatt Gentleman's Kit
Bundle Trundle
Genuine Veeder 10,000-Mile Cyclometer
Osmond Handlebar Speed Indicator
Coldwell Bicycle Coupler
Kanine Konfounder
Washington Taylor Dog's Scare
Keogh Body Shield
Jansen Handlebar Revolver
Instruction Belt
L.A.W. Combination Sprocket Lock
Victory Pedal Bell
Hall Automatic Whistle
Clear the Way Horn
Schumacher Acetylite

1990s

Silca Impero Pump
CO_2 Cartridge Tire Inflator
Blackburn Racks
Karrimore Panniers
Madden Rocky Handlebar Bag
Astra Nautics Polyethelene Box
Kirkland Faspack Seat Pack
Live Chin Wire Basket
Burley Lite Child Trailer
Bike Burro Touring Box
Kryptonite Rock Lock
Cobra Links
Loc-a-Wheel
Basta Click 3000
Cinelli Cork Ribbon Handlebar Tape
Onza Bold Bar Ends
Ritchey True Grips
Power Grips
Stereo Tune Tote
Cellular Phone Pack
Piggy Back Waterbottle Cage
CamelBak Drinking System
Bike Stream Hands Free Drinking System
Cateye Cordless Cycle Computer
BioScan Heart Monitor
Avocet Altimeter
Bike Hike
Power Point Saddle Pad
Flit Controls Aero Shifter Mounts
Gorilla Brake Beefer
Bluemels Mudguard
Splash Mate Mudguard
Bullseye Derailleur Pulleys
Uni-Disc Wheel Covers
Halt Dog Repellent
Third Eye Helmet Mirror
Handlebar End Mirror
Pedastyle Bikes Up and Away
Thule Car Roof Bicycle Carrier
Graber Guardian Trunk Mount
Bike Kase Travel System
Wheel Safe
Jog-a-Lite Pants Clip
Ampec Belt Beacon
Brite Lite Halogen Light System

CYCLE CAMPING EQUIPMENT

Camping equipment for a three-week tour.

Handlebar and saddle bags
(with shoulder or back straps)
Front and rear panniers
Tent and drop cloth
Sleeping bag and pad
Water bottles and carrier
Camp light and batteries
Lighter or matches
Camp stove and fuel
Mess kit (pot, plate, cup)
Cooking and eating utensils
Multi-purpose knife (can opener)
Cooking scrubber and cloth
Food storage bags
Towel, wash cloth, handkerchiefs
Body soap, toothpaste
Toilet paper, sanitary napkins
First aid kit, sunscreen, lip balm
Maps, compass, map holder
Notebook, pens, address book
Reading material, radio
Camera and film
Sewing kit and duct tape
Spare bike parts and tools
Bike lights
Expandable straps

TOOLS

Tools for maintaining, repairing and building cycling machines in their approximate order of necessity. Both metric and inch measures are required for the serious bike mechanic. Bicycle riders should start at the beginning of the list, "overhaulers" should start at the end:

Patch kit	Repair stand
Tire irons	Bench vise
Screwdrivers	Hacksaw
Adjustable wrenches	Files (flat, round, medium, coarse)
Allen wrenches	Fixed cup wrench clamp
Liquid lubricant	Freewheel vice clamp
Grease	Chain whips
Oily rags	Wheel truing stand
Cable cutter	Wheel dishing gauge
Tape measure	Spoke tensiometer
Spoke wrench	Vernier caliper
Chain rivet extractor	Metric ruler
Chain stretch measure	Fork alignment tool
T-wrenches	Dropout alignment tool
Seat wrench	Derailleur alignment tool
Channel pliers	Rear triangle alignment bar
Vise-Grips	Headset cup press
Needlenose pliers	Metric taps
Cone wrenches	Electric drill and bits
"Third hand" or toe strap	Grinder (stone, wire, cloth)
Foot pump	Air compressor (vacuum and blower)
Tire pressure gauge	Solvent tank
Presta-Schraeder valve adapter	Rubber gloves
Schraeder valve core remover	Protective eyewear
Needle and thread	Painting box
Tire talc	Baking oven
China marker	Crown race cutter
String	Head race mill
Adhesive tape	Adjustable level and angle tool
Ball-peen hammer	Frame building jig
Rubber or plastic mallet	Fork building jig
Scissors	Tubing mitre
Needle-nose grease gun	Tubing mandrel
Enclosed chain scrubber	Torch
Freewheel remover	Gas and oxygen tanks
Pedal wrench	Anvil
Crank bolt wrench	Protractor and compass
Crank puller	Forge
Bottom bracket tool set	Drawing board
Headset spanner	Pencil and paper

Motor-Powered Ingenuity

Bicycles brought to society an industry of innovative manufacturing techniques, an active movement for better roads, and a popular means of personal mobility and freedom. In the process, they laid the foundation for the development of motorcycles and automobiles. The development of steel tube frames, ball bearings, chain drives, differential gears, pneumatic tires, as well as mass production techniques and specialized machine tools, sheet metal stamping, and electrical welding—all of these were technological innovations of the bicycle industry that were key elements in the development of motorized vehicles. While carriage makers were often allied with horse interests, cycle makers were better equipped to expand into the manufacture of motor vehicles and the majority of early automotive engineering talent came from bicycle mechanics and racers.

Countless inventors applied steam, electric, or gas-powered engines to cycling machines as far back as the 1860s. Most of the well-known names in the auto industry got their start in the cycling world: From Germany, the Adler Co., Carl Benz, Adam Opel, and Ferdinand Porsche (Steyr-Puch); from France, Paris-Roubaix winner and spark plug king Albert Champion, Clément Trochard, Alexandre Darracq, Albert De Dion, André and Edouard Michelin, and Armand Peugeot; from England, Herbert Austin, William Hillman, Harry J. Lawson (Humber), Henry Leland, Henry Morris, J.K. Starley (Rover), and George Singer; from the U.S., Vincent Bendix, Charles and Frank Duryea, Henry Ford, R.P. Gormulley & Thomas Jefferys (Rambler), William Knudsen (Ford and General Motors), Hiram Percy Maxim, Ransom Olds, Albert Pope, Sylvester Roper, Alexander Winton, and John North Willys.[22]

Michaux-Perreaux cyclomotor (top).
Daimler motor cycle (above).
Benz motor tricycle (left).

As early as 1869, Pierre Michaux fit a Perreaux steam-powered engine to his *vélocipède*, and in the 1880s the Frenchmen Albert De Dion and Armand Peugeot built heavy tricycles with Serpollet steam engines. These proved too heavy and inefficient compared to the two-cycle one-cylinder gasoline-powered engines which were first successfully applied to a velocipede by Gottlieb Daimler in 1885, and to a tricycle by Carl Benz in 1886. During the 1890s, the Panhard et Levassor car became the prototype of the four-wheel automobile, while the De Dion-Bouton tricycle was the most popularly priced motor vehicle in France and England. Electric motors were more prominent in America until the legendary "Spindletop" oil gusher of 1901 in Beaumont, Texas, launched the widespread use of petroleum in the U.S. By this time, the automobile industry in Europe, England and the U.S. was beginning to separate itself from its bicycling roots.

Hiram Maxim, chief engineer of Albert Pope's Columbia Automobile Company and a maker of machine guns, described the situation in his autobiography *Horseless Days* (1937):

> The reason why we did not build mechanical road vehicles before this [1890], in my opinion was because the bicycle had not yet come in numbers and had not directed men's minds to the possibilities of independent long-distance travel on the ordinary highway. We thought the railway was good enough. The bicycle created a new demand which was beyond the capacity of the railroad to supply. Then it came about that the bicycle could not satisfy the demand it had created. A mechanically propelled vehicle was wanted instead of a foot-propelled one, and we know that the automobile was the answer.[23]

Motor-powered "enginuity" continued through the twentieth century, with motor-assisted bikes, trikes, and HPVs equipped with small gas engines and electric motors, with batteries and solar panels. As more motor vehicle makers have pursued lightweight and efficient vehicles, many are using components and data from bicycle technology.

Henry Ford with his bicycle.

FLYING MACHINES

Similarly, motorized flying machines were pioneered by bicycle makers such as the Wright Brothers and Glenn Curtiss. Orville (1871–1948) and Wilbur (1867–1912) Wright became enthusiastic cyclists when they bought a pair of safety bicycles in 1892, and later that year they opened a bicycle repair shop in Dayton, Ohio. By 1896, they had begun manufacturing their own line of bicycles, such as the Wright Special, the St. Claire, and the Van Cleve. As bachelors and members of the League of American Wheelmen, their lives revolved around "nuts and bolts." Soon they became intrigued by the flying experiments of Otto Lilienthal, the German aeronautical pioneer who died in 1896 as a result of a crash landing with his glider. Bicycling and flying had something in common, as James Means suggested in the *Aeronautical Annual* (1896): "To learn to wheel one must learn to balance. To learn to fly one must learn to balance. Why not begin now?"

By 1900 the Wright Brothers' seasonal cycle business was financing their experiments with gliders and kites. Using their unique form of bicycle ingenuity, they determined the principles of wingwarping as Wilbur was idly twisting a long box of bicycle inner-tubes. To understand the effects of air pressure on wing forms, they used one of their St. Claire bicycles with a third wheel mounted horizontally in front of the handlebars that held two upright airfoils. As the airfoils moved through the air, the brothers studied different airfoil shapes and positions, and later they built a small wind tunnel in their shop to perfect their data. After several glider flights during 1900–1902 at Kitty Hawk, North Carolina, Orville developed two lightweight air-cooled twelve horsepower engines, which were mounted on their Flyer, and on December 17, 1903, he made the first controlled motor-powered flight by a human being.

Meanwhile, in Hammondsport, New York, the aviation pioneer Glenn Curtiss (1878–1930) was a talented teenage bicycle racer and bicycle messenger for Western Union who went into business for himself at age 22 by opening a bicycle shop. Curtiss began building a crude one-cylinder gasoline engine, using a carburetor made from a half-pint tomato can, and installed it on one of his bicycles. In 1903, the G.H. Curtiss Manufacturing Company was selling bicycles and motorcycles, and Curtiss set a world speed record for motorcycles going nearly 64 mph for one mile. A few years later he built a 40 horsepower V8 engine and set another motorcycle speed record of 136 mph. Eventually his engines became sought after by aircraft makers, and in 1908 his company made a profit of $120,000 building aircraft. With World War I, Curtiss' business skyrocketed, with some $170 million in orders from the British and U.S. governments for flying boats, flight trainers, and engines. Even as a millionaire, Curtiss customarily rode to work on his bicycle.[24]

4 Cycling Machines

Tandem monocycle, 1882.

A man, in my view, cannot spend his entire life making bicycles. He can modify them, he can make bicycles with two wheels, three wheels, four wheels, one wheel, underwater bicycles, flying bicycles, but at some point he wants to make something different.
　　—Yevgeni Yevtushenko, poet

Naming the Bicycle

Throughout its history, in its various shapes and incarnations, the bicycle has collected a long list of names which help illustrate its ubiquity. Naming an invention can be difficult because it should be a perfect fit, a "living word" that relates the function and character of the device. As the invention evolves in technology and culture, the name must continue to "live" or else be replaced.

To describe early bicycle-like machines, many inventors, critics, and scholars combined various root-words until the Franco-Greco-Latin word "vélocipède" (*velox*: "fast" + *ped*: "feet") became the first international name. The velocipede itself became a root-word for creative additions such as "velocipedomania" (a social phenomenon), "velocipathy" (a natural exercise involving general development of every muscle of the body), "velocinasium" and "velocipedarium" (indoor cycling halls), "velocipedestrienne" (a female cyclist), "velocipedagogue" (a professor of cycling), "velocipedestrination" (the act of cycling), "velocipedraniavaporiana" (hot and heavy breathing while cycling), and the 40-letter word that competes with the longest of all English nouns, "velocipedestrianisticalistinarianologist" (one who studies the study of studying cycling).

The word "bicycle" appeared on an 1869 British velocipede patent by J.I. Stassen. In a few years, the name was commonly applied to highwheelers. "Bicycle" (a two-wheeled velocipede) became a root for an activity, such as "bicycled," "bicycling," and "bicyclism" (the art of bicycling); for a person, a "bicycler," "bicyclian," and "bicyclist;" and for anything pertaining to or connected with the nature of bicycles, "bicyclic," "bicyclical," "bicycular," and "bicycle kick" (in soccer, a kick made with both feet off the ground and moving the legs as if pedaling a bicycle). The root of "bicycle" is "cycle," with "cycling," "cyclism" (practice of the cyclist), "cycler," "cycleman" (one who cycles), "cycledom" (the world of cycles and cyclists), and "cyclometer" (cycle odometer). Cycle also appears in the middle of some bike-related words, such as "amphcyclotheatrus" and "gymnocyclidium" (velocipede riding schools), and *Encycleopedia* (a book about cycling).

自行車

دراجات

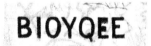

BIOYQEE

Among the world's languages there are many concise, living root words, such as *velo* (French), "bike" and "cycle" (English), *bici* (Italian), *cykel* (Swedish), *fiets* (Dutch), *rad* (German), *rower* (Polish), *sepeda* (Indonesian), and *birota* (Latin: "two-wheeler"). The word "bike" (and "byke") in Scottish predates the bicycle, yet its meaning and use is somehow similar: "a crowd or swarm of people," as in "the lads about me biket."[1] The Flemish author Stijn Streuvels described the naming of the bicycle in *Memories* from his *Collected Works*:

I think of our Flemish word "rijwiel" for "bicycle." Has any machine ever become so popular, so widespread in so short a time, and have we ever had more difficulty in finding a name for it? The new machine was like a revelation, everyone wondered how something so simple could have remained unknown for so long, why it had taken so long to discover it. Each nation gave it a name of its own in their own language. The French had little trouble with this and, as always when they have to name something new, they took a piece of Greek and a piece of Latin and stuck them together, giving us the "velocipede."

For everyday use, however, this name proved too long and too cumbersome for something so speedy, and they shortened it to "velo." We Flemings, however, who seldom take the trouble to invent a new word and prefer to borrow from our neighbors, but then try to find some kind of related concept in the foreign word, changed it into "vlosse-peerd" (literally: "floss-horse" or "floss-machine"). The authorities, however, produced "rijwiel," "schrijwiel," "trapwiel," "wielpeerd" and finally "fiets," which in Holland at least proved to be the "living word." The English went about the task in their customary rational manner and came up with "bicycle," "wheel," or simply "cycle," which became the real name, the true name. The practical Germans started with "Fahrrad" and ended with "Rad."[2]

The growing family of cycling machines inspired many attempts to rename and categorize them. The name "human-powered vehicles" came about as a generic way of making the point that people can transport themselves with their own energy in unlimited ways. Many people feel this is not a "living" phrase, even though the human is combined as driver and power source. As a vehicle it opens up possibilities and reflects a new paradigm for cycling machines. Like many phrases of its day, it's been replaced by its initials, HPV, which some folks thought was DOA. Mike Burrows describes the HPV dilemma in "My Other Bike Is a Recumbent" from *Encycleopedia 1993/94*:

Mention the initials HPV to the average person and you usually get a blank look. Mention them to a cyclist and you will either get a beaming smile and be told they are the greatest, or a growl and some mutterings about going under lorries.

Another way of naming cycles appeared at a New York bike conference in 1989, when Mary Frances Dunham proposed "a terminology for the universe of Motor-Free Vehicles—Morfs." She described Terramorfs as land vehicles, Mermorfs for the water, Airmorfs for flight, and Ideomorfs propelled by thoughts. If 100 years from now there is a further synthesis of body, mind, and machine in cycles, we humans may become "biocyclists" riding "cybercles."

INTERNATIONAL NAMES

Albanian: biçikletë
Arabic: bisiklaat, bisiklaataat
Australia: bush bike
Cameroun: pating bamileke
Czech: bicikl, kolo
Danish: cykel, liggecykel, sofacykel (recumbent)
Dutch: fiets, loopfiets, tweewieler, hoge bi (high-wheel), dreiwielfiets (trike), ligfiets (recumbent), zweefiets (flying bike), fietskar (bike trailer)
English: bicycle (two-wheeler), bike, cycle, machine, trike, tricycle, three-wheeler, wheel, push bike, boneshaker (velocipede), balance (high-wheel), penny farthing (high-wheel), sociable (multi-cycle), tandem (bicycle built for two), rickshaw, pedicab, (passenger cycles), HPV (human-powered vehicle), funny bike (aero bike)
Esperanto: bicikleta
Flemish: fiets, rijwiel, schrijwiel, trapwiel, vlosse-peerd, loopfiets
French: vélo, vélocipède, cycle, bicyclette, engin, cyclisme (cycling sportif), cheval de bois (swift-walker), cheval mécanique (velocipede), grand-bis (high-wheel), aviette (flying bike)
Gaelic: da'chasach, ceffyl, heaarn, deurod
German: Fahrrad Fahrad, Rad, Radeln, Dreirad (two-wheeler), Zweirad, Laufrad (swift-walker), Tretkurbelrad (veloicepede), Hochrad (high-wheel), Klapprad (folding bike), Liegerad, Sesselrad (recumbents), Kurzfahrrad (short bike), Rikscha (rickshaw)

Hawaiian: ka'a paikikala
Indonesian: sepéda, bersepéda
Irish: rothar, gearran, iarainn
Italian: bici, bicicletta, due ruote, monociclo (monocycle), triciclo (trike), dupletta (tandem), michaudina (veloicipede)
Japanese: ji-ten-sha
Kikuya: baithikiri, maithikiri, mũbria
Korean: cacénke
Latin: birota
Latviska: divritenis, ritenot
Lietuviu: divratis
Lingua Franca: bersable, bercagle
Magyar: kerékpar
Norwegian: bicykkel, sykle, sykkel, velosipéd
Polish: bïka, rower
Portuguese: bicicleta
Romanish (a Swiss dialect): velo, bicicletta, cuorsa cun velo (bike race)
Rumanian: bicícleta
Russian: velociped
Serbo-Croat: točak, velosiped, bicikl, jahati
Slovak: bicykel, dvojkolo
Spanish: bicicleta, biciclista, bicicletista
Spanish (Uruguay): chiba
Swahili: baisikeli, boda boda (bike taxi)
Swiss German: Velo
Swedish: cykel, bysicles, bicykel, velociped
Tagalog: bisikleta
Tahitian: pere o'o taatahi
Turkish: bisiklet, bisikletle, gitmek
Ukrainian: velociped

The Family of Cycles

The family of cycling machines includes anything human-powered or hybrid-powered (human-powered with motor-powered assist), with any number of wheels, hulls, or wings, that provides go power for mobility or ergo power for work. There are roughly fifteen general categories of cycling machines and about 100 specific types. Most of these machines have been mass-produced, although some are built in limited numbers, some are one-of-a-kind prototypes, and a few are ideas yet to be built.

Cycling machines are categorized in many ways: by their intended uses, by the numbers of wheels and riders, by the kinds of cycling positions, and the kinds of drive mechanisms. Many cycles overlap categories as they are adapted for other uses and copied by other makers: for example, mountain bikes are used for speed and utility, and Pedersen bikes are being built one hundred years after Pedersen's original.

Most kinds of cycling machines are described in this chapter, except the evolutionary types in Chapter 2 (Velo Development), and those mentioned in other chapters. Generally, the word "bike" is used to describe a two-wheeler and "cycle" is used for all other vehicles and tools with any number of wheels and human-powered mechanisms.

Kinetic Sculpture by Duane Flatmo.

CATEGORIES AND TYPES OF CYCLING MACHINES

Evolutionary Cycles
Manumotive carriages
Pedomotive carriages
Swift-walkers
Velocipedes
Velocipede carriages
Dicycles
High-wheel bicycles
Tricycles
Sociable cycles
Multi-cycles

One-Wheelers
Monocycles
Spherical cycles
Unicycles

Practical Cycles
Safety bikes
Roadsters
Classic bikes
City bikes
Folding bikes
Touring bikes
Ten-speed bikes
Recumbent bikes
Bantam-polo bikes
Tandem bikes
Multi-bikes
Combination cycles
Hand cycles
Tricycles
Recumbent trikes
Tandem trikes
Pedal carriages

Utility Cycles
Carrier cycles
Trailers
Trailer cycles
Pedicabs
Rail cycles
Utility cycles
Military cycles

Speed Machines
Road bikes
Track bikes
Aero bikes
Streamlined bikes
Streamlined HPVs
Downhill bikes
Motor-pace bikes

All-Terrain Cycles
Cyclo-cross bikes
BMX bikes
Mountain bikes
All-terrain cycles
Ice-snow cycles
Wind cycles

Show Cycles
Stunt bikes
Low-rider bikes
Kinetic sculpture
Exposition cycles
Musical cycles

Human-Powered Watercraft
Aquatic cycles
Amphibious cycles
HP boats
HP submersibles

Human-Powered Aircraft
Aviettes
HP airplanes
HP helicopters
HP airships

Exercise Cycles
Rollers
Stationary cycles
Ergometers
Exercise machines

Human-Powered Tools
Shop cycles
Farm cycles
Power generators

Hybrid-Powered Cycles
Moped cycles
Motors

Spin-Offs
Walking machines
Skates
Scooters
Skateboards
Wheelchairs

Children's Wheels
Velocipedes
Bikes
Hi-rise bikes
Midget race bikes
Trikes
Pedalcars

One-Wheelers

In the family of cycling machines, one-wheeled vehicles are the ultimate embodiment of the human being unified with a wheel. One-wheel vehicles come in three basic formats: monocycles, with the center of gravity inside the wheel; spherical cycles, with the center of gravity inside a sphere; and unicycles, with the center of gravity above the wheel entirely. Monocycles and unicycles have an unstable equilibrium in both longitudinal (forward–backward) and lateral (sideways) motions. Spherical cycles tend to have a stable equilibrium in lateral motions, but this depends on the design of the sphere. The unstable longitudinal equilibrium of these cycles can be stabilized, depending on the skill and position of the rider.

MONOCYCLES

It is believed that a wheel with a diameter somewhat larger than the person who is cycling inside it can gain enough momentum to overcome its unstable equilibrium. Dozens of monocycle inventions appeared before the twentieth century but very few made it beyond the patent office. More often than not, inventors admitted that "the vehicle crashed badly on its first trial run, and proved unsatisfactory." Sir Richard Lovell Edgeworth, an inventor of the telegraph, described making a walking wheel in his *Memoirs* of 1820:

The machinery which I intended to employ was a huge hollow wheel made very light, within side of which, in a barrel of six feet diameter, a man should walk. Whilst he stepped thirty inches, the circumference of the large wheel, or rather wheels, would revolve five feet on the ground; and as the machine was to roll on planks, and on a plane somewhat inclined, when once the *vis inertiae* of the machine should be overcome, it would carry on the man within it, as fast as he could possibly walk. I had provided means of regulating the motion, so that the wheel should not run away with its master. I had the wheel made, and when it was so nearly completed as to require but a few hours' work to finish it, I went to London for Lord Effingham, to whom I had promised, that he should be present at the first experiment made with it. But the bulk and extraordinary appearance of my machine had attracted the notice of the country neighbourhood; and taking advantage of my absence, some idle curious persons went to the carpenter I employed, who lived on Hatch Hare common. From him they obtained the great wheel, which had been left by me in his care. It was not finished. I had not yet furnished it with the means of stopping or moderating its motion. A young lad got into it, his companions launched it on a path which led gently down hill toward a very steep chalk-pit. This pit was at such distance, as to be out of their thoughts, when they set the wheel in motion. On it ran. The lad withinside plied his legs with all his might. The spectators, who at first stood still to behold the operation, were soon alarmed by the shouts of their companion, who perceived his danger. The vehicle became quite ungovernable, the velocity increased as it ran down hill. Fortunately the boy contrived to jump from his rolling prison before it reached the chalk-pit; but the wheel went with such velocity, as to outstrip its pursuers, and, rolling over the edge of the precipice, it was dashed to pieces.[3]

Since the 1970s, several monocycle-like vehicles have appeared that use extra wheels for stability. Examples include the monocycles with trailing wheels designed by Arthur Lidov of New York, and by Naef Fridolin of Switzerland. A tandem "Big Wheel" was built in 1983 by two Americans for an employee design contest in Japan for the automaker Honda. Another stabilized monocycle rolls on a monorail in a cycling amusement park in Tokyo.

Big Spokeless Wheel Bike, by Arthur Lidov, 1978.

Spherical Cycles

Around 1884, a transparent spherical walking device was proposed by "one of the foremost manufacturers of velocipedes in France." While sitting inside this hermetically sealed sphere containing 140 cubic feet of air sufficient for a two-hour trip, the "sphero-velocipedist" could make walking and leaning movements to go forward, backward, to turn right or left, and even traverse small rivers. The idea was reported in the Dutch magazine *De Natuur*:

> Imagine a hollow sphere made of some transparent, solid and not too fragile material, five to seven feet in diameter, and provided with a circular opening large enough to permit a person to enter, which opening can be closed with a convex door in such a manner as not to interfere with the spherical shape of the whole.
>
> In the centre of this sphere there is an iron shaft, with a double right-angled bend and dished ends into which there fits a metal ball. This ball presses against the wall and forms a socket-joint with it. Due to the bends in the shaft, the centre of gravity is not in the geometrical centre of the sphere so that the seat attached to the shaft will always point downwards while remaining horizontal whatever the position of the sphere may be.[4]

Spherical velocipede, 1884.

During the epic periods of bicycle ingenuity, a few open-air spherical kinetic sculptures have been built with circular tubing in a space frame design, and various enclosed spherical cycles have appeared as drawings that were never patented or built.

Otto Dicycle, 1880.

Giraffe unicycles.

UNICYCLES

Unicycles are one-wheel vehicles with unstable equilibrium that have been ridden by people of all ages, including the blind and "at least one senior citizen who had never even mastered the bicycle."[5] In his book *Anyone Can Ride a Unicycle*, Jack Halpern claims: "Women seem to enjoy a distinct biological advantage when it comes to unicycling, as they are free from any supererogatory excrescencies." Unicycles first appeared with velocipedes around 1869 and were used later by vaudeville performers at the turn of the century. Eventually they developed into two types: the short ones with cranks fixed to the wheel, and the tall ones with extensions of fixed-gear chain-drives, known as giraffe unicycles. Giraffes come in various sizes and shapes, including mini-wheelers with six-inch tires, and the rooftop variety with the saddle over 30 feet high. Some giraffes have tandem riding positions, zig-zagged chain patterns, or they use sets of wheels acting as gears instead of chain-drives.

Several production model unicycles, both standard and giraffe, have been made by American Eagle, Columbia, Matthews, Miyata, Oxford International, Penguin, Schwinn (until 1992), and Sturdee. Standard unicycles typically use a 20- or 24-inch wheel and require a straight fork. Variations include the Pony-Saddle, the Kangaroo, the Big Wheel, the Double Ultimate, and the Ultimate unicycle, which is the most difficult to ride because there is no fork or seat, just a wheel, cranks and pedals. Learning to ride requires soft ground and an assistant to catch one's fall. Some unicycles come equipped with training wheels. The basic idea for the rider is to keep the wheel's hub and the saddle in line under the center of gravity while pedaling.

DICYCLES

Dicycles have two wheels, just like bicycles, but dicycle wheels are mounted side-by-side, whereas bicycle wheels are mounted in-line. On dicycles, side-by-side lateral equilibrium is stablized, but forward-backward longitudinal equilibrium is unstable—the opposite of bicycles. Dicycles evolved around 1870, utilizing a carefully balanced center of gravity, special driving mechanisms, and one or two additional stabilizing wheels. The most famous of these is the Otto Dicycle invented by E.C.F. Otto in 1880 and built by BSA. Gradually, dicycles became rare, so that today bicycle makers rarely talk about dicycles, and no one seems to be marketing one.

Practical Cycles

Practical cycles are all the wheeled vehicles whose basic function is to transport people on roads and paths. Included are cycles with various kinds of seating positions and driving mechanisms, with two or more wheels, and one or more drivers/passengers. This category includes folding bikes designed for compact stowage, combination cycles for joining bikes to make special ones, and hand cycles for physically challenged people.

SAFETY BIKES

Safety bikes are the two-wheelers that gained popularity around the 1890s and continue to be the standard shape of bike through the twentieth century. Traditional safety bikes have diamond-shaped steel tube frames, pneumatic tires, and inch-pitch fixed-gear chain drives.

ROADSTERS

Roadsters are modern bikes that began appearing around 1900 with the development of coaster brakes and internal hub gears. Described in the bike industry as either lightweights, middleweights, or heavyweights, they include the elegant Pedersen truss-frame roadster, the sturdy Schwinn balloon-tire cruiser, the streamlined Bowden Spacelander, and the generic English three-speed, all of which continue to be produced today.

The traditional diamond-frame roadster dates back to the Marsden Golden Sunbeam Two-Speed Roadster (1902), one of a long line of English "garden bicycles," and three-speeds made by Rudge, Raleigh, and Pashley. America's balloon-tire cruisers, made by Schwinn, Murray, and Rollfast, are called classic bicycles by collectors. One-speed and multi-speed roadsters evolved throughout the world with different features and recognizable styling. The bikes of Japan, Holland, and Germany usually come fully equipped, and the bikes of China, India, and Mexico are made more durably. They are perhaps the most widely used adult bikes today. The Low Cost Bicycle (1994), a prototype by Market Village Technologies of Colorado, is designed to cost $15 and carry up to 50 kilos. It has a one-piece frame, front-wheel-drive, plastic wheels, and tires recycled from cars.

The Dursley-Pedersen bicycle is a distinctive roadster that was developed in 1893 by Mikael Pedersen (1855–1929), a Danish engineer living in Dursley, England, and is still reproduced and ridden by many enthusiasts. The bike has a space frame design, based on the Whipple-Murphy bridge truss, made of fourteen separate narrow diameter tubes, joined in 57 places, making 21 triangles throughout the bike. Central to the design is the suspended hammock saddle which transfers a cushioned, sometimes swaying, stately ride. The truss was originally woven from 45 yards of silk and an adjustable buckle allowed variations in saddle tension.

Dursley-Pedersen roadster, 1893–1990s, with Whipple-Murphy bridge truss.

Pedersen produced about 8,000 bikes around the turn of the century and developed a lightweight folding bike for military use. The century-old Pedersen is a connoisseur's bike that has been modified by various builders. In 1978, Jesper Sølling, a metalshop worker in an alternative community in Christiania, Denmark, revived the original frame plans and has refined the design with modern components. With three co-workers, they currently produce about 700 Copenhagen Pedersens per year, including about ten tandems. Pedersens are popular in Germany, with makers such as Michael Kemper in Düsseldorf, and in England, where admirers met in Dursley to celebrate the 100th anniversary of the Pedersen patent application.

The Bowden Spacelander was developed by Benjamin Bowden (1906–), a British-born automotive designer, for a "Designs of the Future" competition in 1946. After several "cursed" attempts at production in Britain and South Africa, Bowden began production in 1960, but he lost money as only about 522 were shipped. They had a fiberglass body and sold for $89.50. Originals are a valuable rarity today, selling for about $5,000 to $15,000. In the 1990s, licensed replicas that cost over $4,000 are being produced by Bowden Industries in Lawrence, Kansas.

City Bikes

City bikes, town and country bikes, metro bikes, commuter bikes, hybrids—these are practical variations of the roadster designed for easy daily transport in cities and suburbs. Some are built for easy riding, such as the low-frame Fitness bike (1990) marketed by NordicTrak and the Utopia Ergorad (1990) by Inge Wiebe of Germany. Others have suspensions, such as the plastic-wheel Sprick Comfortable (1984) of Germany and the twenty-inch wheel Radical by Gerritsen and Meijers of Holland. And some are designed for the future, such as the cross-frame Herkules 2000 (1951) of Germany and the prototype Batavus Double Orange (1993) of Holland. For urban riding in the U.S., cyclists often use fully-equipped mountain and hybrid bikes, while bike makers offer the Specialized Milano (1993) and the Trek MetroTrack. Hybrid bikes are a popular cross-breed, which combines the frame geometry of a mountain bike with somewhat faster, narrower tires of lightweight roadsters.

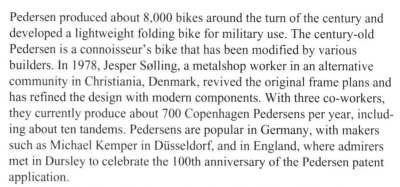

Bowden Spacelander, 1946–1990s.

Utopia Ergorad.

Herkules 2000.

FOLDING BIKES

Portable or folding bikes allow people to carry or stow their wheeled vehicles in a smaller, less cumbersome package than standard bicycles. They provide easier access into buildings and elevators, and into other means of transport, such as trains, planes, boats, buses, and cars. Many kinds of practical folding bikes have appeared in the past hundred years, including small-wheels, large-wheels, tandems, and trikes, and recent innovations in design and components improved their efficiency.

The earliest folding or collapsible bicycles include a few velocipedes and high-wheelers, and they developed increasingly for soldiers to carry on their backs around the turn of the century. Probably the first of the modern small-wheel variety (fifteen-inch, 375 mm) was the well-equipped Van Wagtendonk-Fongers folding bike made in Holland in 1898. The rare fifteen-pound Dursley-Pedersen Military bicycle of 1900 had a folding front fork and wheel. The French military used a folding bike named for its creator, a Captain Gerard. With a joint halfway along the parallel top and down tubes, the two halves could be folded or separated, and the seat was located directly over the rear wheel axle.

Large-wheel folding bicycles usually have frame tubes that separate or swing joints that fold together. Many were developed for military use, such as the Bianchi-Fiat Bersagliere gun carriers (1914) and the BSA Parabike (1916) for paratroopers. Revived versions of the oval-shaped BSA folding bike include the Trussardi (1982) from Milan, and the Galaxe (1986) by Finn Wodschow and Steen Erik Snitkjœr, now built by Niels Keld Madsen in Denmark. The frame has narrow tubes with folding joints, and the bike can fit wheels of 700c or 28-inch size. Luxury features include the Brooks B66 saddle, front hub brake, and Woodguard fenders, chainguards, and hickory rims. Mountain bikes that fold include the Montague BiFrame (1989), the Dahon Mountain Classic (1991), the Worksong (1986), and the Diamant Handy Bike (1994), with a stainless steel frame. To make any quality bike separate for portability, the Bicycle Torque Coupling System attaches to cut apart frame tubes and fastens together with stainless steel screw joints.

Small-wheel open-frame folding bikes were popular in the early 1960s for cycle makers such as Raleigh, Peugeot, and Myata. These bikes have twelve- to twenty-inch wheels and a swing joint along the single low-slung tube. To fit adults properly, the seatposts and handlebars are extra long, and to have a big enough gear with small drive wheels, the chain-wheels are larger. The next step in portability came with bikes that could fit into a small suitcase-sized bag. One of the first was the Italian Pocket Bicy. It had twelve-inch wheels and a double sprocket system allowing the rear wheel to fold into the space frame.

Today's small-wheel folders include the Bickerton, the Dahon, and the Brompton. The aluminum Bickerton Portable was developed in the mid-

Van Wagtendonk-Fongers folding bike.

Galaxe folding bike.

Bickerton folding bike.

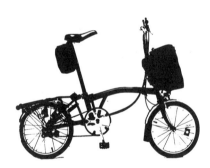

Brompton folding bike.

1970s by Harry Bickerton, an aircraft engineer for Rolls-Royce and DeHavilland. It has a fourteen-inch front wheel and a sixteen-inch rear, and weighs eighteen pounds. The aluminum box-shaped main tube has a swing joint, and the fold-away handlebars are widely adjustable. Its light weight and flexibility made it comfortable to ride at fairly high speeds over varied terrain, and several Bickertons were used for long distance touring. The Bickerton came quickly to the mass market. Though it went out of production in the mid-1980s, it is being revived in 1995.[6]

The Dahon Folder was developed in 1973 in California by the Chinese-born engineers Henry and David Hon, and it came to market in 1983. The original was a twelve-inch wheel, all steel, Taiwan-made bike, equipped with fenders, rack, kickstand, pump, generator lights, bell, tool set, and caster wheel for rolling when folded. It was one of the world's smallest adult bicycles when folded, measuring 28 x 20 x 8 inches, and it took about a minute to fold and unfold, with quick-release levers and knobs requiring no tools. It weighed over 30 pounds, and cost about $250. Dahon now offers about four small-wheel models, including the Classic 16, the Stowaway, and the Mariner. The Brompton folding bike was developed by Andrew Ritchie of London. He began the project in 1975, and after a batch of prototypes were made in the early 1980s, some of the original buyers invested in the company, and production began in 1988. It folds into a 22 x 21 x 10 inch clump in about twenty seconds.

There are several high-performance small-wheel portable bikes in production. Perhaps the best are designed by Alex Moulton, who pioneered the small-wheeled non-folding bike trend in 1962. The Moulton AM14 Jubilee introduced in 1987 weighs about 26 pounds, costs nearly $3,000, and uses a Reynolds 531 space frame which has a kingpin that separates the two halves of the bike for fitting into a large carrying case. It has fourteen speeds, seventeen-inch high-pressure tires, and front and rear suspension systems. The high-performance Bike Friday folders, by Alan and Hanz Scholz of Eugene, Oregon, include the 22-pound, twenty-inch wheel, sixteen-speed, 531 Reynolds frame, $1,300 Pocket Rocket road racing bike, the 24-speed Pocket Llama mountain bike, the New World Tourist, and the 40-pound Two'sDay Tandem. Options include the TravelCase (22 x 29 x 10 inches) which fits the twelve-inch wheel TravelTrailer.

Folding bikes intrigue product designers more than most cycling machines, and many folders have appeared in design competitions that try to inspire the "Bikes of the Future." Although few go past the idea stage and make it to market, some make it to market before the idea is complete. While experienced cyclists can tell good from bad, some designers seem to believe that function follows form. Bikes that balance both innovative materials and "easily collapsible" features include the 22-pound plastic Strida by Mark Sanders of England and the eighteen-pound aluminum Microbike by Otto Linander and Sven Hellestam of Sweden, which was sold at the Museum of Modern Art Design Store in New York.

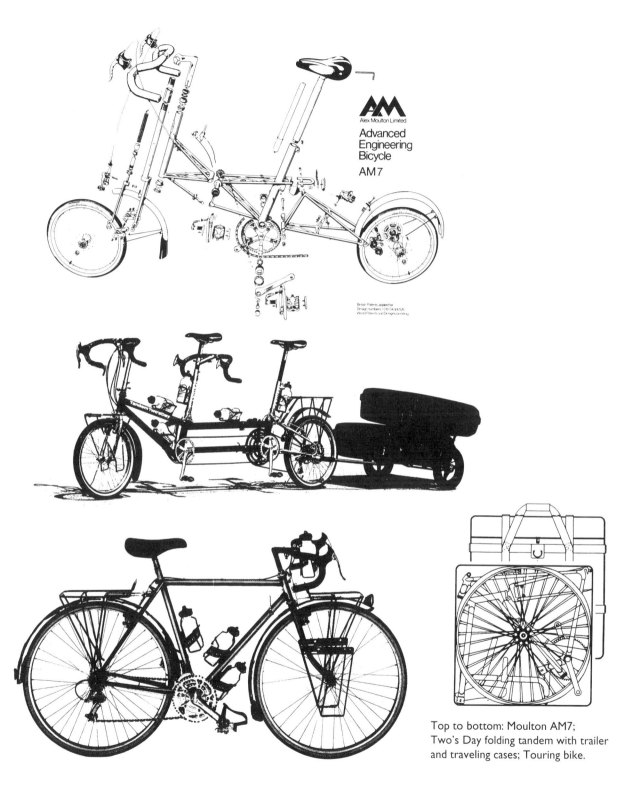

Top to bottom: Moulton AM7;
Two's Day folding tandem with trailer
and traveling cases; Touring bike.

Thanet Silverlight.

Lightning P-38.

TOURING BIKES

Touring bikes are durable, lightweight road or off-road bikes assembled with high-quality components and equipped with racks and panniers for carrying touring and camping supplies. Packs are positioned behind the seat, in front of the handlebars, and on top and along the sides of front and rear racks, with the purpose of distributing the weight of the cyclist and the load between the wheels (about 40 to 45 percent on the front, 55 to 60 percent on the rear) and keeping it as low as possible. Touring bikes in France and Britain have been built according to "official" specifications of touring organizations, called *Randonneur* and *Fédérale*, with fenders, lights, and tool kits. Touring bikes include the three-speed Adler Berg und Talrad (1949) from Germany, the Rene Herse (1960s) from France, and the Bilenky Midlands (1994) from Pennsylvania.

Ten-speed bikes were a popular American variation of the touring bike first marketed in the 1960s and superseded by mountain bikes and hybrid bikes in the 1990s. Ten-speeds were widely used for transport and touring, but with low-quality components, drop handlebars, and fewer accessories, they were somewhat impractical. The classics of this genre include the Schwinn Varsity (1962) and the Sears Roebuck "Ted Williams Quality" Free Spirit (1970).

RECUMBENT BIKES

Recumbent bikes are two-wheelers designed for sport and transport and categorized by length, position, and drive system. Long wheelbase (LWB) recumbents have the front wheel extending in front of the pedals and a wheelbase of 55 to 70 inches, making a long, stable bike. They are about equally popular with short wheelbase (SWB) recumbents, which are compact, quick-steering bikes that have the pedals over or in front of the front wheel, and a wheelbase of 35 to 45 inches. Compact long wheelbase (CLWB) recumbents and semi-recumbent bikes have a shorter LWB configuration with higher seats, smaller wheels, and a wheelbase of 45 to 65 inches. LWB recumbents include the Easy Racer Tour Easy (1982) by Gardner Martin, the Roulandt from Holland, the foldable Linear aluminum bike produced by Steve Hansel, and the Radius Peer Gynt by Andreas Fortmeier and Peter Ronge of Germany. SWB recumbents include the Lightning by Tim Brummer, the Kingcycle by Miles Kingsbury of England, and the Angletech/Counterpoint Presto by Jim Weaver. The Vision R-40 and R-42 by Advanced Transportation Products can convert to either LWB or SWB.

Semi-recumbent bikes include the ReBike (1993) by Kathy Skewis, the EZ-1 (1994) by Easy Racers, the Danish Sofa-Cycle (1960s), and the Villiger (1980s) from Switzerland, with partial fairing, fenders, and stowage beautifully integrated in the body design. Low-rider recumbents, or *Ultrateifleigers* in German, include the Flux Z-Pro bike by Christian Uwe-Mischner of Germany, with partial fairing, and the Kingcycle Wasp, with front-wheel-drive.

Rear-wheel-drive (RWD) recumbents are more common than front-wheel-drive (FWD) recumbents. FWD recumbents usually have shorter wheelbases and chains, and they take longer to learn how to ride. They come in two formats: with the crankset fixed to the front forks, which makes the handlebars turn with the pedals, as on the bikes built by John Stegman of South Africa, or with the crankset fit to the driver's frame, which has fixed pedals and a twisting chain when the front wheel turns, such as the Bevo bike by Klaus Beck and Hans Voss of Germany. The innovative Flevo bike (1988) by Johan Vrielink of Holland, a FWD central steering recumbent, is known as a "zen bike" because the rider must totally relax. The Flevo can convert into a load-carrying trike. Variations from Holland include the semi-recumbent Cha-Cha bike by Bram Moens and Bernd Zwikker, and the Swing Cycle Chinkara by Rob Hofman. The Lean bike (1993), by Harald Kutzke and Norbert Nattefort of Germany, is a prototype sixteen-inch wheel suspension recumbent based on the position of a car driver, with tilting-seat steering.

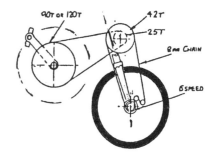

Above, double chainset on Kingcycle. The lower half twists when turning the front wheel. Below, Bevo bike, a front-wheel-drive semi-recumbent; Flux Z-Pro low-rider recumbent.

Flevo bike

BANTAM-POLO BIKES

These are a mixed breed of bike that are fun to ride and allow for special maneuverability. They include the early bantam bikes, bikes with small-wheels or short-wheelbases, and semi-recumbent bikes. The first bantam bikes were the Crypto Bantam and Bantamette (1891), for men and women, which had 24-inch wheels and epicyclic FWD hub gears. Setting the style for polo bikes were the Velocino (1939) from Italy and the Union Strano (1958) from Holland, with a twelve-inch front wheel, a 24-inch rear wheel, and a long, swept-back stem that positioned the bullhorn handlebars above the saddle. This quick steering, short wheelbase design has been replicated in semi-recumbent form in Clive Buckler's Wedge bike (1993). The Funfiets (1992), by Derk Thijs of Holland, is a portable twenty-inch wheel bike designed to ride with the "hands off." It has a three-speed coaster brake, a single steering bar, a quick release steering damper, and front brake lever placed behind the saddle. The rider's freed hands can be used to push the knees for more power.

Funfiets, for no-hands riding.

TANDEM BIKES

Tandem bikes or "twins" are available in four seating formats: the popular in-line format, with the captain in the front seat and the stoker in rear; the side-by-side format, usually with one side steering and the other side with fixed handlebars; the Janus format, or Pushmi-Pullyu, with the cyclists back-to-back facing opposite directions (Janus was the mythic two-faced Roman god of beginnings, guardian of gates and doors, and the Pushmi-Pullyu was a Doctor Dolittle creature); and the back-to-front format, or reversed forward stoker tandem, with the riders face-to-face. Many kinds of bikes have been made into tandems, including roadsters, folding bikes, touring bikes, racing bikes, and recumbents. The Co-Pilot tandem (1975) made by Meyland-Smith in Denmark, allows a child-sized front rider to steer the bike along with an adult-sized rear rider.

In-line tandems are usually set up with in-phase cranks, with front and rear pedals fixed to the same point in the stroke, but some tandems are set up with out-of-phase cranks, where the stoker's pedals are at 90 degrees of the captain's pedals. In-phase pedals are easier for mounting and climbing, and out-of-phase pedals offer smoother spinning, with less tandem sway and bike-straining peak force because there is no dead center. To design a more comfortable and smaller wheelbase tandem, Bill Patterson, an HPV professor at Cal Poly in San Luis Obisbo, California, developed the prototype Wyms two-wheel-drive recumbent folding tandem with twenty-inch wheels. The stoker's rear-wheel-drive operates independently of the captain, who has a fixed-fork front-wheel-drive that allows hands-free steering.

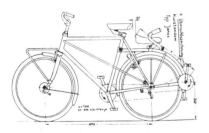

Janus or Pushmi-Pullyu tandem.

MULTI-BIKES

Multi-bikes follow after two-wheel tandems in the family of cycles, with triplets (three-cyclists), quadruplets (four), quintuplets (five), sextuplets (six), septuples (seven), octuplets or octopeds (eight), nincompooplets (nine), decemtuplets (ten), and trigintapedes (31). A famous ten-rider bike during cycling's Golden Age was the Oriten made by the Orient Cycle Company in 1896. It was 23 feet long and weighed 305 pounds unloaded, and about 1,500 pounds loaded. The "Longest Push Bike in the World" is 22.86 meters long (75 feet), seats 40 people, with 39 pedals and one passenger, weighs about three tons, and was built in 1984 in Queanbeyan, Australia.

COMBINATION CYCLES

Combination cycles, convertible trikes, and trailer bikes are special attachments that make single bikes into tandems, cargo trikes, and quadricycles. Single bikes have been converted into tandems since the Invincible Tandem and the Ivel Safety of the 1890s. Bikes can be made into trikes featuring dual front wheel Ackermann steering with the Newton Trike Conversion Kit, and two-wheel trailers can replace rear wheels on the Flevo bike to make a cargo trike. Bicycle coupling devices connect two bikes side-by-side to make tandem quadricycles, such as the Coldwell Bicycle Coupler (1890s).

Above, Coldwell bicycle coupler. Left, Burley Rock 'n Roll tandem with Allsop Softride suspension for the stoker. Lower left, Trailer bikes combine to make bike train; Below, Child-carrier bike converts to pedicab trike.

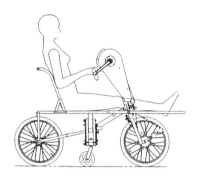

Handbike with parallel crank arms.

Sunburst Tandem, with hand drive in front and pedals behind.

HAND CYCLES

Hand cycles offer alternative kinds of mechanical drive for people with limited strength in their legs. They include bikes, trikes, and wheelchairs with hand-crank and rowing mechanisms. Used for transport, touring, and competition, hand cycles offer recreation and health benefits beyond the expectations of their users. There are about 25 hand cycle manufacturers in North America, with many one-of-a-kind developments by individuals and physical rehabilitation centers.[7]

The Handbike was developed in 1980 by Doug Schwandt at the Veterans Administration Medical Center in Palo Alto, California. It is a two-wheel recumbent with two more caster wheels that swing down for easy boarding. To improve steering and reduce the effort expended, both crank-arms rotate in the same position—unlike the cranks of a standard bike that have one pedal at the top of the stroke and the other at the bottom.

Hand-powered tricycles feature front-drive wheels, off-camber rear wheels (about nine degrees) for extra stability, hands-on backpedal brakes, and carrier racks. New England Handcycles, the oldest manufacturer in the U.S., offers the 24-speed aluminum Trike, useful for road touring and racing. The Rowcycle is a fast tricycle that combines the use of a sliding seat and three-speed lever bars for propulsion. It steers by the rider shifting his or her weight in the seat, and it is adaptable for paraplegics, quadriplegics, and amputees. The Roeifiets (1988) is a high-performance arm- and leg-powered recumbent developed by Derk Thijs that has won HPV races in Europe. The Rowbike (1993) is a long wheelbase recumbent with a hand-powered lever- and chain-drive mechanism made by Scott Olson of Minnesota, founder of Rollerblade Inc.

Many two-wheel tandems are suitable for people with disabilites, such as the Sunburst Tandem by Doug Schwandt. This was the forerunner to the Opus III by Counterpoint Conveyance, an eighteen-speed tandem bicycle in which the front rider sits recumbent, with hand or foot cranks available. The rear rider sits upright, with an unobstructed view of the road.

TRICYCLES

Tricycles, trikes, and three-wheel vehicles are designed for sport, transport, utility. They are categorized by the placement of the wheels, by the number of wheel tracks, and by the steering and drive mechanisms. The traditional variety of three-track tricycles are built with one wheel in front and two wheels in the rear (1+2), and Kendrick-style trikes have two wheels in front and one behind (2+1). Two-track trikes may have a central wheel on one side and two on the other side, front and rear (1+1+1). Trikes with two-wheel-drive and a differential usually track and turn better than one-wheel-drive vehicles, especially since many roads are off-camber and tilt up in the center for drainage. The Victorian by Peter Taylor of England is a 2+1 tandem trike with Ackermann steering, and the custom-made Longstaff Tandem trike is equipped like a traditional high-performance road bike.

RECUMBENT TRIKES

Recumbent tricycles and practical HPVs are designed for sport and transport, and categorized by the vehicle's body (open, semi-faired, fully faired), by the driver's position (semi-recumbent, recumbent, low-rider), and by the driving mechanism. Practical HPVs in production include the Leitra (1985) by Carl Rasmussen of Denmark, a 70-pound town and country trike with a snow-proof, fully-faired body, and the Windcheetah Speedy by Mike Burrows, with a joy-stick handlebar and a full range of fairings. The Thebis trike, by Robert and Peter Perkins of Canada, has the crankset as part of the front wheel hub. The prototype Twike (1989) from Switzerland is a two-seater faired coupe with tandem belt-driven transmission and optional electric motor-drive. The Sinner, a 35-pound aluminum recumbent trike from Holland, allows another Sinner to be hitched behind, as a trailer trike with the extra front wheel as cargo.

PEDAL CARRIAGES

Pedal carriages are tricycles and quadricycles built for tandem and sociable cycling. These vehicles evolved from the velocipede carriages and sociable cycles of the 1870s and 1880s that predate automobiles. The magazine *Cycling* described these vehicles in 1892:

> They were called double tricycles because they were double the weight of anything else of their kind, because they required double the exertion to propel them, double the time to clean, double the money to buy, and also for the less important reason that they carried two persons.... These engines were more generally known as sociables chiefly because after a few miles they made the two riders thoroughly unsociable.

A wide range of three- and four-wheel pedal carriages are currently produced for easy-going recreation. These include the Honeymooner tricycle by Bachtold Bros., with dual cranks for side-by-side pedaling, and the Beach Buggy 2+2 quadricycle by the Original Surrey Company of Texas, with a canopy, battery-powered lights, and stereo system. Four-wheel pedal carriages with rack and pinion steering include the single-seat ForeRunner by NordicTrak, and the two-seat Quadracycle with automobile-style steering wheel. The $3,000 Jomark Bus has four seats, each with pedals, brakes on all four wheels.

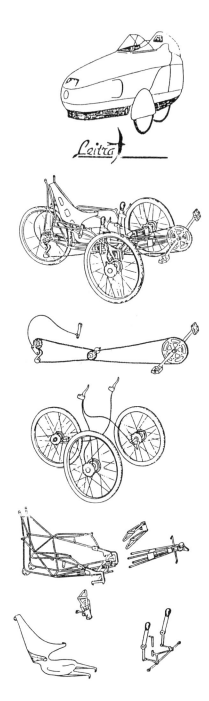

Above, Carl Rasmussen's Leitra trike with its components. Left, NordicTrak Forerunner.

Utility Cycles

Utility cycles, or human-powered utility vehicles (HPUVs), are often the hardest working members of the cycle family. They have multiple wheels and multiple uses, carrying cargo and people in quantities beyond what is practical on a standard bicycle. Along with traditional carrier cycles, utility cycles include various kinds of trailers, rail cycles, pedal-carts, emergency cycles, military machines, and camera bikes.

CARRIER CYCLES

Cargo-carrying cycles come in a variety of shapes. Among cargo bikes, there are duplex carriers with heavy racks front and rear (New-Hudson), small-wheel low-gravity front carrier bikes (Royal Enfield), and long-wheelbase front loader bikes, such as the Long John by Smith and Company-SCO, the Long Emma by Pashley, and the Long Haul by Jan Van Der Tuin. Among cargo trikes, there are side-car carriers (James), rear platform carriers (Oxtrike), semi-recumbent rear carriers (Lucic), box-shaped front loaders (Gundle), and front loader dumpsters (HP Research). Among four-wheel cargo cycles, there is a pedal-powered forklift, called the Super Lift 500, made by Japan Steels. Carriers have been equipped with wicker baskets, mail bags, grocery boxes, bottle racks, plastic dumpsters, cooking stoves, and insulated refrigerators.

Royal Enfield low-gravity carrier bike.

Many carrier cycles are made by specialized companies such as Worksman Cycles of New York and Pashley of England, and by numerous intermediate technology development groups in Europe, Latin America, Africa, and Asia. The Oxtrike, developed by Oxfam, was one of the first HPUVs developed in the West specifically for use in non-industrialized countries. It is currently being manufactured in a dozen small workshops in several countries.

TRAILERS

Bicycle trailers are an easy way to pull additional passengers and cargo. Their advantage is in keeping extra loads lower to the ground with less stress on the bicycle and its stability. Trailers usually hitch to a bicycle at the seat post, or to one of the rear stays. They typically have two twenty-inch wheels and are about 30 inches wide with steel or aluminum frames and platforms or seats that can hold one or more children or grocery bags up to about 100 pounds. For wet weather, trailers such as the Burley, Equinox, and Winchester have tent-like structures with windows or screens. The Cycle Tote trailer has an electric, battery operated drum brake that weighs 25 pounds and cost about $675 in 1992. Side-cars for passengers and cargo also attach to bikes for extra stability. The Springer side-bar dog tether lets dogs run with their master and do a little pulling.

Ivy Tradesman Carrier
Ice Cream model, 1930s.

Trailer bikes attach to other bikes and have additional seats and pedals to tandems and triplets. These include the Adams Trail-A-Bike (1990) from Canada, the Islabikes Trailerbike (1989), and the two-seater Cresswell U+2 trailer trike from England.

James Sidecar Bi-Carrier Cycle, 1924.

Burley trailer.

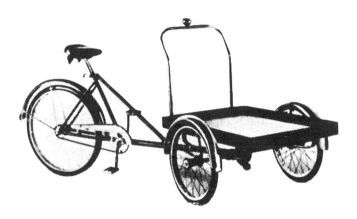

Worksman Platform tricycle, 1990.

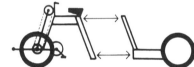

Multi-purpose carrier trike becomes pedal-powered workstation.

Japan Steels Super Lift 500 pedal-powered forklift.

PEDICABS

Pedicabs are pedal-powered tricycles and quadricycles designed to carry non-pedaling passengers to serve as human-powered taxicabs. They are named by language and land: *chaise-roulante* in French; rickshaw and trishaw in English; *tricyclo* in Latin America; *lancha* in Malaysia; *becak* (say bay-jack) and *roda tiga* in Indonesea; *jinrikisha* (human-powered-vehicle) and *rintaku* in Japanese; and *samlor* in Thailand. The two-seat bicycle taxis in Uganda are named *boda boda*, because motor vehicles coming from Kenya have not been allowed to cross into Uganda since the mid-1960s, so drivers shouted "Border Border" to attract travelers.

Passengers sit either in front of the driving cyclist (Indonesean-style), behind the driver (Chinese-style), or in enclosed side cars (Filipino-style). Most have wicker seats or padded benches and weatherproof canopies. In India, Pakistan, and Bangladesh, artists have decorated rickshaws with painted murals, tassles, and metalic fringes. Western-made pedicabs often have fiberglass bodies and stereo systems, such as the Paradise Pedicab of Hawaii and the Trans Canada Pedicab of Vancouver. In China, pedicabs are built as miniature school buses for transporting children. Various designs for pedal-powered buses have seats for over a dozen passengers, each with the option of pedaling. Most pedicabs in Asia have changed little since the 1930s. To improve their efficiency in Bangladesh, the Canadian International Development Agency helped two village factories build lighter and stronger passenger and cargo vehicles that reduce a driver's effort by some 30 percent.[8]

Top to bottom: Indonesean-style pedicab with passengers in front; Chinese-style pedicab with passengers behind; Chinese school pedicab; Right, American-style pedicab, with lights and sound system.

RAIL CYCLES

Rail cycles are designed to ride on railroad tracks, fence rails, and elevated monorails. Because metal railroad tracks have such smooth surfaces and gentle grades they offer an ideal low-resistance path for human-powered vehicles. Rail bikes are usually set up with a bicycle mounted on one rail with extra flanged guide wheels to keep the bike in line with the track. The bike is supported by a triangulated cross bar with one or two flanged guide wheels connected to the opposite rail. This keeps the bike balanced and upright, with very little steering required at curves and junctions in the track. The earliest rail bikes were built specially for track maintenance and more recently have been used for recreation since there are over 40,000 miles of neglected track in the U.S.[9]

With lightweight safety bicycles, rail attachments were made portable so track inspectors could also ride on mixed-traffic roads. The rail attachments included an additional front fork with flanged guide wheels that could be raised and lowered for road or rail, and a folding side frame with a small roller wheel. When the cyclist arrived at the tracks, the triangulated frame was connected near the seat post and the rear wheel axle, with the flanged roller leaning against the opposite track. Telescopic frame poles adjusted to different gauges of track. Recent variations include guide wheels made with double flanges and quieter plastics, with mounts at a 45 degree angle to the track. An alternative is using two bicycles connected side-by-side on each rail with guide wheels to keep them on track.

Three and four wheel rail cycles were develeped for railroad workers in the 1880s. The Sheffield Velocipede Hand Car, made in Michigan, was a 125-pound wood and iron vehicle with both hand and foot lever-drive mechanisms. A similar vehicle was used in the 1890s for track inspectors in Russia to prevent sabotage of the Czar's train. It had iron wheels with rail flanges and weighed about 110 pounds.

The 1890s bicycle craze inspired two kinds of bicycle railroad systems—one for riding on fence-rails, the other with the cyclist suspended above ground. The Mount Holly & Smithville Bicycle Railroad was developed by "Professor" Arthur Hotchkiss for commuters traveling along the Rancocas Creek from Mount Holly, New Jersey, to the H.B. Smith Manufacturing Company. The riders used modified cycling machines with a twenty-inch wheel driven by the treadle mechanism used on the Smith Star bicycle. Some 3,000 people rode it on opening day September 13, 1892, but with only one fence-rail, riders had to dismount when encountering someone traveling in the opposite direction.

Hotchkiss bicycle railway, Smithville, New Jersey, 1892.

A few suspended bicycle railroads appeared around 1893 as amusement rides along the New Jersey shore in Atlantic City, Ocean Beach, and Gloucester. Hanging a couple of feet over the ground from dual ɪ-beam fence-rails, these pedal-driven railroads offered the sensation of flight. The original Smithville line was closed in 1898 and a few years later, W.G. Bean brought a fence-type bicycle railroad from New York to his

native Blackpool, England. Called the Mono-Rail Velocipede, it served as a popular amusement until about 1910. In the 1930s, the Wuppertal railway in Germany used two-wheel cycles on a suspended monorail.

In 1992, a prototype human-powered railway was developed by Jim Kor, an industrial designer and editor of *HPV News*. Called the Skyway Transportation System, it includes single-rider 80-pound streamlined HPVs with four wheels and solid rubber tires that ride on aluminum tracks in elevated, enclosed rail tubes with wind pumped into them for attaining average cruising speeds of 40 mph. As a kind of Personal Rapid Transit (PRT), Kor envisions vehicles that can string together for more efficiency, and a pollution-free network of smooth gradients, curves and interchanges suitable for long commutes and large parks.

Pedaltrain by Steven M. Johnson, from *Public Therapy Buses*, 1991.

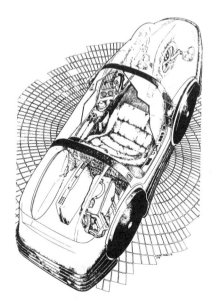

Design for the Skyway Transportation System, by Jim Kor.

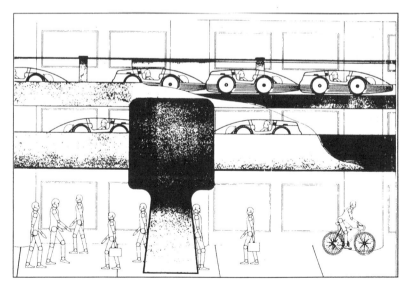

UTILITY CYCLES

These human-powered utility vehicles are designed for special purposes, such as street vending, firefighting, providing health care, tree-climbing, surveying, photographing, and advertising.

Around 1900, some tradesmen put their entire shops on wheels, and their vehicles were called "Applied Bicycles."[10] At Coney Island, there was a tricycle barbershop complete with a standard barber's chair. In Berlin, a wheeled tobacco shop had a glass cigar case and a battery operated electric sign for the café nightlife. In Paris, tricycling street pianists mounted the keyboard of their hurdy-gurdy at the handlebars, and in New York, a "Perambulating Electrician" converted an old wagon coach "according to bicycle usage," and set-up a workbench, an anvil, and a full kit of tools for doing odd jobs. Today, in New York, there are a few roving knife and scissor sharpeners who ride around pedal-driven grinding wheel attachments, and some nomadic bike mechanics who carry their shop on bike trailers.

Many utility cycles have been used for emergency situations. These include the Schoedelin Fireman's Quadricycle used in Paris in the mid-1890s, which had four riders and four wheels. Supposedly, it could reach a fire in one-fourth to one-third the time required by a horse-drawn fire carriage. After arriving at the fire, the men would drop the kickstand, uncoil the hose, connect it to a pump, and hop back on the pedals for pumping the water with a force that could shoot 75 feet into the air. A single-rider fire-cycle with a coil of hose contained within the center of the frame was made by BSA in 1905 for firefighters in the British petroleum industry.

British Petroleum's BSA firefighting bike with hose coil, 1905

Bicycle ambulances have appeared throughout the bicycle's history. Some were long stretchers with tandem riders at both ends, and others were built on rear loading tricycles with enclosed cabins. The Simonis Bicycle Ambulance was a folding bicycle that could be converted "in three minutes" into a two-wheeled hand-cart stretcher for rescue work in British coal mines. Lightweight stretcher trailers for carrying patients to health care centers in remote areas were built by IT Transport (UK) in the 1980s after an original design used in Malawi.[11] In the 1990s, Matteo Martignoni of the Institute for Transportation and Development Policy (ITDP) developed the Haitian Hauler bicycle ambulance, and after much political turmoil, he formed the Laboratwa Esperance in Deschapelles, for Haitians to learn vehicle building. In Denver, the Department of Health and Hospitals developed an All-Terrain Medical Unit (ATMU) in 1990 with mountain bikes carrying oxygen packs, cardiac monitors, and other medical equipment for paramedics working crowded events where motor vehicles have limited access.

In the field of agriculture, the human-powered tractor offers a cleaner vehicle for organic growers. In the mid-1980s, a farm in the Netherlands designed a tandem foot-powered vehicle for planting and seeding. Driving twelve-inch tractor tires geared down to move about six inches per pedal revolution, a cycling farmer sits in a low recumbent position with hands in easy reach of the earth. Various tree and pole climbing tricycles have been invented for harvesting fruit and maintaining telephone lines. These include one from the 1930s seen in the movie *Gizmo*, the Pole Climber from China (1986), and the Cyclopalma from Cuba (1993). Bicycle-powered lawn mowers that attach as trailers have appeared since the 1930s, and one is currently produced by Dynamo Inc. of Colorado.

The Ferguson Cyclograph was developed around 1904 to make a topographic record of the landscape with the surveyor on a bicycle. The instrument was a box holding paper and mounted on the handlebars. A compass was mounted ten inches above the box to protect it against the bicycle's magnetic effects. An eccentric disc on the front hub connected by an oscillating lever moved the paper in a similar speed but in the opposite direction of the bike. As the cyclist turned in any direction, wires from the compass guided the appropriate angle with which the cyclist rotated the paper. An inked wheel, also driven by the front wheel, inscribed the route on paper marked with the known meridians. In practice, the device compared favorably with the lines of roads on official maps, and the intelligence branch of the British government considered its use in China.

Many kinds of bikes and cycles have been equipped for cameras. One of the first pedal-powered cameras was the photographic tricycle for tourists which combined a Rudge Rotary Tricycle mounted with a large format view camera. The whole unit included a tripod and accessory case, and cost around £50. In finding a suitable roadside subject, the photographer-cyclist could either scout around on foot with the camera on the tripod, or simply point and shoot by pedaling and aiming the tricycle.

The cult of the high-wheel bicycle and the growth of amateur photography coincide, and the desire to record cyclists' outings inspired the development of portable cameras which could travel by bicycle. Under the heading "Anthony's Bicycle Equipment," the 1891 photographic equipment catalog from E.& H.T. Anthony and Company of New York offered a $10 dry plate box camera designed to clamp onto the handlebars of a high-wheeler. Using a telescopic support to steady the wheels, with the camera mounted on the handlebars, the bicycle served as a wheeled-tripod with enough height for standing while focusing on the subject. Another popular camera among cyclists was the circular spy camera, a forerunner of today's miniature disc cameras. It weighed about half a pound and was designed to be worn under the coat or vest suspended by a strap from the neck with the lens protruding. The camera had a fixed wide-angle lens of universal focus so the photographer only had to judge the light to time the exposure. There were six exposures per negative with circular images available in two sizes, 1¾ or 2½ inches. They were often advertised in cycling publications and cost around $12.

Around 1900, the pioneering photo-journalist Sumner Matteson carried two cameras and a portable darkroom on his bicycle while exploring Native American settlements around the Grand Canyon. Matteson's Overman Victor Safety Bicycle No. 3 was equipped with a handlebar-

Cyclopalma tree-climbing bike.

Anthony's Bicycle Equipment.

mounted Bulls Eye folding tripod, a Kodak carrying case attached under the top tube, a pocket-sized (3¼ x 4¼ inches) Kodak No. 3 camera, a large format (5 x 7 inches) Kodak No. 5 camera, a flashlamp with flash powder for nighttime photos, a darkroom safe light with wicks, daylight loading cartridges of twelve-exposure roll film, processing chemicals and containers, and "Solio Paper" for making finished contact prints.[12]

The desire to capture the cyclist's point of view has inspired many cyclographers to mount cameras on their bikes and themselves. In the 1980s, sculptor and photographer Kenneth Snelson mounted a sixteen-inch panoramic Cirkut Camera on the rack of his three-speed bicycle and rode around New York searching locations to make 360 degree panoramic pictures that realized his "voyeuristic impulse to see in all directions at once."[13] Mark Forman, an independent filmmaker in New York, mounted a camera to his bike while documenting Alaska's Iditabike race, and eventually patented the Forman Camera Bicycle (1992), suitable for mounting professional quality film, video, and audio equipment. The unique triple-suspension mountain bike, made to Forman's specifications by Boulder Bicycles, has a long, narrow platform for front and rear mounting. Similarly, Bruce Petschek of Seven Generations Video in Boston made the documentary *Way to Go: Bicycles in Cuba* (1994), with a camera and boom microphone mounted on his non-motorized bicycle. Michael Friedland of Colorado developed a helmet mount for lightweight 8 mm auto-focus video cameras, and he rents the equipment ($50 for three hours) through a service called Head Trip.

Probably the most high-tech bike ever assembled is Steve Roberts' Behemoth, which stands for "Big Electronic Human-Energized Machine Only Too Heavy." A mobile telecom work station, this $1.2 million, 350-pound, 105-speed recumbent bike and trailer was developed in 1990 at Roberts' Nomadic Research Labs near Santa Cruz, California, with much of the equipment donated by manufacturers. The Behemoth evolved from Roberts' first generation bike, the 220-pound Winnebiko, which was his home and office during his 10,000-mile adventure into cyberspace, documented in his newsletters, *High-Treknowledgy* and *Nomadness*, and his book, *Computing Across America: The Bicycle Odyssey of a High-tech Nomad*.

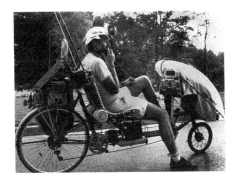

Steve Roberts on his Winnebiko.

Behemoth is equipped with a Qualcomm satellite station with dedicated computer for sending and receiving messages through GTE's orbiting GSTAR satellite. It has a dual band VHF/UHF ham radio, an Oki cellular phone, and a Cell Blazer modem. Among the computers in the front console there is a Sun computer with 207 mb hard drive and CD-ROM drive, a Macintosh with 40 MB hard drive, an IBM-PC with VGA monitor for technical graphics, and a Toshiba laptop, which manages his unique handlebar keyboard, with only ten keys and plenty of macro commands for typing characters, words, and phrases. Another useful feature when cycling is the Brain Interface unit, with ultrasonic sensors on his helmet that move the on-screen cursor by moving his head, and the Private Eye heads-up-display, a tiny helmet-mounted monitor that is easier to read than the console monitors.

For security, Behemoth has a microwave motion detector and Roberts carries a security pager. Whenever he's away from the vehicle, he carries a Manpack briefcase with 10-watt solar panel, laptop computer, and a radio link that allows Roberts to communicate with the bike and those near it, using a speech synthesis and recognition system. If Behemoth is stolen, Roberts can use its navigating equipment, the Trimble Global Positioning System, which computes latitude, longitude, elevation, and speed, to pinpoint the vehicle's location within 50 feet. For entertainment, he has a MIDI music synthesizer, AM/FM/shortwave radio, waterproof Blaupunkt speakers. To power these gadgets, Behemoth's trailer has a 12-volt battery and a 72-watt solar panel array. When Roberts appeared on the Phil Donahue show, Behemoth talked to the audience and before cutting to a commercial, it said "And now a word from our sponsor."

The machine represented herewith opens up a new horizon in the vast domain of advertising, in which it seemed impossible to realize still another innovation.—Revue Universelle (1895).

The tricycle printing press or "Advertising Cycle," was one of those Victorian inventions that combined one good idea with another to make a third idea that may be more or less than the sum of both. It was a tricycle equipped to print short advertising slogans on the street using raised letters on the two rear wheels which came into contact with ink rollers. Behind the saddle were two cubical reservoirs of special ink that fed the ink rollers placed on top of and in contact with rubber tires carrying a message in relief type. The letters were four inches tall and up to about 40 letter spacings were available per wheel. A belt-driven blower cleared the road of dust, but only smooth roads were able to accept the inked message. The vehicle predates Marshall McLuhan's saying, "the medium is the message."

Above, Advertising Cycle, 1895. for printing messages in the road.
Below, Steven Roberts' Behemoth, a mobile telecomunications workstation.

Speed Machines

The most popular question about any bike, besides how much it costs, is "How fast can it go?" The correct answer, which is not so popular, is "How fast can you pedal?" Cycling has many speed records and many ways to say "fastest," depending on the type of cycle and the amount of power input by the cyclist. There are four kinds of fast bikes in cycling—standard racing bikes, human-powered vehicles, downhill bikes, and motor-paced bikes—which correspond to the three kinds of cycling speeds—continuous speed on level ground, maximum speed on level ground, and maximum speed with assistance. Top speed records are determined more by the cycle, and continuous speed records are determined more by the cyclist. Of all speed records, the world hour record is the most fascinating event in cycling. Measuring the distance humans can travel in one hour (kilometers or miles per hour), it corresponds to many human performance factors and many kinds of cycling machines.

Standard racing bikes (road, track, aero, and MTB) are the most common fast bikes because they are used by the world's professional and amateur cyclists. The speed of these bikes is somewhat limited because they are designed according to the standards of cycle sport's governing bodies, the Union Cycliste Internationale (UCI), the International Triathlon Union (ITU), the Ultra-Marathon Cycling Association (UMCA), and the Road Time Trials Council (RTTC) in Britain. Recumbents and human-powered vehicles (HPVs) are the fastest cycling machines for pure record-breaking speed, mainly because there are fewer design limitations specified by the governing body, the International Human-Powered Vehicle Association (IHPVA). HPVs have been banned or segregated from traditional cycle sport, mainly because the group dynamics and human nature of UCI bike racing is somewhat different from HPV racing. Downhill bikes go faster than standard bikes and HPVs because they are assisted by the pull of gravity. Motor-paced bikes, which set the world's land speed record, are the fastest bikes on earth when drafting behind motor vehicles, as they are designed to do.

Butch Stinton and Jan Russell received honorary speeding tickets at the 1979 IHPVA Championships for going over 55 mph in White Lightning. Photo by Ted Mock.

Road Bikes

Road racing bikes are designed according to UCI rules for mass-start road racing, although many are used for recreation and all-purpose cycling. In a sprint on flat land, cyclists can go about 75 kph (47 mph), and downhill they can safely go over 100 kph (62 mph). Featuring skinny tires, drop-handlebars, rim brakes, and multi-speed derailleurs, they traditionally have a diamond-shaped frame and wheels with tubular or clincher tires (700c x 22). Notable road bikes include the three-speed BSA Three Rifles (1935), the ten-speed Bianchi Tour de France (1949), the ten-speed Cinelli Super Corsa (1965), the twelve-speed Colnago Mexico (1980), and the sixteen-speed Specialized Allez (1992). The shape of road bikes has changed relatively little since the 1950s, and most innovations appear in the materials and components. To distinguish different makes when

Road racing bike;
Pursuit track bike;
Six-day race track bike.

brand names were not allowed on the bikes of British amateurs, an unorthodox category of bikes were designed, such as the Hetchins (1934) with Vibrant Triangle curly stays, used for track racing and touring, and the Flying Gate design made by Barnes and Trevor Jarvis Cycles. Road bikes with suspension include those by Moulton, Softride, and LeMond. The latter is a 22-pound titanium bike made by Clark-Kent Cycles with handlebar-controlled front and rear elastomer shocks. The Colnago Ferrari (1989) is a notable prototype, with its carbon composite frame, three-spoke wheels, eight-speed oil-bath gear case, and hydraulic caliper brakes.

TRACK BIKES

Track bikes are designed according to UCI rules for racing on velodromes with a fixed-gear and a backpedal brake. There are different styles and positions for sprint races, mass-start races, time trial races, six-day team races, road riding, and messengering. Cyclists have reached speeds over 80 kph (50 mph) on velodromes, and pacing behind a motor at speeds over 100 kph (+62 mph), usually with a *demi-fond* motor-pace bicycle. Track bikes include those by Cinelli, Pogliaghi, and Schwinn.

The bicycle for track sprinting is heavier and stronger, to withstand the powerful forces of acceleration, with short crank arms for easier spinning. The gear varies from about 88 to 92 inches, depending on the track length and surface. The tandem track bike has stronger wheels and tires, weighs about 45 pounds, and has a gear of about 100 inches. The kilo bike is usually more aerodynamic, with a smaller, lower front wheel and a rear disc, and handlebars that permit better breathing. The typical gear is about 92 inches. The pursuit bike is a light aero bike, with a fixed-gear of about 90 inches. Team pursuit bikes are similar to pursuit bikes, differing only by slightly larger 94-inch gears, and shorter wheelbases to keep the teams tight. In order to take advantage of the pacer's slipstream, the *demi-fond* or stayer's bicycle has a distinctive shape. The front forks are raked backwards and the front wheel is smaller (600 mm diameter) for better steering stability. The saddle is pushed forward, over the vertical line from the center of the crank axle, and supported by a second post on the top tube. Tires are glued and wrapped to the rims to prevent them from rolling off, and the fixed-gear is about 130 inches. Cycle speedway bikes have straight forks, upright handlebars, a low saddle position for cornering, and a one-speed gear of about 45 to 50 inches for quick acceleration.

AERO BIKES

Aero bikes, or time trial (TT) bikes, are standardized road and track bikes designed to reduce aerodynamic drag for timed races. Most are built according to rules of the UCI, the ITU, the UMCA, and the RTTC, and they have gradually changed since the 1980s, with new materials, new aerodynamic and ergonomic components, and new rulings that are responding to bicycle design in the 1990s. Aero bike components include low-profile and monocoque (one-piece) frames, small and large wheels with aero spokes or lenticular discs, aero bars and tri-bars, and forward-position and high-back saddles. Traditional time trial bikes were made lightweight and frictionless, such as the Colnago Windsor used by Eddy Merckx in his 1972 hour record, but without aero bike components they are slower by one to five kilometers per hour.

Radical aero bikes appeared in the early 1980s, in the Tour de France, the World Championships, the Olympics, and the UCI world hour record. In 1984, Francesco Moser used the Moser-Dal Monte aero bike with the first lenticular disc wheels in modern times to set the UCI hour record of 51.151 kilometers, and the U.S. track team used the $40,000 Huffy-Raleigh "funny bikes" developed by Mike Melton and Chester Kyle to win medals at the L.A. Olympics and the Worlds. In the 1986 Tour de France, when Laurent Fignon showed up with a teardrop-shaped high-back saddle on his sleek Gitane Profile TT bike, which provided lumbar support for increased leverage, officials would not allow it. But in the 1989 Tour, Greg LeMond was allowed to use Scott aero bars on his Bottecchia Kronostrada bike. Scientific analysis showed that his eight-second victory over Fignon in the final time trial could be attributed to using those bars and the Giro aero helmet. For an indoor track hour record in 1988, Moser used an aero bike with a large diameter rear wheel (101 centimeters or 39½ inches). Meanwhile, triathlon racing produced a new category of aero road bikes, with the cyclist sitting further forward over the pedals, a position which caused the UCI to vary its standard measure for saddle to crank set-back.

Since 1982, Mike Burrows had been developing a kind of road and track aero bike, called the Windcheetah Monocoque, with a composite cantilever frame and a monoblade fork. When the UCI allowed monocoque frames in 1990, Burrows' bike was refined by Lotus engineers for the 1992 Barcelona Olympics, and called the Lotus Sport "super bike," which Britain's pursuit gold-medalist Chris Boardman used to set a 4,000-meter record of 4 minutes 24.496 seconds. It featured a Mavic 3-spoke front wheel, a disc rear, and a two-piece handlebar with composite wings for accelerations, and flat narrow titanium arm rests for a low-drag aero position. Lotus Sport has adapted the bike for road time trials with a double-blade fork and Mavic aero components, and for mountain biking.

Graeme Obree, an amateur from Ayrshire, Scotland, hit the record books in 1993 with an ingenious new aero position, a forward-prone position with his shoulders resting on the handlebars and his arms tucked in to help push a bigger gear. Obree surpassed Francesco Moser's long-standing hour record by going 51.596 kilometers and won the World Pursuit Championships at Hamar, Norway. Used on the track and the road, Obree's Mark I bike came to be called "old faithful," and featured a 52 × 12 fixed-gear of 116 inches (9.25 meters development), Specialized-Du Pont wheels, 531 tubing, a composite monoblade fork, a narrow Q-factor bottom bracket with bearings from a Hotpoint washing machine, handlebars from a child's BMX bike, and a crank made from a piece of metal found in the street. Obree had another more refined bike made by Mike Burrows, but he opted to use his own. Obree's position has a drag coeffi-

Top to bottom:
Francesco Moser's hour record bike, 1984; Chris Boardman's Lotus Sport pursuit bike, developed by Mike Burrows; Graeme Obree's home-made hour record bike.

Hour record bikes, top to bottom:
Miguel Indurain's Pinarello Espada;
Tony Rominger's Colnago CX;
Catherine Marsal's Corima bike.

cient of about 0.18 and it produces about 25 percent more power output. A modified version was used by 42-year-old Francesco Moser in his tenth anniversary 1984–1994 hour record attempt (51.840 kms).

From Obree's record of July 17, 1993, to the record set by Tony Rominger on November 5, 1994, the UCI hour record advanced 3.795 kilometers or two and one half miles—more than any similar period since the development of the safety bike. The world's four finest time trialists used a variety of aero bikes, all on the 250-meter wood track in Bordeaux, France. Chris Boardman rode 52.270 kilometers using a carbon composite monocoque aero bike made by Corima of France, with Corima four-spoke wheels and a narrow composite handlebar similar to the Lotus Sport bike. Graeme Obree regained the record in April 1994 going 52.713 kilometers on his Mark II bike, a modified original with double-blade forks. The UCI banned Obree's position (but not his records) from road races for safety reasons (he took risks), and from track races (when Obree was at the starting line of the World Championships). Officials referred to Article 49 and rules about unfair advantage, saddle to crank axle set-back, saddle and handlebar type, and that the bike must be "viable, marketable, usable by all types of sporting cyclists." Britain's RTTC allows the bike, along with road and track bikes with single brakes.

Miguel Indurain of Spain, the four-time Tour de France winner, set an hour record of 53.040 kilometers in September 1994, riding a Pinarello Espada ("sword") aero bike, with a thin composite monocoque frame, Campagnolo disc wheels and a solid disc chainwheel, wide ITM tri-bars, and a paint job with horizontal lines intended to reduce drag. Because of his large size (1.86 meters), "Big Mig" has more wind drag than the average racer, and on Bordeaux's 250-meter track, where centrifugal forces apply, he had more mass to pull through the banked curves. Tony Rominger, the Danish-born Swiss star residing in Monaco, who superseded Indurain in 1994 as the UCI's No. 1 ranked cyclist, set two records in October and November using two traditional-style Colnago aero bikes. His second ride of 55.291 kilometers "carried the record into a new era," and it was done on a steel-frame bike built with Columbus Oval CX tubing, featuring Fir composite disc wheels (smaller in front) and narrow ITM aero bars with a position similar to Boardman. Rominger's hour record bikes seemed to validate the UCI's principles by emphasizing human character over technical innovation, even as ingenuity pushed the record to a new level.

Other aero bikes include the Hooker Elite (1991), an eighteen-pound bike developed by the bike racing auto parts makers Gary Hooker and Dave Spangler, the Zipp Designs 2001 (1992) with carbon monocoque frame and the Allsop Softride suspension saddle, and the Look KG 196 (1992), with a carbon-kevlar-ceramic monocoque frame and Aerofin fork, a shock-absorbing needle-bearing headset, and the adjustable Look Ergostem. The X-Bike, a 30-pound prototype by Steve Christ of Innovative Bicycle Components, had the lowest drag in wind tunnel tests at Texas A&M University, but the partial fairing makes it illegal for UCI racing.

STREAMLINED BIKES

Streamlined bikes are standard road and track bikes built with aerodynamic fairings in teardrop and wing-shaped aerofoil designs. A separate category from aero bikes and streamlined recumbent HPVs, they have set various speed records over 80 kph (50 mph) on flat land. They were popular before World War I, in the 1930s when the UCI limited these bikes to a separate category, and again in the early 1970s with the HPV movement. One of the first record-breaking streamlined bikes was the Vélo-Torpille (Torpedo bike), developed in France by Etienne Bunau-Varilla and Marcel Riffard, and patented in Britain in 1912, in France in 1913, and in the U.S. in 1915. The French time-trial specialist Marcel Berthet rode Vélo-Torpille 5,000 meters at 52.3 kph (32.5 mph) in 1913, four miles per hour faster than he managed on a standard bike and two miles faster than the world record. At Berlin's Olympic velodrome, a race for streamlined bikes featured Dickenman in the Brennabor Fisch and Stellbrink in the Goricke Schrapnel (or Bomb), whose wobbly crash appears in an early newsreel featured in the film *Gizmo* (1972).

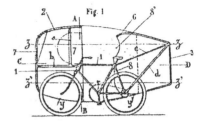

Streamlined bikes were revived in the 1930s, when Oscar Egg, the Swiss cycling star and three-time world hour record holder turned bike designer, built a bike with a streamlined tail called the Vélofusée (Bike rocket). Meanwhile, 47-year-old Marcel Berthet hired Marcel Riffard to build a streamlined body for a standard bike, called the Vélodyne, and on November 18, 1933, Berthet rode 49.992 kilometers, 31 miles in one hour, beating the record set on the open recumbent Velocar bike by nearly five kilometers. Oscar Egg continued building streamlined bikes, including the Sputnik (1961), which was named for the historic Soviet satellite, and had an aluminum streamlined shell fit to a *demi-fond* bicycle with a small front wheel.

In the early 1970s in Southern California, Chester Kyle and Jack Lambie built the record-breaking Teledyne Streamliner, using the standard titanium-frame Teledyne Titan racing bicycle with a long upright fairing, and Paul Van Valkenberg designed the wind-breaking Aeroshell fairing for standard bikes. At first, these new world innovators were unaware of the European history of streamlined bikes, and after a couple of years they discovered they were recycling designs by Bunau-Varilla, Riffard, and Egg. Many kinds of bikes with partial fairings have been made faster for commuting, touring, and HPV racing. The current record of 82.54 kph (51.3 mph) for a full fairing upright bike was set on a small-wheel Moulton AM with Zzipper fairing.

Streamline bike racing in Berlin, 1913.

STREAMLINED HPVS

Streamlined HPVs are recumbent cycles with aerodynamic fairings for racing at speeds over 100 kph on flat land. Although fairings add about ten pounds to the cycle's weight, they have drag coefficients of about 0.1 and less, and they are 25 to 50 percent faster than standard bikes. In the hour record, the fastest HPVs go twenty kilometers further than aero bikes.

The first record-breaking faired recumbent was Georges Mochet's Velocar, which set an hour record of 50.375 kilometers in 1939. Some 35 years later, with the advent of the HPV movement, a new breed of record-breaking vehicles were developed, often with multiple riders and multiple wheels. Even though IHPVA rules are generally open, there are many competition categories, including sprint races and time trials for single and multi-rider vehicles, as well as Le Mans start races, practical vehicle competitions, watercraft races, aircraft demonstrations, and all-terrain championships. Land-based records are usually set on smooth highways, motor speedways, and velodromes, although HPVs uncomfortably surpass the speeds designed for small bike tracks. In Le Mans racing, the racers start standing on the opposite side of the track and must run to their vehicles, climb in, and power away without assistance. These types of races were developed for practicality and as an alternative to flying-start and standing-start races, with cyclists duct-taped into their vehicles needing help to stay upright when stopped.

The top speed record for an unpaced human-powered vehicle was the project goal for many HPV enthusiasts, and as the 100 kph barrier was passed, cumbersome multi-rider quadricycles, such as the four-person Pegasus, were displaced by single-rider trikes, such as Don Witte's Allegro. Single-rider bikes took over in 1984 when Fred Markham rode

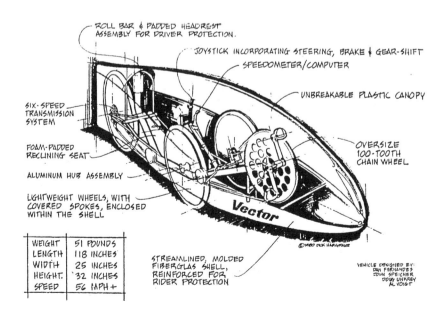

Double Gold Rush powered by Fred Markham and John Howard.

ROLL BAR & PADDED HEADREST ASSEMBLY FOR DRIVER PROTECTION.

JOYSTICK INCORPORATING STEERING, BRAKE & GEAR-SHIFT

SPEEDOMETER/COMPUTER

UNBREAKABLE PLASTIC CANOPY

SIX-SPEED TRANSMISSION SYSTEM

FOAM-PADDED RECLINING SEAT

ALUMINUM HUB ASSEMBLY

OVERSIZE 100-TOOTH CHAIN WHEEL

LIGHTWEIGHT WHEELS, WITH COVERED SPOKES, ENCLOSED WITHIN THE SHELL

Vector

©1980 DICK HARGRAVE

STREAMLINED, MOLDED FIBERGLAS SHELL, REINFORCED FOR RIDER PROTECTION

VEHICLE DESIGNED BY: DAN FERNANDEZ JOHN SPEICHER DOUG UNKREY AL VOIGT

WEIGHT	51 POUNDS
LENGTH	118 INCHES
WIDTH	25 INCHES
HEIGHT	32 INCHES
SPEED	56 MPH +

the Gold Rush HPV on a flat road at high altitude in Mono County, California, going 105.35 kph (65.48 mph) and winning the $18,000 Du Pont prize as the first HPV to go 65 mph or over. Designed and built by Gardner Martin, with Nathan Dean, Alan Osterbauer, Dan Pavish, and Glen Brown, the race model has a frame made of 6061 T6 aluminum, a fairing made of Kevlar and Lexan, wheel covers made of Mylar, and an 84-tooth chainwheel with a six-speed 11–16 cluster, making a top gear of sixteen meters development. Legend has it that helium was pumped into the tires, and oxygen pumped inside the cockpit. This record was surpassed in 1992, by the Cheetah HPV powered by Chris Huber, a pro cyclist on the Coors Light team, who reached 110.60 kph (68.72 mph) on a high altitude road near Del Norte, Colorado. Developed by Kevin Franz, Jon Garbarino, and James Osborn, who worked on an HPV project as engineering students at the University of California at Berkeley, the Cheetah came together in 1990 with a carbon fiber composite fairing and frame, with bonded aluminum inserts along the chain line, Campagnolo disc wheels (small in front), and a double reduction gear system. The Cheetah cuts a slender profile in the wind, and to attain greater speed, HPV designers look to ultra-low recumbents as the next development, such as Matt Weaver's Cutting Edge.

Many elite cyclists have tried the HPV world hour record, which honors technical ingenuity at least as much as athletic performance. In 1989, "Fast Freddy" Markham rode Gold Rush 72.94 kilometers (45.3 miles) for one hour at the Michigan International Speedway. The following year in Britain, Pat Kinch rode the Kingcycle Bean 75.56 kilometers (46.9 miles) at the sea-level racetrack in Millbrook. The front-wheel-drive Bean featured a Reynolds 531 steel frame, and aluminum webbed epoxy-fiberglass fairing, seventeen-inch Moulton wheels with alloy disc covers, a double reduction 186-inch gear (fifteen meters development), and a drag coefficient of 0.08. In October 1994, racer and builder Bram Moens of Holland set the current record of 77.123 kilometers on his M_5 recumbent.

DOWNHILL BIKES

Downhill cycles use gravity to go very fast, on-road and off-road, at speeds over 160 kph (100 mph). Gravity-powered vehicles (GPVs) are customized BMX bikes built for downhill road racing bikes, usually equipped for coasting only, without chains, pedals, or cranks. They are equipped with brakes, aerodynamic fairings, and rear foot pegs. They weigh about 30 pounds, and reach speeds of up to 90 mph. While some makers have tried adding weights, the most important speed factor is aerodynamics. Dan Hannebrink built a winning GPV in 1987 with a semi-prone riding position on a stretched-out Mongoose BMX frame, handle-grips fixed to the front fork, and a Bonneville motorcycle fairing. Mountain bikes are built for off-road UCI downhill racing and for special speed records, which are usually set on hard-packed snow. Most downhill bikes have front and rear wheel suspension, chain tensioners, and sometimes pedals without clips. Streamlined components and motorcycle

Dexter-Hysol Cheetah bike

wheels have been used, but mountain bike purists believe these give an unfair advantage.

MOTOR-PACE BIKES

Motor-paced bikes are specially designed to go fast on various tracks and roads, while using the draft of a motor vehicle to attain speeds over 200 kph (150 mph) on flat land. Motor-paced bikes built for the land speed record began as sturdy *demi-fond* bikes with large chainwheels and evolved with features of road racing motorcycles.

When John Howard set the record of 152.284 mph (245 kph) in 1985 at the Bonneville Salt Flats in Utah, he used a 46-pound, $10,000 bike called the Pepsi Challenger, built by Skip and Vicki Hujsak and developed by Doug Malewicki, an HPV designer who created Evel Knieval's Skycycle. The gearing for a bike that goes 152 mph calls for a double-reduction transmission system, in this case, two Campagnolo chainsets of 70 x 13 and 52 x 16 that make a 376-inch gear that travels 98.5 feet per pedal revolution (30.03 meters development). To turn this gear over and get his legs spinning, Howard had to be towed up to about 60 mph (55 rpm). To reach 152 mph, Howard had to pedal at 136 rpm. For steering, the bike had a 59-degree head tube angle, straight forks with shocks, and a hydraulic steering damper. For control and safety, the bike had a remote control throttle grip that controlled the pace car's speed (Howard could see the road through a window in the car), a single rear cantilever brake, a tow cable release mechanism, and a front bumper bar for high speed braking. The wheels had 36-spoke Akront motorcycle rims, with a Mylar disc on the rear, and 21.5-inch Dunlop road racing tires (V-rated) at 70 psi. In one test, the centrifugal forces of 1600 G's caused an air valve to leak.

John Howard's Pepsi Challenger land speed record motor-pace bike.

All-Terrain Cycles

All-terrain or off-road cycles include many kinds of vehicles built for riding in the dirt (cyclo-cross, BMX, and mountain bikes), on sand dunes (all-terrain bikes), on windswept plains (sail bikes), and on ice or snow (ice-cycles and sleigh-cycles). The question has been asked, which came first, the off-road racer, or the off-road bike? The off-road answer is "Not the chickenshit!"

CYCLO-CROSS BIKES

Cyclo-cross bicycles are the original off-road bikes. They appeared at the turn of the century as safety bicycles with studded tires, and developed in the 1950s with the professional winter sport of cyclo-cross, a combination of bicycling steeple-chase and cross-country running. Cyclo-cross bikes are based on standard multi-speed racing bikes with special features such as a higher bottom bracket for pedal and chainring ground clearance, knobby tubular tires for traction, cantilever brakes for muddy wheel clearance, handlebar-end shifters for hands-on control, and lower alpine gears for pedaling over steep hills.

BMX BIKES

Bicycle Moto-Cross (BMX) bikes evolved around 1970 by combining the bronco style Sting-Ray bikes with features from moto-cross motorcycles. The steel frames tend to be built in one size, with straight forks, a high bottom bracket, and 20- or 24-inch spoked or cast wheels with knobby tires. Stanadard equipment includes a single speed with a freewheel, one-piece Ashtabula cranks, and caliper brakes with motorcycle style levers. The wide upright handlebars have rubber grips, with padded handlebars and top tube. Formula One BMX bikes are equipped with fairings and slick tires for fast road riding. BMX bikes are made by GT (Gary Turner), Haro, Mongoose, and Redline.

MOUNTAIN BIKES

Mountain bikes (MTBs) are "big boy BMX bikes" according to Gary Fisher, one of the pioneers of this popular and influential new breed. Mountain bikes combine elements from classic balloon-tire cruisers, known in the 1970s as "klunkers," with the lightweight alloy components of quality touring and racing bikes. MTBs feature "fat" knobby tires (26 x 2.125 inches) and upright handlebar positions, suitable for off-road racing, heavy-duty touring over rugged terrain, and reliable on-road transport.

Mountain bikes developed considerable ingenuity in frame design, with fat-gauge tubing, shock-absorbing front forks, and various rear wheel suspension configurations. With the first mass-marketed mountain bike, the Specialized Stump Jumper (1982), special component groups appeared, with cantilever brakes with motorcycle-style levers, handlebar mounted gear shifters, and both rat trap and clipless pedal-shoe combinations. Mountain bikes include those made by Keith Bontrager, Joe Breeze, and Tom Ritchey.

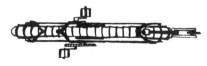

Top to bottom: Dan Hannebrink's
Extreme Terrain bike, Ski bike,
Traction vehicle patent.

ALL-TERRAIN CYCLES

All-terrain cycles are specially designed to negotiate extremely difficult terrain such as sand. They feature pedals with high ground clearance, two or more wheels with wide tractor-style tires, and ultra-low gearing. A two-wheeled example is the 40-pound Extreme Terrain bike, nicknamed the Monster, by Dan Hannebrink, with nine-inch wide tires for cycling on sand, rocks, and snow. The Animas Quadracycle is a prototype two-seat, 150-pound pedal-powered dune buggy developed in 1992 by Greg Fischer of Arizona. With independent drive through a jack-shaft mechanism, 84 gears, and four wheel suspension, it cost about $8,000 to make.

ICE AND SNOW CYCLES

Ice cycles and snow cycles (or ski cycles) have been around since the days of velocipedes, around 1869. *Harper's Weekly* featured an Ice Velocipede that had a front wheel with metal spikes on the circumference for traction, and dual ice skating blades where the rear wheel would normally be. Bray's Velocipede sleigh appeared in 1883 as another spiked single-wheel vehicle with an arching frame that linked with two pairs of sleigh runners front and rear. A saddle was mounted on the frame with handlebars and forks holding the wheel. As the wheel swiveled in the frame, two rods attached to the pedals turned the front runners in the same direction.

In 1885, a chain-driven semi-recumbent Ice Velocipede was developed by J. Hussong of New Jersey. This had two blade runners under the rear spiked wheel, and one blade up front. The rider sat down and pedaled a one-piece crank turning a block chain connected to the rear wheel. Two levers, one for steering and the other for pressure braking into the ice, were placed on each side of the rider. Eventually ice blades, sleigh runners, and snow ski attachments were fit in place of the wheels on normal bicycles. Some are side-by-side tandems with an ice wheel or snow paddle in the rear with two outriding blades or skis for stability. Inventors have tried single bikes with dual sleigh runners providing traction via a complex set of gears linked to the crankset. A pedal-powered Snowped developed by Giles Poirir of Laval, Quebec, mounts to a regular bike, with a crawler track rear-drive and wide ski on the front fork.

THE ICE VELOCIPEDE

WIND CYCLES

Wind and sail cycles use wind power either as a primary means of propulsion, or to assist cyclists. These are most often used for recreation along beaches, sand dunes, dry lakes, and occasionally for crossing deserts. Some of the early combinations of wind power and bicycle ingenuity include cyclists using their clothing to catch the breeze with their feet propped on foot rests, and handlebar-mounted umbrellas on tandems turned sideways for an extra push. In the 1890s, triangular sails were fixed to bicycles in the 1890s with the mast fastened to the forks and the boom angled up so it would not knock over the rider in crosswinds. Then sail tricycles were developed with a recumbent position and the improved stability of three wheels.

The Rans Sailtrikes come in two models, one with a fiberglass frame, measuring about 5½ feet wide with twenty-inch wheels, three-speed gearing with a differential, and an aircraft-style steering wheel. A flexible mast is supported by three cables connecting the vehicle's three corners. The triangular 30 square-foot sail is reefable (adjustable in size), and the boom is secured at the rear end. In a ten mph breeze, the vehicle can reach speeds over 20 mph. Heavier winds can cause a rear wheel to lift off the ground, which is normal and part of the fun. Larger sails have been used on touring mountain bikes for a crossing of the Sahara desert.

Another type of wind-powered vehicle used on the road employs an aerodynamic airfoil for propulsion. One limited production model that costs over $20,000 is a streamlined tricycle with a six-foot high airfoil that arches over the single-seat driver's pod. Pedal-power is used to set the vehicle into motion, and the airfoil then directs wind currents to push the vehicle to speeds up to 45 mph.

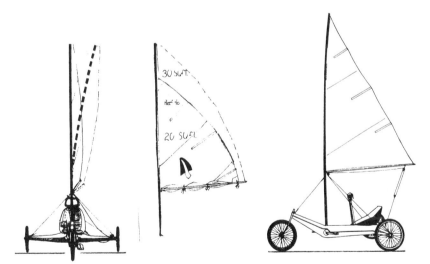

Top, sails mounted for crossing the Sahara desert. Above, HPV with airfoil. Left, Rans recumbent sailtrike.

Show Cycles

Show cycles are designed for having fun and being creative. They include stunt bikes for doing acrobatics, low-rider bikes and kinetic sculpture for showing off, musical cycles for making sound, and exposition cycles for teaching science.

STUNT BIKES

Various types of bicycles have been built with special handling characteristics for field sports and for performing stunts indoors and outdoors. Polo or soccer bikes are designed to be ridden on grass playing fields and have small wheels (sixteen to twenty inches) and a short wheelbase enabling a smaller turning circle. They have low gears for quick acceleration, the handlebars are cut narrower, and the seat is placed further back over the rear wheel so the rider can stand and balance while making shots with a polo mallet. Artistic or circus bicycles are used for performing indoor stunts usually not possible on a standard bike. Stunt bikes have appeared in the circus since the 1890s, and the most artistic bikes have been built in Germany. They typically have a fixed-gear one-to-one drive ratio, with straight rake front forks, no brakes, and a seat that curves up and further back over the rear wheel. The handlebars and stem are one-piece and mounted with the hooks upside-down so the rider can balance on them in various positions. Foot pegs, called dorns, are placed on the forks, the stays, the down tube, and a few other locations for mounting teams of riders on one bike. Bicycles used in tightrope high-wire acts have similar features, but the wheels use the grooves in the rims, without tires, to fit the rope. An indoor version of soccer where the wheels do the kicking, called cycleball, uses acrobatic bikes with upright butterfly-style handlebars and a top tube that extends back so the seat is centered directly over the rear wheel's axle for easy wheelies.

Freestyle BMX bikes are built for balancing tricks and airborne stunts on pavement, grass and special freestyle ramps. These bikes come equipped with foot pegs fixed part way up the front fork, and at the rear wheel axles. The frames have a "kicktailed" platform extending along the top tube under the seat, and steering accessories allow the forks to rotate 360 degrees without twisting the brake cables around the stem. The Freecoaster hub allows the option of a freewheel or coasterbrake.

LOW-RIDER CYCLES

Low-rider cycles are low-slung, highly-decorated bikes, trikes, and trailers, that developed in the 1970s among youngsters and parents in the Chicano community of California, who recycled and streamlined balloon-tire roasters and sting-ray bikes. They are designed with the idea that the closer you ride to the ground, the closer you are to heaven. Some are art works on wheels—all show and no go—with extremely low riding positions—so low that the pedals touch ground, awkward for forward pedaling. Gaining popularity in the 1990s, there are rideable production low-rider bikes, and specialized low-rider frames and accessory makers.

KINETIC SCULPTURE

Kinetic sculptures are unique kinds of human-powered works of art capable of traversing roads, sand, mud, and water. They are usually one-of-a-kind multi-cycles built with new and used bicycle, motorcycle, tractor, and marine parts where both the vehicles and the pilot-artists are wildly decorated. An extraordinary promotional vehicle from 1895 was the Giant Eight-Man Tricycle which weighed almost 1.5 tons. It had to be geared down since the two rear wheels, with pneumatic tires, were eleven feet tall. Hundreds of vehicles have been built for the Great Arcata to Ferndale (California) Cross-Country Kinetic Sculpture Race since it began in 1969. These include Hobart Brown's "Pentacycle," Duane and Micki Flatmo's "The Happy Swanderer," Ken Beidleman's "Nightmare of the Iguana," and George and Jinger's "Counterfeit Cadillac."

Bill Harding, known as "Gene Pool," is an environmental performance artist in New York who created "Drum Cycle," a bicycle built with bongo drums, a cymbal, and a tamborine, which are activated by pedaling and make percussive, multi-phase rhythms, and "Can Suit," a 35-pound coverall made of over 500 aluminum cans which he wears while riding a unicycle.

EXPOSITION CYCLES

Exposition cycles are designed to interact with and educate people in science and art museums, such as at the Exploratorium in San Francisco, where cycling machines show how muscles and gyroscopes work. The artist Margia Kramer created a multi-media installation *Progress (Memory)* (1983) where the spectator could activate a pedal-powered video. Installed at the Whitney Museum of American Art, Kramer described the work as a three-ring viewer-activated video environment that examined the relationships of people and new communications tools. The easy-to-pedal cycle-generator faced a video showing expert testimony on the pros and cons of computer technology, information management, and electronic networks.

Above, Duane and Micki Flatmo's 'Happy Swanderer' on the Kinetic Sculture race program. Far left, Margia Kramer's *Progress (Memory)* at the Whitney Museum of American Art.

MUSICAL CYCLES

Various kinds of bikes and cycles have been designed to play music since the days of the velocipede, when the Hanlon brothers of New York had a traveling show called the *Hanlon Superba*, with acrobats performing music and song. One vaudeville style bicycle act appeared on early television with the "Ed Wynn Show" (1956) in which Wynn's absent-minded professor pedaled on stage playing a harmonium-tricycle with Dinah Shore singing on top. Peter Schickele invented the Baroque composer P.D.Q. Bach as the "forgotten" son of J.S. Bach and performed a piece titled *Pervertimento For Bagpipes, Bicycle and Balloons* at Carnegie Hall in New York. A description of this spoof reads:

> The bicycle is used in several ways. In the second and last movements a siren mounted on the rear wheel sings plaintive melodies; in the Trio of the Minaret, the performer blows on the handlebars as if they were a trumpet; and in the final movement, after the passage of the siren, playing cards are allowed to flap on the spokes of the rear wheel as it turns, thus producing a percussive effect known to every small boy but, until P.D.Q. Bach, unknown to even the most sophisticated masters of orchestration. The first performance in Bach's day of this work was marred when the soloist got a flat tire, but unfortunately Stradivarius made no bicycles, and the modern ones seem to be more reliable.[14]

New music composer Richard Lerman scored two works called "Travelon Gamelon" in which the musicians play bicycles, simulating the sound of Indonesian gamelon music. In one piece, three bicycles are placed upside-down and the spinning wheels are played with violin bows, drum sticks, guitar picks, and fingers. The sound is amplified and mixed through pickups in the bike frame. Another mobile ensemble, called "Promenade," consisted of about 30 bikes rigged for sound to be ridden through the streets. Lerman said that older bikes with looser spokes produce a deeper, more resonant music. The works were videotaped by Skip Blumberg and aired on public television stations.

Rock and roll musician Doug Prose made a cross-country trek in the summer of 1988 riding a "Rockercycle." This was a recumbent bicycle with an 8½-foot-long plastic and fiberglass guitar built around it, and a storage trailer shaped like a huge amplifier, used to promote his debut album, *Power of One* on the Earthsong label.

Human-Powered Watercraft

Since water covers almost three-fourths of the surface of the earth, it is not surprising that there are many types of aquatic cycling machines. These include swimming machines, pedal-powered paddle-wheels, boats, catamarans, proas, hydrofoils, yachts, submarines, and amphibious cycling machines.

AQUATIC CYCLES

The advent of pedal-power inspired some ingenious gadgets for swimming, floating, and sinking. Richardson's Swimming Device of 1880 was a propeller-driven hand- and foot-powered mechanism that allowed a swimmer to move at speeds up to six knots (1 knot equals 1.15 miles). Barathon's Velocipede Lifebuoy of 1895, designed to save lives in shipwrecks, was equipped with hand- and foot-powered propellers for both lift and thrust, an inflatable cushion, a sail, a flag, and a lamp. At the same time, a Submersible Tricycle was designed for riding with an aqua-lung along the bottom of lakes.

AMPHIBIOUS CYCLES

Many aquatic cycles have been designed to ride on land and water. A Swan-shaped amphibious quadricycle was patented in 1883 by H.S. Blanchard of Illinois. In the water, treadle-driven paddles and rotating cork-filled buoys propelled the vehicle and kept it afloat. On the land, the buoys served as drive wheels and supports with the front ones used for steering. In England, William (Jack) Terry built a combination tricycle and canoe. On the road, it was a standard tricycle with a few extra poles and bundles of tarred canvas. For use on water, the two larger wheels broke down into semi-circles serving to form the front, the back, and the hull of the boat, with buoyancy provided by two air bags. In 1883, Terry rode it from London to Dover and then crossed the English Channel in about eight hours. When he arrived in France, he was arrested as a smuggler because of the odd construction of his boat; but all was cleared up, and he reassembled his tricycle and rode to Paris, stopping for demonstrations on canals along the way. Another Channel crossing was attempted in 1894 by a Mr. Pinckert on an amphibious tricycle with large, airtight rubber wheels with fin-like paddles on their sides. After setting off from Cap Gris-Nez, he had to board a nearby vessel when the tide turned against him near the half-way point.

In 1909, a French inventor created a 270-pound amphibious bicycle called the Amphibicycle. It was equipped with two metal pontoons, a propeller driven by the rear wheel, and a rudder extending from the front fork, each of which was lifted for riding on land. Variations on this design have appeared throughout the years, with more efficient and lighter components, such as inflatable or styrofoam floats.

The inclusion of an amphibious category at the IHPVA Championships and a variety of kinetic sculpture races has inspired some curious and innovative vehicles. The Rhino is an all-terrain tricycle built in California

Jack Terry's tricycle-canoe used to cross the English Channel.

Top to bottom: Swan-shaped pedal-paddled boat, Bishop catamaran, Saber proa, and Edie Seacycle.

in 1984 by Robert Hitchcock and Matteo Martignoni which has tandem recumbent seats and wheels for the road and sand or mud. Side struts carry pontoons for water crossings. This 21-speed, 40-pound vehicle has won three kinetic sculpture championships. Other amphibious cycles include the Gila Monster quad, the 2½-passenger Ute trike, the Egret XIII trike, and the Lampi Limo 2½-wheeler.

HP BOATS

Human-powered boats (HPBs) using treadle-driven paddle-wheels first appeared in the 1870s, and then pedal-driven paddle boats became popular in lakes and ponds at public parks, such as the Swan boats at the Public Garden in Boston which were created around 1880. These are still in use in a smaller, more modern form, usually twin-hulled boats with a paddle-wheel in between. Sometimes a single rider mounts the wheel in an upright position, while others have pairs of pedals on both sides for tandem riders sitting in chairs.

By the 1890s, the first pedal-powered propeller-driven catamaran and proa boats were developed. Pedal-powered catamarans are lighter twin-hulled boats with a bicycle mounted in the middle, sometimes without its wheels, driving one or two propellers. The advantages of the pedal-propeller system over a scull or kayak being rowed with oars includes a smoother, more efficient transfer of human-power into propulsion, the use of stronger leg muscles, a greater speed, and a forward-facing position for the cyclist. In the mid-1890s, in a 101-mile race along the Thames River from Oxford to Putney, a three-cyclist racing catamaran beat a three-man university sculling team. The cyclists finished in under 19½ hours, compared to 22 hours for the rowers. At the same time, a pedal-powered proa boat, with one main hull and two small outriggers, was seen in the pages of *Scientific American*. The interest in pedal-propelled watercraft faded for a few generations, perhaps because they could only reach speeds of about ten knots, which is slow compared to boats with diesel and gasoline engines.

Interest in human-powered watercraft picked up again in the late 1970s with more recreational and racing designs such as catamarans, proas, and hydrofoils. Pedal-powered outboard propellers are made to clamp onto the back of small boats, such as Circle Mountain's recumbent unit with shaft-drive. Screw propellers with two or three blades about fifteen inches in diameter are used with right-angle pinion gears to convert pedaling into propulsion. Some propellers are designed to reach up to 90 percent efficiency. Specially built HPBs include the semi-enclosed *Sea Mallard* by Garry Hoyt, the *Whistler* by Jon Knapp, the *Dorycycle* by Philip Thiel, and the fully-enclosed *Waterbug*.

For speed and racing more exotic designs have been developed to eliminate hulls to reduce drag, since every hull design has its inherent speed limit. *The Flying Fish I* and *II* were developed around 1984–86 by Alec Brooks and Allan Abbott in California and have been among the fastest HPBs, with a top speed of about fourteen knots. They use a 5½-

foot wide hydrofoil, or underwater wing, which lifts both the cyclist and the floatation pontoons above the water once it reaches a speed of about six knots. Other unique HPBs include Sid Shutt's *Hydroped II*, a recumbent hydrofoil, Parker MacCready's *Mutiny on the Boundary Layer*, also known as *Pogo Foil*, a flapping or oscillating winged hydrofoil inspired by his work on a radio-controlled pterodactyl, and Theo Schmidt's submerged buoyancy craft.

In 1989, the $25,000 DuPont Prize was offered for the first single-person HPB to achieve a speed of twenty knots. So far, the fastest hydrofoil is the *Decavitator* built by M.I.T. students with a ten-foot air propeller borrowed from the Daedalus project. With double foils, it has three modes of operation. At low speed (up to eight knots), it floats on its kayac-shaped pontoon hull. At high speed (nine to fourteen knots), the pontoons lift over the water and it flies on its double-wing foils. At very high speed (over fifteen knots), it lifts onto its smaller single-wing foil while the larger wing pivots up into a streamlined receptacle. In October 1991, the men's and women's HPB speed records were broken on the Charles River when Mark Drela powered *Decavitator* up to 18.5 knots, and Dava Newman reached a speed of 11.4 knots. In an unofficial record, it reached 19.59 knots.

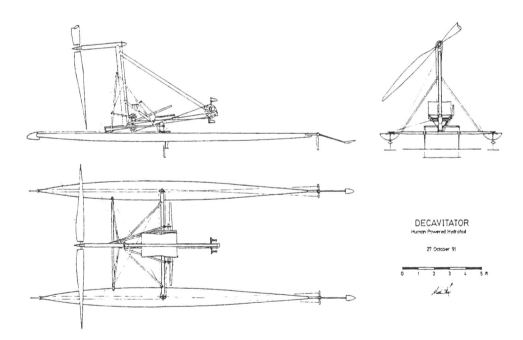

DECAVITATOR
Human Powered Hydrofoil

27 October 91

0 1 2 3 4 5 ft

Above, Alec Brooks and Allan Abbott with Flying Fish II. Right, Decavitator human-powered hydrofoil, drawn by Mark Drela.

HP Yachts

Human-powered yachts (HPYs) are built for making long ocean voyages, usually with a crew of one, so they must be entirely self-contained and "unsinkable." In 1988, Donald Spaulding designed HPY *California* for a possible round-the-world cruise. The 2,600-pound ship features two cycling positions, an upright seat for harbor and fair-weather propulsion, and a recumbent seat when the bowmar hatch is closed. Ventilation is provided during rollovers by hurricane boxes, a system of baffles that draw air through the cabin, which measures eight feet long, five feet wide, and four feet high.

In July 1992, Dwight Collins of Noroton, Connecticut, pedaled the 24-foot HPY *Tango* almost 2,000 miles across the Atlantic Ocean from St. John's, Newfoundland, to Plymouth Harbor, England, in approximately 40 days. Developed by Bruce Kirby, the enclosed skiff was made of cedar and carbon-fiber, and equipped with a global positioning satellite receiver and a desalination unit. Collins set a new record for crossing the Atlantic in a human-powered vessel, surpassing a rowboat journey of 54 days.

A two-person boat is being used by Steve Smith and Jason Lewis in their attempt to circumnavigate the world by land and sea using pedal power. The three-year Pedal for the Planet voyage began in July 1994 in England, with the pedal-powered boat used for crossing the English Channel, the Altantic Ocean, and the Bering Sea. The 26-foot wood boat was designed by Alan Boswell in Exeter, at a cost of about $25,000. A hand-held desalination unit makes drinking water, and solar panels provide power for lights, radio, and navigation equipment. Unlike the upright position on their Ridgeback bikes, the boat's pedal system has a recumbent position, with a Shimano Dura Ace crankset and a 60 × 12 gear driving an eighteen-inch propeller at 300 rpm—top speed five knots.

HP Submersibles

There are two types of human-powered submarines, dry and wet. The dry kind keeps the air sealed in, such as Dave O'Neil's one-man pedal-powered 1,300-pound steel submarine. It can submerge to about 250 feet and has about half an hour of air in the hull with a carbon-dioxide ballast tank for rising back to the surface. The wet kind is a water-filled craft with scuba-equipped divers. This type is easier to build and more popular for research and competition because the divers can usually remain underwater for longer periods. An example among dozens is the two-person *SQUID* (Submerged Quick Intervention Device) built in 1989 by the U.S. Naval Academy in which one crew member pedals while the other navigates.

Human-Powered Aircraft

People have dreamed of flying with their own power for thousands of years and with the development of the bicycle, people began to believe they had wings on their feet. After many pedal-powered attempts, and the development of propeller-driven airplanes, jet engines, and space flight, sometime in the middle of the twentieth century inventors began to take another look at self-propelled flight.

Human-powered flight has evolved through three generations of human-powered aircraft (HPA), in a gradual process of ideas, experiments, competitions, and technological refinements over a timespan of about 75 years. Developments came in small leaps, and there are several flights which can be called the first. Machines being flown today have little resemblance to the first foot-powered flying machines that were conceived in designs by Da Vinci (1485), Blanchard (1781), Quimby (1871), Ayres (1885), Goupil (1885), Holmes (1889), and many others. Morton Grosser, author of *Gossamer Odyssey* (1981), says that: "If every inventor in history who thought of building a human-powered airplane had actually built one, we would probably have run out of airport space long ago."

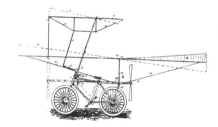

AVIETTES

Flying bicycle competitions began in Paris in 1912 with several human-powered flight prizes. The first of three Prix Peugeot attracted twenty-three "aviettes" by offering 10,000 francs for the first machine to fly ten meters in two directions (to account for wind assist). These aerocycles were mostly jumping bicycles fit with cumbersome wings, so a second prize of 1,000 francs was offered for a one meter flight. The big prize was won in 1921 at Longchamps in Paris by the former cycling sprint champion, Gabriel Poulain, who managed to lift off and glide for almost twelve meters on a bicycle bi-plane with wingspans of six and four meters. The third prize for a two-way flight over 50 meters was never awarded. The Prix Michelin, 2,000 francs for a five meter flight, was won by Paul Didier in 1912 on a flapping wing bike, and the Prix Dubois, 700 francs for a flight ten meters high, was never earned.

HP SAILPLANES

The next developments in human-powered aircraft came from Germany and Italy around 1935. The Frankfurt Polytechical Group offered 5,000 marks for flying around a 500-meter circuit, and its first entry was *Mufli* (for *Muskel Flieger*—"muscle flyer"), a 75-pound high-wing monoplane built by Helmut Haessler and Franz Villinger with a pedal-driven propeller on a front mounted pylon. It was launched by a rubber-cable catapult to heights of about three meters and the pilot pedaled to sustain its glide. In Frankfurt, a Muskelflug Institute was formed, and cyclist-pilots were tested for their human-power output. With a pilot named Hoffmann able to produce 1.3 horsepower, *Mufli* made its longest flight of 712 meters but could not complete the circuit for the prize. Meanwhile, the Italian government offered 100,000 lira for a one-kilometer flight by an

Paul Didier's flapping wing aviette, Paris, 1912

Italian citizen. Enea Bossi, an Italian-American, built *Pedaliante* ("Pedal-glider") which made some 80 flights, half with a catapult launch because it weighed 220 pounds. Though it flew the kilometer, the catapult disqualified it. Neither *Mufli* nor *Pedaliante* survived World War II.

The best-known competitions, the ones that led to genuine human-powered flight, have been the Kremer prizes, sponsored by British industrialist and philanthropist Henry Kremer and the Royal Aeronautical Society of England. The first Kremer prize of 1959 offered £5,000 for flying a one-mile figure-eight course by "a British designed, built, and flown Man-Powered Aircraft." This inspired the development of several planes in England, with the first to fly in 1961 being *SUMPAC* (Southampton University Man-Powered Air Craft), followed closely by *Puffin* developed at the de Havilland Aircraft Co. with the Hatfield Man-Powered Aircraft Club. Both were designed as pedal-propeller driven sailplanes, and the next year John Wimpenny pedaled *Puffin* 911 meters at an average height of two meters, but neither had enough turning ability to complete the Kremer course. Meanwhile, in Japan, a plane called *Linnet* was built at Nihon University with a team lead by Hidemasa Kimura, and in 1966, Munetaka Okamiya was able to fly *Linnet* about 143 meters.

In 1967, with no results in its first eight years, the Kremer prize was increased to £10,000 and opened to international entrants. Also, an additional £5,000 Kremer prize was offered for a ¾-mile slalom course to be flown in both directions within an hour of each other. Another round of planes appeared including *Dumbo*, a large, lightweight plane with independently controllable wings; *Liverpuffin*, made with parts of *Puffin II*; *Toucan* (for "two can fly if one cannot"), a two-person monoplane with the wingspan of a Boeing 707 (43.5 meters); and *Jupiter*, which set a new record by flying more than one kilometer. Once again, there was no progress on the Figure-Eight Competition so Henry Kremer increased the prize to £50,000 in 1973, making it the largest aviation prize thus far.

GOSSAMER WINGS

Kremer's prize inspired the second generation of human-powered aircraft which, at last, started winning some of his money. These flying machines employed unique structural and aerodynamic forms to conform to this scarcely understood regime of flying at slow speeds near ground level. Instead of carrying on with the low drag attributes of sailplane designs, second generation aircraft designers shifted to the use of larger wing areas with external bracings based on hang glider designs, resulting in lower weight and power requirements.

The *Gossamer Condor* developed by Paul MacCready and his team had an aluminum tube frame with a 96-foot wingspan, a front-mounted canard stabilizer, and a twelve-foot diameter propeller. Kingposts with piano wire were used for bracing, and corrugated cardboard covered in Mylar formed the wing's "gossamer" airfoil. With the aircraft weighing 70 pounds and the pilot-engine, Bryan Allen, at 137 pounds, the *Gossamer Condor* won the Kremer Figure-Eight prize in August 1977 with a flight

Mufli flying near Frankfurt, Germany, August, 1935.

of 7½ minutes at an average speed of 10.8 mph. Within a month of this historic achievement, two important events occurred. Henry Kremer offered a £100,000 prize—the largest in aviation history—for a flight across the English Channel, and the first known woman-powered flight was made on the *Condor* by Maude Oldershaw, a 60-year-old grandmother.[15]

The *Gossamer Albatross* was Paul MacCready's sequel designed for the Channel crossing. The *Albatross* used lighter materials such as carbon fiber composite tubing, polystyrene foam wing moldings, Kevlar control cords, and the polymer Berg chain, none of which had been available fifteen years earlier. The pilot's position was moved from recumbent to the standard upright cycling posture based on ergometer tests in which Bryan Allen produced 0.3 horsepower more while pedaling upright. The gearing for churning the propeller through air at about 90 rpm had a 52 × 42 tooth chainset. The main problem was overheating of the "engine" while enclosed within the Mylar and vinyl cockpit. After several flights, crashes, repairs, and re-flights, the 55-pound Albatross gradually withstood longer flights and was equipped with various avionics controls, including a two-way radio for crossing the Channel. On June 12, 1979, Bryan Allen set off from the English coastline at Folkestone, and after a flight of 2 hours 49 minutes, he touched down at Cap Gris-Nez, France, covering 22¼ miles.

A third generation of faster human-powered aircraft has developed in response to another Kremer prize of £20,000 for flying a triangular 1,500 meter course in under three minutes, a pace that required a speed of about 20 mph. This was won in 1984 by Frank Scarabino flying the *Monarch B* developed at the Massachusetts Institute of Technology. Third generation aircraft reflect the experience of previous machines with newer structural materials and more refined features, such as three-axis controls with ailerons, cantilevered structures that eliminate external wires, electronically "tuned" propellers, and energy storage devices.

Bryan Allen flying the Gossamer Albatross across the English Channel, June 12, 1979.

MIT's Michelob Light Eagle flying at Edwards AFB, 1987.

The *Monarch B* led to the Daedalus Project, named for its re-creation of Daedalus' mythical flight with wings of feather and wax across the Aegean Sea from the Greek islands of Crete to Santorini (Thira), a distance of about 74 miles. The *Daedalus* aircraft, named the *Light Eagle*, was also developed at M.I.T. and had a 112-foot wingspan and weighed 70 pounds. Unfortunately, the flight in April 1988 was more like that of Icarus, who, flying too close to the sun, melted his wax wings and fell into the sea. After almost four hours of flight, as the pilot Kanellos Kannellopoulos, a Greek cycling sprint champion, was ten meters from the Santorini beach, a gust of wind snapped the tail boom. The wings buckled, and Kannellopoulos had to swim to shore.

HP Helicopters

Human-powered helicopters are the latest form of aircraft to attract inventors. In 1981, the $20,000 Igor I. Sikorsky Award was offered for a one minute flight three meters above the ground by a human-powered helicopter (HPH). The first HPH flight was achieved in December 1989 by the *Da Vinci III*, the fourth of a series of helicopters developed by students at Cal Poly San Luis Obispo. It hovered for 6.8 seconds at a height of about eight inches inside the school's gymnasium.

The helicopter was powered by a recumbent cyclist whose pedaling turned propellers which were mounted at the tips of the rotor blade to make it turn. To provide lift, the long rotor was constructed in three parts with a carbon fiber spar, foam core ribs, and a mylar skin. Sensors were attached to the four caster wheels of the craft so that a light switched on while it was off the ground. Human-powered helicopters pose one of the most difficult problems since some calculations show that the rotor for an average pilot and craft at sea level would have to be at least 35 meters in diameter.

HP Airships

The first modern human-powered airship was built in 1984 by Bill Watson, a member of the *Gossamer Albatross* team. This 150-pound blimp, called the *White Dwarf*, carried about 6,000 cubic feet of helium, and with an adjustable 64-inch propeller, a 200-pound recumbent cyclist could cruise at about ten mph in windspeeds below five mph. Buoyancy was controlled by jettisoning water to go up, or helium to go down.

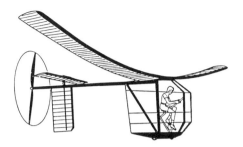

Musculaire II holds the current speed record for human-powered aircraft.

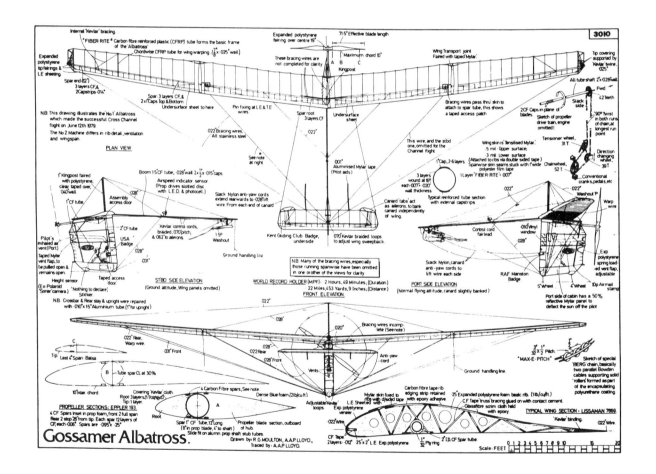

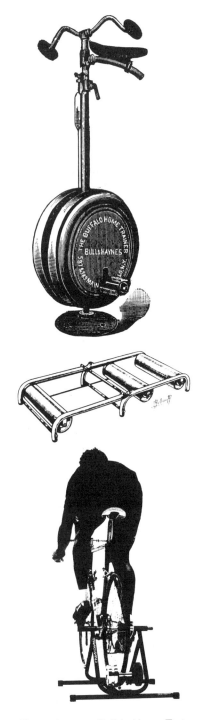

Top to bottom: Buffalo Home Trainer; portable rollers; wind-load simulators.

Exercise Cycles

Exercise cycles offer an excellent means of getting exercise without having to encounter difficult traffic and weather conditions. Exercycles are found in homes, at health clubs, gymnasiums, sports clinics, hospitals, and in space, orbiting around the earth. They come in two basic forms: machines for riding one's own bike, such as rollers and rear wheel stands with load simulators; and machines designed specifically for going nowhere but towards better health, such as stationary cycles and cycle-rowing machines. Exercycles account for almost fifteen percent of the U.S. cycle market, and in the early 1990s there were about two million units sold annually, with over ten million in use. Many accessories are available for simultaneously measuring physical performance and providing entertainment. These are helpful because many cyclists consider stationary cycling the most boring way to ride a bike.

There are many ways to prevent boredom while exercycling, including reading, watching TV, listening to music, and using computers. Athletes have been cautioned against sensory overload on exercycles that masquerade as an entertainment center. It is possible to become mentally fatigued by loud sounds and eye strain before exercise-induced weariness sets in. Just keeping up with the human performance console is enough, with power output, cadence, calorie consumption, breath rate, heart rate, speed, time, and distance travelled nowhere.

ROLLERS

Rollers and training stands for bicycles and tricycles first appeared in the 1870s. Traditional rollers consist of three free-spinning cylinders fixed to a floor frame. Two rollers support the rear wheel, one supports the front, and a conveyor belt connects the rollers so the cyclist must balance while pedaling. Rollers have featured large clock-like dials for measuring the distance traveled, and multiple sets of rollers have been linked together for indoor racing. Training stands with load-simulating rollers allow bikes to be mounted on various kinds of platforms without the need for balancing.

Load simulators use any combination of fans, magnetic discs, liquids, or flywheels to create resistance. Wind-load simulators offer both pedal resistance and a cooling breeze with a pair of cylindrical fans or "squirrel cages" connected to the rear wheel. An exponential and equivalent amount of resistance and wind is produced as the speed increases, thus simulating an outdoor ride. But as speeds increase, the whirling sound of the fans can reach up to 80 decibels of "white noise" at 25 mph. Magnetic-load simulators that use electro-magnetic dampers for resistance are quieter, but the resistance they create is not always comparable to wind-loads.

STATIONARY CYCLES

Stationary exercycles have a variety of shapes and features, and they have been around as long as rollers. The Buffalo Home Trainer of the 1880s was a pole on a platform with two resistance discs attached to pedals, and an adjustable seat with handlebars at the top. It was equipped with a cyclometer that rang a bell at quarter-mile intervals. Household stationary exercycles, such as the Rollfast of the 1930s, used adjustable pressure plates and rollers against a solid tire to make resistance with speedometers, and odometers mounted on the handlebars. The heavy-duty Schwinn Air-Dyne replaces the front wheel with a large fan used to measure the work load by the displacement of air. It has handlebars that act as levers for upper body workouts, with accessories such as a pulse meter and a reading stand. Flywheels weighing from 15 to 50 pounds appear on Tunturi exercycles made in Finland. The AMF Benchmark recumbent cycle, with a magnetic-load simulator, has a sleek design that looks more like furniture than a bicycle.

Some exercycles offer therapy for disabled bodies, and others offer a better upper body workout by combining arm and stomach movements with cycling. Recumbent exercycles offer more leg leverage, with pedals on rotary cranks, or linear tracks, with handlebar levers used for added rowing exercises.

Schwinn Air-Dyne exercises arms as well as legs.

ERGOMETERS

Ergometer cycles are designed to measure cycling performance for science, sport, and therapy. Measurements include power output in watts, pedal revolutions (cadence), pedal torque in foot-pounds, heart rate, oxygen consumption, caloric expenditure, and some can precisely control and repeat a workout. The Cateye Cyclocimulator is a turbo and electromagnetic resistance home trainer that offers a gradient simulator of up to ten percent. The Kingcycle Trainer, by Miles Kingsbury of England, is an ergometer that measures power output in watts, heart rate, percent of maximum heart rate, cadence, calories burned, power to weight ratio, and it is IBM-PC compatible.

Exercycles have been brought aboard the *Mir* Space Station and the Space Shuttles *Endeavor* and *Columbia* to keep the astronauts fit, to prevent muscle atrophy, and to study the physiological effects of zero gravity living. One problem with weightless cycling in the confines of a space craft is that cycling vibrations interfere with other sensitive equipment and experiments. NASA and Lockheed engineers developed the Isolated-Stabilized Exercise Platform (1992) to counteract the motions of cycling, with motors mounted in each contact point.

NASA's Stabilized Exercise Platform.

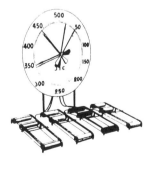

Human-Powered Tools

There are various forms of tools for both work and play which use human power. Some date back to ancient times, while many are a product of modern age bicycle ingenuity. Around 1900, as fossil fuel and electricity was becoming the power standard of the industrial world, pedal-powered tools appeared at the workbench, in the home, and over remote landscapes. Since then, human-powered tools have been developed for use around the world for agriculture, industry, and service trades.

To gain power for performing tasks, people have used their hands, arms, backs, shoulders, legs, and feet with a variety wheels, levers, and pulleys. The age-old foot-powered potter's wheel, which is based on the momentum of a flywheel, has been kicked around for thousands of years and is still preferred for hand-crafted ceramic housewares. The treadle uses the leverage of foot power either in low-torque repetitive actions or in high-torque driving with full weight applications. Treadles can be used throughout the whole garment making process, from cotton ginning and thread spinning to sewing and pressing. Treadles were a prelude to pedals in cycling machines and some of the earliest velocipedes were built at sewing machine factories.

As the bicycle's practical efficiency has become more apparent, many research and development groups concerned about the distribution of the world's energy resources have refined these pedal-powered tools. They are called intermediate technology, because they require some mechanical proficiency but don't need excessive industrial infrastructure. Often recycled from old bicycles and machine parts, intermediate technology has been recognized for its economy, efficiency, and its appropriate use of resources.

Shop Cycles

With the development of the bicycle's pedal-crank and chain-drive around 1880, the pedal-powered revolution began. Pedal power was used for lathes, screw cutters, scroll saws, grinding and sanding wheels, sewing machines, apple cider presses, water pumps for showering, and musical instruments. They supplied enough torque to cut both wood and iron. The Barnes Velocipede Scroll Saw No. 2 sold for $23 while the Barnes Screw Cutting Lathe No. 4½ could adapt to pedal, treadle, or countershaft and cost $65. In one of many testimonials for the Shepard Foot Lathe, a Mr. D.S. Huff stated that: "I think you have made a decided success of your propelling power. It runs very easy with the Screw Cutter thrown in. You could scarcely know you were running a Lathe by foot power."[16]

Farm Cycles

People in less developed lands began adapting pedal-power to their traditional means of agriculture and irrigation. Examples of these pedal-driven mechanisms include winches for hauling or hoisting, Archimedes screws for bringing water upstream, and borehole pumps for pumping well water.

Bicycling magazine offered a $500 prize in 1978 for the invention of

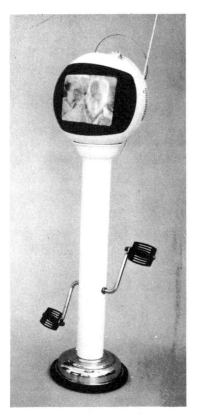

Phil Garner's X-R Vision promises to "turn your software into hardware as you cycle through your favorite TV shows."

the best pedal-powered shredder made from recycled parts which could chop cornstalks, piles of leaves, broccoli plants, and cabbage heads. The contest was cancelled when only two entries were submitted, but when one of the participants threatened to sue, the magazine had to reinstate the contest.

POWER GENERATORS

Bicycle generating stations were used for wireless telegraph corps in Germany and England around 1906. These stationary bikes were connected with a direct current dynamo which produced about 100 watts, enough to transmit messages up to 50 miles over land and 150 miles under water.[17] The portable BSA Cyclo-Generator, built in England for World War II, was used in the field to generate electricity for charging batteries for lights and communications.

Designers and engineers have developed a new generation of pedal-powered workstations, such as Alex Weir's Dynapod, which incorporates a flywheel, and the Rodale Energy Cycle. These consist of a basic pedal-powered unit in which a stationary cyclist sits in an upright or recumbent position with the hands free to perform a variety of tasks. A chain-driven or nylon belt transmission connects to winches, pumps, maize shellers, fruit pitters, grinding stones, lathes, saws, and electrical generators. Human-powered energy is practical for many tools and situations, but to generate the amount of energy consumed in the U.S. by human power, it would take nearly every body pedaling for about sixteen hours per day.

Pedal power drives a dentist's drill where there's no electricity.

Hybrid-Powered Cycles

Rounding out the family of cycles are hybrid-powered vehicles, which combine both motor and human power. A cyclist is a super efficient vehicle because of the power to weight ratio, but some cyclists need more power for steep hills and heavy cargo. Various gasoline- and electric-powered motors are available that attach to bikes and trikes. Sachs makes a two-stroke, one-horsepower, 30cc motor that drives a special cast-aluminum rear wheel at 20 mph or 240 mpg. The Whizzer Motorbike Co. offers a four-cycle, four-horsepower engine that can go 40 mph at about 100 mpg. The Chronos Hammer is an electric motor with a rechargeable battery pack that fits in a waterbottle cage. It drives a rear wheel by a friction roller at speeds up to 15 mph.

Mopeds, or mini-bikes in Japan, are the most common fully-equipped hybrid-powered cycles. Using gas and oil burning internal combustion engines (25 cc to 100 cc), or electric motors and batteries (six to twelve volts), they often lack efficient multi-speed pedaling systems. Moped trikes, known as Tuk-Tuks, are widely used in Asian and Indonesia for passengers and cargo. Innovations in solid state electronics and photovoltaic panels inspired a new breed of solar and electric-powered cycling machines in the 1980s, which were tested in road rally events such as the Tour de Sol in Switzerland. Sir Clive Sinclair of England has produced the electric C5 recumbent tricycle (1982) and the small-wheel Zike bike (1992). The Yamaha PAS and Honda Racoon are power-assist electric bicycles for the Japanese market, and prototypes for the American market include the Specialized Electra Globe (1994) and the folding Minimo by Ross. Motor attachments cost over $500, while complete motor assisted bikes cost $1,000 to $1,500. Rules in Japan and England allow mopeds with a speed limit of 15 mph to be operated as bicycles, not motorcycles.

Yamaha PAS electric-assist bike.

Spin-Offs

Wheels have been fit to the body with various kinds of cycle-like walking machines, wheeled footwear, rollerskates, in-line skates, scooters, skateboards, and wheelchairs.

WALKING MACHINES

Walking contraptions include a device patented in Germany in 1903 made with a pair of six-foot elliptical discs with rotating stirrups for the feet, and a pedal-driven walking machine in which a machine does the walking while a cyclist pedals on top. Another simple, ingenious device is the Walk-A-Cycle, a wheeled walking device that rolls, thus eliminating the need to lift and place a conventional walking aid. It provides a seat for resting, a basket, and a parking brake to keep it from rolling away.

SKATES

Various kinds of wheeled footwear fit into the category of skates. Possibly the first in-line roller skates were Shaler's Flexible Roller Patent Floor Skate, made by O.M. Vail in New York, and advertised in *Frank Leslie's Illustrated Newspaper* in 1861. The Luders Pedespeed appeared around 1870 as a pair of fifteen-inch wheels attached to wooden stirrups that fit under the feet and wrapped around the calves of the legs. Shields were placed over the top of the wheel to protect women's skirts, but this probably did not solve the problem of the wheels leaning into the legs. This was remedied in 1907 with the Koller Wheel Skate from Switzerland in which the axle was attached at a 45 degree angle, thus allowing a dished wheel to support the person's weight. The Tricycle Skate of 1882 had two twelve-inch wheels for each foot that were placed over the axle with a third trailing caster wheel that acted as a balancing and braking device by lowering the heel. This could reportedly reach speeds up to 20 mph. Perhaps the first wheeled footwear to resemble modern skates was the Pneumatic Schaatsen, developed in Holland around 1893. These were like ice skates fit with a pair of six-inch wheels with air-filled tires.

The next step was to add gears and chain-driven mechanisms to skates. A chain-driven "bicycle-skate" made by Paul Jassman of Brooklyn in 1901 used springs and a lever to move a chain connected to the rear wheel. With each foot bouncing between two fifteen-inch wheels to go forward, the skater could pull a long rod to activate a spoon brake on the front wheel. Another two-wheeled chain-driven skate was invented in Germany and called the Foot-Cycle. It had a repetitive up and down motion with the heel advancing a chain that drove a set of gears. Forward pressure with the toes activated a spoon brake on the main wheel which was trailed by a smaller caster wheel.

While some wheeled footwear was fit with small gasoline engines, these complex mechanisms were eventually abandoned in favor of more lightweight roller-skates and scooters. The Skat-Scoota by Sears had two platforms for each foot linked with two s-shaped levers to four wheels. The wheels rolled forward or backward by walking on the platforms.

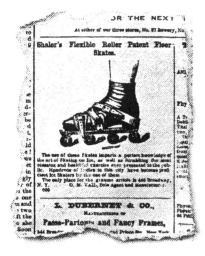

Rollerskates, or quad skates, come with four wheels made of various materials, such as metal, hardened rubber, nylon, polyurethane, and polyethylene. Often used indoors by children, one problem is cuts and scuff marks on floors. Some skates strap around the shoes or feet, while others, now popular with adults, come with form-fitting foam injection boots. The Skatebike is a new bicycle-rollerskate hybrid made by Worlds of Wonder.

In-line skates date back to Shaler's Flexible Roller Patent Floor Skates of 1860, and have become one of the most popular forms of mobile footwear. Known as blades, or rollerblades, for the first popular brand, in-line skates are like ice skates with four or five wheels, about three inches in diameter, with hard and cushion tires mounted in-line under the platform sole of a snug-fitting high-top boot. Bladers can outpace rollerskaters, and can sometimes equal the speed of cyclists on a flat road, but they often take a wider path and burn more calories. Blades require a bit more balance than rollerskates, and they offer a full-body workout. In-line skate racing is similar to cycling, with the effects of drafting apparent in mass-start circuit races. As a sensible form of transport for short hops around town, blades are easier to carry and take less parking space than bikes. As a kind of lifestyle footwear, bladers can be seen rolling around parks, shopping malls, waiting on tables at restaurants, and serving drinks at nightclubs.

Makaha roller skates, 1970s.

Bauer in-line racing skates, 1990s.

SCOOTERS

Scooters typically have two twelve-inch wheels with a long platform and upright handlebars for steering, while some come equipped with brakes. Recent innovations include the Mongoose Pro Miniscoot for freestyle tricks, and the BCA Combo E-Z Mount that combine a bicycle with a scooter-style platform.

SKATEBOARDS

Skateboards developed as wheeled surfboards for concrete and asphalt playgrounds in the late 1950s. Halfway between a scooter and a skate, they are used for acrobatic fun, local transport, curb bashing, moving heavy things, and speeding down hills in a prone position. They became a cult unto themselves as skates evolved into precision wide-track "trucks" and boards became "decks" with "rad" graphics. Accessories include a nose, rails, copers, grips, and lappers. Some skateboards are designed to be propelled without the feet touching ground. The Snakeboard is a recent invention that moves as the rider twists his or her body, legs, and feet on two decks held with a crossbar made of flexible DuPont Zytel.

WHEELCHAIRS

Wheelchairs provide personal mobility for riders seated between two bicycle wheels which they turn by hand, arm, and shoulder muscles. As with bikes, wheelchairs vary in style and weight. A distinguishing feature in wheelchair design is its dependence on the relative ability of the rider—whether he or she needs an attendant or is independently mobile. There are heavy, four-wheel hospital models made with chromed steel and solid tires, lightweight, four-wheel portable models with aluminum frames, and ultra-light, three-wheel racing models with aerodynamic titanium frames and composite wheels. While the heavier models move at a walking pace and have parking brakes to prevent the vehicle from rolling away on slight inclines, the racing models move at speeds up to 18 mph (30 kph) on flat land and come equipped with brakes similar to high performance bicycles.

Hand-cycle units attached to wheelchairs provide an easier and potentially faster means of propulsion. Because the unit can be easily removed, the rider need not change seats when sitting at a desk or table. The Cycl-One models by Quickie Designs of Kent, Washington, offer gearing from three to 48 speeds, with internal hub brakes actuated by backpedaling.

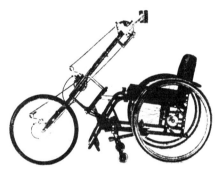

Shadow Cycl-One multi-speed hand-drive attachment for wheelchairs.

Racing wheelchair by Top End.

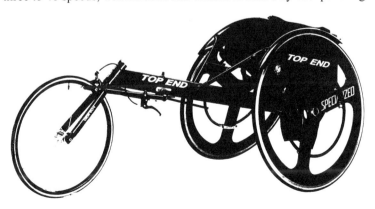

Children's Wheels

Kids bikes, trikes, scooters, and pedal-cars for children are a big part of the family of cycling machines, inspiring some of the most ingenious designs. With their roots in the hobby horse, various generations of pedal-powered wheelers, including velocipedes, tricycles, carriages, and miniature racers, offer children the chance to play with the idea of independent mobility. "Kiddie bykes" have often been built to mimic the wheels of their parents, be they bicycles or motor vehicles. Some bikes are designed for either boys or girls, and animal characters are a popular decorative motif.

The traditional trike, with a larger pedal-driven front wheel and two tiny rear wheels, evolved into four-wheel pedal-powered cars, tractors, and fire engines. Training wheels make two-wheel bikes into four-wheelers for learning the art of balance. From the toy to the ten-speed, the cycle of growth is illustrated by a group of wheelers that suggest not only the imagination of children, but also the future of humanity.

Part Two

Human Power

5 Bicycle Body

The bicycle is one of the least known yet best and safest medicines that exists. There is no more agreeable means of building one's health than bicycling.
     —Jean-Pierre de Mondenard, M.D. (1977)

Body, Mind, Machine

The life force of human bodies powers bicycles. The combination of body, mind, and machine—the cyclist—is the most energy efficient traveler of all, either biological or technological.[1]

BEING HUMAN

Animals, human beings among them, can be described as fuel cells with a brain. Some 300 trillion cells of many different kinds, each one containing its genetic codes for function and reproduction, come together to form one human body. Brain cells are the central processing unit that regulates bodily functions and produces our sense of being alive. Cells are fueled by sunlight, oxygen, water, and various other elements and nutrients found in nature. As cells transform these raw materials into useable energy, humans become capable of perception, thought, movement, communication, invention, and reproduction and are able to enhance their bodies through knowledge and the practice of nutrition, exercise, and healing techniques.

The bicycle is one human invention that has a remarkable compatibility with the body. Cycling has a synergistic effect on people; as human energy flows into the machine, the cyclist becomes empowered by it. Through this lively mechanical appendage, people gain the benefits of economical mobility, a healthy lifestyle, a sense of self-sufficiency, and a means of improving their potential. Bicycles offer the possibility of total health, defined by the World Health Organization as "a state of complete physical, mental, and social well-being and not merely an absence of disease and infirmity."

Bicycles offer a full circle of health for human bodies. They are used for curing illness, for maintaining health, for achieving fitness, and for reaching a maximum level of performance that, as Tour de France cyclists claim, may be harmful for human health. For transport, cycling is one of the easiest means of mobility using the least amount of energy, yet for sport, it is one of the most difficult physical activities, using the most amount of energy. At some balancing point, cycling is one of the best ways to achieve health and well-being.

Benefits of Cycling

Not in 200 years has there been any one thing which has so benefitted mankind as the invention of the bicycle.

—Anonymous physician, c.1900.

When man invented the bicycle he reached the peak of his attainments. Here was a machine of precision and balance for the convenience of man. And (unlike subsequent inventions for man's convenience) the more he used it, the fitter his body became. Here, for once, was a product of man's brain that was entirely beneficial to those who used it, and of no harm or irritation to others. Progress should have stopped when man invented the bicycle.

—Elizabeth West, *Hovel in the Hills* (1977)[2]

What enjoyment to a cramped and warped women's life is the whirl of the wheel, bringing back as it does God's gift of health, and the memory of childhood's delight in out of door activity. With a sense also of rest to the brain, and by raising the thoughts in gratitude above the household cares and drudgery, it gives a woman for one brief while the chance to rejoice in the feeling of liberty and delight in her own strength.

—From *Wheelwoman* (1896)[3]

Quite a large number of our young men, who formerly were addicted to stupid habits, and the seeking of nonsensical distractions and vulgar pleasures, are now vigorous, healthy, energetic, and for the sake of this extraordinary machine submit themselves to an ascetic rule of life, and, induced by taste and passion, acquire habits of temperance, the imperative desire of quiet and regular living, and, most important of all, the steady exercise of self control, by resisting their appetites and doing, without hesitation, all that is required for effectual training.

—Henri Desgrange, Tour de France founder (1895)[4]

The truly extraordinary feature of the bike is that, like the very greatest teacher, it encourages you to find the answers from somewhere deep down inside yourself and not merely take them from someone else. When I began my adventure into myself on my bike I did not need to be told that I had to eat more of the right kind of food. I just knew I had to do it or else my legs would not work. I had never listened to or cared about those long terrifying lectures about the evils of smoking—complete with coloured slides of blackened lungs—but I did know, after some time in the saddle, that I just had to give up cigarettes. I did not need an expensive psychiatrist to tell me why I was depressed since, after a brisk ride, I was depressed no more.

—Tom Davies, *Merlyn the Magician and the Pacific Coast Highway* (1982)[5]

The cycling doctor is rewarded a hundredfold for his exertions by the pleasure of seeing his people at work in the garden or just out for a stroll. They, too, so obviously relish the sight of him taking a dose of his own medicine. Doctors have more than a medical duty to their flock: they should also practice what they preach in their ways of life... Surely by its silence, its simplicity, its efficiency, and its economy the bicycle is the most divine invention of contemporary man. Every doctor should be a cyclist.

—S.L. Henderson Smith, General Practitioner (1976)[6]

CYCLES OF HEALTH

Bicycles stimulate the human body's cyclical process of metabolism, the energy cycle of cells, in which the elemental nutrients we consume produce the energy for our activities. The more the metabolic cycle is activated, the healthier the human being. The health-giving aspects of cycling include its positive effects on breathing, blood circulation, muscle tone, bones and joints, digestion, elimination of wastes, perspiration and cooling, weight control, and peace of mind.

HEART AND LUNGS

Cycling improves respiration because the lungs expand, contract, and grow larger. As more oxygen enters the lungs, the blood becomes richer, its circulation more dynamic. The heart muscle grows stronger and does more work with less effort. As it pumps with more force, fewer pulses are needed to push the blood, and it reacts to increased effort more moderately, with quicker recovery. Blood flows smoothly through arteries and veins and reaches the extremities and all tissues and cells. Cycling is perhaps the most commonly recommended cure for heart diseases and their causes, such as clogged vessels (angina), high blood pressure (hypertension), and irregular pulses (arrhythmias). Heart attack patients can often begin cycling two weeks after their first seizure and achieve a decent level of health after two months. Because cycling is fun and can easily integrate with a person's lifestyle, it is one of the few exercises heart patients keep doing.

BODY SHAPE

Beautiful muscles develop from cycling, as muscles throughout the body exercise they become stronger, quicker, and more supple. With oxygen-rich blood coursing through muscle tissues, they perform with less fatigue. Most positions on a bike use the most powerful muscles of the body, those in the legs, buttocks, and lower back. While the upper body and arms get a good share of exercise from cycling, the abdominal muscles get the least, and they usually need some supplemental workout to keep up with the others, to help breathing, and to support the back.

Bones benefit from muscle contractions, which help to metabolize calcium, and they adapt in relation to the strains of the muscles attached to them. Regular exercise helps minimize the weakening of bones with aging. The joints, tendons and ligaments are also stimulated by exertion, and because the cyclist is supported by the hands, arms, pelvis, and feet cycling is easier on the bones and joints than running or walking, but a bit harder on them than is swimming. For these reasons, swimming and cycling are preferred methods of physical therapy for people with paralyzing disabilities from accidents, arthritis, and polio.

FUEL EFFICIENCY

Cycling improves appetite and digestion as the body makes better use of its nourishment. With an increase in metabolism, the body seems to ask for better foods and cleansing liquids, and this stimulates a more complete processing of nutrients in the viscera. Cycling can be an important treatment for people with diabetes, especially insulin-dependent diabetics who receive a natural boost of insulin from exercise. The elimination of wastes and toxins is enhanced by cycling. Constipation is relieved by exercise, and more toxins pass through urine and sweat. Also, studies have found that of people caught in the polluted air of traffic, cyclists tend to accumulate less toxins than motorists and pedestrians.

AIR-CONDITIONING

Because cyclists ride through an amount of wind roughly equivalent to the heat they generate, bike riding offers an excellent way to keep the body comfortably cool while exercising. Women usually have more sweat glands, which tend to produce less sweat than men, and so have better tolerance for heat. Overheating problems are less frequent in cycling than other sports, because sweat evaporates quickly on the skin, providing better cooling. However, since cyclists can move quickly through different temperature zones, they must protect against developing a cold sweat. With the proper clothing, cyclists can endure extremes of weather.

FAT AND FITNESS

Bike riding can easily be enjoyed by overweight or obese people, known as "Clydesdale cyclists." If a person can pedal a cycle, they are probably in some kind of shape. For those who wish to lose weight, cycling offers a methodical way to reduce body fat. Burning fat is achieved by finding one's maximum and resting heart rate (HR), the number of heart beats per minute, and then making the effort to ride at a heart rate of 60 to 70 percent the maximum. This should be done gradually according to levels of fitness, with the average plan to burn an additional 2,000 calories per week spaced over about three days of workouts.

There are a few myths about losing weight through exercise. One is that exercise increases the appetite, thus reversing any losses. But studies show that exercise increases the body's metabolism several hours after the workout, so more calories are burned during rest and recovery. Another myth is that exercise brings quick weight loss. Actually, at first neglected muscles develop and weight reduction may not occur because muscles weigh more than fat. It takes at least a month of regular workouts (three times weekly) to notice any real change as fat disappears. Women normally have several percent more body fat than men. Vigorous cycling

tends to make both fat and thin people more muscular. There is an extremely wide range of body weights for physically fit cyclists.

REPRODUCTIVE HEALTH

Cycling can improve reproductive functions through better health, and sexual energy is enhanced by general fitness. Vigorous cycling has various effects on men and women. Several studies show that short rides can increase testoterone levels, while long rides decrease it. Cycling is said to increase lust and libido, but it can also make one "too tired" or uncomfortable for sex.

Women racers and tourists may have irregular or absent menstrual cycles, called athletic amenorrhea. For the most part, amenorrhea seems to result from stressful situations, and will disappear. But if it continues for six months or more it can cause permanent ovarian damage. Usually it can be remedied by a little more fat in one's diet, but the safest bet is to consult a doctor.

Pregnant women have been able to carry on with moderately vigorous bicycling up to their eighth month. One prominent racing cyclist, Mary Jane "Miji" Reoch, reportedly rode her bike to the Pennsylvania Hospital in Philadelphia to give birth to her daughter Solange. Regular cycling almost certainly will not harm a fetus, and can help get an expectant mother's body in shape for the strain of childbirth.[7]

Mary Jane Reoch, 1946–1993.

POSITIVE MIND

Cycling stimulates a positive mental outlook through the effects of exercise which bring more blood circulation to the brain. Thoughts, worries, and emotions tend to flow through the mind from the meditative action of cycling on a stationary bike or along the open road. A sense of playful, light-hearted confidence is gained through self-powered mobility, and a cyclist is less likely to feel confined, helpless, or frustrated than a motorist in traffic. People who ride to work often arrive more vibrant and ready to be productive. Cycling eases the stress from other aspects of modern life and it produces a pleasant fatigue that results in a deeper, more restorative sleep.

Ailments of Cycling

In the days of velocipedes, a writer in the *English Mechanic* (1869) claimed: "The exertion required on the bicycle is of too concentrated a nature, and tends to pull one to pieces, rather than to afford a healthful exercise... Bicycle riding, if gone in for to any great extent, results in depression, in exhaustion and in wear and tear... Unless anyone is possessed of legs of iron and thighs of brass, I would strongly recommend him to look before he leaps into the saddle of a bicycle." High-wheel bicyclists probably showed the first symptoms of the use and abuse of cycling. They suffered mainly from headers, rattled joints, and saddle-sores. During the 1890s, when safety bicycles became a popular craze for millions of people, the debate grew louder as some physicians claimed cycling caused insanity, "congested digestion," "chronic disease," damage to the nervous system, and excessive thirst that led to alcoholism.[8]

BICYCLE WALK

Some cyclists have a peculiar way of walking, called the "bicycle walk," which mimics the action of pedaling. Instead of allowing the leg and foot to swing forward and then falling upon it, the "cyclo-pedestrian" tends to lift the foot in a circular motion and pushes it off the ground as if it were a pedal. In an advanced stage, bicycle walk includes a rolling of the shoulder and head, with quick roundabout glances to check the competition or traffic. Thick, slippery shoe cleats were developed to create a modern form of bicycle walk, with awkward tip-toe steps and an occasional sudden slip.

BICYCLE BACK

Bicycle walk was believed to be part of a systemic condition called "bicycle hump" or "kyphosis bicyclistarum." This malady was a result of the infamous bent-over scorcher's position, similar to today's aero-position, in which handlebars were lowered and seats were raised, exaggerating the natural curvature of the spine. The scorcher's position was so radical, it inspired the following verse, from the *Riverside Daily Enterprise* (August 16, 1896):

> He spun upon his waiting wheel,
> His vertebrae thrown out of joint,
> And onward pedalled looking like,
> A great interrogation point.

In New York, one cyclist protested against the scorcher's position by forming the Westfield Non-Scorching Sit-Erect Bicycle Club. Some people recognized its positive effect on speed, and others saw the similarity to the fetal position, calling it egg-shaped. Also, it was noticed that bicycle hump continued when the cyclist got off the bike, in a kind of slouching posture. In San Francisco, Dr. Albert Adams claimed he could not find a single case of spinal deformity because of bike riding and considered the hump an efficient position.

Strains in the neck, shoulders, and arms are common for untrained and elderly cyclists who ride in the typical bent-over position. When the upper body is supported by the hands on the bars and the back is bent forward more than about 45 degrees, the weight of the head, at 15 to 22 pounds, must be held upright to see the road. The natural curves of the upper spine support this position, but when held for more than a few hours under the stress of rough terrain, the strain can worsen from stiffness and aching between the shoulder blades, to numbness, tingling, or spasms in the neck, shoulders, and arms. In most cases, loosening exercises like calisthenics and yoga can relieve the condition, as can strengthening exercises like weight training. Riders can also sit more upright, or switch to a bike with a recumbent position.

Lower back pain from the bent-over position is caused by an exaggerated or reversal of the curvature of the spine, known as lordosis. Leaning forward for long periods places a burden on the muscles supporting the lumbar vertebrae of the spine, causing the lower back to have a sunken feeling, with aches or muscle spasms. The problem is particularly noticeable for beer-bellied cyclists burdened with "Dunlop's disease." The spare tire tube that "done lops" around the waist adds weight which the back must support. Adjustments in posture, loosening or strengthening exercises, dieting, and the application of heat pads on the lower back offer relief. Some cycling teams employ chiropractors to help re-align sore, twisted, and injured bike riders.

BICYCLE FACE

"Bicycle face," "bicycle stare," and "bicycle eye" afflict cyclists today, but must have been more pronounced in the 1890s when the following article appeared in the *Minneapolis Tribune* (July 20, 1895):

Scientists took hold of the matter, and advanced theories about it. One learned man said that the bicycle face was the result of a constant strain to preserve equilibrium. Up popped another scientist who stated that the preserving of equilibrium was purely an instinct, involving no strain, and that if the first man knew a bicycle from a rickshaw he'd realize it. Thereupon the first scientist said that the second had a bicycle brain, and hundreds took sides in the discussion. A prominent bicycle academy instructor here is positive that he has solved the secret. The three component parts of the expression he ascribes to the following causes:

The phenomenon of the wild eyes is acquired while learning the art. It is caused by a painful uncertainty whether to look for the arrival of the floor from the front, behind, or one side, and, once fixed upon the countenance can never be removed.

The strained lines about the mouth are due to anxiety lest the tire should explode. Variations of the lines are traceable to the general use of chewing gum.

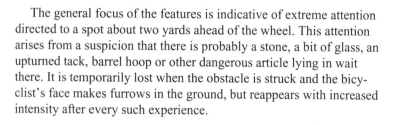

The general focus of the features is indicative of extreme attention directed to a spot about two yards ahead of the wheel. This attention arises from a suspicion that there is probably a stone, a bit of glass, an upturned tack, barrel hoop or other dangerous article lying in wait there. It is temporarily lost when the obstacle is struck and the bicyclist's face makes furrows in the ground, but reappears with increased intensity after every such experience.

Nowadays, when a cyclist's face makes furrows in the ground, it is called a face plant. In the *Fat Tire Flyer* glossary, face plant is defined as: "1. Any cycling maneuver that ends up looking like an attempt to hypnotize an earthworm; 2. Any vegetation growing between chin and hairline." This glossary also includes the "intransitive verb," called "Eat It" and defined as, "To make a sudden and close inspection of the road surface, and use the opportunity to have lunch."[9]

Bicycle face, stare, and eye are caused by road glare from chrome, concrete, and glass, kicked up dust and stones, noxious gases and soot exhaled by motor vehicles, and the attempts of cyclists to see through the back of their heads to prepare for what may come from behind. The use of darkened or mirrored "shades" tends to shield these problems, without providing a solution.

BICYCLE HANDS

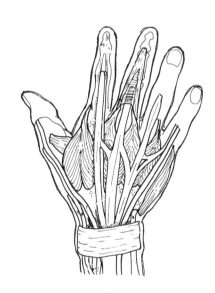

"Bicycle hands" and "bicycle wrists" are well-known maladies for cyclists, particularly those riding long distances in the bent-over position of racers. The condition consists of numbness in the thumbs or fingers caused by the pressure of palms on the handlebar. As the ulnar or median nerves travel from the wrist to the fingers, they can be impinged upon by the pressure of the rider's upper body on the hands. This can be relieved to some extent by padded gloves and handlebar grips, along with a more relaxed grip on the bars and the changing of hand positions, or switching to a recumbent bike.

"Bicycle wrists" is a general weakness in the wrists caused by the strains of holding the handlebars and road shocks. In severe cases, the wrists are temporarily paralyzed, go limp or become swollen, and the rider must be careful of slower reactions or lack of control. This is also known as carpal tunnel syndrome, named for the narrow channel of bone and ligament which the nerves pass through. Before the 1890s, when most bikes had fixed-gears, the action of backpedal braking added strains on the wrists. Lifelong cycling compounds bicycle wrists as calcium deposits form around the bones in the wrists and cause added stiffness.

SADDLESORES

The buttocks and pelvic region are one of the main points of support for body weight on the bicycle saddle, and all cyclists experience some form of discomfort, known as saddlesoreness. On standard bikes, the points of contact are the two ischial bones of the pelvis, called the "sit bones," which are naturally cushioned by small fluid-filled sacs. The tips of these bones are roughly three inches apart for men, and four inches apart for women, so seats are designed accordingly. Recumbent bicycles often have more comfortable bucket-style seats with the contact points shared by the ischium, ilium, and sacrum bones.

To prevent saddlesores cyclists should avoid clothing with seams or elastic bands in the crotch, and shorts or pants should have a soft chamois lining. Some say "nothing should come between you and your chamois," while others recommend the use of talc, baby powder, vitamin-rich ointment or antiseptic cream applied to the skin or the chamois. Chamois should be cleaned regularly, and the natural kind should be kept dry and supple. People who spend a lot of time in the saddle are apt to get calluses or boils caused by friction and irritation. These can become aggravated by hair follicles and rough riding terrain. Women cyclists have also spoken of pain due to "raw vulva." Repeated splashings of cold water on the affected skin toughens it and relieves some pain. Racers have been known to continue riding with severe saddlesores and rely on warm mineral baths, antibiotic ointments, anti-inflammatory medications, and cortisone shots for treatment.

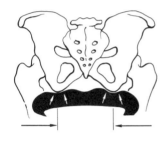

Sit bones have different widths for men (above) and women (below).

BICYCLE KNEES

"Bicycle knees," or "cyclist's knee," is actually a variety of conditions which can cause considerable pain and worry. The knees are complicated, modified versions of hinge joints, consisting of the juncture of four bones: the femur or thigh, the patella or kneecap, the tibia or lower leg, and its "side kick," the fibula. Added to these are the powerful thigh and lower leg muscles, a number of ligaments and tendons, plus two cartilages, the menisci, which act as stabilizers and shock absorbers, with sacs of fluid, the bursae, for lubrication.

In normal use, as the leg bends and extends nearly 180 degrees, the knee joint tends to slide or glide, allowing a small amount of side play. With cycling, the bending and extending of the leg is limited between a range from about ten degrees to 130 degrees, with the foot connected to the pedal in a mechanical motion. Knee-related injuries common in other sports, such as pulled hamstrings, and torn ligaments and cartilages, are less likely in cycling, except as a result of falls.

The majority of knee problems from cycling are caused by improper leg and foot position, excessive force or torque applied to the pedals, and overuse errors from hard training. The limited range of bending or flexion causes the patella to be almost constantly in contact or under pressure with the powerful quadricep muscles. When a cyclist pushes a large gear, or if the seat position is too low, excessive loads on the tendons, which surround the patella, may result in the pain and swelling of patella tendinitis.

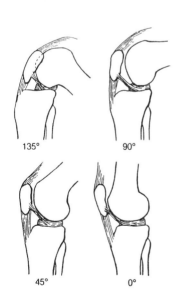

When a cyclist's seat is too high, the overextension of the leg can result in an excessive outward pull on the patella. Cyclists with one leg shorter than the other, abnormally shaped patellas, knock-knees, or poorly aligned quadricep muscles may suffer from a knee condition known as excessive lateral pressure syndrome (ELPS). This can result in chondromalacia patella, a softening or degradation of the knee cartilage, that may require repositioning of the foot-pedal position, or surgery. Crepitation is the slushy or crunchy feeling or sound that can occur with chondromalacia.

BICYCLE FEET

The positions of the feet are important for maintaining healthy knees. Many knee pains are the result of locking the foot into a fixed shoe-cleat-pedal system, and can be relieved by allowing free movement with cleatless shoes and toe clips, or free-floating clipless pedal sytems.

The foot is an active contact point that transmits the body's energy to the pedals, and friction within the shoe causes various problems. Proper fitting shoes with hard soles that distribute foot pressure over the pedals are essential for comfortable and effective cycling. Numbness is a common ailment when narrow shoes pinch the nerves between the metatarsal bones. A narrow or confined toe area, besides being uncomfortable, can also cause toe jamming and bruised toenails. These can be relieved by massage, soaking, and shoe stretching.

Corns, calluses and blisters are also common foot ailments for cyclists. Toe straps can cause friction at the ball or metatarsal joints, resulting in callus buildup or blisters. Straps can be wrapped behind the bulge and blisters can be drained with a sterile needle, followed by warm saltwater soaking, or the application of an antiseptic cream. Tightened shoes and toe straps can cause circulation problems so most cyclists leave them relatively loose except for climbing, sprints, or rough roads. Blisters occasionally appear around the heel below the Achilles tendon and on the tops of the toe knuckles from friction between the shoes and feet during the pedal stroke.

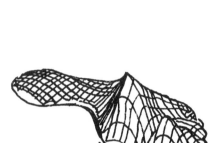

3D representation of peak pressures over foot during normal cycling.

BICYCLE BODY

Many muscle and tendon strains are the result of overuse. Overuse injuries are particularly common for recreational and racing cyclists because they are often active for many hours and days at a time. The best prevention is a daily routine of stretching, calisthenics, and yoga, usually performed in the morning before riding. The recommended exercises for cyclists include sit-ups, push-ups, pull-ups, leg-lifts, head-stands, toe-touching, spine-twists, windmills, cartwheels, backward back bends, and deep breathing exercises.

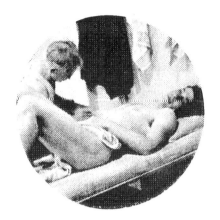

Massage is very important for muscle formation and recuperation, especially after a ride. Self massage can be done to a certain extent, mainly to the feet, legs, buttocks, and arms, but is best with the hands of a professional. There are four basic massage movements performed in sequence, in motions directed towards the heart and lymph glands using some form of lubricating medium such as mineral oil. One reason racing cyclists shave their legs and hips is to make massage easier and more effective. Starting with stroking and rubbing, the hands follow the contours of whole muscles to aid relaxation and circulation. Kneading in a smooth rhythmical squeezing and rolling of muscles aids tone and blood flow. Percussion is cupped hands making rapid slapping blows, and also loose shaking, wiggling or fingering of the muscle for stimulation. Friction is applied in circular movements with fingers and thumbs on the skin around tendons and ligaments to loosen adhesions in joints. Like training rides, a massage should begin as it ends, with gentler actions.

The immune system is usually enhanced by cycling and vigorous exercise, yet the stresses of long distance or high performance cycling can often weaken the body's defenses against bacteria and viruses. A reduced percentage of body fat below the average athletic levels and a lack of water or dehydration tend to make cyclists more susceptible. Preventive techniques include rest and healthy eating and drinking.

BODY HEAT

Cyclists can reach levels of athletic intensity and duration beyond most other activities and sports. Because cyclists tend to spend a lot of time exercising outdoors in all types of weather, they are vulnerable to ailments from overexposure to extreme temperature conditions. The body's average temperature is 98.6 degrees Fahrenheit (37 degrees Celsius) with normal variations of one degree. If the variation is more than five degrees either way, the person is in serious condition requiring medical help. Plus or minus ten degrees is usually fatal.

Hot weather can cause heat cramps, heat exhaustion, and heat stroke. These are the result of the body's inability to regulate excessive heat. Heat cramps and heat exhaustion are relatively temporary conditions that cause muscle cramps, a weak pulse, nausea, and pale, clammy skin. The best thing to do once these symptoms appear is to get off the bike and rest, lying down on cool level ground. Drinking water with salt is recommended.

Heat stroke is a much more serious condition which can easily lead to unconsciousness and death. Symptoms include a flushed red face, dry skin and a rapid pulse. The body temperature becomes dangerously high as the person feels headaches and dizziness. In this condition the rider should lie down with the head elevated; clothing should be removed or cooled off with water, and a doctor should be called immediately.

Cold weather produces a variety of problems for cyclists, mainly because of the increased windchill brought on by the cyclist's passage through cold air at speed. The first symptoms usually begin in temperatures around 40 degrees Fahrenheit, with numbness in the extremities (fingers, toes, nose, and ears) and the joints (knees, ankles, and elbows), which often lack a coating of fat. This can lead to frostbite, the freezing and deadening of tissues which can cause permanent damage or gangrene.

Covering the head is very important because a large percentage of heat transpires from it. Insufficient head protection causes fatigue, headaches, and dizziness. This can be prevented by adequate coverings, such as hats, caps, and facemasks. Gloves, mittens, and boots, with waterproof neoprene and warm linings of down, sheepskin or fleece are necessary in cold weather.

Long exposure to temperatures below freezing can lead to hypothermia, a condition in which the body loses heat faster than it can generate it, and body temperature drops below 97 degrees. This is especially prevalent at high altitudes when a rider gets wet and temperatures fall quickly. Hypothermia begins with shivering, reduced muscle coordination, and slurred speech. Then, as the condition worsens, slower thinking sets in, the person loses awareness, and becomes uncontrollable and irrational. When the body falls below 95 degrees, muscle control, breathing, and heart rate become weaker, followed by unconsciousness and death. The best prevention is to dress warmly, drink warm liquids, eat easily digestible high energy foods such as bananas, and to stop for rest in a warm, sheltered place when the first symptoms appear.

CRASH AND BURN

Most cycling injuries stem from the effects of falling on hard ground. A typical injury is "road rash," "asphalt burn" or skin abrasions from sliding on pavement. This can be partially prevented by wearing two layers of clothing which slide against each other, except in the case of some polypropylene fabrics, which may burn the skin. Racing cyclists shave their legs, buttocks, and hips to ease the process of cleaning bits of road grit from abrasions and in applying and removing bandages. Stretching and twisting while landing causes sprains or torn ligaments in the wrists, ankles, knees, the back, and the neck. These often become swollen and can be treated with soaking, splints, and easing off for a week or so. Dislocations occur when bones are jammed and snapped out of their usual joint socket during hard landings. The symptoms are similar to sprains, but require ice or pain-killers for relocation, followed by a splint and, if necessary, antibiotics.

"Failer." Photograph by Dimitri Korobeinikon.

FRACTURES

The most common fracture in cycling is of the clavicle or collar bone, caused by landing on the shoulder. These can either separate or break, resulting in pain and limited movement. The rider's arm is usually held close to the side and supported in a sling. In high-speed falls or collisions, leg and arm bones can break. Open or compound fractures, in which the bone pierces the skin, require a splint and immediate medical attention to prevent infection. Lacerations or deep cuts from sharp objects are often the result of falls on gravel roads or multiple bicycle pile-ups. Excessive bleeding must be stopped by hand compression or with a tourniquet and ice-packing. Wounds should be cleaned to prevent infection and stitches are often necessary.

HEAD INJURIES

Probably the worst injury for a cyclist is a concussion or fractured skull from impacts to the head. Headaches, dizziness, incoordination, temporary loss of memory, convulsions, vomiting, foaming at the mouth, unconsciousness, and even death can result. In some instances, the person may feel just a little shaken up and proceed riding, only to be hit by spells of dizziness and collapse. A cyclist with a mild head blow should lie down and rest or sleep to allow the brain and nervous system to recuperate. If vomiting occurs with convulsions, the mouth must be cleared out to prevent choking and medical help should be summoned immediately. These days, more cyclists are wearing hard shell helmets for head protection.

Broken helmet, '92 Olympic road race.

Cyclists have come up with ingenious roadside medical methods, such as using bicycle pumps as splints and surgical suction pumps, and using inner tubes as arm slings. Some riders carry pocket-sized first-aid kits, and ride leaders should have a good understanding of first-aid and emergency preparedness.

Cycling Positions

The bicycle must be in harmony with the body for a person to receive the most benefits from cycling. A correct position on the bike brings an easier, safer, and more efficient cycling experience; proper fitting reduces the risk of injury. An important factor in finding a comfortable position is based on gender. Average men and women of equal height have different proportions. Women tend to have longer legs, narrower shoulders, and a wider pelvis, while men have longer torsos and arms, and larger hands and feet.

Thanks to the ingenuity of cycle makers, various kinds of cycling machines are designed to fit various body shapes and abilities. For example, recumbent cycles allow people to ride comfortably in a chair instead of perched on a saddle. On tricycles and quadricycles people don't need to balance on two wheels. Handcycles and rowing vehicles let people who can't use their legs to ride with arm power.

Upright roadster

Touring

Racing (aero)

Semi-recumbent

Supine recumbent

Prone recumbent

BIKE FIT

The following measurements apply for standard foot-pedaling bicycles, including city, road, mountain, and recumbent cycles. It is important for cyclists to refine their position and style by making small incremental changes according to the individual ways of riding.

Bike shops have a few special accessories for measuring the best bike fit, such as the Fit Kit developed by Bill Farrell and the New England Cycling Academy. After years of measuring, Farrell offered a "wacky but often accurate" way to figure the correct length of seat tube for a road bike, by measuring the circumference of a cyclist's head and subtracting two centimeters.[10] The Bio-Racer is a computerized sizing system for standard racing positions from Belgium, and the Personal ProBikeFit software, developed by Jack Harrier, matches frame specs with body dimensions. It measures nine body dimensions and selects from 1,050 bikes, including road, mountain, and track bikes.

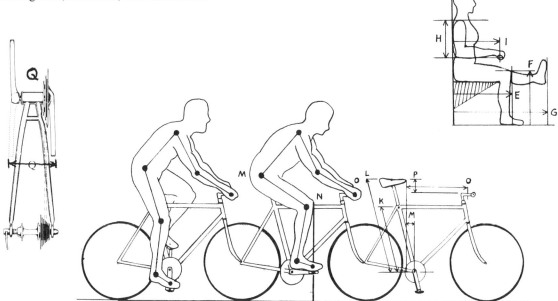

Measures for road bikes:

(J) **standover height**, from crotch to top tube, allow at least 1 to 4 inches.

K) **seat tube length**, usually measured from center of crank axel to center point of seat tube and top tube, multiply inseam (C) times 0.65

L) **seat height**, from center of crank axle to top of saddle, multiply inseam (C) times 0.883, compensate for pedal and shoe thickness.

M) **saddle setback**, on level ground, from center of crank axle to front of seat, in the saddle, align N) plumb line hanging from front of knee cap to center of pedal axle, with crank arms in horizontal position (3 o'clock) and balls of feet centered over pedals, compensate for various fore or aft positions.

O) **handlebar reach**, measure (I) forearm to center of stem, with elbow at front of saddle and handlebar grip at center of stem, compensate for (B) torso and (H) upper arm lengths, and upright or prone positions.

P) **stem height**, from top of saddle to top of stem.

Q) **Q-factor**, width of crank arms at pedals.

Body measures: standing barefoot, back against a wall, hands holding grips.

A) **height**, top of head to floor

B) **torso**, collarbone to crotch

C) **inseam**, crotch to floor

D) **reach**, shoulder to hand grip. Sitting with thighs level to ground, back against a wall, feet flat on floor, hands holding grips.

E) **thigh**, butt to front of knee cap

F) **lower leg**, top of knee cap to floor

G) **leg length**, butt to ball of foot

H) **upper arm**, collarbone to elbow

I) **forearm**, elbow to center of hand grip.

Resistances of Cycling

Cyclists face various elemental forces that affect their human-powered progress. Friction, rolling resistance, gravity, air pressure, and water pressure: these are the natural laws governing a cyclist's speed and energy efficiency. Total resistance is the sum of each individual resistance, which varies widely depending on the kind of cycle, the conditions of the cycling environment, and the speed of the cyclist.

Friction is caused by the cycling machine and the human body. Wheel bearings, pedal bearings, suspensions, chains, and gears cause mechanical friction on the bike, and bone joints, cartilage, tendons, and muscle tissue cause bio-mechanical friction in the body. Friction accounts for 0.5 to five percent of total resistance, but increases substantially if the bike is a pile of junk.

Rolling resistance is caused by the cycling machine and its contact with the ground. The cyclist's weight and the tire's air pressure and treads cause resistance on the bike, while the gradient and surface conditions of roads and paths cause resistance in the environment. Unpaved trails and cobblestones add about ten to 0.8 percent resistance, and asphalt roads and racing tracks add about 0.2 to 0.1 percent of total drag. Rolling resistance averages about ten percent of total drag, and it increases linearly in relation to speed and weight. Slope resistance is calculated by the weight of the cyclist and the machine, multiplied by the gradient of the road, which is measured as a percent of the gain or loss in altitude to the distance. Cycling uphill, a fairly difficult ten percent grade rises 100 meters in one kilometer, and a 25 percent grade (250 meters in one kilometer) is extremely difficult. Going downhill, the slope is a positive force, as a percent of the gradient.

Wind resistance is caused by air pressure on a cyclist's body and bike and is influenced by a cyclist's speed and environment. There are two kinds of wind resistance, form drag and skin friction, that are based on a moving body's shape and surface texture, and measured by the frontal area and coefficient of drag (Cd). Wind resistance increases as a square of velocity with a cyclist's speed, and as a cube of velocity with a cyclist's power output. When penetrating the air, making a headwind in still air, a cyclist must double the energy expenditure for each additional six mph (ten kph). When a headwind of ten mph (sixteen kph) rises, or if a cyclist's speed increases over fifteen mph (25 kph), wind drag increases to 70 to 90 percent of total resistances. Some say the speed of a cyclist and the headwind can be added together to estimate a cyclist's wind speed, so the effort of a cyclist going fifteen mph into a ten mph headwind is the same as going 25 mph in still air. Others say that winds change a cyclist's speed by about half the wind speed, so a ten mph headwind slows a cyclist by about five mph. On a standard bike, a cyclist's body accounts for about two-thirds of wind resistance, with one-third due to the bike.

A cyclist's wind resistance and energy expenditure can be lowered by drafting behind other cyclists and vehicles, by making the body and bike more aerodynamic with fairings, or by cycling at high altitude. In drafting, cyclists benefit from the form drag of other cyclists and vehicles, by following in the low pressure air that eddies behind a moving body. A following cyclist requires about fifteen to 30 percent less energy than a lead cyclist, depending on speed, spacing, and shapes of the two bodies. There are many variables, whether the cyclist rides in traffic at about twenty percent less energy expenditure, in a paceline or echelon (sidewind paceline) at about 25 percent less energy, a pack or peloton (about 40 percent less), or behind a motorcycle (about 40 percent less), a van (about 60 percent less), or a race car (about 100 percent, with a forward push because of the Von Karman vacuum effect).

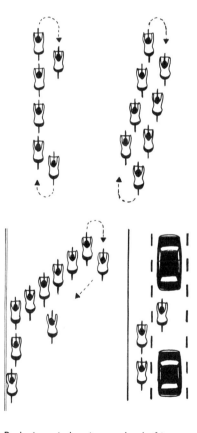

Reducing wind resistance by drafting in a paceline or echelon (top), in traffic (above), behind a motorcycle (far left), or behind a car.

Compared to a standard racing bicycle, an aero bike has five to 25 percent less drag, a fairing on a standard bike has ten to 25 percent less, an open recumbent has fifteen to 40 percent less, and a fully faired HPV has 60 to 80 percent less drag. An in-line tandem has about 50 percent less drag than two bikes, and the two riders use twenty percent less power, making it go about ten percent faster.

As altitude increases, air pressure (barometric pressure) and oxygen content (pressure of oxygen) progressively decrease by about 11.5 percent for each increase of 1,000 meters (3,280 feet) above sea level. Low air pressure results in low wind resistance, so a cyclist at 2,000 meters (6,560 feet) going ten mph (sixteen kph) requires about six percent less effort as at sea level, and when going 30 mph (49 kph), a cyclist requires about twenty percent less effort. Oxygen content decreases by about 23 percent at 2,000 meters, which limits performance, but humans adapt and can acclimatize to high altitude with increased production of blood hemoglobin. At 4,000 meters (13,120 feet) and above, the shortage of oxygen in the air severely limits human performance. In cold weather, air resistance increases by about one percent for every decrease of three degrees Celsius in temperate climates.

Water resistance applies mainly to human-powered watercraft, and depends on the hull shape (if any), the method of propulsion, and the current of the water. On pavement, water provides less rolling resistance, close to edge of slippery, as tires hydroplane over smooth wet surfaces.

RESISTANCES OF CYCLING MACHINES

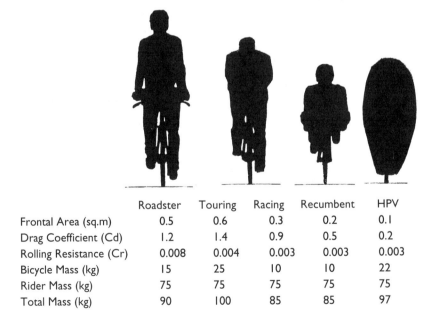

	Roadster	Touring	Racing	Recumbent	HPV
Frontal Area (sq.m)	0.5	0.6	0.3	0.2	0.1
Drag Coefficient (Cd)	1.2	1.4	0.9	0.5	0.2
Rolling Resistance (Cr)	0.008	0.004	0.003	0.003	0.003
Bicycle Mass (kg)	15	25	10	10	22
Rider Mass (kg)	75	75	75	75	75
Total Mass (kg)	90	100	85	85	97

Cycling Clothes

To get the most enjoyment, comfort, and efficiency in cycling it is best to wear comfortable clothing that fits the form and function of bike riding. Cycling clothes are designed for all kinds of bicycle riding, for protection from the elements, carrying things, creating an identity, and promoting messages. Because bikes are usually exposed to weather and road conditions, unlike motor vehicles with heaters, air-conditioners, and enclosed bodies, cyclists can combine their climate controls and protective coverings with healthy body functions and special clothing.

Cycling clothes are made to provide comfort in and out of the cycling position, to give warmth when needed, to allow the skin to breathe, to wick sweat from the skin into the cloth, to prevent rain and moisture from soaking the cloth, and to be easily washable, dryable, and durable. Dressing in layers of clothing that can easily be added or removed is important, because cyclists are often exposed to changing weather conditions. For example, climbing and sweating up a sunny hillside and then descending into a cold, shady hollow can cause cold chills, fatigue, and bronchitis.

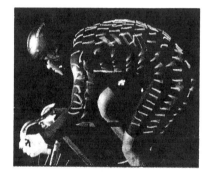

Clothes produce enough wind resistance to affect performance in competitive cycling. Letting your ponytail or long hair blow in the breeze slows you down a little. Like the dimples that help a golf ball fly farther, a textured fabric such as wool has less wind resistance than bare skin. Aerodynamic clothing can reduce resistance by about six to ten percent.

MATERIALS

Many warm-blooded creatures come equipped with natural coverings, such as fur, feathers, and full-body hair. Humans evolved as semi-hairy naked creatures equipped with the ability to fabricate their own coverings. Traditional materials come from plants, insects, and animals, such as cotton, hemp, rubber, silk, wool, leather, and fur. The expansion of chemical industries in the mid-1930s brought a variety of materials for clothing, including synthetic polymer and processed natural fibers. As synthetics emulate or improve upon nature, function determines the form of special clothing for cycling.

DuPont has contributed many synthetic fibers to the world of cycling, including Nylon (1935), Spandex (1937), Lycra (1962), Fortrel, Cordura, Kevlar (1976), CoolMax, Spandura, Supplex, and Thermax (1989). Lycra spandex is an amadine polymer that revolutionized cycling clothes as a light-weight elastic material used in shorts with a blend of 80 percent nylon and 20 percent spandex. Cordura and Kevlar are strong polymer fibers used in gloves, shoes, jackets, packs, and many bike components. CoolMax is a polyester fiber with four wicking channels for staying dry and cool in hot weather.

Other widely used synthetics include Gore-Tex, a windproof, waterproof and breathable material developed by W.L. Gore & Associates. Improved since its debut in 1976, it has a PTFE membrane with "nine billion microscopic pores per square inch, 20,000 times smaller than a droplet of water and 700 times the size of a water vapor molecule." Gore-Tex XRC (Extended Comfort Range) is a thin glossy windproof membrane that provides a "microclimate." Versatech by Burlington is a microfiber polyester yarn used in outerwear. Hydrofil by Allied-Signal is a nylon wicking material used in linings, and Synera is a "no sweat performance fiber" made of polypropylene. Polartec by Malden Mills is plush polyester fleece used as weather-resistant outerwear. Superwash is a treated wool made of 100 percent Australian merino wool.

The question of which fibers are best is often a matter of opinion. Many people refuse to wear fur and leather out of concern for animals. Likewise, with growing concerns for the environment, many people avoid chemically treated and synthetic clothing materials. One solution may be the Synchilla fleece made by Patagonia from the recycled plastic in bottles, polyethylene terephthalate (PET).

The essential clothing recommended for cycling depends on a cyclist's style and the weather conditions. The "must have" cycling clothes are shoes, shorts or pants, jersey, headwear, and gloves. There are a few Golden Rules for cycling clothes. In cold weather, it is best to cover the head, hands, and feet. All but racers should cover their knees in temperatures below 60 degrees Fahrenheit (18°C), and in temperatures below freezing there is little relief for cold extremities except to stop at a warm place before frostbite sets in. The Golden Rules: There is no such thing as bad weather, just bad clothing. Wear bright colors for high visibility, such as a yellow jersey. Only present or former World Champions may wear the rainbow jersey. Always wear a helmet before you crash. Don't sit on your bananas.

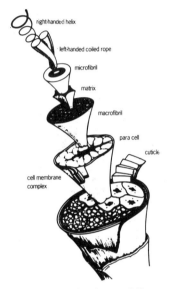

Magnified details of a wool fiber.

CAPS

Cyclists often need to cover their heads with a light, warm, breathable cap for wicking up sweat, shading the eyes and face from sunburn, and reducing the splatter of rain. The traditional cycling cap is a dome-shaped cover with a crescent-shaped bill, made of light or middleweight cotton with an expandable back side. Bills are stiffened with cardboard, which deteriorates in the wash, or with plastic, which becomes warped in a hot drier.

Cycling caps are worn with the bill at the front, back, or side, flipped up or down. On hot days in races like the Tour de France, it is customary to wedge green leaves or lettuce under the cap, for moist cooling and to prevent sunburn. Cycling caps come in many colors and motifs. The traditional design is white with the World Championship *arc-en-ciel* bands centered across the top. Embellished with club colors and sponsor's logos, cycling caps are offered as souvenirs at big cycling events. Alternatives to caps are bandanas, scarves, and headbands, made of terry cloth and spandex, useful for absorbing sweat on the forehead, before it stings the eyes.

HATS

Cycling hats evolved from equestrian and military hats of the nineteenth century with club medallions on the crest. They gradually became soft double-lined woolen hats with small bills and stretch bands that fold up or down to cover the ears. Since the cover is usually stitched from four pieces of cloth, they often come multicolored. Some are made reversible, with nylon on one side for light rain protection. Other popular hats for cycling include the traditional beret; the watch cap, with or without a bee-nie ball; the fleece-lined leather flight cap with ear flaps and optional chin strap; and the American baseball cap worn backwards.

In heavy rain storms, the classic floppy "so'wester" hat provides full coverage, as does any water-repellent urethane-coated hood and cape combo. For colder weather, an assortment of natural and synthetic cloth hats, scarves, and masks are used to cover the whole head, with holes for the eyes, nose, and mouth. In freezing temperatures, fleece lined neoprene masks are used to protect the skin and breathing membranes. The traditional balaclava hat, with a more streamlined cut for cycling, unfolds to cover the ears and neck. Variety comes with all shapes of leather and fur army surplus hats; one company makes a colorful line of synthetic fleece hats with jester-like earflaps, such as the "Rooster-Farian." Folly comes with the multicolored whirlybird beenie, and the air-conditioned hat with solar and wind-powered fans to cool heads.

MASKS

In areas with high concentrations of air pollution, cyclists have begun to use air-filtration masks for protection from particle (dust, soot, pollen) and gaseous (carbon monoxide, nitrogen dioxide, sulphur dioxide, benzene, ozone) contaminants. There are several styles of air-filtration masks, depending on the type of filter and the amount of unfiltered air that passes through the system under the stress of an actively breathing and perspiring cyclist.

The easiest to wear and least effective mask is a bandana; some are specially designed for cycling, shaped to fit around the bridge of the nose, mouth, and chin. Disposable particle and fume filters with elastic head bands made of fine-mesh synthetic cloth are a popular and partially effective option. A couple of lightweight masks which attempt to form air seals have been marketed for cycling, including the plastic and foam Greenscreen and the neoprene Respro mask, which has an activated charcoal cloth developed by the British Ministry of Defense for chemical warfare, and won a technology design award from British Petroleum (BP). The heaviest forms of air-sealed protection are the industrial masks used for working amidst toxic materials, such as the 3M Dust and Mist Respirator. The primary filter normally uses a removable activated carbon fabric which captures most of the ozone and benzene but none of the carbon monoxide.[11] Additional fabric and foam filters are used to capture particulates. Like bicycle helmets, masks are not a cure for the problem, but merely a protective shield.

HELMETS

Cycling helmets come in a variety of forms and functions. For much of the twentieth century, most helmets were for racing, and the most common was the "ribbed" or "hairnet" helmet with padded leather bands crossing the top of the head. Some helmets had multicolored ribs or extra padding at the forehead, the back of the neck, and around the ears. The finest were covered in glossy patent leather. A tradition among Flemish racers was to hang small religious medallions on the front brim near the "third eye," with crosses and saints for heavenly protection.

The risks in motor-paced racing require more substantial protection. The large stayers use helmets with a hard leather or plastic shell and a cork or polystyrene liner. These have a wide brim for mounting earphones for the pacer to hear the rider. Derny pacers and riders have used traditional leather racing helmets. Kei-rin racers developed a uniform style of helmet with a colorful cloth-covered hard shell displaying the rider's number. A variety of helmets from polo, hockey, football, mopeding, and motorcycling have been used for dirt and field cycle sports such as bicycle polo and BMX racing, where the latest innovation is a padded chin shield.

A major development came in the 1970s with the first generation of made-for-cycling helmets with hard plastic or fiberglass shells and expanded polystyrene linings, known as "biscuits." The classic styles include the Skid-Lid (1970), and the Bell Biker (1972) with a DuPont Lexan high-impact thermoplastic shell, a shock-absorbing beaded polystyrene liner, and movable Velcro-fitted foam pads. To cool the head and prevent the "sweat box" condition, helmets featured shapely air circulation vents. By the 1980s, racers began experimenting with aerodynamic helmets on road and track, designed more for speed than for safety. With the formulation of bicycle helmet safety standards by the Snell Foundation and the American National Standards Institute (ANSI Z90.4), a second generation of sleeker and lighter helmets became more popular with molded polystyrene models, such as the Giro Aero and the Specialized Sub-6.

Helmets are available in children's sizes, and decorative helmet covers include the typical colors and logos of helmet makers, clubs, and team sponsors, as well as many animal shapes made by Comic Covers and Narly Noggins, with the faces, horns, and patterns of puppy dogs, cats, tigers, hogs, sharks, bulls, and ducks.

The most popular helmet attachments are rearview mirrors and visors fit to the helmet brim. Silencers are ear shields used to muffle annoying wind noise produced by some helmets. At the 1991 Tour DuPont bicycle race, Greg LeMond wore an eight-ounce Giro Air Attack helmet fit with a two-way radio. Molded into the polystyrene brim was a tiny microphone on a flexible tube, an earphone and a transceiver switch. Wires led from the helmet to a half-pound circuit board and battery pack carried in his jersey pocket. With a range of about a mile, the radio allowed LeMond to keep contact with his coach in the team car and give radio-TV interviews.

Steven Roberts, the wizard of cycle-computing "nomadness," has equipped his helmet to interface with his hi-tech recumbent bike. His Bell Tourlite has a rearview mirror, double Nightsun headlights, a tiny Private Eye Heads-Up Display monitor, a SetCom audio system with a boom mike for dictating to the bike's computer console, earphones for his ham radio and a solar-powered, solid-state 50-watt refrigeration device to cool his head. While riding his bike, Roberts can move his head to control the cursor on his Macintosh computer screen, using a Brain Interface Unit with ultrasonic phase and doppler shift sensors on his helmet.

GLASSES

Various kinds of glasses, goggles, and visors have been used to see properly while cycling. Wearing glasses has rarely been an obstacle for nearsighted or farsighted cyclists, and even those with 20/20 vision use clear, shaded, or filtered glasses for protection from flying bits of sand, snow, gravel, glass, or insects, oily traffic soot, and harmful ultraviolet rays.

Goggles became popular with racing and touring cyclists, beginning with the high-wheel bikes of the 1880s. With glass lenses surrounded by perforated side-flaps and adjustable head straps or ear hooks, goggles shield the eyes from dusty road grit, windy rain, spraying wheels, and stones kicked up by horses, carriages, and automobiles. While most cyclists wore their glasses casually atop their heads when not in use, the "Pedaler of Charm," Hugo Koblet, was known for sporting them on his biceps.

Sunglasses with detachable shadings and colored lenses became popular in the 1950s, especially when Louison Bobet wore a flashy pair with white rims in the Tour de France. Several champion cyclists have worn glasses with distinction, such as Jan Janssen and Laurent Fignon. Cyclists using contact lenses often wear glasses for added comfort and protection, bringing eyedrops for long rides.

Recent developments are lightweight "shades" or "sportshields" with large lenses that combine the features of goggles, being dust-proof and breathable, while offering wider peripheral coverage. Made of ANSI-approved shatterproof polycarbonite or Lexan glass, with an assortment of distortion-less, scratch-resistant, anti-fogging, static-free, and waterproof coatings, lenses block harmful ultraviolet rays and are available with polarized, mirrored, and rainbow-colored filters. Filtered lenses provide an enhanced view of the world by disguising the haze from smog.

Special features include clip-on rearview mirrors with adjustable wire mounts, flaps or screens to protect the nose from exposure, and adjustable straps made of leather, spandex cord, or rubber to keep the glasses from falling off the head. When the cyclist-businessman Robert Zider fell off his bike and bent his glasses, he was inspired to develop "memory glasses," with frames made of the patented alloy called Memorite. If the frames get bent, they can be dipped in hot water to return to their original shape.

UNDERWEAR

An assortment of cycling undergarments are used as a second skin for wicking perspiration, as an extra layer of warmth, and as a supporter for loose and protruding body parts. A lightweight wool T-shirt has the advantages of being breathable, wicking away perspiration and maintaining a temperate climate. Wool works well in all but the hottest weather where loose or mesh cotton is preferred. When cotton is pressed against the skin under layers of other clothing, it tends to collect sweat, causing harmful chilling effects. A popular cycling tradition is to put newspapers (or plastic bags) under the jersey over the undershirt at the top of a hill to keep warm and save energy from the chilling wind on downhill runs.

Different kinds of underwear are used as the temperature drops. In freezing weather, one-piece long johns and thermal double-lined long-sleeve shirts and tights, made of pure or blended cotton, wool, nylon, and polyester, serve as a base for outer layers. Bib-like aprons and mock turtlenecks provide added warmth for the torso and neck.

Cycling is often credited with stripping women of restrictive corsets, but many women support their breasts while riding to minimize bouncing, chafing, and tissue breakdown. A variety of comfortable athletic and cycling bras have become available and most designs are made of cotton/polypropylene blends with Lycra and CoolMax fabrics, without wires or hardware which can cause irritation. They feature molded cups with front-cross support and separation, mesh panels for wicking perspiration, and wide elastic bands circling the lower ribs, allowing better breathing in the cycling position. To prevent slippage, straps are designed in cross-the-back, T-shaped or Y-shaped patterns.

Bike is the trademark of a popular crotch supporter or "jock strap," but these are not recommended for male cyclists because the crude seams irritate the crotch, and the saddle already supports the penis and testicles. Though the penis usually contracts into the crotch on long rides and in colder temperatures, some men wear a soft "cod piece," such as a sock, to prevent the tip from irritation and freezing. A "female fly" appears on bikini briefs by Zanika, with a pull-apart crotch that allows women to "answer Nature's call without the indignity of undressing."[12]

T-SHIRTS

T-shirts and tank tops are popular garments often associated with cycling enthusiasts. T-shirts are commonly made of cotton or cotton/polyester blends, with long sleeves, mid-length BMX-style sleeves, and standard issue short sleeves, and tank tops have the U-shaped sleeveless design. Special features include open-air fishnet fabric and shoulder pads. As a means of expressing a cyclist's individuality, a whole genre of fashionable T-shirt art with bicycling messages has appeared. These include personalized names and slogans, photos, air-brush paintings, logos, and graphics representing bike manufacturers, shops, activists, clubs, teams, races, tours, and rides. T-shirts seem to gather around cyclists, either as collector's items or as old rags for cleaning the bike.

JERSEYS

Cycling jerseys are the traditional shirts for bike riding. They evolved from finely woven wool pullovers, cut extra long to compensate for the cyclist's bent-over position with high collars that button up in front or along one shoulder. Pockets were added across the back and the breasts for carrying identity cards, keys, money, maps, patch kits, rubber bands, tools, sandwiches, sliced fruit, sweet cakes, candy bar wrappers, pocket flasks, tobacco, matches, and found objects. Racing inspired the traditional jersey patterns by Tortelli and Sergal of Italy with horizontal bands, national colors, and embroidered team logos.

With the higher cost of wool since the late-1970s, cotton and wool jerseys have gradually been replaced by equally expensive synthetic blends of polyester, polypropylene, and nylon fibers, and embroidery has been replaced by sublimated printing for graphics. Some riders, known as "retro-grouches," complain of the plastic feeling in synthetics, and the traditional wool jersey has made a bit of a comeback.

Silk jerseys appeared for track racing in the 1890s. A strong, shiny material, silk offered smoother sliding on wooden velodromes. These have been replaced by Lycra-like nylon-spandex one-piece skintight suits. For better aerodynamics, many track racers use rubberized or Ciré-coated nylon suits. The "wet look" has an exotic slippery appearance, but its lack of breathabilty is impractical for all but the shortest events. One-piece suits are contoured to fit tight in the aero position so they are rather uncomfortable for standing upright, and racers often zip or sew themselves into their suits on the starting line. To maximize aerodynamics with breathable materials, Descent's research lab in Osaka, Japan, developed Sei-Ryu Tech. Wind-tunnel tests showed considerable trailing turbulence coming from a rider's shoulders and back, so specially shaped silicon patches were applied to the suit.

JACKETS

There are assorted made-for-cycling outer garments which serve as second, third, or fourth layers of protection from wind, rain, and cold. These include double-thick long-sleeved jerseys, wind parkas, and rain-proof down-filled jackets. Cycling jackets need to have extended arms and backs to compensate for the bent-over cycling position, and be close fitting to prevent excess flapping in the wind. High collars, hoods, and tight cuffs help seal out the cold. Pockets appear on the sides, the back, or the front, kangaroo style.

Various kinds of nylon are used for wind shells, with mesh sides for breathability, and urethane coatings help resist wet weather. For extreme cold, goose down jackets provide the most warmth for the lightest weight, though care must be taken to prevent excess sweat by wearing underneath layers with sufficient wickability.

Armless vests have been popular for cycling since the Victorian days, offering freedom of movement for the arms while keeping the chest warm. Lightweight down or fleece-lined vests are useful in cold weather, and urethane-coated nylon vests with reflective patterns are handy for commuting cyclists.

GLOVES

Cycling gloves provide cushioning, protection, and warmth for the hands and wrists. Traditional cycling gloves stop at the middle of the fingers and thumbs for better manual dexterity. Most use some form of foam padding or gels in the palm to relieve pressure on the ulnar nerve of the wrists. Some have terry cloth backs for wiping sweat, and others come with bright or reflective patches for signaling in traffic. Extra tough material in the palm is also handy for cyclists who wipe their tires of wet road grit.

For colder weather, gloves come with full-length fingers, thicker padding, fleece linings, and water-repellent coverings. Lobster mitts by Pearl Izumi have three "claws:" for the thumb, the index and middle fingers, and the ring finger and pinky. Full-fitting mittens are recommended for maximum warmth.

SHORTS

Cycling shorts have become popular in mainstream fashion, fitness, and sports. Traditionally made of tight-fitting wool—black, for wiping greasy hands—they feature smooth seams and crotch padding made of chamois hide for protection from saddlesores. They are cut at mid-thigh for easy leg movement and muscle support. Preferably, they are held up with suspenders or bib straps, to provide easier breathing without elastic waist bands, and to cover and comfort the lower back. Track racing shorts had special buttons for wearing suspenders underneath silk jerseys that tucked into the shorts. Madison shorts have an inner pocket holding the team racer's hand-sling fob, and extra hip padding to soften crashes. Touring shorts are often designed as loose-fitting recreational cut-offs with extra pockets, saddle-shaped seams, and a chamois-padded seat.

Since the late-1970s, cycling shorts have become more colorful and wool has been replaced with blends of nylon and Lycra spandex. Bib style shorts have incorporated suspenders in the design. Leather chamois have been replaced with synthetic suede, terry cloth, polyurethane foam, and polypropylene liners called Supersuede, Ultrasuede, and Suedemark. The Hydroshort uses a liquid-filled bladder and a terry-cloth lined perforated chamois. Vision shorts by Hind have Scotchlite reflector panels for safe night cycling.

PANTS

Long-legged shorts, leggings, tights, knickers, and trousers have all been designed for cycling. Traditional track suit bottoms were made of wool and worn over a pair of shorts. Some are cut at the ankle and trimmed with the customary World Championship bands, and others have stirrups for the feet. Leggings are separate garments which make shorts into ankle length tights and roll up to fit in a jersey pocket. Knickers are cut below the knee and worn with long socks. They are made of wool, corduroy, and synthetics, and urethane-coated nylon gaiters are used to provide wet weather-proofing. Rain pants are made of urethane-coated nylon or taffeta, and have velcro closures to keep the pant legs from tangling with the chainwheel, cotter pins, or pump clip.

Socks

Socks are usually necessary for foot comfort, hygiene, warmth, and per-spiration wicking. Traditional cycling socks are cut a couple of inches above the ankle, like anklets, and made of cotton, wool, or synthetic blends, such as Cool Max, Thermax, Lycra, Hydrofil and Acrylic. Thin cotton is preferred for hot dry weather, and thick wool or neoprene for cold and wet weather. While the sporting tradition of white socks contin-ues, black socks have an ominous (or naive) character, and logos and col-orful pop-art designer styles are increasingly common. Track racers often ride without socks because bare feet feel more in touch with the shoes and pedals on a fixed gear.

Shoes

The earliest shoes developed for cycling include leather boots equipped with spikes for swift-walking, and chukka boots with thick heels for clutching the velocipede's pedals. Oxford-style leather shoes were light-ened, streamlined, and strengthened in the soles to provide uniform foot pressure. Holes were cut out of the uppers and in the soles so the feet could breathe. For cold weather, linings of cloth, sheepskin, and fur kept the feet warm. Rubber galoshes shielded the rain. Cleats on the soles fit with the pedals with toe clips and straps, giving more control while apply-ing foot pressure in the pedal stroke, especially with fixed-gear bikes.

Cycling shoes for racers and cycletourists developed in the "boot" of Europe. Specialists in Italy created curvaceous form-fitting leather shoes that were usually polished in black, some in patent leather. They were shaped for high arches as well as flat feet. Metal cleats were carefully nailed or riveted into the sole so as not to puncture cyclists' feet. Wooden sole shoes were perfect for wood rim bikes on board tracks. Winter boots came in luxurious fleece-lined models which tried to protect from frost-bite. Low-cut (below the ankle) shoes had long tongues for ankle protec-tion, and layers of animal oils and vegetable creams were applied to con-dition, soften, and waterproof the hides.

Sport shoes for running, football, tennis, and hiking became popular in the 1930s and the wide variety of cycle sports have inspired many shoes, including Cycleball shoes, a kind of handball or tennis styled shoe that developed in the 1950s, and Artistic Cycling shoes, which are like gym-nastic slippers with gripping rubber soles. Polo and Speedway bikers used oxfords, football, and jogging shoes. Since the 1960s a popular kind of multipurpose recreational shoe developed that is suitable for average cycling. These evolved from Keds sneakers, to Spaulding tennis shoes, to Adidas and Puma running shoes, to the Nike, New Balance, and Reebok generation of leisure, fitness, and multi-sport shoes.

In the mid-1970s, special kinds of recreational shoes were developed for cycle touring and commuting. Like running shoes but with harder soles for pedaling, they featured rubber wedges or slots for gripping the pedals, and rubber bumpers on the toe and the sides to protect from pedal clip and strap abrasions. Early models include the Bata Biker, made with canvas and rubber-covered cord, and the leather Avocet touring shoes with Vibram soles.

Touring shoes developed with blends of leather, foam, and polymer fibers for all-purpose riding, walking, and living, and with knobby soles and recessed cleats for all-terrain mountain biking. Some shoes are made lightweight at the expense of durability; one common problem is that the plastic sole insert breaks apart near the pedal cleat from the combined stress of cycling and walking. For off-road cycling, cyclo-cross shoes have spikes that screw into cleats, and mountian bike shoes have gnarly treads and bright colors, such as Nike's Cross Terrain, with amethyst, infrared, powder blue, neon green, and jet black. BMX shoes, known as "skids," are similar to high-top sport shoes.

Since the late-1980s, bike racing shoes have been modernized with synthetic fibers, carbon composite soles, velcro straps. and adjustable foot bindings. The conversion to clipless pedals brought lighter shoes with stronger and smoother uppers, making them easier to cover with cold weather neoprene boot-covers.

PADDING AND LEATHER

Padded clothing and protective leathers are used in several cycle sports including BMX, freestyle, kei-rin racing, and downhill mountain biking events. Based on the designs of motorcycle road and off-road racing, these are made of natural or synthetic leathers and foam-lined plastics. Providing injury protection from abrasions (crash-and-burn) and sharp impacts, they are worn on the shoulders, elbows, hips, and knees.

PACKS

Several kinds of packs and panniers are worn by cyclists, either on the body or on the bike. Cyclists should carry their important personal items on their body, in jersey pockets, musettes or shoulder bags, backpacks, and fanny-packs. Extra food, clothing, books, cameras, and luggage should go on the bike in saddlebags (Karrimore), handlebar packs (Cannondale), rack-mounted panniers (Madden), or frame-fitting cases, to provide a more stable support for the extra weight and to reduce fatigue by freeing the rider from the burden. Some rack-mounted panniers have box-shaped liners, and others can be worn as backpacks for carrying off the bike. The Eco-Sport pack is designed to keep a business suit neat. So-called waterproof and breathable fabrics, such as nylon, Cordura, Gore-Tex, and polyurethane, are not always completely watertight because moisture exists in the air, so air-sealed pouches and luggage are useful for sensitive camera and electronic equipment.

LIGHTS

Lights and reflectors are considered part of a cyclist's clothing when they are worn on the body. Arm and leg lights, waist-mounted flashers, helmet beams, light-emitting diode (LED) panels, and reflective strips, such as 3M's Scotchlite material which is applied to shorts, jerseys, jackets, pants, and shoes all serve to make the cyclist more visible.

CLOTHING FOR TOURING

Clothing carried by a cycletourist for a three-week camping trip, * in winter:

1 cycling cap or helmet
1 cycling winter hat *
1 face mask *
1 pair sunglasses
1 bandanna
1 pair cycling gloves
1 pair long gloves
1 pair mittens *
1–2 T-shirts
1–2 long-sleeve turtlenecks
1 short sleeve cycling jersey
1 long sleeve cycling jersey
1 wind and waterproof jacket
1 weather-proof down jacket *
2 pairs cycling shorts
1–3 pairs underwear
1 set of long underwear *
1 pair cycling leggings *
1 pair cycling knickers *
1 pair knickers socks *
2–3 pairs cycling socks
1 pair wool socks
1 pair cycling shoes
1 pair cycling shoe covers *
1 pair sandals
1 pair boots *

CLOTHING FOR LE TOUR

Clothing packed by a racing cyclist for the Tour de France:

1 road helmet
1 aero helmet
15 cycling caps
1 winter hat
1 face mask
2 pairs glasses
10 wicking undershirts
5 short sleeve jerseys
1 long sleeve jersey
1 time trial skinsuit
2 windbreakers
1 rain cape
1 winter jacket
2 polo shirts
1 track suit
7 pairs cycling gloves
2 pairs winter gloves
1 pair arm and leg warmers
7 pairs cycling shorts
5 pairs cycling socks
2 pairs cycling shoes
1 pair cycling shoe covers
1 pair sandals
1 pair sport shoes
1 suit and tie

6 Energy and Power

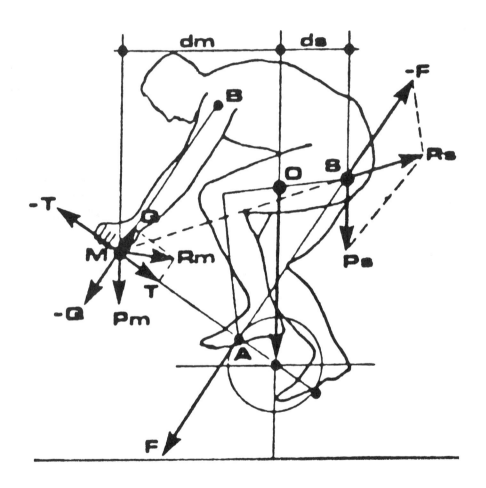

The bicycle is a curious vehicle whose passenger is also its engine.
—John Howard, *The Cyclist's Companion* (1984)

Cycling's Efficiency

Cycling is the most energy-efficient means of travel among animals and machines. Traveling efficiency is based on the amount of energy a body uses to move its weight a certain distance. An easy-going cyclist uses about .15 calories per kilogram per kilometer.

In fuel efficiency, where the amount of calories consumed is compared to the amount of work or output produced, the "human machine" is comparable to the most efficient modern power sources, including fossil-fueled automobiles and power plants. In one study, Chester Kyle and Alex Moulton calculated that the super-endurance riders in the Race Across America (RAAM) consumed about 80,000 calories over ten days, producing about 16,000 calories of mechanical work, for an average efficiency of 20 percent. Moulton added that "Mankind would be hard pressed to make any automotive vehicle as efficient as a man on a bike. Moreover, our fuel is non-fossil, pleasant to consume, and easily renewable."[1]

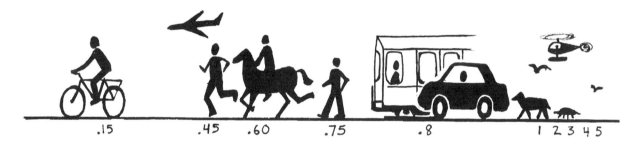

CALORIES PER GRAM PER KILOMETER

Since the studies by Vance Tucker of Duke University, which popularized the super efficiency of cycling, this data has been expressed, not only in the various ways of measuring energy and output, but also in the global context of energy use:

A bicyclist is by far the most efficient traveler—three times more than a horse, five times more than a car, ten times more than a sea gull or a dog or a jet plane, and one hundred times more than a blowfly or a bumblebee.
—From *Bicycling!* (1973)

I eat to ride, I ride to eat. At the best of moments, I can achieve a perfect balance, consuming just the right amount of calories as I fill up at bakeries, restaurants, or ice cream parlors. On the road, I can get about twelve miles to the quart of milk and a piece of baker's apple tart.
—Daniel Behrman, *The Man Who Loved Bicycles* (1973)

CALORIES PER PERSON PER MILE (1984)	
Automobile (1 occupant)	1,860
Transit Bus	920
Transit Rail	885
Walking	100
Bicycling	35

When one compares the energy consumed in moving a certain distance as a function of body weight for a variety of animals and machines, one finds that an unaided walking man does fairly well (consuming about .75 calorie per gram per kilometer), but he is not as efficient as a horse, a salmon or a jet transport. With the aid of a bicycle, however, the man's energy consumption for a given distance is reduced to about a fifth (roughly .15 calorie per gram per kilometer). Therefore, apart from increasing his unaided speed by a factor of three or four, the cyclist improves his efficiency rating to No. 1 among moving creatures and machines.
—Stuart S. Wilson, *Scientific American* (1973)[2]

A bicyclist moving at twelve miles per hour uses only 97 BTUs per passenger mile; a pedestrian uses 500 BTUs per passenger mile walking at 2.5 miles per hour [mass-transit uses 4,000 BTUs; an automobile uses 8,000 BTUs].
—Nina Dougherty (1974)[3]

A cyclist can do 1,000 miles on the food energy equivalent of a gallon of gasoline, which will move a car only some 15 to 30 miles. Facts and figures be as they may, utilizing a 300 horsepower, 5,000-pound behemoth to move one single 150-pound person a few miles is like using an atomic bomb to kill a canary.
—Richard Ballantine (1979)[4]

A rider on a "racing" bicycle going quite slowly could cover a mile with the expenditure of only four calories, while someone on a "roadster" bike going against a twenty mile per hour head wind would use up more than sixty calories... A racing bicyclist at 20 mph can travel more than 240 miles per gallon—of homogenized grade A milk.
—David Gordon Wilson (1987)[5]

A cyclist can ride three-and-a-half miles on the calories found in an ear of corn. Bicycles consume less energy per passenger mile than any other form of transport, including walking. A ten-mile commute by bicycle requires 350 calories of energy, the amount in one bowl of rice. The same trip in the average American car uses 18,600 calories, or more than half a gallon of gasoline.
—Marcia D. Lowe (1989)[6]

Bicycles are 53 times more energy efficient than cars. And you can run them on so many forms of energy: rice, beans, couscous, spaghetti bolognese, it's all the same to a bike.
—From *Colors* (1992)

Food for Cycling

One thing people like best about cycling is that their fuel comes from eating. It is common knowledge that "we are what we eat," but many people tend to choose what they eat according to habit, taste, or convenience. Cycling stimulates the body's metabolism, so cyclists tend to have better than average appetites and a bit more respect for what they put into their bodies. As a cyclist's activity becomes more vigorous, his or her body develops special needs which require an enhanced awareness of nutrition.

It takes about 35 calories to fuel one bicycling mile, equivalent to one banana every three miles. Human bodies require six major nutrients every day, including water, carbohydrates, fats, proteins, vitamins, and minerals. Added to these nutrients are the medicinal attributes of herbs, the balance of enzymes necessary for digestion, the antioxidants which protect against contaminants, and the single most important element—oxygen. The quantity of each nutrient needed depends upon one's health and the amount of energy used.

In everyday activities, people burn about .01 calories per pound of their weight per minute. Thus, a 150 pound person consumes about 1.5 calories per minute, or 2,160 calories per day. With the addition of cycling, which has an enormous range of energy needs, this person might add only 60 calories for an easy-going trip to market or over 6,000 calories if entered in the ultra-marathon Race Across America (RAAM). Professional cyclists competing in races like the Tour de France require an average of 5,900 calories per day, with some riders needing up to 9,000 calories.[7]

FUEL COST PER MILE PER CALORIE:

FOOD	CENTS PER MILE	DRINKS	
Frozen dinner	71.3	Bottled spring water, pint	25.0
McDonalds Big Mac	19.0	Bottled spring water, liter	7.5
Power Bar	23.0	Sports drinks (Gatorade),	10.0
Pizza, slice	11.0	Coca-Cola, liter	10.0
Chocolate bar	8.4	Carbohydrate drink (Ultra-Fuel)	20.0
Banana	7.0		
Fresh Corn	6.0	ENERGY	
Milk	5.7	Gas $U.S. gallon (moped)	0.005
Pasta	4.0	Gas (car)	0.6
Rice	1.7	Solar-electric (Sunraycer car)	0.3

AIR

While people can live two months without food, or about eighteen days without water, life ends after less than five minutes without air. Fresh air contains about 78 percent nitrogen, 21 percent oxygen, and about one percent of mixed gases, including carbon dioxide, argon, neon, radon, ozone, helium, krypton, xenon, carbon monoxide, hydrogen, methane, and nitrous oxide. Along with lead, pollen, and micro-organisms, air contains up to seven percent water vapor.

WATER

Water is present in every tissue and used in every body function—even thoughts would dry up without H_2O. Water weighs about two pounds per quart, and the average body contains 40 to 50 quarts of water or about 65 to 70 percent of total body weight. Blood contains about 83 percent water, and the loss of five percent of body water brings muscular weakness, while twenty percent brings death. An easy-going cyclist needs about ten cups of water per day, and some RAAM riders consume about three and a half gallons (28 pounds) of liquid food and water per day.

CARBOHYDRATES

Carbohydrates are the body's major source of energy, supplying about four calories per gram as fuel for our cells. Carbohydrates come in two forms, complex (natural or whole) and refined (processed or depleted). The complex form supplies a more complete diet. Complex carbohydrates digest easily and transform into a starchy sugar (glycogen) and blood sugar (glucose) used by body tissues for muscle and mental energy, for metabolism of fat, and for forming amino acids from proteins. Cyclists usually maintain a high carbohydrate diet, which builds energy reserves in muscles and the liver, with excess "carbos" converted into fat. Carbohydrates are found in most foods, including grains, breads, cereals, pastas, legumes, fresh fruits and vegetables, tubers, seeds, nuts, honey, jams, pastries, and sugar. The recommended daily dose of complex carbohydrates consists of three servings of grains or legumes, and three or four servings of fresh fruit and vegetables.

PROTEINS

Proteins are basic compounds which continually rebuild our cells, tissues, and organs. They maintain healthy bones, skin, blood, muscles, nerves, and hormones. As enzymes, they serve as catalysts in various chemical reactions in the metabolic cycle. Proteins cannot be stored, so their intake should be spread throughout the day's meals. Excess amounts are converted into glucose or fat, which can be drawn upon for energy. Proteins consist of about 23 amino acids. Fifteen of these are produced by the body, eight of these are the "essential amino acids" which must be present in our food, and one (histamine) is essential for children. For proteins to be useful, all eight amino acids (threonine, valine, tryptophan, lysine, methionine, histidine, phenylalanine, and isoleucine) must be present in the same meal in a certain proportion roughly similar to that found in eggs. These complete proteins are found in eggs, fish, fowl, meats, and dairy products.

People who do not eat meat mix protein sources to form complete proteins, such as soy tofu and brown rice or peanut butter and whole wheat bread. On average, adults need around one gram of protein per kilogram of body weight per day.

FATS

Fats are necessary for many of the body's chemical processes, including the use of fat-soluble vitamins (A, D, E, and K). Fats help protect and support most of the vital organs, acting as an insulator from cold weather and from viral infections. They also serve as a concentrated form of energy by supplying about nine calories per gram, though it is not so quickly available. Many natural sources of fat are over-refined in processing which changes their nutritional character. Fatty acids come saturated and unsaturated. Saturated fats are found in dairy products, fish, fowl, veal, lamb, beef, pork, and in hydrogenated vegetable oils. Unsaturated fats should make up at least three-fourths of one's fat intake. They are found in grains, legumes, seeds, nuts, and their oils such as olive oil, corn oil, safflower oil, sunflower oil, sesame oil, and soy oil. Fats should comprise between 15 to 25 percent of daily caloric intake.

VITAMINS

Vitamins are organic compounds with no caloric value. They are necessary for the process of metabolism and in forming bones, tissues, and organs. Fat-soluble vitamins (A, D, E, and K) need oil or fats to be absorbed and stored in the body. Water-soluble vitamins (B complex, C, and bioflavinoids) are absorbed in water and must be replenished daily since they are not stored by the body. Many recreational cyclists feel the need to supplement their diets with vitamins, and many high level amateur and professional racing cyclists often receive liquid vitamin injections, especially the B complex vitamins which can enhance the transformation of oxygen and nutrients into the kind of energy that the Swami Beyondananda called "Vitamin be one."

Vitamin A is necessary for the growth and repair of the body's tissues, including those of the skin, the mucous membranes, the digestive system, the blood and bones, and the eyes. It is found in green, yellow, and orange vegetables, milk products, fish liver oils.

B Complex Vitamins work together in a proper ratio to break down fats, carbohydrates, and proteins to make them available as energy. They are especially needed for muscular energy in endurance sports like cycling. B complex vitamins are found in nutritional yeast, seed germs, eggs, liver, fish, meat, whole grains, legumes, and vegetables.

Vitamin C is said to do almost everything. It fights sickness, disease, and pollutants. It aids fertility, builds connective tissues (collagen), maintains mental health, and is a natural laxative. And it is useful for athletes and surgery patients in repairing tissues. Vitamin C is found in citrus fruits, sprouts, berries, tomatoes, sweet peppers, potatoes, and raw green leaf vegetables.

Vitamin D helps use calcium and phosphorus to form strong bones and teeth. It makes healthy skin, and is important for the nervous system and kidneys. Vitamin D is found in sunshine, dairy products, egg yolks, seafood, fish liver oils, and fresh green vegetables.

Vitamin E promotes health in muscle tissues, cells, blood, and skin. It is used as an ointment for burns and saddlesores. Vitamin E is found in wheat germ and its oil, whole grains, seeds, nuts, and fresh leafy green vegetables.

Vitamin K helps blood clotting and aids bone development. It is produced by bacterial microorganisms found in the large intestine which are nourished by yogurt and other fermented dairy and soy products.

Bioflavinoids aid the function of capillaries, and they assist vitamin C. They are found in grapes, rose hips, prunes, citrus fruits, cherries, and black currants.

Vitamin P (Urine) is sterile and occasionally used for treating wounds in emergencies such as snake bites.

MINERALS

Minerals serve the body as building materials for bones, tissue, muscle, blood, and nerve cells. They work together to help maintain the balance of fluids and the various bio-chemical reactions in the body. Minerals comprise about four to five percent of total body weight. They can be found in a well-balanced diet including various whole grains, fresh fruits, vegetables, tubers, mushrooms, seeds, nuts, honey, dairy products, eggs, or meat.

Calcium is the primary mineral that forms bones and teeth.

Chromium is an active ingredient in the heart, liver, brain, and in glucose metabolism.

Iodine aids the process of cell metabolism, and the production of the hormone thyroxin.

Iron is an essential oxygen-carrier that works with hemoglobin in red blood cells and myoglobin in muscle tissue.

Magnesium works in the production process of proteins, hormones, muscles, and nerves. Digestion, reproduction, blood formation, and immune system maintenance all require magnesium.

Manganese is active in the production of bones, cartilage, tendons, nerve impulses, metabolism, and sex hormones.

Phosphorus works throughout the body's systems, including the metabolism of energy in muscles.

Potassium helps the functioning of nerve impulses and aids in maintaining proper acid-alkaline balance.

Selenium protects the cells from degeneration.

Sodium (Salt) is necessary for nerve, blood, and muscle functions.

Zinc is important in the production of insulin and sex hormones, and it aids the healing process.

BIKE BITS

DURING A 15 DAY PERIOD BETWEEN MARCH 17 AND APRIL 2, 1977, M. LOTITO OF EVRET, FRANCE, ATE A BICYCLE. HE WAS ABLE TO ACCOMPLISH THIS FEAT BY REDUCING THE MACHINE TO METAL FILINGS.

Eating Guides for Cycling

There are a few general rules for the feeding and watering of cyclists who subject themselves to vigorous or competitive cycling. The basic goal is to maintain a diet consisting of 65 percent carbohydrate, twenty percent fat, and fifteen percent protein. This means that "quack" or "fad" diets high in fat and protein should be avoided, except in the case of careful dietary balancing.

The "law of three hours" says the last whole meal should be eaten at least three hours before intense effort. After eating, blood concentrates in the digestive tract, so less is available for the muscles and the brain. Mixing exercise and digestion risks muscles cramps, nausea, breathlessness, and an increased pulse. The "law of two hours" says to have a whole meal approximately two hours after an effort, to replenish the body for the next day's cycling.

Another set of rules applies to liquid replenishment. One rule says to "drink before you get thirsty," and another says "drink little and often." Water is an extremely important factor in exercise because muscle cells need water to metabolize blood sugars and fats, and the body needs water for cooling as heat rises. Cyclists lose large quantities of water by perspiration, in evaporation by wind on the skin, and in expiration of water vapor released in breathing. During exercise, the loss of water increases with body heat and air temperature, and thirst tends to come only after the body's fluid balance is already upset. Studies show that at least one liter, or four to five cups, of water are needed every hour for hard-working cyclists in temperatures around 68 degrees Fahrenheit (20°C).

Carbohydrate loading is a way of modifying the diet to enhance performance for a specific endurance cycling event. The goal is to increase the amount of glycogen or blood sugar available in the body on the chosen day. The traditional method begins six days before the event by the cyclist using up all his or her stored glycogen, and for the next three days, while still training hard, eating a diet of 90 percent proteins and fats, ten percent carbohydrates. Then, in the remaining days before the event, the cyclist rests and eats a 90 percent carbohydrate, ten percent protein and fat diet. A revised method of carbo loading with more moderate levels of training and eating, recommends carbohydrate intakes of 50 to 70 percent. Carbo loading has little effect on performance until about 90 minutes into an event, and the practice should not be used continuously because it can result in reduced training capacity.

Fasting is occasionally recommended for cyclists who eat large quantities of food and need to give their various systems a chance to rest or clean out toxins. This can be done for one or two days every few months by drinking water and fruit juice while abstaining from all solid food. Cyclists can still go riding but should ease off from long distances or intense training.

A cycling proverb claims that eating less chocolate will safeguard your bicycle from theft, as illustrated by the fact that Spanish people eat less chocolate than any other European nation, and Spain has the lowest incidence of bicycle theft in Europe.

Omnivores

Since cyclists have such diverse and extreme energy needs, they tend to disprove many rigid dietary schemes by showing the remarkable variability of human bodies. For instance, with two cyclists of similar ability, one may have no problem eating fast-food cheeseburgers, diet sodas, and Twinkies, while the other will insist on a meatless diet of whole, fresh foods.

There is evidence that human beings have evolved to be herbivores (plant-eaters), not carnivores (meat-eaters), though cyclists illustrate the widely-held belief that people are omnivores (anything-eaters). The scientific proof for our being herbivores is found in the body's flat grinding teeth, in the long digestive tract, and the salivary enzymes.[8] This suggests that we must be sick if we eat meat—and maybe we are—yet many people seem to thrive on meat, including the group considered the most physically fit athletes in the world, professional cyclists. While these riders may stop at nothing to improve their performance, eating lean meat is still an established part of their extraordinary diets. It makes sense for their needs because it supplies complete protein in a small amount of weight, and some claim it gives them the killer instinct. Nevertheless, there have been several vegetarians in professional cycling and though acceptance at the team meal is a problem, they have been able to balance their dietary needs adequately. One notable vegetarian cyclist is Dave Scott, the six-time winner of the Ironman Triathlon.

There are a few types of vegetarians. Vegans are the strictest, eating only grains, legumes, vegetables, fruits, nuts, and seeds. They do not eat meat, fowl, fish, eggs, or dairy products. Lacto-vegetarians eat dairy products and vegetables. Lacto-ovo-vegetarians eat eggs, dairy products, and vegetables. Pesco-vegetarians eat fish and vegetables, and pollo-vegetarians eat poultry and vegetables. With cycling, sometimes it takes a great deal of preparation to avoid breaking a vegetarian diet, especially on road trips. Food poisoning is a problem for traveling cyclists, especially for tour groups and teams. Bad water, rancid meat, and toxic sauces can cause diarrhea, nausea, migraines, and weakness. Because cyclists need large quantities of food from foreign kitchens, they often bring or become their own chef to ensure food quality.

Energy Foods

Many kinds of athletic food products have been developed, including sports drinks, energy snacks, and liquid food. These are used to supplement the athlete's diet with the extra water, carbohydrates, minerals, vitamins, and proteins needed for vigorous cycling. Gatorade was the first popular sports drink developed in 1965 for football players, and electrolyte replacement drinks, such as ERG by Gookinaid, became popular in the 1970s. In recent years, sports drinks come with mixed ingredients, for supplementing glucose, replenishing carbohydrates, and providing a complete athletic diet for special endurance events. Because cyclists need a high carbohydrate diet consumable during exercise, most energy foods have sugars and carbohydrates, including glucose polymers or maltodextrin, which digests easily, and fructose, sucrose, dextrose, and lactose, which have protein. Mineral salts, such as sodium, help balance fluid and electrolyte loss in sweat.

Meal replacement drinks, such as Ultra Energy, Body Fuel, and Exceed, contain carbohydrates, proteins, fats, vitamins, minerals, and other nutrients, often derived from natural food, but processed and preserved as chemical powders and liquids. Most are designed for ultra-endurance energy or muscle-building, and some are high energy tonics with chemicals found in the process of metabolism, such as coenzyme Q10, which helps produce the energy phosphate ATP, and creatine, which is found in raw meats and human livers and helps extend the lactate cycle in muscles.

FAVORITE FOODS

In cycletouring, people's adventure stories inevitably include discussions of eating. Peanut butter and bananas are the most commonly consumed foods, as found in a survey of cyclists who had ridden across the American continent, by Kevin Kelly in the *Whole Earth Review* (1987). He simply asked: "What did you eat the most of?" Here are some replies:[9]

Peanut butter and jelly sandwiches.
Peanut butter and bananas.
Mountain Dew, bananas, peanut butter.
Bread, peanut butter, yogurt.
Peanut butter and honey sandwiches on whole wheat bread.
Massive quantities of fruit and peanut butter and jelly sandwiches.
Pancakes, also peanut butter and jelly sandwiches.
Granola and peanut butter and jelly.
Bread, cookies, pasta, fruit and peanut butter.
Peanut butter, ice cream, oranges.
Peanut butter and noodles.
Peanut butter.

WHAT ATHLETES EAT, CALORIES PER DAY (*Men's Health*, 1992)

ATHLETE (WEIGHT/LBS)	SPORT	CAL/DAY
Konishiki (580)	Sumo wrestler	18,805
Davis Phinney (165)	Pro road cyclist	8,730
David Robinson (230)	Pro basketball center	5,030
Matt Biondi (210)	Olympic swimmer	4,752
George Foreman (250)	Heavyweight boxer	4,579
Steve Spence (135)	Olympic marathon runner	4,157
Bruce Smith (273)	Pro football defensive end	4,047
Ryne Sandberg (180)	Pro baseball second baseman	3,851

TOUR DE FRANCE DAILY DIET

PRE-BREAKFAST:
1–2 cups coffee or tea
1–2 bowls muesli
or cereal with fruit and yogurt
2–4 slices bread with jam or honey
1 glass dairy or soy milk
vitamin supplements

BREAKFAST:
1–2 bowls rice or pasta
2–3 eggs with ham or cheese
1 plate fresh chicken, fish, or steak
1–2 bottles carbohydrate drink
and water

PRE-RACE SNACK:
4 oz. glucose concentrate
or fruit nectar
1–2 pieces of fruit
2 pieces sweet bread pudding,
or 1 bakery tart
1–2 energy bars
1–2 pannini rolls
(meat, cheese, or rice, and jam)
1–2 bottles carbo drink and water

IN-RACE EATING:
2 musette bags, each containing:
3–4 muesli bars
1 energy bar
1–2 pieces fruit
4 oz. glucose concentrate
or fruit nectar

5 bottles water
5 bottles carbo drink
1 bottle caffeinated cola

POST-RACE SNACK:
3–5 bottles water or juice
1–2 pieces fruit
1–2 bread rolls or biscuits
1 bakery tart

POST-MASSAGE MEAL:
1–2 sandwiches
or 1–2 pieces quiche or pizza
1–2 cups yogurt
1–2 pieces fruit
1–2 bottles juice, carbo drink
or water

EVENING MEAL:
1–2 bowls pasta
or beans with light sauce
1–2 bowls salad
1–2 bowls soup
1–2 plates fresh chicken, fish, or steak
1 plate vegetables and potatoes or rice

DESSERT:
3 slices cheese, or 1 cup yogurt
1–2 pastry desserts
1–2 pieces fruit
1 glass water
1 glass wine

Cycling Recipes

Some of the following recipes are famous in cycledom, others can be found in cycling cookbooks such as Lauren Heffron's *Cycle Food: A Guide to Satisfying Your Inner Tube* (1983) and John Rakowski's *Cooking on the Road* (1980). For cyclists who have spent a good part of a day in the saddle, one basic rule is to double all serving sizes. While offering options for vegetarians and meat-eaters, this selection emphasizes the use of whole, fresh, organically-grown foods.

Avocado Tofu Go Food

This is a cold, refreshing all-in-one meal that can be prepared quickly and easily from roadside markets. Chop each ingredient into bite-size bits and stir them into a large bowl or carton. Can be made lacto-vegetarian, or with fish. Serves 3 to 6.

2 avocados

1½ pounds firm tofu

2 red bell peppers

10 scallion stalks

¾ pounds fresh green vegetables

1 pound cheese and/or fish

6 fresh basil leaves

2 tablespoons mayonnaise

1 tablespoon ground mustard

1 tablespoon tamari soy sauce

1 tablespoon sesame seeds

Pasta alla Carbonara

This popular high carbohydrate meal is found in many cycling cookbooks. Sauté the onions, garlic, mushrooms, etc., in oil, and set aside with the eggs and cheese off the heat. Boil the pasta until tender and strain it. While the pasta is still hot, mix in the eggs, cheese, onion, and mushrooms letting the pasta's heat do the cooking. Serves 2 to 3.

1 pound fresh spaghetti or vermicelli

6 eggs

2 cups parmesan or romano cheese (grated)

6 tablespoons olive oil

salt, pepper, basil

1 onion

2–3 cloves garlic

½ cup mushrooms

½ pound bacon (optional in sauté)

Pedalini bicycle pasta (actual size).

Tour de France Salade

"Pick out one or two of everything, and I mean everything, on the fruit and vegetable counter—bananas, cucumbers, apples, lettuce, oranges, celery, grapefruit, carrots, cherries, plums, pears, peaches, tomatoes, nectarines, green peppers, berries, avocadoes, coconuts, pineapple—cut them up and mix them together. (The only consideration is amount! All of

above would make dinner for 10 or 15; so watch out.) Add slices of cheese, chicken, turkey, ham, lunch meat, sunflower seeds or pumpkin seeds, cashews or mixed nuts, peanuts—salted or not, raw or roasted— any combination you can get that strikes your fancy for protein and variety. Stir in a carton of yogurt, flavored or plain. Even if you don't like it, use it. You won't know the difference. For added zest pick up one of the powdered salad dressing packets—green goddess, Italian, herb, French, anything. Add it to the yogurt whether it's flavored or not. Ignore the instructions that tell you to add the powder to buttermilk, mayonnaise or any other liquid. With the diverse salad mixture you've come up with, you don't need it. And with the yogurt as the base you can safely eat any leftovers for breakfast without fear of food poisoning—at least, we're still alive."

—From the kitchens of *Bicycling!*[10]

VELOWEDGE

This was an all-natural fast-food sandwich sold at the Handle Bar, a concession stand at the Trexlertown Velodrome in Pennsylvania, around 1978. Besides the Velowedge they served apple juice, herbal teas, mixed nuts and seeds, and cookies from the kitchen of Rodale Press. Slice open the pita bread and line the insides with mayonnaise or tahini. Shred the cheese, carrots, cucumbers, peppers, and onion. Mix them with sprouts and wedge this into the pita bread. Serves 2 to 4.

4 pockets whole wheat pita bread
1½ pounds muenster cheese
3–4 carrots
2 cucumbers
2 bell peppers
1 large onion
2 handfuls alfalfa sprouts
4 tablespoons mayonnaise or tahini

PEANUT BUTTER BANANA ROLL

Mix ingredients and eat.

1 cup peanut butter
1 banana
½ cup honey
¼ cup whole grain flour

ROAD BREAD

Mix the dry and wet ingredients separately, then combine. Spread into oiled or buttered pan. Bake at 300°F for about an hour. Cool and cut into pocket-sized squares. Serves 2.

3 cups whole wheat flour
½ cup millet flour
½ cup corn meal
1 cup water, milk, or fruit juice
½ cup honey
¼ cup seeds or nuts
1 teaspoon salt
2 teaspoons baking powder

GORP

Gorp (Good Ole Raisins and Peanuts), trail mix, or "bird seed" can have various ingredients. Just raisins and peanuts usually won't do. Most high energy recipes call for a mixture of nuts, seeds, dried fruit, and chocolate bits. When serving a small crowd, let each person add a cup of his or her favorite ingredient, so the mixture does not suffer from selective picking. No candy, salt, or sulphured fruit is allowed. One cup of each ingredient in this recipe will serve 2 to 4 squirrelly cyclists.

cashews
almonds
sunflower seeds
pecans or walnuts
white raisins
pitted dates
banana chips
carob

GUAYAQUIL FRUIT PUNCH

A sweet tangy drink which has been described as the "nectar of paradise." Use fresh squeezed juices if possible. Serve chilled. Makes 1 gallon.

2 quarts apple cider
1 pint grape juice
1 pint mineral seltzer (or beer)
1 cup orange or grapefruit juice
1 cup lime juice
1 cup berry juice
1 cup pear juice
3 sliced lemons

—BIKECENTENNIAL

The Energy Cycle

The beauty of cycling's energy cycle is that although cycling demands energy from the human body, it also puts energy back into the body.

People have compared the workings of the human body to factories, machines, engines, and transport systems, with body functions likened to assembly lines, pistons, cog wheels, carburetors, radiators, roadways, and gasoline consumption. More recently, the body has been described as a fuel cell, which is a more human likeness, because a fuel cell is an energy-producing device that converts chemical reactions into electricity (to power space shuttles and cars) by electrolytic oxidation with the by-products of hydrogen and carbon dioxide. Energy machines such as internal-combustion engines and electric motors serve to empower many people, and they are symbols of mankind's technological ingenuity. Unfortunately, they are missing what cycling machines have developed—the ability to convert chemical energy to mechanical energy, and to enable the human body to empower itself, through the clean, quiet, renewable, and efficient energy cycle of biological organisms.

In cycling, you input oxygen, water, and nutrients, you output power, heat, and sweat, and you receive feedback on all those factors through perception, technique, and practice. Each cell in a cyclist's body and mind becomes energized in an interrelated cyclical pathway, involving respiration and circulation, ingestion, digestion, metabolism, movement, secretion, as well as observation, inspiration, and motivation. In fact, all activity in living organisms can ultimately be reduced to two basic forms: movement and secretion.[11]

METABOLIC FUNCTION

The most important effects on cycling performance occur in the metabolic cycle. Metabolism refers to the whole output of the various actions and reactions that occur within a cell. The "miracle of metabolism" takes place in each of the body's cells according to their special forms and functions.

With cycling, the whole body's metabolic cycle is enhanced by higher levels of conditioning and performance. The metabolic capacity of the respiratory and cardio-vascular systems determine the metabolic output of muscular activity. Muscle metabolism is the essential power source for body movement and human-powered performance. The functions of the digestive organs determine how the nutrients and waste products of metabolism are recycled or secreted, just as the kind of nutrients, liquids, and "treatments" consumed determines the quality of each metabolic process in the body. Also important is the stimulation of the nervous system and brain cell metabolism, which results in a cyclist's enhanced mental outlook, and in the ability to accept extraordinary challenges, especially in the form of pain and suffering. Many other factors affect the metabolic cycle in cycling, including the resistances of wind and gradient, the extremes of hot and cold weather, and the efficiency of the cyclist's position and pedal stroke.

Cardio-Respiratory Energy

The pulsations of the heart and the rhythm of breathing are the first and last signs of life, and they are the primary means of achieving and measuring a high level of human-powered performance. The cardio-vascular and respiratory systems seem so fragile in the complexity of their functions yet are able to adapt to very difficult working conditions, provided they receive a little respect.

OXYGEN AND BLOOD CIRCULATION

Lungs expand and contract to take in oxygen and expel carbon dioxide. An impulse by the respiratory nerve, either automatic or consciously initiated, forces the expansion of the lungs so that air is drawn into the mouth or nose. Air is filtered and sucked down the windpipe, or trachea, where it branches off at the bronchi and smaller bronchioles into the hundreds of millions of moist air sacs, the alveoli, which are the basic tissues of the lung.

The respiratory and circulatory pathways meet at the alveoli. The expansive alveolar cell membranes are interlaced with both air-filled bronchioles and blood-filled capillaries and provide a thin, wet surface for air and blood to move past each other. Blood is aerated when inhaled oxygen molecules are absorbed by the hemoglobin in the red blood cells, and carbon dioxide molecules are released to be exhaled. Cycling demands and develops an increased capacity of the lungs to absorb oxygen.

Blood is a liquid tissue that consists of plasma (about 55 percent) and three kinds of cells: red, white, and platelets. Plasma consists of water (92 percent) and glucose, fats, proteins, minerals, and hormones. Red blood cells, with their component of hemoglobin (protein and iron), transport oxygen and carbon dioxide to and from the body's tissues. White blood cells guard the body against bacteria, and platelets are necessary for blood clotting.

Blood circulates continuously throughout the body in two types of one-way vessels—arteries and veins. Arteries carry replenished oxygen-rich blood from the lungs to the heart and on to other cells, and veins carry depleted carbon dioxide-rich blood from the cells to the heart and on to the lungs. The arteries and veins taper off into arterioles and venules and finally into tiny capillaries, which have tube walls only one cell thick. By osmosis and diffusion, the capillaries exchange nutrients and wastes in the blood as they interlace cell tissues throughout the body's organs, such as the lungs, heart, muscles, liver, kidneys, skin and brain. In fact, the circulatory system is so complete that the blood sustains those cells which sustain the blood, just as the bicycle sustains its own power source—the human being.

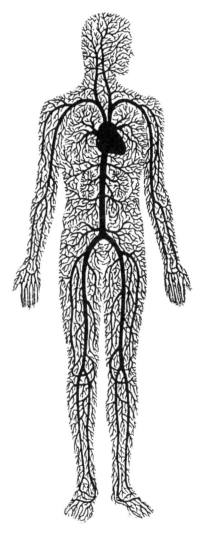

BREATHING

Since heart and breathing rates are the essential means of supplying energy for aerobic metabolism, the cardio-respiratory system receives the most attention from high performance cyclists. Breathing can be enhanced with a few techniques, and it is important to realize that exhalation is just as vital as inhalation, because high concentrations of carbon dioxide in the lungs cause more panting.

Deep breathing, also called "belly breathing," is an easier and more efficient method of exchanging oxygen and carbon dioxide than rapid panting. This involves exercising the diaphragm or stomach muscles to fill and empty the deeper cavities of the lungs with larger and longer inhalations and exhalations. At first, this requires conscious manipulation, sometimes aided by a four-count rhythm (in-2-3-out); eventually it becomes second nature. Deep breathing can also prevent a common result of heavy panting, known as "side stitch," which causes a pain in the side around the rib cage because of cramped, overworked breathing muscles.

It is best to inhale through the nostrils rather than the mouth while cycling at a moderate pace, because this filters, warms, and moisturizes the incoming air. When heavy breathing ensues, nasal inhalation is not adequate for the larger amounts of air required so mouth inhalation takes over. Exhaling should be done fully and quickly through the mouth, except when blowing mucus from the nose. Actually, seasoned cyclists develop the skill to clear their noses fully in one blow, without hands, and with sufficient aim to prevent the mucus from flying into the paths of companions.

There is a slight delay between the time when the muscles start producing more carbon dioxide because of increased effort, and when the lungs respond with heavy breathing. For this reason, cyclists often practice multiple deep-breathing or hyperventilation exercises just before the start of heavy efforts. These are usually done before a sprint, or a hill. However, too much hyperventilating can backfire, causing dizziness and weakness.

HEART RATE

Both heart and breathing rates are important measures for achieving fitness and for serious training. By counting the number of heart beats per minute, cyclists can find their maximum and minimum heart rates (HR), knowledge which is essential for regulating fitness and training programs. Racing cyclists may measure their pulse several times a day, either with an electronic pulse meter, or by fingers placed on an artery (not thumbs, which have their own strong pulse), counting in 15 or 30 second segments to find the number of beats per minute (bpm).

Daily pulse measurements serve as a guide for a cyclist's rate of recovery from workouts of the previous days. Upon first waking, while still in bed, the pulse is measured before making many movements or rising. Then, after falling out of bed, standing up, and taking a nice deep breath, the pulse is taken again, and these two numbers are compared (i.e., 48 bpm and 72 bpm). If the numbers are high, or the amount of difference between the two (24 bpm) is greater than usual, the cyclist has not fully recuperated.

Maximum heart rate is useful since many training programs categorize the level of a workout by percentages of maximum heart rate. For example, if one's maximum heart rate is 190 bpm, and a schedule calls for an effort of 80 percent, this implies cycling at a heart rate of 152 bpm. One way to determine maximum heart rate is to make an all-out effort and record your heart rate, then round it out a bit higher, and that's your max HR. Scientific testing methods which employ interval cycling with a heart rate monitor, such as the Conconi "ramp" test, are more accurate. Another widely disputed method is to subtract one's age from the magic number 220. For example, all twenty-year-olds have a 200 bpm maximum heart rate, and all sixty-year-olds have a 160 bpm max HR.

CYCLING FITNESS RANGE

Comparing an average person to a racing cyclist helps illustrate how the heart and lungs can adapt to hard work. For an average person "at rest" (between hard work and sleep) the heart beats 60 to 80 times a minute, or about 100,000 times a day, for roughly 250 million beats per lifetime. At any given moment, the body contains about five to seven liters of blood within its 60,000 miles of arteries, veins and capillaries, and it makes a circuit throughout the system about once every 20 to 60 seconds.

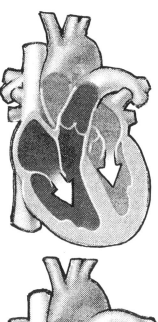

For a racing cyclist, the heart does not necessarily grow into a huge "bicycle heart" as was once believed. Instead, it becomes stronger and more efficient in two ways: by maintaining an increased rate of pumping without tiring (heart rate); and by increasing the volume of blood pumped with each beat (stroke volume).

The resting heart rate of a racing cyclist normally drops to 30 to 40 bpm as each stroke can pump more blood. This slow rate has caused some misunderstandings with untutored health care professionals. For example, the champion cyclist Greg LeMond was once denied a life insurance policy after a cardiac examination until his occupation was taken into account. More than one racer who has entered a hospital for a minor injury has been rushed to intensive care and hooked up to an electro-cardiograph (EKG) after a low pulse rate reading.

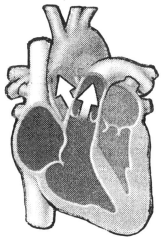

A racing cyclist's maximum heart rate can reach over 195 bpm, and during exercise they can maintain rates over 150 bpm for four to six hours and over 175 bpm for an hour. A racing cyclist's heart can quickly recuperate, going from 160 bpm to 60 bpm in about 30 seconds. Likewise, the volume of blood the heart pumps increases from five to ten liters per minute for an average person, and from 25 to 50 liters per minute for a racer.

An average person has a vital capacity, or maximum air intake, of four to six liters, while a racer's is six to eight liters. "At rest," the average person inhales about six to ten liters of air in about ten to fifteen breaths per minute. For racing cyclists, breathing rates can increase to about 150 to 200 liters of air in up to about 50 breaths per minute.

Muscle Power

Neuro-muscular metabolism moves the pedals on a bicycle. Muscles are bundles of neurons and fibers which are capable of only one movement; a single contraction. The combination of multiple contractions and relaxation in a series of muscle fibers creates the continuous power to move. The impulse for contraction comes from the central nervous system via motor neuron cells that trigger chemical reactions within muscle fiber cells.

The fuel for muscular contraction is adenosine triphosphate (ATP), a high-energy phosphate compound that breaks down into adenosine diphosphate (ADP), an inorganic phosphate, and energy.

AEROBICS AND ANAEROBICS

ATP is utilized in three ways according to the two pathways of muscular metabolism: the aerobic, alactic anaerobic, and lactic anaerobic. The aerobic path uses "slow twitch" muscle cells with red fibers which have oxygen-rich supplies of myoglobin and fresh blood. These fibers produce repetitive contractions suitable for endurance cycling. Within the mitochondria of muscle cells, nutrients such as glucose and fats are transformed by the cycle of combustion (oxidation) in the Kreb's cycle to produce enough ATP sufficient for continuous energy, with the by-products of carbon dioxide and water. This steady-state process is "practically without limit," provided that food and air are available. It is limited by death, disease, injury, or the general or localized fatigue from the gradual build-up of lactic acid.[12]

The anaerobic path uses "fast twitch" white muscle fibers enriched with glycogen, high-energy phosphates, and enzymes, but lacking in oxygen and nutrient enriched blood. These metabolize the muscle's stored energy to make faster contractions suitable for short powerful sprints in cycling. The alactic anaerobic pathway involves splitting the muscle's store of phospho-creatine (PC). This creates small amounts of ATP sufficient for up to about 30 seconds of maximum power. The lactic anaerobic pathway involves the transformation of the muscle's store of glycogen into pyruvate with by-products of ATP and lactic acid, which is well-known for producing muscular pain. This produces power for a few minutes until either the muscles weaken from excess lactic acid or the glycogen is exhausted. Through high intensity training, the lactate cycle can be extended to the point where it provides a limited amount of energy for muscles.

Muscle fibers are not strictly divided into these types. They often contain attributes of both slow and fast twitch fibers, and the metabolic pathways tend to overlap with the fluidity of cycling. For example, a sprint may use 95 percent anaerobic and five percent aerobic, a pursuit may use 50 percent anaerobic-aerobic, and a long ride may use 95 percent aerobic and five percent anaerobic. Power output in cycling is determined by increasing the heart and lung capacity, by developing the muscle's store of myoglobin, glycogen, and high-energy phosphates, and by conditioning a resistance to greater levels of lactic acid.

When cyclists begin pedaling, the first few movements are accomplished by using the oxygen stored in their muscles' myoglobin to initiate the aerobic metabolic process. The aerobic path, with breathing as part of the process, is the typical way of doing continuous work for several hours, such as mountain biking or long road races. When output is increased—during time trials, on fast hill climbs, or when breaking away—cyclists approach their maximum aerobic rate. They begin to run out of breath and become increasingly reliant on lactic anaerobic metabolism, which consumes the muscles' store of glycogen until lactic acids accumulate in sufficient quantities to cause weak and painful muscles. This is the anaerobic threshold (AT), known as the heart rate deflection point, where the two pathways overlap. During the course of a hard race, cyclists will often ride just below their AT, going over the threshold for short efforts, with complete anaerobic exhaustion saved for the final sprint.

Time-trial cycling events are based on combining both lactic anaerobic and aerobic metabolism for maximum power output. In time-trial events such as the hour record or in stage races, where cyclists go 50 to 55 kph, more endurance with high-level aerobic capacity is required, while events such as the kilometer and the four-kilometer pursuit race, at 55 to 60 kph, require increased lactic anaerobic capacity. When muscles are called upon to make a short, vigorous performance, such as the ten-second, 200-meter track sprint, the alactic anaerobic path kicks in. This lasts as long as does the muscles' store of phospho-creatine, and breathing tends to increase towards the end of the effort, in order to stimulate recuperation.

Miguel Indurain at full power, wearing the *maglia rosa* in a Tour of Italy time trial. Notice the deep belly breathing.

CYCLING MUSCLES

Cycling uses some of the most powerful muscles in the body. These include the following muscle groups:

Hips: gluteus maximus (1), gluteus medius (2), gluteus minor (3), iliopsoas (4), and tensor fasciae latae (5).

Quadriceps: rectus femoris (6), vastus laterus (7), vastus intermedius (8), vastus medialis (9).

Hamstrings: biceps femoris (10), semitendinosus (11), semimembranosus (12).

Lower Legs: gastrocnemius (13), soleus (14), tibialis anterior (15), peroneus longus (16), peroneus brevis (17), achilles tendon (18).

Arms: deltoids (19), biceps (20), triceps (21), brachialis (22), brachioradialis (23), extensors of the wrists and fingers (24).

Upper Body: trapezius (25), sternocleidomastoid (26), pectoralis major (27), latissimus dorsi (28), rhomboid (29).

Breathing Muscles: intracostals (30), abdominal (31), diaphragm (32).

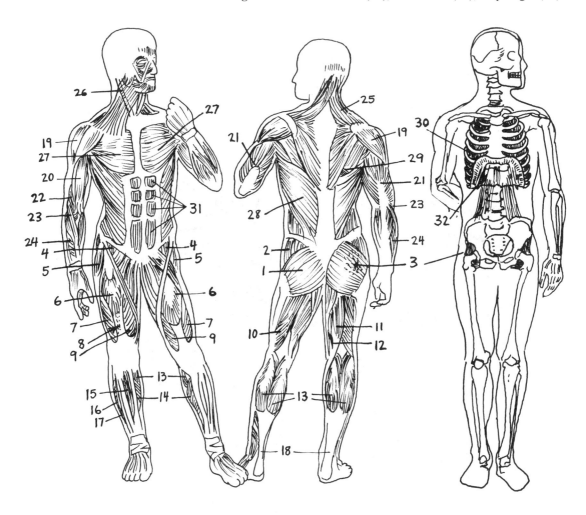

PEDALING

There are four phases of the 360-degree pedal stroke which should come together like clockwork to produce a smooth, round motion.

At the top of the pedal stroke, at twelve o'clock (0°), the foot is pushing forward over the dead center, and the hip flexors, the iliopsoas and tensor fascae latae, are giving way to the hip extensors, the gluteus maximus, media, and minor.

During the power phase of the pedal stroke, at three o'clock (90°), the foot is pushing down and the hip extensors or gluts are joined by the knee extensors or quadriceps, the rectus femoris, vastis laterus, intermedius, and medialis, and biceps femoris, while the sartorius keeps the thigh aligned.

Through the bottom of the stroke, from five o'clock to six o'clock (180°), the hip and knee muscles are at their weakest point and the ankle plantar flexors, the gastrocnemius and soleus begin pushing the foot down and backward. Around six o'clock, the ankle shifts from downward toeing (plantarflexion) to upward pulling (dorsiflexion) with the tibialis anterior and peroneal muscles.

On the "back side" or recovery phase of the pedal stroke (270° to 330°), the upward-pulling ankle dorsiflexors are joined by the knee flexors or hamstrings, the biceps femoris, semitendinosus, semimembranosus, and adductors. From ten o'clock to twelve o'clock (330° to 360°), the hip flexors, iliopsoas, and tensor fasciae latae complete the upward stroke to the dead center.

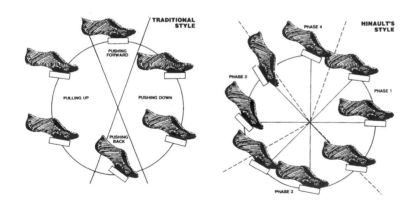

Phases of the pedal stroke.

Various descriptive words characterize the two general styles of pedaling. Smooth or refined pedaling has souplesse, finesse, fluidity, elan, spin, cadence, rhythm, and tempo. Hard or crude pedaling is described as square, choppy, punching, slogging, hammering, wobbly. There is even a French colloquialism that refers to bad pedaling, "*vous pedalez dans le choucroute*"—literally, "you're pedaling in sauerkraut," but meaning, "you don't know what you're talking about."

One occasionally discussed and widely refuted pedaling style is called ankling, in which the ankles help twirl the pedals in a steady flow of power. Most cyclists develop their own style after a bit of experience on the bike and can improve by practicing spinning at high rpms (100 to 120). Jacques Anquetil, one of the five-time winners of the Tour de France, had one of the most beautiful pedaling styles, which by all accounts came naturally. Other successful professional racers have had slightly idiosyncratic styles, and it is difficult to say whether refinement would have hindered or helped them.

PEDAL POWER

Muscular-mechanical output can be measured as energy, work, and power. Each measure has different factors important in understanding the body's metabolic cycle. A calorie, like the British Thermal Unit (BTU), is a measure of energy stored in substances which are available for transformation into work or heat energy. Nutritional calories are stored in foods and body fats and are actually kilocalories (kcal) in physics.[13] Most people store about 2,000 calories (500 grams) of glycogen in their liver and muscles, and about 60,000 calories (ten to twelve kilograms) in fat tissue, little of which is burned during exercise. In the course of aerobic cycling, additional fuel can be supplied at the rate of 250 to 2,000 calories per hour.

Work is the energy necessary to displace a weight a certain distance (force times distance), measured as foot-pounds, newtons, or ergs.[14] In terms of work, the force of pedaling varies throughout the stroke depending on a cyclist's weight, cadence, gear size, duration of effort, and speed. It can range from about 15 to 125 foot-pounds of thrust, with an average thrust of about 20 to 35 percent of a cyclist's weight.[15] That's 40 to 70 foot-pounds of thrust for a 200-pound cyclist in the saddle.

Power is the rate of transformation in energy, equivalent to the amount of calories needed to move a body in a given time (force times distance divided by time). Power is measured in watts (one joule per second) or horsepower (746 watts = one hp). Watts can be converted to calories by multiplying by 3.74, e.g., cycling at 100 watts per hour requires 374 calories. Power output can be estimated from measurements of heart rate and oxygen intake. Fresh air contains around 21 percent oxygen, and exhaled air contains about seventeen percent oxygen, so for an average person at rest, about 0.4 liters of oxygen is absorbed by the lungs per minute. Each milliliter per second of oxygen absorbed by the lungs produces about 4.5 watts of power and eighteen watts of heat.

The average person can produce roughly 75 watts (0.1 horsepower) for several hours, and 225 watts (0.3 hp) for efforts up to a few minutes. A physically fit cyclist can generate about 375 watts (0.5 hp) for several minutes, and 525 watts (0.7 hp) for one minute. Compare that to NASA measurements of first-class athletes who produced 550 watts (0.75 hp) at one minute. Top racing cyclists can produce 375 watts (0.5 hp) at a steady-state aerobic pace for several hours, 750 watts (1.0 hp) for up to ten minutes, and over 1,500 watts (2.0 hp) for flat-out sprints up to about ten seconds.[16] In a one-hour ride, an average person on a touring bike going twelve kilometers burns about 120 calories (at ten calories per kilometer) to produce 33 watts (0.05 hp), while the top racing cyclists can go 50 to 55 kilometers, burning 2,150 calories (at 40 calories per kilometer) to produce about 575 watts (0.77 hp).

Pedal power is a combination of force and velocity (muscle strength and leg speed). Cadence is a cyclist's leg speed, measured in revolutions per minute (rpms). In comparing power and cadence, there is a big difference between optimal efficiency and maximum output. While a slow cadence of 55 to 75 rpm offers the most energy-efficient power output, only a fast cadence of 140 to 160 rpm produces maximum power. Calculating and comparing all these inputs and outputs together allows cyclists to improve their potential and performance.

PERFORMANCE FACTORS IN CYCLISTS

FACTOR	AVERAGE	SPORT	PRO
resting heart rate (bpm)	70	50	30
anaerobic threshold (bpm)	160	175	185
maximum heart rate (bpm)	180	190	195
blood volume (ml)	10	25	50
lung capacity (l)	5	6.5	8
VO$_2$ max (ml/kg/min)	40	60	85
thrust (lbf)	15	30	55
cadence (rpm)	70	90	100
watts (per hour)	50	200	500
calories (kcal)	135	750	2,150
speed (kph)	15	30	50

7 Cycling Performance

Bicycle ergometer measuring volume of oxygen and power output.

Man would seem to be pitilessly analyzed, in the functions and performance of his organs; his bicycle examined bolt by bolt and rendered efficient by the new studies in almost perfect manner; even in racing tactics today every possibility is necessarily considered and defined; little is left to chance.

Thus, it is not surprising that, in a sphere of such great importance for man, the at-times merciless consciousness of modern society is reflected.

Sport is by now inconceivable outside the bounds of science; however we should not deny the danger which is liable to arise from an incorrect understanding of progress.

If sport were to be understood as the raising of a super-race intended for the markets of ambition, it is evident that the objective to which our efforts tend would be humiliating. But this has not been, nor will be, the risk of involution of our sport. It is useless to insist on the presuppositions of willpower, character and morality which have always constituted its strength. Each athlete finds himself faced with such hard and in all cases such diverse difficulties that in the absence of a spirit of initiative, intelligence, and in short personality, success would be impossible.
—Adriano Rodoni, FIAC President, *Cycling* (1972)

No pain, no gain.
—Anonymous

Performance Testing

Cycling is one of the finest activities for improving a person's human-powered potential, and the sport produces some of the world's most physically fit athletes. Cycling requires an athlete to develop a wide range of physical, psychological, technical, and tactical skills. Whether or not a person is endowed with the physical talent or mental competitiveness to become a professional athlete, cycling offers many ways of understanding and attaining peak human performance.

A revolution in sports science and technology has occurred since the 1960s, with the application of refined physiological testing, training methods, nutritional aids, performance gauges, and sports psychology ideas. While many cyclists applied a variety of scientific training and dietary regimes since the 1880s, the majority of cyclists and trainers in the early twentieth century relied on the heroic, intuitive aspects of the athletic personality.

One of the most influential attempts to systematize the "art of cycling" came with the publication of *Cycling* (1972), a complete manual for cyclists and sports managers. This was the culmination of years of experience by professional and amateur racing groups in Italy, a methodology described by the authors as "the doctrine of the Italian School, already considered one of the best in the world."

Sports science has collected considerable data on human performance. Bicycle racers routinely undergo a variety of physical tests that measure body type, fitness level and basic potential. Combined with performance data of cycling machines, the net results of such tests allow a near-perfect model of actual human-powered performance.

HUMAN PERFORMANCE DATA

BODY
Age
Gender
Height, meters
Weight, kilograms
Fat content, percent of body weight
Liquid body weight (LBW)
Proportions, percent of body limbs
Urinalysis

CARDIO-VASCULAR
Heart rate (HR)
beats per minute (BPM)
Anaerobic threshold (AT)
Maximum heart rate (MHR)
Blood pressure (BP)
Blood circulation rate
Blood cell count (BC)

RESPIRATORY
Vital capacity (liters)
Breath volume
Breathing frequency (BF)
breaths per minute
Inhalation/exhalation
volume per minute (MV)
Air equivalent of oxygen (AEO$_2$)
Oxygen uptake (VO$_2$)
liters per body weight per minute
Oxygen uptake maximum (VO$_2$ MAX)
Carbon dioxide output (VCO$_2$)
Respiratory quotient (RQ)

MUSCULAR
Muscle content,
percent of body weight
Contraction rate, seconds
Fiber count
Fiber ratio, percent of muscle type
Lactate levels

BIOMECHANICAL
Pedal–saddle position
Pedal width, Q-factor
Pedal thrust, power cycle
Pedal thrust, maximum
Cadence (RPM)
revolutions per minute
Power output (HP) horsepower
Power output, maximum

VEHICULAR
Cycle weight, kilograms
Total weight
Mechanical friction
Rolling resistance
Frontal area, square meters
Wind drag, kilograms
Coefficient of drag
Development, meters
Speed (KPH) kilometers per hour
Energy consumption, calories

VO₂ MAX

Maximum volume of oxygen uptake, or VO_2 max, is the best test of cardio-vascular efficiency. The test is not a particularly comfortable experience and usually involves indoor cycling on an ergometer or running on a treadmill with increasing resistance or workload to the point of total physical exhaustion. The subject wears a heart rate monitor and a breathing mask connected to a machine that analyzes the air inhaled and exhaled, thus measuring the amount of oxygen consumed. The resulting value is a calculation of the uptake of oxygen in milliliters per kilogram of the cyclist's body weight in minutes, or VO_2 ml/kg/min. Average healthy people have VO_2 max values of 35 to 55 ml/kg, recreational cyclists reach values of 55 to 80 ml/kg, and elite racing cyclists attain values of 75 to 95 ml/kg. For real-world outdoor cycling, portable breathing machines have been mounted on roadster bikes for testing average cyclists, as well as being carried in support cars with air tubes attached to racing cyclists while training.

The VO_2 max test provides useful data for measuring human-power potential, including maximum functional heart rate, anaerobic threshold, and maximum power output in watts. As with most tests, VO_2 max is not an absolute indicator of racing performance. For example, one cyclist may have a high value but lack the refined preparation or mentality to perform at maximum output. Another cyclist, with a lower value, may be able to consistently ride close to the maximum, faster than the cyclist with a higher potential.

On-road testing of VO₂ (volume of oxygen), from *Cycling Science*.

PULSEMETERS

Pulsemeters or heart rate (HR) monitors measure a person's heart beat or blood pulse. Since the mid-1980s, they have been made to be worn while cycling and have become a popular training tool. With electrode skin attachments, such as chest straps, earlobe clips, fingertip slots, and handlebar pads, they connect by wire or wireless transceivers to electronic monitors with liquid crystal display readouts on wrist watches and handlebar-mounted cyclometer units. Computer Instruments Corp. (CIC) offered ten types of Polar pulsemeters in 1991, with the $450 Polar Cyclovantage featuring ECG chest sensors; a cyclometer measuring cadence, speed, distance, and time; an 8-hour memory of past performance data which can playback on the watch, or download into another computer with the $500 Polar Interface software, modem, and cable.

POWER GAUGES

Numerous biomechanical and ergometric devices have been developed for measuring pedal stroke and power output. A problem with many measuring devices is that they inevitably change whatever they are measuring, and additional measuring devices are often needed to test their accuracy. In laboratory testing, the natural effects of cycling are often missing, such as wind resistance and its cooling benefits, road surface variations, and the sensation of speed. More accurate cycling performance data are possible with the development of on-bike power meters for outdoor cycling, but at the cost of extra weight.

To understand and improve the cyclist's pedal stroke a variety of dynamometers have appeared since the 1890s. Various mechanical data had been collected by the 1960s and 1970s, when scientists at the Japan Bicycle Research Association and the Biomechanics Laboratory at the Institute of Sports Medicine in Rome began to develop on-bike electronic dynamometric devices that could transmit data through telemetric radio signals. Mounted to road racing bikes for on-road tests, the Italian dynamometer pedal measured both the vertical and horizontal forces applied throughout the pedal stroke.[1]

Look MAXone power meter, above, with strain gauge hub and handlebar-mounted computer.
SRM Powermeter, right, was used by Yvonne McGregor, below, when setting the women's hour record of 47.411 km in June 1995.

Because power output (in watts or horsepower) is a more direct measure of human performance than heart rate or VO₂ capacity, several kinds of power meters and bicycle ergometers have been developed. Power meters for on-bike use include the Balboa Power Pacer, the Look MAXone, and the SRM Powermeter, all developed in the early 1990s. The Power Pacer and MAXone consist of special rear wheel hubs with strain gauges for measuring torque and microprocessors that convert signals to readable data displayed on handlebar monitors. In addition to power output, speed, cadence, and distance, a cyclist's caloric expenditure can be calculated. The SRM Powermeter (for Schoberer Rad Messtechnik), patented by Ulrich Schoberer of Germany, and initially tested by the German national cycling team, consists of a special crankset with strain gauges and deformation elements which transmit signals to a handlebar-mounted Powercontrol computer. Several hours of data can be stored in the Powercontrol unit, and downloaded to another computer with SRM software for printing out performance tables useful in training. The unit cost about $5,300 in 1993.

Cycle ergometers have advanced since the 1970s, as the parameters of human performance expanded when sports doctors discovered the extraordinary fitness of cyclists such as Eddy Merckx. Perhaps the greatest cyclist of all time, Merckx raised the bar by riding an ergometer "off the charts" for an entire hour at 0.62 horsepower (455 watts) without reaching exhaustion. As legend has it, the ergometer was supposed to cause total exhaustion for top athletes in ten minutes. Estimates of Merckx's peak power output for one hour range between 485 and 600 watts. The new generation of high-performance ergometers allow cyclists to ride their own road or track bike, while tracking performance data such as watts, VO₂ rate, heart rate, cadence, speed, and caloric expenditure. Ergometers used by top cyclists for testing and training include the Racermate CompuTrainer, the Kingcycle Trainer, and the Schwinn Velodyne. The CompuTrainer constists of a rear wheel stand, an electronic load simulator, a handlebar controler, and a link to a TV or computer via the Nintendo system. Race courses with variable wind and grade conditions are displayed along with a competitor, either computer-generated or another cyclist on a CompuTrainer stand. With its SpinScan feature, a graph simulates power output by each leg through the pedal stroke. The Computrainer is as entertaining as it is useful. Because there is a competitor it can measure another important human performance factor, the desire to win.

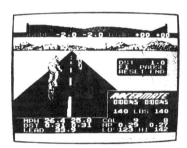

Computerized training with the Racermate CompuTrainer.
Top, real competitor, above, simulated competitor, below, SpinScan graph.

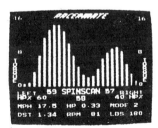

Performance Training

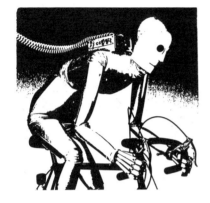

To reach his or her best, a cyclist must train physically and mentally. Training has been defined by the "Italian School" as "a program of repeated tests that will produce progressively increasing efforts in order to stimulate the physiological processes of adaption of the body organism and assist the increase of the physical, psychological and technical capacities of the athlete, so that the performance during competition can be consolidated."[2] For cyclists there are three basic types of training levels, each with different goals.

The first cyclist rides to maintain a decent level of physical and mental fitness. This person fits cycling into an otherwise busy lifestyle, either as a daily means of transportation for commuting or errands, or for two or three fitness rides per week for a total of about 50 miles. The second cyclist rides for personal achievement and a relatively high level of fitness for occasional touring or competition. This person devotes a considerable amount of time on vigorous rides about three or four times a week for a weekly average of 100 miles. The third cyclist rides to achieve the maximum level of performance necessary for competitive cycling. This person's lifestyle revolves around a dedicated training and racing schedule with endurance and interval workouts that average 150 to 600 miles per week.

Methods of training can be broken down into various time spans ranging from a lifetime to a few minutes. Training programs are based on age or phase of life, seasonal or year-round periods (macro), weekly training schedules (micro), and daily exercise routines.

PERIODIZATION

Most training is based on gradual improvement through a process known as periodization. Periodization usually has four sequential phases spread throughout a year, which are also divided into several smaller periods. These periods include general preparation, conditioning, special preparation, and competition.

The main variables of these training periods are volume (accumulated time or miles) and intensity (levels of effort or speed). Most training programs serve as guidelines for which individuals must adapt their own goals and traits. The general idea is to achieve a level of fitness and conditioning necessary for recovery from regular near-maximum exertions, with the added goal of finding the optimal training load. This plan will stimulate improvement to the point of attaining peak form without the negative effects of overtraining.

The first task in training begins with general preparation, or pre-athleticism. This is especially important for beginning cyclists, and in different ways for experienced cyclists starting a new season. For beginners, a basic understanding and development of the various forms of metabolism and a coordination of cycling skills is undertaken. Beginners are advised to pedal with low gears and rapid spinning, often with a fixed-gear. To prevent early burn-out, youngsters should not begin serious training until the age of sixteen or so, and to avoid muscle injuries, there are age-based gear limits in racing. Through practice (volume) a gradual improvement in muscular and aerobic efficiency is achieved. It may take a few weeks or a few months depending on athletic condition and riding time (volume). For experienced cyclists, the first period often involves participation in other vigorous activities, such as swimming, ball games, cross-country skiing, running, and mountaineering, coupled with weight training and calisthenics. It often occurs during an off-season layoff of three to twelve weeks.

The next level is conditioning, with the emphasis on volume and developing aerobic efficiency. Experienced cyclists continue exercises such as weight training and calisthenics, and return to the bike with long rides occasionally combined with sprints and climbing (intensity). The mileage (volume) reaches its highest level towards the end of this phase, which lasts about twelve weeks.

In the third phase, called special preparation, emphasis shifts from volume to intensity. The training techniques of intervals, climbing, sprints, motor-pacing, and long slow distance rides are combined within each week's schedule, while weight training is curtailed. For experienced cyclists this phase may overlap with the competition period as preparation for a peak event. This period lasts about six to eight weeks.

During the competition period, lasting up to about 45 weeks for amateurs and professional cyclists, training is used to supplement racing activities. A combination of intensity and volume is used to maintain fitness and to reach peak form for a particular event. For most athletes, peak form can be attained only once, or at best twice per season, and it may last one to four weeks.

Training Exercises

Interval training is a system of fast and slow riding in designated and repeated periods which permits a precise amount of recuperation. They may be sprints or time-trialing "jams" at racing speed on flat or hilly terrain, measured in time or distance. For beginning cyclists, the intervals can be spaced so the slow recovery period is two to three times longer than the fast period of effort. Eventually the two periods can become equal in duration.

Speed play, or *Fartlek* training in Swedish, is a free-form method of training, described as "cat's play," usually done in groups of cyclists who have already developed a higher level of fitness. The idea is to relax and have fun while making spontaneous jumps, jams, or sprints. It is used to prevent boredom from stricter training regimes, to sharpen reactions, and to adapt to random variations in pace typically found in racing.

Kermesse training, or criterium training, is used to develop speed, strength, and bike handling ability. This is done in groups around a circuit of roads over a certain number of laps, usually at or near racing speed with sprints out of corners and at sign posts or road marks which simulate prime sprints. For racing in breakaways or periods of intense jamming, cyclists practice exchanging pace in echelons or drafting lines for wind protection. Rather than simulating races, many cycling clubs or regional associations promote mid-weekly training races which serve this purpose. Motor-paced training is used to simulate racing speeds, and for developing leg speed for sprinting, and long jams.

Long slow distance training, also known as LSD training, or over-distance training, involves riding at a steady-state aerobic pace for about six to ten hours. The object is to create endurance and condition the body to feel comfortable on the bike for long periods. Some cyclists ride extra miles before and after races.

Cycling Lifestyle

Factors which affect a cyclist's ability to succeed in the sport are outlined as follows:

Mechanics: mechanical, rolling, and air resistance, terrain gradient.
Biomechanics: saddle, handlebar, and feet positions, pedal style.
Physical Condition: nutrition, medication, preparation, training, massage.
Psychological Condition: personality, tenacity, flexibility, visualization, moral behavior, non-cycling activities.
Competition: quality of opponents, type of course, race tactics, personal potential, confidence.
Community: teammates, sponsors, promoters, coaches, family, friends, fans, press.

"Life in the fast lane" is an appropriate definition for the lifestyle of a professional cyclist. The career statistics of Felice Gimondi, rated as one of the top fifteen cyclists of all time, illustrate this fast pace. These were compiled by the Italian cycling magazine *Bicisport* when Gimondi formally retired in 1978 at the age of 37, after a career spanning eighteen years, fourteen as a professional:

• Gimondi cycled 551,250 miles, enough to circle the globe about 22 times. He averaged 22,800 miles of racing and 15,000 miles of training each year.
• He started 2,548 races, won 145 stage races and classics, finished second 100 times, and received about 1,000 victory kisses.
• He drank 6,225 bottles of liquid during races and received 3,696 musette bags of food. He consumed 61 million lira worth of steak.
• He lost 13,737 pounds of sweat, or about 83 times his body weight. He received 140,000 minutes of massage and took 2,520 injections of various medications. He went through 290 anti-doping controls.
• He used 98 bikes, putting only five out of commission, four road and one track. He used 5,000 tubular tires, 420 jerseys, 280 pairs of gloves, and 380 pairs of shorts.
• He boarded 258 airplanes, and slept in 3,360 hotels around the world. He traveled to races by airplane twenty percent of the time, by car 78 percent, and by train two percent.

Felice Gimondi.

Sport Psychology

A common saying in cycling is that "winning is ten percent sweat, and 90 percent psych." Human beings normally use only a fraction of their potential brain power. Most people agree that the winners of bike races are determined by three factors: luck, fitness, and desire. For winners, these often come together as a result of complete preparation: "Genius is in the details."

Because the sport of cycling is so important to some, techniques beyond physical training are used to improve performance, such as various psychological techniques, based on the psychophysiological principle. Every change in physiological state is accompanied by an appropriate change in the mental-emotional state, which, conscious or unconscious, is accompanied by a corresponding change in the physiological state. Psychological exercises for cycling include biorhythms, visualization, and mantras.

Refined methods of training offer a means of studying and applying biorhythmic behavioral patterns. By repeated intensive awareness of pulse rate, breathing patterns, and states of mind, cyclists can follow and manipulate their optimal periodic training and racing rhythms. Visualization is a process of mental or physical exercises used to prepare oneself for extraordinary efforts such as racing. One system, visuo-motor behavior rehearsal (VMBR), involves relaxation, practice of imagery, and the use of the imagery for strengthening psychological or motor skills. By concentrating on an imaginary sequence of events, such as sprinting or breaking away, while tensing the appropriate muscles, a "well-controlled copy of experience" is formed which can be used when the actual experience occurs.[3] Mantras, or autogenic training phrases, are a way of recuperating, building confidence and psyching up by using a series of words or phrases for relaxation and activation. Mantras such as "I am," or "bicycle" are used for relaxation or meditation, while activation phrases, such as "I feel life and energy that makes me feel alive and powerful," or "I will win," help to psych up the racer. Meditation, or semi-conscious relaxation can create a sense of revitalization and centeredness which many cyclists find beneficial. This sensation also develops by cycling itself, through the meditative aspects of steady-state aerobic exercise.

Nobody Is Perfect Yet

As imperfect creatures, humans tend to strive for perfection, especially in sports where athletes expect the best of themselves. But few are endowed with the perfect heart, lungs, or legs, or the unsurpassable talent, dedication, or will to win. Nonetheless, with the synergy of human power, people of all abilities have the opportunity to be champions in their own ways. Many athletes have overcome severe disablties to become "super-abled" champions.

Sports Medicine

In modern sports, the history of cycling demonstrates the most wide-spread use and abuse of substances or medicines designed to increase human performance. The use of stimulants, pain killers, muscle-building hormones, and other chemical compounds for sports is called doping. Bicycle racing is extremely tough on the body and mind, and success offers enormous rewards of fame and fortune for a professional cyclist who becomes a champion. Many racers have the desire to boost themselves beyond natural limits, and in doing so have turned the sport into a notable testing ground for sports medicine.

The definition of doping has been a controversial subject with many varying opinions. One view is that anything taken to artificially enhance performance is dangerous, cheating, and unethical. This raises the question where to draw the line between food and drugs, with plants, vitamins, caffeine, and cough syrup. Another view is that cyclists must be able to treat themselves not only for common ailments, but also for those which arise because of the extraordinary demands of racing. This creates problems interpreting the subtle difference between treatment and enhancement. A third opinion says that doping is part of the evolution of the species, and that racing cyclists are capable of deciding whether or not to explore the frontiers of medically-enhanced performance. The problem is that the advantage goes to the cyclists with superior sports doctors, and that when performance-enhancing drugs are used incorrectly, they can destroy health rather than build it.

To avoid the stigma of the word doping, racers tend to use code words like "vitamins," "treatments," "medication," or "balancing." The following definition of doping is the one most commonly applied for amateur cycling in Europe:

Doping is the administering to a healthy person, or the utilization by the same person of substances extraneous to the organism, of physiological substances in abnormal quantity or by abnormal channels, having the scope of artificially increasing the performance of the person when participating at a race. Some psychological processes [i.e., psychotherapy, hypnosis] created to increase performance may also be considered doping.

When an athlete is injured or ill, he can only be treated by a doctor or under his own responsibility. Only the doctor is able to authorize if the injured or ill athlete, under treatment, can take part in a race. Nevertheless, if the prescription contains any agent or substances of any nature, dosage, preparation or method of administering it that for its effect could change artificially or unfairly the performance during the competition, the athlete must not participate in the race.[4]

LESSONS FROM HISTORY

Sports doping has been around since the first major bicycle races in the 1890s. The first notable death due to doping was the Englishman Arthur Linton shortly after he won the 1896 Bordeaux-Paris race. He had mixed a trimethyl-amphetamine into his drink. At the Six-Day races in New York, cyclists were known to try concentrated caffeine, cocaine, sugared ether, and nitroglycerine.

In the first half of the twentieth century drugs like "the bomb," a potent amphetamine, were used to help cyclists override their fatigue. Many drugs did not raise the level of fitness but instead blocked information between the muscles and the central nervous system, allowing excessive physical force to be applied with damaging results. Doping was an open secret as some racers carried around enough pills, vials, syringes, and vitamins to constitute "a small pharmacy."[5]

Cyclists and their trainers were fairly naive about the drugs they used, but the residual effects became apparent as some cyclists seemed to grow older faster. Some famous cyclists came forward to tell of their scandalous survival from drug abuse, with impassioned warnings to those who might be foolish enough to follow their path. Their experiences inspired pity and criticism. Antoine Blondin described the public's mixed emotions during a 1960s drug scandal in the French sports newspaper *L'Équipe*:

> As sports fans, we prefer to dream about angels on wheels, Simon Pures somehow immune to the uppers and downers of our own pill-popping society. There is, all the same, a certain nobility in those who have gone down into God-knows-what hell in search of the best of themselves. We might feel tempted to tell them they should not have done it, but we can remain secretly proud of what they have done. Their wan, haggard looks are, for us, an offering.[6]

Since the mid-1960s, national and international cycling federations began to institute anti-doping rules and tests for major races. While the incidence of positive test results (showing traces of drugs) was reduced from about 40 percent in the 1960s to about six percent in the 1970s, this did little to stop the use of performance-enhancing drugs.[7] The controls may not be strict enough, since it is estimated that at least 75 percent of professional cyclists have used some form of banned substance. Some say that a rider is at fault only if he or she is caught. Various national sports federations have regulations beyond the UCI rule. Erroneous test results and suspicious suspensions have been used for and against cyclists for nationalistic purposes. Cyclists have been caught cheating, and legend has it that the Tour de France produced the world's first pregnant man, who submitted his wife's urine for the drug test.

Each anti-doping test is fairly costly, with a price tag of $30 to $100 per test. A sample of urine, 100 milliliters, is usually collected, with half being used for the first computer-aided chemical analysis. If this shows positive, containing a banned substance, the other half is tested. Stimulants, steroids, cortisone, and masking drugs are the most common substances searched for nowadays, while recreational drugs such as hallucinogens or cocaine are rarely used in cycle racing.

Because the Tour de France is the most arduous race offering the greatest prize in cycling, it has suffered the most well-publicized doping scandals over the years. Tom Simpson's death during the infamous 13th stage of the Tour de France on July 13, 1967, was a major incident which brought the doping issue into the news, resulting in attempts to change cycling's bad image.

Tom Simpson was Britain's finest road racer of the day; in 1962 he was the leader for part of the Tour, in 1965 he was World Champion, and early in 1967 he had won the classic Paris-Nice race. It was already 80 degrees Fahrenheit in the early morning when the Tour left Marseilles for the barren volcanic slope of Mt. Ventoux, the "Giant of Provence." A Belgian reporter noted that Simpson looked tired and asked him if it was the heat. He replied, "No, it's not the heat. It's the Tour."

After seven miles of climbing, Simpson slipped behind the pace of the leaders and kept trying to bridge the gap. Suddenly he dropped further back and began weaving across the road. Then he collapsed, and was surrounded by spectators. In whispered gasps, he uttered his famous last words: "Put me back on my bike." The spectators lifted him back on the seat and got him going again. Again he zig-zagged on his bike and fell; this time into a coma. While receiving oxygen and a heart massage, Simpson was flown by helicopter to a hospital in Avignon and his death was announced at 5:40 P.M. from artificially induced heat stroke. His jersey pockets held three vials. Two were empty and one contained tablets of Stenamina and Tonedrin. The autopsy showed that he had ingested amphetamine, methylamphetamine, and cognac. The following year, the Tour was sponsored by Vittel mineral water, it was named the "Tour of Health," and mandatory drug testing was implemented.

The year 1967 had more doping scandals, with Yvonne Reynders of Belgium being denied the women's World Champion road title for using a cough syrup with ephedrine. Later that year, Jacques Anquetil set a new world hour record but was officially denied the record because he refused to show up for the doping test until 48 hours later. He was making a stand against controls or, as rumors have it, allowing time for whatever he had taken to pass through his system. Anquetil was quite forthright on the subject when he retired and became a cycling commentator:

> I do not wish to hear spoken the word "doping." Rather, one must say "treating yourself," and speak of treatments that are not appropriate for ordinary mortals. You cannot compete in the Tour de France on mineral water alone.[8]

Tom Simpson in the Tour France.

In 1968, the Union Cycliste Internationale established two lists for doping controls, one for "hard" prohibited substances, and the other allowing certain "light" substances in limited quantities with a medical prescription. In dope testing at races such as the Tour de France, four or five cyclists are selected each day, usually the top two stage finishers, the overall leader, and two other riders chosen at random. In the first-time offense for a positive test the rider receives a 1,000 Swiss franc fine, a last place finish for the stage, a ten-minute overall penalty, and a 30-day probation. A second-time offense gets a 3,000 Sf fine, disqualification from the race, and a three-month suspension. A third-time offense means a life-time suspension. But all three offenses must occur within a two-year period—therefore if additional offenses occur every three years, each one is treated as the first.

SCANDAL!

In the 1978 Tour, Michel Pollentier was caught attempting to defraud the drug test just as he won the mountain stage up to L'Alpe-d'Huez and took the leader's yellow jersey. Instead of going to the doping control, he went to his hotel room where he put on a long sleeve jersey to hide a small flask containing another person's urine. The flask was taped into his armpit and had a rubber tube running down his arm to his wrist.

What happened when Pollentier arrived at the Tour urinalysis trailer almost an hour late has been told many ways. Apparently the officials allowed him to wear the jersey, despite the rules which state, "The rider shall appear naked from the middle of his back to his knees and with the sleeves of his jersey rolled up." When he could not get the apparatus to work and started flapping his arm, officials removed his jersey and exposed him. Pollentier claimed his specimen was acceptable, but admitted taking Alupent, a prescription treatment for asthmatics. He was thrown out of the Tour, given a two-month suspension, and fined 5,000 Sf.

The whole episode resulted in a scandal as much for the officials as Pollentier. It also raised the question of how racers could treat their ailments, without using medications commonly available for "ordinary mortals," that are off-limits to racers. As Bernard Hinault, winner of five Tours de France, once said: "I went to the pharmacist's to buy a cough syrup for my little boys. Luckily, before I used it myself, I looked at the label and saw it contained substances banned for a professional bicycle racer."

While the list of banned substances has grown longer, it seems the competition is between team doctors and drug testing laboratories. Contemporary sports medicine has emulated the alchemist's search for gold, and the 1980s brought a new set of drugs, and doping scandals. Joop Zoetemelk, a 36-year-old Dutchman known as the "Honorary Frenchman No. 1," tested positive for testosterone while riding his fifteenth Tour de France in 1983. He appealed, claiming that his body produced excess amounts of hormone, but this failed in court. Zoetemelk sued the Tour organizers to clear his reputation, and after several appeals with expert

MICHEL POLLENTIER

medical testimony he won his case, just as he was retiring.

A major scandal was revealed five months after the 1984 Los Angeles Olympic Games. Seven members of the U.S. cycling team, four who won gold, silver, and bronze medals, were found to have blood boosted by the risky method of transfusion. At the time, neither the U.S. Olympic Committee nor the U.S. Cycling Federation had ruled it illegal, and there was no definite way to test for blood boosting. Because these were amateur Olympic athletes ("Simon Pures"), and because of the Cold War, with the U.S. boycotting the 1980 Moscow Olympic Games and the Soviet bloc reciprocating in the 1984 Los Angeles Olympics, the controversy played out in the press, with the following opinions appearing in *Sports Illustrated*:

> We weren't gonna fall behind the Russians or East Germans anymore. So instead we'll just stoop to their level of immoral and artificial ways of winning, eh...?

> You know where we were in the Dark Ages. You know where we are now. Nobody says we wear white gloves.

> Maybe the U.S.O.C. should be accused of blood boosting for establishing a training center at 6,000 feet.

> Maybe a few words should be added to the Olympic credo: "No additives, no preservatives, no artificial anything."[9]

In July 1988, the 75th edition of the Tour de France received another major shock when race leader Pedro Delgado tested positive for a masking drug. He was reprieved on a technicality, and eventually won the race, making a mockery of doping controls. The drug in question was probenecid, a steroid-masking drug used to obscure traces of an active illegal substance for doping tests. Delgado was reprieved because probenecid had been ruled illegal by the International Olympic Committee late in 1987, but it was not scheduled to be banned by the Union Cycliste Internationale until August 1988. The scandal was a painful lesson for a novice Tour official who said: "I know today that the letter of the law can replace its spirit and that one can play with the rules. So, today, I'm ashamed and, perhaps tomorrow, I must ask my children not to get too involved in competitive sports."[10]

The synthesis of new performance-enhancing drugs appears to have no end. Another "killer" drug called EPO appeared around 1989, and was believed to be responsible for the death of several Dutch cyclists from heart failure. EPO is an undetectable substance derived from a naturally occurring hormone which boosts the production of oxygen-carrying red blood cells. Since it causes blood clotting, it can also cause heart attacks. For a time, it seemed the most commonly used drugs were anabolic or cortical steroids which build muscles with testosterone hormones. They are used to enhance training during the winter, for races without testing and in controlled races with the use of masking drugs.

Many cyclists continue to speak out against the use of drugs. Paul Kimmage, who stopped racing after four years with the professionals, wrote *A Rough Ride* (1990). He questioned the sanity of a sport where an athlete's heart pounds six to seven hours each day for three weeks at a time, and a system that seems to promote drug taking. North American racing stars Andy Hampsten and Greg LeMond are known to ride drug-free, while some team managers claim their riders compete on "bread and water." Meanwhile, in preparation for the 1992 Olympics, the makers of Nuprin, a popular "pain relief formula" containing the banned substance ibuprofen, became sponsors of the U.S. Olympic Cycling Team. Halfway through the 1991 Tour de France the leading Dutch PDM squad, with three riders in the top ten, had to pull out of the race due to team sickness—at first described as "food poisoning," or "bad air conditioning," but reportedly from poorly handled intravenous treatments of intralupid, a legal prescription dietary supplement.

TREATMENTS

The following medications or treatments have been used by racing cyclists to improve performance:

Stimulants mimic adrenaline, both in their chemical structure and effects. Doses of five to twenty milligrams take away the feeling of fatigue, especially sleepiness. They can cause insomnia, anorexia, high blood pressure, and cardio-circulatory collapse. They do not aide endurance or recuperation.

Hormones can aid weight loss, strength capacity, muscle development, and can cause a feeling of euphoria. Side effects on vital organs include nausea, edema, hair growth, change of voice, increase of the libido. For men, they can cause atrophy of the testicles and impotence, hepatitis, hypertrophy of the prostate, and hardening of the epiphysis. For women, hormones cause irregular menstruation and virilization.

Cardio-respiratory aids stimulate the central nervous system and act on both the cardio-vascular and respiratory systems. Some drugs cause increased awareness and concentration capacity, some increase the frequency and depth of breathing, and some dilate blood vessels while increasing the contracting force of the heart. Generally cardio-respiratory aids increase metabolism, while delaying fatigue. They tend to be more benign than other drugs, and many appear in common cold or asthma remedies.

Masking drugs have little performance-enhancing effect when used alone. Instead, they are combined with an illegal active substance, with the effect of either concealing the active drug, or producing a new substance which does not appear as an illegal drug.

Blood boosting is a method of improving performance, especially endurance, by up to ten percent by increasing the number of oxygen-carrying red blood cells in the athlete's cardio-vascular system. There are

TOP 40 BANNED SUBSTANCES

1. Amphetamine
2. Methamphetamine
3. Dimethamphetamine
4. Benzphetamine
5. Ethylamphetamine
6. Fenfluramine
7. Norfenfloramine
8. Furfurylamphetamine
9. Furfurylmethyl-amphetamine
10. Metoxyphenamine
11. Phentermine
12. Mephentermine
13. Chlorphentermine
14. Propylhexedrine
15. Aletamine
16. Cyclopentamine
17. Methylphenil
18. Pipradol
19. Phacetoperane
20. Pipethanat
21. Phenmetrazine
22. Phendimetrazine
23. Diethylpropione
24. Prolintane
25. Pyrovalerone
26. Phencamphamine
27. Tranylcypramine
28. Pemoline
29. Cypenamine
30. Strychnine
31. Ibogaine
32. Ephedrine and derivatives
33. Heptaminol
34. Aminophenazenol
35. Bemegride
36. Leptazol
37. Nikethamide
38. Anabolic Steroids
39. Cortisone
40. Crotetamide

three basic ways of blood boosting: reinfusion, transfusion, and low-pressure or altitude training. In reinfusion, about a pint (or unit) of an athlete's blood is drawn from the body nine or ten weeks before an event and then it is spun down in a centrifuge to concentrated red blood cells. This is held in cold storage, and during the time preceding the event, the body naturally replenishes the missing blood. A few days before the event, the athlete receives a reinfusion of the stored red blood cells. In the transfusion method, blood is not removed from the athlete's system. Instead, someone else's same type concentrated red blood cells are added to the recipient's, usually a close relative. Blood boosting (also called blood packing or blood doping) was prohibited in 1985 and is difficult to detect. A natural way to get the effects of blood boosting is to live at higher altitudes (5,000 to 10,000 feet). The lower concentration of oxygen at high altitudes causes hypoxia, which brings on headaches and dizziness, known as altitude sickness, for which the body compensates by producing more red blood cells, equivalent to about one additional pint. Other ways to simulate high altitude blood boosting is to breathe low-pressure air through a mask while training, or sleep in a low-pressure oxygen chamber.

Electrical stimulation is a method of applying an electrical charge to enhance neuro-muscular conditioning. By stimulating muscular contractions and the pathways to the brain, it is used to strengthen muscles and to help recover from injuries. This "shock treatment" involves doses of about 50 to 220 milliamps through electrodes placed on specific muscles of the body. The doses are given in sessions up to several minutes each, for several weeks. It can produce some pain, and possible localized neuron damage. It is more often used in sports such as weightlifting, with improved results. One electronic neuro-muscular product, called the Shogo Motion Enhancer, is a surgically implanted microprocessor which decreases inter-synapse reaction time within the nervous system (somatic) of the nearby muscle. The small $3,000 unit claims to monitor and increase muscle frequency up to five times normal cadence.[11]

UCI PROHIBITED SUBSTANCES

The prohibition of substances includes narcotics and their salts and by-products which are governed by international regulations. Many common over-the-counter drugs contain prohibited substances, including Alka-Seltzer Plus, Dristan, Nyquil, and Sudafed. Ma Huang, a natural Chinese herb found in tea blends, contains ephedrine.

Part Three

Bikeable Planet

8 Global Bicycles

Tianjin, China, 1990. Photograph by Mary Francis Dunham.

*In a world so transformed by the automobile that whole landscapes
and lifestyles bear its imprint, a significant fact goes unnoticed. While
societies the world over define transportation in terms of engine
power, the greatest share of personal transport needs is met by human
power.*

—Marcia Lowe, *The Bicycle: Vehicle for a Small Planet* (1989)

Bicycle Migrations

The bicycle evolved during an age of great expansion for humanity. When
the first swift-walkers appeared, nearly two hundred years ago, the world
was populated with less than one-fifth the number of people living today,
and landscapes were only beginning to be transformed by industrial
development. Transport and communication was measured in days,
weeks, or months, carried out by walking, riding horseback, with animal-
drawn carriages, river boats, and ocean-going vessels. Most people's daily
experience was limited to their local village or homeland.

According to David Pilbeam, director of the Peabody Museum of
Architecture and Ethnology at Harvard University, the bicycle has had "a
major impact on the population structure of humans."

> We often ignore the fact that the most significant invention certainly in
> recent human history, maybe in human history, is the bicycle. Before
> the invention of the bicycle, most people married someone who was
> born no more than ten miles from where they were born. Now the aver-
> age marriage distance for the vast majority of people around the world
> who still ride on bicycles and don't drive around in BMWs or
> Mercedes is more like a hundred miles. That means the average breed-
> ing population is radically expanded so that the degree of genetic out-
> breeding as opposed to relative inbreeding has changed very signifi-
> cantly and this is already having an effect on the genetic structure of
> populations, on the physical structure of populations. That still has a
> way to work its way through and it is changing the effects of natural
> selection in ways that are simply not estimable at the moment.[1]

During this population growth and expansion, bicycles spread throughout
the globe. Pre-industrial European colonialism had already been under
way for a few centuries when swift-walkers first appeared in western
Europe and began to be shipped in small numbers around the world.
Within five years of the velocipede's invention in the 1860s, it was
exported from Germany, France and England to every continent of the
globe. Records show velocipedes were shipped to Cairo, Perth, Rio, San
Francisco, and Yokohama. These were followed by the arrival of sociable
tricycles, high-wheelers, and safety bicycles, a few of which were constructed by indigenous cycle makers. One notable potentate who acquired
a Rudge tricycle in 1883 was Solhikoff, His Highness The Moharana
Sahib Bahadur of Oodypore.

Velocipedes came to Japan through
the Westernized port of Yokohama.

The safety bicycle migrated with colonial expansion. Bicycles came to many "primitive" areas as British, French, and Dutch armies ventured into other people's lands. As a means of independent mobility, bicycles accompanied the pioneers of the last frontiers. When white men explored Africa, bicycles provided transport where narrow paths and thick forests blocked access. Bicycles were also used by white men in exchange for Nigerian slaves. In late nineteenth century, only the few Nigerians who had profited from the slave trade owned bicycles, until the twentieth century, when English bikes were introduced in the market by more conventional means. In the 1890s, "bush bicycles" were a big part of the gold-drush activity in the outback of Western Australia, and in the klondike rush of Alaska. In the frenzy to claim property in the native Cherokee land that is now Arkansas, bicycles were used by the white American settlers.[2]

"Cooly" trishaw, 1883, migrated from England to India with the British East India Company.

Methodist missionary J.J. Methvin with bicycle in Kiowa country.

As peoples of various cultures discovered the bicycle, their customs often influenced its function in society. One of the earliest advocates of the bicycle in Beijing was the last emperor of the Qing dynasty, Pu Yi (1906-1967), who came to the throne as a young boy.

He used to scoot around the Forbidden City with his long Qing queue flying in the breeze. To smooth his ride he ordered court officials to remove the high wooden thresholds at the doors between rooms and corridors which his ancestors had believed were able to keep out demons. The last emperor maintained his strong interest in the bicycle even after he became an ordinary citizen of New China, only then he was able to ride freely around the streets.

Before 1949 not many ordinary folks could afford this prohibitively priced, new-fangled gadget—this bicycle that had to be imported from Britain or Japan. Only after Liberation did the majority of the population begin to make their moves on bicycles. And they made those moves on a steadily increasing variety of brands—of steadily increasing quality.[3]

With the spread of bicycles at least one place was named after them. Bicycle Lake in the Mojave Desert in California is an example. It now lies within the Fort Irwin Military Reservation, which has restricted access. There are a couple of explanations for the name according to Erwin G. Gudde, author of *California Place Names*:

The intermittent lake has become well-known because of the army anti-aircraft range here, which is named after the lake. The story that an unfortunate traveler left a bicycle here while attempting to cross the desert was confirmed by Washington W. Cahill, a long-time official of the borax company, who told L. Burr Belden that the teamsters of the company found a rusty bicycle here around 1890. However, according to an old resident of Barstow, the young men of Daggett in its flourishing days used the lake for bicycle races when it was dry. In 1957 an aerial photograph, taken by pilot Don Krogh and widely published, shows a corpse lying beside a bicycle in the Mojave Desert not far from the lake.[4]

Ripley's—*Believe It or Not!*

"BICYCLE TREE" ON Vashon Island in Washington State, A DOUGLAS FIR TREE *HAS GROWN AROUND A BICYCLE* EMBEDDED IN ITS TRUNK!
SUBMITTED BY RALPH & WILLIAMS, JUNEAU, ALASKA

新到上海跑自行車

Global Cycling

In 1994 there were about one billion bicycles in the world. Placed in a single line, they would circle the globe 35 times. These were offset by about 500 million cars, and another 150 million trucks, buses, motorcycles, and tanks.[5] Over 100 million bicycles were produced that year, outnumbering cars three to one. With about 5.6 billion people in the world, there is one bicycle for every sixth person.

Bicycles are used throughout the world for transport (70 percent), recreation (29 percent), and competition (one percent). Adult cyclists outnumber children (under sixteen) by about two to one, and while estimates vary, women ride bicycles as often as men.

The majority of the world's bicycles are made and used in Asia, where human-powered vehicles "transport more people than do all of the world's autos."[6] The industries of China, India, Taiwan, Japan, and Thailand produce over 75 percent of the world's bicycles. In China, known as the "Kingdom of the Bicycle," 1987 bicycle production outnumbered total worldwide automobile production. Bicycling is the primary means of land transport, other than walking, and traffic controllers see an average of 10,000 cyclists per hour pass the busiest urban intersections. In the city of Tianjin, with over four million people, they count up to 50,000 cyclists per hour.[7]

In Asia, non-motorized, human-powered vehicles have a huge role serving as load-carrying light trucks and passenger-carrying taxis. Called "paratransit," these include cycle rickshaws, trishaws, pedicabs, palanquin, and becaks. In Bangladesh, pedal-powered trishaws move more heavy goods than all the motor vehicles combined. In the capital of Dhaka, rickshaws account for half of all passenger trips in the city, employing some 140,000 people.

Despite the economic value of human-powered vehicles, several local governments have tried to phase out non-motorized vehicles in attempts to reduce traffic congestion and stimulate motor vehicle use. When the city of Jakarta, Indonesia, dumped about 100,000 becaks into the Java Sea, advocates of non-motorized transport from around the world formed solidarity movements, including protests at the United Nations in New York.

In Japan, every other person owns a bicycle and the 1980 census counted some 7.2 million bicyclists who rode to work, or to commuter rail stations, making fifteen percent of total trips. To reduce the clutter of bicycles parked at stations, called "bicycle pollution," legislation required railways to supply ample bicycle parking. By 1989, there were 8,600 official and private parking sites, with dozens of multi-story automated bicycle parking structures.[8]

Recreational cycling in Japan has grown with the development of bicycling vacation resorts. Japan has a special kind of parimutuel bicycle track racing, called *Kei-rin*, with more events and competitors than in European cycle racing. In the 1978–79 season there were some 36,000 races watched by 37.5 million fans who wagered about $5.5 billion in bets. The money is distributed to the bettors (75 percent), to public welfare (fifteen percent), and to maintain the sport (ten percent).[9]

Western Europeans are the biggest bicycle users in the industrial nations. Communities in the Netherlands, Denmark, and Germany are called "bicycle friendly" because of their balanced use of bicycles for transport, recreation, and sport. Cycling facilities such as bike lanes and parking sites, along with traffic calming and intermodal transit links, have encouraged people to use bicycles for 20 to 50 percent of all urban trips.

As the birthplace of the bicycle, Europe has an abundant bicycle culture in the arts, in industry, in recreation, and in cycle racing. The European sport produces the world's most physically fit professional athletes, and the Tour de France ranks as the world's largest annual sporting event, in terms of budget, duration, and worldwide spectators. The globalization of Le Tour in the late 1980s was reflected by its first American winner, Greg LeMond, whose name is most likely derived from the French *le monde*, meaning "the world."

In the United States, which some call the "Kingdom of the Automobile," and where a gallon of gasoline costs less than a gallon of bottled water, bicycles have been used more for recreation. In 1992, there were about 100 million cyclists, with more females (55 percent) cycling than males, and more adults (55 percent) cycling than children. About 31 million people rode at least once a week, and 4.3 million were regular bike commuters. Recreational riding was the most popular way of using the bike (about 70 percent), with four million participants in cycling events, and 250,000 cyclists (0.3 percent) involved in competive cycling.[10] Since the 1970s, the majority of the world's international bicycle tourists have come from North America.

In Africa and Latin America, the bicycle hangs in the balance of rich, poor, and middle class. In Mozambique, people with bikes are said to have *jinga*, a way of "moving in style." In Mexico, the name *Pueblo bicicletero* ("bicycle village") refers to small, impoverished, backward towns where bicycling is still the main means of transport. Several regions of Africa and Latin America have heavy bicycle use, but in general, governments tend to stigmatize bicycles as an undeveloped "Third World" means of mobility. While many leaders enjoy the prestige of cars and new highways, they do so on the backs of their people, who often rely on walking instead of cycling for essential transport.

Brazil and Mexico have prosperous bicycle industries, and Nicaragua and Cuba have growing bike industries. Competitive cycling ranks as the second most popular sport in Latin America and Colombian cyclists are national heroes who have globalized the Tour de France.

The former Soviet Union and Eastern European countries, have a great variety of bicycle uses. In cities such as Moscow, where public mass transit is widely used and the number of motor vehicles for private use has traditionally been limited, bicycles are rare—the mayor once described

The Tour de L'Ile in Montreal is the world's largest annual bike ride, with 40,000 cyclists.

cycling as "good way to commit suicide."[11] In smaller cities, such as in Hungary, bicycles are used for roughly half of all trips to work. With the fall of the Berlin Wall and the centralized Communist Party, and with rising economic and environmental problems, it remains to be seen whether Eurasian countries restructure with the bicycle in mind.

Russia and Poland have substantial bicycle industries, and bicycle races such as the Peace Race (Prague-Warsaw-Berlin) produced athletes that consistently dominated international amateur cycling until the late 1980s, when many integrated with Western European professionals. Various kinds of indoor cycling activities developed in Eastern Europe, such as Cycle Ball, Artistic Cycling, and circus cycling.

Throughout the world, bicycles offer people a means of self-empowerment. As transport, human-powered vehicles are clean, quiet, healthy, safe, quick, economical, space-saving, and self-sufficient. When compared to automobiles, bicycles represent the most logical, sustainable means of daily travel. With growing issues such as over-population, land-use, economic viability, energy efficiency, and environmental degradation, the bicycle enters the twenty-first century as the vehicle for the future.

COST OF BICYCLES

The relative cost of a bicycle varies throughout the world. While bicycles are used mostly for transport, in many countries they are classified and sold with sporting goods. And while many view bicycles as a vehicle for poor people, import duties are often levied on bikes as luxury items.

About 80 percent of the world's people can afford a bicycle, while only ten percent can afford a car. China produces the most bicycles, yet for the average worker in China's bicycle industry, the cost of a typical adult roadster ($50 to $75) represents about two and a half months of pay.[12] In India, where one in 12.5 people own a bicycle, the price ($60) is equivalent to one month's wages. In the Soviet Union in 1985, a simple bicycle cost about half a month's wages, with imported sports models three times higher. In North America, the cost of a typical adult bicycle ($300) amounts to less than a week's worth of average pay, while the cost of buying and maintaining a typical automobile consumes over two months of the average income.[13]

Child with bike wheel, United Arab Emirates, by Mathias Oppersdorff.

BICYCLES AND AUTOMOBILES IN SELECTED COUNTRIES, 1985–1988[14]

COUNTRY	BICYCLES (MILLIONS)	AUTOS (MILLIONS)	BIKES PER AUTO	BIKES PER PERSON
China	300.0	1.2	250.0	0.27
United States	103.0	139.0	0.7	0.42
Japan	60.0	30.7	2.0	0.49
India	45.0	1.5	30.0	0.06
West Germany	45.0	26.0	1.7	0.74
Mexico	12.0	4.8	2.5	0.16
Holland	11.0	4.9	2.2	0.79
Australia	6.8	7.1	0.9	0.42
South Korea	6.0	0.3	20.0	0.15
Argentina	4.5	3.4	1.3	0.16
Egypt	1.5	0.5	3.0	0.03
Tanzania	0.5	0.5	1.0	0.02

BIKE AND AUTO PRODUCTION IN SELECTED COUNTRIES IN MILLIONS[15]

COUNTRY	1986-87 BICYCLES	1986-87 AUTOS	1991 BICYCLES
China	41.0	0.004	36.0
Taiwan	9.9	0.20	7.7
Japan	7.8	7.89	7.8
United States	5.8	7.10	7.6
Soviet Union	5.4	1.33	
India	5.4	0.15	7.7
France	4.5		
West Germany	2.9	4.37	4.9
South Korea	2.6	0.79	1.5
Brazil	2.5	0.68	2.3
Indonesia	1.0		2.0
Italy	1.6	1.71	
Poland	1.3	0.30	
United Kingdom	1.2	1.14	1.1
Canada	1.2	0.81	
Thailand	0.7		1.0
Others	10.5	6.54	
World Total	99.0	33.01	100.5

CARGO CYCLES AND PEDICABS WORLDWIDE, 1988[16]

COUNTRY	ESTIMATED NUMBER
India	1,700,000
China	750,000
Bangladesh	700,000
Indonesia	300,000
Vietnam	150,000
Colombia	100,000
Chile	100,000
Burma	60,000
Laos	50,000
Nepal	50,000
Europe	20,000
Thailand	15,000
Philippines	15,000
Malaysia	10,000
Pakistan	10,000
Argentina	10,000
Brazil	10,000
Mexico	10,000
North America	10,000
Dominican Republic	10,000
Kampuchia	5,000
Pakistan	5,000
Japan	5,000
Korea	5,000
TOTAL	**+4,200,000**

WORLD BICYCLE AND AUTOMOBILE PRODUCTION IN MILLIONS, 1950–1994[17]

YEAR	BIKES	AUTOS
1950	11	8
1951	12	7
1952	12	6
1953	13	8
1954	14	8
1955	15	11
1956	16	9
1957	17	10
1958	18	9
1959	19	11
1960	20	13
1961	20	11
1962	20	14
1963	20	16
1964	21	17
1965	21	19
1966	22	19
1967	23	19
1968	24	22
1969	25	23
1970	36	22
1971	39	26
1972	46	28
1973	52	30
1974	52	26
1975	43	25
1976	47	29
1977	49	30
1978	51	31
1979	54	31
1980	62	29
1981	65	28
1982	69	27
1983	74	30
1984	76	30
1985	79	32
1986	84	33
1987	98	33
1988	105	34
1989	95	36
1990	95	36
1991	95	35
1992	100	35
1993	100	35
1994	100	35
TOTAL	**2,129**	**1,016**

PERCENT OF DAILY TRIPS BY CYCLING
IN SELECTED CITIES, 1989[18]

CITY	PERCENT OF DAILY TRIPS
Tianjin, China	77[a]
Shenyang, China	65
Groningen, Netherlands	50
Beijing, China	48
Delft, Netherlands	43
Dhaka, Bangladesh	40[b]
Erlangen, Germany	26
Odense, Denmark	25
Tokyo, Japan	25[c]
Moscow, Russia	24[c]
Delhi, India	22
Copenhagen, Denmark	20
Basel, Switzerland	20
Hannover, Germany	14
Manhattan, U.S.	8[d]
Perth, Australia	6
Toronto, Canada	3[d]
London, England	2
Sydney, Australia	1

[a) non-walking trips; b) trips by cycle rickshaw
c) cycling or walking to work; d) vehicle trips]

COST OF BICYCLES IN SELECTED CITIES, 1985–1992

CITY, COUNTRY	CURRENCY	COST OF BIKE	DAYS WAGES
Havana, Cuba	Peso	65–150	3–12 days
Copenhagen, Denmark	Kroner	2,000	10 days
Estonia	EEK	800–2600	90–275 days
Ethiopia	Dollar	390	1,100 days
Guangzhou, China	Yuan	1000	60 days
Amsterdam, Holland	Guilder	200–6,000	2–30 days
Shanghai, China	Yuan	200–400	30–60 days
Tianjin, China	Rmby	300–600	30–60 days
London, England	Pound	150–3,000	2–30 days
Chicago, U.S.	Dollar	150–4,000	2–30 days
Zanzibar, Tanzania	Shilling	15,000–20,000	350 days
Zambia, Kasama	Dollar	160–180	110 days

9 Transport

As part of our transport revolution is it not time we stopped riding our bikes and began to drive them? Similarly, who ever drove a car? They ride them! Words matter.
　　—Andrew Shrimpton, *Bike Culture Quarterly* (1993)

Developing Roadways

Roads are the veins and arteries of civilization, as pathways for social contact, trade and commerce, tourism and adventure, religious pilgrimages, and military conquest. Oceans and waterways supplied much of the long distance transport needs in the development of civilization, and the foundations of land routes were laid by empire-building Chinese, Ottomans, and Romans. Land transport remained virtually unchanged before the nineteenth century as roads were intended for walking, horseback riding, and animal-drawn wheeled carriages. Settlement patterns were based on the "walking city" as people lived close to their markets and workplaces.

In the pre-industrial period, French roads of gravel and cobblestone were considered the finest. The founding of the École des Ponts et Chaussées in 1747 trained civil engineers in road building, and the establishment of a law in 1836 required local governments to maintain roads through taxation. In England, John McAdam and Thomas Telford developed roads with more level grades and smoother, tougher tar and gravel surfaces, known as macadam. There was a brief "highway renaissance," but this slowed with the development of steam locomotives around 1840. In the U.S., the eastern states were linked by private and public turnpikes, such as the Boston Post Road from Massachusetts to Georgia, and the National Pike over the Appalachian mountains. Western territories were reached by various trails, such as the Santa Fe Trail, the Oregon Trail, the Mormon Trail, and the gold-rush crowded California Trail. Railroads became the first modern means for transporting people and freight on land over long distances. Carriage and stagecoach use declined as railroad companies in England and America acted to stifle further development of roadways.

Swift-walkers and velocipedes offered the first individual means of wheeled mobility, but they had difficulty gaining ground on sidewalks, bridlepaths, carriage routes, toll roads, railroads, and forest trails. Velocipedes were outlawed in many areas, particularly in cities where horse-drawn railcars were popular. Modern roadways took shape with the further development and use of mechanically-driven bicycles in the late 1870s, followed by electric trolley systems in the 1880s. Eventually, the motorcycles and automobiles of the 1900s fostered the growth of highways and exclusive "freeways," which transformed the landscape and living patterns of many people.

High-wheelers and tricyclists had discovered the fastest means of individual mobility. At first, they had to overcome jealousy, prejudice, and poor road conditions. Cyclists battled with carriage drivers and toll gate keepers for their right to roadways, which were often not in the public domain.

The condition of rural and urban roads brought tales of adventure, hardship, and anecdotal whimsy. A wonderful description of English high-wheel cycling is told in Andrew Ritchie's *King of the Road* (1975):

> The loneliness of those roads is past all belief to those who never cycled over them and only know the whirl of traffic that congests the highways today. Perfect quiet reigned out in the country, miles would be covered without meeting a vehicle, and those that *were* met were mostly farmer's wagons slowly drawn by heavy horses.... On these early runs they were really exploring, they were adventuring into what was to them the absolutely unknown. Every bend in the road was full of pleasant speculation as to what was round the corner; the uncertainty as to the state of the roads and certainty of some riders having headers made each run an adventure.
>
> The surface was sometimes macadam, nearly always so in larger towns, whilst in the southern counties, it was either sandy gravel or chalk. In summer every road became very dusty if a wind blew, and if the dry weather was at all prolonged the sand roads became terribly loose and cut up.... In wet weather, the macadam, and to a lesser degree, the chalk, became very slippery and accounted for many croppers, whilst the sand would be lifted up by the splash of the water into pedal and other bearings; any chain-driven machine suffered intensely, the block chains simply sucking in the grit until they became so gorged with it they were literally incapable of bending and were little short of bars of solid metal.[1]

In America, road conditions inspired a folktale that first applied to horse-back travel, and was retold after high-wheelers arrived in the late 1870s:

> A cyclist riding in a rural district once came upon a large mudhole in the road where another wayfarer was stuck in the mire right up to his neck. When the cyclist asked the stranger if he could be of some assistance, the wayfarer refused, saying that he was perfectly safe since he was mounted on the seat of his high-wheel bicycle.

Another report came from Karl Kron in his book *Ten Thousand Miles on a Bicycle* (1887). During a ride from Michigan to Virginia in 1883, he claimed that 60 miles was the longest he could ride a high-wheeler without dismounting due to poor conditions. Rudyard Kipling described New York's streets in the magazine *Outing* (1892) as "first cousins to a Zanzibar foreshore," with "gullies, holes, ruts, cobblestones awry, kerbstones rising from two to six inches above the level of the pavement; tram lines from two to three inches above the street level; building materials scattered half across the street; lime, boards, cut stone, and ash barrels generally and generously everywhere."[2] Thus, the condition of roads could be summed up in rhyme:

Wholly unclassable
Almost impassable
Scarcely jackassable![3]

Bicyclists had a major impact on the development of modern roads because they required better roads than horse-drawn carriages. Beginning in the 1880s, bicycle manufacturers, clubs, and periodicals in England, Europe, and America organized and agitated for improved roads. Two groups in England, the Cyclists' Touring Club and the National Cyclists' Union, formed the Roads Improvement Union in 1886 and published the influential booklet *Roads, Their Construction and Maintenance*.

   Cycling machines revolutionized the idea of personal transport by bringing the open road within reach of thousands of people. The use of bicycles in England caused what may be the first migrations of people from city centers to suburban towns. *Bicycling News* reported this phenomena as early as 1878: "To working men it is an incalculable boon, for it enables them to live further away from their work, and to substitute for themselves and their families a cheap and healthy home at a moderate distance from their town for the expensive insalubrity of the urban rookery. The social importance of this benefit can hardly be overestimated."[4]

   In the U.S., the bicyclists' desire for improved roads had great success as it coincided with farmers' discontent with the railroad monopolies that didn't provide suitable farm-to-market routes. The League of American Wheelmen (LAW) was founded at a Memorial Day meeting of over 150 cyclists on May 31, 1880, in Newport, Rhode Island. Charles E. Pratt, a patent lawyer, public official, and bicycle writer, was elected its first president, and C. Kirk Monroe, editor of *Harper's Young People*, was named first commander. The League's charter stated it was founded "to promote the general interests of bicycling; to ascertain, defend and protect the rights of Wheelmen; and to encourage and facilitate touring."[5]

Taking a header in a sinkhole.

Pioneers of American cycling on the Wheel Around the Hub ride in Boston, September 1879. Left to right: Charles Pratt, Albert Pope, L.H. Johnson, Josiah Dean, Geoffrey Fairfield. Photo by Walter Kendall.

The first task was to repeal a series of regional bans against bicycling. A successful test case occurred in 1880 against the Haddenfield Turnpike in New Jersey. A major victory was the drafting and the passage of the New York State Liberty Bill of 1887, which opened public roads and parkways to bicyclists. This was followed by the formation of a Committee on the Improvement of Public Highways in 1888, and the circulation of a pamphlet called "The Gospel of Good Roads" which showed the contrasting condition of roads in Europe with those in America, and preached the "Good Roads Sermon," advocating the economic benefits of road building. One version of the "Good Road Sermon" appeared in the St. Augustine, Florida *News* (1896):

> Do you know a Good Road Sermon when you hear it? If you do, here is one in a nutshell. On the poorest of earth roads, not muddy, but sandy, a horse can drag twice as much as he can carry on his back; on a fair road, three and a half times as much; on a good macadamized road, nine times as much; on a smooth plank road, twenty-five times as much; on a stone trackway, thirty-five times as much, and on metal rails, fifty-four times as much. Those who use roads can therefore make money by improving the roads rather than buying new horses every year.
>
> Yes, and further, if you have sandy roads, you may possibly get one new settler per year; if you have fair roads, two; good smooth stone or shell, fifty or more! One little city in this state has recently completed miles of beautiful roads about the city, and the number of ten-thousand-dollar homes going up in that town this year is amazing. Good roads work all around, and for the benefit of all.[6]

The number of cyclists in America grew from 100 in 1878, to about 50,000 in 1889, to over five million in 1898, mainly because more women were riding bicycles. The largest bicycle makers, such as Albert A. Pope and A.H. Overman, helped support the good roads movement as it became a national political issue in the 1890s. Manufacturers financed most of the early bicycle periodicals through the national and regional chapters of LAW, which published the monthly *Good Roads Magazine*. That publication later combined with the *LAW Bulletin*, and was called the *LAW Bulletin and Good Roads*, with the motto: "The Road is a creation of man and a type of civilized society."

Good Roads was published for ten years, with a photography contest of "stuck in the mud" pictures, and directions for making stencil kits with official LAW road markers for cycling routes, the forerunners of modern road signs. The editor, Sterling Elliot, once remarked: "It was the wheelmen who started the good roads movement, for the reason that the carriage makers didn't know about it. The horses knew about it, but couldn't talk."[7]

As the bicycling lobby grew, Pope and Overman used their political and economic clout to help LAW petition Congress to form the

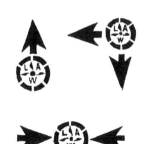

LAW road signs.

Department of Agriculture's Office of Road Inquiry in 1893, which eventually became the Office of Public Roads. Meanwhile, LAW supported the founding of the National League for Good Roads by General Roy Stone, and a course at the Massachusetts Institute of Technology in road building techniques for civil engineers. In 1894, *Harper's Weekly* reported that 90 percent of the nation's highway advocates and builders belonged to LAW. It was the bicycle equivalent of the American Automobile Association (AAA).

New Jersey was the first state to pass a law requiring the state and counties to pay ninety percent of road building costs if two-thirds of the landowners wanted a road. By 1892, voters agreed to spend $20 million for road building, and the result was an increase in rural property values and a hastening of postal deliveries. It helped reduce what Albert Pope called the "billion dollar a year tribute to mud."

The good roads movement brought the development of modern road maps. As bicycle touring became popular, members of regional LAW chapters drew up and distributed maps illustrating favorable routes, road conditions, and safety tips. These were published in touring guide books and in bicycling supplements of local newspapers. Cyclists were also responsible for correcting errors in direction and distance on signposts and milestones, by means of their cyclometers.

Cyclists' parade in Washington, D.C.

LAW MEMBERSHIP, 1880-1898

1880	44
1881	104
1882	179
1883	390
1884	558
1885	774
1886	1,206
1887	1,528
1888	1,888
1889	2,482
1890	3,560
1891	4,827
1892	6,997
1893	9,416
1894	11,915
1895	24,724
1896	66,522
1897	121,267
1898	141,532

In 1898, LAW's membership reached its all-time peak at 141,532. Cycling became an overwhelming fad in big cities of America, Europe, and England for "princesses and commoners" alike. The American bicycle market was fully saturated and controlled by powerful industrialists who were taking a new interest in motor vehicles. Automobiles had just begun to appear, and although it would be several years before their widespread use, General Roy Stone proposed a "Grand Highway" to run across the U.S. linking the two north-south routes, the Boston Post Road on the Atlantic coast, and El Camino Real (The King's Highway) on the Pacific.

Thus, LAW's good roads movement helped lay the foundation for the automobile age, with the development of interstate highways and the transformation of landscapes and lifestyles. But, unlike the automobile, which shaped the landscape to its needs and then kept drivers and passengers from experiencing it, the bicycle encourages enjoyment of nature. As J.B. Jackson, founder of the journal *Landscape,* said:

[The bicycle] stood for independent locomotion, movement through a world which most urban Americans had hitherto seen only through the windows of a streetcar or train, or on foot. Free locomotion became an attribute of the individual. It offered, in short, an individual, unstructured experience of the environment, combined with healthy exercise and a very mild exhilaration from rapid motion.

The bicycle had, and still has, a humane, almost classical moderation in the kind of pleasure it offers. It is the kind of machine that a Hellenistic Greek might have invented and ridden. It does no violence to our normal reactions: it does not pretend to free us from our normal servitudes to the environment, steep slopes, rough or treacherous surfaces have to be avoided; weather still matters a great deal.[8]

Cycle Ways

The basic needs of cyclists—safe routes for riding and secure places for parking—are much easier to provide than are those for motor vehicles, which require more land for roads and parking, more taxes for infrastructure, and more costly resources for energy. Yet, there is often a catch-22 situation in developing cycling facilities. Planners often don't see the need for better cycling facilities. And without these already in place, there is less incentive for people to get into the cycling habit, especially when motor vehicles rule the way.

There are three basic types of roadways for cycling: mixed-traffic roads, bike lanes, and cycle paths. Transport planners have used various systems of bikeway classification. Most commonly, Class I bike routes are separate bike lanes or cycle paths, Class II routes are marked bike lanes on mixed-traffic roads, and Class III routes have posted route signs but no special lane other than the road shoulder. Other kinds of roadways for cycling include greenways, traffic-calming zones, auto-free streets, veloways, and railways. Appropriate facilities vary according to each region's landscape and the transport needs of the community. Each path has its own set of pros and cons, with strong feelings for and against it within the cycling community.

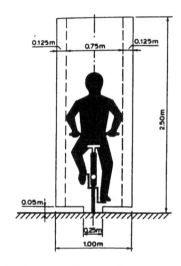

Designers' profile of cyclist.

MIXED-TRAFFIC ROADS

Mixed-traffic roads are all the highways, expressways, divided roads, city streets, suburban boulevards, country lanes, and bridges that combine cyclists with motor vehicles, with no special lane for cyclists. These are the most prevalent type of roads, constructed of gravel, cobblestone, macadam, asphalt, concrete, dirt, and recycled broken glass. Narrow margins for cyclists, rough pavement edges, potholes, sewage grates, railroad tracks, and roadside debris make safe cycling difficult.

Opinions vary about mixed-traffic roads. They are more dangerous for some cyclists, who feel squeezed between a lane of motor vehicle traffic and the edge of the road, where soft shoulders, parked cars, and road debris cause problems. Other cyclists believe mixed-traffic roads are the only place for cycling vehicles, that separate cycle paths push cyclists off the road, and that mixed-traffic roads can be calmed by bike traffic. Some demand the right to ride two or more abreast, taking just as much space as drivers and passengers in a car are allowed. Bern, the capital of Switzerland, has pioneered the integration of bike traffic with motor vehicles.

Most cyclists prefer not mixing with motor vehicles that are 10 to 50 times their size, 20 to 100 times their weight, move at two to seven times their speed, and make noise and pollutants. In certain situations, cars and trucks provide a few benefits for cyclists. Motor vehicles tend to clear a path in the road, as their wind helps pull cyclists like a paceline, and sweeps aside broken glass, sharp rocks, and thorns, which collect on the road shoulder and in bike lanes. By edging out into a clear lane of traffic,

and drafting with motor vehicles, cyclists are often able to maintain equal pace with traffic at speeds of 15 to 30 mph.

BIKE LANES

Bike lanes are separate marked lanes along mixed-traffic roads that are intended only for cycling. Most bike lanes use the same road bed as motor vehicle traffic, and are separated by a painted line in the road, about three to ten feet wide (one to three meters), along the side of the road going in each direction of traffic. Other kinds of bike lanes use raised curbs, metal fences, concrete barriers, divider strips of grass or plantings, and mixed paving surfaces to help separate cyclists from motor vehicles and pedestrians.

Bike lanes are the most economical means of giving cyclists their own share of the road. By providing a lane for human-powered vehicles, road safety is improved with minimal structural changes. To encourage cycling, some people feel that bike lanes should be mandatory for all major streets, avenues, expressways, and country roads. Reconfiguring roads for bike lanes may require a trade-off between lanes for driving and parking, with older, narrow roads posing the greatest problem, since buildings and property lines placed there often border directly the shoulder of the road. Poorly designed bike lanes often direct cyclists onto sidewalk space dedicated to pedestrians, or force cyclists into motor vehicle traffic when the lane is blocked. For these reasons, and because bike lanes can become congested with slow-moving cyclists, more experienced cyclists prefer bike lanes to be optional.

Below, overflowing bike lane in Denmark, 1985. Photo by Bo Hansen.

CYCLE PATHS

Cycle paths are roads or trails designed primarily for cyclists and other non-motorized traffic. They come in various forms, as side paths that follow mixed-traffic roads and highways, or paths that take their own route through towns, parks, along rivers and canal towpaths. They may be paved roads or unpaved trails, with or without pedestrian use. Many cycle paths have been converted from older secondary routes, abandoned railroad lines, fire trails, and bridle paths. Cycle paths usually offer the most pleasant surroundings for cycling, being separated from the risk, noise, and foul air of motor vehicle traffic. Compared to roads designed for motor vehicles, cycle paths require less space and maintenance. They enhance nearby property values and the public's regard for the landscape, as cycling brings people closer to their surrounding environment.

The problems with cycle paths include a lack of a well-defined separation for pedestrians, skaters, and cyclists, the hazards of people moving at different speeds, the accumulations of debris due to poor maintenance, and the degradation of wilderness trails due to poor management. Cycle paths are especially dangerous at crossings of mixed-traffic roads that lack adequate rights of way, warning signs, and smooth gradings. On long, narrow pedestrian-cycle paths on bridges, cyclists may be required to dismount and walk. Some think this is unrealistic and counterproductive, since a person walking a bike takes more space and time than a mounted rider. In many places, caution signs, speed limits, and path markings are disobeyed.

To survey and maintain cyclepaths in Berlin, inspectors ride with dictaphones and cameras. Cycleways in Berkshire, England, have automated detectors to count cyclists. On trails in Marin County, California, park rangers began using radar detectors in 1990 to catch mountain bikers breaking the fifteen mph speed limit.

Cycle paths show promise in developing countries because of their lower cost. In 1985, the government of Ghana began to realize that motorized transport was failing to meet the needs of moving people and goods, and with assistance from the World Bank and Intermediate Technology Transport they proposed to build low-cost rural roads for non-motorized vehicles, on the scale of cycle paths, but sufficient for an occasional truck or car. The road building costs were estimated at about $2,400 per kilometer, compared to $30,000 per kilometer for conventional roads, and $50,000 to $100,000 per kilometer for American-style highways.[9]

Veloways are an advanced form of cycle path, like freeways for cycling. They are non-stop expressways built specifically for bikes with multiple lanes for fast and slow cycling and overpasses or underpasses for crossing freeways and waterways. Many cycle paths approach the conditions of veloways for short segments, but few have been developed for distances over ten miles. The future of veloways looks promising, as transit planners and designers envision rail systems with human-powered trains. Other unique kinds of cyclepaths include the indoor bike path fea-

tured at the Sustainable Lifestyles design conference in Rotterdam in 1993, and the 50-mile London Ring Main tunnel used by Thames Water workers in 1992. Cycling in the traffic-free 2.5-meter illuminated tunnel, workers averaged speeds of 15 mph, faster than traffic on the road.

GREENWAYS

Greenways combine bike lanes and cycle paths in wide-ranging routes for urban, suburban, and rural areas. Combining the English greenbelt and the American parkway, greenways connect people with places by interlacing a region with scenic recreation and transport routes that pass through parks, residential neighborhoods, and industrial parks, along waterfronts, gardens, and schools. Greenways are a natural evolution for metropolitan areas, allowing people easy access to open spaces in their daily travel. Greenways are often mixed-use paths, populated by walkers, runners, skaters, children's strollers, equestrians, novice cyclists—good for scenic touring. Seattle's twelve-mile Burke-Gilman Trail is the busiest multi-use rail-trail in the U.S. Built in 1973, it has improved the quality of life along the route, where property values rose by six percent, and many experienced cyclists have "graduated from Burke-Gilman."

Greenway networks and international cycle paths are a growing trend. In the U.S., a 500-mile continuous linkage of greenway from Boston to Washington, D.C. and beyond was tested in 1992 by a coalition of cycling and walking groups, and in Europe, a 2,000-mile linkage of cycle paths in England, Holland, Germany, and Poland has been mapped.

TRAFFIC-CALMED STREETS

Traffic-calmed streets, called *Verkehrsberuhigung* in Germany, are designed to reduce speed and congestion in residential and urban areas by limiting the use of motor vehicles. They rearrange traffic in favor of non-motorized vehicles and pedestrians by using speed bumps, landscaped barriers, raised street crossings, and bollards, called *amsterdammers* in Amsterdam. The Dutch *woonerf*, or "residential yard," which originated in Delft, is a kind of street where precedence is given to children and adults who use the whole street as a courtyard. Textured pavement distingishes sidewalk from road, and planted trees and sculpture gardens serve as barriers, while parking lots are located in outlying areas. All traffic speed is limited to less than ten mph, making it unsuitable for fast cycling.

Auto-free streets further restrict motor vehicles, either entirely, or according to specific traffic schedules. They are used in city centers to improve pedestrian mobility and air quality, often evolving into busy market malls with limited cycling allowed. While some shopkeepers fear that auto-free means a loss of business, the problem is often of rising rents as auto-free becomes upscale. In residential neighborhoods, auto-free streets are used to encourage cycling by providing essential routes for the exclusive use of bicyclists. Since the 1980s, the cities Amsterdam, Vienna, Bordeaux, Florence, Singapore, Hong Kong, and Mexico City have installed auto-free zones to promote cycling.

NEW YORK AND LOS ANGELES—1890 TO 1990

New York City and Los Angeles are North America's largest metropolitan areas. With contrasting climates and landscapes they illustrate the evolution of cycle facilities from the Golden Age to the present.

Cyclists ruled the roads during the bicycle's heyday in the 1890s, but in cities they had to share the public ways with horse-drawn wagons, electric trolleys, an occasional horseless carriage, as well as pushcarts, wheel barrows, animals, and pedestrians. The many disputes prompted the idea of special cycle paths. In New York, the favorite cycling routes included Riverside Drive, which followed the Hudson River on Manhattan's upper west side, the Central Park loop roads, which officially permitted cycling after 1880, and the smooth, scenic roads on Staten Island, reachable by ferry boat. In Manhattan and Brooklyn, several fancy townhouses served as cycling club headquarters with indoor parking and gymnasiums for instruction and winter recreational cycling.

The first major bike path in America was Brooklyn's Coney Island cycle path, going from Grand Army Plaza through Prospect Park, along Ocean Parkway to the beachside boardwalk at Coney Island. Originally landscaped by Frederick Law Olmstead and Calvert Vaux, the path was 7½ miles long, fourteen feet wide, and made of crushed limestone. It opened on June 15, 1895, with a huge parade consisting of some 10,000 cyclists including political and social luminaries, 300 cycling militiamen, and three little girls pedaling "in white costumes with sashes that bore the proud name of the Brooklyn Good Roads Association."[10] The route was so popular that one month after opening, it was widened to seventeen feet and milestones were added. In the following seasons the path was made twice as wide and rebuilt with a firmer foundation. By 1920, the road was given over to motor vehicles.

Grandiose plans for Manhattan included an elevated cycle path to be built as an upper deck on the Ninth Avenue railway from Harlem (uptown) to the Battery (downtown), as well as a system of elevated roads and pedestrian walks that allowed cyclists full use of ground level streets.

First anniversary parade on the Ocean Parkway Bicycle Path, 1896.

Wilshire Boulevard, Los Angeles, 1918–1972, before and after the impact of the automobile.

At the turn of century, the Los Angeles area had over 30,000 bicyclists and several cycle paths, such as the beachfront route in Santa Monica. Then a proposal came to build the Pasadena Cycleway, a $187,500 elevated toll-road to go nine miles in a smooth grade from Pasadena to Highland Park, down the picturesque Arroyo Seco, following the Los Angeles Hills into the city of Los Angeles. Led by a company formed by Horace Dobbins, future mayor of Pasadena, and Henry H. Markham, former governor of California, construction began in March 1898.

A description of the cycleway appeared in *Scientific American* on July 14, 1900. The four-lane bike path was to have woven wire railings painted dark green, with the elevated riding surface made of 1.25 million feet of Oregon pine. Overhead incandescent lights placed at intervals of 200 feet were planned, with the terminal stations of Moorish design, one placed near the Green Hotel in the business district of Pasadena, and the other at the Plaza in Los Angeles. There would be facilities for renting bicycles and motorcycles, a repair shop, and a casino halfway along the route. The toll for the cycleway was ten cents per day. After two years and the completion of about 2½ miles, the Southern Pacific Railroad forced a court injunction to halt construction. Apparently, the railroad feared the cycleway would take away business from their Pasadena to L.A. line, which charged 25 cents to transport a bicycle.

In the following years, the North American transportation landscape was restructured to serve the needs of corporate shareholders instead of the common good of society. In the 1930s, a diversified holding company called National City Lines, controlled by General Motors, Standard Oil, Firestone Tire, and others, became involved in a successful, but illegal plan to buy, bankrupt, and dismantle America's independent intercity electric railways.[11] To stimulate the sale of more motors, oil, and tires, thriving electric trolley and train lines were replaced by poorly-run diesel bus services, causing many people to choose private cars, and pushing overland freight from rail trains to tractor trucks and highways. In L.A., a fertile valley was turned into highways, oil rigs, gas stations, and parking lots; in New York, major transport systems were shaped by power brokers and semi-private public authorities, such as Robert Moses' Triborough Bridge and Tunnel Authority, with little regard for the good of the public.

By 1990, New York and Los Angeles had to face the problems of a monolithic transport network dominated by motor vehicles. In Los Angeles, highway congestion has badly affected social relations, economic prosperity, air quality, and the ability to ride a bicycle. Although New York City has about 40 percent of the public transit service in the U.S. with electric subways and diesel buses, the highway and bridge infrastructure is crumbling as heavy trucks ply the streets because the city lacks rail freight service. Of New York's 38 major bridges and tunnels, 30 allow access for bikes, yet only a dozen are considered safe and pleasant enough for all but hardcore cyclists. Major crossings such as the Verrazano and Throgs Neck bridges were built without pedestrian-bicycle paths, and the Whitestone Bridge and Outerbridge Crossing had their non-motorized paths removed for more motor vehicles.

With the current renaissance of cycling, city planners have shown some interest in developing cycling facilities to help rehabilitate their transport situation. In 1990, an estimated 75,000 people cycled every day in New York City. Of a total 6,300 miles of streets and highways, only 111 miles are designated bike routes (a 56 to 1 ratio), including 45 miles of separate cycle paths, 50 miles of marked bike lanes, and 16 miles of routes with posted signs. In Manhattan, the ratio of lanes dedicated to motor vehicles, pedestrians, and cyclists is 111:33:3 for north-south routes, and about 1,000:300:0 for east-west routes.[12]

In 1974, the old Coney Island cycle path was reconstructed by converting the bridle path to a bike path that runs along Ocean Parkway. In 1987, it became part of a larger network called the Brooklyn-Queens Greenway, one of many "emerald necklaces" of accessible open spaces under development in the metropolitan area. Intended to link the Atlantic Ocean with the Long Island Sound, the 40-mile greenway passes through thirteen parks (including the Kissena velodrome) in the two most populated boroughs of New York City. Ocean Parkway is a six-lane boulevard with two landscaped medians and two frontage roads, for a total of eight motor vehicle lanes, four parking lanes, four pedestrian walks, and one bike lane for two-way traffic. On the path, cyclists must negotiate troublesome curb-cuts at each cross-street and heed motorheads who, in New York style, think they have the right to turn in front of cyclists and block the bike lane while waiting to cross the boulevard. Experienced cyclists choose the frontage roads with problems of parked cars, driveways, and gridlock.

Los Angeles is a sprawling megalopolis renowned for its freeway culture that inspired the saying, "You are what you drive." The region is the source of the best and worst cycling conditions, home to many recreational cyclists who often drive to their cycling sites. Although 40 percent of all commuting trips are estimated to be under five miles, bike commuters represent about one-third of one percent of the city's population. L.A. cyclists use nearly a hundred miles of cement-lined flood control channels as bike paths. These dry creek beds are, at best, comparable to veloways; but they are full of debris and criminal activity. Officially prohibited but informally allowed thanks to laissez-faire policy, the routes are a bureaucratic breakthrough for kids on BMX bikes and commuters on mountain bikes.

South Bay Bike Path, Los Angeles, 1990. Photo by Peter Meitzler.

A major bike project is the West Los Angeles Veloway, a multi-lane bicycle freeway to serve the University of California community. First envisioned in 1976, the project has been in the planning stage for many years, led by Ryan Snyder, a transport planner from Westwood. By 1986, some $132,000 had been spent by L.A. County, Caltrans, and UCLA in feasibility studies for the originally proposed $32 million, eight-mile elevated path to be used by about 6,000 cyclist per day.[13] After additional traffic studies and an environmental impact report, the veloway was scaled down to a four-lane, two-mile elevated path costing $7 million to

$10 million. The veloway would rise seventeen feet to span Wilshire Boulevard, Veteran Avenue, and Sepulveda Boulevard, with two additional segments to cross the San Diego Freeway, and several on-off ramps able to accommodate some 4,300 riders at any time. By contrast, it was estimated that building another parking garage for automobiles near the UCLA campus and the shopping area in Westwood would cost $30,000 per space, and serve less than one-tenth the people as the veloway.[14]

Los Angeles has taken the lead in the U.S. for air-quality initiatives that point toward the twenty-first century. The plan is to phase in low- and zero-emission vehicles (ZEVs) at a ten percent rate of about 300,000 cars, vans, and trucks by the year 2000. Another intiative by the South Coast Air Quality Management District (SCAQMD) requires companies with over 100 employees to offer incentives for bicycling, car pools, and transit use. Of the first 800 companies to be approved, 270 provided bike racks, 166 set up shower and locker rooms, 152 organized employee cycling clubs, and six supplied free loaner bikes.[15]

Bike messenger, New York City, 1898. Photo by Alice Austen.

Traffic

Traffic is the complex phenomena of people and things moving from point A to point B. A science of chaos and control, traffic is a manifestation of nature and civilization that affects people socially, economically, and personally.

A condition of traffic that works to the benefit of cyclists is the fleeting moment phenomena. When various vehicles or bodies are in continuous motion, when traffic is happening as it should, the roadway is empty for all but a small fraction of the time, with no two bodies taking the same space at the same moment. This open space enables cyclists, who take little room and can maneuver quickly, to "shoot the gap" by moving through other forms of traffic.

Unfortunately, traffic does not always happen as it should, with congestion and accidents as an inevitable consequence. For many years it seemed logical that more roads for motor vehicles would ease congestion, so traffic planners, government officials, and the highway lobby went on a road building spree. The result was more congestion. This is an example of Braess' paradox, also known as the "traffic paradox," a statistical theorem that came to light in 1968 with the work of Dr. Dietrich Braess of the Institute for Numerical and Applied Mathematics in Münster, Germany.

Dr. Braess found that when one street was added to a network of streets, all the vehicles took longer to get through. The reason traffic slows is that when drivers are in crowded conditions and a new street is opened, the opportunity inspires more drivers to crowd their way toward the open road, thus adding congestion. This is consistent with the principles of game theory: if everyone participating in a game plays selfishly, everyone loses.

In studying the traffic paradox, mathematicians have also found that it works the opposite way, that closing streets to traffic actually reduces congestion. When drivers realize an area has limited access, they tend to find a more suitable means of access, or avoid passing through it altogether. For these reasons, traffic calming and auto-free zones can reduce congestion, as well as air pollution, noise, and the costs related to motor vehicle accidents.

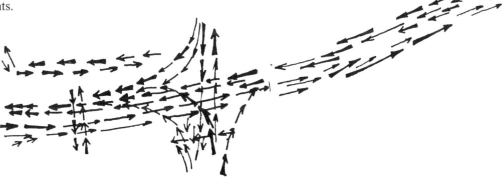

CYCLING SOLUTION

Bicycling is ideally suited for solving many environmental, economic, and psychological problems caused by motor vehicle traffic. Bicycles provide a better transport environment in terms of land use and air quality, they save time and money, and offer personal health and well-being.

The amount of land given to motor vehicles is astounding, almost half in typical American cities, 45 percent in New York, and 60 percent in Los Angeles, compared to 20 percent in London. Bicycles use land more efficiently than automobiles by moving more people in less space. Yet other forms of transport move even more people than bicycles, as shown in the following table:

ROAD CAPACITY BY MODE OF TRANSPORT
PEOPLE PER HOUR PER ONE METER WIDTH LANE[16]

MODE (AVERAGE MPH)	PEOPLE
Auto in mixed traffic (15)	120–220
Auto on freeway (45)	750
Bicycle (10)	1,500
Pedestrian (5)	3,600
Suburban Rail (30)	4,000
Bus in separate lane (25)	5,200
Urban Rail (25)	9,000

The perception that bikes are slow is often disproved in traffic. On open roads, bikes usually lag behind motor vehicles, but in city traffic, where motorists often average less than 10 mph, bikes can be the faster mode. Commuter races held in various cities around the world have proved this. By competing for the best time from Point A to Point B, bicyclists usually beat mass transit riders and motorists.

At the 1st Invitational Commuter Race held in San Fransico in 1971, three people raced six miles across town during the morning rush hour. The cyclist's time was 19:09, the streetcar rider placed second in 31:20, and the motorist finshed last at 31:58.[17] In a televised New York City race in 1991, from downtown Brooklyn to midtown Manhattan, a woman on a three-speed bike beat both the subway rider, and a motorist, who not only arrived much later (with plenty of excuses) but also had to spend additional time and money on a parking space. In a six-mile race in Brazil, the cyclist came first in 32 minutes, followed by a car (40 min.) and a bus (50 min.). In a 1½-mile taxi race in Amsterdam in 1994, a rickshaw beat a car by one minute and charged half the fare. When people time themselves on their own commuting routes, taking all the alternative modes (car, taxi, bus, train, running, skating, cycling, etc.), the results are one of the most encouraging aspects of bicycling.

Cycling is much less stressful for the body than driving in traffic. According to a University of California study, motorists in traffic have higher blood pressure, and they become easily frustrated, often displaying negative moods and more aggressive behavior. On the other hand, cyclists arrive at their destinations more alert, with less hypertension and a healthier cardio-vascular system.[18]

A surprising attribute of cycling is that a cyclist's bloodstream can accumulate less carbon monoxide than a motorist's. Studies reported separately by the U.S. Department of Transportation (1977) and the *British Medical Journal* (1979), measured levels of toxins for travelers on high-density roads. The DoT's study showed concentrations of pollution are higher in traffic than on the nearby roadside. Furthermore, despite receiving equal amounts pollution, levels of carbon monoxide in the cyclists' blood rose 1.7 percent, while it rose 2.1 percent for motorists. The reason is that a cyclist is actively inhaling, exhaling, and eliminating toxins. The DoT study involved ten men making commuter trips of 30 to 60 minutes over a 29-day period with eleven "pollution alert" days, when carbon monoxide levels reach over 60 parts per million (over 300 ppm can cause loss of consciousness).[19]

Accidents

Bicycle accidents have a variety of causes, all of which can result in serious injury. While many accidents are indeed random events, most accidents are caused by cyclists themselves, and most fatalities result from collisions with motor vehicles. Along with failures in manufactured bike parts, many accidents are a fault of "the system" in communities lacking serious cycling awareness or safe places on the road for cyclists. U.S. statistics show that about 50 percent of all accidents are caused by cyclists falling by themselves. About seventeen percent are caused by collisions with motor vehicles, sixteen percent are caused by collisions with other cyclists, eight percent by collisions with dogs, and nine percent by everything else. Among cycling facilities, separate bike paths are considered the most dangerous, followed by high-density mixed-traffic roads, and low-density roads.[20] The question remains whether this is because more cyclists use bike paths, or bike paths are poorly designed, or bike paths are simply not necessary.

Cyclists have many ways of describing their accidents. These include "the ground hitting the cyclist," from road hazards like loose gravel, wet leaves, slippery rail tracks, patches of ice, buckled pavement, and deep potholes. "Things which get in the way" include shrubs, trees, posts, railings, animals, pedestrians, other cyclists, parked cars, and their suddenly opened doors. "Things which hit cyclists" include many of the above, especially people driving motor vehicles recklessly. "Accidents waiting to happen" are inherent dangers found in various traffic situations, faulty bikes, and inept cyclists. Group rides can be especially dangerous, if cyclists are inexperienced and lack understanding, communication, or trust in one another. Experienced cyclists have a saying: "Let's not meet by accident."

ACCIDENT RATE PER MILE BY TYPE OF CYCLIST

CYCLIST	MILES PER ACCIDENT
Serious Mountain Biker	1,000
Child (1–16)	1,500
Young Adult (16–25)	2,000
Club Cyclist	10,000

"The Door Is Always Open"
by the San Francisco
Department of Public Art
CRITICAL MASS, 1992

Many experienced cyclists are able to travel thousands of miles for several years without a serious fall. They learn to avoid all possible hazards by knowing the capabilities of their vehicle and developing the habit of constant attention. Some cyclists claim to have acquired a sixth sense, or an ability to foresee and prepare for inevitable dangers, such as slippery surfaces or dangerous motorists. Other cyclists claim to be fearless of falling because they know the proper way of crashing.

Bicycle crashing is a popular subject for cyclists who debate about the use of helmets, pedal cleats, suspensions, and the correct ways of falling. Toe-clips and straps may seem dangerous to inexperienced bike riders, but most serious riders say they add to safety by keeping the feet from accidentally slipping from the pedals. According to theories of crashing, pedals with toe-clips and tight straps work like a seat belt by keeping the rider with the bike, while clipless pedals work like ski bindings by releasing the rider from the bike. Cycling physiologist Edmund Burke noted these differences in *Bicycling* (May 1991):

> Most riders seem to prefer the seat belt approach. The thinking is that your attachment to the bike will keep you from sliding or rolling as far, which will minimize abrasions. Other riders say you're better off tumbling away from the bike, where it's less likely you'll break bones and torque knees by becoming entangled with machinery.... The problem is that crashes happen so fast you can't control how you fall. Many cyclists will give you complex advice on how to do it right and protect yourself. This is baloney. When the moment comes, you're on the way down before you know what's happening.

Still, cycling experts speak of the art of crashing. Chris Carmichael, 1992 U.S. Olympic Team Coach, describes a "crash training" program, where cyclists begin practicing rolls and somersaults on mats and grass, and proceed to falling off slow-moving bikes on harder ground:

> Falling comes easy to all of us, but falling properly is an art. If you train yourself to avoid the natural impulse to stick your hand out, you have a chance to tuck your shoulder in and roll. The force of landing is spread rather than concentrated on one spot.

Bicycle spokesman Richard Ballantine sums it up:

> ...when I suddenly find myself flying through the air upside- down I am automatically loose, looking to tuck and roll when I hit. If you do not know how to fall, try to have someone with training—fighting experts, skydivers, skiers—give you pointers. I find that fast woods riding with an old trasho bike is useful.[21]

INJURIES AND FATALITIES

People in the U.S. have the mistaken perception that bike riding is more dangerous than car driving. Statistics show that less than two percent of all traffic deaths involve bicyclists, even though they comprise about five percent of traffic. Each year in the U.S., about 0.5 percent of all cyclists (550,000) are injured and treated in hospital emergency rooms. Two-thirds of those treated are under fourteen years of age. Less than four percent require further hospitalization. In 1991, 86 percent of all cyclist fatalities were male, although they are only 45 percent of all cyclists. Of all cyclists' fatalities, 96 percent involved collisions with motor vehicles.[22]

Since 1977, about 880 cyclists per year have been fatally injured—1980 was the highest (965), 1983 the lowest (830). Among all cyclist deaths, the percent of adults (21 and older) has recently increased. In 1977, about one in five cyclist deaths involved adults. This increased to over one in three in 1989, and by 1991 to over one in two. By comparison, about 7,000 pedestrians and 48,000 motorists are fatally injured in traffic accidents each year in the U.S., more than half of all accidental deaths by any means. Comparing the death rates is difficult because accident reports compiled by police or traffic officials often have discrepancies, and the definition of a road death varies from "at the scene of the accident" up to "within 30 days of the accident." In calculating which vehicles are safest by comparing traveling modes, deaths per population is incomplete information without considering deaths per vehicle, deaths per trip, and deaths per mile or kilometer.

Rules of the Road

If you can pick yourself up off the ground, you can pick up the art of cycling. For the untutored cyclist, obstacles and hazards are found in the road, on the bike, and from other kinds of travelers. Effective cycling is knowing how to handle these obstacles. Because cyclists are such a diverse assortment of people, not all see things the same way, and the methods of handling obstacles change from one cyclist to another.

John Forester's books, *Effective Cycling* (1993) and *Bicycle Transportation* (1984), provide instructions for safe cycling technique, with guidelines for organizing safety education programs in communities intended for individuals, bicycle education coordinators and transport planners. The Effective Cycling program is sponsored by the League of American Bicyclists (formerly LAW) and has many regional disciples. Forester is a pioneer in the U.S., having taught a University of California course, held in Palo Alto, for traffic planners and regional bicycle coordinators, called "Traffic Engineering for Bicycles."

John Forester, past president of the LAW and author of *Effective Cycling*.

Forester is a fourth-generation cyclist, the son of the English novelist C.S. Forester (*African Queen*) and a former president of LAW. Once described as "America's most militant bicyclist," he is a former resident of Palo Alto, the bicycle-friendly city which is my hometown.[23] As my cycling wings were developing, I remember seeing him riding in traffic on Middlefield Road, where bike lane signs told cyclists they *must* ride on the sidewalk, and he made them change it to *may*. He carried the burdens for me and my friends, young speedsters with unruly ways, as we often thought: "There's John Forester—let's make a good showing and slow down a bit for the stop light."

Forester introduced two controversial concepts about cycling, one that needs to be taught, the Vehicular Cycling Principle, and another that needs to be overcome, the Cyclist Inferiority Superstition. The Vehicular Cycling Principle is based on road sharing, with cyclists taking a lane of traffic and knowing how to handle themselves there. Promoting education of adult cyclists as well as children, it favors bicycle parking facilities rather than special bike lanes that marginalize cyclists, which brings on the Cyclist Inferiority Superstition.

According to Forester, this inferiority superstition is a widely-held opinion that cyclists are dangerous to themselves and to motorists. It is what forms American bicycle transport policy, and it is cured only by successful experience cycling in traffic.[24] In a "bicycling efficiency" test he devised which was based on legal and effective cycling techniques and scored on a scale of one to 100, Forester found that many serious and experienced riders scored 98–100, while the average Palo Alto cyclist scored 54, and Berkeley cyclists scored 83. His strident views frighten careful cyclists, who want separate bike lanes and cycle paths, and restrict daring and freewheeling cyclists who like to set their own rules. His influence is clear as many cycling Rules of the Road urge riders to merge with lanes of mixed-traffic.

TRAFFIC LAW

Throughout the world, vehicles drive on both sides of road. In most of Asia, continental Europe, and the Americas, people usually drive on the right; in Japan, Australia and Britain, they drive on the left.

Of all the traffic laws for cycling, two rules stand out as the most important and controversial. According to the *Uniform Vehicle Code* (1992): "Every person propelling a vehicle by human power or riding a bicycle shall have all of the rights and all of the duties applicable to the driver of any other vehicle, except as to those provisions which by their very nature can have no application." This law gives cyclists the rights and responsibilities to join most kinds of traffic just as any other vehicle. For some cyclists, it inspires freedom from tolls, stop signs, roadblocks, and unnecessary laws. Sadly, it provides no incentive for transport planners to provide facilities, such as building freeway bridges for motor vehicles, pedestrians, and cycles.

Another article of common law states: "Whenever a usable path for bicycles has been provided adjacent to a roadway, bicycle riders shall use only such path, and shall not use the roadway." Here the controversy lies in the key word "usable," because many cyclists prefer to choose for themselves whether a bike path is usable. The law often restricts cyclists from maneuvering outside paths that are dangerous, poorly maintained, or blocked by traffic, and allows traffic enforcers to ticket cyclists for doing so.

Licenses are usually required for cyclists in two ways: for the vehicle and for the person. Most regional authorities throughout the world require bike licenses. In the U.S., these are often issued by police or fire departments at a cost of about $2 to $6 for the life of the bike. When cyclists demand their right to the road, this often becomes an arguing point for motorists who are quick to ask: "Have you got a license?" While most motorists must take lessons and pass official tests to drive, this rarely applies for cyclists. One of the benefits of the Effective Cycling program is a certificate of graduation from a nationally recognized cycling course, useful in court. Since the late nineteenth century, authorities in Europe and Asia have required cyclists to be licensed, pay road taxes, or carry a permit for operating a bicycle. In China, permits are required for cycling, and children under twelve are often restricted from riding on the road. In most countries, licenses are required for racing cyclists, as well as for commercial cyclists making deliveries or carrying passengers.

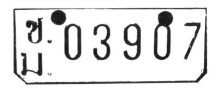

Bicycle licenses, top to bottom: Dutch bike, 1931–32; Indonesian pedicab; New York bike messenger; New York car.

I SHARE THE ROAD — BICYCLES BELONG

Ten little bike riders,
In a single line,
One swerved out to pass,
Now there are nine.

Nine little bike riders,
Not inclined to wait,
One ignored a stop sign,
Now there are eight.

Eight little bike riders,
Out until eleven,
One went without a light,
Now she's in heaven.

Seven little bike riders,
Cutting up for kicks,
One got too "fancy,"
Now there are six.

Six little bike riders,
Eager and alive,
One didn't signal,
Now there are five.

Five little bike riders,
Hurrying to the store,
One dashed out the driveway,
Now there are four.

Four little bike riders,
Carefree as could be,
One didn't check his brakes,
Now there are three.

Three little bike riders,
Distracted by the view,
One hit a parked truck,
Now there are two.

Two little bike riders,
Having lots of fun,
One rode against traffic,
Now there is one.

One little bike rider,
Who's still alive today,
By following the safety rules,
He hopes to stay that way.

CHILD SAFETY

Children are often unable to understand traffic, and they suffer the most bicycle accidents of all age groups. Half of all cyclist deaths are children under sixteen, and the highest death rate is among 10–16 year-olds. Most people learn how to ride a bike as children, and by steady progress they learn how to maintain a bike and maneuver in traffic. Many public and private agencies offer guidelines for bicycle safety programs, school education, and registration for children. Motor vehicles have a major role in bicycle education, as suggested by a slogan on a safety brochure by the Vermont State Police: "Today you are riding a bicycle, but soon you will be driving a car." *Time* magazine (1986) repeated the same message when writing about Greg LeMond: "In the U.S., cycling is what kids do after Santa Claus brings them a bike and before they get their driver's license."

Sprocketman was a super-hero of bicycle safety designed to teach kids the subtleties of cycling. Developed in 1978 by John E. Williams, editor of *Bicycle Forum*, with the Urban Bikeway Design Collaborative, Sprocketman was fashioned after Spiderman, and appeared in comic books, at bicycle rodeos, and on television. He showed kids how to look drivers in the eye, how to watch their shadow in the headlights of passing cars for safer night riding, and how to discern the "Twelve Hazards" facing cyclists. In the 1990s, the Teenage Mutant Ninja Turtles served as role models for child safety.

Teaching children bicycle safety through scare tactics has been popular in the United States. One discouraging set of safety tips, supplied to the New York State Governor's Traffic Safety Committee by the Outdoor Empire Publishing Company, illustrates the curious fate of "Ten Little Bike Riders:"[25]

RULES OF THE ROAD

Cycling's Rules of the Road depend upon various factors—whether one is learning or experienced, and whether one has a passive or assertive character on a bike. Just as traffic inspires both control and chaos, both passive and assertive cycling styles may be considered the right and wrong ways to ride.

PASSIVE RULES

Ride with traffic, not against it.
Obey all stop signs, stoplights, and traffic laws.
Signal all turns and use proper turning lanes.
Ride in a straight predictable line. Don't zigzag in and out of parked cars.
At busy intersections give everyone the right of way and walk the bicycle across the street.
Don't pass other vehicles in stopped traffic. Be patient and wait your turn.
Ride defensively. Be courteous and allow cars to pass or turn in front of you whenever possible.
Don't cycle two abreast when cars are present.
Never hold on to another vehicle to hitch a ride.
Carry only the number of passengers that the bike has seats for.

Keep both hands on the handlebars at all times.

When riding over wet metal surfaces, such as slippery railroad tracks or manhole covers, ride in a straight and smooth path, don't turn or pedal hard.

Never ride a bicycle that's in poor condition.

Carry a repair kit.

Don't make repairs while standing in the road.

Never ride with anything in your mouth.

Always wear a helmet.

Use a horn or bell, not a whistle.

When riding in darkness always use lights front and rear, and wear reflective clothing.

If you have a dispute with an irate motorist, calmly explain that you are obeying all the rules of the road which includes the right to share the road.

ASSERTIVE RULES
(USE AT YOUR OWN RISK)

Always remember that humanpower is more sacred than motorpower.

Look, listen, and premeditate. Use your sixth sense. Know where you and other vehicle drivers are going.

Ride in traffic when your speed matches that of motorists.

Ride two abreast if you can maintain a pace at the minimum speed limit. Pairs or small groups of cyclists should maneuver as a unit, separating only for obstacles.

Don't yield to honking motorists trying to exceed the speed limit.

Don't allow cars to pass and then turn in front of you. Watch their tires for quick turns. Speed up and force them to stop, or bang on their fender and roof to make them think they've hit you.

Obey stop signs and other traffic rules only when necessary for public safety, to prevent ticketing, or according to the customs of the road.

Use hand or body signals when changing lanes, turning, or swerving for obstacles.

For left turns, move into traffic lanes and signal when cars are present.

When traffic slows or stops, proceed through, passing on either side. Watch carefully for opening doors and quick turns.

Give plenty of clearance for opening doors of parked cars. Make eye contact with people in traffic.

Look into windows or rear view mirrors to know the actions of drivers or passengers.

When riding against the flow of traffic, try to yield to those with the right of way.

Pass cars on winding descents on the left side.

Practice your bike handling skills by riding on all types of surfaces, such as dirt, sand, gravel, wet leaves, etc.

Carry two forms of identification, your real ID for emergencies, false ID for police.

THE TWELVE HAZARDS:

1. Drivers making quick turns.
2. Potholes.
3. Loose ground.
4. Opening vehicle doors.
5. Careless pedestrians.
6. Fiesty animals.
7. Railroad tracks.
8. Big and fast vehicles.
9. Parallel sewer grates.
10. Careless cyclists.
11. Vehicles moving backward.
12. No bell or helmet.

Find the twelve hazards…

Bicycle Parking

Beside safe places to ride, the most important facilities for encouraging cycling are secure places to park where people live, work, play, shop, and use other kinds of transport. Bicycle parking comes in a variety of forms, both indoor and outdoor. There are automated bike parking towers in Japan, bike lockers in California offices, bike garages in European train stations, sign posts on the sidewalks of New York City, and trees found along cycle paths.

Adequate bicycle parking depends on the needs of the community. Where bicycling is encouraged, the first problem is how to accomodate hundreds or thousands of bicycles needing to be parked, secured, and easily accessed. Some cyclists have concerns about weather, others worry about vandalism and theft. There are places where bike locks are not needed, and places where the thieves are at your back and a complex strategy is required for safe outdoor parking.

The obstacles to adequate indoor bicycle parking are often legal and psychological, with fire codes and building managers defining bicycle access and parking as safety hazards or socially unacceptable. In North America, bicycle advocates have initiated the most developments in bicycle parking facilities. Two useful reports for understanding the variables in bicycle parking and choosing the right system are *Bicycle Parking* (Santa Clara Valley Bicycle Association, 1983) by Ellen Fletcher, and *A Comparative Study of Bicycle Parking Racks* (City of Ann Arbor, 1980) by Tom Pendelton. *Bicycle Parking* describes the cyclist's lot in a quote by Darryl Skrabak:

> Perhaps the greatest impediment to urban bicycle use is a dearth of secure bicycle parking and storage. A bicycle might provide ideal city transport, but it is no good if, at one's destination, the bike isn't welcome inside, but can't be left outside due to risk of theft. This unhappy situation is met nearly everyplace: the post office, libraries, shops, stores, shopping centers, museums, etc. These places might as well hang out "bicyclists unwelcome" signs.

A bicycle takes about fourteen square feet (1.3 sq. meters) to be parked in a rack on the ground, and 1,000 bicycles take up almost half an acre or 20,000 square feet, with extra space necessary for retrieving them. About twelve bicycles (or 3.33 tricycles) can fit in the same space as a parked car. In urban areas where cars are often given space on public roads or parking lots, a car parking space costs from $5,000 to $20,000, compared to $500 for a fully enclosed bicycle locker. Also, the high cost of car parking tends to be hidden in the U.S. economy, because many city and county building laws require large developments to provide free car parking, with the construction and maintenance costs being tax deductible for developers.

Unlike car parking, bike parking spaces can be flexible. In urban areas, bikes are often parked ad hoc against fence rails, street poles, "no parking" signs, parking meters, fire hydrants, garbage cans, mail boxes, gates, scaffolding, and young trees. Bicycle racks are often designed to double as public sculpture, but as Fletcher says, "Bicycle parking is more likely to be used if it looks like bicycle parking."

Outdoor bike racks provide the least security by attaching the bike to a stationary object. Such racks are useful for quick bicycle parking close to the rider's destination, as on sidewalks near shops, in apartment building lobbies, and in guarded parking garages. They take shape as ribbon racks, "dish racks" (or wheel-mounted racks), hitch posts with "O" rings, and metal railings attached to buildings. The Ribbon Rack, designed by Steven Levine and made by Brandir International, won a design award from the Industrial Designers Society of America, and illustrates the "less is more" design problem. The beautifully shaped rack has curving, modular metal pipes that provide space for five bicycles when attached at only one wheel. But when attached at both wheels, with the bikes lengthwise, they hold only two bikes.

John Dowlin, of the Bicycle Parking Foundation, installing a rack in Philadelphia. Photo by Elizabeth Perry.

Developments in Philadelphia show how cyclists can help solve their own parking problems. After attempts in the early 1970s by Ralph Hirsch and the Greater Philadelphia Bicycle Coalition to pass city legislation requiring buildings to provide bicycle access, and developers to include a reasonable amount of bicycle parking space based on occupancy, the Coalition was given thirty Ralley Racks to install throughout Philadelphia. The Coalition was surprised when racks were refused at the Penn Central railroad's 30th Street station, with the excuse, "If we put out bike racks, people will use them, and then when their bikes get stolen, we'll catch the flak."[26] In 1980, the Coalition received a foundation grant to purchase and install more bicycle racks. John Dowlin, of the Bicycle Network and editor of *Network News*, became the Coalition's bicycle parking coordinator. While considering parking sculpture in terms of "bicyclic still life," "urban realism," and "please park" configurations, they found a simple hitching post designed by David Rulon, a University of Pennsylvania architecture grad-student. The Bicycle Hitch-2 holds two bikes with both wheels and costs less than $100 with an optional chain. According to *A Comparative Study of Bicycle Parking Racks*, the Hitch-2 fits the most number of bicycles and locks, and was rated the least complicated and most preferred by the bicyclists surveyed.

Indoor parking racks, outdoor bicycle lockers, and check-in guarded security systems provide the most security. They protect the bike from theft, vandalism, and weather, and are useful for long-term parking, such as at home, at work, or in shops, theaters, museums, public centers, rail stations, and airports. Indoor parking racks include rows of upright "dish" wheel racks, metal hooks for hanging bikes by one wheel from the ceiling, and vertical wall racks for mounting several bikes, with the ability to lock both wheels and the frame.

Bicycle lockers are fully-enclosed locked parking modules that are only accessible to the person with the key. These mini-garages are about 2 x 1.5 x 1 meters in size with the bike positioned vertically, or horizontally, and can be placed outside near other parking sites. Some of the first bicycle lockers were developed by the Bike Commuters of the Environmental Protection Agency (BEPA), a cycling club formed in August 1975. Using federal funds, they were able to install 60 enclosed bicycle parking lockers and shower facilities at the EPA headquarters. The problem with bike lockers is their versatility as storage space. In downtown Oakland, dozens of bike lockers at the Bay Area Rapid Transit station served as shelter and storage for the possesions of homeless people.

Bicycle check-in systems allow the cyclist to leave their bike with an attendant who guards the bicycle in a secure place. They are usually found at rail stations and college campuses, sometimes using remote video systems, or key accessed gates, with a small fee charged by hourly, daily, monthly, or membership rates. In Long Beach, California, a full-service bike parking facility was built adjacent to public transit. With two employees, it has 130 enclosed, guarded parking spaces, and rental and

repair facilities.

Bicycle parking towers in Japan are the latest design in check-in systems. They are used to prevent what was called "bicycle pollution," when parking places at commuter rail stations became crowded with bikes. Since the 1970s, Japan has based its commuter transport system on railroads that link suburban household neighborhoods to urban business centers, with many people using bicycles to get from home to the train station. As the number of bicycles crowding around rail stations grew, in 1980, when Tokyo ranked second to Moscow worldwide in rail passenger trips per person, the government passed legislation and provided funds to build ample bicycle parking. Due to limited free space and city land that costs several thousand dollars per square foot, the Japanese found that by stacking their bicycles twenty abreast and 22 stories high, they could fit 440 bikes on a 750 square foot plot of land. About a dozen private companies built thousands of multi-level parking garages with automated check-in and storage facilities. By 1990, some 8,700 facilities were providing parking space for about 2.2 million bikes, with the capacity for 2.7 million bikes.

Mini skyscrapers containing only machinery, these parking towers have locking "dish" or platform racks for securing and moving bicycles within the building by automatic conveyor-elevator machinery. The cyclist rolls his or her bike into an empty rack and secures the handlebars to the conveyor arm. Using a key, or membership card that allows a computer to record the identity and time, the cyclist can watch the machine take the bike into the building, and retrieve it in less than a minute when there is no waiting line.

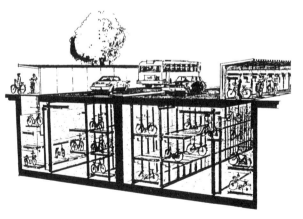

Intermodal Access

Whether people travel for work or play, when provisions are made for bicyclists to have access to trains, buses, trolleys, cars, planes, ferry boats, and ships, it enhances the usefulness of each traveling mode. The linkage of bicycles and pedicabs with public transit can widen the range of travelers and transport services, provide door-to-door convenience, and fill the gaps between the various places people go.

Michael Replogle, World Bank consultant and founder of the Institute for Transportation and Development Policy (ITDP), is a good resource on intermodal bicycle transport, having written many significant books and reports on the subject, including *Bicycles and Public Transport* (1984) and *Linking Bicycle/Pedestrian Facilities with Transit* (1992). In the latter he states: "As a strategy for holding down transit costs while boosting ridership, saving energy, reducing air pollution and traffic congestion, slowing global warming, and preparing for future oil-supply interruptions and cost escalation, the improvement of pedestrian and bicycle linkages to transit is among the most cost-effective approaches."

TRAINS

Bicycles interact with trains in a variety of ways, including bicycle feeder routes to train stations, access aboard trains, park-and-ride bicycle parking sites, and bicycle rental facilities. Throughout the world, most railway operators allow bike access aboard trains, either as luggage in special cargo cars or within the passenger cars. Most railways require bicycle permits or a special handling fee of $1 to $5. Some offer racks or straps for securing bikes, while others allow only folding or packaged bikes.

The potential for trains has been neglected in North America in favor of autos, buses, trucks, and above all planes, the busiest form of public transit. Most railways allow bikes, including the Bay Area Rapid Transit (BART), the Southern California Rail Authority, Canadian Public Railroad (STCUM), the Metropolitan Boston Transit Authority (MTBA, known as the "T"), the Metropolitan Atlanta Rapid Transit (MARTA), and the Washington, D.C., Metro inter-urban train. Beginning in 1962, the first modern inter-urban train to allow bicycle access was the PATH system, connecting New York and New Jersey via tunnels beneath the Hudson River. On PATH's larger companion, the New York City subway system (MTA), bikes are allowed aboard trains at off-peak hours. In 1992, CalTrain, which runs 77 miles along the San Francisco Peninsula, introduced a "California Car," designed to carry four bikes per car, twelve bikes per train (at off-peak hours), and two years later some 6,000 cyclists had CalTrain passes.

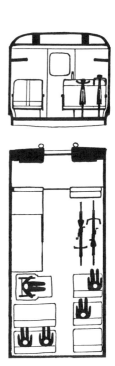

Park-and-ride systems, where cyclists park their bikes and ride a train, are in use throughout the world. Europeans use bicycles for ten to 55 percent of all trips to train stations, and Japanese usage has grown to 21 percent, while Americans use bikes for five to ten percent of commuter rail travel. Switzerland (40 percent) uses a combination of trolleys and trains

New York City subway. Photo by
Michael Spano, MTA.

and bike park-and-lock systems adjoining station platforms. The
Netherlands has seen the growth of suburbs with less dependence on cars.
On any given day, 35 to 50 percent of all access to rail stations is by bicycle, making it the dominant access mode. Throughout the Netherlands,
there are about 175,000 bicycle storage spaces with 70 percent occupancy.[27]

Some cyclists make a two-bike commute, using one bike on the home-
side ride, and the second for riding to and from the destination station. At
commuter rail stations in Silicon Valley, California, some 40 percent of
bicycle lockers are used for overnight parking, for mobility from the station to work and school.

Bicycle rental facilities at transport depots are useful for business and
recreational travel. Many bicycle rentals are available at bike shops and
parks, but with no way to get there travellers are more likely to rent bikes
at the train, plane, bus or boat depot. In Europe, most railroads operate
bicycle rental services. Some require the purchase of a ticket, or a deposit
on the bike. In Italy, bicycle clubs often operate such services. The
Deutsche Bundesbahn (German Federal Railroad) rented some 2,500
bicycles to 70,000 tourists in 1975, and by 1985 roughly five percent of
all passengers were using the service.

Access on trains is an important issue and bicycle activists have some
creative ways of making their point. In 1987, thirty members of the
London Cycling Campaign attempted to board a British Rail (BR) train
and invited the news media. Whole bikes were rejected by BR officials—
only folding bikes that fit in the overhead luggage carrier were allowed.
Bikes were packaged in brown bags and rejected. One bike was dismantled and the parts were attached to its owner who wore the rear rack like a
hat. Rejected. Finally, the cyclists were reduced to "folding" a bike using
a hacksaw to cut and bend it into a compact package, which was allowed.

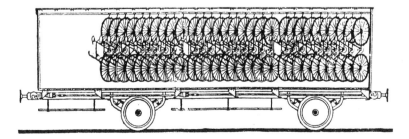

In Australia, a cyclist named Shelby Rightjake, from Duckmaloi, Victoria, offered his "Creative Solutions to Train Troubles" in *Australian Cyclist* (January 1990):

1. Make a bike that folds into a pram with a blow-up (inflatable) baby.
2. Travel in pairs, one takes the wheels and the other the frames. See, just new parts. Only don't sit together.
3. Wear extra large lycra shorts under a Scot's kilt, stretch the shorts over the bike before getting the ticket and pretend it's your bagpipes.
4. Bribe an adult with two accompanying children to take the bike because as an accompanied child, the third child is free.

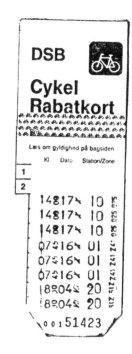

BUSES

Buses, trolleys, and passenger vans often carry bicycles, on front- and rear-mounted racks, trailers, roof racks, in storage bays, and the passenger compartment. Bike-carrying bus services are operating in many North American cities such as Montreal, Dallas, Phoenix, Tucson, San Diego, Los Angeles, Santa Barbara, Portland (Oregon), and Seattle.

Front-mounted racks with capacity for two bikes cost about $300 to $500, and can be watched by the bus driver. In Phoenix, after a test run in 1991 of 45 buses on three routes which attracted over 1,000 cyclists per month, the program was extended to all routes with some 350 municipal buses getting front-mounted racks. The racks were designed and built by Phoenix Transit, and bike loading takes about 60 to 90 seconds. In 1994, Seattle began to put front bike racks on all 1,200 of their buses. Rear-mounted racks, which allow up to six bicycles locked in a vertical position, are a bit more susceptible to damage or vandalism. When racks are not avaiable, bikes are often stored on the roof, as on motor homes.

For carrying more bikes, several transit systems use hitch trailers hitched to buses or vans. In San Diego, Caltrans used an eight bicycle bus trailer, built in the 1970s by David Eggleston of San Diego State University, on routes crossing the Coronado Bridge, which restricted access for cyclists. Before this service was implemented, the only way for bicyclists to cross the bay was to go about twenty miles out of their way.

The Santa Barbara Metropolitan Transit Authority also tried the Eggleston method, with trailers for fourteen bikes on an express route between the University of California campus and downtown. Dr. Eggleston said, "When I began work on this project, I thought that the engineering and construction of the trailer would be the most difficult problems in getting the system going. It turned out that the political and financial problems were much harder and took much longer to solve." It took eight months to change a law prohibiting trailers towed by buses. By 1981, using both racks and trailers, some 42,000 bus passengers traveled with bikes in Santa Barbara. Of those surveyed, 80 percent would not have taken the bus otherwise, and 30 percent would have used a car. The extra maintenance costs of providing this service amounted to about ten cents per bike.[28]

Germany offers the *Fahrradexpreß*, or "Bicycle Express" buses for tourists in several regions, including Wiesbaden, Bonn, Bremen, and Wuppertal. Using reconditioned buses with the back seats removed for storing bikes on hooks, the service runs on weekends and holidays, connecting various recreational bike routes in the country. In 1989, the Allgemeiner Deutscher Fahrrad Club (ADFC) offered a bus and trailer service that carried up to 42 cyclists to fifteen vacation sites in Germany.

PLANES

Most airlines in the U.S. carry full-sized bicycles as luggage for a fee only if they are contained in boxes or bags, and many airports are accessible only by bicycle-unfriendly freeways. As bike traveler Arlene Plevin says:

> Don't ask me why golf clubs, skis, huge boxes, and unwieldy suitcases that more closely resemble a piano fly for free and bikes do not. Don't ask me why as a cyclist flying with a well-packed bicycle, you have the privilege of paying $25 to $50 for taking your bike in one direction and sign away your right to claim damages.

While the policy of packaging bikes may prevent damage during shipping, thus limiting the carrier's liability, it presents an obvious inconvenience for the cyclist who wants to ride to and from the airport. When a box is available, usually for a fee, it requires tools and time to dismantle the bike. When the person reaches his or her destination, there is often no convenient way to store the box for the return trip, so another box is necessary.

Many types of bike crates, wheel boxes, and padded bags are available for people who travel regularly with bicycles. Approximately the size of two large suitcases, with casters for easy handling, these not only protect the bike, but they also provide extra room for packing tools, spare equipment, and clothes, often serving as a single piece of luggage. Most airline freight compartments are pressurized, so there is no need deflate tires except to prevent possible tire punctures.

The need for a shipping box is questionable. For many years European cycle racers and tourists have traveled by train or plane without bike boxes. They simply detach their wheels and pedals, strapping them with the handlebars to the frame, with axles placed in the front and rear forks to prevent damage. With care and padding, it is fairly rare that wheels are bent or frames scratched or dented. Many cyclists think the bicycle receives better handling when it is exposed.

In the last five years, airlines such as Delta and Continental have offered a special seasonal pass to members of U.S. Amateur, an affiliation of several sports federations. Since North American touring and racing cyclists are frequent flyers, the pass allows their bikes aboard free of charge.

BOATS

Ferry boats and ocean liners often provide the easiest mode of transport for bicycles. For a small fee, bikes can be wheeled into either passenger areas or large holding areas, some of which supply parking racks. On ships that transport motor vehicles, the only problem is the noxious fumes emitted from idling engines. On smaller boats, such as yachts and sailboats, folding bikes are especially useful for mobility on shore. On some large ships, bicycles are ridden on deck for maintenance and exercise.

CARS AND VANS

Cars and vans are probably the most popular mode of transport for the bikes of recreation and sporting cyclists. Bikes are carried inside the passenger compartment or the trunk, safe from the elements, either folded or with wheels detached. On the outside, bikes are mounted on hook racks fit to the rear bumper with straps and locks, or on roof racks, stacked flat and tied down for minimal wind resistance, or with the bike held upright on its wheels, or upside down held by the seat and handlebars. Roof racks used by racing teams are the most sophisticated, allowing several bikes to be carried upright, ready to ride, with additional forks for spare wheels. With the bikes subject to wind, sand, insects, pollution, and vandals, a variety of coverings and aerodynamic fairings have been developed for protection.

Transport Cycles

Since the development of carrier cycles in England in the 1870s, human power has been used by postal and newspaper deliverers, grocers, bakers, dairies, fishmongers, poulterers, butchers, confectioners, hosiers, milliners, chemists, and many other tradesmen. These cycles offered the cheapest method of distribution, often increased business efficiency, and gave employment and responsibility to neighborhood youngsters. In *At Your Service: A Look at Carrier Cycles* (1983), John Pinkerton describes the cycles as popular fixtures of street life. In 1939 alone, there were 4,000 Stop-Me-and-Buy-One ice cream tricycles in London.[29]

In America, the United Parcel Service started delivering letters and packages, in 1907, with six teenagers who used two bicycles.[30] With the rise of motor vehicles in industrial nations, carrier cycles were often replaced by motorized tricycles, vans, and light trucks, as was the case with Western Union messengers, who used bicycles until 1940. In rather quiet and innocuous ways, carrier cycles continue to be used in various business, factory, and industrial situations by maintenance engineers, electricians, supervisors, and safety inspectors carrying tools, spare parts, and paperwork.

Cargo cycles are currently used at hotels, airports, construction sites, breweries, oil refineries, auto factories, electric generating plants, aerospace manufacturers, and shipyards by companies such as Anheuser-Busch, International Paper, Exxon, Texaco, General Motors, Chrysler,

DOONESBURY

G.B. Trudeau, 1990,
Universal Press Syndicate.

Mexico City newspaper delivery.
Photo by Frans Stoppelman.

Martin-Marietta, and Boeing. On a grass-roots level, utility trikes are also handy at community parks, gardens, and waste recycling centers, such as the Village Green in New York City.

Able to transport loads of 200 to 750 pounds at an average speed of eight mph, cargo cycles increase the time and cost efficiency of individual workers by roughly 66 percent over walking, and can save more than $20,000 per vehicle per year compared to motor vehicles. Cargo cycles provide a healthful exercise for riders, and don't emit harmful quantities of carbon monoxide, hydrocarbons, sulphur dioxide, and particulates where people are working. For some situations, they have the advantage of being noiseless, vibrationless, and non-sparking.[31]

At the extensive Newport News shipyards near Norfolk, Virginia, human-powered vehicles have been used since the 1930s, with some 2,245 utility cycles in use in 1988. Moving people and things around the 2.2-mile waterfront site, they are quicker than trucks and reduce traffic congestion and the need for parking spaces. They are highly valued by workers, with one department frequently "borrowing" the wheels of another. As one foreman said, "They don't steal them, they misappropriate them. I could almost be a king with those bicycles. I could trade them for anything I want."

Human-powered utility vehicles are even more crucial in developing countries because they fill the gap between walking, which is time consuming and lacks load carrying capability, and motor vehicles, which can cost more than 30 times the average per capita income. As intermediate technology, pedal power enhances mobility with an informal, flexible, low-cost, energy-efficient means of transport. Sadly, many transport authorities in developing countries have often been concerned with motor vehicles and highway routes rather than supporting a more appropriate cycling infrastructure.

Load-carrying bicycles, tricycles, and trailers are utilized in many of the basic needs in life: in agriculture, for transporting tools, fertilizer, seeds, and produce; in domestic chores, for transporting water, fuel, and market goods; in health care, for transporting doctors, patients, and medical supplies; in business, for transporting letters, parcels, materials, and as mobile market stalls; and in education, for providing access to schools by teachers and pupils. Non-motorized vehicles can improve the world.

China shows the full capability of human-powered vehicles. They carry newlyweds' dowries, hat racks, bales of hay, stacks of furniture, live geese and ducks, refrigerators, television sets, piles of bricks, generators, tractors, cast-iron bathtubs, piles of foam rubber mattresses, scrap metal, used bottles, mounds of refuse, bouquets of retail bicycles, heaps of carcasses, flayed heads of cattle, bags of unbroken fresh eggs, and monkeys in cages. A personal account by a Chinese postal worker, Yang Yuliang, describes how "Postal Wheels Bring People Together:"

It seems postal workers never say goodbye to people. Day after day I ride my green bike down the same familiar streets and lanes, bringing a newspaper to Grandpa So-and-so and a letter to Aunt This-and-that. I'm 32 now. I came to work at Beijing's Xisi Post Office soon after I graduated from senior middle school and have been a postman for some ten years.

Delivering letters is a physical exercise involving many parts of the body. We pedal along with both legs, one hand holding the handlebar while the other draws out the next batch of letters. Our brains have to memorize the addresses of each family, while our mouths are busy calling out, "Letter for the Zhangs! Newspaper for the Wangs!"....

At 6:00 P.M. the rush-hour traffic is in full flow. By this time I've finished my last mail round, and my bicycle joins the stream of homeward-bound commuters. Riding along, I often think how much of the rest of my life will be spent on bikes. I pedal up and down the same places morning and afternoon, day after day. Sometimes I long for a change. But when I remember the comradeship of our team, the excitement when I bring a special letter that someone's waited for, I begin to like my job again. Society can't do without us. My bicycle wheels link thousands of families![32]

Above, blockprint of mail carrier in China. Below, cargo cycle dispatch center, Airborne Express in New York City. Photo by Bill Waltzer.

PEDICABS

Taxi driving is called the "second oldest profession," and pedicabs, or pedal-powered taxis, provide the major socio-economic benefits of affordable mobility, easy-to-learn employment, healthy exercise, pollution-free transport, and personable service. In Asia, these vehicles support millions of landless peasants and their dependents, supplying the largest portion of land transport in many cities and rural areas.

In Singapore, cycle rickshaws are an institution. Pedal-powered rickshaws replaced the man-drawn, runner-pulled vehicle in about 1880, and by 1900 there were 20,000 drivers with 9,000 vehicles. Through the years, millions of tourists have used the vehicles, including the actor Charlie Chaplin, who said, "I like its simplicity. It puts one at ease, it gives me a good ride and makes me relax after a day's hard work." In 1986, a government traffic official said, "Since it is part and parcel of our heritage and since it is still of use especially for the tourist trade, we will preserve it." In Calcutta, there are some 75,000 rickshaw drivers and the advocacy group Unnayan estimates that pedal-powered drivers earned nearly $300 per year, well above the average income.[33]

According to Rob Gallagher, author of the massive, compelling book *The Rickshaws of Bangladesh* (1992), there were about 700,000 rickshaws in Bangladesh carrying passengers and cargo in the late 1980s. These employed nearly one million drivers and 250,000 owners and mechanics (the latter known as *mysteris*). Five million people (4.5 percent of the population) depended on rickshaws for their subsistence, and rickshaws contributed 35 percent of the revenue from the transport sector to the economy (GNP), more than double the motorized sector. By the year 2000, the number of rickshaws in Bangladesh is expected to reach one million. In the capital of Dhaka, only 88,000 rickshaws were registered by the Dhaka Municipal Corporation, yet the true number was estimated at 150,000 to 200,000. They accounted for half of all vehicles, 70 percent of passenger trips, 43 percent of passenger miles, employing an estimated 400,000 people. Every day, about seven million passenger trips of eleven million miles were made by rickshaws in Dhaka. When Gallagher asked a friend how many rickshaws there were in Dhaka, he was told a story (which I've paraphrased here):

King: How many rickshaws are there in the country?
Advisor: Sir, I will tell you. If you do not believe me, you can always count them.
King: Fool! Off with your head if you give the wrong answer. Tell me at once!
Advisor: There are exactly 999,999. If you find less, then some have gone away. If you find more, then some are visiting.
King: Clever man, keep your head!

Handlebar decorations and hood ornament on Dhaka rickshaws.

Unfortunately, the bias against human-powered vehicles produced a major tragedy in Jakarta, Indonesia, when the city government limited the number of becaks (rickshaws) in the 1980s. Citing such reasons as traffic congestion, the indignity of the job, and the desire for more motorized vehicles, over 100,000 becaks were confiscated and dumped into the Java Sea "to provide a habitat for nutritious crustaceans."[34] From a peak of about 90,000 rickshaws in the early 1970s, the number of vehicles was reduced to 40,000 in 1983. Some were recovered, sold, and nicknamed "sea becak," and although more kept reappearing, the number of officially allowed becaks was reduced to about 8,000 in 1990.

The city's plan eventually backfired because the drivers had a significant role in the economy. They serviced areas not covered by buses at reasonable rates. The drivers, who are often urban migrants, were provided a relatively lucrative livelihood, earning roughly $3.50 per day. More than a civil servant makes, this was enough to send a portion to their families in their native villages where work is meager. Despite the seeming powerlessness of the drivers, political pressure against the ban mounted.

The Association of Jakarta Pedlars, representing 2,000 becak drivers, took their protests to the parliament, and Jakarta's governor, Wiyogo Atmodarminto, apparently had some difficulty explaining the logic of the plan. Eventually, he was forced to publicly apologize for the heavy-handed tactics. As the controversy became news around the world, a daughter of President Sukarno supported the drivers. The international network of bicycle activists applied pressure, even at the Indonesian Consulate in New York City. Meanwhile, some drivers still ply the side roads at night where, as one driver says, "the police no longer come so frequently. Now there are fewer of us and the money is better, at least 10,000 rupiahs ($5.50) a day."

Pedicab services are found in North American cities such as Annapolis, Baltimore, Charleston, Denver, Key West, Louisville, New York, Oakland, and San Francisco. Since the 1980s, the Barbary Coast Pedicab Company has carried tourists around Fisherman's Wharf in San Francisco for an average fare of $4. Operated by Jeff Sears, with drivers renting cabs for about $35 per day, he had up to 45 pedicabs in use without a major accident. In 1986, the city government set standards for vehicle safety, driver licensing, and insurance requirements, and Sears' insurance company would not renew his $1 million liability policy. Temporarily forced out of business, he became "the latest victim of the insurance crunch."[35] In 1993, Sears was again going strong, though he got competition from newer pedicabs ventures in San Francisco and across the bay in Oakland. In the town center of Giessen, Germany, near Frankfurt, pedicabs shuttle passengers free of charge while the drivers' wage is paid with revenue from advertising displayed on the vehicle.

Cycling Communities

Several communities around the world are considered bicycle utopias because they provide outstanding facilities for cyclists. Cycling communities such as those in China, Holland, and California transcend such factors as geography, climate, political ideology, personal income, and industrialization. What really distinguishes these cycling societies from their non-cycling neighbors is enlightened public opinion and strong governmental support.

CHINA: KINGDOM OF THE BICYCLE

China is the country where hundreds of thousands of people in cities use human-powered transport, filling wide boulevards with cyclists. While the bicycle traffic in Beijing has become legendary, the city of Tianjin has the most bicycle traffic in the world.

According to Cheng Yi, a traffic control chief in Beijing, most roads are being built or converted to park-like, three-lane boulevards, with middle lanes reserved for motor vehicles, and side lanes, each about seven meters wide, for bicycles. Spaces between lanes will be planted with trees shrubs and flowers. On several existing main roads, space for bicycle traffic has been widened. When two parallel roads run close together, one is reserved for motorists and the other for cyclists. In some streets, cyclists observe the system called the "morning and evening tide." Here, rush-hour bike commuters going the same direction at morning and evening are allowed to use motorists' lanes. Cheng Yi says, "We look forward to the day when, with the Chinese people's livelihood improving further, everyone will have his or her own bike, but that will bring more problems which will stay with us until there is a really big leap in new road building." Another official account, called "Early Morning Traffic Shift," by Wang Heng, a traffic officer in Beijing, appears in *Lives of Ordinary Chinese* (1988):

> Today it's Zhang Shuijun's and my turn to be on duty at Xidan Street, one of the busiest intersections along Chang'an Avenue, Beijing's main street. At 5:50 in the morning I cycle westward from our traffic control headquarters to take up my post. Actually, my home is just a ten minute bike ride from the Xidan crossroads, but on weekdays we live at headquarters, ready at any time to go to the scene of an accident or handle other jobs.
>
> At 6:00 sharp we switch on the traffic lights and lower the glass windows on the traffic control kiosk. Today I'll take first turn in the kiosk, while Zhang takes up his position on the traffic stand in the center of the broad avenue. Especially in rush hours, the automatic lights need to be supplemented by hand signals from the man on the traffic stand to ensure a smooth flow of vehicles. When the motorcades of foreign diplomats pass through, we control the lights by hand.
>
> By 6:30 the flow of bicycles has become really heavy. From now to

8:00, when most government offices and enterprises start their day, traffic is dominated by bikes and buses carrying people to work. After that cars from the various units out on business, taxis carrying tourists, trucks and other vehicles are more common.

From 7:00 to 8:00 every morning over 10,000 bikes stream past the Xidan intersection. Traffic is much more congested these days, mainly because road building cannot keep abreast of fast developments in the economy, tourism, etc. The city now has over 300,000 motor vehicles, five million bikes and tens of thousands of motorcycles—an additional headache for us. The heavier flow has brought more traffic accidents and added to our burdens.

The city government has taken certain measures—such as keeping trucks off the Third Ring Road during daylight hours and forbidding left turns at Xidan and other intersections—which have helped a lot. In the past several years we haven't had a single serious accident at our post. But we're still looking forward to the pedestrian overpass which is planned for the Xidan crossing.

Rush hour, Shanghai, China, 1989.
Photo by Wang Gang Feng.

In China's cities, a bicyclist's average speed is eleven kilometers per hour (6.8 mph). In the city of Tianjin—with 154 square kilometers, 4.4 million people, 3 million bikes, and only 122 traffic signals in 1990—the average speed increases to thirteen kilometers per hour (8 mph). Tianjin uses only 4.8 percent of the land for streets, unlike Western cities that use 40 to 60 percent. The narrow streets favor cycles because many were built to be non-interchangeable—without through routes—by settling colonies that wanted to discourage strangers from passing through their neighborhoods. In trips to and from work in 1990, the modal split (the percentage each traveling mode is used) was 74.6 percent by bike, 10.6 percent by walking, 12.3 percent by bus, and 2.5 percent by all other means—a phenomenon that grew from a 1980 split of 56.2 percent cyclists and 29.5 percent pedestrians. Some 6.1 million bikes were produced in Tianjin in 1989, the home of the Tianjin Bicycle Manufacturing Group, China's largest maker.[36]

In facing pressure from developed nations to use more motor vehicles, the Chinese were able to justify their decision to emphasize bicycle transport. If China were to pave over as much land per person as has the United States (about 600 square meters per person), they would give up some 64 million hectares, equal to 40 percent of the country's crop land.[37] As one citizen reports:

> Foreign observers have different views about the "King of the Road." Some think it is fine for China to increase its bikes rather than private cars—in their minds is the energy crisis and the dangers of pollution in developed countries. Also, they argue, cycling is good exercise. But some may just think that the Chinese have to do with bikes because they are unable to produce enough cars—that it reflects China's relative poverty and backwardness.
>
> In fact, bikes are not primarily used in China to save energy or to avoid pollution. China is a developing country, motor vehicles, compared to her vast population, are still few, and the overwhelming majority are publicly owned. Some urban construction experts think public transport is always preferable to individual cars, judging by the problems the latter have brought in developed countries.[38]

China has begun shifting its bicycle policy in the 1990s. With the lure of Western companies and the aid of multinational development banks, its transport officials are planning for more motorization. In 1993, Mayor Li Ziliu of Guangzou (Canton) planned to ban bikes and motorcycles from the center of town. But after a huge outcry and over 700 letters of disapproval, the ban was delayed four months and limited to one cross-town route during business hours. Yet costly permits and taxes on bicycles and parking are rising compared to those for motorists. In the 1980s, China's motor vehicle production grew at a rate of fourteen percent, averaging about 400,000 vehicles per year, with 500 kilometers of expressway built. In the early 1990s, the auto production growth rate has doubled, to about

Rural road near Guanghou. Photo by George Bliss.

28 percent, averaging one million per year. By 1993, China became a net importer of oil, and with about seven million motor vehicles, 350,000 privately owned, it had 1,400 kilometers of expressways and over a million kilometers of paved highway. By the year 2000, motor vehicle production is expected to be three million per year, and there will be another 15,000 kilometers of expressway, some with bicycle routes.[39]

HOLLAND: CIVILIZED CYCLING

With fifteen million people living within about 16,500 square miles, the Netherlands is one of the world's most densely populated countries. As an example of what the future may bring, the country has the most cars per square mile and the world's most intensive agriculture. The Dutch have a long cultural tradition of cycling for transport, recreation, and sport, and although cycling declined somewhat after the second World War, it has resurged with the energy and environmental awareness of the 1970s.[40] Over the years, several public media campaigns have promoted cycling and reduced auto use. A 1986 campaign offered a reward of 1,000 guilders ($400), equivalent to the savings, for cycling instead of driving all trips under five-kilometers for two years. In a series of television commercials in 1990, people were offered incentives to recycle their car for a bike, and reminded to lock their *fiets*.

Between 1975 and 1985 the Netherlands spent some $230 million to construct or improve cycleways and parking facilities at rail stations. More than ten percent of highway construction funds were devoted to cycling projects. By 1986 there were about 13,500 kilometers of cycleways, with a substantial portion being direct, uninterrupted routes that skirt motor vehicle routes. Cycling makes up about 30 percent of all trips made in the nation, and in cities such as Groningen (50 percent) and Delft (43 percent), the percentage of cycling trips out-ranks all other modes of transport, including walking, motorcycling, driving, and mass transit. In 1992, some 3.65 million bikes were on the road each day, and each Netherlander cycled 853 kilometers (530 miles) per year.

The city of Delft (pop. 65,000) has evolved from the layout of a medieval town into a modern city which originated the *woonerf* residential traffic calming zone. In 1979 the city sought to improve cyclists' facilities and reduce auto use with the Delft Cycle Plan. The widely documented plan was based on various-sized networks of cycleways derived from the town's form and structure that connect residential areas, business districts, transport depots, work sites, and schools.

Innovations include cycle path underpasses and bridges for crossing motor vehicle roads, one-way mixed-traffic roads with two-way lanes for cyclists, paving curbs that favor cyclists and act as speed bumps for motorists, traffic-activated signals that detect cyclists, and *Ofo*s or "blown-up" zones where cyclists are permitted to wait at traffic lights in front of cars. As a result, people shifted their mode of transport to cycling for over 40 percent of their trips, with the total amount of kilometers ridden by cyclists increasing by about seven percent. Each day, the inhabi-

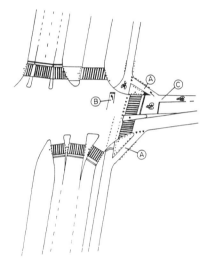

Dutch intersection designed for bike traffic, with A) free right turns, B) left turn waiting zone, C) 'blow up" waiting zone in front of cars, called *Ofos*.

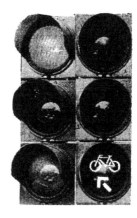

BICYCLING MAGAZINE'S
BEST AND WORST
CYCLING CITIES (1990)

THE TOP TEN:
1. Seattle, Washington
2. Palo Alto, California
3. San Diego, California
4. Boulder, Colorado
5. Davis, California
6. Gainesville, Florida
7. Eugene, Oregon
8. Montreal, Canada
9. Madison, Wisconsin
10. Missoula, Montana

THE WORST THREE:
1. New York City
2. Orlando, Florida
3. Pittsburgh, Pennsylvania

tants of Delft cycle over 425,000 kilometers, a total equivalent to riding ten times around the globe.[41]

The Dutch Bike Masterplan of 1992 allocates $133 million from 1992 to 1996 for bike projects and research into wind barriers, bikes on trains, and collective city bikes. Goals include substituting auto traffic for bikes, increases of 30 percent in cycling kilometers from 1986 levels by 2010, fifteen percent increase in train-bike use, 50 percent decrease in cyclist deaths, fewer stolen bikes, and complete integration with traffic and transport plans by 1995.[42]

CALIFORNIA: A STATE OF BICYCLE MIND

When *Bicycling* magazine listed its top-ten North American cities for cycling in 1990, the state of California had three in the top five: Palo Alto (No. 2), San Diego (No. 3), and Davis (No. 5). The distinguishing feature of these cities is that they are college towns. Since the mid-1970s, Davis (pop. 45,000) was considered "Bike City U.S.A." as the nation's most "bicycle friendly" place with 25 percent of all local trips made by bike and some 30 percent of all roads having bike lanes or cycle paths. By the mid-1980s, Palo Alto had risen to the top rank and there was a certain amount of rivalry, as seen in editorials such as Ray Hosler's "Best Bike Town Listing Leaves Davis Spinning its Wheels" in the *San Francisco Chronicle* (December 12, 1988).

Palo Alto (pop. 56,000) is described as an affluent, educated community which borders the extensive grounds of Stanford University. The San Francisco Bay Area is blessed with a temperate climate, mostly dry and sometimes very foggy. With a flat landscape in town, Palo Alto has access to rolling hills and long climbs on country roads crossing the Santa Cruz mountain range towards the Pacific Ocean about 30 miles away. Within a 100-mile radius of Palo Alto, including Davis, Marin County, Santa Cruz, and Monterey, there is probably more bicycle activity than anywhere else in the world.

In the mid-1970s, Palo Alto was the home for a large number of bicycling activists and technical innovators, including City Council member Ellen Fletcher (*Bicycle Parking*), former LAW president John Forester (*Effective Cycling*), Jobst Brandt (*The Bicycle Wheel*), Eric and Jon Hjertberg (Wheelsmith), and Tom Ritchey (mountain bike pioneer). At the public high school I attended there, an alternative physical education class allowed our group of cyclists the time to ride and to share experiences with other students.

Meanwhile, the city began developing a system of 40 miles of cycleways, roughly one-fourth of its total street mileage. After the first year of the system, when it was not yet fully implemented, bicycle use increased by fourteen percent, and bike accidents on major roads dropped by almost a fifth.[43] The centerpiece of this network is the two-mile Bryant Street bicycle boulevard featuring barriers for cars but not bikes.

The city has taken several progressive steps to enhance cycling, spending roughly $1 million in the 1980s, mostly from state grants. City employees are reimbursed seven cents per mile for using their bicycles on city business; large building developments are required to provide ten percent of all parking for bicycles, with racks or lockers; street repairs must adhere to bicycle smoothness standards; and middle school students receive on-road bicycle education classes. At the two CalTrain commuter rail stations connecting San Francisco and San Jose, bike parking lockers have been installed which rent for $4 per month and have long waiting lists. Though the Southern Pacific railroad refused to carry non-folding bikes in the 1980s, the new company, CalTrain, introduced its bike-accessible California Car in the 1990s.

With a workday population of about 70,000, several large employers in Palo Alto now provide incentives for bike commuting. For example, the Alza Corporation pays its bicycle commuters $1 for each day they ride to work. Employees at Hewlett-Packard are provided parking facilities with showers and clothes lockers, and the Xerox Research Center goes further by offering a hot towel service in their shower rooms, resulting in twenty percent of their employees cycling to work, one of the highest rates in the U.S.[44] However, in the 1990s, the overall number of bike commuters from Palo Alto dropped by over 40 percent, while the number of solo car commuters rose, due to factors such as longer distances to travel, increased congestion for cyclists, and an aging population.

Future Designs

The Congress recognizes that bicycles are the most efficient means of transportation, represent a viable commuting alternative to many people, offer mobility at speeds as fast as that of cars in urban areas, provide health benefits through daily exercise, reduce noise and air pollution, are relatively inexpensive, and deserve consideration in a comprehensive national energy plan.

These encouraging words appeared in a 1980 energy conservation study by the U.S. Department of Transportation. The study described the low awareness and acceptance of bicycle use, the lack of bicycle facilities, the lack of skills and knowledge related to safe bicycle use, the lack of communication and coordination, and the inadequate funding for bicycle transportation projects.

The study showed that if these obstacles were reduced or eliminated, there would have been three million more bicycle commuters than the estimated 470,000 people who commuted by bike in the U.S. in 1975. Almost twenty years later, in 1994, there were an estimated 4.3 million bike commuters in the U.S., out of a total of about 100 million commuters. Some of those obstacles have been eliminated, as cycling is growing and bicycles are beginning to be called the vehicles of the future again.

Social Changes

Today the world is at a crossroads regarding transportation planning. Politics and economics are crucial factors in the development of any transport mode or system. Cycling represents the most logical, independent, economical, and ecological way for most people to transport themselves in daily life, but without the industrial infrastructures on the scale of motor vehicles, cycling lacks the political and economic power of the oil-driven motor vehicle industry.

What people want in the future—better facilities for cycling, pleasant places to walk, easier ways of using public transport, and more efficient kinds of motor vehicles—appears to be at odds with the profit-driven goals of corporate industries. Because bicycles link so many people and places, they are likely to be the central movement in a whole system of interacting modes.

Future vision of big city pedicabs from the 1950s. Painting by Ed Emsh.

Many people believe we need a transformation of our landscape from an emphasis on space and the mechanics of acceleration to a topography of places. Instead of a *space-age* projection of lines, speed, and numbers, we need a *place-age* topography of human values. With cycling, the idea is to go fast enough to cross the forest, yet slow enough to smell the trees.

In the late 1980s, the Green Party in Germany included a coalition of bicycle activists that offered a transport policy with solutions to problems in current and future systems. Their plan is based on the following points: 1) Better land use; 2) Shift to non-motorized and public transport; 3) Equal rights for all transport forms; 4) Priority for pedestrians and bicycles for personal transport; 5) Move freight from road to rail.

A study of three German cities (Gladbeck, Luenen, Troisdorf) by Socialdata, a non-governmental think tank, showed the contrasting ideals of people and politicians. While 77 percent of the people favored a bike-friendly city over a car-friendly city, only 33 percent of the politicians and officials favored a bike-friendly city—and they figured that 37 percent of the people would favor a bike-friendly city. Another study compared the real transport system with the perceptions of two groups—ordinary people and politicians and opinion makers—asking people from these groups to estimate the local transportation modal split, including non-motorized transport (walking and cycling), personal motor vehicles (motorcycles, cars and vans), and public transport (buses and trains).

PERCEPTIONS OF MODAL SPLIT

	WALKING AND CYCLING	PRIVATE MOTOR VEHICLES	PUBLIC TRANSPORT
REAL LIFE	39%	54%	7%
WHAT ORDINARY PEOPLE THOUGHT	18%	66%	16%
WHAT POLITICIANS AND OPINION-MAKERS THOUGHT	16%	67%	17%

The transportation vision in France seems to be changing. In the late 1960s, President Georges Pompidou said, "Paris must adapt to the automobile," and most of the country followed. Daniel Behrman, a correspondent for the *International Herald Tribune*, wrote in his book *The Man Who Loved Bicycles* that "no Paris newspaper has yet gotten around to explaining to me why I spit black solid particles in Paris and nowhere else, not even New York. Paris was once civilized, now it's dieselized." Another person wrote in *The New York Times* that "there are no more adult French people: they have all turned into cars." To reduce energy use in the mid-1970s, a French transport official suggested that "government should give free bicycles to anyone who trades in their motor-vehicle license. Everyone over 65 years of age should receive a bicycle." By 1990, Paris had the highest amount of carbon monoxide of major cities listed by the World Health Organization. The city government began

looking for a new masterplan, such as traffic calming plans which have been implemented in Bordeaux with roughly half the roads reconfigured to favor cyclists and pedestrians. Hélène Desplats, a Bordeaux city council member said, "The idea that one can adapt a town to suit the car is absurd and the equivalent of killing off a city."

Developing nations face the dilemma of reaching for progress, as presented by Western standards, while failing to recognize the full benefits of bicycles. The problem is compounded by occasional suspicions that intermediate technology projects promoted by industrial nations come not out of generosity, but to limit competitive progress in developing countries.

TECHNICAL CHANGES

As human-powered vehicles continue to evolve, and while the world's population grows, few vehicles are likely to multiply as fast or have the flexibility of the human-powered variety. Name another vehicle that goes on sidewalks, roads, and freeways; inside bedrooms, kitchens, garages, gymnasiums, velodromes, shopping malls, office buildings, and factory sites; in cars, trucks, trains, buses, boats, ships, planes, and spacecraft; through paths, forests, meadows, beaches, and glaciers; and in rivers, lakes, bays, bogs, and oceans.

Visions of the bicycle give us clues to the future forms of transport. Bicycle makers have ideas that include hybrid human-powered cars, genetically engineered automatic cycling machines, passenger-powered transit buses, and wind-assisted veloway trains on rails, while car makers have ideas of supercars and lightweight vehicles that use HPV technology. Mobility may be divided into two types: robot-driven vehicles for moving freight and passengers, and human-powered vehicles for personal trips. As motor vehicles make the shift towards a sustainable power source for the twenty-first century, mopeds, cars, vans, buses, and trucks are likely to evolve with a mix of power sources, including internal combustion with cleaner gasoline and natural gases, and electricity with coal, nuclear, hydro, solar, wind, hydrogen, and human power.

Robert and Peter Perkins of British Columbia, makers of the Thebis tricycle, describe a possible future for their human-powered vehicle in an essay called "The Mall City" (1990). Tricyclists would move inside and outside of supermalls, containing shops, theaters, restaurants, condominiums, parks, offices, and factories. The trikes could pass freely through air doors and up gently sloping ramps, with "quiet, clean parks and buildings laced with cycle paths, the natural outdoor environment completely integrated with the moderated indoor environment; people once again face-to-face with one another in a relaxing and pleasing social atmosphere, free of noise and pollution."

A prediction made at the dawn of cycling's Golden Age, called "The Bicycle—A Hundred Years Hence" (*Toronto Globe*, June 14, 1893), shows how much was expected of the bicycle:

The roads will be prepared especially for bicycles, the grades being very slight.... The roads will be kept clean, as by that time the horses will found be only in zoological gardens. The improvement in the rider will be equally marked. From the continued and increasing use of the wheel a race of people will be evolved that will take to cycling as readily as a foreign immigrant does to politics.... We may expect an average speed of 30 miles an hour on the road and 60 miles on the track. The use of the machine will be universal.

Children will be taught to ride as they are now taught to walk. The suburbs of our great cities will extend from 60 to 100 miles in every direction. All patents will have expired, and such large quantities of bicycles will be manufactured that the cost will be nominal and within reach of all. There will be no more crowded tenement houses. The artisan, who will work only four hours a day, will live with his family in a cosy little home in the suburbs, where he can see the sunshine and breathe the fresh air. The use of the wheel will have so improved the stamina and physique of the race that the only cause of death will be old age and accidents.

Everyone will own a bicycle. Those intended for distance travel will be run by small but powerful storage batteries, which may be charged at automatic electric stations by connecting the battery to a dynamo and dropping a coin of small value in a slot. With machines of this character it will be possible to attain a speed of 150 miles an hour.

The bicycle will not be used in war for the simple reason that as dyspepsia will be unknown, everybody will feel so well and be so good-humoured and disinclined to quarrel that there will be no one to go to war.[45]

Left, a vision from Inner City Cycles, Glebe, Australia.

10 A Political Tool

Slogan from the Dutch Fietserbond: Go Bicycling!

*Few articles ever used by man have created so great a revolution in
social conditions as the bicycle.*
    —United States Census Report (1900)

Socialism can only come riding a bicycle.
    —José Antonio Viera-Gallo, Assistant Secretary of Justice, Chile

Ideologies

The bicycle has become a political tool, due to its social, egalitarian
nature, serving all alike. Democratic, socialist, and communist cultures
have all produced flourishing bicycle communities. Bicycle uses vary by
country and ideology, from the official prohibitions on cycling in parts of
North Korea, Saudi Arabia, and the United Arab Emirates, to official
encouragement in the Netherlands. Democratic societies such as the
United States, which emphasize personal liberties and free markets, tend
to develop innovative approaches to bicycles for the benefit of recreation
and business. Communist societies such as China, which emphasize community cooperation and government control, tend to develop practical
approaches to bicycles in more structured ways. Social-democratic societies such as the Netherlands, which blend public and privatization, tend
to develop innovative and practical approaches to bicycles in ways that
reflect a special understanding of the bicycle's social nature.

    Cuba is an example of a small country that is geo-politically situated
between two powerful ideologies. As a small thorn at the foot of its capi-
talist neighbor, the U.S., Cuba embraced communism through the economic support of the U.S.S.R. This situation is reflected in Cuba's vehicle
traffic, where Soviet-built cars and trucks mix with old American vehicles
leftover from before the U.S. trade embargo. In 1980, the country had
about one motor vehicle per 5,000 people, and as in most developing
nations progress was measured in horsepower, despite the high price of
importing oil and motor vehicles on the economy and the island's environment.

    In 1990, the breakup of the Soviet Union caused cutbacks in oil ship-
ments, and Cuba's leader, Fidel Castro, addressed the energy crisis with a
program called "Special Period in Time of Peace." Cuba's transportation
system was restructured to emphasize bicycles for personal transport,
based on the plans of Eugenio Balari, a government economist. By 1993,
about a million practical bicycles were imported from China, and bike
lanes were installed with traffic signs reading *Atención! Ciclos en la Vía*
("Attention! Cyclists in the Road"). Bikes were assembled at factory-
schools, such as the Cuban-American Friendship Technology Institute,
and cost about 125 pesos, over half the average monthly salary, with a 50
percent student-worker discount available. Balari describes the bicycle as
"a king's gift... No one's complained, everyone's happy, everyone wants
one. Just look at the advantages. One, they save energy—that's the main
thing. Two, they're practical, convenient. Three, they help protect the

Bicycles are used as symbols for political parties in Nepal and Bangladesh.
Writing on the wall in Kathmandu
(top) reads "Vote for the Bicycle
Party." Photo by Robert Kelly, 1991;
cartoon from *The Dhaka Daily Star*,
1994.

environment, right? No pollution. Four, they're less noisy; they contribute to the pacification and tranquility of the city. Five, the exercise and health benefits. Six, they improve your psyche by letting people see the city in a fuller and more beautiful way, not cooped up in a car. I see it as an advance, a progress. Everything it represents is positive."[1]

Cuba held a bicycle conference in 1993, where North American bike advocates saw a Havana bus factory being converted to a bike factory. Future plans include the development of a domestic bicycle industry, with a system for supplying parts and repairing bikes, as well as new bike traffic regulations and parking sites.[2] Though some would like to see Cuba go motorized, its movement toward bikes supports the logical and sustainable trend of promoting cycling for economical and environmental transport in developing countries.

Havana, Cuba, 1993. Photo by Cindy Arlinsky.

BIKES OVER LIMOS

The appeal for "bicycles over limousines" by ranking politicians is a popular way that bicycles have been used as a political symbol. Claiming a preference for bicycles—an economical, clean, and egalitarian mode of transport—many a conservative or liberal, communist or democrat has declined a costly, pompous, chauffeur-driven limousine. Most famous was the proclamation made by Kim Il Sung, the late Premier of Northern Korea, who once said he preferred to use his bicycle instead of traveling in a western-style motorcade. Similarly, in the U.S., a Connecticut state Governor, Ella Grasso, did not want to keep a limousine, and said she would put the honorary car license plate, No. 1, on her bicycle.

Limousines have evolved from decorative royal carriages into ominous black automobiles, symbolizing an amount of power and privilege that is clearly at odds with the idea of democratic public service. A few politicians make a point of driving common used cars, while others are proud to say they bicycle to work whenever they can. However, politicians are well-known for talking out of both sides of their mouths, saying different things to different people.

Once in a while an honest politician comes along, usually riding a bike. Bud Clark, the Mayor of Portland, Oregon, who became known for the "Expose Yourself to Art" poster in which he exposed himself to a nude statue wearing only a rain-coat, stood up for his jovial manners and habit of riding a StumpJumper mountain bike on city business. Quoted in the *International Herald Tribune*, he said: "I'm not a funny man. I'm a serious man... I'm a conservative. I know you have to have money in the bank to pay your bills. People who think I'm an eccentric misjudge me. Everyone in the world is different. That's what makes it wonderful. I've been riding a bicycle for a long time."[3]

Several U.S. Presidents have been cyclists, such as Franklin Delano Roosevelt, who cycletoured in his youth before being stricken by polio as an adult; Dwight D. Eisenhower, who cycled at the advice of his physician Dr. Paul Dudley White, a well-known bike advocate; and Jimmy Carter, who rode regularly at the Camp David weekend retreat. Ronald Reagan was not a cyclist, but he once appeared selling Schwinn bicycles and a bicycling paperboy is shown in one of his "Morning in America" TV commercials.

George Bush, the 41st U.S. President, was known to bicycle while serving as Ambassador to China from 1970–76. In a letter to John Dowlin of the Bicycle Network (June 4, 1975), Bush wrote: "The more I think about our U.S. domestic transportation problems from this vantage point of halfway around the world, the more I see an increased role for the bicycle in American life. Obviously, some terrains make it more difficult, obviously some climates make it more difficult; but I am convinced after riding bikes an enormous amount here in China, that it is a sensible, economical, clean form of transportation and makes enormous good sense."

When George Bush became President he returned to Beijing in 1989.

Mikhail Gorbachev as a cyclist, 1989, from Specialized Bicycle Co.

Trade was increasing between the two countries and a diplomatic exchange of gifts occurred between him and Premier Li Peng. George and Barbara Bush received his and her bicycles, while the Pengs received a pair of cowboy boots with American and Chinese flags. Shortly thereafter, in Beijing's Tiananmen Square, students on bicycles were massacred by the Chinese army during democratic uprisings.

In the 1992 Presidential campaign, former-candidate Eugene McCarthy said it was "like a sprint race" with the riders going as slow as possible in early laps. President Bill Clinton has made his inevitable political bike rides, in Massachusetts on a Merlin titanium mountain bike, with Congressman Joseph Kennedy III, who is one of the highest ranking pro-bike polititians, and in California with his wife Hillary, on Specialized beach cruisers, with and without helmets. In his *Washington Post* column, bike advocate Colman McCarthy urged vice president Al Gore to "Leave The Limo At Home," saying he would be king of the road if he biked to work. Bikes are a subject not found in Gore's enviromental book *Earth in the Balance*.

Many people wonder when there will be a woman U.S. President. One of the first "lady candidates" was Belva Ann Lockwood, a lawyer from Royalton, New York, who ran for President with the Equal Rights Party in 1884 and 1888. When a photograph showed her campaigning on an English tricycle, she told the press: "There is a principle behind that picture. A tricycle means independence for women, and it also means health." In 1884 she received 4,149 votes in seven states, while Grover Cleveland won the election with 4.9 million votes. Lockwood helped pass the law allowing women to practice before the U.S. Supreme Court.

George and Barbara Bush with bikes in Beijing, China, 1975. Photo from Bicycle Network.

Fatcat by Al Scott.

Human Rights

Bicycles have been one of the most important tools for people to exercise their individual human rights. As ideal vehicles for creating a sense of freedom and equality, and as a way of connecting people who are empowered and mobilized by its use, bicycles have had a major impact on lifestyles, especially in the realms of women's emancipation and class struggles.

Since the days of velocipedes and high-wheelers, human-powered vehicles have offered men and women a means of moving freely through the world in a healthy way. Roads opened the landscape and expanded horizons for people of all social classes, who realized social and intellectual development from bicycles.

In the late nineteenth century it was suggested that society was divided into two classes of people: those who rode bicycles and those who did not. As bicycles evolved those who first rode bicycles were more often men of the upper class—the nobility, aristocrats, and wealthy people. For those who did not ride bicycles, it was not always by choice. As bicycles were not easily affordable or acceptable for the majority of people until the 1890s, the question was raised: "Who should ride?"

Bicycles encouraged a new kind of social behavior that changed the roles and relations of men and women. The modern women's movement dates back to the 1850s and has sought equal rights and opportunities for women in a male dominated world. Before the 1890s, women were generally denied the right to ride bicycles alone. Though they certainly rode cycling machines such as tricycles and side-saddle velocipedes, with some women participating in races and acrobatic exhibitions, there were various social restrictions that inhibited cycling for women, including chaperons, corsets, and beliefs suggesting that cycling was immoral, unfeminine, and unhealthy.

With the development of the pneumatic tire safety bicycle women discovered a vehicle for breaking away from these restrictions. Women realized the benefits of cycling for creating independence, health, comfortable fashion, and informal etiquette, and a "New Woman" emerged wearing "rational" dress. Bicycles became linked with the women's movement as a powerful tool for emancipation and suffrage.

The question of women riding bicycles became a much discussed and controversial subject in the mid-1890s:

> Now that the bicycle has arrived, with the new woman seated in the saddle, it has suddenly become the deep concern of the prophets and seers to tell whither the wheel is carrying the woman. It behooves us to settle this burning, scorching question before it has gone a century farther.
>
> Mrs. Elizabeth Cady Stanton proclaimed some time ago that woman was riding to suffrage on the bicycle. Latterly a reverend gentleman in

Poster for Liberator Cycles et Automobiles, 1899, by Jean de Paleologue.

Advertisement for Elliman's
Embrocation shows a fact of life: men
are more dangerous than women.

"New Woman" looking like an old man.

Atlanta has consulted the oracle of his own wisdom and has procaimed to the world that woman was riding to the devil. Possibly this is the only clerical form of stating Mrs. Stanton's discovery. However that may be, Mrs. Reginald De Koven's idea of the matter, as expressed in the August *Cosmopolitan*, is quite different. She is very certain that the bicycle is to be the panacea for woman's ills, physical, mental, moral and imaginary. "To men, rich or poor," she says, "the bicycle is an unmixed blessing, but to women it is deliverance, revolution, salvation."
—from *Wheel Talk* (1895)

I can't see but that a wheel is just as good company as most husbands two years old. I would as lief talk to one inanimate object as another; and I'd a great deal rather talk to one that can't answer than one that won't. I'd rather imagine a sympathetic response in a bright and shining handlebar than know it doesn't exist in a frowning man, who yawns or starts when I ask him a question.

As for health, I am certain that a great many old maids will hail the advent of the bicycle as a rare substitute for the prescription so many doctors administer: "If you would only marry and have a family to care for your health would be all right." Compare a wheel with a family in this respect. You can make your wheel tidy over night, and it never kicks off its shoes the very last minute, and never smears itself with molasses. When you are ready you can start. No little elbows are stuck in your ribs; there is no wiggling; screams at the cars or at the candy stores. You glide along, silently, smoothly, swiftly. There is exhilaration and nerve tonic in the very spice of danger, the need to look sharp, the chance of adventure.

Another great superiority of the bicycle lies in the fact that you can always get rid of it when you wish. You can roll it in and stand it up in a corner, and there it stays. It will neither follow you around or insist on receiving attention at inconvenient moments. When it gets shabby or old you can dispose of it and get you a new one without shocking the entire community.
—Ann Strong, *Minneapolis Tribune* (1895)[4]

Such historians as record the tides of social manner and morals, have neglected the bicycle. Yet would it be difficult to deny that this "invention of the devil," as Swithin Forsyte always called it because "a penny-farthing" had startled his greys at Brighton in 1874—has been responsible for more movement in manners and morals than anything since Charles the Second. At its bone-shaking inception innocent, because of its extraordinary discomfort, in its "penny-farthing" stage harmless, because only dangerous to the lives and limbs of the male sex, it began to be a dissolvent of the most powerful type when accessible to the fair in its present form. Under its influence, wholly or in part, have wilted chaperons, long and narrow skirts, tight corsets, hair that would come down, black stockings, thick ankles, large hats, prudery and fear of the dark; under its influence, wholly or in part, have bloomed week-ends, strong nerves, strong legs, strong language, knickers, knowledge of make and shape, knowledge of woods and pastures, equality of sex, good digestion and professional occupation—in four words, the emancipation of woman. But to Swithin, and possibly for that reason, it remained what it had been in the beginning, an invention of the devil.

    —John Galsworthy, *Forsyte Saga* (1922)[5]

As women entered the workplace in larger numbers with better opportunities, some were employed in the shops and factories of the bicycle industry. Beginning in the 1920s, and especially during World War II, women dispelled the stereotype that men were more mechanically-minded by taking jobs as bicycle wheel- and frame-builders. Lucille Redmann worked as a welder and brazer at the Schwinn Bicycle Co. since the mid-1930s. In the 1980s she and another woman were building top-of-the-line Paramount racing bicycles. Many women have run bike shops, and some shops in Europe and the U.S. are operated solely by and for women. In sports, the 1980s brought the first Olympic cycling events for women, and stage races such as the Tour de France Feminin.

    In some societies, where sexism and cultural practices discourage women from cycling, the women's movement has greater obstacles to overcome. Karen Overton, of the Bikes for Africa development project in Mozambique, asked the residents of Beira why so few women ride bikes. They claimed that "women don't know how... It's not ladylike for women to spread their legs... Riding isn't easy in a *capulana* (the traditional dress)... Women are afraid to ride... They can't be trusted because they may ride off and have affairs... The man of the house deserves to ride a bike more than the woman." While some husbands encourage their wives to get a bike so they can ride it, the community grows more supportive when bicycles deliver more goods to market and provide for better health care and educational services. In a country where women spend up to 1,650 hours per year for basic transport and men spend only about 530 hours, the cycling women save over 330 hours per year.[6]

Lower prices for bicycles in the 1890s allowed people of all economic classes to enjoy the adventures and exercise of cycling on the open roads. James McGurn, author of *On Your Bicycle* (1987), describes the bicycle's impact in realms of individual rights and class struggles, and how the ethos of wanderlust mixed with conservative authoritarian forces in Germany. There were over 500,000 cyclists in Germany in the 1890s and the German Cycling Federation represented some 500 bicycle clubs. German cyclists had to know the various laws in each region, as many roads were off-limits for cycling, including half of all Bavarian roads. In some provinces cyclists had to ride in single file, ten meters from each other, and they were required to carry a bicycle identity pass that could be withdrawn by police officers. Furthermore, middle-class cyclists who ventured into some rural districts faced resentment and abuse. McGurn writes: "The freedom, mobility and privacy of the bicycle were more than the authorities would tolerate. Significantly, Germany was one of the first nations to provide bicycles for its policemen and local militias—agents of social control."[7]

The Worker's Cycling Federation: Solidarity (*Arbeiterrafahrbund: Solidarität*) was founded in Germany in 1896, and by 1913 it had grown to include some 150,000 members constituting a group of cooperative bicycle factories and shops, with a circulation of 167,000 for its newspaper, *The Worker Cyclist*. Members were described as "the Enlightened Patrols of Social Democracy," and "the Red Hussars of the Class Struggle." They organized recreational and sports activities, and used their bicycles for distributing pamphlets and political electioneering. To evade identification they would throw handfuls of leaflets at crowds as they cycled past.

The idea of socialized cycling in Germany continued with the rise of National Socialism and the Nazi Party, which used the bicycle in propaganda, such as in the "Day of the German Cyclist" which took place in 1933, in bicycle parts laden with swastikas, and in Leni Riefenstahl's influential film, *Olympia*, which depicted blonde-haired, blue-eyed athletes. The film shows two Frenchmen and a Swiss winning medals in the 1936 Berlin Olympic road race.

As James McGurn relates, the movement traveled abroad, particularly with the Clarion Fellowship in Britain, which formed the Clarion Cycling Club. Led by Robert Blatchford and calling themselves "Clarionettes" and speaking "Clarionese," which involved shouting "Boots!" and "Spurs!" when passing one another on bikes, the group's hobbies and utopian ideals included cycling, literature, music, arts and crafts, rational dress, feminism, vegetarianism, and farming. Blatchford wrote that "Beneficial as women's suffrage has been I should place it second to the pneumatic tyre in the general life of our working people."

Economics

Although there are about twice as many bikes as cars worldwide, and bikes are a basic accessory of daily life for about one-tenth of the world's people, bikes have had a relatively quiet influence in global economics, except during the heydays of cycling, when bicycles attained popular status.

Cycling accounts for $50 billion to $100 billion in annual sales and services worldwide, straddling several realms of business, including manufacturing, clothing, sports, tourism, and transport. China produces the most bicycles of any nation. Making only 14,000 bikes in 1949, the year Mao Zedong and the Communist Party took control, and 1.1 million in 1958, the year of the Great Leap Forward, the bike industry has expanded to produce about 40 million units per year since 1987. In 1991, China's production was split between state-owned factories (40%) and foreign joint-ventures (60%), and as domestic demand was estimated at 30 million bikes, over seven million bikes were exported to Europe, the Americas, Indonesia, and Korea. The state-owned factories include one in Shanghai that makes the Phoenix brand, and another in Guangzhou making the Five Rams brand.

The China Bicycle Company (CBC) of Guangzhou was founded by Jerome Sze, a Hong Kong businessman and early player in Deng Xiaoping's special commercial zones. The company, which is traded on the Shenzhen stock exchange, began making bikes for Western firms such as Schwinn in the 1970s, and has expanded with access to China's domestic market and its cheap labor (with one-tenth the labor costs of Europe and one-twentieth of Japan). In the 1990s, the CBC opened a new factory in Shenzhen, making its own Diamond Back bikes, and those of its competition, Schwinn, Specialized, and Scott. In 1992, CBC was rated one of the top ten foreign investment enterprises in China.

Taiwan is the world's second largest producer, making almost ten million bicycles in 1987 and about seven million in 1993. Taiwan makes over 70 percent of the bikes sold in the U.S. The biggest Taiwanese bike makers are Giant Manufacturing Company and Merida Industry Co., producing their own brands and supplying bikes to Schwinn, Raleigh, and numerous others. Japan has Shimano Industrial Corp., the world's largest bike component maker, and an annual domestic demand of about eight million bikes. After yen shock raised prices in the late-1980s, Japan's bike production has dropped below seven million in the mid-1990s, as it imports a million bikes a year, mostly from Taiwan. Japan's bike exports dropped from a million units in 1980 to 110,000 in 1993, as fewer bikes were shipped to Europe and North America and more went to Southeast Asia.

BALANCE

...an essential key to a smooth ride in bilateral trade relationships.

According to the *Guinness Book of World Records*, the largest privately owned bicycle manufacturer is the Hero Cycles Company of India, which produced roughly 2.5 million bicycles in 1987, about 40 percent of the Indian market. Founded in 1956 by the Munjal family, the company makes all the components, except tires, tubes, and resin products, at its factory in Ludhiana, Punjab. The bicycle industry in India has grown from the process of assembling British imports to a group of self-sufficient companies named the "Big Four," (Hero, Atlas, Avon, and TI Cycles) which exported some $37 million in bikes and parts in 1980.[8]

Before 1990, when the Soviet and East German (GDR) bicycle industries were state-owned, bikes from those countries were known for their bad quality. Most of the Soviet Union's poorly made bikes came from a centralized factory in Charkov, Ukraine. The German magazine *Eulenspiegel* (1989) described "unroadworthy" new bikes from the GDR's "People's Factory," with rear wheels mounted the wrong way around, spokes protruding from nipples that punctured tires, badly assembled brakes, rubbing chainsets, and non-functioning lights. Three-speed hubs were not available, and since the 1950s cyclists have crossed illegally from East to West Germany to purchase them. Quality bikes were sold in Western department stores for foreign currency. Since the destruction of the Berlin Wall, Western investors have bought interests in the East German bike industry, or set up subsidiaries. In 1993, the Mitteldeutsche Fahrradwerke was producing Shimano-equipped city and mountain bikes, such as the Boss, made of fine wood and leather, and advertised as "the only alternative for bankers and stockbrokers who wish to convey themselves in a manner which befits their standing in life."[9]

The distribution of bicycles varies throughout the world. In India, where one in 12.5 people own bicycles and production does not keep pace with the need, bicycle frames and parts are shipped from the manufacturers directly to the bike dealers for assembly in shops with no middleman distributors involved. In China, since 1949 the central government has controlled distribution of bicycles by community-based cooperatives which award bikes to exemplary citizens. Then around 1980, with a gradual wave of "liberation" in the country, bicycle manufacturers were given greater freedom to distribute at least one-third of their products both locally and for export.

In the U.S., mass merchants sold 71 percent of the retail bike market in 1993, valued at about $875 million, while independent dealers sold about 29 percent, valued at $684 million. However, independent dealers sold more bike parts and accessories, valued at $926 million (excluding clothing and repairs), compared to mass merchant sales of $310 million and mail order sales of $300 million.

The bike industry has become a global market since World War II, with producers in Asia, Europe, and North America balancing their fortunes on fluctuating exchange rates, labor costs, and tariff restrictions. To help England after the war, the U.S. Congress cut duties on English roadsters from eleven to 5.5 percent. So as not to compete with America's balloon-tire bikes, they were specified to 1) weigh less than 36 pounds; 2) have wheels 63.5 centimeters or larger; 3) allow clearance for tires no wider than 1.625 inches. Imports totaled about 1.3 percent of the U.S.

market until 1949, when England devalued the pound from $4 to $2.80, and the lightweight English three-speed, formerly an expensive bike, became affordable to a wider market. By 1955, imports grew to over 40 percent of the U.S. market, and President Eisenhower signed an import law that increased taxes on heavyweight bikes, with less taxes for light-weight European bikes, which increased in popularity in the 1960s and 1970s. Tariffs on hybrid bikes are being disputed in the 1990s because these bikes have characteristics of both heavyweights and lightweights. Tariffs on imported tires were cut in half by 1970, and the Carlisle Tire and Rubber Co. became the last U.S. manufacturer of bike tires.

Frank W. Schwinn, president of Schwinn Bicycle Co. from 1933 to 1963, brought many sales innovations the bike market. The "Schwinn Plan" began in the 1950s and built a loyal network of distributors, dealer-ships, and mechanics to increase the brand-name value of Schwinn bikes, by keeping the Schwinn name off discounted mass merchant bikes, and preventing those bikes from being sold in Schwinn stores. In 1967, the Supreme Court ruled in *The U.S. vs. Schwinn* that such restrictions were illegal. Although there was no apparent price fixing, Schwinn reduced their distributors and retailers, and allowed stores to sell other brands and interchangeable parts. Schwinn reached its peak market share of over 25 percent in 1950 and its peak sales of 1.5 million units in 1974. Though it was not the largest U.S. bike maker, Schwinn set the standard for quality. In 1990, Schwinn was rated among American consumers as the best-known name of all sporting goods (297th of all brands, between United Air Lines and Doublemint gum) in a market survey by Landor Associates of San Francisco.[10]

Schwinn's third generation was led by the great-grandson of Ignaz Schwinn and nephew of Frank Schwinn, Edward R. Schwinn Jr., who became company president in 1979 at age 29. The Schwinn family lost control of the 97-year-old privately-owned company after filing for bank-ruptcy in October 1992. The public record showed revenues of $195 mil-lion, debts of $82 million (almost half unsecured), a sinking market share of less than seven percent, and 1,838 anxious Schwinn dealers. Schwinn's problems began with a United Auto Workers strike in 1980 that brought the gradual shutdown of its historic Chicago factory. Schwinn invested in a new factory in Greenville, Mississippi, that cost millions and was even-tually closed in 1991. Schwinn's best managers departed in the late-1980s, and the company reduced its supply from Giant Manufacturing and bought shares of another supplier, the China Bicycle Company. Another bike factory investment of the late-1980s was Schwinn-Csepel, a joint-venture with Csepel Works in Budapest, Hungary. At first, Schwinn was praised for positioning itself to exploit the Eastern European market, but later it was criticized as a money-losing diversion.

In January 1993, the Schwinn Bicycle Company was sold for $40.75 million to the Scott Sports Group, headed by a pair of successful "vulture investors," regarded as the best management team available, Sam Zell of Zell/Chilmark Fund L.P., a Chicago-based partnership, and Charles

Waterbottle from the new Schwinn Bicycle Company.

Ferries of Scott USA, an enterprising Idaho-based ski and bike maker. The Schwinn family trust received about $2.5 million and the contents of the Schwinn museum, which became the Bicycle Museum of America curated by James Hurd in Chicago. The Paramount name went to Scott, and the Paramount factory in Wisconsin went to Richard Schwinn and now produces Waterford Precision Bicycles. The China Bicycle Company received full debt payment from its Schwinn-owned stock, while unsecured creditors, such as Schwinn pensioners, were said to be the biggest losers. Scott Sports Group moved the Schwinn Bicycle Company to bike-friendly Boulder, Colorado, with the new slogan: "Established 1895. Re-established 1994."

ECONOMICAL TRANSPORT

The bicycle offers the most economical means of travel. Compared to walking, cycling saves time. Compared to driving, cycling saves money. Compared to anything living or man-made that moves, cycling saves energy. *Time* magazine summed it up in an otherwise bike-bashing article titled "Scaring the Public to Death" (1987):

> A marvel of efficiency, the bicycle is also cheap, handy, nimble. It can sprint like a cat, then stop on a dime and give you nine cents change. It is easy to ride and speedy enough for any sane short-distance traveler. In the typical bumper-to-bumper city creepathon the bike can outrun a Porsche.

Most indicators point to transport as a major factor in economic growth and prosperity, with the sales and profits of the auto and oil industries as a popular measure. This applies to industrial nations, where the auto and oil industries account for one of every six or seven jobs, and in developing countries, which were supporting motor vehicle growth rates of from nine percent (Pakistan and Thailand) to 26 percent (Kenya) per year in the 1990s. It is estimated that about half of the world's earnings are motor vehicle-related.

Some institutions help create the perception that bicycles have a minimal economic impact. For example, a 400-page World Bank report of 1985 called "China Transport Sector Study" failed to mention the important role of bicycles. Likewise, for many years the U.S. Department of Commerce placed bicycle sales data under the category of toys, until bikes started outselling cars in the 1970s. In Latin American countries such as El Salvador, bikes are classified as sporting goods rather than as vehicles, so imported bikes are taxed as luxury items. With the global recession of the early 1990s, there has been a policy shift towards inclusion of non-motorized transport.

Transportation has an enormous cost on the economies of both developing and industrial nations. Surveys in rural Kenya showed that 90 percent of all trips are made by walking (four percent are by bicycle), with the majority being three to six hour trips by women gathering water and firewood, using about one-fourth of their daily energy. With the use of cycling machines, they could save roughly two to four hours per day.

The U.S. spends more on transport than on food or housing, accounting for fifteen to eighteen percent of the gross national product (GNP), and sixteen to 22 percent of personal expenses, while Japan spends about nine percent of their GNP on transport. The U.S. spends less than one percent of all transport funds for cycling and non-motorized vehicles, whereas the Netherlands spends about ten percent.[11]

The auto, oil, and highway infrastructure has various subsidies, incentives, and hidden costs, such as the servicing of road accidents, the loss of productivity due to traffic congestion, the health damage caused by air and noise pollution, the tax abatements for parking facilities, and the travel expenses paid by business and government. The total cost of driving in the U.S. in 1990 was estimated to be roughly $5.50 per gallon, about $4 more than the cost of gas at the pump. These subsidies allow the automobile to flourish in a rigged market that contradicts free market ideology.

Travel expenses are hidden subsidies widely given to motor vehicles that have only recently been offered to bicycles. They illustrate the bicycle's low operating cost and its growing political-economic value. In early 1975, James Berryhill, a cyclist who worked with the U.S. Bureau of Outdoor Recreation in Atlanta, Georgia, put a travel expense claim of 60 cents for a twenty mile trip by bicycle from the Fort Worth, Texas, airport to an official speaking engagement. Despite the fact that this amounted to three cents per mile, compared to seventeen cents per mile for a car, government officials refused to pay because the Travel Expense Act of 1949 allowed only motor vehicles. Meanwhile, Bob DuVall, of the California Department of General Services, asked the state for reimbursement from two years in the mid-1970s for expenses while traveling by bicycle on the job to various inventory sites. DuVall's claim amounted to $49.05 for 1,625 miles. He pushed it to a vote in the State Legislature where it passed and was signed by Governor Jerry Brown. Since the 1980s, more businesses and regional governments have created incentives for employees to use bicycles to save money, to increase energy efficiency, and to reduce insurance rates by having healthier workers.

Courtesy of GE Capital

COST OF TRANSPORT—BIKES VS. CARS

In 1976, the cost of owning and operating a car for ten years was about $18,000, compared to the cost of owning and operating a bicycle which was $450.[12] In 1990, the average U.S. retail price of a car was $13,581, and the cost of a bike was $385. The cost of operating a car in the U.S. averages 58 cents per mile, while the cost of operating a bicycle is one to five cents per mile. U.S. households spend about twenty percent of their annual income on owning and operating cars.[13]

In 1990, the average cost of a car in developing countries amounts to 30 years of personal income, while the average cost of a bicycle is six months. One hundred bikes can be produced for the same amount of energy and resources as one mid-sized automobile. The number of cars that have been trashed since 1946 in the U.S. totals 288 million.[14]

Of all urban trips in the U.S., 43 percent are under four miles, and 67 percent are under eight miles. If one in every four motorists traveling four miles or less (eleven percent of all urban trips) switched to bicycles they would save 2.5 billion gallons of gasoline per year, worth about $4 billion. The reduced cost to society would be an estimated $15 billion. In Britain, if one in every ten motorists traveling under ten miles switched to bicycles they would save nearly 600 million gallons of oil per year.

Since 1956 the 42,000-mile Interstate Highway System has cost over $230 billion to construct. With another 800,000 miles of road eligible for federal aid between 1980 and 1990, annual U.S. spending for highways nearly doubled from about $8 billion to $16 billion.[15] The American Lung Association estimates that the annual health care costs and loss of productivity due to vehicle pollution is between $4 billion and $93 billion. University of California researchers estimate that more than 30,000 deaths per year in the U.S. are caused by respiratory illness related to motor vehicle air-pollution.[16]

Environmentalism

The environment is an all-encompassing phenomena, with the elements of earth, air, and water combining as a whole organism to influence the quality of life for all creatures. Likewise, the environment and the quality of life are influenced by issues of a political, ideological, economical, and human rights nature.

Humanity's role in nature is at the heart of the enviromental issue. On one hand there is a religious, technological belief that man is separate from nature, that he can control and dominate it to suit his needs. On the other hand is the holistic, ecological belief that humans must understand and cooperate with nature because we are part of it.

One of the major benefits of the bicycle is that it is an ecological vehicle. The bicycle is considered by most evironmentalists as the most appropriate means of mobility for humanity, being an intermediate or "ecotopian" technology that is relatively clean, quiet, and healthy. The bicycle's environmental attributes have been recognized since its beginnings, but in recent generations the importance of the bicycle has grown with the concerns for the health of the planet and its inhabitants.

For the past hundred years, industrial civilization has been formed and fueled by petroleum. While auto and oil production was the economic lubricant for industrial nations, the Organization of Petroleum Exporting Countries (OPEC) was formed in 1960 by a group of oil-producing non-industrialized countries, that eventually grew to include Algeria, Ecuador, Gabon, Indonesia, Iran, Iraq, Kuwait, Libya, Nigeria, Qatar, Saudi Arabia, the United Arab Emirates, and Venezuela. During the energy crisis of the early 1970s, OPEC's members acted as a cartel to raise oil prices, which caused gasoline shortages, inflation, and economic problems for oil-importing countries in Europe, Asia, and North America.

OPEC was supposedly conceived of as an environmental organization by one of its main founders, Juan Pablo Pérez Alfonzo. He believed that selling oil too cheaply was bad for consumers, resulting in the premature exaustion of a non-renewable resource. For producing countries, oil was a national resource which should not be squandered today at the expense of future generations. The only way to stop the industrial nations of the West from wasteful consumption was to raise oil prices so high that they would be forced to limit oil imports and conserve. As Pérez Alfonzo grew disillusioned with oil politics and OPEC, he described oil as "the excrement of the devil," and said "I have always been an ecologist first of all. I live for my flowers. OPEC, as an ecological group, has really disappeared. Cars are a cosmic curse and should be replaced by bicycles. Electricity ought to be replaced by candles, and petroleum by wood." The *Washington Post* reported that, "the idea of OPEC as the promoter of bicycles seemed an unlikely image then. But Juan Pablo was merely ahead of his time."[17]

By 1990, transportation used about 67 percent of all petroleum products in the U.S., an amount that has increased from about 50 percent in 1970. Industrial and household applications of oil account for 25 percent of its total use, making food packaging, fabrics, ointments, printing inks, asphalt, building materials, and bicycle parts. By 1990, annual oil consumption per person in North America was about 1,050 gallons, the highest in the world. Per capita consumption in Japan was about 600 gallons, and Europeans used an average of 500 gallons.[18]

Anne Hansen's bicycle, 1990.

Because cycling burns calories instead of petroleum, it contributes almost nothing to oil pollution, except for the solvents and lubricants used to produce and operate bikes. Burning fossil fuels such as gasoline or diesel fuel releases carbon dioxide, carbon monoxide, and other noxious chemicals and particulates into the air that are partly responsible for acid rain, climate change, and the loss of the protective ozone layer. Motor vehicles are the single largest source of air pollution, with passenger cars accounting for more than thirteen percent of the total carbon dioxide emitted worldwide from burnt fossil fuels, equivalent to more than 700 tons of carbon per year. Accidental oil tanker spills dump an average of 125 million gallons into the sea each year, and another 750 million gallons are either flushed into the sea by routine cleaning of oil tanks, or spilled into the environment by "do it yourself" mechanics changing the oil in their car.[19]

AIR POLLUTION BY MODE OF TRAVEL
GRAMS PER PASSENGER MILE[20]

Mode	Hydrocarbons	Carbon monoxide	Nitrogen oxides
Bicycle	0.00	0.00	0.00
Rail	0.01	0.02	0.47
Bus	0.20	3.05	1.54
Car (1)	2.09	15.06	2.06
Carpool	0.70	5.02	0.69
Vanpool	0.36	2.42	0.38

After the Exxon Valdez oil spill in 1989, the bicycle presented itself as an environmental solution. An advertisement by the environmental group Greenpeace, which pictured the tanker's captain, stated: "It wasn't his driving that caused the Alaska oil spill. It was yours." Another ad by the Cannondale bicycle company read, "Let's take Exxon to the cleaner's. Ride a bike to work today." *USA Today* reported that response to the ad was high, though mixed. A couple of Exxon employees who owned Cannondale bikes wanted refunds, while other readers complained about the unnecessary apostrophe in "cleaner's."

NOISE POLLUTION

Noise pollution is another environmental problem to which cyclists contribute almost nothing, yet they suffer many of the effects of other people's behavior. Road traffic is the major cause of noise pollution in urban and suburban areas, from tire friction, combustion engine noise, horns, alarms, and sirens. In the Central London Noise Survey (1990), which tested 400 sites in the city, 84 percent of the noise was attributed to traffic. More than a third of the people questioned in the survey were disturbed by traffic noise at home, while one in five were disturbed by traffic noise outside.[21]

Noise is an invisible but stressful pollution that is difficult to access.

For one thing, the decibel scale which measures sound is a non-linear logarithmic progression where an increase in three decibels (dB) doubles the noise intensity. Because of the way the brain perceives sound, a person's impression is that ten dB doubles the subjective loudness of noise. Our impression of sound is further complicated by the resentment factor, in which we perceive loudness especially if the sound is unpleasant. About 150 dB will cause the ear drums to pop, and 100 dB for many hours every day for several years is enough to cause hearing loss. At a noise level of 60 dB the maximum distance for conversation is two meters. When noise rises to 80 dB the distance decreases to twenty centimeters, and at 90 dB conversation is reduced to shouting into each other's ears.

The health effects are such that about 60 percent of people are "highly annoyed" by noise levels of 80 dB, and sleep patterns are disturbed by noise levels of 40 dB or more. High levels of traffic noise are likely to make people aggressive, quarrelsome, fatigued and more accident-prone. When coupled with the stress of traffic, the effect can be devastating in terms of safety and human relations. By law, most motor vehicles are allowed to generate up to about 80 dB, depending on the country. While many motor vehicles provide sound-proof enclosed interiors with radios, music, and phones, the noise of traffic and sirens has increased. Electric vehicles promise a quieter solution for cars and trucks by eliminating the sounds of combustion. However, for cyclists there is one benefit from the noise of motor vehicles. The bike rider in the street without a rearview mirror can detect the approach and relative speed of a motorist coming from behind by sound.

BIKE POLLUTION

Human-powered vehicles may be nearly pollution-free in use, but the process of manufacturing and selling them produces considerable amounts of garbage and hazardous waste. These include the processing of raw materials in bicycle manufacturing, the energy consumed in their distribution, and all the packaging and marketing materials produced for promotion.

As a product of the Industrial Revolution, bicycles have evolved with the expansion of high-tech manufacturing processes. Widely described as a low-tech self-sufficient device, the modern bicycle has components that require a relatively sophisticated level of industrial processing in their construction. As progress continues with bikes made of exotic alloy metallurgy and chemical or petroleum based resins and fibers, the nature of the bicycle's manufacturing waste has changed.

The Consumer Goods Hazardous Waste Study of April 1988 describes the typical hazardous wastes generated in the manufacture of ten-speed bicycles. The report was submitted by Science Applications International Corporation for the New Jersey Waste Facilities Siting Commission. A "hazardous waste" is defined by the Resource Conservation and Recovery Act (RCRA) as:

a solid waste, or combination of solid wastes, which because of its quantity, concentration, or physical, chemical or infectious characteristics may cause, or significantly contribute to an increase in (human) mortality or an increase in serious irreversible, or incapacitating reversible, illness, or pose a substantial present or potential hazard to human health of the environment when improperly treated, stored, transported, or disposed of, or otherwise managed.

The report analyzed parts of a low-cost bike including the carbon steel frame, the chrome plated wheels and handlebars, the rubber tires and tubes, the ABS plastic (acrylonitrile-butadiene-styrene) pedals and seats, and the paints and lubricants used. The manufacture of a complete bicycle involves at least 35 hazardous wastes listed by the U.S. Environmental Protection Agency (EPA) such as spent solvents, sludges, and furnace dusts, and numerous organic chemical by-products. Since each component may be made of various materials such as steel, anodized aluminum, titanium, epoxy resin carbon fiber, rubber, plastic, foam, lycra, and leather, each component adds another hazardous industrial process. The bike in the study generated this partial list of toxic elements with their EPA hazardous waste number:

Emission control dust/sludge from the primary production of steel in electric furnaces. (K061)

Spent pickle liquor generated by steel finishing operations of plants that produce iron or steel. (K062)

Spent halogenated solvents used in degreasing: tetrachloroethylene, methylene chloride, 1,1,1-trichloroethane, carbon tetrachloride, and chlorinated fluorocarbons; and sludges from the recovery of these solvents in degreasing operations. (F001)

Spent non-halogenated solvents: xylene, acetone, ethyl acetate, ethyl benzene, ethyl ether, methyl isobutyl ketone, n-butyl alcohol, cyclohexanone, and methanol; and the still bottoms from the recovery of these solvents. (F003)

Spent non-halogenated solvents: toluene, methyl ethyl ketone, carbon disulfide, isobutanol, and pyridine; and the still bottoms from the recovery of these solvents. (F005)

Dissolved air flotation float from the petroleum refining industry. (K048)

Slop oil emulsion solids from the petroleum refining industry. (K049)

Heat exchanger bundle cleaning sludge from the petroleum refining industry. (K050)

API separator sludge from the petroleum refining industry. (K051)

Tank bottoms (leaded) from the petroleum refining industry. (K052)

Wastewater treatment sludge from the production of pigments. (K002-K008)

Bottom streams from the wastewater stripper in the production of acrylonitrile. (K011)

Bottom streams from the acetonitrile column in the production of acrylonitrile. (K013

Bottoms from the acetonitrile purification column in the production of acrylonitrile. (K014)

Bicycle Activism

Bicycles have their own political agenda developed from the ideas and actions of bicycle activists. By promoting widespread bicycle use through the various social benefits of cycling such as equality, economy, ecology, and exercise, bicycle advocates are both loved and loathed in the eyes of the public and in the ranks of the cyclists whom they seek to represent. Bicycles symbolize both conservative ideals and revolutionary movements, and bike advocates and activists illustrate these two components by working through conventional and radical methods.

Within the bicycling community, conventional application of political pressure includes manufacturers lobbying legislators for favorable trading conditions, and national or local groups pressuring public officials for cycling facilities through letter writing campaigns and meetings with public officials and planners, backed by educational programs in safety, consumer protection, and legal aid. The more radical methods of making political statements include public rallies and human-powered "direct action" protests through street theater, road blockades, and civil disobedience for rights of way, backed by leafleting, manifestos, and worldwide networking.

Bicycle activism grew in the early days of cycling with national groups such as the Cyclists' Touring Club (1878), the League of American Wheelmen (1880), the Algemeen Nederlandsch Wielrijdersbond (1883), the Italian Touring Club (1895), the German Cycling Federation (1895), and the Danish Cyklist Forbund (1905). The original agenda was oriented towards all aspects of cycling, including road development, rights of way, touring camaraderie, and in some cases race promotion. Many of these groups still flourish, and many more groups have sprouted, especially in the 1970s, because of increased bicycle use and the awareness of the bicycle as a solution to many community problems.

Bicycle activists have formed groups all around the world which reflect the environmentalist's motto, "think globally, act locally." International conferences such as Velo-City and Pro Bike, unite bicycle activists for sharing news, activities, and ideas with national and regional cycling advocacy groups. The European Cyclists' Federation (ECF) was formed in Copenhagen in 1983 as a result of the first Velo-City International Cycle Planning Conference held in Bremmen, Germany, in 1980. By 1987, the ECF represented over 25 national organizations linked to another 700 regional groups with a combined membership of about 250,000 bicycle activists, for the purpose of promoting cycling within the European Community.

Given the dual nature of political activism, with "hot-blooded reformists" and "level-headed realists," once in a while the ideologies of cyclists conflict with one another. This was illustrated in an article called "Points of View: Considerations for Cycling in the Future," in *Bicycle USA* (January 1990). The opinions of Alan Streater and John Forester

raised the issue of environmentalism in relation to cyclists' rights, causing what one letter writer described as an "identity crisis on the subject of advocacy."

It all boils down to why you started riding a bicycle in the first place. If you're like me, you started riding a bike because you're a penny-pinching cheapskate, and you don't want to pay for a car. And when you're a cheapskate, the only thing worse than spending money is spending it on something you don't want to support anyway. For me that means not wanting to support air pollution, oil spills, parking lots... I could go on indefinitely, but you've heard it before.

That's right, I'm one of those blasted environmentalists for whom an anti-car attitude is the whole point for riding a bike. Recreation is a kind of afterthought—I figure I already put air in my tires, so I might as well go for a ride.

On the other hand, a substantial portion of us were drawn to the sport primarily for recreation—fitness, neato high-tech equipment, whatever. Recreation-oriented cyclists are bound to put a different spin on their advocacy from environmentally-oriented cyclists.

Nonetheless, we're still on the same team and we even need each other. You realists out there are valuable as liaisons with the more traditional elements of our society, but the anti-car people are capable of shaking, motivating, and inspiring.[22]

Street theater is a popular form of bicycle activism involving lively public demonstrations with imaginative non-violent methods of protest. One of the more original practitioners of street theater has been Montreal's Le Monde à Bicyclette, a cycling advocacy group founded in 1975 and led by "Bicycle Bob" Robert Silverman and Claire Morissette. On the occasion of their tenth anniversary in 1985, Morissette recounted "Ten Years of *vélorution*," in the group's popular newspaper, *Le Monde à Bicyclette*.

Calling themselves "*vélorutionaires*," "*vélo*-Quixotes," and "*vélo*-holy rollers," the group drafted the "Cyclist's Manifesto" and presented it and a bicycle to Mayor Drapeau. To protest the carnage caused by cars, they argued before the Canadian Radio and Television Commission for the restriction of auto advertising, saying that cars are more harmful than cigarettes and hard liquor. They blocked the entrance to the Montreal Auto Show wearing gas masks, using stretchers, bandages, and crutches, calling it "Ambulance Theatre." To protest the amount of land used up by motor vehicles, "Space Demonstrations" were held with cyclists making automobile-sized "space frames" of wood and wire for their bikes. While parading along St. Catherine Street, participating "like everyone else" in the chronic traffic congestion, they discovered how "the scandal of space monopolized by one rider was so much more flagrant than the same space taken by one driver that those in cars blew their cool and charged recklessly at the cyclists. One motorist even drove up on the sidewalk with all four wheels to pass."

Morissette also wrote about the episode when some cyclists went to jail for painting their own path on the public road:

> Strange how simple it seems to go to the moon and pick daisies, yet almost impossible to develop a network of cycling paths—even a few routes—downtown, in front of our homes and to the doorstep of our workplaces.
>
> It cost us nothing more than a few gallons of paint when we decided to create a "do-it-yourself" north-south line one hot summer night on 1978. The following day a green line swung happily down Saint Urbain Street and Marie-Anne Street, the very same strange green hue that stained the soles of certain smiling cyclists present at the ribbon-cutting ceremony.
>
> These same stains gave us away when in June 1980, and then in September of the same year, the police caught us green-handed. Certain individuals were acquitted by their judges who saw the nobility of their cause. Others were treated as dangerous criminals by a judge with questionable political connections and sent to Bordeaux prison to serve their sentence. At Le Monde à Bicyclette, this "do or die" attitude is a way of thought and action. From their cell, the incarcerated cyclists could at least dream of the cycling path in North Montreal.
>
> On the order of Mr. Niding, Drapeau's right-hand man, (found guilty, several months later, of having his $200,000 house built as a "favor" by one of the Olympic Games contractors), several gallons of paint were also bought but, instead of extending our cycling paths, he had them covered with a grey matching the rest of the urban drabness.[23]

Friends of the Earth keeping cycle lanes open, Cambridge, England, 1987.

Lacking access for cyclists to cross the St. Lawrence river by subway or on the city's five bridges, on Easter holiday in 1981 a cyclist, Philip Coutu, dressed as Moses in white robes and read the Ten Bicycle Commandments (Thou shall not kill, Thou shall not pollute...) and attempted to part the waters. As a result of the group's activities, bike racks were installed on buses, access was provided on trains, and bridges were opened for pedestrians and cyclists.

Tooker Gomberg, an Edmonton city councilor and cycling advocate, went on a "Pollution Solution" tour of ten North American cities in 1990. Sponsored by a $10,000 grant from the Canadian government, with the purpose of reducing acid rain, Gomberg led various groups of activists wearing gas masks and white anti-toxic body suits who handed out "environmental tickets" to gridlocked motorists. He told the press in Washington, D.C.: "The bicycle is so small and quiet and innocuous. So we have to raise the profile and stick the bicycle on the agenda. It's all well and good to write letters and to phone elected representatives and to be polite. But this street theater is useful too."[24]

"Critical Mass" occurred in 1993, as cycling gained more attention and funding in government spheres, and new cyclists joined the *vélorution*. Seeking a new approach to direct action in traffic-congested cities, cycling activists discovered the idea of critical mass. Defined as the minimum amount of people required to make something happen, it was based on the bike traffic in China, shown in Ted White's video, *Return of the Scorcher* (1992), where cyclists crossing busy roads at uncontrolled intersections would gather enough mass to stop opposing traffic. Critical Mass rides began in the San Francisco Bay Area and New York City in 1992, and a "chain reaction" occurred as they spread to cities throughout North America to Havana, Barcelona, and Poznan, Poland. Groups of five or five hundred cyclists would meet as an "organized coincidence" after work at rush hour and create a "bike clot."

Critical mass rides have generated new slogans of bike protest, as in: "We don't block traffic, we are traffic," or "We don't block traffic, we open minds," and they have added new meaning to words like "corking." It operates by "xerocracy" with rides announced by flyers, phone trees, e-mail, and zines such as *CM Missives* and *Hey! Get Out of Our Way!* Not all motorists or cyclists are happy to see Critical Mass, as there are sometimes actions of provocation and assault. A mass ride around Berkeley in July 1993 veered onto the I-80 freeway, where the police staged a Critical Mass arrest of 63 cyclists.

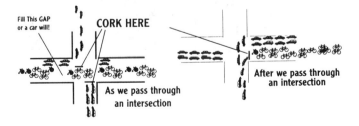

Environmental ticket (above); Instructions for "corking" an intersection (right).

Bikes Vs. Cars

There is a certain antagonism between cyclists and motorists and their vehicles. Many bicycle activists believe the biggest threat to cycling and to the human species is embodied by the motor vehicle in its present state. Yet not all cyclists dislike motor vehicles. There are many similarities in cycling and car culture and many cyclists are just as thrilled by cars as by bikes. When *Bicycling* magazine surveyed its readers on their favorite cars, perhaps to encourage its auto advertising, one cyclist wrote, "At last, a survey I can get excited about."

Automobiles offer personal convenience and power, but many benefits commonly attributed to them, such as speed, safety, unlimited mobility, economic growth, and sex appeal, are proving to be false myths. Furthermore, many automobile problems, such as congestion, danger, pollution, and noise, can be improved upon. There is nothing inherently wrong with motor vehicles that are clean, quiet, quick, compact, healthy to use, safe, economical, logical, and personable. As it is, the only vehicles with those attributes appear to be the human-powered kind. The following statements illustrate the many sides to this controversy:

> Government must help to eliminate cars so that bicycles can help to eliminate government.
> —Kabouter slogan, Holland (1967)

> The bicycle wins if it does not lose, the automobile loses if it does not win.
> —New York City graffiti (1984)

> "Cyclophobists and Motophobists"
> The "cyclophobist," or bicycle hater, is a well-known though rapidly disappearing type. Since he can no longer vent his spleen upon the bicycle he must seek other victims, and the motor vehicle offers him his next opportunity. The "motophobist," or automobile hater, is already developing abroad, where motor vehicles are becoming common. The prevalence of the petroleum motor, and its concomitant odor, gives him his excuse for abuse, but his ignorance of the fact that motor vehicles are driven by other power than petroleum sometimes makes his "motophobia" ridiculous.
> —Anonymous (1898)

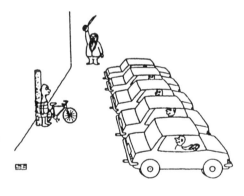

> The ordinary horseless carriage is at present a luxury for the wealthy; and although its price will probably fall in the future, it will never, of course, come into as common use as the bicycle.
> —*The Literary Digest* (1899)

"Principal Arguments That May Be Marshaled Against Bicycles"
1. Bicycles are childish.
2. Bicycles are indignified.
3. Bicycles are unsafe.
4. Bicycles are un-American.
5. I don't like the kind of people who ride bicycles.
6. Bicycles are unfair.
7. Bicycles are good exercise.
    —P.J. O'Rourke, *Car and Driver* (June 1984)[25]

"Bicycles are Model Citizens"
I ride a bicycle—not because I hate General Motors but haven't the courage to bomb an auto plant. I don't do it as a gesture of great stoicism and personal sacrifice. I am not even engaged, necessarily, in an act of political protest over that company's responsibility for most of the air pollution by tonnage in the United States.
 It's like finally giving up cigarettes. You just wake up one morning and realize you don't want to start the day with another automobile. Cigarette smoking is not a pleasure, it's a business. In the same way, you finally come to realize that you don't need General Motors, they need you. They need you to drive their cars for them. You are driving for Detroit and paying them to do it. Automobiles are just a part of your life that's over, that's all. No hard feelings. You've just moved on to something else. From now on you just use their buses, taxis and rental cars when they suit your convenience. You don't keep one for them that you have to house, feed and water, insure and care for.
 You ride a bicycle because it feels good. The air feels good on your body; even the rain feels good. The blood starts moving around your body, and pretty soon it gets to your head, and, glory be, your head feels good. You start noticing things. You look until you really see. You hear things, and smell things you never knew were there. You start whistling nice little original tunes to suit the moment. Words start getting caught in the web of poetry in your mind. And there's a nice feeling, too, in knowing you're doing a fundamental life thing for yourself: transportation. You got a little bit of your life back!
                —Nicholas Johnson, *The New York Times* (1973)

"Energy and Equity"
The model American male devotes more than 1,600 hours a year to his car. He sits in it while it goes and while it stands idling. He parks it and searches for it. He earns the money to put down on it and to meet the monthly installments. He works to pay for gasoline, tolls, insurance, taxes, and tickets. He spands four of his sixteen waking hours on the road or gathering resources for it. And this figure docs not take into account the time consumed by other activities dictated by transport: time spent in hospitals, traffic courts, and garages; time spent watching automobile commercials.... The model American puts in 1,600 hours to

get 7,500 miles: less than five miles per hour. In countries deprived of a transportation industry, people manage to do the same, walking wherever they want to go.... What distinguishes the traffic in rich countries from the traffic in poor countries is not more mileage per hour of lifetime for the majority, but more hours of compulsory consumption of high doses of energy, packaged and unequally distributed by the transportation industry.

Bicycles let people move with greater speed without taking up significant amounts of scare space, energy, or time. They can spend fewer hours on each mile and still travel more miles in a year. They can get the benefit of technological breakthroughs without putting undue claims on the schedules, energy, or space of others. They become masters of their own movements without blocking those of their fellows. Their new tool creates only those demands which it can also satisfy. Every increase in motorized speed creates new demands on space and time. The use of the bicycle is self-limiting. It allows people to create a new relationship between their life-space and their life-time, between their territory and the pulse of their being, without destroying their inherited balance. The advantages of modern self-powered traffic are obvious, and ignored.

—Ivan Illich, *Toward A History of Needs* (1973)

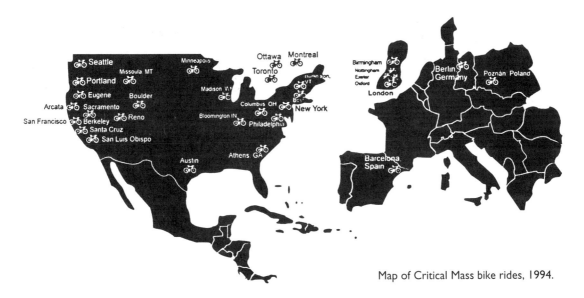

Map of Critical Mass bike rides, 1994.

11 War and Peace

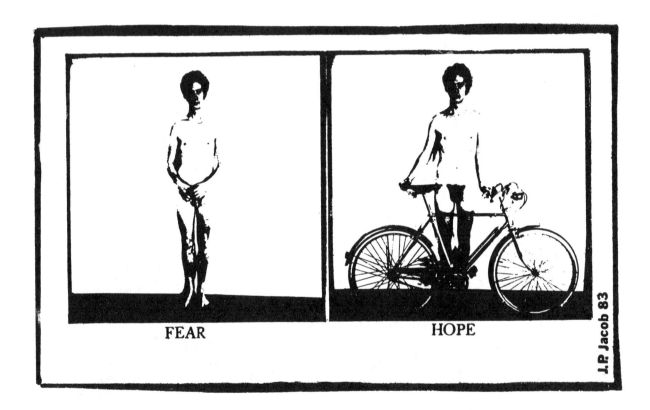

The 5th battalion of cyclists sent from the front has arrived at Tsaryoke. A joint meeting was held, and it was discovered that among the cyclists not a single man was found willing to shed the blood of his brothers, or to support a government of bourgeois land owners, said a commissioner, panting and covered with mud from his ride.
—John Reed, *Ten Days that Shook the World* (1919)

Military Machines

From bicycles to nuclear weapons, machines can enhance and destroy our lives, work for and against our well-being. They allow for a "good servant but a bad master," as Jacques Ellul observed. The bicycle, in its two-wheeled way, shows how a device that is inherently life-giving and peaceful can get drafted into the service of death, destruction, and deceit.

Bicycles have a long history of uses for offensive and defensive military actions. As swift, silent, and self-sufficient vehicles they have been applied in combat, reconnaissance, smuggling, riot control, guerrilla warfare, and resupply networks. Cycles have carried revolvers, machine guns, canons, munitions, explosives, poison gas detectors, communications equipment, food, shelter, medical supplies, and wounded or dead soldiers.

The essential character of military bicycles has been their ability to inspire surprising, ingenious tactics. Often underestimated by traditional military planners who tend to favor larger, more powerful weaponry, the impact of military bicycles has been ignored and lost in modern stories of warfare, which often describe reality with technical jargon and nationalistic slogans. For the American military this lesson became especially meaningful during the Vietnam War. In *Bicycles in War* (1974), the authors Martin Caidin and Jay Barbree describe how after many years of underestimating the impact of bicycles in combat by the U.S. war machine, and despite forewarnings from French military experiences in Vietnam, a David-and-Goliath situation developed when America's multi-million dollar weapons systems were unable to deter the Vietcong bicycle resupply network. In 1967, the U.S. Foreign Relations Committee heard the indications of a stalemate situation caused by Vietcong bicycles. When Senator William Fulbright remarked, "Why don't we bomb their bicycles instead of their bridges? Does the Pentagon know about this?" it brought a round of laughter in Congress.

PARA-MILITARISM

Bicycles have a longtime relationship with military technology and culture. Around 1870, when the Prussians were forming an empire, French velocipede makers such as Compagnie Parisienne stopped building bicycles to store military equipment for the Franco-Prussian War. When Paris was under siege in January 1871, Rowley Turner, the cycling entrepreneur, supposedly missed the last train out of town and was able to escape under fire on his velocipede. The growing bicycle industry moved to Britain and initiated an alliance between the makers of bicycles and weapons, known as "the Military-Industrial Bike Rider Complex."[1]

Cyclists became a new kind of "mechanized infantry" in 1875, when the armed Italian militia, known as the *bersaglieri*, utilized high-wheel bicycles in large-scale maneuvers which duplicated battle conditions. Using bikes equipped with lanterns, mounted rifles, ammunition, and knapsacks, the cyclists, averaging about 12 mph, carried dispatches to isolated units in the field. By the 1880s, the French, Austrian, and British militia also formed cyclist battalions. The English movement was led by Colonel A.T. Saville, a Professor of Tactics at the Royal Staff College in Camberley, who commanded the 26th Middlesex Cyclist Volunteer Rifle Corps in 1888 with a collection of 361 men ranked by their machines: High Wheelers, Safeties, and Tricycles.[2]

French soldiers (above right) with velocipedes, 1870. British regiment (right) using convertible tandems.

Militarism was a major part of the high-wheel bicycle craze in the 1880s, when men's cycling clubs were often fashioned around para-military activities. These included uniforms in club colors with emblems of rank and mileage, and regimented wheeled marches with banners and bugle calls. Clubmen wore gaiters, stockings, knickers, jackets, and caps, and carried pistols, swords, clubs, flags, trumpets, messenger bags, and mess kits. Most of the bugle calls used in organized high-wheel bicycle marches were derived from horseback cavalry, such as the Cavalry Tactics Manual of the U.S. Army.

Bicycle ingenuity in the 1890s inspired many experiments with military cycles. The League of American Wheelmen (LAW) was involved in the promotion of military cycles, and one bugling wheelman was Lieutenant Howard A. Giddings, who commanded cycle maneuvers with the Connecticut National Guard in 1891 using Columbia bicycles and Colt firearms—both manufactured by Albert A. Pope. These wheelmen developed an innovative formation by crouching behind their upside down machines with the wheels spinning to frighten approaching cavalry horses. This was called a "zereba" or "zariba," after the Sudanese thorn-bush enclosures. Giddings later wrote the *Manual for Cyclists: For the Use of the Regular Army, Organized Militia, and Volunteer Troops of the United States* (1896).

In the 1890s, Major Royal Page Davidson of the Northwestern Military Academy in Wisconsin organized sixteen cadets into a cycling corps. They practiced scaling walls in full battle gear with bicycles strapped to their backs, and journeyed from Chicago to Washington, D.C., via the National Pike to present their message to the Secretary of War.

The biggest advocate of military bicycles was Major General Nelson A. Miles, a cyclist involved in the LAW's Good Roads Movement and an "Indian fighter" who led troops that defeated several nations of Native Americans including the Cheyenne, Kiowa, Comanche, and Sioux. Miles organized the 25th Infantry Bicycle Corps in 1896 with Second Lt. James A. Moss as the (white) commander of an "all-Negro" corps. In the summer of 1897, Moss led 21 men on an arduous 1,900 mile, 34 day journey from Fort Missoula, Montana, across the Continental Divide to St. Louis, Missouri. They rode 32-pound Spaulding bicycles equipped with Goodrich tires, Christy anatomic saddles, tandem spokes, reinforced forks, carrier racks, frame-fitting bags, and quick-release rifle clips. Each man carried about 27 pounds of supplies including mess kit, canteen (often filled with whiskey), rifle, ammunition, blanket, half a shelter (the other half was carried by a buddy), and food supplies which were picked up every few days. The next year saw the outbreak of the Spanish-American War, and the 25th Infantry Bicycle Corps was increased to 100 cyclists. After most U.S. troops pulled out of Cuba due to sickness, the 25th Infantry performed riot control duty in Havana. The black cyclists worked 24-hour duty by surrounding crowds and forming bicycle barricades, and they reportedly never had to fire their weapons, not even a warning shot.

Fongers bicycles, used by the Dutch and Dutch-Indian army. Seven-foot tall poster by F.G. Schlette, 1915.

The balance of power is so nicely adjusted that the chances in the coming conflict will be governed by efficiency in detailed operations. The bicycle will weigh in the scale. We are told somewhere that for want of a horseshoe nail a battle was lost. In the next war, for want of a bicycle the independence of a nation may be forfeited.
—W.C. Whitney, U.S. Naval Secretary (1896)

Bicycles were getting serious attention in military circles and inventors responded with new designs and uses for cycling machines. Around 1896, two kinds of specially equipped bicycles for laying and retrieving telegraph wires under combat conditions were developed by Captain R.E. Thompson of the U.S. Army Signal Corps and by Leo Kamm, a German living in London. By 1898, the U.S. Army had commissioned several military cycles from the Pope Manufacturing Co., including a Columbia safety mounted with a 40-pound Colt automatic machine gun, an in-line Columbia tandem equipped with two Colt quick-action revolvers, a twelve-shot rifle, a set of signal flags, and two bundles of blankets and overcoats, and a side-by-side Duplex tricycle featuring a mountain cannon.

Various folding military bikes appeared around 1900, including the cross-frame model designed by a Captain Gerard for the French Army, and the 18-pound, 28-inch wheel, collapsible hammock-saddled Dursley-Pederson designed by Mikael Pederson in Dursley, England, and built for, but never used by, the British Army. In the Boer War of 1899 in South Africa, a native remarked after first seeing the bicycle, "Trust the English to invent a way of travelling while sitting down." The bicycle's success in the Boer War led many other countries to adapt bicycles for military purposes, including France, Germany, Italy, Belgium, Russia, Switzerland, Japan, and China. Other kinds of military cycles include bicycle trailers for large guns, tandems that converted into ambulances, the BSA fire-fighting bicycle, a British cyclograph bicycle for map making, and various portable cycle-generators used to supply power for battlefield communications and lighting.

Many military machines were made to order for governments by companies that made bicycles and arms. These include Pope's Columbia and Colt in the U.S., BSA (Birmingham Small Arms) in Britain, Fongers in Holland, National Arms in Belgium, NSU and Adler in Germany, Condor in Switzerland, Bianchi and Fiat in Italy, with Peugeot and the St. Etienne industry in France. A century later, the linkage of bicycle and arms makers continues, as military contractors apply today's technology to racing bicycles and human-powered vehicles.

Bicycles in Battles

By the time of World War I (1914–1918) most of the world's big armies were using bicycles. Known as the Great War, the conflict involved some 65 million service people, with about thirteen million killed and twenty million wounded. It is estimated that the French and Belgian forces employed 150,000 bicycle troops, while the British had 100,000, the Germans and Turks used about 125,000 each, and the American Expeditionary Force brought 29,000 bicycles when they arrived in 1917.[3]

Among the various battles on the Western and Eastern fronts, both sides shared victories with bicycles, although the increasing industrialization of the war, with motorcycles, tanks, aircraft, and poison gas, overshadowed the bicycle's role. Among the Allies there were differing opinions on how bicycles should be used, such as the attitude of the American Expeditionary Force, which used bicycles merely for communications, reconnaissance, supplementary transport, and recreation, and the Belgians, who formed bicycle commando units with several hundred volunteers that launched demolition raids on railroads behind enemy lines.

One notable battle was the sneak attack in September 1914 by 200 soldiers of Germany's First Bicycle Company, Rifle Battalion, on the Marne River bridge at Mont St. Père. Equipped with bicycle-mounted machine guns and trailers of dynamite, the advance guard of German cyclists surprised the protecting force of 4,000 French soldiers, and destroyed the bridge, slaughtering 444 Frenchmen and losing only five of their own, while returning with a unit of French troops as prisoners. By the end of the war, more than 6,000 bicycle troops were killed in combat, about 8,000 were seriously wounded, and tens of thousands more were listed as missing or taken as prisoners.[4]

In the aftermath of World War I, the military use of bicycles spread to smaller wars. British troops utilized bicycles in Ireland during the Easter Rebellion. When the Irish Republican Army (IRA) formed in 1916 to fight for independence from Britain, bicycles were used in their guerrilla warfare tactics. IRA cyclists quietly worked nights sabotaging communication lines, bridges, railways, and targeting British police and military stations.

In China there were over 200,000 bicycling troops, and bicycles were employed by rival groups during the Nanchang Uprising in 1927. The Russian army developed an innovative solution to sentry duty over the cold, vast landscapes by forming bicycle-man-dog units in the 1930s. Troopers mounted bicycles with fat tires and specially-trained dogs ran beside them with a leash that was either hand-held or mounted near the rear wheel. The dogs could maintain the same pace as a cyclist traveling cross-country, and while sniffing out any danger they guarded the men as they slept. Bicycles had a role in the Chaco War of 1932–1935 between Bolivia and Paraguay over the oil-rich Gran Chaco. With World War II on the horizon, the major powers sent observers, and this reportedly influ-

enced the Germans and Japanese to build up their bicycle forces.

Though World War I was called "the war to end all wars," World War II suggested that war is an inevitable consequence of industrial nationalism and imperialism. As Joseph Stalin was negotiating with Winston Churchill, he said, "This is a war of engines and octanes. I drink to the American auto industry and the American oil industry."[5] When the war began it seemed that powerful armed machinery would be the dominant factor, but as it developed the bicycle's role gained in importance. Because many records of the bicycle troops were lost, scattered, or destroyed as the war played out across the globe, the role of the bicycle in World War II has been "greatly understated."[6]

On the European fronts, bicycle troops were deployed from Norway to North Africa. In the Pacific theater, some 50,000 soldier cyclists were utilized by Japan in the jungles from the Malay Peninsula to Burma. The Nazi *blitzkrieg* ("lightning war") used a combination of rapid and continuous assaults by tanks and armored personnel carriers on the ground, covered by bombers in the air, with cyclists in advance and rear positions. Germany utilized cyclists in chemical warfare units that specialized in securing places attacked by the poison gas of Allied forces. The riders carried impermeable suits with gas masks, hoods, boots, and gloves, and their bikes were equipped with frame-mounted chemical detection and identification kits.

Bicycles were particularly useful in the German invasion of Norway, where the icy and rugged terrain was less suited to blitzkrieg methods. While covered by powerful tanks, the heavily armed cycle troopers with grenade launchers and light machine guns were able to move along narrow trails and mountain passes to defeat the Norwegian defenses.

Both sides dropped large numbers of paratroopers equipped with folding bicycles behind enemy lines for sabotage and espionage. A widely seen British War Department film warned citizens to look out for German paratroopers in disguise, with the scene of an enemy soldier dressed as a Catholic nun who rides a folding bicycle and hides a gun beneath her habit.

In occupied France and Belgium, hundreds of underground resistance teams on bicycles were so successful with surprise explosions, fires, and killings that the German command in Paris banned the use of bicycles at night. A nearly perfectly planned and executed raid by British commandos occurred in February 1942 when Major John Sheffield led a unit of cyclist-paratroopers to demolish a heavily defended and strategic German radar installation along the northern French coast near the village of Bruneval. The commandos were dropped at night equipped with grenades, explosives, machine guns, ammunition, and folding bicycles. They completed their mission in about two-and-a-half hours, passing through machine gun crossfire, and leaving the radar in flames. When they were picked up on the beach by the British Navy, they had only one fatality, with seven wounded, seven left behind, while taking three prisoners.

While the American armed forces brought about 60,000 bicycles overseas, none were assigned to combat duty. Just as in World War I, their bicycles served for supplemental transport, communications, and recreation. Many G.I.s (government issue, or ground infantry) used captured or abandoned bicycles, of which there were thousands piled along French roads, for rapid retreats from the enemy. Since the occupying Germans escaped Holland on Dutch bikes, they are still being asked to "Give back my grandmother's bike."

Dr. Clifford L. Graves, an American who founded the International Bicycle Touring Society and served as a major in a surgical unit on the Belgian-German frontier, described how the bicycle he bought in London on the black market saved his life in a risky retreat during the Battle of the Bulge on December 16, 1944. Finding himself on a dark road face to face with the driver of an advancing German tank squadron, he was luckily mistaken for one of the German soldiers who had been deployed in American uniforms.[7]

Huge supplies of energy and manufactured goods were expended during the war, so many countries had to ration bicycles, clothing, and oil. In Britain, a small controversy arose when the National Committee on Cycling was informed that cycling capes and leggings were not considered as essential clothing and replacement coupons were not available. In Paris, the few nightclubs that stayed open during the Occupation reportedly used pedal-powered dynamos driven by racing cyclists for lighting. Entertainment was provided as the lights brightened and dimmed according to the racers' stamina.[8]

As the war was raging in Europe, the second Sino-Japanese War was being fought from 1937 to 1945 over large areas of Eastern Asia and the Western Pacific. As Japan attacked, invaded, or occupied major parts of China, the Philippines, Hawaii, Thailand, Burma, Malaysia, Singapore, and Indonesia, they joined with the Axis powers of World War II. Under the leadership of General Tomoyuki Yamashita, known as the "Tiger of Malaya," Japan deployed a force of 50,000 bicycle troops equipped to carry rifles, light machine guns, mortars, explosives, food supplies, spare parts, and medicines.

As part of a plan to take over the Dutch East Indies, on the same day, December 7, 1941, the Japanese attacked Pearl Harbor in Hawaii, Hong Kong, and the Malay Peninsula. Landing a fleet of ships on the northeast coast of the Malay Peninsula near the Thai-Malaysian border, and led by the "Tiger," they came with 60,000 soldiers and 20,000 bicycles. Their main objective was the strategic British colony of Singapore at the south. The British forces, which were led by Lieutenant General A.E. Percival, outnumbered the Japanese three to one and were expecting a naval offensive on Singapore, since the dense tropical jungle of the Malay Peninsula was believed to be an impassable barrier.

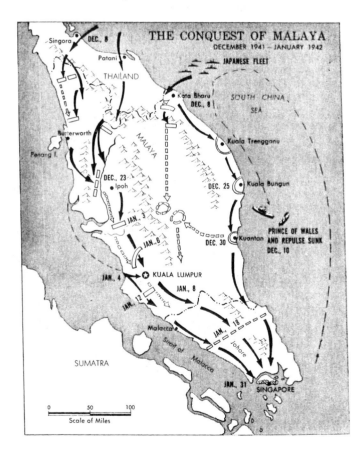

Nevertheless, the Japanese army advanced 700 miles in 70 days. Along the way, the cyclists waded across rivers while holding their machines over their heads. When they had flat tires, they would remove the tires and tubes and ride on the rims, which mimicked the sound of tanks. They would climb trees at night and open fire on the enemy at daybreak. And their most notorious trick was to set off firecrackers and explosive charges creating a barrage that convinced the British that they were under attack by a larger force. By the time they arrived at Singapore, where the fixed guns were pointing out to sea, they took over 4,000 prisoners and General Percival surrendered.

In August 1945 Japan surrendered, and as the Japanese withdrew from Indochina, French rule was restored and the forces of Ho Chi Minh renewed the fight for Vietnamese independence. Under the leadership of General Vo Nguyen Giap, Ho's Army, the Viet Minh, used the bicycle tactics of General Yamashita.

General Giap developed a network of combat supply using bicycle transport. By strengthening the frames and forks of their French Peugeot bicycles, and using cargo sacks and bamboo poles for steering, his men created a war machine that could carry over 500 pounds of supplies. Some 200,000 bicycles moved through jungle roads hauling nearly a hundred tons of rice, arms, and medical supplies per day to stockpiles in caves and tunnels surrounding the heavily defended French camp, known as the *facilité*, located at Dien Bien Phu.

When the battle broke out at Dien Bien Phu in the spring of 1954, the French commander General Henri-Eugene Navarre grossly underestimated what the bicycle porters could carry, and overestimated the effectiveness of the French pilots. While the French dropped time-delayed bombs, the guerrillas used buffalo to clear the roads, thus providing an extra supply of meat. After the airstrip was destroyed, and the fortress at Dien Bien Phu was surrounded by the Viet Minh, the U.S. military reportedly offered to detonate a nuclear weapon there, but the French declined and eventually surrendered.

After the fall of Dien Bien Phu, the Geneva Conference divided Vietnam at the 17th parallel with the paradoxical situation of a communist democratic republic in the north and a U.S.-backed anti-communist government in the south that canceled national elections. Guerrilla warfare ensued in the following years with the formation of the *Viet Nam Cong San*, or Vietcong, and it increased into a full scale war with the arrival of 550,000 U.S. troops in the 1960s.

Bicycles had a special role in the war, as the Vietcong infiltrated deep into the south to the capitol city of Saigon, using hundreds of bicycles in random terrorist bombings. Explosives were packed within the hollow bicycle tubes, detonators were fit beneath bicycle seats, and battery or generator-powered timing devices were installed within bicycle headlights. The bicycles were parked in crowded public places, and at the set time, or when the wheel was moved, the bicycle would explode.

The Vietcong used bicycles in resupply networks along the Ho Chi

Vietcong bicycle supply route.

Minh Trail. A resident of Hanoi said that "Whoever invented the first bicycle could never imagine what the Vietnamese have done with it. We can carry whole families, piles of vegetables, and stocks of weapons." Meanwhile the U.S., having learned the lessons of the French, commissioned Colonel B.F. Hardway of the U.S. Advanced Research Projects Agency to study the elimination of the Vietcong bicycle transport system, and the Battelle Memorial Institute in Ohio determined that American commandos on bicycles could work with the South Vietnamese to stop the flow. The Pentagon dismissed the idea of Americans on bicycles, and so long as they could not go after the Soviet and Chinese sources of supply, without risking the advent of a third world war and nuclear annihilation, the war turned into a stalemate, with the humiliating withdrawal of U.S. forces in 1973.

Today, the bicycle seems inconsequential compared to the proliferation of nuclear weapons. Yet the bicycle's ability to empower the individual can also make it a formidable part of any nation's army. The development of mountain bikes has inspired another machine for military action as some makers have outfitted small battalions of troops, including the Swiss Army and even the Peace Corps. No matter how future conflicts take shape, it seems likely that bicycles will continue to be there, so long as people are still around to ride them. James Berryhill, a cyclist who served in Vietnam, says:

> It is easy to view the bicycle as an essentially benign device, removed from potential involvement in geo-political conflicts. This attitude is both foolish and particularly American. Of all the major powers, only the United States has never used the bicycle exclusively as a tool of war. Moreover, for generations we have associated its use with recreation and play and have rarely considered it a serious mode of transportation, in or out of war.
>
> Perhaps it is this attitude that causes us to ignore the military potential of our own technology—a mistake that could have serious results if the technology is passed to irresponsible hands. The bicycle has been an instrument of war in the hands of any political and military groups needing its capabilities. Viet Cong or American, Nazi oppressor or French Resistance, the bicycle doesn't care; it stands ready to carry any and all to victory.[9]

Road Wars

For many communities the real war is closer to home, as various sorts of violent behavior occurs on public roads and places. Road wars seem to have begun as soon as there were roads. Cyclists in the late 1880s demonstrated their strength as road warriors while organizing solidarity in the growing good roads movement. The disputes were in part a battle for rights to the roads, and in part a class war between poor country farmers and rich city wheelmen. The spokes of the high-wheelers excited and upset horses and other farm animals, and carriage drivers would sometimes whip passing cyclists or drive them off the road or into trees and walls. There were various anti-cyclist thugs and bike-bashers who would lie in wait for riders. They placed roadblocks of trees and rocks, or strung a cord or rope across the road between two trees, usually at night. Occasionally cyclists would get beaten, robbed, raped, or have their bicycles battered. These criminal groups were particularly active on the open roads of Germany, Belgium, and the Netherlands, where they were known as *velo-kannibalen*.

The Sower, by Charles Addams, for Simon and Schuster.

One protection against the *velo-kannibalen* was a handlebar revolver which fit inside the hand grip and could be fired while riding. Spray guns were designed to shoot liquids such as water, ammonia, ink, or acid at dogs, horses, and thugs. While cycling magazines covered self-defense tips, long-distance tourists often had to carry conventional firearms.

With the development of the pneumatic-tire safety bicycle a frequent attack against cyclists became the placement of tacks in the road. Whether tacks fell off horseshoes, or people intentionally threw in them in the road, which has been done at races, in the Golden Age of cycling it was such a problem that someone suggested that bicycles held a magnetic attraction, causing tacks to fall off people's shoes. Hence, it was proposed that a magnet should be attached to the front of a bike, like a locomotive's cattle catcher.

Surely the greatest tolerated crime and cause of carnage on the road is due to motor vehicles used as deadly weapons. Since the first fatal car crash in 1899, motor vehicles have killed over 2.5 million Americans and permanently injured 43 million. The Humane Society estimated that in 1990 more than one million animals were killed every day on U.S. roads. The *Green Lifestyle Handbbook* claimed that motor vehicles kill more animals than the fur trade and animal experimentation industry combined, and more deer than hunters. Throughout the world, some 700,000 people are killed each year in traffic and ten million are injured. Nobody likes to admit that more people have been sickened, wounded, and slaughtered by cars, trucks and buses than in all the wars of the twentieth century.[10]

An article titled "Violence on the Highway Increases" in the journal *Traffic Safety* (July 1979), began to raise the issue of traffic-related violence. Jan Bowers stated that, "All over the country more and more traffic-related altercations are leading to violent disputes. Some incidents involve the cars as weapons." A deputy chief of police in Houston, Texas, suggested that in a car, "The man who is very small becomes just as large as the man that's six-foot eight. And if you try to be nice in traffic, that little-bitty man might take that big man on, because he's got this bomb with him, this big automobile." Psychiatrists think this behavior occurs with people who associate their ego with their driving and are in tight control of their emotions, but with no outlet for expression. When they get behind the wheel of a powerful automobile there is a feeling of frustrated physical performance when confronted by blocked traffic situations.

Though various studies on the nature of traffic violence have been compiled, very little was done until Los Angeles suffered from an outbreak of "freeway gunmen" in the late 1980s. Even the World Champion cyclist Greg LeMond was randomly shot at while training in the foothills of the Sierra Nevada Mountains. In a letter to *The New York Times* (March 1989), titled "How Bicyclists Can Protect Themselves," Andy Clarke of the LAW noted that, "Objects that are thrown from a vehicle are, in most states, considered to be part of the vehicle—making the offense that of hit and run. Cyclists should record the license number of any reckless driver or passenger and report the incident to the police."

In 1988, bicycle activists in Toronto set up a non-profit 24-hour telephone hotline for bicycle accident "survivors," called Cycle Watch. The volunteer response team provided support and legal information, giving referrals to lawyers and expert witnesses, and recorded a detailed accident report for creating a statistical data base. In their first year, they dealt with about three accidents a day from a variety of tourists, commuters, racers, couriers, and occasional riders during the cycling season.[11]

The serious consequences of traffic violence appear in various urban upheavals and riots, such as those in Los Angeles over the Rodney King verdict and in New York at the deaths of Gavin Cato and Yankel Rosenbaum. Its pervasive nature can be found in American culture, with the comedy of George Carlin's anti-biker skit, "Bicycles and Joggers," and in the fantasy of Richard Cohen, from *The Washington Post Magazine* (1988):

> I want to kill a bicyclist. I want to hit one of them with my car, knock him off the road, send him spilling over the curb, tumbling out of control. I want to see the bike go flying and then—this is my fantasy—I stop the car, get out and so do all the other drivers. They cheer me. They yell "hooray!" and then they pick me up and carry me around on their shoulders. And then they take me to the District Building, where they have a ceremony for me.

In the United States there is a fundamental problem in a legal system that allows many fatally reckless driving incidents to be judged and tolerated as accidents or misdemeanors. For example, when a motorist rams into a cyclist, the law says the motorist is guilty of having an accident, or reckless endangerment, depending on the motorist's intent. The reality for many cyclists is that the motorist committed assault with a deadly weapon, a crime that rarely applies to drivers in the U.S.

There is also a double standard in the U.S. legal system, in which injured cyclists are more likely to lose in accident-related court cases. According to a study by Verdict Research, Inc., from 1988 to 1990 roughly 45 percent of cyclists who were injured in collisions with cars and brought their case to court were awarded money for damages. This was compared to 67 percent of motorcyclists who received a jury award, and 63 percent for all liabilty cases. While an estimated 85 percent of all liability cases are resolved by pre-trial settlements, it was reported that insurance companies representing motorists in cases involving cyclists preferred taking their case before a jury. Insurers are aware of the bias against cyclists, and juries are more likely to empathize with the motorists who hit cyclists than the cyclists who are hit.[12]

Cycling advocates have a way of revealing how these double standards apply in the real world. Steve Stollman, a pedestrian and cycling advocate in New York City, points out that "If anyone walking along the sidewalk were to make deafening noises, spew poisonous gas into innocent faces, and threaten people with a deadly weapon, they would be arrested. Yet, a few feet away, on the public roadway, it is considered normal behavior." A 1994 press release from the pro-bike group in Germany (ADFC) noted that "There has been no known case of a cyclist failing to see a motorist and killing him in the resulting collision."

Most traffic situations that pose a danger can be anticipated by cyclists through attention, education, and experience, but one big problem is the erratic drunken driver. The combination of petroleum in the engine and alcohol in the bloodstream makes a deadly weapon, with the power of hundreds of horses and the weight of thousands of pounds of armor. Anti-drunk-driving groups like Bicyclists Against Drunk Driving (BADD) formed political lobbies which brought Breathalyzer tests for drivers, and a partial ban on alcoholic beverage advertising. While stricter laws are being enforced, more and more severe alcoholics have been stripped of their driver's licenses, and this has brought them onto bicycles "trying to get to the bar any way they can." This has brought "a new headache" on American roads. Drinking alcohol was involved in one-third of the bicyclist fatalities studied between 1989 and 1991 by the Johns Hopkins Injury Prevention Center in Baltimore and in almost half the fatalities of men aged 25 to 34.[13]

One strange but true story is that of Joe Cyran, a New York State Trooper who set out on a solo cross-country bicycle trip to raise money for two brothers from Utah who had been paralyzed in separate accidents due to drunken drivers. In May 1990, Cyran flew to Los Angeles, assembled his bike at the airport, rode to the beach to dip his rear tire in the Pacific Ocean (a cross-continent cycling tradition), and then turned around and headed east for Atlantic City in New Jersey. After 21 grueling days, he was just 38 miles from his goal when he was struck by a car that crossed four highway lanes, driven by a man accused of having alcohol and cocaine in his blood.

Cyran was flung through the car's windshield and out a side door. He was flown by helicopter to a trauma center in Camden where he spent three months undergoing twenty operations, nearly losing a leg. His fiancée said: "Many people promised to pray for him, and the week after the doctors were discussing the amputation, the leg began to heal." He suffered from nightmares about his bike trip with a sudden ending, which he worked out by reliving the experience from photographs of the accident scene.

Six months later Cyran was back on a stationary bicycle riding 75 to 100 miles about three times a week. He says: "There have been 250,000 deaths caused by drunk drivers in the last ten years, and if you multiply this by ten people who may be affected by each death, then I believe we are a country of walking wounded due to drunk drivers."[14]

Helmets

What do you call a cyclist who doesn't wear a helmet?
An organ donor.

Because they are safety devices used in life-and-death situations, a controversy surrounds the use of helmets involving personal freedom and public policy, health care and traffic safety, risk-taking and risk-prevention.

Many people, including those who rarely ride bicycles, believe helmets are a necessary component for safe cycling, and that governmental legislation should make helmets mandatory for all cyclists. Some people think helmets are bad medicine, claiming that they discourage people from cycling, and that the best way to save lives is to get everyone cycling. Others claim that the proper use of the brain and the bicycle serve the same purpose as helmets. In the middle are those who believe helmets are necessary for special cases, such as children, group rides, and most racing events, but that no law should mandate them for everyone, allowing for personal choice.

Helmets are a relatively new accessory for the average cyclist. Bicycle racers were the first to use helmets because danger and risk-taking is a normal part of the sport. Padded leather and hard-shell helmets gradually appeared in track, road, cyclo-cross, and especially in motor-paced cycle racing events, but only a few racers, some cycletourists, and people with weakened or fractured craniums used helmets in non-competitive situations. In the 1970s and 1980s, more and more average cyclists began to wear soft- and hard-shell helmets, as many North Americans took to cycling on inferior bikes and found traffic systems with motor vehicles and road conditions too dangerous for cycling without a helmet. In the 1990s, while mandatory bicycle helmet laws for children and adults have been enacted in the U.S., Canada, Australia, and New Zealand, the vast majority of the world's cyclists do not wear helmets.

The first hard-shell helmets for cycling, nicknamed "brain buckets," were rather heavy, hot, and unfashionable. People wanted to know what worked best and what safety standards should be applied, and some people wondered what the world had come to when those using the most logical vehicles—cyclists—had to add a bit of armor to protect themselves.

The scientific testing and rating of helmets for motor vehicle racing began with the Snell Memorial Foundation, which formed in 1957 after race car driver Peter Snell suffered a fatal head injury. The foundation developed standards for motorcycling and auto racing helmets in the mid-1960s and set bicycle helmet standards in 1980. Since then, numerous testing laboratories have sprung up, and most industrialized countries have set standards for bicycle helmets. The U.S. has four standards-setting organizations, the American National Standards Institute (ANSI), the American Society for Testing and Materials (ASTM), the Safety Equipment Institute (SEI), and the Snell Memorial Foundation.

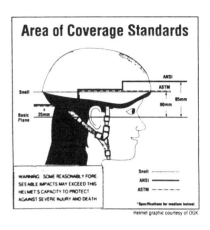

Area of Coverage Standards

In the Snell test, helmets are placed on a dummy head form and dropped from a height of about three meters onto a flat or curved anvil. An accelerometer inside the head assembly at its center of gravity measures peak deceleration, or negative acceleration, in G forces (1 G = earth gravity at sea level). The Snell safety standard limits G forces to 285. In a head crash at the speed of 25 mph, a cyclist may receive over 1,000 G forces. In such a head-on impact, the wearer of a ribbed leather helmet may receive as much as 700 Gs and a typical expanded polystyrene (EPS) foam helmet allows about 150 to 250 Gs.

Helmets, like many safety devices, change the physical dynamics of crashing, as well as the psychological factors in risk-taking. One test, which reveals a possible helmet-induced injury, shows the amount of friction the helmet creates in sliding, which can cause neck and spinal injuries. In this case, hard-shell helmets that slide are recommended over soft-shell EPS foam helmets that grip. In terms of risk compensation, many people wearing helmets feel more confident and ride with less care, knowing that in the event of an accident their risk of head injury will be reduced. There are also those who say, "I paid for it, now I'm gonna use it!" Most helmet makers recommend replacement of helmets after the first crash or if cracks appear. Helmets are relatively cheap to make, but rather expensive to buy, in part because of the high overhead costs, including testing, certification, insurance, lobbying, and promotion. The bicycle helmet industry has grown rapidly as more cyclists choose to wear helmets or are legally required to wear them.

Bicycle helmet advocacy groups have influenced the public safety debate by emphasizing the most harmful consequences of cycling—instead of the healthy consequences—and by promoting the use of a safety device that reduces the impact of accidents, rather than reducing accidents with preventive measures such as safer roads and public education. The opinion of most helmet advocates is that helmets can save lives and injuries, and because the public must share the especially high medical and legal costs of bicycle-related head injuries, the public must be required to wear helmets when bicycling. As for children, society must

protect those who cannot make decisions on their own.

Helmet advocates have used statistics to bolster their opinion. For example, *The New England Journal of Medicine* reported that bicycle helmets are 85 percent effective in preventing head injury. A study in the Journal of the American Medical Association (December 4, 1991) reported that head injuries account for 62 percent of all bicycling deaths and 32 percent of all visits to emergency rooms. Children under fifteen suffer 41 percent of all bicycling head injury deaths and 76 percent of all non-fatal head injuries. The *JAMA* report suggests that one life per day in the U.S. could be saved by universal helmet use.[15] National Safe Kids Campaign says that 75 percent of all cyclist deaths involve head injuries, and 70 percent of all hospitalized cyclists are treated for head trauma. According to a 1988 poll by the makers of Cheerios, a sugar-sweetened cereal, 65 percent of American kids under seventeen years favored making a cycling helmet mandatory for their age group. Bikecentennial said that helmetless riders on the TransAmerica Trail in the mid-1970s suffered concussions at the rate of one every three days, while nobody wearing a helmet received a serious head injury.

A problem with these statistics—and a problem with helmet laws—is that they emphasize one part of a whole issue. In the realm of public health, studies in Britain and Denmark show that the lifetime health benefits from bicycling far exceed the years of life lost to bike accidents, by ratios of ten to one and twenty to one. Bicycle-related head injuries occur about 0.05 percent of the time and cyclists are no more at risk than other road users. In fact, in many places the percentage of bicyclist deaths and injuries is lower than the percentage of bicycles in traffic, and is lower than pedestrian and motorist deaths and injuries. The European Cyclists' Federation estimates that more accidents and injuries would be prevented if the money to equip all bicyclists with helmets were spent on safety education and improved cycling infrastructure.

The big problem with helmet laws is that they discourage people from cycling and gaining the health benefits of cycling. Australians were the first to have universal (all ages) mandatory helmet laws in 1990, and New Jersey was the first U.S. state to rule it illegal for anyone under fourteen to ride without a helmet, with $25 and $100 fines for the first and second offenses, which is waived if the child gets a helmet. California enacted a helmet law in 1994 for people under eighteen. In Australia, discretionary cycling has fallen off by 25 to 50 percent. In some cases, the percent of decline in head injuries (32 percent) did not keep pace with the overall decline in cyclists (36 percent), so the risk of head injury actually increased for the remaining cyclists, as roads generally without cyclists can be more dangerous for the few remaining cyclists. At first, bicycle dealers profited from increased sales of helmets, but with the decline in cyclists, some have had to close shop.

Certain public roads and wilderness trails require helmet use. On mountain bike trails, where cyclists take the role as the threatening mechanical vehicle, a helmet is useful for avoiding self-inflicted injuries.

Many cycling groups will not allow helmetless riders to participate in their organized rides, because of the dangers of large packs with cyclists of varied experience and to reduce their insurance rates. Racing cyclists have fairly well-defined laws for helmet use, yet they often dislike helmets the most. The Union Cycliste Internationale (UCI) requires helmets for mountain biking and track racing, but not for professional road racers, leaving rule-making to the national federations, the majority of which require some kind of helmet. In 1991, the UCI tried to require hard-shell helmets for all road races except individual time trials, but this failed after protests at Paris-Nice and the Tour de France, when racers chose to ride helmetless and pay the 300 Swiss franc fine ($195), complaining that helmets are too hot and awkward.

Law and Order

In the realm of law and order, bicyclists are victims, survivors, perpetrators, accomplices, witnesses, and enforcers. The crimes include manslaughter, assaults, robberies, fraud, smuggling, victimless social behavior, and acts of civil disobedience.

Bicycles provide an ideal vehicle for smuggling, as secret documents and other small amounts of contraband can be hidden in the handlebars and frame tubes. An Irish tale relates how a "shapely lass" frequently passed British road blockades on her bike and was usually allowed to pass freely by enamored guards. One time she stumbled and her bike fell with a heavy thud. While the guards tried to lift it, she fled, and they found the frame tubes filled with gold she was smuggling for the IRA.

A similar deception occurred at the U.S.-Mexico border when a man regularly bicycled from Mexico carrying a large sack. Each time he was stopped and searched, the sack was found to contain nothing but sand. In desperation, a U.S. Customs agent begged the man to confess what he was smuggling, even offering immunity from prosecution. With a wry smile, the man whispered: "bicycles."[16]

Some of the notable crimes committed on bicycles include an attempted purse snatching by a cyclist who was beaten off by an 87-year-old New York City woman with an umbrella. Bicycling bank robbers hit several mid-western banks including a drive-thru teller. A seven-year-old boy in San Carlos, California, collided on his bike with an official city truck and was sued by the city for $13,000 in damages to the driver. While traveling to the Great Wall in China, an American diplomat's motorcade was hit by a girl cyclist who died of her injuries. The police ruled the driver responsible, fined them $12,500, and the diplomat was expelled from the country.[17]

An insurance fraud case was uncovered in which a bicycle rider and his accomplice were accused of a scheme to defraud an insurance company out of $30,000 in false claims. Their plan was to fake a collision with a rental car. The cyclist spread blood and glass on the roadway, cut himself in several places, broke his own teeth, and finally checked into a hospital.

DAILY NEWS
New York's Hometown Newspaper   Tuesday, October 6, 1992

BICYCLE HITMEN

3 teens gunned down in 'pedal-by' shooting

STORY ON PAGE 3

Bicycle Killer Guns Down Cop

Swiss Protester Run Down

ZURICH, June 20 (Reuters) — A cyclist who sat down on a busy roadway to protest traffic was run down and and badly injured by a car today.

The rider was caught after his fourteenth fake accident, and eventually pleaded guilty.[18]

In Ft. Lauderdale, Florida, a cyclist rode his bike to a McDonald's fast-food restaurant around midnight and found the front doors closed and the drive-thru window open. The window clerk told him to leave, that they served only motorists, and the cyclist persisted, claiming that they were discriminating against him as a bicyclist. As cars began stacking up, McDonald's management had him arrested, and after spending a night in jail, he was released when friends posted the $25 bail. After *The Miami Herald* reported the story, it gained national attention and played out in the AP, UPI, and CNN news services.[19]

In Washington, D.C., at DuPont Circle, on June 12, 1992, the United States Park Police conducted a confiscation raid against bike messengers hanging out after work. The black-suited SWAT team enforced a little-known law requiring bike registration as a ruse to clear the couriers from the park. Police blocked park entrances, jumped benches, and confiscated fifteen unregistered bikes—thirteen from couriers, two from bystanders—loading them into idling vans. One courier was arrested, and one officer allegedly pointed his baton at the chest of a courier and shouted "Drop the fucking bike!" The courier replied: "It's not loaded." Although non-registration is a $5 traffic offense, in this case it was treated as a criminal offense. By paying a $25 fine, the couriers gave up their right to stand trial. With attention from *The Washington Post* and support from the American Civil Liberties Union, the Superior Court returned the fines and dismissed the criminal charges.[20]

Bicycling reported that a misguided bike enthusiast named Roy Clarence Rose was captured thanks to a "Wanted" notice that appeared in their magazine. Rose was wanted in several states for felony bike theft, check fraud, and parole violations, and was known to be wandering around in a stolen VW bus with a stolen credit card. He was a "wannabe," acting as a world-class racer with a few national team jerseys, expensive bikes, and the ability to swindle expensive merchandise from bike shop employees and cyclists. When the owner of the Free-Flite Cyclery in Atlanta spotted Rose in his shop, he checked the issue of *Bicycling* and called the detective in Colorado assigned to Rose's case. When the cops came, they showed Rose his picture in the magazine, and "his jaw dropped."[21]

The use of illegal behavioral and recreational drugs is a part of society that generates a large underground economy. In America, marijuana has been the largest cash crop since 1980. While the drug trade usually goes on behind closed doors, in many cities it flourishes on the streets where drug dealing is often carried out on bicycles. An "increasing use of bicycles to transport illegal drugs" was noted by Boston Police Detective John Ulrich, who once chased and arrested a drug runner who "abruptly turned onto a side street after sighting his police car." Although "angel dust" was found on the suspect the case was dismissed when the judge ruled that "turning sharply onto a side street" was no reason for an illegal search, seizure, and arrest.[22]

COPS ON BIKES

Since the mid-1980s and with the development of mountain bikes, many American cities have had success in fighting street crime and narco-trafficking by employing uniformed and undercover police on bicycles. Typical equipment includes a .38 caliber revolver or nine millimeter semi-automatic handgun, an eight-pound kevlar bulletproof vest, handcuffs (which often double as bike locks), a short stick (a portable club), a police radio, a first-aid kit, a citation book, and a badge.[23]

Known in Boston as BOPS (Bicycle Oriented Patrol Squad), to replace the old acronym COP (Constable On Patrol), these bicycle-mounted units have several advantages over patrols in squad cars or on foot. They are far less expensive to operate than motor vehicles, they offer greater mobility than foot patrols, they allow more personal contact with citizens and neighborhoods, they provide aerobic exercise for stereotypically over-weight police officers, and, of particular interest for cycling advocates, they legitimize the bicycle as useful transportation.

The *Police on Bikes Survey Report* published by the LAW in 1991 listed over 500 bicycle-mounted police units in the U.S. According to Lt. Charlie Davidaitis of the Las Vegas Metropolitan Police, the cost of outfitting a bike patrol of fifteen riders with equipment and uniforms amounted to $18,000 in 1990, with annual maintenance costs of $120 per bike. In contrast, the price of one patrol car was $23,000, with annual maintenance costs including fuel about $7,000 per car. Davidaitis said that between May 23 and September 8, 1990, the Bike Team handled 850 service calls and 941 reports; they stopped and "spoke" to 1,396 people and 1,440 vehicles; they issued 1,058 misdemeanor citations, 943 traffic violations, and made 49 arrests for felonies, 308 for misdemeanors, and recovered sixteen stolen vehicles.[24]

New York City Housing Police, 1992.
Photo by Anita Bartsch.

Police have been on bicycles throughout the world for the past hundred years. The first bicycling policemen were traffic officers used in parks and on streets of cities in the 1890s to apprehend speeding cyclists, known as "scorchers." These crackerjack bicycle patrolmen were the elite members of the police force. Cycling patrolmen were instructed to catch up with offenders and then cut in front of them, forcing them to stop. For this purpose, the New York City police hired the racer-stunt rider Charles "Mile-a-Minute" Murphy, but the pursuing policeman became such a menace that it was recommended that each police bicycle be equipped with a continuously sounding bell. Cycling cops also chased after runaway horses, as well as some of the early motorists, including the comedian W.C. Fields, who, according to *The Boston Globe* (1902), was "arrested for fast driving... while racing down North Broad Street last evening... by Bicycle Patrolman John Ulrick." A few bicycling patrolmen were reportedly killed in the line of duty.

Bicycle policeman pulls over motorist, 1900. Photo from National Archives.

The idea of police on bikes drew a certain amount of ridicule. One midwest newspaper reported that: "The spectacle of the staid, sober,

heavyweight policemen of this city breaking their necks and the injunction against profane swearing while learning to master their vicious steeds will be a show that will stand almost any admission the city may please to charge for it. The treasury reserve will be raised away above the low water mark by hiring a hall and giving this exhibition under a reasonable scale of prices."[25]

In 1968, *Law and Order* magazine reported the use of bike patrols at suburban shopping centers in Long Beach, California, and Birmingham, Alabama, where half a dozen sheriff's deputies had shotguns strapped to their bikes. Long Beach Police Chief William J. Mooney claimed that the use of the bicycle "set a fantastic record for a two-man team. For street crime, purse snatching, mugging, general malicious mischief, teen trouble areas—it's the most effective police method we've found."[26]

NEW YORK LAW

For the past fifteen years I've done most of my daily bike riding in New York City, where the cycling conditions tend to mirror the city's public image. Despite the worst ranking by *Bicycling* magazine's 1990 poll of cycling cities, and the infamous "Bike Ban" of 1987, over 75,000 people ride bikes in the city every day. They find that the size, topography, and chaotic liveliness make New York, if not a "bicycle friendly" town, then a place nonetheless worthy of the fight for that honor.

Street traffic in New York is a special kind of chaos in which the rules of the road are formed by the instincts of people moving with contrasting interests. Stereotypes abound, as there are impudent, seemingly blind jaywalkers, wrong-way delivery cyclists, outlaw bike messengers, unionized truckers, oppressed taxi drivers, uninsured commercial vans, speeding government vehicles, and the mayor's lawless police. A "Talk of the Town" piece in *The New Yorker* magazine called "Anarchy Without Malice" serves as primer for cycling in Manhattan:

> Most bicyclists in New York City obey instinct far more than they obey the traffic laws, which is to say that they run red lights, go the wrong way on one-way streets, violate cross-walks, and terrify innocents, because it just seems easier that way. Cycling in the city, and particularly in midtown, is anarchy without malice: anarchy as a way around the usual obstacles, anarchy that seems at once graceful and suicidal, anarchy in quest of the improbable. It is cheap and thrilling, and it enables a person to journey from Point A to Point B without being held hostage by the MTA.[27]

In 1987, a famous episode in the annals of the bicycle occurred when Mayor Edward I. Koch announced an experimental three-month bike ban in the central business district of midtown Manhattan, on Fifth, Park, and Madison avenues, between 31st and 59th streets, daily from ten A.M. to four P.M. Responding to pressure from various groups, the Mayor tried to put the ban into effect in spite of the law. The bike ban took effect on August 31 for only one hour before a temporary restraining order issued

by the State Supreme Court stopped it, the result of several lawsuits brought against the city by a coalition of bike messengers and bicycle activist groups. Ten days later, the court permanently voided the bike ban, because the city had not followed proper procedures in notifying the public.

The main targets of the bike ban were the city's commercial bike messengers. A free-spirited, hardworking group, they have been described in the media as "folk heroes," "urban cowboys," "speed merchants," "kamikazes," "the despised," "rough riders," "road warriors," "unmoved movers," and "killer bikers." The average messenger is said to be threatened or hit by a bus, car, truck, or pedestrian at least once a day, but they are harder to kill than a cockroach on the Upper West Side. Although the bike ban treated messengers essentially as political pawns, a few got the chance to voice their dilemma. In a letter to *The New York Times*, "For the Bicycle Messenger, No Roadbed of Roses," Seth Amgott wrote that, "Like the Jews of medieval Europe, messengers make an objective contribution to the local economy, but are viewed as utterly foreign, existing tenuously on official tolerance punctuated by specific harassment. Some of us on the margins of traffic are from the margins of society as well, lacking tact and communication skills, and would not otherwise be in corporate midtown—or decently employed. We, as well as pedestrians, deserve better peripheral vision."[28] Another *Times* opinion piece by David Paler, titled "I'm a Bike Messenger, and I Break the Law," said, "Why? Because I can get away with it. The streets of New York have become a free-for-all, apparently devoid of law."[29]

The bike ban was also regarded as an attempt by City Hall to sidestep normal law enforcement channels, including a 1984 law requiring all messenger companies to issue identification cards and license plates. The messengers were employed with independent contractor agreements, and their companies, with names such as Speedy, Dash, Rush, Born to Run, Prometheus, Chick Chack, Rough Riders, Streetwise, One Track, Unique, and We Are the Best, often evaded liability for worker's compensation and health or accident insurance. The bike ban generated several fierce editorials, and reached bicycle activists around the world. Murray Kempton wrote in *Newsday*:

> My bicycle is a regular companion of my semi-professional rounds and has contributed vastly to my peace of soul.
>
> There are reports that the mayor's posture has been stiffened by the exhortations of Police Commissioner Benjamin Ward. The commissioner can be excused his discontents, because he is oppressed, like so many of us, by a dirty little secret: His department does not enforce the traffic laws.
>
> If, to take an instance, the census were a guide, we could expect at least 40 percent of the drunken driving arrests in New York State to be made in New York City. Yet the actual percentage does not approach that; one year it was down to one in five.... Patrol cars regularly disdain

the regulations their department appoints for private vehicles and, as a class, show an indifference to the rules of the road approached only by mail trucks, MTA buses, and automobiles operated by municipal chauffeurs.

Nothing has done more to loose whatever tenuous hold the tenets of socialism still have upon me than my engagements with vehicles owned by public agencies.

But the experience has brought a new appreciation of the anarchist ideal of balance of nature achieved by free men with no intervention from the state. The New York traffic system has approached that dream; and justice demands the concession that the bicyclist, as a new force, is an intrusion upon this celestial harmony. The solution is not to suppress him avenue by avenue but gently and firmly to guide him to adjustment.[30]

Bike messengers have developed a popular cultural identity in the 1990s, being the subject of film (*Quicksilver*) and television (*Double Rush*), and with their own World Championship, begun in Berlin in 1993. Amid a growing awareness of their usefulness in mainstream and informal business, cycle couriers in Denmark are well-paid fully-insured professionals. In 1994, messengers in New York and Washington D.C. began negotiations for joining the Teamsters Union (AFL-CIO), and a preliminary vote among New York's couriers was 89 for, 89 against.

Empowered by the bike ban victory, New York's leading bicycle advocacy group, Transportation Alternatives (TA) grew to become one of the nation's largest regional groups, with over 3,200 members in 1994 and an expanded mission that includes bike, pedestrian, transit, and auto-reduction issues. TA won many victories for cyclists, and in defending rush-hour access on the bike-foot path of the Queensboro-59th Street Bridge in 1990, it won a landmark decision. Judge Laura Safer-Espinoza ruled that by blocking motor vehicles allowed on the foot path during bridge maintenance, the cyclists proved that their "direct action" was justified to prevent imminent public harm: to cyclists and pedestrians, to all New Yorkers because of motor vehicle exhaust, and to the U.S. Constitution because it provides the right to travel freely over public roads. Former N.Y.C. Transportation Commisioner Ross Sandler testified that the city had failed to restrict motor vehicle traffic, and had violated the national Clean Air Act since 1970 because "a very powerful coalition of unions and business leaders were opposed to any kind of restrictions."[31]

Transportation Alternatives faced one of cycling's biggest dilemmas—pedestrian and cyclist conflict and how to share rights of way—in a divisive piece of legislation drafted by City Councilor Charles Millard in 1992 that allowed the confiscation of commercial cyclists' bikes for sidewalk cycling or any traffic offense. Laws already prohibit sidewalk cycling, but they were not being enforced on the cyclists delivering hot food in Millard's wealthy Upper East Side "silk stocking" district. With most of the City Council blindly supporting the bill, TA's leaders at first

Murray Kempton, *Newsday* columnist, by Victor Juhasz.

Bike messenger 'surfing the traffic.'
Photo by Jean-Jacques Marquety.

Logo from *Road Kill*.

supported the bill in hopes of winning pedestrian rights and getting equal enforcement of laws banning double- and triple-parked motorists and highway speeding—the reason so many cyclists go on the sidewalk in the first place. But TA then recognized a gross infringement of civil rights aimed at its heart—the bike messenger—and decided to come out against the bill. TA's indecision caused fallout from people on both sides of the issue, even from those who share the same vision.

Not everyone agrees on the best ways to create order in public places where cyclists conflict with pedestrians, motorists, and other cyclists. In the pecking order of mixed traffic, safe cyclists give the right of way to every other traveler: to slower, lighter "vehicles" (pedestrians first, then wheelchairs, skaters, and bikes); and to faster, heavier vehicles (trucks, vans, cars, and motorcycles). Consequently many cyclists find a way by making their own rules, and even those who make the laws break the rules when cycling. Jean Gerber, a French cycling advocate and a Strasbourg city councilor, describes one solution: "We make sure that our journeys involve the shortest routes, without recognizing certain institutionalized hinderances here and there, such as traffic lights and one-way streets; but we are neither immature nor irresponsible."

Bicycle Theft

People often describe the psychological effect of bicycle theft in terms of losing a lover or friend, and many compare the experience to being raped, because it is a personal violation that goes widely unreported and makes one suspicious of other people. Bicycle theft is a big part of bike culture and Vittorio De Sica's Academy Award-winning movie *The Bicycle Thief* (1949) shows the dramatic nature of this crime in its full social cycle.

Precise statistics on bicycle vandalism and theft are not easily available, because investigators estimate that more than half to three-fourths of all incidents are not reported. According to an FBI Crime Report of 1980, bicycle theft accounted for ten percent of all larcenies in the U.S., with an estimated 2.6 million stolen bikes in 1979.[32] The theft rate per capita in the U.S. (1.1 per 100) is about twice as high as in Germany and Denmark, and five times higher than in Japan.[33] Furthermore, a U.S. Department of Transportation study showed that one in four frequent cyclists have a bicycle stolen, that less than one-fifth of stolen bicycles are restored to their owners, and that twenty percent of all theft victims stopped cycling, at least temporarily, as a result of the experience.[34]

Like many large cities, New York has a severe crime problem and bicycle theft is part of it. Often associated with the drug trade, there are about 8,000 bicycle thefts reported per year, with an estimated 90 percent of all thefts unreported, for an approximate total of 80,000 stolen bikes per year. Much of New York City lacks adequate bike parking facilities, there is no enforcement of bike registration, and the police department has other things to keep it busy. Theft victims are often advised to "forget about it." The thieves are thick in New York, and to prove it, the

Kryptonite Lock Company introduced the "breakable" Rock Lock with an insurance plan that did not apply to New York City, and the "unbreakable" New York Lock, which did. Bicycle thieves hide on bridges for ambush and they drive around in vans using pipe cutters, sledge hammers, crow bars, and, supposedly, quick-freeze freon gas. As some arrests indicate, there is a thriving interstate black market in stolen bicycles, and on St. Mark's Place they will take your order for a "hot" bike.

Every cyclist has a horror story. Central Park bicycle thieves once ambushed an early morning amateur bike race, which included an unarmed off-duty police officer, taking several thousand dollars in equipment. On the Upper West Side, a 30-year-old bike thief was killed when the bike's owner gave chase and knocked the thief down, slamming his head against the curb. No charges were filed. Murray Kempton wrote in *Newsday* (October 2, 1988): "The Theft of My Bicycle is a triennial street festival, came round again Thursday, and I observed its recurrence, as my civic duties ordain, with a quiet interval of meditation upon developments in the war on crime since last I was called upon to celebrate my return to casualty status." An editorial in *The New York Times* described how Port Authority workers at the World Trade Center broke a lock and "towed away" a bicycle because it lacked "curb appeal."

In Brooklyn, known as "America's Hometown" and "the People's Republic of Brooklyn," Gonzalo Delgado was cycling in Prospect Park when he witnessed a woman on a bike get struck by lightning. He set down his bike and with the help of a parks officer immediately set to work applying cardiopulmonary resuscitation (CPR) to the unconscious woman. Delgado learned CPR in the military but never had a chance to try it. When he went to his bicycle for his water bottle he discovered it had been stolen with two saddle bags, his keys, money, tools, a radio, and a paddle ball set. After his story was featured on *Live at Five*, a TV news show, a stockbroker offered to buy him a new mountain bike. Another news item from Brooklyn in 1988 read:

> A bicycle was stolen from in front of a Carroll Gardens store on Wednesday, July 13 while the bicycle's owner was inside buying a bike lock, said 76th Precinct police. The 28-year-old victim told police she went into the store at Court Street and Fourth Place at about 10:45 A.M., leaving the brand new $271 Peugeot ladies' 10-speed outside, said police. When she came out, the bike was gone.

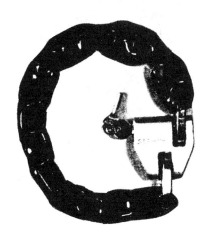

Facing these obstacles, New York City cyclists have developed ingenious ways to park a bike. The city's several thousand bicycle messengers display the most innovations, probably because they collectively ride on over a million dollars' worth of equipment, their bikes costing anywhere from a day to two weeks of pay. For outside parking, messengers remove anything of value that cannot be fastened down, including pump, bottles, cyclometer, seat and wheels. Brakeless fixed-gear track bikes, with the least components, are best. Seats are secured with bicycle chains wound around the seat rails and frame stays. Padlocks secure quick-release levers to the frame as a lightweight solution for stolen back wheels. Messengers came up with the idea of using a plumber's T-shaped pipe joint to deter thieves with pipes and crow bars breaking U-shaped locks. Some cyclists try to sabotage their bikes, making them fall apart before thieves can get away, by releasing hub axles. Using two or more different types of locking systems is the safest method. The idea is to hinder the thieves by requiring them to have extra tools or time. Some cyclists stamp, engrave, or hide their names and numbers (phone, address, I.D.) on various parts of their bike, making it positively identifiable in case of theft and return. Most of this doesn't apply if you ride a piece of junk.

Many countries, states, counties, and cities require bicycles to be registered and licensed just like motor vehicles. Bikes are fit with license plates, or stamped with a maker's serial number, so that if or when they are stolen and recovered, the police might be able to identify them. Also, many bicycle shops put a durable emblem with their address on the frame which can help to identify the owner. In Denmark, the bike advocacy group Dansk Cyklist Forbund set up a computerized registry for stolen bikes that has encouraged police action and reduced theft by as much as 23 percent in Copenhagen. In the U.S., bicycle security companies such as the National Bike Registry, Inc., have "shifted into high gear." The Sacramento, California, company charges fees of $3 to $25 for cyclists to be on an ownership database useful for police investigations.[35]

"Too bad these bikes weren't registered with the **National Bike Registry!**"™

Of the five bikes stolen from me, two have been returned. In one case, my Volkswagen containing two racing bikes was stolen at a motel near Auburn, California (each bike was worth as much as the car). When the bikes were found weeks later in a San Francisco bust, the police were able to return the bikes by calling the shop named on the bike. The shop recognized the description and told the police who owned it.

For cyclists, bicycle registration has its pros and cons. Some cyclists see it as the only hope for recovering a stolen bike, while others see it as hopeless red tape. An informal benefit of a lax bike registration system is that loads of recovered bikes become available at police auctions for low-cost recycling.

Bicyclists' Golden Rule: *Never buy a stolen bike.*

TEN COMMANDMENTS OF BIKE THEFT PREVENTION
I. Remember that your bicycle, no matter what type or condition it is in, is valuable and sellable merchandise to the bike thief.
II. As you ride, be alert for the possibility of an ambush.
III. Ideally, never leave your bike outside, locked or otherwise.
IV. If you park your bike outdoors, don't leave it for long.
V. Outdoors or indoors, even in your home, lock your bike to something.
VI. Keep up with the latest anti-theft techniques by sharing horror stories with other cyclists.
VII. Be on the lookout for bike thieves. Anywhere many bikes are regu-

larly parked you will eventually find bike thieves.

VIII. Register your bike, and carry its I.D. and serial number on your person.

IX. Report your stolen bike to the police, registered or not. Carry the police report number with you in case you spot the bike.

X. Don't be afraid to press charges against the individual who bought your stolen bike. Bike theft would largely cease if people stopped buying stolen bikes.[36]

GLOBAL BIKE THEFT

In Vancouver, Canada, 468 bikes were reportedly stolen in 1980, and 2,149 in 1984, with a dollar value of $2 million, exceeding bank robberies. In London, 25,541 bikes valued at £10 million were stolen in 1992–93. That was 250 fewer than the previous year, the first reduction in a decade. The average insurance payout was £300. Fewer than 700 bikes were returned, while many others were thought to be sold abroad. In Britain, 222,242 bikes were stolen in 1992–93. In Copenhagen, over 101,000 bicycles were reported stolen in 1989 at a cost of $1.7 million. In China, a 29-year-old bicycle thief, Xiao Guoqi of Guangdong, was sentenced to death for stealing 74 bikes on his own, and 37 bikes with an accomplice who was sentenced to 13 years in prison. In Japan, where few bicycle thefts are unreported, the number of stolen bikes doubled from 1970 (115,000) to 1980 (246,000). Abandoned bikes are the real problem in Japan, which had over one million discarded bikes in 1990.

FREE BICYCLES

A popular utopian plan for encouraging cycling while trying to solve the problem of bicycle theft is the idea of free bikes. These are basic bicycles available free of charge for anyone to ride around as long as they want, with the condition that the bicycle always be returned to a common parking place so someone else can also use it freely. The idea questions the concept of private ownership and seems to come only to social-democratic communities, including Holland, Switzerland, Italy, Denmark, and Portland, Oregon.

In Amsterdam in 1967, a community group called Provos proposed the White Bicycle Plan in which the city purchased 20,000 bicycles, painted them white, and set them out in public places to be used as free transport. The plan was led by Luud Schimmelpenninck, an Amsterdam City Councilor and vehicle inventor. It was a social welfare program associated with the hippie movement and the "happenings" of the art world, and documented in the film *Sex, Drugs and Democracy* (1994). The song "My White Bicycle," by Steve Howe and his rock group Tomorrow, became one of the anthems of 1967, and the free bike idea is part of the utopian society described in Ernest Callenbach's *Ecotopia* (1975). The plan worked for a while, until the bikes suffered from selfish vandalism and theft. A similar plan is currently in place at the Hoge Veluwe National Park in Holland.

In Geneva, 125 pink bicycles were provided for free public transport in 1986 by the Geneva Youth Association's Liaison Group. Anyone could use the bikes provided they stayed within the city limits and parked the bikes unlocked in an obvious spot for others to use. The youth group was responsible for maintaining the bikes and hoped to increase their numbers to 500.[37] In 1987, city officials in Milan donated 500 yellow bicycles to citizens for a weekend traffic reduction experiment. When the weekend was over, almost all of the bikes had been stolen. In 1994, a civic group in Portland, the United Community Action Network (UCAN), placed about 100 yellow bicycles for free use around town. Hanging from the saddle of each recycled second-hand bike is a sign that reads: "Free community bike. Please return to a major street for reuse by others. Use at your risk. Repair or pickup call ...."

In 1991, some 5,000 rental bikes carrying advertising from sponsors were planned to be parked in 900 specially-equipped bike racks throughout Copenhagen by a company called Bycyklen. Users were to insert a coin worth twenty kroner (three dollars) into a slot on the bike to release it from the rack. When the bike is relocked to a similar rack, the deposited coin is returned. The bikes are called *Bycyklen*, a play on the words *by* (city) and *cycklen* (bicycle). They are built with non-standard parts to prevent theft, and are easily recognized. Ole Wessung, one of the organizers, described what inspired the plan: "People are screaming about pollution and the Copenhagen municipality wants a car-free city. So here's the alternative. I had enough of getting my bicycles stolen. Five of them have disappeared within three months." When questioned about the likely fate of the bikes, Wessung said, "Everyone can see it's a Bycyklen. If you are spotted 200 kilometers away from Copenhagen, you're either a good rider or a thief."[38] The system had yet to be fully implemented in Copenhagen by 1994, but *Bycyklen* could be found in a few suburban locations.

Bicycles for Peace

If you asked a bicycle, it would probably not want to go to war. Appearing merely as a servant for military strategy, the bicycle's natural instinct is in creating a peaceful world. Since few people see the same peaceful solution for whatever it is that brings them to fight one another, the bicycle plays many roles as a peace-maker.

Perhaps the most popular peace-making activity is the sport of cycling, as some people believe athletes channel aggressive, tactical, and nationalistic behavior into a regime of healthy civilized competition. Another activity is local and international tours organized for peace and understanding, where bicycles allow people to experience cultures unlike their own. With humanitarian aid projects, bicycles create an independent economical alternative.

People do not always agree about what a peaceful world would be. Slogans used in global political affairs show this confusion, with "peace-keeping forces" armed covert soldiers, "freedom fighters" imperialist oppressors, and "Pax Universalis" a multi-national weapons trade. When people bring up the issue of the use of force and the right to bear arms, bicyclists have registered diverse opinions. When *Bicycling!* magazine published a piece about gun control in America, here was one reply:

> Recently I came across an article on "Bicycle Riders" in a car magazine which was stupid and offensive. The writer, of course, had never ridden a bicycle, and his only love seemed to be the automobile. Now, *Bicycling!* gets into the act with guns... As for guns, it may well be that everyone will have to own a gun for protection in the future. It may be the only way to survive! Crime is going up, NOT down. And if the state of the world is any indication, "peace" is a long way off. My only advice is that you must learn the mechanics, rules and laws in owning and using guns. Cars and bicycles can kill just as easily as guns. In any argument where people are unable to control their emotions, *any weapon* in their hands will kill—a knife, axe, bicycle frame or even a gun. I prefer to be shot; it's less painful and more humane.... *Bicycling!* and other magazines are [for enjoyment]. No matter what your hobby or sport is, enjoy it. Put-downs are only for the jerks that have no hobby. Say something nice or say nothing at all; that way you'll make friends, not enemies.[39]

The peace-making aspects of bicycle racing appear to be cloaked in diplomacy and international regalia, and because sport is often based on nationalistic allegiances, it continues to be politicized. The Peace Race was first held as a "celebration of peace" after World War II, and gained notoriety as a means of creating solidarity between Prague, Warsaw, and Berlin, the principal cities of this popular amateur Eastern European stage race. Cyclists from Africa, Asia, India, and the Americas have been allowed to participate, thus receiving several days of torture from the superior local amateurs.

War and political terrorism has interrupted many races, such as the decade of missing years in all the European Classics, Tours, and Championships during both World Wars, the massacre of Israeli athletes at the 1972 Munich Olympic Games, and the East-West Cold War Olympic boycotts at Moscow and Los Angeles. Occasionally there are demonstrations that serve as roadblocks to stop the newsworthy European races and help to settle labor or social disputes. Some races attempt to maintain a semblance of peace while under fire or near the mobilization of front-line warfare such as the Tour de Vietnam in the early 1960s. In response to South Africa's apartheid regime, several international sports federations instigated a boycott from the mid-1960s until 1991. Teams from South Africa couldn't ride the World Championships or Olympics, and foreign riders were mostly restricted from racing there.

Peace Rides

When the year 1984 arrived and George Orwell's fictional Big Brother seemed to be alive and in control, people recognized the fundamental absurdity of the Cold War nuclear arms race, where one Trident submarine had the power (24 megatons or eight times the amount of explosives used in World War II) to destroy every major city in the northern hemisphere and less than one percent of the U.S. and Soviet arsenal (totaling 18,000 megatons) was enough to change the climate and turn civilization into a post-apocalyptic dark age.[40] In this scenario the bicycle or human-powered vehicle would be the only modern means of transport to survive widespread loss of natural, industrial, and communications resources.

Bicycle tours and bike-a-thons have been organized to promote peace and disarmament, such as the Bike for Peace tours of 1983 and 1986. These were "people to people" exchange programs offering Eastern and Western trips for riders traveling from Kiev to Prague and from Montreal to the United Nations headquarters in New York. In 1984 the Lifecycle for a Nuclear Weapons Freeze was a Seattle to Washington, D.C., bike ride led by fifteen cyclists that attracted thousands more en route. The Pilgrimage to Pantex was a bicycle journey from various southwestern U.S. cities that converged in early August 1984 at the Pantex Nuclear Weapons Assembly Plant near Amarillo, Texas. This was the central point for nuclear arms production known as the place "where the end of the world begins." One notable participant was John Stockwell, a former CIA agent who rode a recumbent Tour Easy bicycle, built in Freedom, California.

On the Pilgrimage to Pantex, Bob Henschen of the War Resisters League reported that, "The choice of bicycles turned out to be a stroke of genius. We felt our willingness to pedal through the summer heat for our cause won us the respect and support of even conservative folks. The media loved the bicycles too. We were covered by practically every newspaper we came near, often on the front page, and television stations covered us so well that people already knew who we were when we arrived in

Wright—Scripps-Howard Newspapers

their town."[41]

In January 1986, 51 nuclear disarmament activists were arrested for blocking buses entering a Trident submarine launching celebration in New London, Connecticut. While protesters fell limp when they were arrested for civil disobedience, ten men and women chose not to give their names to police. They remained in jail and were given the names John Doe and Jane Doe. Three of these, two Johns and a Jane, held out for over a month when the judge ordered the district attorney to find their names so the Does could be released. Jane hoped to sue the state for false arrest, one John was identified by photos at previous protests, and one was a 23-year-old bicycle repairman from Massachusetts. His boss, a bicycle shop owner, called the district attorney saying "Spring is coming, and I need to have him back." The D.A. said, "Tell who he is, and if he acknowledges it, he can come out." The bike shop owner refused. This last John Doe said he was worried about losing his bicycle repair job, but he was more worried about nuclear weapons.[42]

In Ireland an annual weekend bicycle ride called the Maracycle was organized by Cooperation North, a group promoting non-violent solutions to the differences between Catholics and Protestants and the northern and southern republics. Two groups of cyclists, in Belfast and Dublin, traveled the hundred-odd miles to each other's capital cities. Over 5,000 riders took part in the 1987 Maracycle, and according to American participant Michael Verdon, most of the Irish "found Belfast far different from what they had expected: no bomb craters, no diving for cover, no army patrols. Instead, they saw a provincial city whose inhabitants, like themselves, enjoyed their pint of Guinness and a good chat. In other words, they saw people, real people living in a real city. If only for that, the ride was a success. Bringing the two sides together was a step toward creating mutual trust—and eventually peace—in Northern Ireland. It also opened a new chapter in the history of the bicycle, now a peacemaker."[43]

Once in while the bicycle fits the peaceful solution so perfectly that it startles people. It can be a wonderful manifestation of clear logic, human kindness, and economic sustainability that grows out of wartime and brings out the quintessential truth of the situation. This happened in Nicaragua with the Bikes Not Bombs (BNB) project founded by Michael Replogle and Carl Kurz of the Institute for Transportation and Development Policy (ITDP). As the war between the "democratic" U.S.-sponsored Contra rebels and the "communist" Sandinista government was destroying the country of Nicaragua, between 1984 and 1990 the Bikes Not Bombs group sent more than 4,500 bicycles to Nicaragua. North Americans donated new and used bikes, parts, and tools to over 30 local Bikes Not Bombs members in the U.S. and Canada. The material was shipped and assembled in revitalized Nicaraguan bike shops, and sold to education, health, food, and development workers. BNB chose to sell the bikes instead of giving them as charity to create a long-term sustainable development project rather than an unhealthy dependence on foreign aid.

In an economically devastated country efficient transport is essential, and *No Bombas, Sí Bicicletas* workers seeded a growing independent bicycle repair and manufacturing industry that received none of the millions of U.S. dollars in "humanitarian aid" used to fund and execute the Contra war. As more teenage Nicaraguans became wounded and disabled veterans, many were outfitted with wheelchairs and employed in the bicycle industry. The group eventually expanded to other oppressed nations including Mozambique and Haiti, and is currently active in the Boston area. When Bikes Not Bombs was featured by Bill Moffett in *Bicycle USA*, the LAW's magazine, it generated a major controversy among the readers. While most of the article was a friendly travelogue of the Bikes Not Bombs activities with matter-of-fact descriptions of a country during wartime, only the first and last sentences made a partisan political statement.

> I have never bought the argument that Nicaragua threatens United States security, but something *must* be happening in that part of the world for it to be in the news every day.... Although Nicaraguans generally detest American policy towards their country, they have the political sophistication to distinguish between the American people and the policies of the present American government. We were made welcome, and many of us hope to return.
>
> —Bill Moffett, "Bikes Not Bombs For Nicaragua."[44]

But this was enough to rouse many reader responses:

• I was dismayed to find that the league magazine had been used by Bill Moffett to promote the virtues of Communist Sandinista Nicaragua. Apparently Mr. Moffett is part of the peace-at-any-price group which would allow Russian and Cuban expansion on our continent. Let us keep *Bicycle USA* a magazine for the benefit of bikers in the image of the good old *LAW Bulletin*.

• Mr. Moffett's first paragraph, in which he doubts Nicaragua's threat to the United States, indicates he is still ignorant about the Sandinista government and Nicaragua even after a trip down there. The rest of the article amounts to Communist propaganda. As I read it I began to see red. My rising anger was fueled by realizing I had helped pay for this piece!

• The bike committee of the Appalachian Mountain Club's New York-New Jersey chapter believes that cycling is a nonpartisan activity. It is counterproductive to the spirit of the cycling fraternity to encourage any political viewpoint whatsoever except that directly related to furthering the cause of biking. Those who think otherwise should be compelled by group policy to express their views through proper political parties and political action groups and not be allowed to employ the forum of the cycling press for their own agenda.

• I would hope that LAW members have as strong a passion for the democratic process, free speech, and open discussion as they do for bicycling. You'd expect it; why else join an organization that represents bicycling in the political arena?

• "Bikes Not Bombs for Nicaragua" brings out a lesson I learned long ago: You can't beat the bicycle for penetrating a country and learning its profound truths. It also shows that the closer you get to an event, the more remote its reality becomes from the version presented by the mass media.

• I was so pleased to read Bill Moffett's moving article, "Bikes Not Bombs For Nicaragua." As Moffett made poignantly clear, Nicaragua is not our enemy, and the U.S. war against that country must be stopped.

• I recently declined to renew my LAW membership due to the sexist name change. After reading "Bikes Not Bombs For Nicaragua" in *Bicycle USA*, I have changed my mind. Thanks for the great information.[45]

The Persian Gulf War of 1991 was another instance where the bicycle appeared to be part of a peaceful solution. Bike advocates claimed that America's involvement in the war was due to the extra petroleum that had needlessly been consumed by not riding bikes. It was estimated that if the number of American bike commuters had doubled to seven million, they would save as much oil as was imported from Kuwait to the U.S. Amidst various reactions to the war, such as bicycle rallies featuring both patriotic yellow ribbons and provocative American flags embellished with the Nazi swastika, one peaceful letter to the editor of *The New York Times* by Kenneth W. Morgan, a professor of religion, brought a note of human-powered reconciliation.

Once, in Damascus years ago, when I was strolling along the street called Straight—wondering whether it is truly the most ancient street in the world that has served continuously as a marketplace—I watched as a man who was riding slowly through the crowd on a bicycle with a basket of oranges precariously balanced on the handlebars was bumped by a porter so bent by a heavy burden that he had not seen him. The burden was dropped, the oranges scattered and a bitter altercation broke out between the two men, surrounded by a circle of onlookers.

After an angry exchange of shouted insults, as the bicyclist moved toward the porter with a clenched fist, a tattered little man slipped from the crowd, took the raised fist in his hands and kissed it. A murmur of approval ran through the watchers, the antagonists relaxed, then people began picking up the oranges and the little man drifted away. I have remembered that as a caring act, an act of devotion there on the street called Straight by a man who might have been a Syrian Muslim, a Syrian Jew or a Syrian Christian.

Now that our American bicycle has been bumped and oil supplies are being spilled, and angry, unseemly insults and threats have been exchanged, and war has broken out with the possibility of the loss of myriad lives while millions stand by in horror, when and where can we turn for someone to kiss the American fist, so we can pick up the pieces and go peacefully together along our way?[46]

12 Cycle Sports

On the road to Luchon, 1971 Tour de France. Eddy Merckx of Belgium (right) pushes the pace with Luis Ocana of Spain (left) in the *maillot jaune*, Dutch champion Joop Zoetemelk (obscured), Lucien Van Impe of Belgium (standing), and Bernard Thevenet of France (Peugeot). Each of these riders won at least one Tour de France.

Cycling—the sport of the century—mechanization which, together with the marvelous nature of man, triumphs over time and space.
   —La Gazzetta dello Sport

Cycling Events

The bicycle has its most awesome manifestation in the world of sport. By combining the body, mind, and machine, cycling offers people a way of challenging themselves, their environment, and their equipment. Balancing the dynamics of both individual and team sports, competitive cycling has a wide range of events. From stories of pioneering individual physical achievements, to the fanfare and colorful regalia, to the progress of bicycle technology, team sponsorship, media coverage, and event specialization, cycling has become a remarkable expression of human nature.

   Cycling takes form as a popular athletic ritual and a complex commercial enterprise. At the summit is the Tour de France, the world's largest annual sports spectacle. This international stage race has the most live spectators, and arguably the world's most physically fit professional athletes. According to many sources, bicycle racing has ranked second only to soccer in terms of world-wide participation for the past fifty years. Since the 1980s, cycling has experienced growth and globalization, with new events such as mountain bike races and triathlons, and in the 1990s cycling may have the largest number of competitive participants of all sports. The bicycle's special synergy with the human body allows a wide range of sporting events like no other physical activity:

Sprint race—the ten-second tactical speed race.
Kilometer race—the one-minute-plus test of anaerobic strength.
Pursuit race—the four-minute threshold of aerobic power.
Hour record—the sixty-minute benchmark of human power.
Mountain race—the two-hour struggle of power and skill.
Road race—the seven-hour competition of the aerobic work day.
Six day race—the hundred-hour grind of speed, skill, and teamwork.
Ultra-marathon race—the ten-day round-the-clock human performance.
Stage race—the three-week battle for the fittest athletes and teams.
World cup series—the year-long award for best all-round athlete.

CYCLING EVENTS

EVENT (BIKE)	TIME per event	DISTANCE metric	COMPETITORS per event (per team)
TRACK RACING			
Match Sprint (track)	10 sec	200 m to 1,000 m	2 to 4
Tandem Sprint (tandem)	10 sec	200 m to 1,000 m	4 to 6 (2)
Olympic Sprint (track)	1 min	1,000 m	(3 to 4)
Individual Time Trial (aero track)	1 to 2 min	500 to 1,000 m	1
Pursuit (aero track)	3 to 5 min	3,000 to 5,000 m	2
Team Pursuit (aero track)	3 to 5 min	3,000 to 5,000 m	8 (4)
Points (track)	30 to 90 min	25 to 100 km	20
Keirin (track)	30 min	5 to 10 km	9 to 20
Motor-Paced (demi-fond)	1 to 60 min	500 m to 100 km	4 to 6 (2)
Madison (track)	1 hour	40 to 50 km	10 (2)
Omnium (track)	6 hours	200 m to 100 km	50
Six-Day (track)	60 to 100 hours	1,000 to 2,000 km	10 to 16 (2)
ROAD RACING			
Individual Time Trial (aero road)	10 min to 4 hours	5 to 150 km	1
Team Time Trial (aero road)	2 to 4 hours	60 to 100 km	(5 to 10)
Criterium (road)	1 to 3 hours	30 to 100 km	25 to 150
Kermesse (road)	2 to 5 hours	60 to 200 km	25 to 150
Place to Place (road)	3 to 8 hours	50 to 300 km	50 to 250
Stage Race (road)	2 to 23 days	300 to 4,000 km	100 to 250
Hill Climb (tt road)	10 to 90 min	10 to 25 km	25 to 500
Triathlon (aero road)	1 to 10 hours	25 to 180 km	25 to 2,500
Rando (touring)	1 to 10 days	300 to 1,200 km	25 to 3,000
Transcontinental (aero road)	5 to 20 days	5,000 to 10,000 km	25
OFF ROAD RACING			
Moto-Cross (BMX)	3 to 60 min	1 to 20 km	2 to 50
Speedway (track)	5 to 120 min	5 to 75 km	3 to 25
Trials (MTB)	2 to 10 min	10 to 100 m	15
Downhill (MTB)	3 to 15 min	4 to 15 km	10 to 20
Dual Slalom (MTB)	2 to 10 min	2 to 10 km	2
Cyclo-Cross (cross)	1 to 2 hours	15 to 50 km	25 to 250
Cross Country (MTB)	1 to 2 hours	15 to 50 km	25 to 250
Stage Race (MTB)	10 to 50 hours	100 to 500 km	25 to 200 (5)
RECORDS			
Slow Record (trick)	1 to 5 days	less than 10 cm	1 to 5
Speed Record (all types)	15 to 30 sec	1 to 2.5 km	1 to 10
Hour Record (all types)	1 hour	20 to 75 km	1
24-Hour Marathon (all types)	1 day	400 to 1,200 km	1
SPECIAL EVENTS			
Messenger Race (road, cargo)	5 to 60 min	2 to 50 km	10 to 100
Polo Match (polo, MTB)	45 min	10 km field	6 to 12 (4)
Cycle-Ball (trick)	30 min	5 to 15 km gymnasium	6 to 12 (4)
Artistic Cycling (trick)	30 min	100 m gymnasium	1 to 250
Unicycling (unicycle)	10 sec to 1 hour	100 m to 10 km	1 to 250
Bicycle Derby (clunker)	1 to 4 hours	5 km playground	3 to 50
Kinetic Sculpture (HPV)	30 min to 3 days	5 to 50 km	50 to 100 (2 to 10)
Human-Powered Flight (HPA)	5 min to 4 hours	1 to 100 km	1 (10)
Human-Powered Watercraft (HPB)	5 min to 50 days	1 to 4,000 km	1 (5)

Nineteenth Century Racing

Ever since bicycles were developed, people have been inspired to race them. Early tales of the "wheele for one to run races in" from 1665 evolved into a story in the French paper *Le Siècle* of 1802 reporting célérifère races up and down the Champs-Elysées, where the "betting was lively." Horse racing was an early influence, as a goal for speed and in styles of racing. On an English hobby horse of 1819, a rider was said to defeat a four-horse coach in a race from London to Brighton by half an hour. In Bavaria on April 20, 1819, some 26 swift-walkers took part in a ten kilometer race from Munich to Nymphenburg Castle and back. The winner, a Mr. Semmler of Munich, finished in 31 minutes 30 seconds— no faster than a person can run.[1]

When pedals were attached to the wheels of velocipedes, they became a sporting vehicle for athletes and acrobats. On May 31, 1868, the first track race was held by the Véloce Club de Paris at the Parc de St Cloud. The velocipedists wore colorful jockey caps and silk jackets, with high leather boots. The 1,200 meter race was won in 3 minutes 50 seconds (averaging 18.7 kph) by the Englishman James Moore, who lived in Paris across the alley from the Michaux's shop at Cité Godot-de Mauroy and was taught to ride by Ernest Michaux. Later that year a women's race took place at the Hippodrome du Parc Bordelais in Paris.

The first major long-distance road race was held on November 7, 1869, covering 123 kilometers (76 miles) from Paris to Rouen. The race was organized by the editors of *Le Vélocipède Illustré*, one of the first magazines devoted exclusively to cycling. They received 325 entries, but with stormy weather on the morning of the race, only 109 riders, including twelve women, showed up to sign in and pick up their route map at the Compagnie Parisienne des Vélocipèdes in Paris. Because of a false start, the organizers delayed some of the riders and divided the field into two groups departing thirty minutes apart. Though James Moore began in the second group, he caught and passed the leaders, arriving in Rouen after 10 hours 45 minutes to win the large first prize, a 1,000 franc note. Count de Castera and J. Bobilier finished together in a tie for second place fifteen minutes later, though they started in the first group. "Miss America," reportedly from England, was the first woman finisher, 22nd overall, in 17 hours.[2]

While the Paris-Rouen race became the forerunner of the classic *ville de ville* (town to town) road course, James Moore went on to set an hour record of 14 miles 880 yards riding an Ariel high-wheeler in 1873. He became the first unofficial "Champion of the World" by winning races in 1873 and 1874 at Wolverhampton, in 1875 at Paris, and in 1877 at Toulouse. Velocipede clubs in France, Italy, and England organized a variety of events such as competitive touring rides, speed trials, and steeple-chase races. When velocipedes evolved into high-wheel bicycles, the sport drew more racers, spectators, and venues for competition. Racers

James Moore (right) and Count de Castera after the Paris-Rouen race.

Logos of the sport:
UCI through the years, FIAC, and
Italy's FCI.

competed on roads and tracks, in groups, or alone against the clock. Popular events of the 1880s were the one-mile sprint, the hour record, the 24-hour marathon, and the cross-country multi-day race.

ORGANIZING THE SPORT

The growth of cycling activities engendered national and international governing bodies for racing. Charged with the power to set the format, rules, schedules, and categories, these groups were part of the development of "rationalized sports." Given the differing opinions on the nature of athletics and sport, it took several years to decide who would take control, whether to accept amateurs or professionals, to measure in meters or feet, and to discriminate by age, gender, race, and bike design.

In 1892, the International Cyclist Association (ICA) was formed by the national federations from Great Britain, the United States, Canada, France, Belgium, the Netherlands, Germany, and Italy. Both the ICA and the national federations had to rule on the rise of professionalism at a time when most groups were aligned for amateurs, though some allowed professionals. When the Italian federation allowed its cyclists to cash in their gold and silver trophies, the ICA restricted Italians from international races. The ruling was inspired by the British, who had added Wales and Scotland as ICA voting members, and it infuriated the Italians, who saw their crest missing from the gold-embroidered ICA World Championship banner. A great dispute ensued and some federations allied with the Italians, who reacted by withdrawing their professionals and "true amateurs" from championship races.[3]

On March 14, 1900, a group led by the Italian and French federations formed the Union Cycliste Internationale (UCI), which became the main governing body for conventional bicycle racing in the twentieth century, with headquarters in Geneva, Switzerland, and with French as the official language. Professional and amateur cycling was governed by subsidiaries of the UCI, the Fédération Internationale de Cyclisme Professional (FICP) and the Fédération Internationale Amateur de Cyclisme (FIAC), in conjunction with the International Olympic Committee (IOC), which organizes the Olympic Games and regional Games such as the Pan-American, Asian, Pan-African, Mediterranean, and Commonwealth Games.

In the 1990s, historic changes have occurred in the governance of UCI cycling. Led by its Dutch president Hein Verbruggen, in 1992 the UCI agreed with the IOC to allow professional cyclists in the 1996 Atlanta Olympics. On January 1, 1993, the UCI was restructured, the FIAC and FICP were dissolved, and professional and amateur racing has gradually become one category called "open." With over 150 affiliated national cycling federations in the UCI, five continental confederations were formed to represent Europe (with fourteen votes), the Americas (nine votes), Asia (nine votes), Africa (seven votes), and Oceana (three votes).

Through the years, national cycling federations formed along the lines of the amateur versus professional issue. In Britain, the Bicycle Union (BU) was formed in 1878, sharing jurisdiction with the Amateur Athletic Association (AAA) with strictly amateur rules. It was renamed the

National Cyclists' Union (NCU) in 1883, and continued to ignore professional racing, while banning women's racing, and eventually discouraging and banning road racing altogether, thus condemning British cycling to years of isolation from European road racing.[4] The NCU was challenged by the British League of Racing Cyclists (BLRC), formed in 1942, which held road races outside the NCU realm. In 1959, the NCU and BLRC came together to form the British Cycling Federation (BCF) which governs UCI racing for pros and amateurs. In France, the Union Vélocipèdique de France (UVF) began organizing races in 1881 and riders could accept cash prizes up to 2,000 francs. The name has since been changed to the Fédération Française de Cyclisme (FFC).

In the U.S., the League of American Wheelmen (LAW) formed its Racing Board in 1881, which sanctioned events mostly for amateurs, while affiliated with the Amateur Athletic Union (AAU), which formed in 1888. Because of limitations for professionals, such as the ban on Sunday racing, a number of competing organizations formed, beginning in 1893 with the National Cycling Association (NCA), known as the "Cash Prize League." In the late 1890s, the American Cycle Racing Association (ACRA) was run by and for promoters, and the American Racing Cyclists Union (ARCU) of 1898 was for pro riders. By 1900, the LAW relinquished racing jurisdiction to the NCA, and in 1912 a group of time-trialing New York and New Jersey clubs formed the Inter-Club Amateur Cycle Road Racing League of America. This was the predecessor of the Amateur Bicycle League of America (ABLA), formed in 1920 to pursue Olympic gold. In the late 1930s, the AAU performed a coup by nullifying the NCA's Olympic affiliation, which fell into the hands of the ABLA. Professional racing withered with the NCA, and returned with the Professional Racing Organization (PRO), formed in 1968 to be the UCI-FICP affiliate. Meanwhile, the ABLA reformed itself to be a better UCI-FIAC affiliate, and became the United States Cycling Federation in 1975. After changes in ownership, PRO became the United States Professional Cycling Federation (USPRO) in 1983, and after many disputes, USPRO will join the USCF in 1995, as the UCI will recognize only one federation from each country for all categories.

In Belgium, the Fédération Vélocipèdique Belge (FVB) was formed in 1882 in Brussels, and became the Ligue Vélocipèdique Belge (LVB), known to the Flemish as the Belgische Wielrijdersbond (BWB). In Holland, various cycling activities were brought under control in 1883 by the Nederlandsche Velocipedisten Bond (NVB), which two years later became the Algemeen Nederlandsche Wielrijders Bond (ANWB). With the expanding differences between touring and racing, the Nederlandsche Wielren Unie (NWU) was formed in 1899, and later renamed the Koninklijke Nederlandsche Wielren Unie (KNWU). In Italy, the Union Velocipedist d'Italia (UVI) was formed in 1884 in Como, and eventually became the Federazione Ciclistica Italiana (FCI) with headquarters in Rome. In Germany, the Bund Deutscher Radfahrer (BDR) began in 1884, and when the country was split during the cold war, the Deutscher

National federation logos: top to bottom; France, Holland, Belgium, and Germany.

Above, cycling logo from the first modern Olympic Games, 1896. Below, Olympic rings.

CITIUS · ALTIUS · FORTIUS

World Champion's rainbow jersey, with bands in blue, red, black, yellow and green.

Radsport Verband (DRV) was formed for amateur racing in East Germany.

Most races in the early 1880s were organized by bicycle clubs, and various private organizers took the initiative to claim a "World Championship." The first series of championships were held in Leicester, England, beginning in 1886, and by 1889 they were organized by the LAW. The first all-male amateur ICA World Championships were held in 1893 on the occasion of the World's Fair at Chicago, followed by the first professional World Championships in 1895 at Cologne. The first modern Olympic Games were held in 1896 at Athens and bicycle racing shared the program with other sports such as the discus throw, wrestling, and the marathon. There were six events for men, including a one-lap 333.3 meter time trial, a sprint race, a mass-start ten kilometer race, a paced 100 kilometer race, a twelve-hour race, and an 87 kilometer individual road race. Along with championship races, cycling's international and national governing bodies have kept lists of records, complete with distances, times, dates, places, riders, and other details. Bicycle historian James McGurn commented on this phenomena in his book *On Your Bicycle* (1987):

> The keeping of international records, which began around 1880, made it possible for, say, an Australian cyclist to compete against a Norwegian who had died before the Australian was born. Competitors and spectators became "sports numerate." They fell within the spell of a competitiveness expressed in statistical calculations and tabulated results. They applied themselves, personally or vicariously, to the single-minded pursuit of improved performances measured in fractions of a second.

THE RAINBOW JERSEY

One of the best creations of the UCI is the rainbow-colored World Champion's jersey. With the "colors of every flag, of every nation," similar to the Olympic rings, the rainbow jersey is a brilliant trophy worn by cycling's annual champions of the world. Like the mythic rainbow, it is awarded with a gold medal at the end of each championship race. In 1994, there were some 78 world titles in track, road, and off-road racing, but the UCI plans to soon limit those to 55 events. Traditions have grown around this basic bicycle symbol. In Italy it is known as the *maglia iridata*, or more passionately, the *maglia sognata* (dream jersey). In French it is the *maillot arc-en-ciel*, in Dutch the *regenboog trui*. The rainbow jersey is clean white and the colored bands appear in a special pattern—blue, red, black, yellow, green—so as not to offend any important countries, and to distinguish it from the Olympic order—blue, yellow, black, green, red. For pros and amateurs the jersey has horizontal stripes 25 centimeters wide, while the junior's jersey has v-shape stripes around the shoulders. Only current official champions may wear the jersey in their event, and former champions may wear smaller bands as trim on their sleeves and collars. Cycling's rainbow bands appear on bike parts and clothing, and unofficial rainbow jerseys are sold to anyone with gold at better bike shops for $60 to $100. Considering the evolution of racing jerseys with bright day-glo pop-art graphics on team uniforms fashioned around sponsors logos, the rainbow jersey continues to stand out in the crowd.

RACING VENUES

Unlike pure athletic events, such as running, fighting, or swimming, cycling was one of the first sports to include an element of technology, other than a ball or a stick. As the bicycle and the sport evolved, technology has had a profound effect on the nature of cycling. The machine helped define the venues for racing in terms of terrain and distance, and as a means of demonstrating the potential of bicycle technology for sport and transport, competitive events were supported by the bicycle industry. In the final decade of the nineteenth century, when the pneumatic-tire bicycle reached its modern form, there was an explosion in the types of racing events. As the machine age took full form in the twentieth century, with motor-pacers, fairings, freewheels, and gear-changers, the question was raised, "Is this a race for man or machine?" Hence, the rules defining the bicycle's shape and technology became standardized for UCI racing.

Bicycle racing became a unique spectacle as cyclists had the speed to beat horses. The high-wheel cyclist was competition for the trotting horse, and with the pneumatic-tire bicycle, an athlete could—at last—go faster than the thoroughbred racer. An account of this important feat appeared in *Harper's Weekly* (1894):

> For the first time in world history a man has propelled himself a mile purely by muscular exertion faster than the muscles of any other living creature ever carried it over the earth's surface. As a triumph of human development this achievement is therefore unique, and worthy of record quite apart from its interest to the sportsmen.[5]

Another element in the sport's development has been the attraction of cycling for the public. During the bicycle's Golden Age in the 1890s, the sport was a popular part of the social scene in Paris, London, Berlin, Milan, and New York, with cycling topics flourishing in the press. As people discovered a fascinating pastime in the sport, the bicycle industry supported the cycling press, which in turn promoted the expansion of cycling events.

France had about a dozen bicycle touring and racing journals, including the daily newspaper *Le Vélo* with a circulation of 80,000 in 1894. While covering cycling's social events, touring rides, and technical innovations, the press got behind race organization, sponsoring the first *ville de ville* road races and stage races, including Bordeaux-Paris (*Véloce Sport* and *Le Vélo*), Paris-Brest-Paris (*Le Petit Journal*), Milano-Torino (*La Bicicletta*), the Tour de France (*L'Auto*), and the Giro d'Italia (*La Gazzetta dello Sport*). Through the race reports in the press, the emerging cycling stars became mythic figures whose seemingly impossible exploits were followed closely by the public.

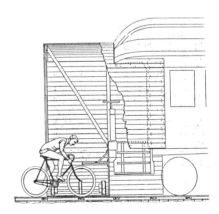

Charles 'Mile-A-Minute' Murphy, top, racing with a horse, and above, behind a locomotive on the Long Island Railroad.

The first Bordeaux-Paris road race was organized by the Vélo Club Bordelais and *Le Véloce Sport* in May 1891. Twenty-eight riders covered 572 kilometers and the Englishman George Mills finished first in 26 hours 34 minutes and 57 seconds, with Montague Holbein coming second more than an hour later. As the racers sought increased speed and endurance while exploring the advantage of drafting, they were paced by other cyclists stationed along the route. Paced-racing was a popular form of competition that developed both on the road and the track in the 1890s. The Bordeaux-Paris tradition carried on into the twentieth century with riders being paced by motor-bikes, automobiles, and eventually, special trainers on mopeds, called dernys, *brom-fiets*, or *entraîneurs*, a distinctive manifestation of man using the motor as a basic component for advancing human-powered performance.

Inspired by the success of Bordeaux-Paris, the editors of the popular magazine *Le Petit Journal* organized another unique road event in September 1891, Paris-Brest-Paris. This was a longer race of 1,200 kilometers, from Paris to the western tip of Britanny and back. For the competing pneumatic tire makers, the race was a means of proving which was best, with Charles Terront riding a Humber bicycle with Michelin tires, and Laval on a Clément with Dunlops. As spectators lined the route, some saboteurs threw tacks in the road. Terront finished first, after five flat tires, in 71 hours 22 minutes, followed by Laval at one hour, and Couilliboeuf at 24 hours. Less than half the 206 starters made it to Paris, and the last rider arrived ten days later. The race was not held again until 1901, and it continued its ten-year tradition until 1951, when race distances were limited by the UCI, and the event became a randonnee, a competitive touring ride.

Charles Terront is often described as the first sporting hero of France, which, according to Ernest Hemingway, became "the most *sportif* country in the world—*La France Sportive*." Terront set the pattern as the poor working-class fellow who rose to fame and fortune through his achievements in the world of professional cycling. He began racing by renting wooden velocipedes. On a high-wheeler he finished second to George Waller in the six-day "Long Distance Championship of the World" held in 1879 on a flat board track at Agricultural Hall in Islington, England. He adapted successfully from the high-wheeler to the safety bicycle, and besides winning the first Paris-Brest-Paris, he rode from St. Petersburg, across Germany and Belgium, to the Buffalo Velodrome in Paris in 14 days 7 hours.

One of Terront's notable contributions to the sport was in the realm of "*besoins physiologiques*"—the need of the cyclist to relieve his or her bladder or bowel while in the midst of a long-distance race. Terront was the first to use a rubber bicycle inner tube attached to his frame for urinating. Other cyclists have used sponges, towels, and empty bottles. Some men mastered the art of pissing while pedaling a fixed-gear or freewheeling on their bicycles, and women performed quick squats by the side of the road, or learned to pee while standing like the men. Traditionally,

Charles Terront, the original *sportif*.

cyclists stop at public facilities in town, or according to recent rules, in the bushes outside of towns. In open country, cyclists in less of a hurry kneel behind their bikes and pretend to fix their gears.

By the turn of the century, more and more bizarre long-distance cycling events appeared as reality and fiction. In the U.S., William Randolph Hearst, publisher of the *San Francisco Examiner* and the *New York Journal*, organized a cross-country ride in 1896 called the *Journal-Examiner* Yellow Fellow Transcontinental Bicycle Relay. Perhaps an inspiration for the Tour de France, the 3,500-mile San Francisco to New York ride was named after the "Yellow Kid" cartoon character and featured yellow-clad two-man teams riding fifteen-mile relays that finished in thirteen days and 29 minutes. The French poet Alfred Jarry created a "Ten-Thousand-Mile Perpetual Motion Food Race," in his 1902 novel *Le Surmâle* (Superman). This was a surreal 16,093-kilometer race from Paris to Vladivostok between a locomotive, a six-man cycle team, and superman, who won on a chainless bike. The cycle team included a dwarf, a negro, a dead Jew, and a *New York Herald* reporter, who rode a quintuplet bicycle with a counterweight trailer. Their fixed-gear development was 57.34 meters and their food was strychnine and alcohol.

RACING WOMEN

Early on, women's velocipede racing was described in chauvinistic or derisive terms. Athletic performances were considered mere entertainment. But with the popularity of the safety bicycle in the 1890s, women's racing grew to a level of competition and professionalism that closely matched the men's sport. Women cyclists took to the roads and tracks in Europe, Britain, America, and Australia. There were mixed races, where women could ride with the men, and separate races, where elite professional cycling women traveled the international circuit. While women compiled various world records and were awarded various championship titles, the UCI did not officially sanction World Championship events until the 1950s, nor Olympic events until the 1980s.

In the U.S., many women of the Century Road Club set long-distance records on the road, such as Jane Lindsey of Long Island, who in 1899 rode 800 miles in 91 hours 48 minutes, and Marguerite Gast of Germany, who in 1900 was ordered to stop in the middle of a 5,000 mile record by the Nassau County, New York, District Attorney who considered it "improper, immoral, and illegal to make such an exhibition on the public highway." She had already covered 2,600 miles in 12 days 7 hours 55 minutes. On the tracks, the notable women racers around 1895 included Clara Grace of Scotland, Frankie Nelson of the U.S., who won the first American women's six-day at Madison Square Garden, and Hélène Dutrieu of France, who rode an hour record of 39.190 kilometers, and was later awarded the Légion d'Honneur for her exploits in aviation. Two famous protégées of the manager "Choppy" Warburton were "Lisette" (Amélie le Gall), a French farm girl who dominated women's professional racing in France, Britain, and America, and Louise Roger, the 1898

"Women's World Champion."[6]

TRACK RACING

While road racing became the dominant venue of cycling in the twentieth century, around the turn of the century track racing was the world's most popular and sophisticated sport. Track racing flourished in Europe, North America, and Australia, as the cycling stars were the highest paid athletes in the world, and the indoor and outdoor tracks attracted more fans than other sports, including America's supposed national pastime, baseball. The venues for track racing began expanding with the evolution of horse-tracks to bicycle velodromes. Bicycle tracks allowed spectators to see the riders through the whole race, while the organizing promoters, clubs, and municipalities could charge admission to make a profit. Horse racing tracks or hippodromes served as the first tracks, with the surface smoothed out, or with smaller infield ovals and boardwalks as bicycle tracks. In 1884, the American H.E. Ducker, known as "the P.T. Barnum of cycling," built one of the first velodromes at the Hampden Park horse track in Springfield, Massachusetts, where the Springfield Bicycle Club Tournaments were held on the smooth record-breaking one-third-mile cement track.

The racing scene at the Springfield Tournaments illustrates the social impact of cycling. Over 20,000 spectators crowded the grounds made festive by colorful banners, musicians, and a hot-air balloon. There were practice heats in the day with League meetings and parties at night. The *Springfield Daily Republican* reported that "in the evening bicycle gossip was all that could be heard anywhere. Bicyclists owned the town...and considerable betting was seen.... On the third floor [the LAW headquarters] there was an informal 'smoker' and all the means for affording the devotee of the weed delight, from a cob pipe to cigarettes, were there in abundance."[7] Similar scenes could be found in Paris, where four velodromes were opened in the early 1890s—the Vélodrome Parc des Princes, the Vélodrome d'Hiver, the Vélodrome des Vincennes, and the Vélodrome Buffalo. The Buffalo track was named for Colonel William F. Cody's "Buffalo Bill Circus" which was staged at the site, known as the "Buffalo grounds."

In the 1890s there were over 1,000 licensed racers in the U.S., and over 100 tracks surfaced in gravel, dirt, cinder, cement, or wood. Among the events held on these tracks were one-third-mile sprints, one-mile scratch races, 5- to 50-mile paced-races, and the grueling six-day races. Because outdoor bicycle racing was difficult during the cold winter months in the Northern Hemisphere, and because of the year-round devotion by spectators and competitors, the sport went indoors as wood velodromes were constructed inside auditoriums. One of the more famous indoor banked tracks was built around 1895 in Madison Square Garden at the former site of P.T. Barnum's Hippodrome in New York City.[8]

Two forms of track racing developed in the 1890s: paced-racing and the six-day. The first pacers were cyclists, usually riding in groups, trading pace on tandems, triplets, quadruplets, and even longer multi-rider bicycles, called *humaine entrâineurs*, and nicknamed *artillerie à pédales* in France. Teams of professional pacing cyclists were provided by bike makers, or hired by the elite professional riders for events such as the flying-start sprint, the two-team pursuit, the 100-lap, and 50-mile race. To increase "dead air" for the record breaker, the last pacer closest to the rider would sit upright, opening a large coat, or attaching a wind screen to the bike. Excitement and danger came as two sets of pacers changed the lead. The style reached an early peak with Mile-A-Minute Murphy's ride behind a locomotive on the Long Island Railroad. Paced racing was featured in the first UCI World Championships, and by the twentieth century, human-pacers were replaced by motor-pacers on steam and gasoline-powered motor-bikes, providing even greater speed, danger, smoke, noise, and thrills.

Chaine Simpson poster by Henri de Toulouse-Lautrec, 1896.

Vel d'Hiv poster by J. Cancaret, c.1900.

The first six-day style track races of the late 1870s and early 1880s were held in England on portable flat board tracks with about eight laps to a mile. They were long-distance events of continuous cycling held indoors and outdoors at regional fairs as a kind of "traveling circus" promoted by tavern owners and bookmakers. By 1889 the event was revived in America, with indoor races of 120 hours. They were called six-day races because of the prohibition on Sunday racing for the observance of the Sabbath. The spectacle usually began with a prologue exhibition on Saturday night and the official start early Monday morning. It continued for six days, twenty hours per day, until Saturday night, with the object of the race being to accumulate the most miles or laps on the track. Interspersed along the way were sprint prizes offered by sponsors and spectators, and separate short-distance pursuit races.

The early six-day was a world of its own, as the riders circled the track day after day, like squirrels in a cage. The press often focused on the bizarre, and perhaps for the same reason the public came in droves. Fans arrived in the afternoon, became an enthusiastic crowd in the evenings, and drifted out after midnight, with only the die-hards remaining through the quiet hours of the morning. In the track center, along with the officials, there were the rider's cabins or tents for resting or sleeping, with cots, cooking stoves, and a wash pail. Electric lights were strung across the ceiling casting confusing shadows as the riders rolled around the track. Spectators could sit at infield trackside tables for drinking and dining, while hearing race announcements from megaphones mounted on tripods and music from the bandstand. The arenas were filled with tobacco smoke, and the scene inspired heavy betting, bad language, and pickpocketing. Riders maneuvered on wooden tracks with tight, uneven banking. Some tracks had no outer guard rail and some riders flew right over the edge. As crashes became "so numerous that keeping count of them was out of the question," the boards would splinter, causing even more trouble for the riders. Opposition to the "cruel sport" grew quickly, with newspaper accounts of racers suffering hallucinations, wrapped in blood-soaked bandages and taking dope while being pushed onto the track by greedy promoters. By 1898, state laws were passed in New York and Illinois which resulted in the two-man team format of modern six-day racing. Here are comments by the *New York Times* from 1897 and 1898:

It is a fine thing to demonstrate that a man astride two wheels can, in a Six-Day race, distance a hound, a horse, or a locomotive. It confirms the assumption, no longer much contested, that the human animal is superior to the other animals. But this undisputed thing is being said in too solemn and painful a way at Madison Square Garden.

An athletic contest in which the participants "go queer" in their heads, and strain their powers until their faces become hideous with the tortures that rack them, is not sport, it is brutality. It appears from the reports of this singular performance that some of the bicycle riders have actually become temporarily insane during the contest, while all of them are sore, cross, and distorted. Permanent injury is likely to result from the attempt to perform any task that is beyond the limits of what a man can undergo and make up for in one night's sleep. Days and weeks of recuperation will be needed to put the Garden racers in condition, and it is likely that some of them will never recover from the strain.

The knowledge that a man can propel himself 1,769 miles in 110½ hours is purchased too dearly when it costs the reason and the physical well-being of the person who imparts it.[9]

Charles W. Miller, 1899.

Among the track stars who emerged in the 1890s, the sprinters were considered the "fastest human beings on earth" with riders such as Willie Windle, A.A. Zimmerman, Major Taylor, Edouard Jacquelin, and the legendary Frank Kramer, who reigned until 1918. The best middle-distance and paced-racer was Jimmy Michael from Wales, the five-foot speedster known as "Midget Michael" who represented the "new breed" of sober, dedicated, and highly paid athlete. The early six-day stars were Charles Miller and George Waller.

Cycling's first international star was Arthur Augustus Zimmerman (1869–1936), known for his graceful style and rapid sprint. Born in Camden, New Jersey, he began racing in the late 1880s, riding a Star high-wheeler with a lever-driven 54-inch gear, and on a safety bicycle he became the "Champion of America, Europe, and the World" in 1893. Nicknamed "Zimmy," "The Flying Yankee," and the "King of Speed," he set a 100-meter record going 66.6 kph (41 mph), a bewildering velocity for a cyclist. As an amateur he won over 100 races in 1893, and his prizes totaled over $20,000, including fifteen bicycles, fifteen rings, fifteen diamonds, fourteen medals, two cups, seven studs, eight watches, one city lot, six clocks, four scarfpins, nine pieces of silverware, two bronzes, two wagons, one piano, and according to rumor, one coffin, from a British promoter who wished not to see him win another race.

Zimmerman was most popular in Paris, where the artistic society that followed cycle racing accepted him. In the *Revue Franco-Américain* of June 1895, Tristan Bernard characterized Zimmerman as a new sensation at the track, "with henna bleached hair, a worn-out jersey, his socks falling below his ankles, his fine head with a powerful nose, with nonchalance, and his mouth forming a vague grin, he walked in an awkward manner, distinguished by a winged presence." Reporters described Zimmerman as "a free-ranging, loose-training natural athlete" who "daily and nightly joined in every boyish prank." Some wrote of how he smoked cigars and partied with friends late into the night before big races. Other accounts describe his modern methods, with his dedication to training, diet, and massage. With Frank Bowden of Raleigh, he wrote a primer for racing called *Points for Cyclists with Training* (1893). He wore the winged-wheel emblem of the New York Athletic Club on his jersey, and he designed bicycles, equipment, and clothing with the brand name

Henri Toulouse-Lautrec, *Zimmerman and his machine*, 1894.

"Zimmy," thus being one of the first athletes to cash in on his famous name. After a victorious trip to Australia in 1896, he gave up racing to run a hotel on the New Jersey shore.

MAJOR TAYLOR

One of the most compelling cycling stars of this era was Major Taylor (1878–1932), nicknamed the "Ebony Streak," the "Black Zimmerman," and *le nègre volant*. Major Taylor was the first athlete of African-American heritage to establish world records, the first to be a member of an integrated professional team, and the first to have commercial sponsorship. His career was marked by his speed, his skin color, and his religious convictions. In a sport that has very few black champions, Taylor remains the finest black cyclist of all time, and one of the greatest cycling heros. His story is fascinating because although he rose from humble beginnings to international acclaim, at the end of his life he was almost forgotten.

When Major Taylor was about 50 years old, he published his autobiography, *The Fastest Bicycle Rider in the World: The Story of a Colored Boy's Indomitable Courage and Success Against Great Odds*. This has been reprinted, and several other recent books and films have portrayed his singular career. These include an Australian TV movie, *Tracks of Glory: The Major Taylor Story* (1992), a children's book called *Bicycle Rider* (1983), by Mary Scioscia and illustrated by Ed Young, and Andrew Ritchie's *Major Taylor: The Extraordinary Career of a Champion Bicycle Racer* (1988), which provides much of the following history.[10]

Marshall Taylor was born near Indianapolis, November 26, 1878, the grandchild of freed slaves. He grew up during the bicycle boom, at a time when opportunities for "colored" people were controlled in America by a power structure in which racism was upheld by the "separate but equal" code. Because of what he called a "freak of fate," Marshall lived for several years with a wealthy white family as a companion to their boy. Instead of living around their stables, he was raised inside their home, with clothes, a tutor, and a bicycle. When the family moved, Marshall returned to his parent's farm and got a job delivering newspapers by bicycle. When he was about thirteen years old, Taylor was hired by the bicycle shop Hay and Willits in Indianapolis to do odd jobs and publicity work performing an exhibition of trick cycling while wearing a military uniform, which is the origin of his adopted first name, "Major." After fondling the gold medal of an upcoming ten-mile road race promoted by Hay and Willits, Major was coerced into racing. He was in tears at the start, where he had a fifteen minute handicap on the scratch group. He took an early lead, and at the halfway point, with a one-mile lead, Tom Hay dangled the gold medal in his face, and Major decided to go all out for it. At the finish he won by about six seconds.

Taylor became "stuck on bicycle riding." In 1894, he worked at a more established bicycle shop giving cycling lessons, and he became the house boy for Louis "Birdie" Munger, a former record-breaking high-wheel racing star and maker of lightweight racing bicycles. Munger let Taylor take part in activities with the all-white Zig-Zag Cycling Club. He introduced

Taylor to several racing stars who traveled the cycling circuit and stayed with Munger while in Indianapolis. When his hero A.A. Zimmerman came to town, Taylor met him at the train station and watched him set the mile record of 2 minutes 12$_{4/5}$ seconds.

Since its charter, the rules of the League of American Wheelmen were not specific about a member's skin color or ethnic origins. As bicycles became widely available and the club's membership grew, more and more African-Americans wanted to join. Amidst much debate and lobbying, the question whether or not non-whites should be allowed to join the LAW was brought to a vote. An amendment to ban non-whites passed, but because of widespread protests, they could still race as non-members in LAW-sanctioned events with friendly promoters. The Colored Wheelmen's Association was formed, with the growth of all-black clubs, such as Taylor's See-Saw Cycling Club.

In 1895, Munger and Taylor moved to Worcester, Massachusetts, where Munger started the Worcester Cycle Manufacturing Company with a group of partners that eventually had offices on Wall Street. Taylor joined the all-black Albion Cycling Club and could train at the YMCA, unlike in Indianapolis. After his eighteenth birthday, in November 1896, Taylor turned professional and received a "baptism by fire" as his first race was the Madison Square Garden Six-Day. He won the Half-Mile Handicap against Eddie "Cannon" Bald and Tom Cooper, and finished eighth overall with 1,786 miles. This was his first and last experience with marathon cycle racing. Instead, he specialized in the pure short-distance sprint races.

With his success in the Garden against Bald and Cooper, the main rivals of his early career, Taylor became a controversial celebrity as he traveled the national cycling circuit for professionals, described in *The Referee* (1896) as the "supreme court of racedom," where the "pick and flower of American speedsters daily measure their relative standing in the racing world, to enter which is the fondest ambition of every young racer." As Taylor rose through the top ten of the 1897 American sprint championship series, winning at Waverly Park, New Jersey, Manhattan Beach, New York, Harrisburg, Pennsylvania, Portland, Maine, and Cleveland, he began to receive rough treatment from many other riders, who formed a combine against him. The hostility reached a peak in a close finish of the one-mile race at Taunton, Massachusetts, when a loser attacked and strangled Taylor into unconsciousness. As the circuit moved South in the late fall season, Taylor was barred from completing the championship series. Race promoters would reject him, or the white riders refused to race with him. Nevertheless, "Majah" was crowned the 1897 "Colored Sprint Champion of America." That same year, Major Taylor's mother, Saphronia Kelter, died in June. She inspired his religious faith and his strict observance of the Sabbath, his reason for not racing on Sundays. Before her death he promised that he would lead a Christian life, and after her death he re-affirmed this by writing in his diary: "Embraced Religion, January 14, 1898."

The 1898 season began with a "complete revolution in the methods, style, and quality of cycle racing in the U.S." Taylor obtained a contract with the American Cycle Racing Association (ACRA), a professional group of riders and promoters who co-existed with the LAW. The ACRA riders included Taylor, Jimmy Michael, Fred Titus, and Edouard Taylore, with an additional forty to fifty riders hired as pacemakers. Taylor wanted to go south for pre-season training, but some riders in Florida would not allow Taylor to join them. After a skirmish in Savannah, Georgia, where he out-paced a group on a triplet, Taylor received an infamous letter: "Mister Taylor, If you don't leave here before 48 hours, you will be sorry. We mean business. Clear out if you value your life—signed White Riders." A high point came at Asbury Park, New Jersey, where the retired A.A. Zimmerman met Taylor at the train station, and saw him beat the "Big Four," Bald, Cooper, Gardiner, and Stevens, in the one-third-mile sprint final. In August at Manhattan Beach, Taylor set a pair of world records in the one-mile race from a standstill, the fastest being 1 minute 41 2/5 seconds (35 mph). In September, as Taylor stood in second place behind Bald in the American championship series, a conference of the professional riders lead to the formation a new racing organization, the American Racing Cyclists Union (ARCU). Taylor had to decide between the LAW, which more or less supported his racing, and ARCU, which supported Sunday racing, and was attracting the real competition. As his main rivals either led or joined the "outlaws," Taylor first refused to sign with ARCU, but then joined.

In the two final championship races, Taylor found himself deceived by the ARCU promoters. At St. Louis, they extended the racing to Sunday due to rain, and at Cape Girardeau, Missouri, the local promoter, Henry Dunlop, had promised hotel accommodations for Taylor, which turned out to be the home of a black family nearby. Dunlop refused to honor his agreement and Taylor decided the contract was broken so he left the race in disgust. On the morning of the race, Dunlop stopped Taylor at the train station, and explained that black cycling fans had put up $400 in prizes to see him race. Without Taylor, Dunlop's promotion would collapse. Taylor later wrote, "They told me, that if I failed to ride in the races that afternoon they would see to it that I was barred forever from the racing tracks of the country."

Taylor returned to setting world records with the support of the Waltham Manufacturing Company. Waltham was well-known for its Orient bicycles and multi-cycles, and they collaborated with the Sager Gear Company on the development of chainless bicycles for racing. Sager offered Taylor $10,000 to lower the flying start one-mile record below 1 minute 30 seconds. Although he did not get below that mark, in two rides he set a new world record at 1 minute 31 4/5 seconds. By the end of 1898 Taylor held seven world records from the quarter-mile to two miles.

Taylor was on more solid ground for the 1899 season as he rejoined the LAW and had the backing of his sponsors, the Waltham-Orient-Sager bicycle company. A Stearns steam-powered pacing tandem was gradually developed, with many break-downs and leaks, and Taylor entered into a pioneering duel with Eddie McDuffie over the motor-paced mile record. On June 30, McDuffie broke Taylor's human-paced mile record behind a Stanley steam-tandem, the same day that Charles Murphy made his "Mile-A-Minute" ride on the Long Island railroad. Finally, Taylor's pacing machine worked properly and on August 3, he set a new mile record of 1 minute 22⅖ seconds, taking five seconds off McDuffie's time.

While there were parallel American championships, the ICA ruled that only the LAW could represent the U.S. for the 1899 World Championships held in Montreal at the Queen's Park track. Taylor won the one-mile sprint championship over Tom and Nat Butler before a crowd of 12,000 fans. He was the second black World Champion of any sport, nine years after the boxer Jack Johnson, and decades before the track hero Jesse Owens and the baseball player Jackie Robinson. This was Taylor's last World Championship race during the prime of his career, since future championships in Europe were held on Sundays. Taylor finished the season winning the LAW American Sprint Championships, and in another duel with McDuffie, he set a new mile record of 1 minute 19 seconds using a 121-inch gear. He won 22 races in 29 starts, and earned over $10,000, though he claimed to have been cheated out of $2,000 by promoters who "forgot" to pay him. With his earnings, Taylor bought a house in Columbus Park, an affluent neighborhood in Worcester, and though the protesting white residents offered to buy back the house for $2,000 more than he paid, Taylor refused, and the "battle closed with the enemy in possession of the field."

In 1900 the LAW relinquished racing control to the NCA and its subsidiary ARCU, and Taylor was again "at mercy of his enemies," the racist clique that had suspended him at the Cape Girardeau race. Meanwhile, Taylor received an offer of $10,000 plus winnings to ride in Europe from Victor Breyer and Robert Coquelle of *Le Vélo*. He turned it down, because he would not ride Sundays. When asked why, Taylor responded: "It is a matter of conscience. It makes no difference how many ministers you quote me, it is the way I feel and believe about it. I reckon it is because of my early teaching. I still haven't outgrown what I was taught. I believe in the saying that 'a mother's prayer will last forever,' and I honestly believe it's my mother's prayers that are standing by me now." Finally in late May, ARCU reinstated Taylor with a $500 fine owing to the Cape Girardeau incident. By most accounts, the white riders capitulated because the public wanted to see Taylor and his presence brought more money to the sport, and because they did not want to be accused of being afraid of the "dusky duster."

Taylor won the year-long American championships, his first in open competition over a new rival, the first-year pro Frank Kramer. In the fall, instead of attacking the paced mile record, he worked up a vaudeville act which toured Massachusetts. He played the mandolin and piano while singing, and rode indoor roller races with Charles "Mile-a-Minute" Murphy. A crowd of a thousand fans gathered at the window of a

Major Taylor on a chainless bike.

Hartford bicycle shop as he set a record time of 43⅗ seconds for a mile, equivalent to 82.5 mph. He completed the year in a match sprint race at Madison Square Garden with his long-time rival Tom Cooper, whom Taylor beat in two heats.

In January 1901, Taylor agreed to an offer by Breyer and Coquelle to compete in Europe from March to June, with no Sunday racing, for $7,200 plus winnings. Shortly before leaving, he became engaged to Daisy Morris, who had entered his life the previous fall. She was the beautiful daughter of a black mother and a white father. She was educated at a private school and lived in Worcester with her relatives, the Rev. and Mrs. Louis Taylor. Major Taylor took the fastest trans-atlantic luxury liner "across the pond," and received royal treatment in France. At the Café Espérance, a cycling cafe on the Avenue de la Grande-Armée, known as *L'Avenue du Cycle*, where old champions, trainers, journalists, and promoters gathered over bottles of wine, Taylor met his rival Edouard Jacquelin, the 1900 World Sprint Champion. They became "fast friends," and complimented each others' legs. Taylor was invited to lunch with Count Albert de Dion and visited the de Dion-Bouton automobile factory. While following the Bordeaux-Paris road race in the open seat of a Dorsay automobile with a journalist from *Le Vélo*, he was "greeted with tumultuous applause all along the route. Peasants and cyclists lined the roadside waving to the American. Maurice Martin asked Taylor to sign his name on pages of his reporter's notebook and Major threw the sheets into the air as they passed by."

Paris was considered the world's cultural center and sports capital at the time, and Parisian *cyclisme* had developed sophisticated tactics with a sense of aesthetic style. In the sprint race, while Americans preferred to see a mad dash and complained of "loafing," the French enjoyed the tactical waiting games and quick spurts. Likewise, Taylor was appreciated more in France as a public hero with a mysterious physical talent. Taylor was featured in a long, illustrated article in *La Vie au Grand Air*, where he described getting used to people staring at him, how he liked to play the piano and mandolin, and his reasons for not racing on Sundays. His style was analyzed, he and his bike were measured (he had an 88-inch gear), and he was x-rayed by French doctors who agreed he was "a human masterpiece," except that "his thighs were a little over-developed." Andrew Ritchie describes his historic impact:

> Taylor's success in France was among the earliest examples of the elevation of an athletic star to the status of a popular hero. Bicycle racing was an emerging mass spectator sport of a new kind, in need of stars and heroes, and the fact that he was exotic and had charisma and mystique made Taylor perfect star material—a superb performer, disciplined, down-to-earth, good-humored, and intelligent, an underdog who had triumphed over adversity. Yet, at the same time, he was unique and somehow untouchable and incomprehensible, like a visitor from another planet.

Taylor toured sixteen cities in France, Germany, Denmark, Belgium, Italy, and Switzerland, winning some 42 times. The highlight of 1901 was the pair of match sprint races between Taylor and Jacquelin at the Parc des Princes velodrome. Jacquelin won the first match in two heats, but on his victory lap, he foolishly thumbed his nose, presumably at the pro-Taylor crowd. Major won the revenge match in two heats. After the race, at the Chalets du Cycle in the Bois de Boulogne, Jacquelin proposed a toast of champagne, and Taylor replied, "With pleasure, but you know I only drink water." But Taylor took a sip of champagne and exclaimed, "Awful! Horrible!" while pushing the glass aside.

When Taylor returned to America, he needed to recuperate and got a doctor's waiver to take a rest from racing. Since he was under contract with the NCA, they fined him $100 for each failure to appear, saying "Sick or well, you must ride at each National Circuit meet." When Taylor resumed racing, Frank Kramer already had 30 points towards the American championship series, and by the end of the year, Kramer won with 72 points over Taylor's 64.

Major and Daisy were married during the first days of spring 1902, and it was the subject of a ten-page article in *The Colored American* magazine with Daisy on the cover. Taylor received a multi-year contract from Coquelle and Breyer and prepared for an international tour in which he would circle the globe twice in two years. Taylor crossed the Atlantic without Daisy for his second European tour and returned in the summer for the American championships. Because Taylor would not ride the World Championships held on Sundays, he openly challenged the winner to a match race. In 1902, one week after Thorwald Ellegaard won the title in Rome, Taylor "annihilated" the Danish star in two heats in Paris. His racing in America became more sporadic as he faced difficulties finding a suitable hotel room and dealing with his main rivals, the powerful combine of Frank Kramer, Iver Lawson, and Floyd McFarland. A new sprint championship format allowing up to four riders in a race, resulting in better opportunities for Taylor's opponents to block or "pocket" the "colored cyclone."

In December 1902, Major and Daisy crossed the Pacific for his first tour of Australia during the racing season of the Southern Hemisphere. On their arrival in Sydney, the Summer Nights Amusement Committee met them with a cheering flotilla of boats in the harbor, where thousands of fans called his name, and a reception was held with the mayor. Bicycle racing was very popular in Australia, and Taylor helped boost enthusiasm as the world's most famous and highest paid athlete of the time. In three months of racing in Sydney, Melbourne, and Adelaide, he earned almost £4,000, equivalent to a lifetime's wages for the average Australian worker. On his second Australian tour, Taylor's contract included a large sum of cash, all expenses paid, plus winnings and a percentage at the gate. The *New South Wales Baptist* described the "Thirty Thousand Dollars for Conscience Sake," the amount of money Taylor lost by not racing on

Taylor and Jacquelin before their match at Parc des Princes, Paris, May 1901.

Sundays. "For years this man of deep and strong convictions has been preaching to the sporting world a silent but eloquent sermon of example."

Taylor was haunted by the appearance of his American rivals, Lawson and McFarland, who helped spread racism amongst the Australian riders and promoters. At Melbourne, Lawson fouled Taylor in a match sprint, causing a serious crash which left the "Worcester Whirlwind" stunned and lacerated. Lawson was suspended for a year and won the World Championships at London in 1904.

From Australia, the Taylors sailed for Europe via the Indian Ocean and Suez Canal, for his third season based in Paris. In September 1903 they returned to Worcester, with sixteen pieces of baggage including a motor-cycle and a French automobile, and after a short rest, they returned to Australia in November 1903. Taylor finished the 1903–1904 season after almost 100 races, and the family set sail for San Francisco with a "small menagerie," including a kangaroo, several colorful parrots, and a cocka-too, which had been taught to say "Major." Finally returning to Worcester in May 1904, Daisy then gave birth to Major's only child, a daughter named Sydney for her place of birth. The stress of Taylor's career took its toll, and as he settled back in Worcester with his family he assumed a period of semi-retirement from June 1904 to March 1907. Taylor returned to Paris in 1907 with a contract from Coquelle, and the sponsorship of Peugeot and Michelin. Though he started off over 25 pounds overweight, he regained fitness to meet two new French sprinters, Gabriel Poulain and Emil Friol. At the end of the season, when he had proven his ability to come back by beating Poulain, he turned down offers to ride in Australia and announced his retirement. Nevertheless, Taylor returned again in 1908 and continued the "familiar cycle of the peripatetic athlete, constant overnight traveling, living out of a suitcase, training, massage, meeting their press." Sometimes Daisy and Sydney accompanied him, sometimes they stayed in Paris.

In 1909 Taylor returned to Paris for his sixth and last European tour. He was accompanied by his longtime teammate and trainer Bert Hazard, but Daisy and Sidney stayed home. Coquelle's influence had waned and he gave Taylor an ultimatum—either race on Sundays or not at all. So Taylor finally succumbed, and compromised his religious convictions to make a living in his final cycling season. He was a former champion con-tinuing well past his prime, and his performances no longer graced the sports headlines. The letters to his family illustrate his situation: "Now love and kisses and God's blessings to both of my sweethearts from your poor, weary, homesick, lonesome, tired and most worn out, discouraged, fat, disgusted, but *game and true* husband, and that does not begin to express how I feel." Before leaving France, he beat the World Champion Victor Dupré in his hometown.

After hanging up his racing wheels for good, Taylor had accumuiated an estimated $75,000, and was looking for a way to get involved in the automobile industry. He applied to the Worcester Polytechnic Institute but was rejected because of his lack of a high school diploma. Taylor had an idea for a metal sprung automobile wheel, and joined with Fred Johnson of Iver Johnson to form the Major Taylor Manufacturing Company to develop and produce his invention. The company failed and Taylor undertook a series of smaller business ventures, such as the Excello Manufacturing Company, makers of automobile oils and lubricants. By the early 1920s, Taylor was the proprietor of "Major's Tire Shop" which replaced and repaired car tires. He could no longer support his family in their comfortable lifestyle, and he began selling Daisy's jewelry and his pieces of property. Eventually he sold their house, and the Taylors moved into a more modest apartment in Worcester, where Major began writing his autobiography, which he paid to have published by the Commonwealth Press of Worcester in 1928. The book was dedicated to Louis Munger, who died the following year. Major and Daisy had drifted apart and after she moved to New York, Taylor went to Chicago at the invitation of an alderman. While living in the YMCA, he sold copies of his book door to door.

In 1932 when his health began to suffer, he was admitted into Provident Hospital, but was moved to a charity ward at the Cook County Hospital, where he died on June 21 of "nephrosclerosis and hypertension with chronic myocarditis." Since nobody came to claim his body, Major Taylor was buried in an unmarked "paupers grave" at the Mount Glenwood Cemetery, outside Chicago. In 1948 a proper burial was given by a group called the Bicycle Racing Stars of the 19th Century Association, based in Chicago with about 200 members. With the philanthropy of Frank Schwinn, Taylor's remains were exhumed and placed in a distinguished location in the cemetery's Memorial Garden of the Good Shepherd, with a service attended by Taylor's first supporter Tom Hay. Another concrete monument in Indianapolis is the Major Taylor Velodrome, which opened in July 1982. The plaque on his grave described his life:

Daisy Major and Sydney Taylor, about 1906, from Andrew Ritchie's *Major Taylor*.

WORLDS CHAMPION BICYCLE RACER
WHO CAME UP THE HARD WAY
WITHOUT HATRED IN HIS HEART
AN HONEST, COURAGEOUS AND GOD FEARING
CLEAN LIVING GENTLE-MANLY ATHLETE
A CREDIT TO HIS RACE
WHO ALWAYS GAVE OUT HIS BEST
GONE BUT NOT FORGOTTEN

Track Racing

Velodromes are the cathedrals of cycledom, sacred gathering sites for demi-god cyclists and their true believers. On most days of the week, velodromes are relatively quiet places where individuals or groups of devotees silently practice the sport. At special times, the ritual reaches a sublime moment, when masses of thousands of enthusiasts share in a passionate celebration of cycling. A sense of purity comes from riding a gracefully banked velodrome with a fixed-gear bicycle. There is usually an ideal racing speed for each velodrome, depending on lap length, track surface, turning radius, and degrees of banking. At this speed the riders achieve a wonderful equanimity with the bike and the track, and the setting provides the conviction to achieve peak performance in a measurable quantum.

Velodromes can be outdoor open-air tracks, semi-covered stadiums, or indoor arenas, with various facilities based around the action on the track. Outdoor tracks are usually aligned so the afternoon sun is not in the riders' eyes on the straight-aways. Tracks have access from outside to the infield via underground ramps, overpasses, or a trackside gate for crossing during breaks in the racing. Within the infield, closest to the finish line are the official's stands, for the judges, the commissaires, and the photo-electronic timing equipment.

The infield may include small warm-up circles, riders' quarters, mechanics' pits, a medical station, rest rooms, press tables, concession stands, and landscaping. The riders' quarters may consist of tents, lounge chairs, semi-private cabins around the infield, or subterranean rooms built under the velodrome. At the outer edge of the track are the front row seats and the spectators' elevated stands with special box stands provided for the race organizers, the announcers, and the press. A scoreboard shows the rider's numbers, placings, and times. Various other sports and recreational facilities often surround velodromes, including showering rooms, equipment rooms, gymnasiums, and playing fields.

Indoor track during a six-day race.
Photo by Graham Watson.

VELODROME BUILDING

One of the most famous modern tracks is the Vigorelli Velodrome in Milan, Italy. Known as "Vel Vig," and the *piste miracle*, it was completed in 1935, and earned the title as the world's fastest outdoor semi-covered track at sea-level. Scores of world records have been made on the 333.3 meter wood track, including sixteen hour records. The surface was made of pine boards, in 2- x 2-inch, twenty-foot long slats, placed in line with the direction of travel. The wood was cut piece by piece from the centers of trunks of trees grown in a particular stand of Siberian pine. The pine grew slowly there, making the wood more dense, and without knots or splinters. This kind of wood made a racing surface as firm and smooth as possible.[11] Racers were able to use the lightest tires, such as the Clement No. 0 made of fine silk with smooth white rubber that weighed 75 grams, held 200 psi, and wore out after about an hour of racing.

The Vigorelli Velodrome has had many exciting moments and weathered many challenges as the world's best track. During World War II it suffered bomb damage but was quickly repaired to serve as the finish line for classic road races, such as the Tour of Lombardy and the Giro d'Italia. As the track of choice for record breaking, the Vigorelli was challenged by Rome in 1960, and surpassed by the high-altitude tracks in Mexico City (built for the 1968 Olympics) and Colorado Springs (1982), and the sea-level track at Bordeaux (1989). The Vigorelli was refurbished for its 50th anniversary in 1985, and the first meet was a five kilometer pursuit race in which Francesco Moser of Italy beat Greg LeMond of the U.S.

When Italy began building for the 1960 Rome Olympics in 1956, the City of Rome issued a directive: "Rome must be faster than Milan, no expense must be spared." In order to improve upon the Vigorelli Velodrome, every aspect of track design was examined. Herbert Schurmann of Germany was in charge of design and construction. With four years to develop the track surface, Professor Giordano of the National Wood Institute in Florence traveled the world in search of the best wood for Rome's hot and humid climate. He collected 25 samples, and placed them at the site to be exposed and analyzed for three years. The wood was selected so as not to hold or absorb water, or to expand or shrink with changes in weather. The choice was *Afzelia Doussie*, a rare African hardwood from French Cameroon that came in four-foot diameter, 40-foot long trunks. The finished 400 meter track "nestled into its custom-designed stadium like a piece of hand-made furniture."[12] The first world record for the track was the 1,000 meter time trial of 1:07:27 set by Sante Gaiardoni of Italy, and in October 1967, Ferdi Bracke of Belgium set the sea-level hour record of 48.093 km at Rome.

Herbert Schurmann, with his father Clemens and his son Rolf, built a family tradition of designing the world's finest velodromes. In all, the family has designed well over 100 tracks around the world. In the 1920s, Clemens Schurmann was a bicycle racer and an architect. He was known as one of the few riders to wear a helmet, a condition set by his wife after too many falls on his head. His first track was completed in 1926 for a

Carpenters assembling a portable wood track.

bicycle club in Krefeld, near Düsseldorf, that wanted a safe, wooden open-air track. One of his worst tracks was built in a narrow exhibition hall in Berlin in 1949. The building had 6,000 seats and the track had long straights and tight turns with the inside radius of only fifteen meters. The turns were so tight and steep that a rider at full speed felt four G-forces of centrifugal gravity. After three riders were killed by breaking their forks at the same point coming out of a turn, it was time for major surgery on the track. This was how Herbert got into business at the age of 24, working days and nights with his father to correct the Berlin turns. Since then, the Schurmanns never build tracks with less than 16.5 meter radius turns. Schurmann tracks vary in size from 133 to 400 meters, with turns banked from 32 degrees to 52 degrees. They are in most Western European countries, as well as in Colombia, South Korea, Panama, and Tasmania.

TRACK MARKINGS

Modern track racing comprises about four basic formats: championship events, omnium events, six-day races, and keirin races. Championship and Olympic events take place on velodromes of varying length and width, about 200 meters to 500 meters long and five to nine meters wide, with 333.33 meters as the standard length. The racing track is marked with a standard set of lanes and distances for different kinds of racing according to the rules of the UCI.

There are usually four colored stripes circling the track marking lanes and several perpendicular lines marking distances. "The finish line for any Championship," reads the UCI rules, "shall consist of a four centimeter wide black line painted on a 72 centimeter wide strip in such a way that 34 centimeters of white show on each side of the black which shall be mat." The lanes are concentric, parallel rings, crossing under the finish line, from the infield up the width of the track to the balustrade. The major distance lines cross the entire width of the track, such as the finish line, the two red pursuit lines on opposite sides of the track, and the white sprint line 200 meters from the finish. Other smaller markings serve as starting points for the kilometer (1,000 m), the mile (1,609 m), and other distances.

The inside lane is the legendary *Côte d'Azur* or blue band, named for the region where the Riviera meets the Alps. Cycling's *côte d'azur* is usually a sky-blue colored band over 70 centimeters wide, lying at the bottom of the banking, on the flat inner oval of the track. It serves as a neutral zone for slow riding, where no racing should occur. The racers inevitably dip into the blue band, using the whole track in sprints, or taking the shortest line around the track. To prevent this in timed distance races, foam blocks are placed at five meter intervals around the turns at the edge of the blue band. The riders can hit the blocks without disruption, but if they hit too many there is cause for disqualification.

Next to the blue band is an open space about 20 centimeters wide usually used for marking distances, and then a four centimeter wide black stripe known as the pole line, which represents the actual measurement of the track, and the inner boundary for the pole position, which is exactly 70

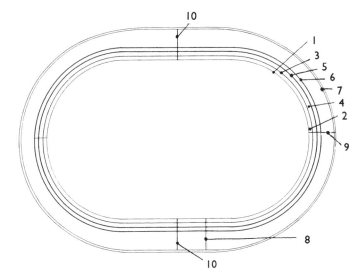

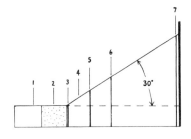

centimeters wide. The outer boundary of the pole position is marked by a four centimeter red stripe, known as the sprinter's line. Finally, about one-third of the way up the width of the track, there is a blue stripe known as the stayer's line, used primarily as the inner boundary for motor-paced events. The balustrade is usually a guard rail or fence over 85 centimeters high. On tracks with nothing to stop the rider from going over the banking into the landscape, a black holding line marks the edge of the track.

CHAMPIONSHIP TRACK EVENTS

The UCI has made changes to Championship and Olympic track racing in the 1990s. Professional and amateur men have been combined into an open category, the tandem sprint and motor-paced events have been dropped, and new events include the Olympic sprint, a 50-km madison-style team race, and a 500-meter individual time trial for women.

MATCH SPRINT - *Vitesse* (Open, Women, Junior Men, Junior Women): This is a race of two or three laps, depending on the length of the track, for a distance of approximately 1,000 meters. While the last 200 meters are timed, the only real objective is to cross the finish line first. This is a race of pure speed, tactics, and regimen. The riders proceed through a series of matches for best of three heats, with the winners going to the semi-finals and on to the finals, where two riders engage in a best of three match for first and second place. The semi-final losers proceed through a series of *repêchage* heats to decide third and fourth place.

Two or more riders start each heat together. By the drawing of lots, one rider is chosen to start from a position closest to the pole line and to lead for the first lap. The advantage is often for the rear rider not only because of drafting, but also because the rear rider can easily see his or her opponent. For the second heat the rear rider must lead the first lap, and if there is need for a third heat, the lead rider is again chosen by drawing lots. The rear rider may take an early lead, but this is rare. Once the riders have passed the first lap, the race is open, and as the riders jockey for position, the speed can vary from a motionless track stand, known as

Track Markings:
1. Inner track
2. Blue band
3. Black pole line, track measure
4. Pole position
5. Red sprinters line
6. Blue stayers line
7. Black holding line
8. Finish line
9. Sprint starting line
10. Pursuit starting line

surplace, to a gradual wind-up to a flat-out sprint. In the last 200 meters, the first rider to take the pole position must stay within that boundary. Another rider can pass the pole rider above the sprinter's line but they must give reasonable space before "closing the door" and taking over the pole position. With the riders sprinting all out, oftentimes shoulder to shoulder, there are many intimidating moves.

The track stand is a curious exercise in the fastest race of cycling. The technique is a kind of *séance* where the riders come to a stand-off and play a tense war of nerves. Using the fixed-gear and the banking of the track, the riders perform a balancing act, where the object may be to force the other rider into the lead, to entertain the crowd, or to surprise the opponent by gaining a jump-start on the sprint. During some track stands the lead rider may pedal backward, trying to change places with the rear rider, but they may not move back more than twenty centimeters. Riders are also able to "walk" their bike by hopping up and down the banking to change their angle or advance their pedals to a more favorable position. The longest moments of *surplace* have exceeded one hour.[13]

As a "chess match on wheels," with the whole track as the kingdom of the sprinters, there are many strategic moves available. The lead rider can make a mock track stand by braking with the gloved hand on the front wheel, following the pedals but without applying backward force, causing the opponent to slow, giving the lead rider an advantage. A rider can "box" or "pocket" his or her adversary by riding with closely overlapping wheels, or by edging against the rail or the pole line, so that the only way out for the rear rider is to slow and turn down or up the banking. The front rider can weave up and down the banking, trying to catch the second rider slowly going up the slope, while at the same time being in position to accelerate rapidly on the down slope. The rear rider can lag behind high on the banking, only to take off and pass the lead rider at a speed impossible to latch onto. A rider can lead out the sprint moving towards the sprinter's line but not crossing it. As the opponent comes around on the top, the leader may apply maximum speed while holding the opponent to the longer outer path around the turn. Then, with a quick jump into the pole position at the perfect moment and by "throwing the bike" at the finish line, he or she may win. Sprinters are usually graced with natural speed, well-developed fast-twitch muscles, and a crafty, courageous temperament.

TANDEM SPRINT (Open): Similar to the match sprint, this event has two riders on one track bike comprising each team. Because of higher speeds, this is often a longer race of about five laps for approximately 1,500 meters. Tandem riders must share with their teammates a mastery of sprinting ability and a special understanding of racing tactics. The captain (front steering rider) supplies confidence through calculated decision making, while the stoker (rear power rider) provides the collaborative response with a powerful kick while checking opponents. The riders communicate through the pedals of the fixed-gear with subtle body language.

Sprinters doing a track stand.

KILOMETER TIME TRIAL - *Kilo* (Open, Junior Men): This is a 1,000 meter individual time trial (about three laps), with riders starting from a standstill and the winner having the fastest time. When the rider is fixed to his bike at the start in the pole position, an official blows a whistle and the rider has five seconds to cross the start line which begins the clock. The race is a long, grueling sprint that takes about a minute or more, somewhat longer than a cyclist's anaerobic capacity at about 45 seconds. Towards the finish a kind of physical wall appears and a certain amount of aerobic power is called upon. There are two or three phases in the kilo: the powerful accelerating sprint of about 200 meters; the middle stretch lasting about 650 meters; and the grueling finish in the remaining 150 meters. Depending on a rider's attributes, one may start fast and "float" his speed for a finishing burst, and another may start moderately fast, gradually increasing the pace so that nothing is left at the finish. As the riders generate incredible force, while struggling for oxygen to produce their last dash of energy, they try to maintain a straight line as close as possible to the pole line to save fractions of seconds. Kilo riders are usually the biggest, most muscular cyclists, often sharing the same events and attributes as the sprint and tandem specialists.

Cycling's muscle event, the kilometer time trial.

500 METER TIME TRIAL (Women, Junior Women): Same as the men's kilometer time trial but half the distance for women.

INDIVIDUAL PURSUIT (Open, Women, Junior Men, Junior Women): The length of this race varies depending on category. In championship racing, junior men and women ride 3,000 meters (about nine laps) and professional and amateur men ride 4,000 meters (about twelve laps). Before 1993, professionals rode 5,000 meters (about fifteen laps). Two riders start from a standstill at opposite sides of the track, with one rider ending the race at the finish line. The riders attempt to catch each other, because if one succeeds the race is won. While this result is more frequent on small tracks (250 meters or less), the riders are usually equally matched, so they go for the best time. The tactical strategy of the pursuit race often takes form as a schedule of lap times which the riders attempt to equal or better. Progress is measured by coaches or trainers, who record lap times and the time differential with opponents. The coaches call out "splits" every lap or kilometer, and signal as the riders are "even," "down," or "up" on a winning schedule. To calculate the average lap time for a pursuit, the race distance in whole laps, plus any partial lap for odd-sized tracks, is divided by the desired time, less three seconds to account for the starting acceleration. For example, with a five minute schedule for a 4,000 meter race on a 333.3 meter track, the distance is twelve whole laps. The first lap would be 27.75 seconds and the each remaining lap is 24.75 seconds. According to the attributes of the riders, such as those with a fast start and a strong finishing kick, the lap times are adjusted. Pursuit riders are specialists who combine the speed skills of track racing with the endurance capacity of road racing. They include the

Steve Hegg winning the 1984 Olympic pursuit.

"fast-on-the-flats" road riders, known as *rouleurs*, who excel in circuit races and time trials, and the middle-distance "trackies" who ride points races, keirins, and six-days. Many pursuiters spend several months in special preparation for an annual championship race.

TEAM PURSUIT (Open, Junior): Similar to the Individual Pursuit, the teams consist of four riders in a tight formation, with each rider on his own bike. The team's time is recorded when the third rider crosses the finish line. If one team catches the other, they win the race, otherwise they ride for the fastest time. The teams must function as a close-knit unit, requiring a high degree of specialization, that can take over a season of preparation. The teams exchange pace at the banked turns, either every lap or half-lap (on tracks over 250 meters), as the front rider goes straight up the banking at the turns, and then swings back down in line behind the last rider. Almost two meters of forward progress are lost as the lead rider swings up.

POINTS RACE - *Cours aux Points* (Open, Women, Junior Men, Junior Women): In championship races this is a 100 to 150 lap event (about 30 to 50 kilometers), with points awarded every five laps (not less than 1.5 kilometers on small tracks), and the winner earning the most points. The riders start together positioned on the track according to placings in preliminary heats. The intermediate sprints are awarded thus: five points for first place; three points for second; two points for third; and one point for fourth. Points are doubled for the sprints at the half-way mark and at the finish (10, 6, 4, and 2 points). If there is a tie in the final tally, the intermediate sprints are counted, and if there is again a tie, the final sprint counts.

In the madison race, one teammate relieves another with a handsling. Photo by John Chay, Trexlertown Velodrome.

KEIRIN (Open): This is a recent addition to championship racing, inspired by the *keirin* style of competition in Japan. The UCI event is a ten-lap race for nine riders who fight for position behind a motor-pacer. With one lap to go, the pacer swings out of the way, and the riders have a mass sprint for the finish.

MADISON RACE - *L'Américain* (Open): Teams of two riders compete in a 50-kilometer race. The teammates take turns on the track, with one below the stayers line throughout the race, and the other high on the banking. They exchange places either by a hand-sling or by grabbing a hip fob, a handle, small baton, or towel rolled tightly in the teammate's shorts.

WORLD RECORDS

There are many world records in track racing, known as *Records du Monde sur piste*. Before the changes of the 1990s, the UCI listed over 60 world records on outdoor tracks (*en plein air*) and indoor tracks (*sur piste couverte*) at sea-level (*niveau de la mer*) and high-altitude (over 600 meters) for professional and amateur men, and women. While cyclists still consider these distinctions, the UCI now recognizes an open category for men, and all tracks are considered equal. Each track has its own lap record, from a standing start (*arrêté*) or a flying start (*lancé*). Cycling's "record of records" is the individual hour record (*record de l'heure*).

OMNIUM EVENTS

Omnium events include a variety of popular and traditional races. They are similar to six-day races and may include championship events. Omniums can be held on a wider range of tracks, from small 100 meter indoor velodromes to larger than 600 meter outdoor ovals. They provide an entertaining program for spectators, and more events for a wider range of cyclists.

HANDICAP RACE: This is a sprint or medium-distance race where the riders start at various intervals around the track and compete for a common finish line. Handicap races are usually based on distances such as the kilometer, the mile, or 50 to 100 laps. The riders are assigned starting positions or times of departure, determined "in accordance with an appraisal of merit adopted by the jury." This formula allows the beginners, veterans, women, and slower riders to compete with the fastest racers. Known as the "scratch" group, the top-seeded riders start last and go the whole distance, while trying to chase and pass all the handicap riders on the track.

ELIMINATION RACE - *Miss and Out, Devil (Take the Hindmost)*: This is an exciting variation on the points race. Instead of awarding points for the first riders at the intermediate sprints (five to ten laps), the last rider is eliminated at each sprint. In this way, the race is at the rear of the pack during the sprints, as a wave of riders try to squeeze past each other across the line. The "devils" are the hindmost riders who miss and must

Photomontage of Roger Riviere, world hour record holder, 1957–1967.

bow out. As the race follows its course the field dwindles down to a few fast riders who finish in a match sprint. Sometimes one or more steady, strong riders who lack a quick sprint may breakaway during the race.

AUSTRALIAN PURSUIT: This is a medium or long distance race in which several riders start out at handicapped intervals around the track and pursue each other. When a rider is caught he or she must pull out. The race continues either until the last rider is caught, or until a specific distance is covered. In some versions, teams of two riders pursue each other while exchanging pace as in a madison race.

MOTOR-PACE - *Demi-fond*, *Stayer* (Open): Formerly a world championship event, these are races of 40 to 100 kilometers or one hour, with the riders being paced by motorcycles or mopeds. The teams of motor-pacers and paced riders begin in a mass start formation with riders catching the pacers' slipstream and staying close to the stayer's line. Teams may not ride more than three abreast above the stayer's line, and they may not pass another team below that line. Both the pacer and the paced ride cycling machines that are commonly known as stayer's bikes. The big pace-making bikes are motorcycles with engines ranging from 500 to 1,000 cc, with long handlebars reaching back to the tip of the seat, allowing the pace-maker to stand on footboards in an upright position. A special helmet with ear phones is worn by the pace-maker to hear the paced rider, along with a regulation uniform of black leather jacket, pants, and boots. Behind the rear wheel is a roller bar, 60 centimeters wide, 33.5 centimeters above the ground, and usually 40 centimeters behind the rear wheel, which the paced rider stays close to and may safely touch. Another smaller kind of moped, called a derny, or *brom-fiets*, is used for pace-making on smaller indoor tracks or on the road. These mopeds have an engine no larger than 100 cc, sometimes with a fixed-gear that requires pedaling. Instead of a roller bar there are mudguards or fenders, and the pacer wears cycling clothes with a vest.

FLAT TRACK RACING

Flat track racing includes events held on asphalt running tracks, grass tracks, and cycle speedways. A unique kind of flat track racing in the U.S. is the Little 500, an annual springtime race held at Indiana University and named after the Indianapolis 500 auto race. The relay race has student teams riding 200 laps (50 miles) for men and 100 laps for women. In San Francisco's Golden Gate Park, on the running track of the Polo Fields, a group of fixed-gear enthusiasts held a series of Outlaw Races in 1993. Grass track races date back to the nineteenth century and are still held on grass-covered running tracks in Britain. Requiring special handling skills in high-speed turns to prevent skidding, the omnium-style events include handicap races, an eight kilometer championship race, and tricycle races.

Cycle speedway developed as a generation of post-World War II youth known as "skid kids" took to dirt and paved speedway tracks on bicycles. The British sport, which is not affiliated to UCI cycling, has been organized by the Cycle Speedway Council since 1971, with almost a hundred clubs and some 2,000 participants competing from April to October on the National Grand Prix circuit at about 75 tracks throughout England, Wales, and Scotland. The tracks are flat, unbanked ovals about 75 to 110 meters per lap and five meters wide, often with a shale surface and an inside curb of concrete. There are both individual and team races for men, youth (under 21 years old), juniors (under 18), and schoolboys (under 16), with sponsorship and publicity provided by breweries and newspapers, such as the *Daily Mirror*. The individual races or heats consist of four riders doing four laps. The riders start from a standstill and sprint for the first turn to get the advantage of the inside line. To achieve the greatest speed in the bends, the riders usually trail their inside, left foot to prevent skidding out. Most of the top riders are over thirty years old, and they wear gloves, long-sleeve jerseys, and long tights or pants for protection from falls.

Six-Days

The modern six-day race with two-man teams was a very popular sport in America from 1900 until about 1940, and continues as a wintertime professional circuit in Europe and Australia. During the peak years of the American six-day in the 1920s and 1930s in New York and Chicago, the riders would go about 120 to 140 hours from Sunday night to Saturday night. Among the thousands of spectators who frequented the races were Al Capone, Babe Ruth, Bing Crosby, and Mary Pickford. Six-day veteran Alf Goullet (1892–1995) described the event in 1926 for the *Saturday Evening Post*, when he was paid $1,000 per day for racing:

> The Six-Day bicycle race is the most grueling contest in athletics because of its sheer monotony. If we weren't mercifully so built that we quickly forget our sufferings, I don't believe there is a man in the world who would ride in more than one. It takes toll of every muscle in the body, of the stomach, of the heart, and while it is being ridden, the mind. In the past fifteen years I have ridden in 24 and the only way I can think of describing the riding is as one infernal grind.

The "jams" are the essence of the race, as riders increase the pace or jump into the lead trying to steal laps on their opponents. As soon as the jam begins the relief riders leap out of their cabins around the infield and hop on their bikes. By picking up speed while high on the banking, the fresh riders swoop down into the fray, squeezing between narrow gaps of riders while making a flying exchange with their tired teammate. A faulty swerve, a closed gap, a touched wheel, or a slippery section of track leads to a massive pile-up of riders and bikes. The six-day stars of the 1920s and 1930s were a tough bunch. Through the course of his career, Bobby Walthour reportedly broke his left collarbone eighteen times and his right collarbone 28 times. He required 46 stitches on his legs and 69 stitches on

Alfred Frueh, *Bicycle Race,* 1920. Courtesy of the Graham Gallery.

his face and head. He suffered 32 fractured ribs, eight broken fingers, and one broken thumb. He was considered fatally injured six times and pronounced dead three times, only the last being final. "Old Ironman" Reggie McNamara had a similar history in a career of 117 six-day races from 1913 to 1936, supposedly leaving a tooth imbedded in a board track after a bad spill. Alf Goullet, known as the "Australian Bullet," set the all-time distance record for a six-day by riding 2,759 miles and two laps in 146 hours with Albert Grenada at Madison Square Garden in 1914. William "Torchy" Peden of Canada was a 6-foot 2½-inch 220-pound red-haired athlete who won some 38 six-day races between 1932 and 1940. Other popular stars included Alf Letourner of France, Franco Georgetti of Italy, Gerard Debaets of Belgium, and the German duo Gustav Kilian and Heinz Vopel.

Over the years the six-day format has gradually changed, under the guidance of the Union Internationale des Velodromes (UIV), with more frequent events and shorter, faster races. The current six-day series goes from October to January, with races in Paris, Dortmund, Frankfurt, Grenoble, Monaco, Munich, Perth, Ghent, Vienna, Zürich, Copenhagen, Bordeaux, Milan, Cologne, Bremen, Rotterdam, Stuttgart, Antwerp, and Moscow in 1992. Attendance for a six-day race ranges from about 25,000 to 100,000 spectators, with the program varying from track to track, usually including sprints, pursuits, derny-pacing, and madison-style team racing. The final standings are based mainly on laps accumulated in madison and motor-paced races, and partially on points awarded in primes and special sprints. The last night often provides the most intense racing. As one team may be leading the lap count, another team may have more points. If the points leaders can regain those laps, they win the race. The daily schedule includes afternoon and evening racing sessions. At noon the riders climb out of bed, stretch, eat breakfast, and then get massaged. The race goes from about 2 P.M. to 5 P.M., and then the riders usually eat their main meal, get another massage, and take an hour-long nap. Re-awakening to discussions of strategy, they are prepared by the masseur, and resume racing from about 7 P.M. to 8 P.M. until about 2 A.M. After the nightly awards, showering, massage, and a few sandwiches, they climb back into bed by about 4 A.M.

The all-time top six-day winner is Patrick Sercu of Belgium, known as the "Flemish Arrow," with 88 victories in 223 sixes from 1965 to 1983. As a road rider, Sercu won the *maillot vert* (green points jersey) in the 1974 Tour de France. In February 1995, Danny Clark of Australia tied René Pijnen of Holland for second place with 72 lifetime six-day victories. Pijnen was at times either Sercu's teammate or rival during the 1970s and 1980s. While suffering from breathing problems at one point in his career, Pijnen's doctor recommended he try smoking cigarettes to build tolerance for the smoke-filled six-day arena.

Madison Square Garden, 1938.

Keirin

Japan has created a form of professional track racing that is the world's richest cycling circuit, and has gambling as a primary part of the promotion. Named keirin for "racing wheels," the enterprize is a highly-regimented series of parimutuel sprint events organized by the Japanese Keirin Association. Each year the circuit lures almost 40 million spectators who wager more than $5 billion at some 36,000 races held at 50 private and municipal open-air velodromes called *Keirin-jo*. Some 4,200 keirin cyclists in nine separate categories earn an average of $35,000 per year, with the top ten riders averaging $270,000. To become a licensed keirin racer the athletes must pass six months of rigorous training at a special school called the *Nihon Keirin Gakko*.[14]

Keirin was born in post-war Japan as the country was undergoing reconstruction and an outlet was needed for working-class society. The first four races were organized in November 1948 in Kokura City with some 50,000 betting spectators. In the following year, as the number of races increased, the annual attendance climbed to seven million, and by 1959 there were over eighteen million keirin fans. According to the original plan, 75 percent of the money raised from bettors is paid back to them in earnings. The remaining 25 percent goes to the private groups and municipal authorities who operate the velodromes, to the rider's expenses and earnings, and to the public welfare, such as schools, public buildings, nursing homes. Each *Keirin-jo* sponsors about a dozen meets per year, with each meet split into two series of events lasting three days each. There are several events for each category of rider, such as Special Prestige, All-Star, Memorial, and Kokusai events in which world class foreign riders may compete. Each event ranges from 1,000 to 4,000 meters, most often in massed start races, with handicaps and tandem events added for variety. The velodromes vary in size from the international standard of 333.3 meters, with the majority at 400 to 500 meters per lap. The track surfaces are wide and there is a noticeable absence of advertising compared to Western velodromes. Many *Keirin-jo* have 30,000 to 40,000 seats, including private VIP boxes. Officials are mounted on fifteen-foot high towers around the track while video cameras also monitor the racing.

When the ritual begins, two groups of women sweep the track moving in opposite directions toward the start-finish line where they ceremoniously bow. Then the riders step out and as they are announced they also bow. The nine competitors wear traditional uniforms with corresponding numbers and colors. Number 1 wears a white jersey; Number 2 black; Number 3 red; Number 4 blue; Number 5 yellow; Number 6 white with black; Number 7 white with red; Number 8 white with blue; and Number 9 blue with red. The stripes or stars on their shorts represent their class. Their track bikes are nearly identical to prevent any technical advantage which may affect the odds.

As the nine competitors line up in starting blocks, a tenth pacemaker or "rabbit" wearing dark colors is placed further up the track. When the starting pistol is fired the riders chase the pacemaker and begin jockeying for position. With about a lap and a half to go, the pacemaker swings off the track and the riders begin winding up for the final sprint. After the finish, a white flag indicates all clear and the race results appear on the scoreboard. If a breach in the rules is spotted a red flag is held out and the spotting officials bicycle to the finish line where the judges make their ruling. Then the crowd has 30 minutes to collect their winnings, place their bets on the next race, and grab another sake, beer, or snack.

With men comprising 99 percent of the spectators, gambling appears to be at least as important as the sport. The admission price is about 50 yen with the minimum wager at 100 yen—less than one dollar. Some twenty newspapers and magazines cover the racing odds, and about 600 oddsmakers are authorized to sell their tips at the velodromes. To prevent any possibility of race-fixing, riders are sequestered at hotels for three days prior to each race, with exceptions made for a rider to attend a relative's funeral. One of the luckiest bets was made on April 4, 1973, when a man won 2.3 million Yen (almost $9,500) on a 100 Yen "win and place" wager.

Koichi Nakano, nicknamed "Mister Keirin" and "Nakano of the World," is the most successful track cyclist of all-time. Besides his record streak of ten consecutive World Professional Sprint Championships from

1977 to 1986, Nakano entered a total of 1,236 races from 1975 to 1992, winning 666 races and earning an estimated $10 million in career prize money. A keirin director once remarked, "If people come to watch Nakano and Inoue instead of betting on them, this will ruin our industry." Many keirin riders continue their pro racing careers for 25 years, such as Nakano's father, Mitsuhito, who was still racing after his 50th birthday. The keirin school, in the resort area of Shuzenji, on the Izu peninsula, is a modern facility built in 1968 comprised of housing for 250 cycling students and their teachers, with classrooms, a gymnasium, a roller racing building, a vast calisthenic yard, and two velodromes. Twice a year, in the spring and fall, some 800 hopefuls compete in an intensive six-month program designed to build the physical, mental, moral, and technical expertise necessary to gain one of the 125 berths into the keirin circuit. The rookie begins at the lowest class, called B-2, and must perform well to be promoted to the S-class which offers the most prestigious races and the highest earnings. Since the late 1980s, many world-class track cyclists from America, Europe, and Australia have raced in the lucrative keirin circuit. In New Mexico, keirin racing is being considered since the state legislature approved bike race gambling in 1991.

Above, Keirin racing.
Below, Koichi Nakano retired in 1992 as the worlds greatest track cyclist. He won ten consecutive world pro sprint championships (and about $10 million).

Road Racing

Road racing is the most complete realm of cycle sport with a variety of events for amateur and professional men and women cyclists. The European-based professional cycling circuit ranks at the top of modern road racing, with the season from early spring to late fall, including the Classic *ville de ville* races, the international Tours, and the annual World Championship events. Many champions emerge with several ways to appraise them, including World Cup winners, World Champions, Tour winners, and the UCI's computerized ranking system.

WORLD ROAD CHAMPIONSHIPS

The World Road Championships are the crowning races of the season. Usually held in the late summer or fall, they are hosted by a different country each year, in conjunction with the World Track Championships. Riders are selected by their national federations, instead of their club or trade teams, and the rainbow jersey is the main prize. The main event is the massed-start individual road race, which is usually held on a hilly fifteen-kilometer (ten-mile) circuit. The pro race began in 1927 and goes 250–270 kilometers (160 miles), the amateur race began in 1921 and goes 165–200 kilometers (120 miles), and the women's race began in 1958 and goes 90 kilometers (55 miles), though the race was only about 60 kilometers before the mid-1980s. Juniors, masters, and veterans (men and women) ride 60–100 kilometers and their events have been held at separate times and places. The individual time trial event began in 1994 and goes about 40 kilometers for men and 30 kilometers for women. The team time trial event began in 1962 for four-man teams going 100 kilometers and in 1987 for four-woman teams going 50 kilometers. It was last held in 1994, and usually run on flat highways in an "out-and-back" route.

Despite the fact that the World Championships are one-day races, with riders subject to the chance of flat tires or flat legs, the top riders inevitably appear on the victory podium. Even when an "unknown" wins, they often say "I knew I could," and their careers rise to new heights. Like the *maillot jaune* of the Tour de France, and the *maglia rosa* of the Giro d'Italia, there is prestige as well as a burden to carry with the rainbow jersey, as its wearer is constantly watched by other riders, the press, and the fans. In past years, rumors have circulated suggesting that the rainbow jersey is jinxed, since a few World Champions suffered injury while wearing it. A notable tragedy was the death of Jean-Pierre "Jempi" Monseré, the charming 22-year-old 1970 pro road champion, in an early season Belgian kermesse race in 1971 due to a stray car on the course.

Eddy Merckx, 1974 World Pro Road Champion.

MILAN-SAN REMO

Milan-San Remo, known as the *primavera*, is the first major classic of the spring. The race covers about 300 kilometers from Milan, the unofficial capital of Italian cycling, to the Riviera city of San Remo. The climbs include the Turchino Pass at 150 km, the Capo Melo and Capo Berta at 250 km, la Cipressa at 275 km, and finally, the Poggio San Remo, just six kilometers from the finish. The most historic exploits have occurred on the climb and descent of the Poggio, and on the old Via Roma along the Mediterranean coast into San Remo.

PARIS-ROUBAIX

The spring classic Paris-Roubaix is considered the most tortuous and chancy of races. Known as *L'Enfer du Nord*, or The Hell of the North, the race begins in Compiègne, usually in cold, wet, and windy weather, and takes a purposeful route over flat highways that gradually become a series of narrow, winding cobblestone paths, with twenty sections of muscle-pounding *pavé* some 50 kilometers long, often slippery, muddy, and plagued by punctured tires. On finishing at the Roubaix velodrome after 270 kilometers and eight hours the riders have a rather famous worn-out look, which they bring back from the depths of cycling's abyss, with mud-splattered faces, shocked eyes, and wrenched muscles. The race proceeds with increasing speed as the battle for the front echelons forces the pace. When the road deteriorates the primary tactic is to survive. Out of 200 starters, about 50 riders are able to finish. There is usually a bit of chance in the race, as the lead changes when riders in breakaways fall behind from punctures or crashes, and chasing groups make passing attacks. The Paris-Roubaix trophy is a cobblestone fixed to a plaque, and it appears that pieces of the race route have become collectors items. When a large patch of cobblestones from the deepest parts of the Hell of the North were found missing, police detectives suspected it was the work of souvenir hunters.

Cobblestone roads of Paris-Roubaix, and the winner's cobblestone trophy.

GIRO D'ITALIA

Founded in 1909 by Emilio Colombo, the Tour of Italy is a professional stage race that ranks just behind the Tour de France in prestige and difficulty. The race is organized by the Italian sports daily *La Gazzetta dello Sport*, which is printed on pink newspaper, the reason for the Giro's pink leader's jersey, the *maglia rosa*. Spanning the months of May and June, the race has about 22 stages over 4,000 kilometers. The route varies from year to year, usually including mountain stages in the Alps and the Dolomites, which have had unpaved roads for many years. While the race normally stays within Italy, the 1973 version traveled into seven countries of the European Common Market, starting in Belgium, and crossing into Holland, Germany, Luxembourg, France, Switzerland, and Italy.

Il Giro has rich traditions for the passionate Italian cycling fans, known as *tifosi*, and more than one Pope has blessed the race. In the early years the winner was based on a system of points instead of time. Alfredo Binda, Fausto Coppi, and Eddy Merckx share the lead as five-time winners, while both Binda and Merckx have held the *maglia rosa* from start to finish. The Giro's first foreign winner did not arrive until 1950, with Hugo Koblet from Switzerland, known as the "Pedaler of Charm" for his aristocratic nature. Unlike most cyclists who preceded him, Koblet mixed with high society. He married a ballerina, and was reportedly offered a Hollywood movie role. In 1988, Andy Hampsten became the first, and so far the only American winner in a race that had severe blizzard conditions on the Gavia Pass. As in most major Tours, there are several jerseys and classifications to be won, including the purple *maglia ciclamino* for the points leader, the green *maglia verde* for the *gran premio della montagna* (King of the Mountain), the white *maglia bianca* for the youngest rider, and the blue *maglia azzurra* for leader of the combined classifications.

PEACE RACE

The Peace Race was once considered the world's biggest and toughest amateur stage race. Since its start in 1948, it has been jointly promoted by the newspapers of the principal cities along its 2,000 kilometer route: Prague, Warsaw, and East Berlin. It is a Tour de France-style event, with long climbs over the Tatras mountains, individual and team time trials, stage finishes in stadiums crowded with 90,000 spectators, and a yellow jersey for the leader. By tradition, the route changes from year to year, each city having the honor of staging the start and finish, with occasional excursions into Belorussia and Moscow. Over twenty international teams usually participate, with Western European riders dominating in the early years. As Eastern Bloc cyclists were required to remain amateur throughout their careers, they came to dominate international amateur racing, and the Peace Race provided the supreme proving ground for road riders from East Germany, the Soviet Union, Poland, and Czechoslovakia. Because of the nuclear disaster at Chernobyl, the 1986 race had only 60 riders compared to the usual 200. After the Berlin Wall crumbled in 1989, many top Eastern Bloc riders joined the European professional ranks and the Peace Race has become a pro-am event.

Topograph of the 1972 Giro d'Italia, from the start in Venice (checkered flag) to the finish in Milan (stop sign). The Cima Coppi, named for Fausto Coppi, is the highest peak each year.

RIDERS AND TEAMS

Road racing has various techniques and tactics used by individual riders and their teams, which creates sociological structures unique in sport, with opposing cyclists forming cooperative associations during the competition. The techniques include the routine, automatic skills such as racing in pacelines and multiple echelons, and handling feeding zones and mechanical difficulties. The tactics include solo and group breakaways, with counter-attacks and team blocking and chasing, as well as pacesetting for climbs and lead-outs for sprints. Team strategy is a main factor in organized sports, and in road racing, team tactics are what separate the *dilettanti* from the pros.

As of 1990 there were roughly 1,000 professionals and about 100,000 amateurs on the European cycling circuit, with the vast majority belonging to professional teams and amateur clubs. In 1990 the Fédération Internationale de Cyclisme Professional (FICP) listed 883 riders from 31 countries who scored points in sanctioned events. There were 57 professional teams and 104 independent riders. In addition to riders, teams are usually comprised of a chief sponsor or owner, a manager or *director sportif*, a technical manager, a coach or *entraîneur*, a riders' attendant and masseur or *soigneur*, a mechanic, a doctor, a press agent, and occasionally a chef. The cost of operating a team ranges from $500,000 to several million dollars. The estimated annual budget for the La Vie Claire squad in 1986 was $3.5 million, nearly ten times the cost of an average team in 1980. By 1991, the leading Italian team Gatorade-Chateaux d'Ax had an $8 million budget, with the average team less than half that.

Among the great amateur clubs there is the Athlétique Club de Boulogne Billancourt (ACBB) of France which dates back to 1924 and has celebrated "over ten thousand victories." Since 1964 it was sponsored by Peugeot, and by 1984 "the old lady was remarried" to Renault. In Russia, the Locosphinx team based in St. Petersburg and led by coach Alexander Kuznetsov has consistently produced international riders who found success in World Championships and pro-am racing. Following the international success of Colombian amateurs in the mid-1980s, the national squad became a professional team sponsored by Varta (a battery maker) and Cafe de Colombia (coffee) with a $1.5 million budget.

The pros are generally divided into two categories: the elite leaders who are capable of winning and attract most of the fame and fortune, and the team players, known as the *équipiers*, *domestiques*, *gregarios*, or "water-carriers," who sacrifice their ambition in service of the leaders. A survey of French professional racers was taken in 1983 by *Le Miroir du Cyclisme*. It showed the seasonal changes in the peloton (the field of cyclists, or main bunch in a race), with new riders emerging, old ones quitting, and others changing teams. Over half the riders started racing by their fifteenth birthday, with 97 percent receiving approval from their family. Most of the riders turn professional by the age of 22, and most are gone before they are 30 years old, although successful riders usually continue into their mid-30s. The turnover rate is about 25 percent per year.

Most of the riders (75%) were in their first three seasons, and 90 percent had ridden for no more than two teams. Half the riders had only a one year contract.

Money was rarely discussed openly in cycling circles because of the disparity in wages between average riders who were poorly paid, and top stars who supposedly "rolled in the dough." Following the trend in other pro sports in the 1980s, cyclists' pay has increased and become a popular topic. At the time of the survey, half the French peloton said they were paid only 4,500 francs per month, less than $500 and somewhat higher than the Socialist government's *salaire minimum*. Twenty-two percent said they were paid 6,500 francs, and only ten percent received over 10,000 francs. Team leaders were paid up to 100,000 francs per month, while the super stars, such as Bernard Hinault and Laurent Fignon, earned over 250,000 francs in salary alone. In the 1990s, cyclists' salaries increased roughly ten times those of the 1980s.

Professional cyclists can add to their base salary by winning races or by contributing to team victories. Most professional races have relatively small cash prizes. While the winner of Paris-Roubaix received about $1,500 in 1983 and $30,000 in 1990, there are generous placings distributed fairly for everyone who finishes. Added to the race prize list are various *primes* (say "preems") or sprint prizes that are planned or spontaneous gifts along the race route. These can add up to considerable sums of money for sprinters or those who escape the peloton in solo breakaways. Most teams traditionally pool their prize money with an equal cut for all. This practice is favored because it inspires team performance and dispels jealousy. To provide incentive, team owners or managers give bonuses for important victories.

Appearance fees are another way for professionals to earn extra money riding their bikes. Some circuit races, time trials, and kermesse races charge admission to spectators while paying appearance fees to selected riders. This is based upon the rider's "gate appeal." The average rider in the mid-1980s received a starting fee of about 1,000 to 2,500 francs, while the winner of the polka-dot jersey in the Tour de France could demand 6,000 to 10,000 francs.

A third way to get rich by cycling is through the endorsement of products or groups. These range from bicycle-related endorsements to celebrity appearances in advertising campaigns. Most endorsements are allied to the rider's team, with bicycle and clothing makers, or by acting as an ambassador for the team sponsor. The turning point towards stardom comes with endorsements for *extra-sportif* sponsors, which can double a star rider's earnings.

When professionals stop racing, a variety of fates await them. Depending on star status and interests, cyclists can choose to stay with the sport, as officials, team managers, journalists, broadcasters, promoters, and of course, as bicycle makers, marketers, or shop keepers, the most common post-cycling career. Many riders become coaches, hired by teams, holding cycling clinics, or volunteering advice for youngsters.

Some former racers retire completely, living as country gentlemen, or seeming to dissipate with their memories, like war veterans. A few champions have run successful businesses unrelated to cycling, several have run for political office, and others have had difficulties with the law, such as Rik Van Steenbergen who was arrested on drug charges, or Louis "Toto" Gérardin who was caught smuggling 1.5 million French francs into Switzerland.[15]

The two-time Paris-Roubaix winner Marc Madiot once said: "When you choose to become a professional, you have to be young, and either naïve or a megalomaniac. As for me, I was young, just seventeen, naïve and, most of all, crazy about cycling."[16] French professionals often give *amoureux fou du vélo*, or "crazy love for the bike" as their primary reason for racing. Glory, money, and social mobility—as a way off the farm or out of a factory job—are other key incentives. Many riders complain about the competitive calendar, saying that it lasts too long and there are too many races too close together. Most riders spend between 15 to 25 hours per week in training, some as much as 35 hours per week. The pros average about 25,000 kilometers per year in training alone or with the team, and about 50,000 kilometers per year traveling in cars to and from races. Sitting confined in cars for long periods is particularly troublesome for cyclists because their legs are cramped.

Many riders spend less than four days per month at home during the season. In terms of their marital and sexual relations, it is often suggested that the riders should abstain from sex as much as possible during the racing season, while some coaches recommend the stabilizing influence of a spouse. During the Tour de France, riders are required to sleep with their teams. One anecdotal story resulted from an interview given by Sean Kelly of Ireland, the world's highest ranked professional during the mid-1980s, who married his childhood sweetheart, Linda Grant. Kelly reportedly said he never made love six weeks before the Tour de France and one or two weeks before a one-day classic race. According to the reckoning of Kelly's compatriot, Paul Kimmage, that would mean that Mrs. Kelly is still a virgin (the Kellys had twins).[17]

Given the nature of constantly traveling athletes, abstinence may or may not always be possible, and there have been some notable playboys amongst the peloton. By tradition, the wives of racers were rarely allowed to follow the races in support cars, but this policy has changed in recent years with the passing of chauvinistic attitudes. The same tradition has applied for women racers, except if their husbands are also their coach, as it is with Jeannie Longo and Patrice Ciprelli.

WOMEN'S ROAD RACING

Various classics and national Tours for women racers have developed since the first World Championship race won by Elsy Jacobs of Luxembourg in 1958. Yvonne Reynders of Belgium and Beryl Burton of Britain dominated women's road and pursuit racing in the 1960s, with seven World Championship titles each, and Keetie van Oosten-Hage of Holland won six World titles in the 1970s. When seventeen-year-old

Beate Habetz won the 1978 World's road race in Brauweiler, Germany, it was a dream come true. She lived in a nearby village and the course included part of her morning newspaper delivery route. Beryl Burton, OBE, is one of the superwomen of cycling. Known as "BB," her specialty was the race against the clock, in the British tradition, and her lack of a quick, powerful sprint was compensated by her ability to set a fast, steady pace. In 1967, Burton rode 277.25 miles in a twelve-hour time trial and became the first woman to break a man's record in RTTC history, beating the record by almost six miles. Her 100 mile record of 3 hours 55 minutes 5 seconds, set in 1968, still remains unbroken in 1995. Supported by husband Charlie, she was once rivaled by her daughter Denise, who became a world-class cyclist. Burton continues to race and her competitive spirit has survived breast cancer.

The Tour de France Féminin began in 1984 with eighteen stages over 620 miles and was won by Marianne Martin, the first American to win a Tour. The same year, the Los Angeles Olympics featured a women's road race for the first time with Connie Carpenter and Rebecca Twigg of the U.S. winning gold and silver. Jeannie Longo of France is perhaps the greatest champion of women's cycling—the *campionissima*. Competitive and controversial, she prevailed during the 1980s by winning both the World Championships and the Tour de France three consecutive times. She set the UCI hour record for women, going 46.352 kilometers in Mexico City, and after a brief layoff around 1990, while serving on the Grenoble city council, she came back using her married name, Jane Ciprelli. Before the 1992 Barcelona Olympics, she battled against the Fédération Française de Cyclisme (FFC) in the French Supreme Court for the right not to use national team equipment. In the 92-kilometer Olympic

Jeannie Longo, the '*campionissima*.'

Beryl Burton, 'the British Joan of Arc.'

road race, while fighting against negative racing, when other riders played follow the leader, in the final kilometers Longo was caught unaware that Kathryn Watt of Australia had already made the winning breakaway. When Longo made her solo attack, she faced the grim reality that somebody else was already up the road in first place. Occasionally accused of chasing down her French teammates, Longo has won twenty top-three medals in championship racing in track, road, and mountain biking from 1981 to 1994.

In 1985 the Tour de France Féminin was lengthened beyond the maximum distance allowed by the UCI, and to get around this ruling the race was organized in two parts. Of the 72 starters, including a team from China, 65 riders finished, and 36-year-old Maria Canins won the *Challenge Maillot Jaune* over Jeannie Longo. In 1990, the race was replaced by the European Community Tour, won by nineteen-year-old Catherine Marsal, who became World Road Champion later that year in Japan. In America, the Power Bar International Challenge, formerly the Ore-Ida Tour, is known as the world's toughest women's stage race, but because of its excessive distances, with eleven stages of up to 90 miles, it was denied international status in 1991 by the FIAC and UCI. Jim Rabdau, the race promoter, told *VeloNews* that, "We're not going back to where we started. The biggest complaint about women's racing five years ago was that it wasn't aggressive enough. You can't get aggressive in a 40-mile race." Several amateur and professional mixed-gender and women-only teams have been formed, such as the French Euro-Marche team, and the American Team Lycra, Weight Watchers, Lowrey's, Sundance-Fuji, Celestial Seasonings, and Team PMS. Leontine Van Moorsel of Holland brought glamour and grit to the sport after winning the 1991 and 1993 Worlds and being offered to pose for sexy magazines. In 1992, she won the E.C. Tour as well as a new stage race, the Tour Cycliste Féminine.

MONDIALIZATION

The European road racing scene has become a global village as more and more classic and championship races have top-ten finishers from ten different countries. Nationalism is a prominent aspect in sport and many people want to know which country has produced the most winners. In combined World Championship road events (pro, amateur, women, team), by 1990 Italy and Belgium were nearly equal with over 30 rainbow jerseys each, followed by France and Holland with about twenty, with the U.S.S.R. and East Germany at about fifteen. Among the professionals, it is close between Italy and Belgium, with France third, followed by Holland, Spain, Germany, and Switzerland. According to the Belgian journalist Bernard Callens, from 1965 to 1977 Belgian cyclists won more international classics and tours than the rest of the world combined. Of the 78 classics and 39 tours held in those years, Belgians won 58 percent, Italians won fifteen percent, the Dutch won ten percent, and the French, Spanish, and Germans each won six percent. Those years coincide with the career of Eddy Merckx who won 27 percent of the races. Trends show a decline in Belgian racing through the 1980s, with the return of France and the rise of English speaking champions. The 1990s have been marked by a renaissance in Italy and Spain, and the rise of champions from the countries of the former Soviet Union.[18]

Amateur road racing is a global sport that developed in different ways depending on the sporting customs and rules of the road for different countries. There have been national tours and stage races in many countries and regions, including Algeria, the Baltics, Bohemia, Burkina Faso, Chile, Costa Rica, Cuba, Egypt, Greece, Guadeloupe, Guatemala, Martinique, Nigeria, Peru, Poland, Puerto Rico, Slovakia, Syria, Taiwan, Turkey, Vietnam, Yugoslavia, and China with the Tour of the Great Wall.

Britain's role in continental pro racing has been relatively small compared to its contribution to the development of the bicycle. This is partly because of England's early proclivity for amateur racing, and partly because of various nationwide bans on road racing. The result was the growth of time trial events, making it possible to compete on the road in an individual, single-file format instead of mass-start group racing. As a reflection of British culture, these are refined specialty events governed by the Road Time Trials Council, which organizes the Best-All-Round (BAR) series with the most popular distances being 10, 25, 50, and 100 miles.

The British League of Racing Cyclists (BLRC) staged the first modern-day, continental-style mass-start road races in England, such as the Tour of Britain, which began in 1952 and became known as the Milk Race. The United Kingdom and Ireland share a wide variety of racing events, including a small professional circuit, the Olympic-format Commonwealth Games, and World Cup road races on the international calendar. World-class professional champions have included Graham Webb and Tom Simpson from Britain, and more recently, the Irishmen Sean Kelly and Stephen Roche, who "strive to be the best in the world, not the best of the Irish."[19] Kelly was the world's top ranked pro in the mid-1980s, and Roche captured cycling's "triple crown" in 1987 by winning the Giro d'Italia, the Tour de France, and the World Road Championships in the same year. The only other rider to accomplish this was Eddy Merckx in 1974. All the time trialing has paid off for Britain with the arrival of Graeme Obree, from Scotland, and Chris Boardman, from the Wirral, near Liverpool. As an amateur, Boardman won the 1992 Olympic pursuit and set a world hour record. As a 26-year-old neo-pro in 1994, he won the prologue *maillot jaune* in the Tour de France and the inaugural World Championship individual time trial in Italy.

Australia has a long history of racing going back to the Boneshaker Club of Melbourne which promoted its first race in 1869. Amateur and professional racing organizations were formed during the 1880s and 1890s, with Victoria (Melbourne) and New South Wales (Sydney) being the strongest regions. Most of Australia's professional champions have been in track events, including Reg McNamara, Bob Spears, Sid Patterson (who won over $500,000 during the 1950s), Gordon Johnson, John

Stephen Roche, triple-crown winner in 1987.

Nicholson, Gary Sutton, and Danny Clark. Australia's world-class Tour de France road riders include Sir Hubert Opperman, known as "Oppy," who won Paris-Brest-Paris in 1931, Russell Mockridge, a double Olympic gold-medalist in 1952 who was killed in a race, and Phil Anderson (born in Britain), the first Australian to wear the *maillot jaune* in 1981.

By 1980 Australia had some 120 amateur clubs with 6,500 competitors. The Australian professional class ranked second to Japan's keirin circuit with some 1,200 racers, but because a majority of races were handicaps, the competition was not quite at the European level. However, during the 1980s three Australian races gained international status. The fourteen-stage Sun Tour, begun in 1952 and sponsored by the Melbourne *Sun-Herald*, has become Australia's premier professional event. The Commonwealth Bank Classic, first held in 1982, travels down the east coast from Queensland to Sydney and has become a world-class amateur stage race. The 228-kilometer Grafton to Inverell road race, known as the "Mountain Classic," began in 1961 and was included on the UCI international calendar in 1982. In nearby New Zealand, the Tour of the North Island, sponsored by the New Zealand *Post*, rounds out the season of racing down under.

The New World

Road racing in North America suffered a worse fate than in Britain during the growth of European racing through most of the twentieth century. But the current rise of internationalism, beginning around 1975, along with innovative races and technical developments, has helped dozens of talented American and Canadian cyclists reach the world class level. By 1990 North Americans were taking a leading role in setting new standards for the sport.

Through the first half of the century, Americans preferred track and six-day races over road races. After World War II, the United States was considered a "Third World country" in cycling. The best that America could produce was merely a struggling group of amateur Olympic cycling teams which had few hopes of winning medals. Professional bicycle racing was about as foreign to the American dream as communism. Just when the road racing scene was at its lowest, the situation began to improve in the 1960s—as things could only get better.

At the World Championships, Jack Simes, future president of USPRO, won a silver medal in the kilometer track event in 1968, and Audrey McElmury won the rainy women's road race in Brno, Czechoslovakia in 1969. With more Americans getting on ten-speeds during the bike boom in the 1970s, the antiquated ABLA became the modernized USCF in the UCI mold. As the level of competition improved, particularly with riders from the Northern California-Nevada district such as Mike Neel, Jonathan Boyer, George Mount, and Greg LeMond, Americans began to set their sights on the daunting, refined European professional circuit.

Sheila Young and Sue Novarra began winning their rainbow jerseys in the women's sprint in 1973, and George Mount and Mike Neel made breakthroughs that seem insignificant today, but were incredible in 1976.

Jonathan Boyer and Greg LeMond at the 1982 World Championships.

Mount finished sixth in the rainy Montreal Olympic road race, and Neel placed tenth in the World's pro road race in Italy. Jonathan Boyer, known as "Jacques," or "Jock," had amateur victories riding for the ACBB and U.S. Créteil in France, and turned pro in 1977 with Lejeune-BP. Boyer finished fifth in the World's pro road race in 1980, and became the first American to enter the Tour de France in 1981, finishing 32nd, 59 minutes behind Bernard Hinault. Meanwhile, Greg LeMond was beginning to show his incredible natural talent and ambitions by winning gold (road), silver (individual pursuit), and bronze (team time trial) at the 1979 Junior World Championships in Buenos Aires. That same year, the Academy Award winning movie *Breaking Away* brought public attention to the sport in the U.S., and for many cyclists of this generation it was the quintessential (if not corny) coming-of-age story about youngsters finding an identity through the dream of European bike racing.

Mike Neel.

LeMond lost his chance to earn Olympic gold because the U.S. boycotted the Moscow Games, so he signed a pro contract with Cyrille Guimard's Renault-Elf-Gitane team in 1980. According to legend, LeMond won Guimard's admiration in his early European years by throwing his bike at a service car after waiting ten minutes to change a flat tire. By 1982 he had won the pro-am Tour de l'Avenir by ten minutes, the greatest margin in the history of the "race of the future." Later that year his rivalry with Boyer reached its peak at the World Championships when Boyer was leading in the final kilometers. LeMond chased and caught Boyer for the lead, but was passed by Giuseppi Saronni of Italy. LeMond finished second with Boyer tenth. The following year LeMond won the World's in a solo breakaway at Altenrhein and ended the season leading the year-long Super Prestige competition. Meanwhile, the 7-Eleven team became the first American-based team on the European pro circuit. Managed by Jim Ochowicz and coached by Neel, they introduced the first woman *soigneur* on the racing scene, Shelley Verses.

Jonathan Boyer.

In Boulder, Colorado, the Red Zinger Classic became the race that helped put America on the international cycling calendar. One of the youngest events to be called a "classic," the race was organized in 1975 by the former disc-jockey Michael Aisner, and sponsored by Celestial Seasonings, the maker of herbal teas with a popular hibiscus and rose hips blend called Red Zinger. Featuring such grueling stages as the Morgul-Bismark, it gradually attracted top amateurs from Colombia, the Netherlands, Cuba, East Germany, the Soviet Union, Australia, New Zealand, and Japan. With the growing cost of staging the race, in 1980 the Coors Brewery from Golden took over sponsorship and the race's name was changed to the Coors Classic. The event evolved from a five-day amateur race to become a fairly controversial thirteen-day pro-am race. It traveled as far-away as San Francisco and Hawaii, and featured cycling's pro superstars Bernard Hinault and Greg LeMond. The race was last held in 1988, when Coors withdrew its title sponsorship.

Greg LeMond, 1979.
Photo by Robert F. George.

Colorado Springs became the mecca of U.S. racing in the 1980s, as the site of the U.S. Olympic Training Center, the USCF headquarters, the

Lance Armstrong, 1993.

record-breaking high-altitude 7-Eleven Olympic Velodrome, and the 1986 World Championships. American road racing is known for shorter circuit races, called criteriums, and there have been several attempts to promote a Tour of America, by the Tour de France organizers, by Donald Trump, the real estate and casino developer, and by David Chauner's International Cycling Promotions. When Trump's debts grew too large, his Tour de Trump was sponsored by the DuPont company and became the popular Tour DuPont, a twelve-day 1,600-kilometer stage race from Delaware to North Carolina.

By 1990 there were some 34,000 licensed amateur racers in the USCF with about 40 percent over the age of 40. In 1994, there were 206 USPRO riders. Lance Armstrong, from Plano, Texas, has replaced LeMond as the top U.S. rider in Europe. In his first year as a pro, riding for America's flagship team, the powerful Motorola squad (formerly 7-Eleven), Armstrong won the million dollar prize Thrift Drug Triple Crown (a three-race series that included the USPRO national championship), the eighth stage of the Tour de France, and the cold, rainy World Championships in Norway. Winning alone, he beat superstar Miguel Indurain and became the second youngest man to win the world pro road race.

The National Cycling League (NCL) is a new development in the 1990s, with a series of city-based professional teams, a format similar to the North American sports of football, baseball, and basketball. Begun in 1989, the team franchises include the Chicago Wind, Gotham Ghosts (New York), Houston Outlaws, Los Angeles Wings, Miami Wave, Pittsburgh Power, San Diego Zoom, and Seattle Cyclones. In 1993, the NCL expanded to Europe with the Amsterdam Flying Dutchmen, London Lancers, and Milan Forza.

Tour de France

Le Tour is a household word for the world's greatest spectacle dedicated to cycling. The Tour is the grand test of human power, and it offers many insights into human nature. The Tour has a history as long as its route and its supporting caravan of characters. In recent years, it is estimated that over one billion people follow news of the Tour each year and about twenty million people watch the Tour on the roadside. Of all international sports events, the annual Tour ranks only behind the Olympic Games and the World Cup in football (soccer), which happen every four years. All together, it embodies a supreme athletic competition and an enormous commercial enterprise.

The Tour de France has inspired many pseudonyms. To the French, it is traditionally the *Grande Boucle*, or Grand Loop. In its best years it is a *Tour de Force*, in its worst a *Tour de Farce*. During a particularly hot year, it was named the *Tour de Furnace*. As an example of a commercial sports event and a race for big money, it was dubbed the *Tour d'Argent*, or *Tour de Francs*. After a doping scandal it was named the *Tour de Pharmacie*, and to make amends, the following year it was christened the *Tour of Good Health*. With the increasing clamor of competing sponsors and broadcasters it was more like a *Tour de Babel*, and one journalist called it the *Tour de Trance*. When American Greg LeMond won the race, *L'Équipe* called it *Le Tour du Nouveau Monde*. As the race became more international and modern, its official name was changed to simply *Le Tour*.

When the Tour makes its way around France, in about 22 stages and 4,000 kilometers, during the vacation month of July, it captivates the countryside as an expression of the *sportif* lifestyle. According to legend, nothing has stopped the Tour but war, but the race has also been shortened by extreme weather, and delayed by union strikes, riders' protests, railroad crossings, and wild bears in the route. The Tour is a beautiful display of athletes at their peak. For the riders it is one of the hardest, most overwhelming accomplishments in their lives, and 1988 Tour de France winner Pedro Delgado said of the Tour, "This is the war of the cyclists. That's what we call it." For three weeks of consistent effort—climbing, time trialing, sprinting, and descending—the riders eat, sleep, and live the Tour, often making it the central object of their season. Recuperation is of utmost importance for the riders, so special care and feeding is taken. Thus, it is said that "*Le Tour de France se gagne au lit*"—The Tour is won in bed.

Société du Tour

Prestige and money is what separates the Tour de France from all the other races. The event is organized by the Société d'Exploitation du Tour de France, a subsidiary of Groupe Amaury, publishers of the sports newspaper *L'Équipe*, the general interest paper *Le Parisien*, and the cycling monthly *Vélo Magazine* (formerly *Miroir du Cyclisme*). *L'Équipe* (The

Team) is the post-war descendent of *L'Auto*, the original sponsor for the race, which was printed on yellow paper, the origin of the *maillot jaune*. The Société promotes several major cycling events, with a permanent staff of about 40 people. Until the 1980s, it shared offices with the publishing empire at 10 rue du Faubourg in Montmartre, Paris. It then moved to new headquaters at 2-4 rue Rouget de Lisle in Issy-les-Moulineaux.

The race was ruled by its founder Henri Desgrange until 1936, when leadership passed to Jacques Goddet, race director, and Félix Lévitan, director general. As a pair, they saw the race become one of the biggest commercial sporting ventures, "a publicity banner that stretches 4,000 kilometers." In the 1980s critics began complaining that the Tour was becoming an antiquated provincial carnival, with over fifty competing sponsors, most of them unknown outside of France. By 1988, the race organization was modernized and streamlined by a new team of managers with Jean-Marie Leblanc at the helm. The total annual revenues have grown, from about $1 million in the 1970s when the race had a "constant and variable" budget deficit paid by the newspapers, to a profit-making $20 million budget in 1991. The prize in Paris for the *maillot jaune* in 1991 was about $385,000, with the overall prize list of $2 million.

The money to finance this extravaganza comes from four main sources. Location fees are paid by the stage towns, which can recoup the money by charging admission at the start-finish and by the increased commerce and recognition the Tour caravan brings. Advertising fees are paid by companies which participate in the publicity generated by the Tour, such as the special prize categories, the publicity caravan, the concessions, and the supporting equipment. Media fees are paid by television networks for broadcast rights. And entry fees are paid by the professional teams to cover the cost of food and lodgings provided by the Tour organization.

The cost to be a stage town in the Tour has ranged from about $15,000 in the 1970s to over $1 million in the 1990s, with increasing costs for sites outside France. In this category, the biggest sponsor has been the French real-estate developer Guy Merlin. For companies that participate in the Tour promotion there are several categories of sponsorship. In 1985, Coca-Cola replaced Perrier as the official Tour "water" with a bid estimated at $1.5 million. As one of the principal sponsors, Coke paid about $2 million in 1990. For the same prestige and money, Crédit Lyonnais serves as the bank of the Tour and the sponsor of the *maillot jaune*, with the opportunity to appear on the winners' podium and the promotional caravan. The main transport sponsor is Fiat, which supplies many of the cars, vans, and trucks for the official caravan. Second tier sponsors pay between $150,000 and $1 million, and include timing, copying, and medical services. When Hewlett-Packard provides computer systems for statistics on the race, the HP logo appears during each day's coverage on international TV broadcasts.

The Société's broadcast rights have increased dramatically over the years, with worldwide distribution over radio and TV, with the French TV

Company mascots, such as Michelin's Bibendum, are part of the Tour's publicity caravan.

network Antenne-2 providing the feed beyond Europe. The 1980s brought contracts from major TV networks in the U.S. (ABC and CBS), Canada (CBC), Japan (NHK), and Colombia (RCN). Through a system of rights exchanges, the Tour is broadcast to Morocco, New Zealand, and Eastern Europe. CBS paid $1 million to do five 40-minute telecasts in 1986, and by 1991 the total TV revenues amounted to $5 million. Teams gaining the honor of riding the Tour pay about $35,000, which helps cover the cost of the food, beds, and transport for the twenty people (racers and crew) comprising each team.

The Tour de France is considered its own sovereign state—complete with its own bank, the only one in France open on Bastille Day; its own police force, the motorcycling gendarmes of the Garde Républicaine; and its own citizens, the entourage of roughly 2,500 participants, including officials, riders, team managers, reporters, photographers, mechanics, doctors, masseurs, sponsors, and sales people who work full-time during the Tour. It is a kind of media bubble that moves around France.

The Tour caravan consists of about 900 vehicles which use over 200,000 liters of gasoline and oil. The promotional caravan has about 365 vehicles, each of which pay about $7,500 to participate, such as the Michelin stunt motorcyclists wearing Bibendum costumes, the Catch insecticide cars with huge dead insects on the roof, the Crédit Lyonnais army jeeps stuffed with its mascot, a huge teddy bear. Any number of free samples and concessions are provided along the route, with ice cream cones, candy, caps, headbands, newspapers, and tire patches. Covering the race are some 1,500 accredited media workers using 550 vehicles including cars, motorcycles, and helicopters. They consist of 600 journalists, 150 photographers, and 750 technicians, representing 300 publications, 30 radio networks, and fifteen TV networks from over 25 countries. Some 20,000 police and gendarmes are used to clear the road of traffic and spectators, while 50 Garde Républicaine gendarmes on motorcycles and eight officers in cars control the entire race caravan. The Tour's police force costs about $250,000. At each stage, about ten kilometers of crowd control fence is constructed and dismantled. An average of 1.3 spectators are killed watching the Tour every year, but rarely by a cyclist.

About 200 riders compete in the Tour, using 4,500 musettes (feed bags), 20,000 water bottles, 10,000 liters of drink, 20,000 pieces of fruit, 300 bicycles, 1,300 wheels, and 2,000 tires. The teams are provided with four vehicles, including two sedans, one station wagon, and one mini-bus, and many teams bring their own equipment-carrying bus. The entourage sleeps in about 600 rooms, with the cost of lodging for three weeks at about $125,000. Besides the team doctors, the Tour's medical crew consists of three doctors and three nurses, with three ambulances, two cars, and a motorcycle.[20] Traditions along the Tour route include spectators having picnics, bakers displaying commemorative pastries, and racers being allowed to sprint ahead of the peloton to stop and greet their family.

The Tour de France has become a part of culture as countless people have described the race, from the feminist Colette to five-time winner Bernard Hinault. The Tour is described as "the greatest sporting event in the world" in Ernest Hemingway's novel *The Sun Also Rises* (1926). Hemingway was a big fan of cycling, and his wife, Pauline, followed some of the 1938 Tour on a motorcycle with photographer Robert Capa. In his book *A Moveable Feast* (1964)—which makes another good name for the Tour—Hemingway wrote that "I have started many stories about bicycle racing but have never written one that is as good as the races are both on the indoor and outdoor tracks and on the roads." Red Smith, the popular sports columnist for the *New York Herald-Tribune*, followed the Tour in 1960 and reported: "There is nothing in America even remotely comparable to it. We think the World Series claims the undivided attention of the United States, but there is a saying here that an army from Mars could invade France, the government could fall, and even the recipe for sauce Béarnaise be lost, but if it happened during the Tour de France nobody would notice." He depicted the crowds waiting on an obscure mountain road as on "a barren knob not close to anything or anybody, yet it looked like the bleachers in Yankee Stadium on a good day with the White Sox."[21] Gabriele Rolin became the Tour's first woman journalist in 1975 covering the race for the French newspaper *Le Monde*. She described the race from a woman's perspective in "A Woman Among the Wheels:"

> Men invented war so they could be among themselves. In peacetime, they have bike racing. Here they can escape from their wives, mistresses, mothers, mothers-in-law... This is their drug and their refuge. What right do women have to share in it?... If the men jealously guard their game, it is not only because they wish to protect the weaker sex, but also because they wish to continue living in their happy ignorance, not only about women, but about unemployment, the threat of the Russians and the latest crisis in Portugal. With the race they can return to infancy.[22]

Ralph Hurne's novel about the Tour de France, *The Yellow Jersey*, is an underground classic described as "the greatest cycling novel ever written." Showing the "sex, drugs, and rock'n'roll" of the sport, the book was published in 1973 with two different endings, one for the American market, and one for the English.[23] *The Yellow Jersey* involves the comeback of a retired British pro, Terry Davenport, a "sensualist, bon vivant, radical, and cyclist extraordinaire," who manages a Belgian team with the young star, Romain Hendrickx. Davenport claims that, "For me, the Tour is the real race because it is the nearest thing to life, outside life itself... I hate the Tour, yet it fascinates me..."[24]

The title of Samuel Beckett's play "Waiting for Godot" may derive from the Tour de France and its race directors Félix Levitan (who was once called God) and Jacques Goddet, whose appearance in the lead car for some 50 years became a fixture of French culture, as their arrival with the *maillot jaune* was anxiously awaited for millions of roadside cycling fans. According to biographer Deirdre Bair, Beckett "encountered a large group of people standing on a street corner one afternoon during the annual Tour de France bicycle race and he asked what they were doing. '*Nous attendons Godot*' they replied, adding that all the competitors had passed except the oldest, whose name was Godot."[25]

Film and video probably comes closest to expressing the beauty of the Tour de France, and the images of spinning wheels, struggling heroes, colorful fanfare, and dominating landscapes inspire many young and old cyclists onto their bikes. Among the most artful documentaries of the Tour are Louis Malle's *Vive Le Tour* (1961) and Claude Lelouche's *Pour un Maillot Jaune* (1965). Attempts have been made to turn Ralph Hurne's *The Yellow Jersey* into a Hollywood movie. Shortly after the book was published in 1973 the film rights were bought by producer Gary Mehlman. With co-producer Carl Foreman several screenplays were developed for Universal Pictures and Columbia Pictures, which took it the closest to fruition in 1985 with a projected budget of $20 million. Based on a script by Colin Welland (*Chariots of Fire*), they hired Michael Cimino (*Deer Hunter*) as director, Jorgen Leth (*La Course en Tête*) as director of photography, and 50-year-old Dustin Hoffman (*Tootsie*) cast as the protagonist, Terry Davenport. Columbia bought film rights for the 1984 and 1985 Tours from the Société du Tour de France, and with Hoffman and Cimino following Frenchman Bernard Hinault, Leth shot 150,000 feet of film, which Mehlman described as "probably the most exciting bicycling footage that's ever been seen."[26] With American Greg LeMond's Tour victories in the late-1980s, the "Yellow Jersey" story was beginning to imitate real life, and by 1990 the Cannon Group owned the story, Mehlman still had hopes, and there was talk of a movie adaption of Greg LeMond's life story.

The Tour is the subject of song and music, such as the French classic "Chante Tour de France" and the electronic soundtracks, *Tour de France* (1987) and *Tour de France: The Early Years* (1990) by American TV celebrity John Tesh of CBS, who claimed: "The sport of cycling changed my life. Everything I do is based on the passion I learned from the Tour de France." The race is featured on special issue postage stamps, and board games including one in English named Yellow Jersey, and one in French called Le Tour. Showing the fantasy of many young cyclists, the movie *Pee-Wee's Big Adventure* (1985) begins with Pee-Wee Herman (Paul Rubens) waking from a dream of winning the Tour de France.

The birth of the Tour de France in 1903 has been compared with other historic events of the same year, including the first motor-powered flight by the Wright Brothers, the Nobel Prize awarded to Marie and Pierre Curie for their pioneering work with radioactivity, the filming of the first Western movie in America, and the Serbian revolution which instigated World War I. In France at the turn of century, another set of social and political events had an effect on the creation of the Tour. These were the events surrounding the Dreyfus Affair. Captain Alfred Dreyfus was a French Jew accused of giving secrets to the Germans. People took sides on the issue as testimony revealed his innocence during the prolonged trials. Anti-semitism grew. The Roman Catholic Church supported the prosecution; Émile Zola, a fan of cycling, wrote his famous essay "J'accuse" defending Dreyfus. The issue caused a split at the French daily cycling newspaper, *Le Vélo*, as the pro-Dreyfus editors were led by Pierre Giffard, and the anti-Dreyfus financial backers were led by the automobile industrialist Count Albert de Dion. de Dion withdrew his support from *Le Vélo* and started a rival newspaper, *L'Auto-Vélo*. With added backing from Michelin and Clément, the newspaper was printed on yellow paper.

Henri Desgrange (1865–1940), who was already known for his effusive style of cycling journalism, was appointed editor of *L'Auto-Vélo*. Desgrange was a retired racer (the world hour record holder in 1893–94) who lost his job at a law firm because a client complained that being a cycling champion was incompatible with the dignity of the legal profession. As the rival newspapers vied for circulation, a copyright suit in 1903 by Giffard forced *L'Auto-Vélo* to drop the *Vélo*, thus retaining the name *L'Auto*. At the same time, Georges Lefèvre, an assistant to Desgrange, came up with the idea of the Tour de France over a business luncheon of *choucroute* at the Brasserie Zimmer, in Paris, known today as The Madrid, where a plaque commemorates this historic moment. The idea was described by Desgrange as a "super race," of exceptional distance, "to create news and capture the imagination," "to force the human body to go to the extreme limits of its capabilities, in such a way as to measure the relative worth of the riders and to stupefy the public."

The first edition of the Tour de France was a six stage, 2,428 km race from Paris through Lyon, Marseille, Toulouse, Bordeaux, Nantes, to the finish in Paris. The six stages took nineteen days because extra rest days were needed for all the riders to finish each stage and for news of the results to reach the public. Georges Lefèvre served as starter, time keeper, supervisor, and journalist. He described his job: "I had to take the train with my bicycle... join the racers on the road in the middle of the night... start them... ride along until we reached a major train station where I could jump on an express and get to the finish line before the first rider. After the stragglers arrived hours later, I had to compose the contents of a full newspaper page."[27]

Of the 60 riders who started in the Paris suburb of Montgeron at the Café Le Réveille-Matin (Cafe Morning Call) on July 1, 1903, at 3 P.M.,

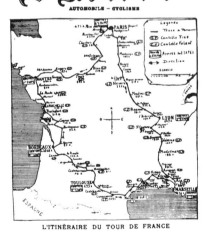

L'ITINÉRAIRE DU TOUR DE FRANCE

Tour de France route, 1903.

only twenty finished at the Parc des Princes velodrome in Paris. Maurice Garin won the race, taking four stages and a prize of 6,125 gold francs. Lucien Pothier finished in second at 2 hours 49 minutes, and Hypolite Aucouturier won two stages but was disqualified for "organized assistance." On the last stage, Aucouturier's supports planned to take revenge in an ambush, but Garin switched jerseys, and passed unnoticed. Garin was born in Italy and raised in France, and became known as *le petit ramoneur* because his father sold him into the chimney-sweep trade for a wheel of cheese. He was the first of many *Géants de la Route*, the giants of the road.

The first Tour was a success, but the 1904 race was a nightmare as spectators and supporters became more involved in the event. Because the long stages required the races to start around 2 A.M., much of the riding was done in darkness. Throughout the route, tacks were thrown on the road and barricades of trees were set up. In a stage on the Col de la République near Saint-Etienne, French fans knocked an Italian off his bike, and when the support cars arrived guns were drawn. Desgrange wrote, "The Tour is finished; this second edition is the last..." The following year the route was altered by making more stages of shorter duration, eliminating most of the night riding, and adding the first mountain pass, the Ballon d'Alsace. By 1907 bicycle manufacturers other than Peugeot and Alcyon, which monopolized the race, began to sponsor riders and follow in team cars. No mechanical assistance could be provided, the riders had to finish each stage with the same bike they started on, making their own repairs, carrying spare tires, and they could not dispose of any equipment enroute. Derailleurs were still developing and were not allowed by Desgrange who believed they were "contraptions unworthy of real men." Typically, the riders had a rear wheel with two sprockets for the flats and the hills, and to change gears they had to get off the bike and turn the wheel around.

In 1910, the Tour journeyed into the Pyrenees mountains, with mud and gravel paths with potholes, falling rocks, sheer cliffs, and wild bears. As one legend recounts, Desgrange was waiting for the riders after their climb of the Col d'Aubisque. As the leader came rolling by, he spat at Desgrange and called him an "assassin." Desgrange took it as a compliment.[28] In 1911 the Tour climbed the Alps over the Col du Galibier at 2,650 meters elevation, known as the "Judge of Peace." Émile Georget was first over the summit, the only one who actually rode the whole way up without walking the bike. The state of the art was tested with the epic exploits of Eugène Christophe before and after World War I. Christophe was the first to wear the *maillot jaune* when it was introduced by Henri Desgrange in the midst of the 1919 Tour. Christophe is one of those riders who never won the Tour, but should have. Known as the "old Gaulois," he captured the sympathy of the fans with his dedicated tenacity, and his famous almost-but-not-quite performances. Christophe recounted one of his famous exploits, how he repaired his broken forks while leading the 1913 Tour in the Pyrenees:

Eugene Christophe.

All of a sudden, about ten kilometers from Ste Marie de Campan down in the valley, I feel that something is wrong with my handlebar. I cannot steer my bike anymore. I pull on my brakes and stop. I see my fork is broken! I can tell you now that my fork was broken, but I would not tell you at the time because it was bad advertising for my firm.

So there I was, left alone on the road. When I say the road, I should say the path. All the riders I had dropped during the climb soon caught me. I was weeping with anger.

I was getting madder and madder. As I walked down I was looking for a short cut. I thought that maybe one of these steep pack trails would lead me straight to Ste Marie de Campan. But I was crying so badly I couldn't see anything. With my bike on my shoulder, I walked for all those ten kilometers.

On arriving in the village I met a young girl who led me to the blacksmith on the other side of the village. M. Lecomte was the name of the blacksmith. He was a nice man and he wanted to help me, but he was not allowed to. The regulations were strict; I had to do all the repair by myself. I never spent a more wretched time in my life than those cruel hours in M. Lecomte's forge. Members of rival cycling firms had been sent to keep a close watch on me. M. Lecomte was only allowed to give me verbal guidance. A young boy helped me handling the bellows, for which aid I was fined. After three hours repair I was able to continue on an uncertain and rather unsafe bike. I had lost the Tour de France.[29]

Christophe is remembered by roadside plaques at the site of Lecomte's forge, on the Col du Galibier, and his name, along with Lapize and Binda, became inscribed on the majority of the toe clips and straps of many future generations of cyclists. The first World War stopped the Tour for four years (1915–1918), and interrupted the careers of a generation of cyclists. Among those who survived were Christophe and Philippe Thijs, the first three-time Tour winner and one of a string of Belgians that dominated the Tour before and after the war. The 1920s saw the arrival of the Pélissier brothers, Henri, Charles, and Francis. They were lead by Henri, the eldest, known for a powerful temper that inspired victories at Paris-Brussels, Paris-Roubaix, Paris-Tours, Bordeaux-Paris, Milan-San Remo, and the Tour of Lombardy. His temper also lead to his tragic death at the age of 46, when a fight with his wife caused her to shoot him with his revolver. In describing the Tour, he once said:

It's a crucifixion, and the way to the cross has fourteen stations. We suffer on those roads... do you want to know how we keep going?... cocaine for our eyes, chloroform for the boils, and pills—we ride on dynamite.[30]

Henri Pelissier.

Tour riders became known as the "Convicts of the Road" after Henri Pélissier was fined for throwing off his long-sleeved jersey. When he won the 1923 Tour on the Galibier pass, Desgrange glorified his victory:

> Henri Pélissier has given us today a spectacle that ranks as art. His victory has the classicism of a work by Racine, it has the beauty of a perfect statue, of a flawless painting, of a piece of music destined to be remembered by all those who hear it
>
> We saw him climb using the full range of his abilities, from the force of his legs to the acumen of his mind. It was the surety of his judgement that allowed him to win the stage by taking advantage of Bottechia's poor timing to change gears. You might say Pélissier knows how to play his instrument.

Henri Pélissier saw it differently:

> What form Desgrange has! He merits entry into the Académie Française, and me, to read him, I should be buried in the Pantheon. I wonder if old Desgrange, who supposedly follows the Tour, actually saw me, for I spent a long time on foot, at the side of Bottechia under a burning sky, pushing the bike with one hand and with the other swigging from a bottle and sharing it with my companion, who was worse off than I. We struggled in a daze, like two soldiers lost in the desert, and if you had passed in our proximity, I, like anyone in my place, would have treated you as a murderer!

By 1929, Desgrange's old and pure Tour was pressured to change with advances in commercial team sponsorship and technical improvements, including the derailleur gear changer. Difficulties arose in the caravan of cars, jeeps and motorcycles as some 25 journalists covered the entire route, including the first radio broadcasters, Jean Antoine and Alex Virot. Desgrange had formed teams based on nationality, causing mixed alliances between riders who belonged to trade teams most of the season and nationals teams for the Tour de France and World Championships. In a decisive stage on the Galibier in 1930, André Leducq of France fell behind Learco Guerra of Italy. On the descent, the pursuing Leducq crashed twice, breaking a pedal and losing some fifteen minutes. Leducq sat there, "contemplating his surroundings in a desperate effort to regain full consciousness." He was picked up by the French national team, and over the last 75 kilometers into Evian, they caught Guerra, who was known as the *locomotive humaine*. Leducq won the sprint for the stage, and went on to win by fourteen minutes over Guerra.

In 1936, when Jacques Goddet and Félix Levitan took over the race organization, Henri Desgrange's initials "HD" became the Tour's logo on the *maillot jaune*. A decade later, after World War II, *L'Auto* changed to *L'Équipe*, and the Tour was being dominated by the exploits of the Italian star Gino Bartali, known as "Gino the Pious" for his devotion to

Jean Robic, from a cartoon by Pélos

Catholicism, and *Il Vecchio* for his long career. Jean Robic, known as "leather head" for his helmet, *Biquet* for his goat-like appearance, and *Jean le Têtu* for being stubborn, became the first rider to win the Tour in 1947 without wearing the *maillot jaune* until the finish. Known for climbing, in the Pyrennees he gained almost eleven minutes on the race leader René Vietto. With three days to Paris, in an extra-long 138 km time trial, Vietto blew up while Robic moved up to third place in general classification behind Pierre Brambilla. Few believed Robic had a chance on the flat roads into Paris but on the final day, on a hill outside Rouen just 75 miles from the French capital, Robic attacked and gained the *maillot jaune* with a 3 minute 58 second lead. This became known in Tour history as "*Le miracle de Bon-Secours.*"

Fausto Coppi (1918–1960) of Italy emerged in the 1940s as the greatest cyclist of his time, the first true *campionissimo*, credited with modernizing training techniques and racing tactics. By appearances he was an unlikely champion, with a lanky build and beak-shaped profile that gave him an impoverished look. Yet those who saw him ride consistently spoke of something unique and spectacular about his style. Raised on a farm near Novi-Ligure, he was a scrawny, unhealthy boy whose mother kept him indoors much of the time. As a youngster, he ran errands for a butcher shop, and he was given a custom bicycle by an uncle, a captain in the merchant navy. Coppi's talent was nutured by the blind trainer and masseur, Biagio Cavanna, who inspired him to reach for the top.

Starting with the pros as an independent, Coppi won the Giro d'Italia in 1940, and set a world hour record at Vigorelli one week before his 24th birthday. Then he entered the Italian army and was sent to Tunisia in North Africa, where he was taken prisoner by Allied troops under Britain's Field Marshall B.L. Montgomery. On returning to war-torn Italy, Coppi was married. His success continued in 1946 with wins at Milan-San Remo, the Grand Prix des Nations, the Tour of Lombardy, and a second to Bartali in the Giro d'Italia. In 1949, after winning Milan-San Remo and the Giro, Coppi won his first of two Tours, ahead of his main rival and Italian compatriot Gino Bartali, who won the 1948 Tour a decade after his first win. Early in the race Coppi had lost eighteen minutes and was ready to quit. His team director Alfredo Binda kept him in, and on a stage into Aosta, Italy, Coppi took the *maillot jaune*, finishing in Paris with 10 minutes 55 seconds over Bartali.

Coppi's later career was marked by controversy and tragedy. After his brother, Serce Coppi, was involved in a disputed tie in the 1949 Paris-Roubaix, Fausto dusted the great Belgian champion Rik Van Steenbergen in the 1950 Paris-Roubaix, but the following year, in the Tour de Piemonte, Serce Coppi was killed. Meanwhile, Fausto shocked his Catholic fans when he separated from his wife, and they learned that his training rides were an alibi for meeting his married lover, Giulia Occhini, known as the "white lady." Occhini was imprisoned for bigamy and Coppi received a suspended sentence, and she had to give birth to their son Faustino in Argentina so the boy could have his father's name. Coppi

Fausto Coppi,
the original *campionissimo*.

won the World Road Championships in 1953 at Lugano when he was 34, and continued racing until late 1959. Some think he raced for too long, saying that he relied on dope to keep his body going. At the beginning of what was to be his last season, on a winter racing and hunting safari in Upper Volta, West Africa, he caught malaria and was rushed home to Italy where he died on January 2, 1960. At his funeral, thousands of fans lined the procession, and some kissed the ground where he passed.

After five years of foreign domination, Louison Bobet, the stylish Breton who abandoned his first Tour and earned the name "Cry-baby," fought back to become a three-time Tour winner and a favorite of the fickle French fans. In Bobet's second victory of 1954, with the Italian National team absent, he dominated on the Col d'Izoard in the Alps over pure climbers such as Federico Bahamontes, Ferdi Kübler, and Jean Mallejac. Later that year he won the hilly and rainy World Road Championships at Solingen, Germany, and he made an unsuccessful attempt on Coppi's hour record.

In 1953, just as Bobet's career was reaching full speed, the nineteen-year-old upstart, Jacques Anquetil (1934–1987) arrived on the scene by winning his first of nine Grand Prix des Nations, the unofficial World Championships for time trialing. Anquetil was the master of the *contre le montre*, the race against the clock, and he became the first five-time Tour winner. He had a graceful pedaling style and amazing powers of recuperation, being known for staying up late, drinking and partying, apparently with little effect on his performance the next day. He was not always loved by his countrymen, and held controversial opinions on doping.

Anquetil won his first Tour in 1957 by dominating the strong French team in the time trials. The following year he quit in the Jura mountains; he finished third in 1959 behind Bahamontes and Anglade; he bowed out of the 1960 Tour after winning the Giro; and he began his record of four consecutive wins in 1961. The Tour adopted the trade team format in 1962, and Anquetil's *plus belle victoire* was winning two mountain stages in 1963.

The 1964 Tour was Anquetil's record-breaking fifth victory and closest finish. He held a fourteen-second lead over Raymond Poulidor at the start of the final 27 km time trial from Versailles to Paris. With a twenty second time bonus for the final stage winner, if Poulidor could match himself against the world's finest time trialist, he would win the Tour. The riders started in traditional order, reverse of the general classification, the leader Anquetil going last. With about three kilometers to go Poulidor had closed to within three seconds of Anquetil, making Poulidor the leader on the road. But in the final kilometers Anquetil's lead increased, and with the bonification, the bonus seconds subtracted from a stage winner's time, he won the Tour by 55 seconds.

Raymond Poulidor, known as "Pou-Pou" by his admirers, had another nickname that summed up his career: "The Eternal Second." Spanning the years of Anquetil and Eddy Merckx, Poulidor became a popular character for his consistent top placings with few major victories. Though he never

Jacques Anquetil (left) and Raymond Poulidor on the Puy de Dome.

won the Tour or got to wear the *maillot jaune*, he finished in the top three of the Tour eight times (1962–1976), and won Milan-San Remo, Paris-Roubaix, the Tour of Spain, and the Super Prestige Trophy in 1964.

Another close finish came in the 1968 Tour, when Jan Janssen of Holland took the *maillot jaune* on the final stage from Herman Van Springel of Belgium. At Melun, Van Springel started the final 55 km time trial into Paris with a sixteen-second lead. By the halfway point, Van Springel had gained five seconds, but in the final kilometers Janssen's pace increased and he finished the stage with a 54-second margin, to win the Tour by 38 seconds. Van Springel knew this was his last chance to win the Tour, as he sobbed, "Next year Eddy Merckx will ride."

Merckx's entry into the 1969 Tour was anxiously awaited, especially for Belgian fans who had not had a winner since Sylvère Maes in 1939. Known as the "Cannibal," Merckx had already won the World's, Paris-Roubaix, the Giro, and many expected him to race in previous Tours, but he waited until he was a more full-grown 24 years old. Merckx took the *maillot jaune* early on, when the team time trial came to his hometown of Woluwe-St Pierre, but passed it to his teammate Julien Stevens. While Merckx chased down all breakaway attempts, reporters said that only Felice Gimondi was racing to win, all the rest were racing to see Merckx defeated.

After the Ballon d'Alsace climb on the seventh day, Merckx held a four-minute lead. On the tenth stage in the Alps, Merckx faltered as Rene Pingeon gained time over the Forclaz Summit to win the stage at Chamonix, but Merckx's overall lead increased, with Pingeon at five minutes, Poulidor at seven, Janssen and Gimondi at eight, Rudi Altig at ten, and Lucien Aimar at sixteen minutes. Over the Portillon Pass to Luchon, Merckx's challenger, Gimondi, collapsed, adding another two minutes to "King Eddy's" lead. The British pro Barry Hoban joked with the press how Gimondi and Poulidor were fined by race officials for hanging onto a support truck during one of the major climbs. He said they also had to fine Merckx because he was pulling the truck up the hill. For most spectators the race was over, and nobody expected Merckx to continue increasing his eight-minute lead. That would be foolish and risky. Yet that is just what Merckx did. The historic seventeenth stage in the Pyrenees to Mourenx-Ville-Nouvelle had four mountain passes, the Peyresourde, the Aspin, the Tourmalet, and the Aubisque. On the descent of the Tourmalet with 140 kilometers to go, Merckx broke away alone, and instead of recuperating for the last Aubisque climb, he continued on to the verge of collapse and won the stage. On July 20, Merckx won the final time trial, and at the Vincennes Municipal Velodrome in Paris his lead was awesome. He became the only rider thus far to win the points, mountains, combine, and yellow jerseys.

The Tour's second five-time winner, Merckx continued to dominate with victory margins that averaged about ten minutes, and the record career-total of 34 stage wins. His closest rival was Louis Ocana (1945–1994) of Spain, a talented climber and time trialist who challenged

Eddy Merckx, in the 1969 Tour.

1969 TOUR DE FRANCE
1. EDDY MERCKX
   4,079 km in 116 hrs, 16 min, 2 sec.
2. Rene PINGEON at 17 min. 54 sec.
3. Raymond POULIDOR at 22 min, 13 sec.
4. Felice Gimondi at 29 min, 24 sec.
5. Andres Gandarias at 33 min, 40 sec.
10. Jan Janssen at 52 min, 56 sec.

Merckx in the 1971 and 1972 Tours, and finally won in 1973, when Merckx skipped the Tour after winning the Tours of Spain and Italy. In 1971, on the eleventh stage from Grenoble to Orcières-Merlette, Ocana "knocked out" Merckx by nine minutes, and took over the *maillot jaune*. Then, in a rainy fourteenth stage into the Pyrenees, on the dangerous descent of the Col de Mente, Ocana was "knocked out" of the Tour as the race radio announced:

> Riders are splashing through the water and mud... Brakes are useless... Visibility almost nil in blinding rain... Ocana crashes... The *maillot jaune* is on the ground... So is Merckx. Merckx is quickly away. Ocana still not back in race... Agostino crashes same place as Ocana... Merckx crashes again... The *maillot jaune* is still on the road and appears to be unconscious. The ambulance is on its way....

The generation of riders who followed in the shadow of Merckx got their chance at victory in the late 1970s. Frenchman Bernard Thevenet won twice, in 1975 when the Tour finished on the Champs-Elysées for the first time, while Belgian climber Lucien Van Impe and the Francophile Dutchman Joop Zoetemelk each won once. Zoetemelk rode a record sixteen Tours in an almost consecutive streak from 1970 to 1986, winning in 1980, finishing second six times, and missing only the 1974 Tour.

Bernard Hinault, the feisty Breton known as the "Badger," became the third five-time Tour winner with his well-rounded ability in climbing, time trialing and sprinting. Winning his first Tour in 1978, Hinault ranks among the finest cyclists of all time, as the 1980 World Pro Road Champion and three-time Giro d'Italia winner, despite his troubling years of tendinitis and knee surgery. Hinault's toughest competition came from his sometime teammates, two-time Tour winner Laurent Fignon from Paris, the youngest winner since 1904, and Greg LeMond, originally from Los Angeles, a three-time Tour winner.

The 1984 Tour began this historic three-way rivalry with Hinault wearing the new Mondrian-styled colors of Bernard Tapie's Look team, with defending champion Fignon in the *maillot jaune* and LeMond in the 1983 World Champion's rainbow jersey, both on Cyrille Guimard's Renault-Gitane team. Hinault was going for his fifth win, Fignon his second, and LeMond was in his first Tour. Hinault took the *maillot jaune* in the prologue, so Fignon had to wear his French champion's tri-color jersey. But Fignon, nicknamed the "Professor," flew through the Alps and regained the *maillot jaune* with three mountaintop stage wins. On the famous climb to L'Alpe d'Huez, Luis Herrera of Colombia became the first South American to win a Tour stage. L'Alpe d'Huez is one of the Tour's mountain climbs rated "beyond category." It was first introduced on the route in 1952, and some 250,000 spectators congregate at the top of Route 211 with its 21 switch-backs. At Paris, the final standing was Fignon in yellow, followed by Hinault at 10 minutes 32 seconds, and LeMond third at 11:46, wearing the white jersey as top neophyte.

Miroir du Cyclisme, 1984 Tour preview, with Greg LeMond, Laurent Fignon, Joop Zoetemelk and Bernard Hinault.

Greg LeMond on the Champs-Elysées in Paris, 1989. Photo by Darcy Keifel.

With Fignon out due to tendinitis, and LeMond on Hinault's La Vie Claire-Look team, the 1985 Tour saw the height of the Hinault-LeMond rivalry. At 30 years of age, this was Hinault's chance to equal Merckx and Anquetil. LeMond was reportedly promised equal leadership so he could go for the win if Hinault faltered. But when the opportunity arrived, after Hinault crashed and broke his nose at Saint-Etienne, Paul Koechli, La Vie Claire's director sportif, told LeMond to hold back so Hinault would remain in the lead. In Paris, with five Tour victories, Hinault said, "Next year I will ride to help another La Vie Claire rider win. Hopefully that rider will be Greg." The Tour had become truly international as the top fifteen riders came from eleven countries, with a Frenchman, an American, two Irishmen, an Australian, two Spaniards, two Colombians, a Canadian, an Englishman, two Dutch, a Swiss, and a Belgian.

Despite Hinault's promise to help LeMond win in 1986, he put up a fight for a record-breaking sixth Tour victory, but LeMond won on his own, becoming the first American to win the world's biggest bike race. LeMond achieved his goal and then tragedy struck. In April 1987, while turkey hunting in a remote region of Placer County, California, LeMond was accidently sprayed by shot-gun pellets fired by his brother-in-law. He lay bleeding for nearly an hour before a CHP helicopter air-lifted LeMond to the U.C. Davis Medical Center. The doctors reported that in another twenty or thirty minutes he would have bled to death.

LeMond's recovery was slowed by an appendectomy and a broken wrist. As 1987 turned into 1988, with meager performances and two missed Tours, LeMond was relegated to the less powerful ADR team for the 1989 season. Showing only a little hope in the Giro d'Italia, his chances for the 1989 Tour seemed almost nil. Yet this turned out to be one of the most exciting Tours of all time, as LeMond and Fignon traded the *maillot jaune* five times, with LeMond trailing Fignon by 50 seconds going into the final historic stage, a 24.5 km time trial from Versailles to the Champs-Elysées. Most experts believed that anything could happen, but on such a course it was unlikely LeMond could gain the necessary two seconds per kilometer over Fignon to win the race. While the Frenchman let his blond ponytail fly in the wind, LeMond used an aerodynamic helmet and triathlon handlebars, taking every advantage available except one. He chose not to hear his split times until the Champs-Elysées, so he could concentrate on going all out. In the end, LeMond beat his longtime rival by 58 seconds averaging 34 mph, and he won the Tour by eight seconds, the smallest victory margin in Tour history.

Later that year, LeMond went on to win the rainy World Road Championships in Chambéry, France, and was named Sportsman of the Year by *Sports Illustrated*. With a three-year $5.5 million contract with Roger Legay's Z team, he won the 1990 Tour without winning a single stage. LeMond has been criticized for winning only the Tour and Worlds and quitting the rest, yet he revolutionized the sport by raising riders' salaries and adding international appeal. The 1992 Tour celebrated the unity of the European Community by going into seven E.C. nations, including Spain, Belgium, the Netherlands, Germany, Luxembourg, and Italy. Jean-Marie Leblanc of the Société du Tour said, "Before, the Tour increased nationalism. Now, this Tour is contributing to help the nations get closer." However, a 1994 survey by *Vélo Magazine* showed that 62 percent of 821 respondents favored a return to national teams.

Miguel Indurain from Villava, Spain, has dominated the Tour in the 1990s. With his powerful Banesto team, "Big Mig" won a record-breaking five consecutive Tours from 1991 to 1995. One of the greatest time trialists of all time, Indurain is known for his calm manner, his fluid pedaling, and his efficient victories. He gains time in a few powerful rides and keeps his lead as his team sets a tempo that limits any losses. Indurain's challengers include the Italians, Claudio Chiappucci, known as the "Devil," who made feisty attacks but lacked speed against the clock, and two-time World Champion Gianni Bugno, who described Indurain as "extra-terrestrial ... of another world." Three-time Tour of Spain winner Tony Rominger of Switzerland was favored in 1994 when the Tour route was supposedly designed for him to beat Indurain, with the toughest mountain stages in the final week. But Rominger's Colorado-based high-altitude preparation was of little help in the Pyrenees when he got stomach sickness, abandoned the Tour, and saw Indurain win by 5 minutes 39 seconds over Piotr Ugrumov of Latvia. Rominger was favored again in 1995 after he had demolished Indurain's hour record, but in winning one of the toughest Tours of Italy just four weeks before the Tour began, Rominger had already peaked and finished eighth, 16 minutes 46 seconds behind Indurain. As the 31-year-old Spanish Basque approached a possible sixth Tour victory, commentators questioned how long he could defy the odds and go on without injury, bad luck, or, as happened to Eddy Merckx in the 1975 Tour, a morale-defeating blow from a crazed spectator.

Miguel Indurain in the 1993 Tour.

Campionissimo

Eddy Merckx (top) went 49 kilometers in his 1972 hour record while Tony Rominger (below) went 55 kilometers in 1994. Still, Merckx is considered the greatest cyclist of all time.

There are many champions from different periods in cycling's history, but only one can be called the greatest of all time. The sign of the true champion, the champion of champions, known as the *campionissimo* in Italian, is the ability to repeat victories and stay at the top, even when everyone wants to see a new champion. There is a powerful desire to compare the exploits of champions from each generation, as if all the stars of past and present could compete in one all-time championship race. Ideally, this is what the world hour record would be.

The race for the all-time greatest cyclist can only be held on paper, with intricate points systems comparing levels of competition, fitness, and technology, noting record times over the same roads and tracks, with experts comparing each champion's career achievements, known in French as *palmarès*. Cyclists are measured as *rouleurs*, climbers, and sprinters. Their will to win is analyzed, as is their ability to recuperate from fatigue, injury, and defeat. Because of advances in training methods since the mid-1980s, most experts believe today's racers compete at higher levels of fitness than earlier champions. Some experts think past generations raced under difficult conditions which today's pampered cyclists could not handle if equal levels of technology were applied, while others wonder how ancient champions would handle today's refined methods. Such questions inevitably occur with the UCI world hour record because it provides a relatively standardized format for comparison. Yet "records are made to be broken," and new generations inevitably succeed in surpassing the old records. The greatest race of all time would include, among others, Fausto Coppi of the 1940s, Jacques Anquetil of the 1960s, Eddy Merckx of the 1970s, Bernard Hinault of the 1980s, and Miguel Indurain of the 1990s. Among women, the ultimate race would include Beryl Burton, Yvonne Reynders, and Jeannie Longo.

What separates the greatest champions, known as "*les grand solitaires*," is their ability to consistently ride alone against the clock and at the front of the peloton, faster than the rest of their competition. According to one statistician, Fausto Coppi, the original *campionissimo*, entered 666 road races in his career totaling about 119,000 kilometers. In 58 of those races he rode in solo winning breakaways totaling an estimated 3,000 kilometers where he gained almost three hours. At that rate, Coppi averaged one meter per hour faster than his closest rivals throughout his twenty-year career.[31] By comparison, in Eddy Merckx's seven Tours de France totaling 28,192 kilometers at 35.6 kph, his net gain over his closest rivals was 43 minutes 54 seconds—about 32.8 meters per hour. In Merckx's hour record he gained 778 meters over Ole Ritter, and 3.583 kilometers over Fausto Coppi. After the flurry of hour records of 1994, Tony Rominger gained 2.251 kilometers over Miguel Indurain, 5.860 kilometers over Merckx, and 9.448 kilometers over Coppi.

In the view of most experts, Eddy Merckx has the most prestigious cycling career, and as a legend in his own time, Merckx had to handle the fabulous myth-making which surrounds an athlete of his stature. A story is told of an unknown professional cyclist whose racing career spanned the reign of Merckx. Try as he might, he could never beat Merckx, and it seemed that he was destined to be another anonymous peon in the sport. During one Tour de France he missed a turn on a descent and flew into the void between the mountains. The next thing he saw was the Pearly Gates of Heaven. Saint Peter came out in his warm-up suit and greeted the cyclist. "It has been rough for you," soothed St. Peter, "were it not for Eddy Merckx you could have been one of the greatest of your time." St. Peter told the cyclist not to fear because the Kingdom of Heaven had a Tour of its own. "You shall get your just reward," said St. Peter, "Eddy Merckx is not here yet."

Then St. Peter offered the cyclist a skinsuit made of the very finest material and an indescribable bicycle that weighed almost nothing. The cyclist mounted his celestial bike and entered the Tour of Heaven. Finding himself in the company of some of the greatest cyclists of times past, including Terront, Christophe, Bobet, Coppi, and Anquetil, he felt confident because of his modern training techniques. While leading the race through the Elysian Fields, on the climb of Mt. Avalon, the cyclist was passed by a blur of spinning wheels. Judging by the other cyclist's form he called to St. Peter: "I thought you said Eddy Merckx was not here." "That was not Merckx," St. Peter replied, "That was God. He only thinks he is Merckx."

Eddy's first victory.

Off-Road Sports

Off-road sports are a big part of cycling, with a wide range of events and venues. Many off-road cycling events date back to the nineteenth century, but most developed in the late twentieth century as more roads were paved. Racing events such as cyclo-cross, BMX and mountain biking, are held on mountain trails and dirt tracks and have highly competitive UCI-governed professional riders and world championships. Ballgames and acrobatic events, such as cycle ball, artistic cycling, and bicycle polo, are held on gymnasium floors and playing fields with amateur championships. Many other off-road exhibition sports, such as stunt cycling, unicycling, roller racing, kinetic sculpture racing, and ice-cycling, tend to cross the threshold from legitimate sports to recreation sports.

Cyclo-Cross Racing

Cyclo-cross or *vélocross* racing is a traditional wintertime sport for professionals and amateurs that became a UCI World Championship event in 1950. It is a form of cross-country steeplechase in which the competitors ride, carry, or run with their bicycle along paved and unpaved roads, across fields, through forests, up and down steep embankments, and over natural and man-made obstacles. It is a specialized sport that serves as a way of maintaining fitness, improving bike handling skills, and providing fun during the off-season.

According to UCI rules, cyclo-cross races are carried out on specially selected courses over three kilometers per lap, with a total distance of about 20 kilometers for amateurs and 35 kilometers for professionals. Roughly three-quarters of the course should be ridable on the bike, while at least a quarter should have variable off-road terrain. These are mass-start races, where the start and finish stretch is wide enough for everyone to have a fair chance to take the lead. As the course tends to narrow into a single track, with one path often the fastest line, there must be room for passing, and no artificial obstacle should exceed about 40 centimeters in height. One or more pit stops are provided where the riders can exchange flat tires, wobbly wheels, or broken bikes. The terrain often varies depending on the location and weather, with stairways, river crossings, mushy fields, loose gravel, slippery ice, and muddy puddles. Swiss courses tend to emphasize technical skill, with dismounting, running, and bike handling being the deciding factor, while other courses require more speed, endurance, and traditional cycling ability. Cyclists from Belgium, Germany, and Switzerland have dominated professional cyclo-cross, and Belgian Eric De Vlaeminck holds the record of seven pro world titles. With the growth of UCI-sanctioned mountain biking in the 1990s, there is a year-round schedule of off-road sports. There has yet to be an official women's cyclo-cross world title, and the 1994 men's event was open to pros and amateurs following the UCI's changes.

Eric de Vlaeminck.

BMX RACING

Bicycle moto-cross, or BMX racing, is a worldwide sport that developed in the late-1960s in California as sting-ray bikes were modified in bike shops and garages with knobby tires and beefed-up frames for off-road child's play. Without the influence of traditional cyclo-cross racing, the sport had phenomenal growth in the mid-1970s as BMX clubs and tracks became supported by a flourishing bicycle industry. The founders of BMX racing include, among others, Ernie Anderson, a former moto-cross racer who used bicycles to help teach kids how to handle motorbikes and helped form the National Bicycle Association (NBA), and Scot Breithaupt, who is credited with organizing the first BMX race at a track in Long Beach, known as "BUMS Park" (Bicycle United Motocross Society). He was also the first to win the National No. 1 plate for his bike.

The races, called "motos," are held on dirt tracks about 400 to 1,000 meters long, with ramped starting gates, flat straightaways, rolling mounds for jumping called "table tops," banked gravel turns called "berms," and sometimes added water hazards. Many courses are designed for a single lap race, a sort of sprint with three heats, known as "quarters," "semis," and "mains." There are over 50 categories of riders, including the Pros (AA, A and B), Super Class, and Super Cruiser. The Expert, Novice, Cruiser, and Girls categories range in age groups from over 50 years old (Cruisers) to five years old (Experts).

Among the various organizing groups in American BMX racing, the most prominent are the for-profit American Bicycle Association (ABA) and the smaller not-for-profit National Bicycle League (NBL). Both hold races such as the Summer Nationals, the Grand Nationals, the Fall Nationals, and Winter Nationals. There are over 500 BMX tracks in North America, and major weekend events attract over 600 riders. In the 1980s it was estimated that at least 100,000 BMXers had tried racing, and over half were regulars. The average first prize for A riders is $3,000, and top pros such as Stu Thompsen, Brian Patterson, and Pete Loncarevich have made small fortunes from racing. For winning the 1987 NBL World Cup race, Loncarevich earned $5,000. The NBL was absorbed by the USCF in 1989, and now represents BMX, freestyle, and Formula racing with the UCI. Up to 37 countries participate in UCI-sanctioned BMX, but World Champions are not awarded rainbow jerseys. Besides race coverage on the ESPN sports network, BMXers were introduced to millions of movie goers with the uplifting chase scenes of Steven Spielberg's blockbuster *E.T. The Extraterrestrial* (1982). The sport's off-shoots include freestyle racing, held on small, ramped velodromes; formula racing, held on flat tracks; and gravity vehicle racing, held on long downhill roads.

BMX racing, coming out a berm.

Mountain Bike Racing

Mountain biking, or MTB racing, emerged as a world-class sport in the late-1980s, with the rapid growth of competitive events and the increased level of talent among off-road racers. Mountain bike events have a variety of venues and courses, including stage races, point-to-point races, cross-country races, downhill races, hillclimbs, observed trials, and relay races. Events usually take place at national or regional parks and ski resorts, and the main event is the cross-country mass-start lap race held on courses five to fifteen kilometers long, including unpaved roads, dirt trails, fields and forests, with various sections of mud, sand, rivers, uphill, and down-hill hairpin turns. The pro men ride about 30 to 35 kilometers and the pro women ride 20 to 25 kilometers. Downhill races are executed as individual time trials on steep slopes of one to ten kilometers, or as head-to-head dual slalom races. Observed trials are held on marked sections of trail, 20 to 100 feet long, with imposing mounds, rocks, or logs to hop. Judges and spectators oversee the rider's skill, as the object is to stay on the bike, and never let the feet leave the pedals or touch ground.

Repack race featured on a *Bicycling* magazine poster, 1981. Photo by Wendy Cragg.

GRUNDIG

MOUNTAIN BIKE WORLD CUP 1992 (UCI)

The MTB sport developed in leaps and bounds as enthusiasts in Northern California and Colorado converted their balloon-tire klunker bikes into "fat-tire flyers." From back-woods beginnings, the first mountain bike events were one-speed downhill runs, such as the Repack race, first held in 1976 near Fairfax, California, so-called because the riders had to re-pack the grease in their over-heated coaster-brake hubs. The Repack race results include two dogs who ran down the hill, along with the pioneers of mountain biking, Gary Fisher, Tom Ritchey, and Joe Breeze, who were experienced road racers. The original klunker bikes were too heavy and not geared to climb the hill so the riders would get a lift in the back of a pick-up truck. As the mountain bike industry began to expand in the early 1980s, more events appeared, including the Whiskeytown Downhill, the Rockhopper, the Punk Bike Enduros, the Reseda to the Sea, the Central Coast Clunker Classic, the Sierra Nevada Fatbike Fest, and the Crested Butte Fat Tire Bike Week. In 1983, the casual group of Northern California mountain bikers who had formed the National Off-Road Bicycle Association (NORBA) let Glenn Odell take over leadership and ownership of the organization. A competition committee set up rules and sanctioned races, including the NORBA National Championships, which were dominated at first by Joe Murray and Jacquie Phelan.

By 1986, several other mountain bike racing associations were formed in Britain, Europe, Australia, and Japan. Meanwhile, NORBA experienced a financial crisis over insurance, and was sold to the BMX organizing company, the American Bicycle Association, headed by Bob Hadley. Despite considerable controversy, the sport continued to grow, from about 1,000 members in 1985, to 5,000 members in 1989, when it was bought by the United States Cycling Federation (USCF) for some $210,000. In 1994, NORBA had about 22,500 members, plus some 30,000 one-day license holders. The first "unofficial" World Championships were held in August 1987 at two separate sites. The European event at Villard-de-

Lans, France, featured a cross-country race promoted by the Mountain Bike Association and sponsored by *Winning* magazine, and the American event, at Mammoth Lakes, California, featured cross-country, hillclimb, downhill, and observed trials events promoted by NORBA and sponsored by Raleigh. Ned Overend, a 32-year-old professional from Durango, Colorado, won both cross-country races and the hillclimb, while Sara Ballantyne and Mary Lee Atkins captured the women's cross-country titles. Mammoth Lakes continued as the site for the NORBA Worlds in 1988 and 1989.

The sport was fully sanctioned by the UCI in 1990 and the first official MTB World Championships were held at the Purgatory Resort in Durango, Colorado. Rainbow jerseys were awarded for the men, women, junior, veteran men, and veteran women in the cross-country and downhill events. Durango's "homeboys," Overend and Greg Herbold, won the cross-country and downhill, while the women champions were Juli Furtado, also living in Durango, and Cindy Devine of Canada. Cyclists from 26 nations participated, more than the cyclo-cross Worlds. The World Cup series, sponsored by the Grundig electronics company, began in 1991 and features six downhill races and ten cross-country races held in Spain, Italy, Belgium, England, Canada, the U.S., Australia, and Switzerland.

Ned Overend.

The American John Tomac became one of the most celebrated mountain biking stars, and the sport's first millionaire. In 1991, he won the cross-country World Championships in Lucca, Italy, and he briefly ventured into the realm of European professional road racing as a member of the 7-Eleven and Motorola teams. Tomac began bike racing in BMX, like many American mountain bikers, especially downhill racers who also come from ski racing. Europeans more often crossover from cyclo-cross and road racing. Most of the top mountain bike racers do about 50 to 75 percent of their training on pavement with road bikes.

Europeans have surpassed North Americans, as Henrik Djernis of Denmark won three consecutive World Championship titles in 1992 to 1994, and Thomas Frischknecht of Switzerland won the World Cup in 1992 and 1993, both riding for the Ritchey team. Juli Furtado dominated women's World Cup and NORBA racing in 1993 and 1994 with over 25 victories in almost every race she entered except the World Championships.

INDOOR CYCLING

Indoor cycling consists of two official events, Cycleball and Artistic Cycling, usually held in gymnasiums. Both are UCI-sanctioned World Championship events awarded the rainbow jersey and governed by the International Commission on Indoor Cycling. The sport has a popular following in Central Europe with some 6,000 competitors in Germany.

Cycleball is similar to football (soccer), except that the playing field is about the size of a basketball court and the ball is kicked with the cyclist's wheels. Each game has two fifteen-minute periods and two teams, consisting of two players, one on the court, the other tending goal. The sport dates back the 1890s, and has attracted teams from Austria, Belgium, Czechoslovakia, Denmark, France, Germany, Italy, Japan, Russia, Sweden, and Switzerland. The Pospíšil brothers of Czechoslovakia dominated the sport, winning nineteen world titles between 1968 and 1988.

Artistic Cycling is a form of bicycle gymnastics with competitions for amateur men, women, and juniors who ride in singles or doubles on one bike, and in formations of quadruplets or sextuplets on separate bikes. There are over 700 specific positions or movements, each worth a maximum amount of points that are totaled up during timed performances of six to eight minutes. The competitors submit their routines before the event and points are subtracted for faults, such as improper execution, going out of bounds, or lack of confidence or style.

Over 40 different movements are possible within a six minute routine. The routines include upside-down hand-stands on the handlebars while doing figure-eights (worth 5.8 points), forward wheelies with a partner standing on the shoulders, and riding backward in circles from a wheelie while revolving the handlebars. Special kinds of training equipment, such as stationary bikes, training wheels, vaulting stands with handlebars, and teeterboards for balancing are used to practice routines. Anna Matoušková of Czechoslovakia won several World Championships during the 1960s and 1970s.

Anna Matousková, artistic cycling world champion, 1975. Photo by Pieter Van Damme.

BICYCLE POLO

Bicycle polo is a field sport for teams similar to traditional polo on horse-back, with the object of the game being to score the most goals. The switch from polo ponies to polo bicycles began around 1890 near Dublin, Ireland, and spread to England and the British colonies in India. It was first organized in America in 1897 by a club in Milton, Massachusetts.

The sport is typically played on a football-sized (soccer) field marked with a half-line and two quarter-lines at about 25 yards, and two goal-lines at either end with the goal posts about four yards apart. Each team usually includes four players and a goal keeper, with one or more substitutes allowed by a system of handicaping. The mallet is shorter than in traditional polo, and the ball is about three inches in diameter. It was traditionally made of bamboo, but since these often cracked, requiring several replacements per game, plastic balls and soft balls have been used. The bikes usually have a one-speed coaster-brake drive with a low gear for quick acceleration, and the handlebars tend be narrower than normal. In modern polo, there are two basic rules of play, British and American.

In 1930, the Bicycle Polo Association of Great Britain was formed with clubs and competitive leagues playing for the English Cup. In British rules, the game consists of six fifteen-minute periods, called "chukkas." If a tie results, a "sudden death chukka" is played until one team scores the winning goal. The game begins as the ball is placed in the center of the field and the one player from each team sprints to take possession of the ball. A special kind of British polo bike has evolved, with 26-inch wheels, a studded rear tire, and a curved seat tube to allow for a shorter wheel-base.

The United States Bicycle Polo Association dates back to the 1940s and was revived in 1970 in New York. In American rules, the playing time consists of six 7½-minute periods, with three minute breaks and a

Bicycle Polo—A Mêlée.

Cycle Ball match.

five minute halftime. According to "Forbes" rules, the game is begun as the referee rolls the ball underhand from the sidelines between the players. Any kind of bicycle is acceptable in American rules, and polo bikes with 18- to 24-inch wheels are normally used for maneuverability, though mountain bike polo has become more popular in the 1990s. Bicycle polo is a fast-paced game, often with quick, airborne passes, and hard charging team tactics. Both feet must be kept off the ground while hitting the ball, and although the player may not throw it, they can use their hands or feet to stop the ball. The advantages of using bicycles in polo includes a mount that costs less (horses may cost five to ten times more than polo bikes), and can take more abuse (you don't have to shoot the bike if it gets severely injured). Although the horse may respond better, the "millionaires' shot" (a back-hand shot between the horse's legs) is much safer on a bike.

Cyclothons

Having an appeal that is both unique and universal, this realm of cycle sport explores the ultimate athletic feats of speed, skill, power, and endurance, in a variety of events that tend to have an individual nature, as each cyclist faces his or her own limit of human-powered performance. Combining elements of physics, physiology, and psychology, in an endless pursuit of technical innovation and supreme fitness, these events include the paced land speed record, the multi-sport triathlons, the super-endurance Race Across America, and the Alaskan survival race, Iditasport. These are merely the top of the pyramid. There are many more competitive events, including speed records, brevets, time trials, and ultra-marathon races.

LAND SPEED RECORD

The world's paced land speed record determines the highest possible velocity for a "human-powered" vehicle. The record dates back to the 1890s, with increasingly powerful motor vehicles used to pace the cyclists towards the limits of aerodynamics and rolling resistances. As much a race as it is a stunt, this record tests a rider's *souplesse*, strength, courage, and bike handling ability. It is a relatively short event, carried out over a distance of 1 to 2.5 kilometers, within a time frame of about 15 to 70 seconds.

A variety of pacing vehicles have been used, and in the early years, most riders were powerful world-class sprinters. At the turn of the century, the former World and National Champion Charles "Mile-A-Minute" Murphy rode behind a locomotive, the fastest land vehicle at the time, on a specially constructed board track between the rails of the Long Island Railroad. By 1928, the Belgian kilometer champion Leon Vanderstuyft reached 78.159 mph (125 kph) behind a motorcycle at the Montlhéry race track. Before and after World War II, the popular French-American six-day racer Alf Letourner, known as the "Red Devil," set the record at Montlhéry, and again on the Los Angeles freeway near Bakersfield, riding a specially built Schwinn bicycle with a 252-inch gear behind an open race car with a large vertical wind screen.

The Frenchman José Meiffret (1913–1983) was the most persevering specialist in this bizarre event. He took up motor-pacing at the suggestion of Henri Desgrange, and with a skull and cross bones painted on his wind screen he had several "dates with death" on the way toward five records. In his record ride in 1951 behind a Talbot racing car on a stretch of highway near Toulouse, he hit a bump and was reportedly in free flight for 30 meters. Yet he held on to set a speed of 109.1 mph (175 kph). The following year, he tried to increase his record at the dilapidated Montlhéry track when something went wrong. He crashed at almost 90 mph, tumbling and skidding for over 115 meters, and came to rest as "a quivering mass of flesh." He suffered five fractures in his skull, but managed to survive. There followed a ten-year period of recuperation, during which Meiffret joined a Trappist monastery at Sept-Fonds and wrote his first book, *Breviary of a Cyclist*. Learning of a new freeway at Lahr, Germany, he resumed his flying kilometer record breaking in 1961. Convinced that he could reach 200 kph (124 mph), at the age of 50 he chose a fifteen kilometer stretch of autobahn near Freiburg, Germany, for his last record attempt on July 19, 1962. Riding behind a Mercedes-Benz race car equipped with a microphone system, on a 45-pound bicycle with a 225-inch gear, Meiffret set a record of 127.243 mph (204 kph). In his pocket he carried a note:

> In case of fatal accident, I beg of the spectators not to feel sorry for me. I am a poor man, an orphan since the age of eleven, and I have suffered much. Death holds no terror for me. This record attempt is my way of expressing myself. If the doctors can do no more for me, please bury me by the side of the road where I have fallen.

Meiffret's record was broken by Dr. Allan V. Abbott, a physician and former motorcycle racer, who took the speed record to its ultimate venue, Utah's Bonneville Salt Flats. The Salt Flats are described as the fastest place on earth, with its remarkably flat and smooth pure white crystalline surface at relatively high altitude. Virtually all the world's top land speed records for cars and motorcycles have been set there. Abbott waited until the end of Bonneville's Speed Week in August 1973 to set his record of 138.6 mph (223 kph) behind a modified 650-horsepower 1955 Chevy hot rod. His bike had front shocks, motorcycle racing wheels, and a massive chainring, with a gear ratio of 375 inches. In high-speed motor pacing the Von Karman effect takes hold at about 135 mph. This is a low-pressure air bubble that pulls the rider close behind the pace car. Outside the bubble is Von Karman's shedding, swirling winds that knock the rider side-to-side and back-and-forth. In one test run at that speed, Abbott's front wheel touched the pace car's fairing, and as he fell out of the vacuum slipstream, he hit the full force of wind, equivalent to a free-falling parachutist, which he leaned into to stay on the bike. Within seconds the wind

José Meiffret (top) on his record bike with a 130-tooth chainring, (center) severely injured at Montlhéry in 1952, and (above) behind a Mercedes at 127 miles per hour in 1962.

Allan Abbott.

had slowed him to 50 mph.

John Howard set the speed record in July 1985 at Bonneville by riding 152.284 mph (245 kph). Howard is a 6-foot 2-inch 170-pound athlete who could be described as "Mr. Cyclothon" as a Pan-Am Games Champion, U.S. National Road Champion, Red Zinger winner, Ironman winner, RAAM rider, and veteran mountain biker. Riding behind Rick Vesco's Bonneville Streamliner, one of the fastest gasoline-powered cars, Howard's bike had a radio-controlled throttle which adjusted the car's speed as Vesco steered, and the two could communicate through headsets in their crash helmets. Fred Rompelberg of Holland, the world record holder for the UCI-sanctioned 100 km motor-paced race, has made several attempts to break Howard's record at Bonneville. In October 1988, riding behind a turbo-charged Offenhauser pace car that fishtailed at 142 mph, he crashed and suffered multiple injuries that left him semi-conscious. Finally, in October 1995, Rompelberg reached 167.051 mph (268 kph) at Bonneville, pedaling a 403-inch gear behind Jeff Strasburg's race car. In fitness tests, 49-year-old Rompelberg produced 500 watts, with a maximum heart rate of 176 bpm.

John Howard setting the motorpaced land speed record of 152 mph, Bonneville Salt Flats, 1985.

TRIATHLONS

Combining the three athletic events of swimming, cycling, and running, triathlons have become the fastest growing worldwide sport. Triathlons developed in America in the early 1970s as a handful of athletes sought a more full-bodied sporting challenge. In 1990, when a World Championship event was first held, it was estimated that at least two million amateur men, women, and children had participated in at least one triathlon. At the same time, the U.S. federation, Tri-Fed, had about 30,000 licensed members. With sponsored events on every continent and world-class competitors in countries such as the Netherlands, Germany, Brazil, Australia, New Zealand, Mexico, Israel, Malaysia, the West Indies, and Japan, national teams have begun to form as the triathlon will be featured in the 1996 Atlanta Olympics.

There are several "athlon" style events with both long and short distance races. The Hawaiian Ironman competition began in 1978 as the original endurance triathlon event with a 2.4-mile ocean swim, a 112-mile bike ride, and a 26.2-mile marathon run. This takes about eight or nine hours for the fastest men (compared to about twelve hours in 1978) and about nine or ten hours for the fastest women. Medium distance events have a 1.2-mile swim, a 55-mile bike ride, and a 13-mile run, which takes about four hours for fast men and four and a half hours for fast women. The Olympic distance triathlon consists of a 1.5-km swim, a 40-km bike ride, and a 10-km run, taking about one hour 45 minutes for fast men and two hours for fast women. Duathlons, (also known as Biathlons, but easily confused with the Winter Olympic sport of cross-country skiing and target shooting) usually have a 5-km run, a 40-km bike ride, and another 5-km run, taking about 1 hour 15 minutes for fast men and 1 hour 30 minutes for fast women. Quadrathlons, known as a "Pedal, Paddle, Splash, and Dash," include a canoe or kayak event.

Paula Newby-Fraser.

Time trialing in Hawaii (left) in the 1984 Ironman. Photo courtesy ABC Sports.

The cycling leg of multisport is carried out as a time trial with drafting prohibited. As some events attract over a thousand participants, with the top performers in wheel to wheel competition, disputes have inevitably arisen. In 1994, the International Triathlon Union began to allow drafting by pros in World Cup races. While triathlons are an excellent means of attaining well-rounded fitness, world-class cyclists and swimmers in their prime are not likely to enter such events because the specialized muscles necessary for these sports are considered uncomplementary to each other. This was evident in John Howard's victorious 1981 Ironman performance, as he was able to supplement his meager swimming with strong cycling. Six-time winner Dave Scott is one of the original Ironmen, along with pros such as Scott Tinley and Mark Allen. Among Ironwomen, seven-time winner Paula Newby-Fraser of Zimbabwe and Erin Baker of New Zealand have dominated the sport.

RACE ACROSS AMERICA

The Race Across America, known as RAAM, is an annual trans-continental bicycle race and one of the longest non-stop open races, going from the Pacific Ocean to the Atlantic. By its nature, the race is a grueling test of ultimate endurance. The riders are a unique breed of athlete, requiring tremendous amounts of will power, support, and logistical skill. The race was conceived by John Marino, a former baseball player who injured himself weightlifting after being drafted by the Los Angeles Dodgers. He cast about looking for something to do with his life and discovered the trans-continental cycling record in the *Guinness Book of World Records*. Marino set out to lower the record, which he accomplished in 1978 going from Santa Monica to New York in 13 days, 1 hour, 20 minutes, taking four hours off the record of Paul Cornish. He tried again in 1979, and in 1980, with a film company documenting his ride, he lowered the record to 12 days, 3 hours, 41 minutes.

As interest in ultra-marathon cycling increased, Marino organized and rode the Great American Bike Race with John Howard, Michael Shermer, and Lon Haldeman, who rode the 2,968 miles in an amazing 9 days, 20 hours, and 2 seconds. After an ownership dispute with his co-founder, Marino changed the event's name to the Race Across AMerica in 1983, and with ABC television coverage, Haldeman won again. Haldeman, from Harvard, Illinois, has held five transcontinental records and cycled across the country about 25 times. In 1984, over 5,000 spectators watched the start and some 3,500 cyclists joined for the first fcw miles. Pete Penseyres, an electrical engineer, won the race and made a detailed accounting of his winning effort, which he described as one-third physical, one-third mental, and one-third crew. In a total of 229 hours 13 minutes, he spent only 23 hours 5 seconds off the bike:[32]

When Jonathan Boyer won the race in 1985, he showed how it might compare to the European pro circuit and the Tour de France. His successful tactic was to get a bit more sleep per night and rely on his world-class speed to make time. A common experience among RAAM riders is having hallucinations, and Boyer described one of an old woman standing

RAAM TIME

Cycling	206:12:55
Sleep	17:57:30
Bathroom	2:06:15
Rest	1:33:30
Changing Clothes	57:10
Bike Maintenance/Flats	22:25
Navigation Problems	4:15
Total	229:13:00

along the road clutching a handbag that held something he needed. That year was a high point of public attention for the race, as the NBC-TV network coverage of the race won an Emmy Award, and the video was featured on trans-continental airline flights.

Susan Notorangelo, who married Lon Haldeman, is a two-time winner in the women's division. By 1991, she had crossed the U.S. seven times on bike. Casey Patterson is a mother of three who won the 1987 RAAM at the age of 43. She started cycling in 1981, when her son Kyle Sharp built her a mountain bike, and she won her first race. Prizes and sponsorship for the race have varied from year to year, and the cost of each rider's support crew and equipment, including a mobile home and liquid food, can reach over $15,000 for the two-week journey. While Rob Kish set the current RAAM record in 1992 of 8 days 3 hours 11 minutes (averaging 14.9 mph) on a course from Irvine, California to Savannagh, Georgia, the cross country record was set by Michael Secrest in 1990, going from Huntington Beach, California to Atlantic City, New Jersey in 7 days 23 hours 16 minutes (averaging 16.2 mph).

IDITASPORT

Originally called Iditabike, this is a 210-mile endurance race held in association with the Iditarod dogsled race and begun by Mountain Bikes of Alaska. The event takes place in February, when the days are short, with a route that goes from Knik Lake, to Big Su Station, along the Yenta river to Skwentna, and back via Rabbit Lake, passing through frozen muskeg swamps, scrub pine forests, and along snow covered rivers in Alaska. The riders must carry survival equipment, including a sleeping bag, signal flares, a whistle, food, a tent or bivy sac, and a stove with fuel.

The first two years, 1988 and 1989, were won by Mike Kloser of Vail, Colorado, and an "Ass-Backwards" award was given for exceptional backcountry navigational skill. The race was cut short in 1990 when blizzard conditions had riders walking for most of their route, earning the race nicknames "Iditapush" and "Ididntbike." The winner, Dave Ford, used a specially designed "Icycle quad bike" with double-track wheels front and rear. The event was renamed Iditasport in 1991, and racers could choose to use cross-country skis, running shoes, snowshoes, or mountain bikes. Rocky Reifenstuhl finished first among cyclists (second to ski-skater Bob Baker) and his wife, Gail Koepf, won the women's division. Combined, they won fifteen ounces of pure gold. With warm weather in 1993, the course record of 15 hours 17 minutes was set on bike by John Stamstad of Ohio.

13 Recreations

"Cycling" by Frank Patterson, June 1920.

The bicycle is its own best argument. You just get a bike, try it, start going with the thing and using it as it suits you. It'll grow and it gets better and better and better.
　—Richard Ballantine, *Bicycle* (1991)

Fun and Discovery

People of all ages and physical abilities can find many ways to have good times on a bike. The world of recreational cycling offers a variety of activities that are fun, challenging, enlightening, and sometimes silly. Whether one prefers to ride alone, with family, friends, or in large groups, the things to do on a bicycle are almost limitless. There are bicycle rodeos for learning how to ride; nature trips, treasure hunts, and mystery map rides for discovering places; group touring rides for fresh air fun and meeting all kinds of people; eating and drinking tours for sensual plea-sure; bicycle demolition derbies for releasing frustrations; round-the-world tours for adventure and understanding; and various bicycle stunts for testing the limits of human-powered ingenuity.

　Cycling is among the most popular physical activities in the U.S. In 1976, an A.C. Nielsen poll found that bicycling was the second most pop-ular recreation, behind swimming and ahead of fishing, camping, and bowling. In 1987, the President's Commission on the American Outdoors placed bicycling fifth (46 percent of Americans do it), behind walking (84 percent), picnicking (76 percent), swimming (76 percent), and fishing (50 percent). The National Sporting Goods Association ranked sports partici-pation in 1992:[1]

DISCOVERY RIDES

Bike riding helps develop a person's sense of discovery. Children often lead the way in discovery, with playful stunts such as bike riding with no hands, blind-folded, or while flying kites. Many cyclists are drawn to dis-cover every street, path, alley, trail, abandoned railroad, bridge, tunnel, and highway in their area. Some cyclists ride as far as they can go, keep-ing records of mileage, making their own maps, and reporting all potholes and road hazards to the authorities. Others like to circle the perimeter of towns, counties, states, countries, and continents.

　A bike allows people to discover many beautiful places to play, picnic, swim, fish, and hunt. Some cyclists use a nature field guide to discover the plants, birds, animals, and insects in different regions. Cyclists can rediscover the world by studying old pictures and maps, and following the path of historic journeys. Bike riders bring sketchbooks, cameras, and recorders to capture their surroundings, making stories, movies, or jour-nals.

　Discoveries are found in bicycle shopping, as cyclists browse in farm-ers' markets, yard sales, antique dealers, book stores, and bicycle shops. In bicycle partying, cyclists discover food and drink, pedaling from café to restaurant, and pub to club. At bike rallies, cyclists discover the unified power and diversity of one another, often dressing in costumes, carrying

SPORTS PARTICIPATION

ACTIVITY	PARTICIPANTS
1. Exercise walking	67.8
2. Swimming	63.1
3. Bicycling	54.6
4. Fishing	47.6
5. Camping	47.3
6. Bowling	42.5
7. Weight lifting	39.4
8. Billiards	29.3
9. Basketball	28.2
10. Aerobic exercise	27.8
11. Golf	24.0
12. Motor Boating	22.3
13. Volleyball	22.1
14. Running, Jogging	21.9
15. Hiking	21.6
16. Softball	19.2
17. Darts	18.8
18. Hunting w/firearms	17.8
19. Tennis	17.3
20. Roller Skating	16.8
21. Baseball	15.1
22. Football	13.5
23. Target Shooting	12.3
24. Calisthenics	11.5
25. Alpine Skiing	10.8

[Participants in millions; 19.2 million people belonged to health clubs; In-line skating and cross-country skiing, about 10 million.]

signs, and making chants.

In cycling treasure hunts, each participant is given a list of things to search for during the course of the ride. These things may be discovered or retrieved depending on the imagination or humor of the organizer. Some people look for natural formations, historical places, or architectural landmarks, others find plants and flowers for study, or metal and glass for recycling. A traditional variation of the treasure hunt theme is to give the riders a set of clues with which to find a buried treasure.

Mystery map rides are a good way to develop a cyclist's skills in map reading, orienteering, and geography. Riders set out alone or in teams, without a map, but instead with separate sets of clues giving directions for meeting places. When everyone meets they can compare their adventures. A variation is to give the riders outline maps which show natural topographic features without the roads, borders, or man-made landmarks.

Question and answer rides emphasize observation instead of direction finding. Riders may start in groups with a common set of questions about landmarks to be passed en-route (i.e., origins of street names). The ride leader may be the only one who knows the route and the answers. The other riders try to fill in the answers, though the shrewder riders mark their answers some distance from the observation point, so as not to draw attention to their discovery. At the end everyone gets to compare their answers. The cycle paper chase is another kind of discovery ride, in which "hares" leave scraps of paper or markers on the trail for "hounds" to follow.

Youngsters can learn the art of cycling at bicycle rodeos. Photo courtesy of Errol Toran, Transportation Alternatives.

Bicycle Rodeos

Bicycle rodeos have nothing to do with roping cattle, but they do involve "steering" and riding skills. They are a way of teaching cycling to children through an assortment of bicycle maintenance tips, road safety lessons, obstacle courses, and competitive trials. Bike rodeos are usually organized by local clubs and schools, and held in empty parking lots or closed streets, where there is little traffic. Some rodeos attract thousands of kids and the organizers must be prepared with enough volunteers, traffic cones, signs, props, score sheets, megaphones, T-shirts, refreshments, portable toilets, and first-aid supplies. There is usually a celebrity Master of Ceremonies, a police officer or city official for licensing bicycles, an informational display, plus films, videos, or some form of additional entertainment.

Most bicycle rodeo programs offer courses for beginners and intermediate level bike riders. Along the course there are as many as ten different "stations" which the riders must pass through in a specific amount of time. Each rider gets a card with his or her name and score, and each station offers a certain amount of points which add up to a total score. Sometimes prizes are awarded for top scorers in categories by age or experience. The biggest obstacle for rodeo organizers, besides keeping up with enthusiastic children, is in creating a learning experience instead of a competitive event or a course in "follow the leader." The following Rodeo Stations are adapted from *The AAA Skills Test and Bicycle Rodeo Guide* by John Williams and Dan Burden:[2]

Parents' Orientation Teaches parents what they need to know to teach cycling skills to their children, and how to be better drivers themselves.

Bike Shop Teaches kids the basics of bicycle fitting and maintenance.

Seeing and Being Seen Teaches kids what to watch out for and where they're going.

Chaos Corners Teaches kids to handle their bikes among other riders within an enclosed area.

Demon Driveway Teaches kids how to avoid the biggest cause of accidents by looking out for traffic before riding into the street from hidden driveways.

Crazy Crossroads Teaches kids to stop at stop signs and street crossings.

Who's There??? Teaches kids to look around and behind themselves while maintaining a straight line.

Dodge-em Drive—Thread the Needle Teaches kids how to deal with an assortment of roadway obstacles and hazards such as rocks, potholes, slippery streets, parallel gratings, opening car doors, and jaywalkers.

Panic Stop Teaches kids how to handle their brakes in quick-stop situations.

Hazard Quiz Teaches kids to think about traffic safety with the cartoon, "Find the Twelve Hazards."

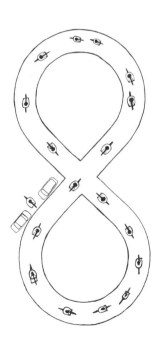

KLUNKING

Something about cycling inspires some riders to trash their bikes. For whatever reasons—to test a bike's durability, to strive for the brink of control and disaster, or just to see how much crazy fun can be achieved on a bike—there is a powerful desire for some cyclists, usually young males, to aim for abuse rather than avoid it. Given various names, such as "klunking," "bike fights," "knockabout," "bumper bike," "derby," "gonzo," "war bikes," and "bike tossing," these activities are executed with all kinds of second-hand bicycles, including balloon-tire cruisers, BMX, mountain bikes, and, especially, department store lemons. While klunking looks like a destructive, wasteful, two-wheeled demolition derby, there is a certain benefit since riders learn better bike handling skills by practicing to survive various ways of crashing.

A typical klunking derby includes the exciting figure-eight formation, where the riders follow each other around the loops with increasing speed. When the riders meet at the intersection, or "hot box," they may try to dodge the others or go for the "the kill," resulting in a quick sprint or a broadside crash. The knockabout exercise involves riders trying to topple each other while doing track stands, usually with their feet clipped to the pedals. When someone falls, his or her bike becomes open game for everyone else to pounce upon. The art of klunking is to have a few good crashes without totally crippling the riders and bikes. One exception (for the bike) is the bike toss, or bike stacking, which is often the grand finale for most big klunker gatherings.

At the annual "International Green Mountain Bike Toss" held in Vermont, the riders get pleasure from thrashing, flogging, and torching the kind of bike they love to hate, the department store ten-speed. Described as "cyclo-sadism," the object is to throw the bike the farthest, with points awarded for parts lost on impact, as well as the speed, originality, and artistry of the toss. In the 1985 Bike Toss, a spring-loaded catapult was used by the Fat City Cycles crew, capable of lobbing a bike 60 feet and slam-dunking it five inches into the earth, almost enough for a proper burial.

The rules for the Vermont bike toss require that the bike be reasonably functional, weighing over 32 pounds, with no more than two components made of aluminum alloy. Rusted vise-grips and dull screwdrivers are the only tools permitted, and wearing a helmet is reason for disqualification. The winner gets his or her name on the perpetual trophy, second place receives a Wald 17th anniversary gruppo (a set of cheap components), third place gets one department store bike, and fourth place gets two.[3]

Being There

"Untitled" by Peter Cummings:

The dry gray ribbon road unrolls
beneath insistent wind.
I'm working hard to cut it clean.
No thoughts on my mind.

There is no goal I aim to reach,
no purpose in the ride.
The motion makes the world again
from the circle and the line.

Whirling Dervish ecstasy uncoils
like the opening of a rose.
It wakes to dance to the steady beat
of dragonfire sighs.

I think I've drunk the liquid gold,
the change is deep and clear.
The transmutation of the soul
by the alchemy of air.

On a bicycle your destination is where you are. Cycling brings an expanded sense of *place* while traveling through *space*. Through the powerful experience of the journey, cycling opens up the body and mind to the surrounding landscape, the elements of nature, and the whole feeling of being there.

Unlike passengers in cars, trains, buses, or planes, which are enclosed and separated from their environment, cyclists are better able to see, hear, smell, feel, and know the world around them. Moving at a variety of speeds with the most efficient means of mobility, cyclists can rush past the landscape or stop to smell the flowers. Feeling the thrill of balancing the body on two wheels brings the sense of flight through air and space, and being involved with place brings the sense of passion for the landscape and its adventures.

TOPOPHILIA

Josh Lehman describes the enhanced awareness of place, space, and landscape geography in an essay called "From Space to Place: Discovery by Bicycle" (*Bicycling*, January 1979). Lehman is a long-time cycling advocate; when he became Bicycle-Pedestrian Program Manager at the U.S. Department of Transportation in 1989, he was one of the few people in the Federal system (of some 100,000 DOT officials) working exclusively for cycling at the time. In his essay, Lehman speaks of "the romance of the road," the "love of the land," and "topophilia: the affective bond between people and place or setting. Such love is born of bicycling." He describes how "feeling the thrill of bodily exertion and the simultaneous thrill of involvement with the world, a strong sense of place is readily developed. Though mere words cannot accurately describe the parallel sensations of moving and being in place, many bicycling writers have summarized the spirit.... Being a bicyclist and being a geographer are so often the same. Bicycling allows more than simply being better attuned to the surroundings." In *Fahrrad und Radfahrer* (1890), Wilhelm Wolf wrote "How greatly does cycling ennoble one's spirit, heart and frame of mind! When the cyclist roams freely on his steely steed in the godly world of Nature, his heart rises and he admires the splendor of Creation." Many cyclists wonder: "Without wet and windy weather will we wither?"

Many people have described cycling's Golden Age, when personal travel and tourism became popular. Maurice de Vlaminck (1876–1958) was a professional cyclist in the late 1890s before he became a landscape painter, one of the colorful, expressive Fauves. His favorite subject was *The Road*, and he paints a picture of early cycletouring in his memoirs of 1938, *Tournant Dangereux* (Dangerous Corner):

> For me, the discovery of the outside world dates from my acquisition of a bicycle. I spent whole days on the high-road. I tasted dust; rain poured down on me; I struggled against the wind. With my cycle I was able to visit places never dreamed of. The horse was dethroned, carriages despised. One could lunch in taverns hitherto unknown, and ride along forest paths and up little tracks.
>
> It is to the bicycle that I owe my first love of the open air, space and liberty. Thanks to my bicycle I saw for the first time the whole of the valley of the Seine from Chatou to Havre, Mantes, Bonnieres, Rouen, Duclair and Tancarville. All this countryside was calm and peaceful. Tourism did not yet exist; it was being born.
>
> The strongest emotions I have experienced were a result of those days, spent on the high roads or on the hill tops whence I could see down into the valleys on to the roofs of houses which I felt I could reach out and touch with my hand.

In *Bicycling for Ladies* (1896), Maria Ward wrote that "The alertness and quickness of perception that bicycling cultivates seems marvelous. A road, previously accepted as ordinarily good, becomes full of pitfalls that the wary learn to avoid.... You are continually being called upon to judge and to determine points that before have not needed your consideration, and consequently you become alert, active, quick-sighted and keenly alive." Mark Twain offered a similar message in his essay "Taming the Bicycle" (1886): "I had been familiar with that street for years, and had supposed it was dead level: but it was not, as the bicycle now informed me to my surprise. The bicycle, in the hands of a novice, is as alert and acute as a spirit-level in the detecting of delicate and vanishing shades of

Maurice de Vlaminck.

difference in these matters. It notices a rise where your untrained eye would not observe that one existed; it will notice any decline which water will run down."[4]

Such a place is found on a large scale near Lone Pine, California, at the foot of Mt. Whitney. The landscape appears to be flat, but it lies on a huge tilted plane of about 80 miles between Death Valley, the lowest point on the North American continent at 292 feet below sea level, and the highest point on Mt. Whitney at 14,300 feet. As with a headwind, cycling there seems a bit difficult in one direction and very easy going the opposite way.

Circulations of heavenly bodies that make day and night, and wind and weather, provide special effects for cycling. Some cyclists like to ride toward the sun as it rises in the East, making a circuitous route when the sun is at its zenith to return towards the sun as it sets in the West. Cyclists touring the globe can go in north-south directions to chase the summer, or temperate climes. Going east to west, they cross time zones to make the day longer. According to meteorologists, as the sun heats the earth the wind often changes direction by the early afternoon and settles to a calm by evening as it cools. In congested areas, pollution levels rise during the afternoon and reach a peak around evening rush hour. The evening is special because it is often quiet and balmy in summer. Night turns the air into a soft cushion, darkness is perceived as a blur of time and space.

-BIKECENTENNIAL

Touring Ways

Tourism is considered the world's largest business, with some 420 million global travelers, and cycletouring is a global activity with millions of riders joining thousands of local and internationally organized bike rides and group tours around the world. Most large cities and many small towns have cycling clubs with weekly and annual bike rides. Hundreds of travel groups lead bicycle tours over most regions of the globe for pleasure, culture, cuisine, and adventure, and there are dozens of classic challenge rides and competitive tours held on traditional cycling routes in Europe, North America, and Australia. The International Youth Hostel Federation (IYHF) is the world's largest shelter provider for cycletourists with over 3,500 hostels in some 60 countries, many located in the most scenic regions.[5]

Cycling vacations have seen rapid growth in the U.S., where bike tour operators' revenues were estimated at 30 to 60 million dollars in 1992. Backroads Bicycle Tours of Berkeley, California, began in 1979, and by 1994 they had sold about $15 million in fully-supported tours, providing food, lodging, and specially-equipped sag wagons. Many groups organize bike-a-thons and century rides that raise funds for causes and charities by counting miles and dollars. Others offer "hike, bike, and paddle" sports, or kinetic sculpture races with creative amphibious human-powered vehicles. Individuals have used the bike for adventuresome trekking, especially in wilderness survival situations, with sail-bike desert crossings and

bike-mountaineering feats. The 1990s have seen increased awareness of the ecological and cultural consequences of cycletouring, as widespread automobile and jet travel contributes to pollution, resort hotels plunder local resources, and insensitive tourists get serviced by local people.

America's biggest cycletouring resource is the Adventure Cycling Association, formerly called Bikecentennial, a non-profit service organization founded in 1973 by Greg and June Siple in the bicycle-friendly town of Missoula, Montana. 1976 was the inaugural year of the 4,235-mile TransAmerica Bicycle Trail, which Bikecentennial had developed and mapped. That year, some 2,000 cyclists completed the journey through America's heartland while another 4,000 cyclists rode smaller portions. Growing with the bike boom, Bikecentennial developed The National Bicycle Trails Network, with 42 maps covering 17,000 miles of bicycle routes in 33 states and Canada. They organize tours and publish maps and touring directories, such as *The Cyclists' Yellow Pages*.

Touring is the subject of the most books about cycling. In 1990, there were some 400 bicycle route maps and tour guide books covering North America in print. For the past century, there has been a steady outpouring of cycletouring adventure stories. Maps for cycling come in various forms, including fold-up pocket maps made of weatherproof paper, urban planning charts, and strip-map books, in which a specific route is closely marked with turn points, signs, distances, topography, landmarks, and facilities for food and shelter. The scales of maps suitable for cycling range from close-up (1:50,000) walking-sized maps showing structures and geologic details, to the cross-country (1:250,000) highway route maps, which tend to be more auto-oriented.

SELECTED LIST OF CYCLETOURING MAPS

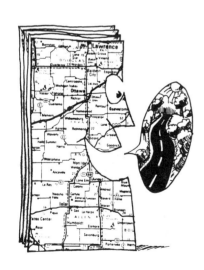

Australia: Bicycle Institute of New South Wales.
Europe: Michelin Route Cartes, 1:200,000 (1 cm = 2 km).
Belgium: Geocart Series, 1:100,000 (1 cm = 1 km).
Denmark: Dansk Cyclist Forbund (DCF) Cykelferiekortet 1:510,000 (1 cm = 5.1 km); DCF Route Series, 1:100,000 (1 cm = 1 km).
England: Ordnance Survey Routemaster Series, 1:250,000 (1 in = 4 mi); Ordnance Survey Landranger Series, 1:50,000 (1 in = 4 mi); London Cycling Campaign Cycle Route Maps, 1:21,477 (3 in = 1 mi).
France: IGN Green Series, 1:100,000 (1 cm = 1 km); Fédération Français de Cycletourisme.
Germany: Kummerly + Frey Series, 1:250,000 (1 in = 4 mi).
Ireland: Ordnance Survey Series, 1:126,720 (1 in = 2 mi).
Italy: Touring Club Italiano Series, 1:200,000 (1 cm = 2 km).
Netherlands: Royal Dutch Touring Club Series (ANWB), 1:100,000 (1 cm = 1 km).
United States: U.S. Geologic Survey 7.5-minute Topographic Series, 1:24,000 (1 in = 2,000 ft); Bikecentennial National Bicycle Trails Network, 1:250,000 (1 in = 4 mi).

GROUP RIDES

For those who like to express their cycling passion in large groups, there is the Tour de L'Île in Montreal, the world's largest annual single-day urban bike ride. Some 40,000 cyclists fill the streets along a 68 kilometer (45 mile) route that departs and arrives at the foot of Mont Royal on the Avenue du Parc. The ride has become an institution and celebration that goes on rain or shine. Writing in *The Montreal Gazette* (1993), James Mennie described the biggest challenge of the ride:

> It is a test of strength and endurance, of the ability to focus the mind on a single objective. Around you are hundreds of cyclists, some owning ultralight, state-of-the-art examples of cycling technology. Others ride heavyweight, rusting, mud-splattered tangles of steel and chrome that have been in the family for years. But it makes no difference what kind of bike you've brought because in the Tour de L'Île, everyone is equal. If you have what it takes to hold on until the end of the line, you know that sooner or later the threshold that has been edging closer to you minute after mind-numbing minute will be passed. You know that sooner or later, you, too, will be able to use the portable toilet.[6]

Other big city rides include New York's Five-Borough Bike Ride with up to 23,000 cyclists going about 42 miles, the Rosarita–Ensenada on the California-Mexico border, the Sydney to Gong ride in Australia, the Tuesday evening mass rides in Rio de Janeiro, Brazil, and the London to Brighton classic in Britain.

In France, one of the most traditional cycletouring events is the Journée Velocio, named after Paul de Vivie, the pioneering cycletourist, derailleur inventor, and editor of *Le Cycliste* who took the name Velocio. Each July near Saint-Etienne, several thousand men, women, and children participate in the timed hill climb along Route 82, marked as the *Rue Paul de Vivie*. At the summit of the Col du Grand Bois, marked by Velocio's granite memorial, the organizers provide a picnic lunch of *charcuterie* and *vin*. The road has an altitude gain of 548 meters in thirteen kilometers (averaging 4.2 percent), and though the event is not considered a race, awards are given to the oldest riders. The ride was founded in 1922, with the expressed purpose of "Living a day in the fresh air, tasting the pure joy of an effort well done, and admiring the beauties of nature, far from the petty masquerades of humanity." Velocio himself rode his last Journée in 1929, making the climb in 1 hour 12 minutes at the age of 75. People remember him by chanting «*Viva Vivie.*»

Some rides specialize in sampling regional cuisine, such as the Hungry Peddlers in New York City and the wine country tours in California, France, and Italy. Veterans' parades are for riding and displaying antique bikes. And there are many events for insomniacs on wheels. In St. Louis, the largest annual nightime bicycle event is the Moonlight Ramble. It began in 1961, and each year several thousand cyclists ride under August's full moon, the Grain Moon. In 1989, the ride coincided with a

LE TOUR DE L'ÎLE DE MONTRÉAL

Paul de Vivie, known as Velocio.

Oksana Yonan (above), and her heart-shaped tour of Ukraine (right).

JOURNEY OF THE HEART 1991

New York City's Five-borough bike tour, 1986. Photo courtesy American Youth Hostels.

lunar eclipse. Other midnight rides include the Death Valley by Moonlight in California, and the Hoosier Ultra Marathon Overnight Ride in Indiana (HUMOR).

Cross-state tours are a popular recreation in the U.S. Most states have organized multi-day camping rides, which have become known by their curious acronyms. These include the AFBRAAM (Annual Fit-Fest Bike Ride Across America), BAMMI (Bicycle Across the Magnificent Miles of Illinois), BAI (Bike Across Illinois), BAK (Biking Across Kansas), BRAT (Bicycle Ride Across Tennessee), BRAG (Bicycle Race Across Georgia), GBAAWR (Great Annual Bicycle Adventure Along the Wisconsin River), PAC (Pedal Across the Continent), PALM (Pedal Across Lower Michigan), RAIN (Ride Across Indiana), SAAGBRAW (Sentinel Active Americans Great Bike Ride Across Wisconsin), STP (Seattle to Portland), TOBRAW (The Other Bike Ride Across Wisconsin), TOGIR (The Other Great Iowa Ride), TOSRV (Tour of the Scioto River Valley), TRAI (Tandem Ride Across Iowa), TRANE (The Ride Around New England), TRIRI (The Ride In Rural Indiana), and the 200—100 (200 miles on Route 100 across Vermont from Canada to Massachusetts).

RAGBRAI, *Des Moines Register*'s Annual Great Bicycle Ride Across Iowa was begun in 1973 by friends of newspaper columnists Donald Kaul and John Karras, and by 1980 there were over 8,000 riders. The group dynamic of this ride is to see and be seen. Riders dress up in club jerseys, personalized T-shirts, and even costumes. A group called Team EATS claimed they could always take seconds at the feed stops, and a rider carried a warning sign: "This cyclist chews tobacco." Glenn Ingram, who rode five RAGBRAI tours into his 80s, until he died of brain cancer, wore custom T-shirts each year, saying: "I'm 79 and doing fine," "Just turned 80 and still with the same sweet lady," and "Just take care of your body, you only have one."

Bike-a-thons are a popular way of raising funds for a variety of charities and causes. Bike-a-thons in the U.S. had an estimated gross income of almost $2 billion in 1990. The TransAmerica Bicycle Trek is one of the largest coast-to-coast fund-raising bike rides in the U.S. Organized by the American Lung Association, it travels 3,357 miles from Seattle to Atlantic City, and raises about $1.5 million per year. In San Francisco, the gay and lesbian club Different Spokes has promoted the Aids Bike-A-Thon, raising some $2 million since 1985. To document the health effects of children five years after the Chernobyl nuclear explosion in 1986, Oksana Yonan, from Minneapolis, cycled in a heart-shaped 1,600-mile route through the radiation-scarred Ukraine. The 46-year-old artist called her mission the "Journey of the Heart."

COMPETITIVE TOURING

One of the oldest and biggest endurance rides is the Paris-Brest-Paris randonnée, known as "PBP," which celebrated its 100th anniversary in 1991. The ride began as a race held every decade, and since 1951 it was changed into a randonneur event held every four years. It is called a

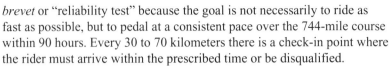

brevet or "reliability test" because the goal is not necessarily to ride as fast as possible, but to pedal at a consistent pace over the 744-mile course within 90 hours. Every 30 to 70 kilometers there is a check-in point where the rider must arrive within the prescribed time or be disqualified.

Among the hardest one-day rides are those with a lot of mountain climbing. The Tour of the California Alps, formerly known as the Markleeville Deathride, is a 145-mile journey over five mountain passes, including Ebbetts Pass (8,730 ft), Carson Pass, (8,573 ft), Luther Pass (7,740 ft), and twice over Monitor Pass (8,314 ft), totaling 15,000 feet of climbing. Other rides with 15,000 feet of climbing include the Terrible Two (200 miles), Climb to Kaiser (160 miles), and the Sherman Pass Challenge (155 miles). While the century (100 miles) is a challenge for most people to ride in a day, and a double century (200 miles) stretches the limit for many experienced cyclists, the triple century (300 miles) marks the threshold of the ultra-marathon 24-hour cyclist. California has the most long rides, with the Bay Area Triple, the Los Angeles Wheelmen Triple and Quad, the Ventura to Vegas (300 miles), and the 1,000-kilometer Wandervogel ride.

Mountain biking has several challenging rides with particularly rugged conditions. The Resurrection, known as the "Rez," is a 40-mile mountain bike single-track trail ride over 3,000-foot Resurection Pass on Alaska's Kenai Peninsula, from Hope to Cooper Landing, promoted by Mountain Bikers of Alaska. The Fort McChip Muffaloose Trail Randonneur, first held in 1989, is a 126-mile ride in northern Alberta. It is held in February when the temperature drops below zero and darkness reigns for eighteen hours of the day. Much of the route is on "ice roads" from Fort McMurray to Fort Chipewyan. In Europe, Africa, and Australia, the tougher mountain bike events are called Raids, or "Extreme, Far-Flung Off-Road Adventures." These include the Corsica Bike in France, an orienteering race organized by StarBike; the Raid Atlantique–Mediterannée; the GrandRaid Cristalp, the world's longest non-stop MTB race from Verbier to Grimentz; the Velo Vert Trophy, with the destination revealed at the start; the MadaRaid in Madagascar, which includes a rickshaw race; the Safari Sportif du Kenya; the Dynasties Rally in Egypt; and the TransAustralia five-day, 250-kilometer ride.

TRAIL RIDING

The popularity of mountain biking has brought many cyclists off roads and into the wilderness where trails offer serene, scenic, and challenging terrain. The bicycle's expansion into natural areas is an inevitable development as mixed-traffic roads have become congested and dangerous. Trekking into the wildnerness has brought many disputes between the rights of people on foot and on horse, and mechanical vehicles. In this realm, the bicycle is seen as a threat by causing accidents, land erosion, and congestion.

The definition of wilderness varies widely as people think the earth should be cultivated for health, enjoyed for recreation, exploited for profit, or closed forever. The Wilderness Act of 1964 created a "wilderness"

designation for protecting specific federal lands, and among its provisions is the rule that "There shall be no use of motor vehicles, motorized equipment or motorboats, no other form of mechanical transport," defined in Federal regulations as "any contrivance propelled by a non-living power source." With the growth of mountain biking, the U.S. Forest Service redefined mechanical transport in 1984 to prohibit bicycles in wilderness areas, and the following year the Sierra Club eliminated the distinction between bicycles and motor vehicles, claiming that the "operation of off-road vehicles is presumed to be detrimental to land resources and human safety."[7]

As more and more land authorities banned cyclists from singletrack trails, defined as five feet wide or less, while allowing cyclists on less-than-scenic unpaved fire roads made for off-road motor vehicles, more and more off-road cycling groups formed in the U.S. to secure access to public lands, to develop bike-friendly trails, and to oversee their maintenance and proper management. In 1983, the National Off-Road Bicycle Association (NORBA) began to organize mountain bike racing, and several off-road advocacy groups had formed, such as the Concerned Off-Road Bicyclists Association (CORBA) in 1987, and the International Mountain Bicycling Association (IMBA) in 1988. The IMBA has over 1,000 individual members and 300 affiliated clubs, shops, and companies, while promoting their "Share the Trail" campaign. The Rails-to-Trails Conservancy has helped to convert old railroad routes into trails for cyclists, walkers, runners, hikers, equestrians, and skiers. When it began in 1986, there were about 75 trails in the U.S. totaling some 750 miles. By 1992, there were some 500 trails going 4,700 miles, and the idea of rails-with-trails is growing, with sixteen trails built beside active rail lines in eleven states.

Northern California—the birthplace of mountain biking—has had intense battles over public rights of way, especially with so-called "outlaw" groups such as the Berkeley Trailers' Union (BTU). Near legendary Mount Tamalpais, on land owned by the Marin Municipal Watershed District, mountain bikers created the New Paradigm Trail for low-impact riding. But before a well-publicized eradication project began on the illegal trail, it was reported that people had ambushed it with traps consisting of precariously balanced trees and four-foot deep trenches.[8] In another case, the Bicycle Trails Council of Marin sued the National Park Service (NPS) because of bike bans in the Golden Gate National Recreational Area, where cyclists accounted for 80 percent of trail users. The NPS Trail Plan sought to take away about half of the available paths, and break up existing loops. According to Trails Council attorney Terry Houlihan, the NPS "did not evaluate the recreational needs of the park users in any balanced or quantitative way in making decisions." In the San Francisco region, a greenway system called the Bay Area Ridge Trail, to be completed by 1998, will connect 75 parks and over 400 miles of trails for people on foot, bike or horse. In eleven western states, the Bureau of Land Management manages some 270 million acres and 65,000 roads or trails.

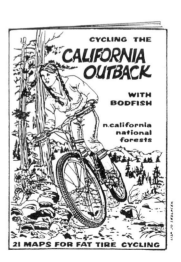

One of its creations is the 128-mile Kokopelli Trail from Grand Junction, Colorado, to Moab, Utah, where the Slickrock Trail was used by over 100,000 mountain bikers in 1994. The Great Divide Mountain Bike Route, planned by the Adventure Cycling Association, is an off-road trail going 3,000 miles from Canada to Mexico.

WORLD CYCLISTS

For many adventurers, the ultimate trip is the round-the-world bike tour. Since the first known round-the-world bicycle tour in the 1880s by Thomas Stevens, thousands of cyclists have circled the globe or cycled large parts of it. The Round-the-World Cyclists Registry keeps track of world cyclists, but some never publicize their exploits, or make it back alive. For some people, the journey around the planet is a once in a life-time accomplishment, for others, it is a part of daily life on the road and just another adventure.

Most people travel west to east. The fully rideable distance near the equator is about 18,000 to 22,000 miles, not much more than the north-south roads from the Arctic Circle to Tierra del Fuego. Many parts of the globe have been off-limits for travel because of warfare or difficult terrain. As travel grows and political boundaries change, new lands have been opened and explored, such as in the Eurasian and African continents. Dick Jensen, of the Perestroika by Bike tour, says: "Nowadays it is possible to cross deserts and climb mountains by bike.... We will not be stopped by an imaginary line in the landscape." While exploring the West African Coast, Adventure Cycling tour leader T'ai Roulston wrote a cycletourists' questionnaire:

> Do you like being interrogated, searched, and asked for bribes by men in uniform? Do you like waking up with 50 children staring in your tent? Would you like to learn a new language every day? Do you like really hot weather and sandstorms? Do you like the taste of iodine in your water? Do you like breeding insects in your skin?[9]

Among the nomads of trans-world cycletouring, there is Albert Leblanc, from Maria, Quebec, who cycled round the world about three times. Along the way he attended the Olympic Games in Tokyo (1964), Mexico City (1968), Munich (1972), and Montreal (1976). Fastened to his handlebars was a hollow globe for collecting donations. His motto, painted on a plywood sign in the main triangle of his frame, read, *Dios, Madre, Libertad* (God, Mother, Liberty).

Dan Buettner, a world cyclist once described as one of America's "most determined cyclists," led a team of four on a 15,536-mile ride from Alaska to Argentina in 1987, earning a place in the *Guinness Book of World Records*. In 1990, his 12,888-mile, 239-day round-the-world Sovietrek Cycling Expedition crossed Siberia, and four riders used 73 tires. In 1993, he completed the 11,877-mile, 272-day Trans-Africa ride, crossing the Sahara desert, going through fifteen countries, 24 tires, 380 flats, eight robberies, and making some 4.7 million pedal revolutions. In the Iteri Forest, Dan waved at a family of baboons crossing the road and the largest one waved back.

Claude and Françoise Herve left the easy security of their home, car, and careers in Lyons, France, to share a globe-trotting adventure of fourteen years and almost 100,000 miles. "Above all we wanted to see with our own eyes what was happening in the world," they wrote. "To travel by bike is a humble, nonaggressive way to get close to people. It is a way of saying we are passing through with no thought of invasion or conquest, but with the simple will to share a part of the road with you."

On April 1, 1980, Claude, a 25-year-old orthopedist, and Françoise, a 21-year-old interior designer, headed to the North Cape of Norway through six countries, and proceeded southeast through Europe from Germany to Istanbul to Greece. They celebrated their first year on the road in Turkey, eating the testicles and eyes of sheep served by tribesmen, and pedaled south into Iraq and Kuwait. They headed to Kashmir, New Delhi, and Kathmandu, living a year in India, including several weeks at a leper's colony near Calcutta. From Singapore they rode through Malaysia and Thailand, where armed bandits tried to rob them (they escaped) and they worked for a year in a Cambodian refugee camp and hospital.

In July 1984, Claude and Françoise flew back to France for several months, and then resumed the hardest and most rewarding nine months of their journey, the 7,000 miles from Hong Kong to Tibet to Beijing to Shanghai. From old China to new Japan, they visited Korea, Taiwan, the Philippines, Brunei, Borneo, Indonesia, and Timor. Landing in Australia's desolate Northern Territory, their road speed increased. In Brisbane, they were met by a large group of cyclists. After eight years on the road, they decided to become three.

Françoise cycled until her seventh month of pregnancy. When Manon was born in New Zealand on September 6, 1988, she had already ridden along for 6,000 miles. The Herves moved their nest to Tahiti, and eventually arrived in Los Angeles in March 1989, heading for Quebec, New York, and Florida, with Manon in a rear-facing Bugger trailer (donated by Cannondale) pulled by Françoise and followed by Claude with a "Baby On Board" sign. By 1991, they were in Central America, having survived mountains, dirt roads, and "anti-gringo" sentiment in Mexico. Reaching Rio de Janeiro in 1992, they settled there for awhile so Manon could go to school. When last heard of they were headed for Dakar, Senegal, and North Africa to that place called home.

The first attempt to circumnavigate the world using pedal power began on July 12, 1994, at the Greenwich Meridian Line (zero degrees longitude) in England. In a project called Pedal for the Planet, Steve Smith and Jason Lewis, both from London, crossed the English Channel in a pedal-powered boat. They then bicycled through France and Spain, before departing from Lagos, Portugal, on October 13, for a pedal-powered crossing of the Atlantic Ocean. Landing in Florida in early 1995, they planned to bike across North America to Alaska, to sail across the Bering Sea to Japan, and to bike across Asia and Europe, returning to zero latitude after three years.[10]

SELECTED LIST OF WORLD CYCLISTS

[Years of trip **Name of Cyclist** (birthdate-Nationality) Countries visited, mileage, type of bike, details, book. Source: Holland Peterson, *International Cycling Guide*, 1980.]

1884–1887 **Thomas Stevens** (1854-GBR) 13,000 miles, Columbia Expert high-wheeler, first world cyclist, *Around the World on a Bicycle* (1887-88).

1890–1893 **Thomas G. Allen Jr.** (1867-USA) and **William L. Sachtleben** (1867-USA) Europe, Asia, America, 15,000 miles, 6,634 by bike, Humber one-speed, *Across Asia on a Bicycle* (1894).

1892–1894 **Frank G. Lenz** (1867-USA) one-speed bike, disappeared in Turkey before completion.

1894 **Annie Londonberry** (nd-USA) one-speed bike.

1894–1898 **Mr. and Mrs. H. Darwin McIlrath** (nd-USA) one-speed bikes.

1894–1904 **William and Fannie Workman** (nd-USA) one-speed bikes.

1896–1899 **Sir John Foster Frazier, S.E. Lunn, F.H. Howe** (nd-GBR) Three continents, seventeen countries, 19,237 miles, Humber one-speed bikes, *Round the World on a Wheel* (1899).

1925–1927 **Kai Thorenfeldt** (1902-DAN) roadster bike, *Round the World on a Cycle* (1928).

1925–1930 **I.S.K. Soboleff** (nd-RUS) Bangkok to Singapore, one-speed bike, *Cossack at Large* (1960).

1930–1950 **Bernard Newman** (1897-GBR) sixty countries, three-speed bike, written over 100 books, *Speaking From Memory* (1960).

1935–1936 **Fred Birchmore** (nd-USA) forty countries, 25,000 miles by bike, 40,000 by boat, Rheinhardt one-speed 43-pound bike (in Smithsonian), *Around the World on a Bicycle* (1938).

1947–1948 **Jesse Hart Rosdail** (1914-USA) Australia, New Zealand, Africa, 46 countries, 11,626 miles by bike, 50 year-old German bike bought second-hand for $7, two-speed coaster-brake replaced by Sturmey-Archer three-speed hub, world's most travelled man, 219 countries, 1,626,605 total miles, *Biking Alone Around the World* (1973).

1949–1956 **Louise J. Sutherland** (1928-NZL) second-hand one-speed bike (£2-10s.) and trailer, first cyclist to follow Amazon from source to sea, *I Follow the Wind* (1960).

1959–1976 **Walter Stolle** (1926-GBR) 159 countries, 402,000 miles by bike, used eleven bikes, *The World Beneath My Bicycle Wheels* (1978).

1960–1964 **Keith Fitchett, Carl Boyer, Mark Follett** (nd-GBR) about 40,000 miles, bikes with trailers.

1960 **Heinz Stücke** (1942-GER) Sahara, three-speed bike.

1963–1977 **Ian Hibell** (1935-GBR) Alaska to Tierra del Fuego, North Cape, Norway to Cape of Good Hope via Sahara, about 100,000 miles, Grubb seven-speed bike, *Into Remote Places* (1984).

1964–1969 **Takafumi Ogasawara** (1944-JPN) René Herse folding tourist bike.

1966 1975 **Hans Drechsler** (1938-GER) 38,000 miles, ten-speed bike, 150 pounds baggage.

1968–1971 **Kunio Katsumura** (1948-JPN) shot and killed by bandits in Thailand after tour.

1968–1973 **Raguhbir Singh** (nd-IND) 108 countries, 93,000 miles, 410 flat tires.

1970–1975 **Wiegand Horst Lichtenfels** (1944-GER) 42 countries, 47,500 miles, 400-pound loaded bike.

1970–1976 **Cyril Proctor** (1905-GBR) three-times around, planning fourth at age 77.

1971 **Ray Reese** (1931-GBR) 13,325 miles by bike in 143 days, Raleigh ten-speed bike.

1971–1972 **Peter Ducker** (1934-GBR) 14,000 miles, American coast-to-coast record en-route, Raleigh Professional, *Sting in the Tail* (1973).

1971–1975 **Lloyd Sumner** (1944-USA) 28,478 miles by bike, Schwinn Super Sport ten-speed, *The Long Ride* (1978).

1971–1979 **Kojiro Hirayama** (1946-JPN) first totally deaf and dumb rider, 300-pound loaded bike.

1973–1977 **George Lindley** (nd-USA) 27 countries, 18,000 miles by bike, 21,000 by other means.

1974–1975 **John Rakowski** (1924-USA) 15,660 miles by bike, 1977–1978, cycled around perimeter of USA, Grade V Browning and Nishiki Competition ten-speed.

1974–1975 **Colin and Veronica Scargill** (nd-GBR) 18,020 miles by bike, Selbach tandem.

1974–1976 **John Hathaway** (1924-CAN) 50,600 miles by bike in 100 weeks, Raleigh Professional.

1974–1976 **Robert Morris** (1954-USA) 32,000 miles, fifteen-speed.

1974–1978 **Motomitsu Ikemoto** (1948-JPN) 24,975 miles, Shimano-equipped bike.

1975–1976 **Bob Ellis** (1946-USA), **Steve Ellis** (1955-USA), **Mark Boyar** (1957-USA), **Matt Rice** (1958-USA) Raleigh Super Course Mark II ten-speeds.

1975–1977 **Michael John Murphy** (1953-GBR) 47 countries, 23,000 miles.

1976 **Dr. William F. Marquardt** (1916-USA) Starting in Wichita, Kansas, intended to follow Thomas Steven's route, killed in traffic in Batavia, New York.

1976–1978 **Wally Watts** (1948-CAN) sixteen countries, 10,000 miles, unicycle.

1977–1979 **Ivar Tønnesen** (1956-DAN), **Mai-Britt Johansson** (1959-DAN) 20,265 miles by bike.

1977–1980 **Michael Manzo, Berthe Laforge** (nd-CAN) 30,000 miles.

1978–1980 **Larry and Barbara Savage** (nd-USA) 23,000 miles and 25 countries, Eisentraut and Follis bikes, three years after trip, Barbara died in a bicycle accident, *Miles From Nowhere* (1983).

1979–1981 **Carmine Militano** (1954-CAN), **Rick Nash** (1954-CAN) ten-speeds, Inuvic (Arctic) to Tierra del Fuego.

1981 **Nick Saunders** (1958-GBR) 16 countries, 13,500 miles by bike, crossed USA in 15 days, *The Great Bike Ride* (1986).

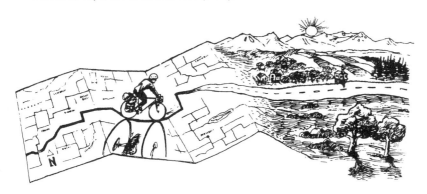

Trick Cycling

The bicycle inspires people to try any number of tricks and stunts. This kind of human-powered recreation balances the realms of play, sport, and theater. Often cited in *Ripley's Believe It Or Not* and the *Guinness Book of World Records*, these tricks encompass death-defying feats, ingenious technical skills, and extraordinary manifestations of human creativity.

The *Guinness Book of World Records* lists several categories for cycling, including largest, smallest, lightest, fastest, slowest, most riders, and most expensive. The world's largest unridable bike is found along a highway in Jiddah, Saudi Arabia. The smallest ridable bicycle has 0.76-inch diameter wheels. In France, twenty-six people rode a 662-pound bike designed by Pascal Esnol that was nearly 50 feet long and had 95 feet of chain. The most people able to ride a standard single-seat bike is nineteen. Brett Schockley rode a 50-foot high, 200-pound unicycle at the University of Minnesota. The world's highest cyclist was Mark Merrony of Britain, who achieved an altitude of 21,030 feet on the south summit of Mera Peak in Nepal.

The world speed record for rollers was set on December 6, 1987, by Jim Baker, an amateur sprinter, who pedaled 129.1 mph at a college basketball game in Tucson, Arizona. The previous record was held by David Lagrys, a British pro sprint champion. Baker used a double reduction 269-inch gear and the roller spun at 9,219 rpm. The slow cycling record is the extreme performance of *surplace*, the sprint racer's balancing act. In 1885, Herbert Owen of the Capitol Bicycle Club in Washington, D.C., balanced on a high-wheeler for 2 hours, 22 minutes. In 1965, 39-year-old Tsugunobo Mitsuishi of Tokyo set a slow cycling record by balancing motionless for 5 hours, 25 minutes. In 1983, Craig Strong of England popped a "wheelie" for 1 hour, 16 minutes, 54 seconds. To set a backward cycling record, Jean Le Greca of France rode 830 kilometers in 21 days averaging 16 kph. Robert Poggio climbed Mont Revard at Aix-les-Bains, rising 1,276 meters in 20 kilometers, in 1 hour 46 minutes 22 seconds, riding backwards without touching ground.

Bicycle eating is probably the craziest of all stunts. This performance suggests the ultimate embodiment of the cyclists' hungry search to become one with the bike. The most famous bicycle eater is the Frenchman Michel Lotito, known as Monsieur Mangetout (Mr. Eat-all). During a fifteen-day period between March 17 and April 2, 1977, he consumed an entire bicycle reduced to metal and rubber filings. He said the chain was tastiest, that "its coating of grease helped it slide down, more easily than, say, the tires."

The 1930s saw the first outbreak of unicycling stunts. Walter Nilsson, a Broadway star known for his unicycling performance in "Hellzapoppin," won a $10,000 wager by riding a high unicycle across the United States in 1934. The following year, the 75-year-old Harry Kramer was giving unicycling lessons at Estes Park in Colorado. Steven McPeak, the "King of Modern Unicycling," rode from Chicago to Las

Hans Rey, expert bike handler.
He got to the top without a foot
touching down.
Photo by Michael Segar.

Vegas on a high "giraffe" unicycle to set a world's record for riding a 32-foot tall unicycle. He married Connie Fullerton on a high wire. In the 1960s, Bill Jenack of the Unicycling Society of America taught a blind man to ride a unicycle, and the man gave "fancy riding performances." Japan has the most unicycling events of any country, with over 10,000 acrobatic and racing competitions held in 1990. The top speed for a unicyclist was set at 20 mph by Troy McKee in 1980, and the U.S. hour record of 15.88 miles (25 kph) was set by Floyd Beattie in 1986 at the Major Taylor Velodrome in Indianapolis.

Freestyle cycling is an off-shoot of BMX racing that has developed into a popular international exhibition sport. Events are held on flat, banked, and steeply ramped rinks, inside arenas, gymnasiums, and at

INTERNATIONAL
UNICYCLING
FEDERATION

freestyle velodromes. On the ramps, the riders gain momentum by riding up and down the slope and then launch themselves into the air, performing a variety of split-second flying maneuvers.

Freestyling has its own "rad" language. Riders are called "deck monkeys" and a "faceplant" is a head first fall. The tricks include: the Helicopter (rotating in flight); the Wind-Shield Wiper (swashing the rear wheel back and forth); the Half-Decade (a backwards rolling headstand); the Elephant Glide (sitting on the bars backwards while "squeaking" the front wheel with the back wheel off the ground); the Locomotive (a semi-standing backwards-infinity-roll wheelie while sitting on the end of the handlebars which are turned 90 degrees); the Trolley (a reverse peg-picker squeaker); the I-Hop (bouncing with the feet planted on the front tire); Hand Pedaling (with one foot on the rear wheel peg, one hand holds the front peg and the other the hand pedals); and the Backyard (riding on one wheel sitting against the handlebars while facing backwards). Ramp tricks include Cancan lookbacks, no-footed X-ups, no-footed one-handers, fakie X-ups, fakie no-footers, one-handed one-footer inverts, one-footed helicopters (an X-up, no-footed cancans), and 540s (a three-quarter rotation).

Cycle-Whirls are ingenious manifestations of cycling that could only have developed around the human-powered vehicle. They are miniature velodromes, less than 50 feet in circumference, that allow cyclists to ride at angles up to 70 degrees. One was supposedly built to be shouldered by a man. Loop-de-loop stunts are usually performed as part of circus acts, such as those by the daredevil named Diavolo and by Les Frères Ancillotti from France, lead by Ugo Ancillotti. More recently, they are part of BMX freestyle ramp tricks. A 60-foot high helical spiral, called the "Circle of Death," was exhibited by Dan Canary at Madison Square Garden in 1903.

The realm of bike jumping includes a variety of venues, including the jumps across chasms or over steep precipices into bodies of water, the free-fall leaps by sky-diving cyclists with parachutes, and the early competitions in human-powered flight. A song was written in 1902 about daredevil A.M. Schreyer, who rode his bicycle down a steep incline into a pool of water at Coney Island. The jumping-off point was 35 feet high and 78 feet away from the four-foot deep water. Raemond Gimmi of Switzerland parachuted at 15,000 feet over South Africa, with a freefall of about 70 seconds. He was equipped with separate chutes for himself and his bicycle. Another rider jumped off Venezuela's Angel Falls, the world's highest waterfall, with a leap of about 2,650 feet.

Freddy Wulf and Lars Bjoern, a pair of photo-journalists from Denmark, staged an underwater bicycle race in a swimming pool. They used 40-pound lead weights to keep from floating and the fastest time for 100 meters was 7 minutes 54 seconds.[11] At the 1991 Interbike Expo in Anaheim, California, Bill Evans of San Diego set a world record for underwater cycling by pedaling a stationary bike 31.5 miles in 5 hours 20 minutes inside a clear-plastic tank filled with 70-degree water. Deana Bodine of San Diego set a women's record by riding 6.5 miles in one hour.

Skydiving on a bike.
Photo by Heinz Schürch.

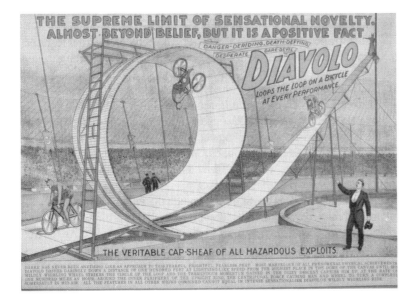

Top left, La Roue Infernale, Paris, 1910.
Photo by Harry C. Ellis, Stephen White
Gallery, Los Angeles.
Top right, Living Cycle Whirl, 1903.
Above, inside a cycle whirl from China,
1970. Left, poster for Diavolo's loop-
the-loop performance, 1904.

Circus Acts

THE WORLD'S LAST AND GREATEST WONDER
ZUILA, THE FEMALE BLONDIN

Bicycles, unicycles, and other kinds of cycling machines are familiar vehicles for performing clowns, tramps, high-wire artists, jugglers, acrobats, chimps, bears, and elephants. The circus is a global entertainment and circus cycling is a subculture, with an estimated one in five circus shows including a bicycle act, combining the realms of stunt cycling and performing arts. From the first balancing acts with swift-walkers and velocipedes of the nineteenth century, to the Chinese "bicycle ballet" at the 121st edition of the Ringling Brothers Barnum and Bailey Circus, circus cyclists can be found in a variety of show places. Throughout the year, at carnivals, fairs, and vacation resort areas, and especially during the peak summer months, there is almost always some kind of bicycle circus act going on nearby.

An improvised circus-style act was performed by the youthful Max and Charles Fleischer, the reknowned cartoonists who created *Betty Boop* and *Popeye the Sailor*. As schoolboys they used an adult-sized bicycle to amuse their neighbors in Brooklyn. One act had both boys riding the bike at the same time, climbing over, under, and around each other, while keeping the fixed-gear turning.[12]

A book called *Bicycle People* (1978) by Roland Geist describes many cycling circus performers. In the 1880s, the Stirk Family was billed as "The Original Trick and Fancy Bicyclists of America." Lead by Professor T. Stirk and Mlle. Flora Stirk, "the greatest child bicyclist in the world," they appeared before the crowned heads of Europe and Phineas Taylor Barnum (1810–1891), who formed "The Greatest Show on Earth" with James A. Bailey. Before the turn of the century, Barnum and Bailey featured several bicycle acts, including Les Frères Ancillotti, the "French Bicycle Experts" who performed daredevil loop-de-loops and juggling acts, and General Tom Thumb (Charles S. Stratton), who rode the world's smallest velocipede at that time. Buffalo Bill's Wild West Show featured the sharpshooting act of Annie Oakley astride her bicycle. Among the vaudeville style acts, there was Professor Bilbo's Olympic Mounted Bicycle Band which played at carnivals in New York.

The Ringling Brothers bought Barnum and Bailey in 1907, forming the Ringling Brothers Barnum and Bailey Combined Shows, and became the world's biggest circus, with cycling acts such as The Great Wallendas from Germany, the Kondovi Troupe from Bulgaria, and the King Charles Troupe from the Bronx, which performed a fast-paced basketball game on unicycles.

Other animated circus cycling acts include the Pallen Bears from Holland, which received top billing with the Sells-Floto circus in the 1920s, and the Marquis Chimps, an act developed by Gene Detroy from Manchester, England, who started with three chimps, Charlie, a ten-year-old female, Enoch, an eight-year-old male, and Candy, a two-year-old female. They came from Central Africa and cost over $1,000 each. Riding

bicycles and giraffe unicycles, they earned about $250,000 a year around 1970, proving that monkey business pays off.

While Charlie Chaplin, the original Tramp, never used a bike in his best-known performances, there is a definite genre that has evolved around the cycling tramp, seen in music halls, poster art, and motion pictures. These performers often start out as clowns, dressing in shabby, torn, or misfit clothes. They mount any kind of pedal-cycle imaginable, including high-wheelers, unicycles, multi-cycles, and especially bikes built to fall apart.

Joe Jackson Sr. and Joe Jackson Jr. carried on a family tradition as the "Cycling Tramps." Joe Jackson Sr. was born Joseph Franz Jiranek in Vienna in 1880, and began his career as a racing cyclist and bicycle polo player. He created a silent comedy act called the "bicycle break-away" and he performed artful stunts on a bike with detachable handlebars. Joe Jackson Jr. continued his father's pantomime in shows such as the Ice Capades. Another former amateur racer and tramp cyclist was Jack Natirboff, "The Bicycle Clown." He directed a "Bicycle Ballet" at the 1939 New York World's Fair and owned the Antique Bicycle Prop Service.

The high wire act is one of the highlights of the circus, and many high wire specialists have included the bicycle in this daring and sublime performance. High wire cycling acts began in the early nineteenth century, occasionally venturing outside the circus arena, with tight wires strung between buildings and natural chasms. The 160-foot canyon at Niagara Falls has been a popular site for cyclists since the famous Blondin crossed it on a velocipede. Frank Donahue, known as "Professor Arion," was a high wire cyclist from Indiana who crossed Niagara Falls safely, but fell to his death at Ridgewood Amusement Park on Long Island in 1897. The 75-foot high wire was charged with 500 volts of electricity and illuminated his costume and bicycle.

"The Great Wallendas," founded by Karl Wallenda with his wife Helen Kreis, had one of the most daring high wire acts known. Wallenda started as a trapeze catcher who developed his own high wire cycling act and eventually joined the Ringling Brothers Barnum and Bailey Combined Shows. His troupe included his children and grandchildren, as well as Luis Murillo, a high wire expert from Chile. One of their creations was the "human pyramid" in which Karl performed stunts while balancing on a beam supported by two high wire cyclists. He usually performed without a safety net, and high winds caused him to fall to his death in 1978 from a wire stretched between two hotels in Puerto Rico.

The culmination of many circus cycling acts, especially among family troupes, is to mount as many people as possible on one bicycle, known as the bicycle ballet. One of the largest families to perform this trick were the Six Frielanis, who appeared at Radio City Music Hall in 1962. Mr. Frielanis held three children and their spouses on his shoulders, while two hung out on both sides.

A beautiful kind of bicycle ballet has emerged from Asia with the cyclists making delicate, flowery formations, described as "the peacock spreading its tail feathers... reputed to be one of the world's miracles."[13] One of today's top circus cycling acts is performed by the Fujian Acrobatic Troupe from the People's Republic of China. Promoted as "Pedalist Perfection: Pedals Pumping, Paragons of Poise Perfectly Perform Paramount Pyramids, Boldly-Balancing on a Bicycle Built for Buoyant Bodies!" they traveled with the Ringling Brothers and Barnum & Bailey Circus and appeared in the 121st edition of the "Greatest Show on Earth" at Madison Square Garden. *The New York Times* reviewer David Richards described how the bicycle acts from China were a gentle respite in a circus that was looking more like "an orgy of exquisite torture."

Clearly, this is no place to evoke the higher values. And that, I think, is why the acrobats from the People's Republic of China register such a novelty. They are polite. Their costumes are prim and on the loose-fitting side. Some are decorated with cloth roses... They don't do bicycle tricks. They do a "bicycle ballet." One by one, then two by two, they climb on a bicycle circling the center ring, until the passenger count is fourteen. Never did a human pyramid appear so light, so delicate, almost like those exotic paper flowers that spring from clam shells, when you drop them in a glass of water. It's a lovely interlude, but it's definitely at odds with the rest of the show, which emphasizes the effort, not the ease, the dazzle, not the decorum.[14]

Bicycle Ballet by the Fujian Acrobatic Troupe, 1991, Ringling Bros. and Barnum & Bailey Circus.

Part Four

Bike Culture

14 Public Image

Victor Cycles poster, 1899.

The bicycle is the most civilized conveyance known to man. Other forms of transport grow daily more nightmarish. Only the bicycle remains pure in heart.
  —Iris Murdoch, *The Red and the Green* (1965)

The ungainly geometry and primitive mechanicals of the bicycle are an offense to the eye. The grimy and perspiring riders of the bicycle are an offense to the nose. And the very existence of the bicycle is an offense to reason and wisdom.
  —P.J. O'Rourke, *Car and Driver* (1984)

Pedaling Fashion

Bicycles have been a major influence on fashion, particularly in the popular development of sportswear that fits active bodies more comfortably. Bicycle history follows the trend towards less cumbersome clothing, which acknowledges the body as a fashion statement in itself. Because cycling is an activity that goes beyond sport into the realm of daily lifestyles, many popular fashions have been inspired by the distinctive forms and functions of cycling clothes.

The first major bicycle fashion for women was the revival of bloomers in the 1880s. These ankle-exposing baggy knickers were originally made in the 1850s by Amelia Jenks Bloomer of Homer, New York, an early activist of the women's movement. They inspired the following rhyme, from *The Wheelmen of 1883*:

Sing a song of Bloomers, out for a ride,
With four and twenty bad boys, running at her side,
While the maid was coasting, the boys began to sing,
"Get on to her shape, you know," and all that sort of thing.

Bloomers evolved into the rational dress worn by the "New Women" of the 1890s. Rationals were slender suits combining knickers, jodpurs, sports jacket, vest, high-collar shirt, and hat. They were revolutionary at the time, though formal and prudent compared to styles today. With the safety bicycle as new mode of mobility, women wanted healthier, less cumbersome clothes. Bicycles brought the demise of those "murderous," "soul-confining" bustles and corsets that "robbed whales of their ribs," pinched women into an hour-glass figure, constricted easy breathing and free movement, subjected women to fainting spells, and jeopardized both mother and child during pregnancy.[1] A commentator in *Puck* magazine of August 7, 1895, claimed that, "The bicycle makers accomplished more for dress reform in two years than the preachers of that cult accomplished since clothes began to be the fashion." In an exhibit of sportswear in 1986 at the Fashion Institute of Technology in New York City, which featured Geoffrey Beene's sequined rainbow jersey pajamas from 1976, Sally

The Rational.

Rational dress, 1890s.

Kirkland described the impact of cycling on fashion in "Sportswear For Everywhere:"

> It is possible that bicycling has had a greater impact on society than any other sport in America except for the automobile. This new and important independence was quickly reflected in bicycling dress. Before the turn of the century, inappropriate trailing skirts gave way to a rising hemline that exposed the calf. Experiments were made with the neglected bloomers of the 1850s and with flapping culottes. Sporty, mannish details prevailed.

Rationals were followed by the pedal pushers of the 1930s, the casual form-fitting pants cut around the knee. Bike shirts had a popular appeal in the 1970s with the colorful stripes, finish line checks, and functional pockets of traditional racing jerseys. In the 1980s, bike shorts became a mainstream fashion trend called "bike chic," and the athletic lycra look continues into the 1990s, even though the dress code for shoppers at Harrods department store in London now bans cycling shorts for men. Fashion reviews of the 1980s attest to this phenomenon:

> Call it cycling chic. Or two-wheel fashion. Or even pedal pants. But the re-emergence of bicycling for fun and exercise is bringing with it a new fashion category—bicycle shorts. In trendy Los Angeles, where casual wear is almost a given, individuals in spandex shorts can be spotted in malls, bars, restaurants and other non-athletic locales. Whether these people arrived on bikes is anyone's guess.
> —*Ad Age* (February 6, 1986)

> They take their cue from the messengers, those ten-speed demons who careen down city streets in record time. But smart cyclists know that Bike Chic demands more than just velocity, so they slip on aerodynamic tights and pull on bright tops to stay visible through the blur of traffic. Here, a Bike Chic look.
> —*Women's Wear Daily* (April 9, 1986)

"Now in the Mainstream: Cyclist's Garb"
Once they were seen only on well-muscled young men who huffed and puffed aboard their racing cycles along switchback roads connecting Alpine villages. They still move in fast company, but not always on bicycle racers.

We're talking about those sleek and aerodynamic Lycra stretch pants, which like the sport of cycling, have become so popular in recent years. These days racing pants—and shorts—can be seen on a variety of non-racing types, including a lot of stylish young New Yorkers who find them both sensual and comfortable in much the same way as jeans are. They also offer a minimalist look, which after a decade of nostalgic fashions seems fresh and sophisticated.

Racing pants come mostly in black, although occasionally a colored pattern can be seen; often, color takes the form of jaunty stripes. The length varies from above the knee to well below it.

Usually the fabric is shiny, but not always. A couple climbing the stairway at Bethesda Fountain in Central Park last week were wearing racing shorts with matte finish. Very sporty.

It almost goes without saying that these streamlined garments—which fit as tightly as anything that isn't skin possibly could—draw attention to one's legs. Certainly the young woman strolling in Soho not long ago was aware of that. She wore a transparent black pleated modesty skirt over her stretch shorts. Good form.

—Bill Cunningham, *The New York Times* (August 23, 1987).

Recreational clothing for cycling enthusiasts has become wildly graphic. Giordana clothing featured Disney stars, Mickey and Minnie, Donald Duck, Goofy, and Pluto on their "G.S. Mickey" collection of jerseys, shorts, gloves, helmet covers, socks, and head-bands. Tommaso's polyester/spandex cycling shorts called Ciao Jeans are printed to look just like worn-out blue jean shorts—without the zipper. Another eclectic, self-reflective jersey-short combo, by New York fashion designer Nicole Miller, has colorful, miniature pictures of bicycles and national and trade teams jerseys on a black background.

Bicycle motifs appear in various kinds of body art, including tattoos, hairdos, and body piercings. Bryan Konefsky, owner of the Connecticut Bicycle Touring Center in Bridgeport, has a Campagnolo Super Record derailleur tattooed on his arm. Shawn Nagel of Rapid City, South Dakota, wore a punk hairdo for the 16th RAGBRAI with a map of Iowa shaved into his scalp and the tour route colored in. Dirk Delmondo, a British fashion designer turned bike designer, wears an earring made of bike chain links.

Biker chic in Central Park, 1987. Photo by Bill Cunningham, *The New York Times*.

Advertising

A popular image with an abundance of positive attributes, the bicycle is widely used in the world of advertising to sell a variety of products and ideas. Bicycles are graced with much symbolism including that of health and fitness, personal freedom, self-sufficiency, social and ecological responsibility, youth culture, and sex appeal.

With these virtues, bicycles have had little trouble selling themselves. Bicycles inspired some of the most beautiful advertising posters at the turn of the century, and today's bicycle boom has encouraged bike advertisers to be ever more ingenious in their sales pitches. Bicycles have also been popular for selling almost everything else that needs selling. Bicycles sell soap, bread, beer, wine, whiskey, cigarettes, medical treatments, fashions, magazines, vacations, furniture, appliances, photographic equipment, computers, automobiles, petroleum products, and nuclear power. Because some of these products represent the antithesis of the

bicycle's virtues, advertisers have used the bicycle to "sell its soul."

The largest arena for advertising is sports, where companies sponsor cycling teams and events. Cycling is considered the first sport to have instituted professional salaries for team participants, who were originally paid by bicycle manufacturers and promoters, and later by non-cycling related (*extra-sportif*) companies. Products marketed with pro teams include automobiles, gasoline, insurance, financial services, business services, public lotteries, telecommunications, computer equipment, televisions, furniture, kitchenware, household hardware, clothing, supermarkets, health foods, beers, bottled water, soft drinks, sausages, ice cream, and candy. With the team colors fashioned around those of the sponsor, the riders appear as human-powered billboards on two wheels.

Cycling events are sponsored by newspapers, civic groups, and many of the same companies that sponsor teams. The travel and recreation industry uses bicycles in their advertising, most often to symbolize good clean fun and a release from the stress of a workaday life. Here the cyclists, usually couples, are riding along quiet country roads with stunning vistas, or on secluded beaches with a distant setting sun.

Advertisers have used several recurring bicycle themes through the years. One of the first was the "New Woman" cyclist, who tends to balance the traditional feminine role in advertising where "sex sells," with her independent movement toward equal opportunity and personal freedom. While her fashions have changed with time, the bicycling woman continues, the advertisers hope, to go shopping.

Another popular theme in America is the old-world European flavor of the bicycle. One recurring image is the cyclist seen from behind, carrying a picnic basket full of groceries. The image probably originated in a memorable photograph by Eliot Erwitt, showing a father carrying his son home from market along a tree-lined country road, which was later copied and carried to extremes. In an advertisement for Stowells Armanac, the rider has three wicker baskets loaded down with some eighteen bottles of wine, and an ad for Bank America Travelers Cheques shows a tottering cyclist carrying a dozen baguettes. One even shows a cyclist carrying a twenty-foot loaf of bread and a few pints of Heineken.

Since marketers have been collecting demographic statistics of consumers, they have watched various age groups pass the generation gap. One of their favorite age groups is that of the Baby Boomers, the children of the post-war population bomb, who came of age during the Hippie youth movement and turned into the Yuppies of the 1980s and 1990s. As this group became part of a health and fitness trend, *Time* magazine set the pace by featuring an athletic thirty-something couple on racing bikes.

> They've Switched Gears. Have You? The chance to sell your health and beauty products to the most vital market of active men and women, 23 million TIME readers. These dynamic Americans just aren't turning to the standard media choices used by advertisers of health and beauty aids. They do come to TIME for the colorful information that keeps pace with all that matters in the 80s. Switch gears and get up to speed with these fast-moving consumers. There's no better place to do it—with power and style—than TIME.

Advertisers have used cycling machines to suit their particular messages. In the business world, tandem or multiple-rider bicycles have appeared in a number of ads, to show unity between foreign trading partners (Republic of Taiwan), to separate one pack of cigarettes from the rest (Kool), or to show how a magazine balances editorial content with advertising pages (*The New Yorker*). One curious image, showing a push-me pull-you tandem with both riders in business suits pedaling in opposite directions on the same bike, was used by an advertising agency to sell itself, suggesting that working with another agency was a "vicious cycle." Unicycles have also been used to symbolize the difficult balancing act of business and industry, typically between profit and people.

There are many mixed messages with bicycles used to create public opinion, often for deceptive purposes. These are especially noticeable in energy industries, such as oil and nuclear power, in which companies attempt to clean up their public image by using the most energy-efficient vehicle on earth. One example appeared in an advertisement for the Exxon Corporation in *Time* magazine (1973), which encouraged Americans to "Use your own energy—save the nation's. Bicycle! Also make a habit of using mass transit. And encourage your friends to do the same thing, too." Another example appeared in an ad for the Shoreham nuclear power plant of the Long Island Lighting Company (Lilco). When two concerned cyclists appear to ask, "Will it poison the air?" Lilco replies: "The answer, of course, is no. Of all available fuels, nuclear is the cleanest. It's an environmentalist's dream. There is virtually no pollution of our atmosphere." The ad makes no mention of the cost ("too cheap to meter"), or the intended disposal site for radioactive waste (which hadn't been decided), or the issue that eventually caused the plant to be shutdown before completion, how to evacuate the area when a meltdown occurs—unless that was the purpose of showing the bikes.

Such cynical treatment towards the public rarely goes unnoticed by cyclists, who gain power by using their own. In 1990, the Ethyl Corporation, maker of a gasoline additive called HiTec 3000 Performance Additive, ran prominent ads in *The New York Times*, *The Washington Post*, and *The Wall Street Journal*, showing a photograph of a street full of bicyclists in China, with the headline, "Some of the alternatives for reducing automobile emissions aren't very practical for America." This outraged energy economist and bike advocate Charles Komanoff, who calculated that the scant number of U.S. cycling trips that displace car trips already saved more gasoline than Ethyl's concoction could if it were used in all of America's 141 million cars.[2]

For many cycling activists, car advertising is considered one of the most disgusting forms of public propaganda. Automobile companies spent some $2 billion on advertising in America in 1990.[3] They are so prevalent in the media they even appear in *Bicycling* magazine, which averaged six car ads per issue in 1993, with no less than 21 auto advertising pages in the March 1994 issue.[4] Cyclists refer to this as "car ad nauseam." In the mid 1970s, when some alcoholic beverages were banned from television advertising, and cigarette ads were required to carry health warnings, a group of bicycle advocates in Montreal associated with Le Monde à Bicyclette, Citizens on Cycles, petitioned the Canadian Radio and Television Commission to ban automobile advertising on the grounds that, like smoking or alcohol abuse, car abuse is harmful to one's health.

In England, despite regulations by the Advertising Standards Authority against auto advertising promoting fast and aggressive driving, members of the Cyclists' Touring Club reported in 1990 that "13 out of 64 car advertisements now breach rules banning undue emphasis on speed."[5] In London, other groups of cycling activists became so frustrated at the increasing numbers of cars, not only in the street, but on roadside billboards, that they defaced, or "corrected" the advertising slogans. One particularly effective graphic image used on auto billboards was the Grim Reaper. An ad for Honda, that read "Perfectly Practical—Practically Perfect" was changed to read "Perfectly Filthy—Practically Stationary." When the Persian Gulf War erupted, cyclists hit car ads with the slogan "No war for oil."

The Cycling Press

There is much to learn and enjoy that revolves around bicycle culture. Invention and technology, travel and fitness, sport and transport, politics and business, passion and spirit—these are among the topics that the cycling press has covered. A reciprocal system drives the public interest in cycling. When bicycles flourish in the public mind, the bicycle industry flourishes, which helps support cycling events and publications, and generates interest in cycling in the public media. The main question regarding *this* cycle is, who leads and follows? The press, the industry, or the people? When bicycles reached their Golden Age in the 1890s, they permeated almost every aspect of daily life in the industrial world. In *A Social History of the Bicycle* (1972), Robert A. Smith describes the bicycle's popularity in the news media:

> When I reached the decade of the 1890s I came upon material unique in my experience as a researcher—not just pages but entire sections of each newspaper were devoted to bicycle news.

The first periodical to specialize in cycling was *Le Vélocipède Illustré*, with issue No. 1 published in Paris on April Fool's Day, 1869. The fortnightly magazine was founded by Richard Lesclide, a personal secretary for the writer Victor Hugo. Though it temporarily ceased in 1872 after 162 issues because of the Franco-Prussian War, it was revived during the Golden Age of cycling. France had the most bicycle touring and racing journals in the 1890s, including two versions of *Le Vélocipède* in Paris and Grenoble, *Vélocipède Illustré*, *Sport-Vélocipèdique*, *Revue Vélocipèdique*, *Véloceman*, *Véloce-Sport*, *La Bicyclette*, *La France Cycliste*, and *Paris-Vélo*. *Le Cycliste* was founded by Velocio (Paul De Vivie) in 1887 for cycletourists, while *Le Vélo* and *L'Auto* competed over racing leadership after the turn of the century. French-language magazines of the 1990s include *Vélo* for sports, *Vélo Vert* for mountain biking, and *Vélocité* for urban cycling.

In the United States, the oldest magazine "devoted to the interests of cycling" is *American Bicyclist*, which traces roots to Frank W. Weston's biweekly *American Bicycling Journal*, founded December 22, 1877, in Boston, "when there were not more than 100 cyclists" in the U.S. In November 1879, it was sold to Edward C. Hodges and became *Bicycling World*, the leading publication during the early years of American cycling, providing a forum for cycling enthusiasts, handling disputes in the industry and sport, and serving as a popular advertising vehicle. It became the official organ of the League of American Wheelmen, taking in *The LAW Bulletin* (1899), *The American Cyclist* (1895), and *The Wheel* (1901). Merging interests with motorcycling, the magazine was named *Motorcycle & Bicycle Illustrated* (1906), and formed the offshoot *Bicycle News* (1915). The Meyers family took over in 1921, renaming it *American*

Motorcyclist & Bicyclist (1925) and acquiring *Motorcyling & Bicycling World* (1930).

When bicycles became popular again in the 1930s, David Meyers received an ultimatum from two prominent American motorcycle makers to chose between bicycles and motorcycles. Meyers chose bikes, and in May 1934 the magazine's title was switched to *American Bicyclist and Motorcyclist*. Subsequent acquisitions include Walter Bardgett's *The Cyclist*, Otto Eisele's *The Cycling Bulletin*, covering news of the Amateur Bicycle League of America (ABLA), and the *NBDA Bulletin*, official organ of the National Bicycle Dealers Association. When *American Bicyclist and Motorcyclist* published its 100th anniversary issue in December 1979, editor Stewart Meyers explained that it was actually two years older, because the traditional founding date was set for *Bicycling World* (1879), instead of the short-lived *American Bicycling Journal* (1877). Once the "world's largest bicycle trade journal," *American Bicyclist* was sold in 1993 to Willow Publishing, and moved from New York to Northbrook, Illinois. Its latest competitors include *Bicycle Retailer and Industry News* (1992), *BDS—Bicycle Dealer Showcase* (1970), and *Bicycle Business Journal*.[6]

Bike magazines and newsletters in the U.S. have grown remarkably since the 1960s. In the 1950s, when American cycling was in the doldrums, only a few special cycling publications existed, such as newsletters by the LAW, the ABLA, the NBDA, and regional clubs. From these beginnings, after three decades of continuous growth, *Bicycling*, the "World's No. 1 Road & Mountain Bike Magazine," has emerged with some 380,000 subscriptions and 2.2 million readers in 1994.

Bicycling's roots come from the *Northern California Cycling Association Newsletter* founded in 1962 by Peter Hoffman and Bill Ziegler, which was renamed the *American Cycling Newsletter* (1964) and *American Cycling* (1965). The magazine was acquired by Harley M. Leete & Co. of San Francisco in 1968, and renamed *Bicycling!* the following year with Hoffman remaining as editor. Competition came from the staid *League of American Wheelmen Bulletin* until early 1972, when *Bike World* was introduced by Bob Anderson of *Runner's World*, followed by the racing-oriented *Northeast Bicycle News* by Barbara and Robert George. In 1973, *Bicycling!* was bought by Allan Hanson of Capital Management Publications in San Rafael, and Gail Heilman became editor. In 1978, when the exclamation point was removed, *Bicycling* was bought by Rodale Press of Emmaus, Pennsylvania, with Robert Rodale as publisher and James "Chuck" McCullagh as editor. In 1990, new offices were established in Soquel, California, to get closer to the mecca of cycling, and in 1994 Mike Greehan and Geoff Drake became publisher and editor.

Northeast Bicycle News started in Brattleboro, Vermont, reporting regional races, and expanded into the national scene, changing its name to *Cyclenews* in 1973, and then *Velo-news* in 1975. Competition for subscribers among ABLA racers came from *Competitive Cycling* (1972), Jim

McFadden's rebel newspaper from Carson City, Nevada, which was transformed into *Cycling USA* (1980), official organ of the USCF. In 1988, *Velo-news* was sold to Inside Communications (Felix Magowan, John Wilcockson, David Walls), publishers of the short-lived, glossy *Inside Cycling* (1987). With offices in Boulder, the redesigned paper became the award-winning, tabloid-sized *VeloNews*. The 20th anniversary issue (March 1992) traced the amazing progress of North American bike racing.

Mountain biking magazines tend to capture the wild passions of cycling and the popular trends in bike marketing. Charles Kelly's *Flat Tire Flyer* (1979) set the sport in motion as a grass-roots vehicle for the Marin County crowd. Then gangs of motorcyclists and BMXers in Southern California took over the consumer market, led by *Mountain Bike Action* (1985), from Hi-Torque Publications in Mission Hills, with the "conservative" Roland Hinz as publisher and the "mountain-biking Jesus," Zapata Espinosa, as editor. Nicknamed "Zap," Espinosa came to cycling via moto-cross. With his product-testing "Wrecking Crew," the magazine was known for telling controversial truths. In the early 1990s, while Zap moved to Rodale's *Mountain Bike* (1989), *MBA* led the industry in advertising pages worldwide, averaging 70 percent ads and 30 percent editorial. More mellow competition came from *Dirt Rag* (1989), published and edited by Maurice and Elaine Tierny in Verona, Pennsylvania, and *Bike* (1994) from Surfer Publications of San Juan Capistrano, California.

From 1972 to 1994, over twenty mass-market bike magazines were started in the U.S., but only about half remain, including *Bicycling*, *Bicycle Guide*, *Winning*, *VeloNews*, *Mountain Bike Action*, *Road Bike Action*, and *BMX Plus*, with a total of about 800,000 paid subscribers. Between 1989 and 1991, cycling magazines had the largest gain in subscribers of all categories according to the Audit Bureau of Circulations, with *Mountain Bike Action* (100,000 in 1992) and *VeloNews* (150,000) in the top four along with *In Health* and *Utne Reader*.

Touring and advocacy publications include *Bicycle USA*, official organ of the League of American Bicyclists, and *Adventure Cyclist*, with Greg Siple and John Schubert, which was formerly *Bike Report*. Technical journals of past and present include *Bike Tech* (1982) from Rodale Press, *Cycling Science* (1989), with Chester Kyle and Edmund Burke, and the International Human-Powered Vehicle Association's *HPV News* and *Human Power*, with David Gordon Wilson. For supine cyclists, there is Robert Bryant's *Recumbent Cyclist News* (1990); for low riders, there is *Lowrider Bicycle* (1993); and for "twicers," there is *Tandem Magazine* (1994).

Britain and Australia both have fine English-language bike magazines for enthusiasts, such as *Bicycle Magazine* (1981) founded by Richard Ballantine, *Cycling Plus* with Andy Idle and Hilary Stone, and *Australian Cyclist*, from New South Wales. The quarterly *New Cyclist* (1988) created by Jim McGurn, became Open Road Ltd.'s *Bike Culture Quarterly* (1992)

Cyklister

Fahr Rad!

with McGurn, Alan Davidson, Ballantine, and Mike Burrows, and its companion, *Encycleopedia*, the annual buyers' guide for the finest cycles around. Covering sports are *Cycling Weekly*, which dates back to 1891, and its monthly sibling *Cycle Sport* (1993), and Tony Doyle's *Performance Cyclist International* (1993). Mountain bikers have *Mountain Biker*; for touring and advocacy there is *Cycle Touring and Campaigning*, formerly *Cycletouring*, and *London Cyclist*, formerly *Daily Cyclist*; historians read *Boneshaker* from Croydon, or *Wheelmen* from New Jersey.

Another way cyclists communicate is through the electronic veloway, with e-mail, bulletin board systems (BBS), and faxes. Using phone lines, modems, and computers, people interested in bikes and cycling can correspond through e-mail, and spend hours reading messages on networks such as the Well, Econet, and on local bike-only networks, such as Bikenet (Missoula), Bikepath (Bloomington), and Bicycle Bulletin Board (San Diego). By the mid-1990s, most large bike groups have gone on-line, along with magazines such as *Bicycling* and *VeloNews*.

In most bike magazines, the April Fools Day issue is something to read carefully for dubious articles. In 1993, *VeloNews* produced *Mountain Bike Distraction*, a spoof of *Mountain Bike Action*, including "gratuitous crash photos," a "Kallmikrazy Roll Cage," the "Ibis Church of the Rotating Mass," the "Litespeed Land Accessor," with defoliator, machete, fence cutter, pump, and tire tool. As a comment on the trend of elaborate liability disclaimers in bike zines, this one stands out:

> WARNING: Much of the action depicted in this magazine is potentially dangerous, embarrassing or just plain stupid. Virtually all of the riders seen in our photos are now paraplegics. Do not attempt to duplicate any stunts that are beyond your own capabilities, unless of course you're trying to impress your betty. Always wear a helmet as advertised in MBD, preserve nature when it's convenient, avoid wilderness areas except when there's a really good singletrack running through, and wear appropriate neon-colored safety attire made by MBD advertisers.

Bicycle messengers have produced a variety of hard-core grass-roots zines which relate their special bicycle mentality. These include such comic books as Jay Jones' *Messenger 29* (1989) and Ed Hilyar's *Skidmarks* (1992), and various newsletters, such as London's *Moving Target*, New York's *I.C.A. Newsletter* (which became *Road Kill*), and San Francisco's *Mess Press* and *Mercury Rising*. *Mess Press* was a one-off zerox zine listing its editor as Joe Courier, with assistance by the "Peon" Mike Bessenger. The whole bike culture scene flowered in San Francisco in 1993, with Xeroxed zines such as *Broken Spoke*, *Mud Flap*, and *Bicycle Siren*.

"Don't kill the messenger"

15 Living and Loving

Love lovers ride bikes! Collage by James Holcomb, 1988.

Are you here alone?
No, I came with my bicycle.

Childhood

For many people, riding a tricycle is among their earliest memories of existence, and for many children, a bicycle plays a big role in the passage from dependency towards self-sufficiency and grown up responsibilities.

A major step in a child's growth can begin with the transition from a tricycle to a bicycle with training wheels. Learning to balance on two wheels may be a scary, awkward, or frustrating experience, but once accomplished through practice and patience, it is a joyous, rewarding moment.

Owning a bicycle is a big part of many a child's development, with the grown-up responsibilities of bike care and repair, and choosing and acquiring the bike that works best. Many youngsters begin to ride hand-me-down bikes shared with siblings, and one's own first bike can be a revelation. When a "Streetwise" reporter asked a handful of people in Palo Alto what their favorite holiday memory was, one person replied: "A bike. I got my very first bike when I was four or five, and I still believed in Santa Claus. I hopped on it and rode it into my parents' room at about 5 A.M., yelling 'I got a bike! I got a bike!' at the top of my lungs. That's my favorite Christmas memory, but probably not theirs."[1]

Oftentimes it is not until a youngster has earned his or her bike that he or she begins to treat it with care. The common childhood scenario of America's baby boom generation was to be given a series of red Schwinn birthday gifts (i.e., a Sting-Ray at seven years, a Varsity at ten, a Le Tour at thirteen). The first thing a kid did was to race down hills practicing crashes at the bottom. A few years later, when he'd paid for a used Frejus, Legnano, Peugeot, or Raleigh with his own paper route and lawn mowing money, the bike was handled with utmost care. Community recycle-a-bike projects provide a good way for children to earn their own bike by learning to repair used and donated bikes.

As a child, Henry Miller, author of *Tropic of Cancer* among other books, considered his bike an "eternal friend he all but slept with." In *My Bike & Other Friends*, Miller recounted how his best friend emerged as a result of his first love:

> Believe it or not, it was my bike. This one I had bought at Madison Square Garden, at the end of a six-day race. It had been made in Chemnitz, Bohemia and the six-day rider who owned it was a German, I believe. What distinguished it from other racing bikes was that the upper bar slanted down towards the handle bars.
>
> I had two other bikes of American manufacture. These I would lend my friends when in need. But the one from the Garden no one but myself rode. It was like a pet. And why not? Did it not see me through all my times of trouble and despair?

HENRY
MILLER

**MY BIKE
&
OTHER
FRIENDS**

(Volume II,
Book of Friends)

...As we spun along (me and my double) I went over these funda-mental facts backwards and forwards. It was like studying a theorem in algebra. And never once did I run into a compassionate soul! I became so desolate that I took to calling my bike my friend. I carried on silent conversations with it. And of course I paid it the best attention. Which meant that everytime I returned home I stood the bike upside down, searched for a clean rag and polished the hubs and spokes. Then I cleaned the chain and, greased it afresh. That operation left ugly stains on the stone in the walkway. My Mother would complain, beg me to put a newspaper under my wheel before starting to clean it. Sometimes she would get so incensed that she would say to me, in full sarcasm, "I'm surprised you don't take that thing to bed with you!" And I would retort—"I would if I had a decent room and a big enough bed."

I took care of my wheel as one would look after a Rolls Royce. If it needed repairs I always brought it to the same shop on Myrtle Avenue run by a Negro named Ed Perry. He handled the bike with kid gloves, you might say. He would always see to it that neither front nor back wheel wobbled. Often he would do a job for me without pay, because, as he put it, he never saw a man so in love with his bike as I was

...After a time, habituated to spending so many hours a day on my bike, I became less and less interested in my friends. My wheel had now become my one and only friend. I could rely on it, which is more than I could say about my buddies. It's too bad no one ever pho-tographed me with my "friend." I would give anything now to know what we looked like.[2]

Bicycling is one of the best ways for youngsters to get to know the world, whether it is the local neighborhood or far-away places. Activities such as club rides, bike racing, and organized touring can transform a child rather quickly into a self-sufficient young adult. An ideal initiation rite for early teens, bicycle touring enables youngsters to leave the nest for a few weeks or months, making new friends and experiencing new places. Franklin D. Roosevelt spoke about his youthful cycling experiences with the International Youth Hostels: "I was brought up on this sort of thing and realize the need for hosteling. From the time I was nine until I was seven-teen I spent most of my holidays bicycling on the Continent. This was the best education I ever had, far better than schools. The more one circulates in his travels the better citizen he becomes, not only of his own country but of the world."[3]

Love and Sex

The line is man
the circle woman.
Bisexual bicycle
carry us on the diamond frame
on the sounds of wheels
by the silent work
of cable chain and gear
to deeper distances.
Link us to our double selves.
　　—Peter Cummings, "Going Bicycle" (1979)

Bikes are often present in the awakening passions of youngsters, in bringing people together for romance, and they appear in some curious marriage traditions. Bikes are sometimes considered a passion unto themselves, and they appear in numerous erotic stories and images which symbolize both the freedom and oppression of various sexual relations. Bicycles are often part of the sexual discoveries of adolescents, as in the following Ozark folktale called "Riding His Cross-Bar:"

> One time there was a country girl and she had stayed pretty late at the swimming hole. Young Tom Harper was fetching her home in the dark and all she had on was a bathing suit, you know how it was done in them days. A boy had a bicycle and the girl would climb on the cross-bar in front of him. This way he could put his arms around her to reach the handlebars. Sometimes he'd go over bumps and make sharp turns so she'd hold on tighter.
>
> Tom was a-riding pretty lively that night and him and her was pretty red-faced and panting when they got to her house. The next morning she was telling the folks about what a wild ride they had through the trails. "I would have fallen off sure" she said, "only I held on to Tom's arms and wrapped my legs around that cross-bar."
>
> The girl's old pappy listened to her a-talking, and after a while he says, "Daughter, if I was you, I wouldn't say no more about holding onto that cross-bar." The girl says that's exactly what happened and surely there ain't no harm in telling the truth. The old man just kind of winked at her. "Daughter," he says, "what you had a-hold of is your own business, and I ain't asking questions, but everybody knows Tom Harper rides a girl's bike."
>
> The girl turned red as a beet when she heard that, because she knew that a girl's bike had no cross-bar, and she had some idea of what she was a-riding on.

Perhaps the most heartwarming aspect of bicycles is their use as a vehicle for traditional romance. Bicycles have been a part of a few rather amusing marriage rituals. In traditional cycling ceremonies, the wedding party meets the bride and groom while holding bicycle wheels instead of bouquets, and tossing ball bearings instead of rice. In China, it is said that a young man must be able to offer his bride "the three things that go round: a watch, a sewing machine, and a bicycle." There are also "certain romantic rules for bicycling," according to Zhou Youma in his "Ode to the Bicycle."

> If a young woman agrees to the offer of a little outing on the back seat of a young man's bicycle, I am told, it is a sign that she will allow him to "court" her. If she hugs the young man's waist tightly as they pedal along, it's a good sign that the courtship is very successful. And, if she sits on the crossbar between the handlebars and the young man, it is definitely time to talk of marriage.
>
> The romance of the bicycle doesn't end with courtship, however. This can be seen from the number of threesomes on bicycles all over the country. The baby is usually on the crossbar in a bamboo chair; papa doing the pedaling; mama on the rear seat. (Passengers are forbidden on bicycles and people have been known to get fines in busy downtown districts, but, generally, and especially on holidays and evenings, the police just look the other way.)
>
> And in a few short years that little tyke will be learning to ride his own bike. Perhaps as a teenager he'll become a speed demon terrorizing the highways, only to mend his manners drastically when he starts courting a girl. Some years more and he'll be the sober father of a family, commuting to work on two wheels, enjoying the passing scene—and complaining about the recklessness of the young![4]

Bicycles are a part of many love songs, and the most popular bicycle song from the 1890s is "Daisy Bell," or "A Bicycle Built for Two." The song was written in 1892 by the Englishman Harry Dacre after an ocean voyage to New York, where a U.S. Customs officer made him pay duty on his bicycle. While complaining about the cost, a friend remarked, "You're lucky it wasn't a bicycle built for two." Something in the way he said it inspired the song, and "Daisy Bell—A Bicycle Built for Two" became a stylish hit in London, while its melody was played at the wedding of the Duke of York.

Harry Dacre, author of "Daisy Bell," or "A Bicycle Built for Two."

(Chorus)
Daisy, Daisy, Give me your answer do!
I'm half crazy all for the love of you!
It won't be a stylish marriage,
I can't afford a carriage,
But you'll look sweet upon the seat
Of a bicycle built for two!

Two years later, Harry Dacre wrote a sequel entitled "Fare-You-Well Daisy Bell," perhaps as his fondness for "Daisy" had waned.

> Fare you well Daisy Bell, I ride alone
> Fare you well sweet-heart, Thus we have to part
> Say good bye, Do not cry
> When your lover's gone
> Now I mean, to have a machine
> Especially built for one.

"Daisy Bell" continues as a sentimental song performed by Mitch Miller, Dave Brubeck, and HAL 9000, the computer in Stanley Kubrick's film *2001: A Space Odyssey* (1968). It also plays in *Spokesong* (1975), an Irish musical play described as "a love affair with a bicycle," with script and lyrics by Stewart Parker. Another love song with a bike in the middle is "Pedal Pushin Papa" (1955) by Billy Ward and his Dominos:

> Any way you like I'll ride your bike if you'll only let me try
> Just tell me when, and I'll begin, a Pedal Pushin Papa am I
> You can ride the bar beyond the stars we'll go sailing through the sky
> Like Jack and Jill we'll get a thrill, a Pedal Pushin Papa am I
> I'll saddle that saddle like Autrey, and bounce along like Fitzgerald,
> and when the trip is over, you'll know that I was there
> So if you decide you want to ride I will gladly be your guide
> Just ask for Dan, the lover man, a Pedal Pushin Papa am I.

Tom Waits crooned about his broken heart in "Broken Bicycles" from the Francis Ford Coppola movie *One From the Heart* (1982):

> Broken bicycles, old busted chains
> Rusted handlebars, out in the rain.
> Somebody must have an orphanage for
> all these things that nobody wants anymore.
> September's reminding July
> It's time to be saying good-bye.
> Summer is gone, but our love will remain,
> Like old broken bicycles, out in the rain.
>
> Broken bicycles, don't tell my folks
> Of all those playing cards, pinned to those spokes.
> Lay down like skeletons, out on the lawn.
> The wheels won't turn when the other half's gone.
> Seasons can turn on a dime
> Somehow I forget everytime.
> For the things that you've given me, will always stay.
> Broken, but I'll never throw them away.

"I KNEW IT"

Scott Friedland.

Many people search for a husband, wife, sex partner, soul mate, or cycling companion through personal want-ads and mating services. When called upon to describe themselves and what they seek, sometimes just "cyclist" is enough, because the word represents a way of life encompassing body and mind, with shared activities and social relations. Cycling personals and mating calls appear in various club newsletters and local newspapers.

> SWF, 25, cyclist, looking for someone who loves cycling as much as I do.

> Smart, left wing, cycling woman seeks smart, left wing, cycling man.

> Handsome SAM, artist, charming and literate, cyclist and cat lover, seeks earthy creative woman with varied wardrobe.[5]

There are various bicycle groups for singles, swingers, gays, and lesbians. Different Strokes is a San Francisco-based club for "bi-cyclists and gay-cyclists" with hundreds of racing and touring members. In San Francisco, an all-women messenger service appeared in 1993 called Lickety Split Delivery, along with a women's cycling zine called *Raw Vulva*. For feminists who want nothing from the opposite sex, there is a popular saying: "A woman needs a man like a fish needs a bike."

Bicycles became involved in the issue of reproductive freedom when anti-abortion protesters used Kryptonite bicycle locks to illegally lock the doors of health clinics, while locking themselves to parked cars. Kryptonite reported calls from police trying to break open the locks. In 1991, when the U.S. Supreme Court ruled that government-funded family health clinics could not give advice on abortions, known as the "gag rule," a group of ten women and one man organized the 4,000 mile trans-America "Reproductive Freedom Ride." Andrea Rose Askowitz said, "Using our own power riding bicycles is symbolic not only of a woman's need to have power over her body, but also of her ability to possess that power. We're not only talking about abortion. We'll talk on a personal level about all reproductive issues and hopefully find some common ground on issues such as caring for a child once it is born."[6]

Lovemaking is expressed in many ways and as a platform for such activity bicycles allow for many positions. Young lovers tend to mount themselves on a single bike, while more mature couples ride a tandem. Opinions differ as to whether the masculine or feminine rider should steer at the front or stoke at the rear. Other couples prefer the side-by-side "sociable" position, such as on the Buddy Bike, though many single riders find more pleasure with their own device. One bicycle maker claimed, "It has been our aim to build a bicycle which a man or woman could ride and still be a Christian. If we have not succeeded you can easily prove it."[7]

During the early days of cycling, as young Victorian women abandoned their chaperons there were countless romantic cycling stories, with

Velocipedienne, by Man Ray, 1950.

titles such as *A Ride for a Wife*, and H.G. Wells' "bicycling idyll" *Wheels of Chance* (1896). Then came the controversial writers of the early twentieth century, with Marcel Proust, who wrote of a "Bacchante with the bicycle,"[8] and James Joyce, who wrote about a "Bisexcycle bunch."[9] Christopher Morley described how bicycling can be a replacement for sexual lust. He suggested that the initials of the Cyclists' Touring Club (CTC), which appeared on British road signs and bed and breakfast inns, were actually the initials for the "Club Terrestre de la Chasteté." He wrote that, "To see before one a forked or meandering road, a wedge-towered Norman church in the valley, to explore the fragrance of lanes like green tunnels, to hear the whispering hum beneath you and the rasp of scythes in a hayfield, all this might well be homeopathic against passion, for it is a passion in itself."[10]

Eventually the automobile, with its infamous back-seat, came to replace the bicycle as the symbolic vehicle of romance. But the sexual revolution of the 1970s, which coincided with the bicycle boom, brought public awareness of sexual behavior. Bicycle T-shirts appeared that read "Put Something Exciting Between Your Legs," "Cyclists Pump Harder," and "Your Pace or Mine."

Movies and theater have included bicycles as part of love scenes, such as in Billy Wilder's mixed comedy *Some Like it Hot* (1959) with Marilyn Monroe and Tony Curtis using bikes in their romantic rendezvous with Jack Lemmon and Joe E. Brown. Threesomes share love and bikes in François Truffaut's *Jules and Jim* (1961) with Jeanne Moreau, in *Butch Cassidy and the Sundance Kid* (1969), with Paul Newman riding Katherine Ross to the tune of Burt Bacharach's "On a Bicycle Built For Joy" (a version of "Rain Drops Keep Fallin' On My Head"), and in Kevin Wade's *Key Exchange* (1980), with sex performed on a bike.

In September 1989, *Bicycling* magazine held a readers' "Sex Survey," which received 1,675 replies, 80 percent from males. It was their biggest response to a survey and their most popular issue ever. Of the cyclists surveyed, 84 percent of those cyclists thought about sex while riding and 66 percent said cycling made them better lovers. Sixty-two percent had suffered from genital numbness on long rides, and 43 percent had postponed rides to have sex. Twenty-eight percent had met a partner through cycling, and fourteen percent had had sexual encounters during a rest stop. While cycling, men were more likely to think about sex than women. While having sex, women were more likely to think about cycling than men. The average respondent cycled 4.41 times per week, and had sex 2.98 times per week.

"Bike riding as little as three miles a day will improve your sex life," wrote Dr. Franco Antonini in the *Sun* (August 24, 1993) after studying 100 couples in Naples, Italy. He found that the act of balancing, the heightened alertness, and the rhythmic exercise stimulates testosterone and estrogen secretion. He correlated the heavy bicycling habits of Chinese, who suffer fewer sexual dysfunctions, with their astounding rate of procreation.

Bicycle seats have the greatest erotic appeal for most sexual persuasions. Pornographers have used the saddle's shape as an obvious phallic symbol with the tip used for pubic stimulation, and lesbians have described a certain kind of affection for the bicycle seat. One rumor reported on the radio claimed that when the actress Jody Foster was attending Yale University she had her bicycle seat stolen at least once a week by her "wimyn" admirers. The poet John Betjman wrote an epigram, which may be relevant:

I think that I should rather like
To be the saddle of a bike

In Nicholas Baker's novel *Vox* (1991), a couple who have never met have phone sex, and the man describes his organs in bicycle terms:

I get so *horny* that I look down at my cock-and-balls unit, and it's like I could take the whole rigid assembly and start unscrewing it, around and around, and it would come off as one solid thing, like a cotterless crank on a bicycle, and I would hand it over to you to use as a dildo.

In M. Masud R. Kahn's "The Evil Hand," the bicycle's sado-masochistic erotic potential is explored:

...I was really quite taken aback to find she had completely undressed herself and was seated naked on the cycle. She asked me with a trembling, excited voice: "What posture shall I take? Please tie my hands to the handlebars." I felt she was taking over my initiative. I went down, found some string, tied her hands to the handlebars, and asked her to stick out her bottom and try to touch one of the parallel pedals. I told her again: "This is a 'contest.' If you fail to touch the pedal, I will give you one stroke per failure with this branch/stick." She replied laughingly: "And if I do succeed, what can I do to you?" I said: "Whatever you please." Well, she couldn't touch the pedal and I gave her one stroke. She tried again and again and I realized I had beaten her nearly ten times. I had also taken off my clothes by now. It was not so much an orgy, as being possessed, without any awareness of her or myself...[11]

Traditional gender-based roles are changing and as women gain more equal rights some men's roles are being tested. *Village Voice* sports writer Joel Del Priore gave an insider's account of a macho cyclist who ran into a female Lycra-clad racer in a story called "Tour de Bergen."

...WHOOSH! She *flew* past me as if I were backpedaling, even turned and sneered. Couldn't have been more than 20 years old, a powerfully built woman, wearing almost the same outfit I had on, riding a different bike (a McDonnell Douglas-Mitsubishi hybrid, I think). She sliced in front of me, opened up a 15-yard lead. I pumped harder, pulled to with-

FROM MESS PRESS

in a few feet of her...and then I saw it. First let's say when it comes to viewing women as objects I generally fall somewhere between Jim McMahon and the Beastie Boys. But on the whole I'm pretty liberated. Yet...damnit, I'll be the first '80s guy to come out and admit it—I get off on women's sweat. There's something about a perspiration stain on the back of a woman's T-shirt, extending down from the shoulders in a V with the point disappearing into her shorts that turns me into one big piece of throbbing gristle. Get me a bottle of Gabriella Sabatini's sweat and I'll start a new religion.

And that's exactly what I was staring at with this amazon in front of me. Something snapped upstairs. My body ripped off the cap of an adrenaline six-pack, a surge of power rocketed into my legs as I pulled even, then exploded past her: God, what a feeling! I thought I was opening up a nice lead but then we hit a hill, I fumbled with the gears. She swept past me again, obviously a great climber.

"BRAZEN WENCH!" I yelled, but she ignored me. The game was on!...

An exit out of the park popped up ahead and by a sort of mental telepathy only bikers can understand we both knew that would be our finish line. I kept the lead another minute but I could feel her closing in for one last charge, her hot sensuous breath on my neck. She was only a bike length behind now but pulling closer...closer...She was practically goosing me, my breath was coming in quick gasps, my brain had degenerated into Cream of Wheat, saliva drooled from my mouth...100 feet...50...25...

Then I saw the light changing, the Mobil Oil truck started to roll into the intersection and—a millisecond of decision time—I hit the brakes and skidded sideways into a bunch of evergreen bushes.

"Nice ass!" she yelled as she detonated through the intersection. She dipped past the truck's front grill, the driver blasted his horn, she gave him the finger, and then she just disappeared down the road.[12]

Bicycle Race, from Queen album, 1978. Courtesy Rainbow Productions.

16 Bicycle Mind

T-shirt, 1975, courtesy of R. Crumb and Triple-E Cyclery.

Act Bicycle!, Speak Bicycle!, Write Bicycle!, Advise Bicycle!, Impact Bicycle!, Meet Bicycle!, Recruit Bicycle!, Persist Bicycle!, Subscribe Bicycle!, Communicate Bicycle!
   —Roger Herz, Bicycle Transportation Action

Ride a bike, ride a bike, ride a bike.
   —Fausto Coppi.

Cycle-Logical People

Cycling inspires ways of life for many kinds of "bicycle people." There may be about a million people in the world who, in one way or another, consider themselves true, hard-core bike lovers, and bicycle people have been stereotyped and categorized by various pundits. These include the machine-minded "techno-freaks" who love all the equipment, the old-time cycle collectors or "veterans" who keep bicycle history alive, the competitive cyclists who ride for bicycle glory, the cycle sport fans, known as *tifosi* in Italy, who follow their heroes, the perpetually pedaling "mileage junkies" who "ride, eat, and sleep," and the bicycle activists who ride for the *vélorution*.

Bicycles fit into many alternative lifestyles, and mountain biking has inspired some notable backwoods folk heroes, such as "Mountain Larry" Hibbard, who lives in the Santa Cruz Mountains. A bicycle cult group called the Wild Mustangs, near Austin, Texas, shares the motto: "Live to Ride, Ride to Live." In creating a post-petroleum culture, they ride klunker bikes and won't wear plastic clothing. A nomad named Kelso from Eureka, California, specializes in delivering verbal messages by bicycle. He was last seen wearing a black pea-coat with felt top-hat, riding a tandem modified for his bedroll, on his way from Arcata, Ca., to Florida, saying, "I love the life I live. When I'm on my bicycle it's like a fish in the water or a bird in the air—it's very similar to flight."[1]

Cycling columnist Sundown Slim described the possible lifestyles for the mostly male "Serious Cyclist." He included the "Basic Jock" racer, "Hardcore Harry" the fanatical cycletourist, "Supertech Sid" who "quotes technical specs to six decimal places," "Mr. Natural" vegetarians who believe crashes are caused by "negative thinking," "Good Old Boy" mountain bikers who sport red bandanas and handlebar moustaches, and "Balloon Tire Bobby" with spiked hair and a ghetto-blaster. He also suggested how to live the life of the "Joe Journalist," "overweight, overage, and underpaid" character who writes a column in bike magazines, "full of clumsy sarcasm about people who actually ride their bikes."[2]

People talk about the addiction of cycling as they would other drug or alcohol habits. Those inflicted call themselves bikeaholics.

Are you late or missing at work because of biking? Does your biking cause financial difficulties for your family and loved ones? Do you

Pee-Wee Herman, from *Pee-Wee's Big Adventure*.

bike to build self-esteem? Do you find yourself biking more and more just to relax? Do you push biking on others, and feel uncomfortable when others don't bike? Do you bike first thing in the morning? Do you bike to forget your problems? Do you resent those who want to stop you from biking?

To describe the special symbiosis people have with bicycles, the Irish novelist Flann O'Brien proposed a kind of "Atomic Theory" in *The Third Policeman*:

> The gross and net result of it is that people who spend most of their natural lives riding iron bicycles over the rocky roadsteads of this parish get their personalities mixed up with the personalities of their bicycle as a result of the interchanging of the atoms of each of them and you would be surprised at the number of people in these parts who nearly are half people and half bicycles.... And you would be flabbergasted at the number of bicycles that are half-human almost half-man, half-partaking of humanity....

Many bicycle people are mentioned somewhere in this book. Some deserve special mention here for being particularly good examples of cycle-logical people.

Alfred Jarry (1873–1907) was a bicycle "Pata-Physician" who wrote two bicycle classics, "The Passion Considered as an Uphill Bicycle Race" and *Le Surmâle*. He was a scorcher with the poetic license of a prophet. His life was short, self-abusive, and tragic, and in his absurd creations we find a bicycle spirit. Jarry created Pataphysics, which he described as "the science of the realm beyond metaphysics, as far beyond metaphysics as metaphysics lies beyond physics—in one direction or another." One of his creations, the Pataphysical Calendar of the *Almanach du Père Ubu*, has a month named *Pédale* and a holiday celebration for Superman, called the *Fête of Saint André Marcueil*, the *ascète cycliste*. Pataphysics allowed Jarry to carry a pistol and drink absinthe or ether, and it allowed him to ride a Clément Luxe bicycle, which he bought on credit and on which he never paid all the installments.

Ellen Fletcher is a fine example of a citizen who has helped make her own region a bicycle-friendly place. Through her involvement in the affairs of local government, serving on the Palo Alto City Council, applying persistent attention to ordinances she helped create, Fletcher helped implement higher standards for bicycle roadways and parking sites in Palo Alto and Santa Clara County, which has influenced other activities in California, North America, and the world at large. John Dowlin of the Bicycle Network once wrote that "Ellen has done as much for bicycling as Greg LeMond, at least in the U.S."[3]

Unlike many politicians who tend to reap power and privilege from

Alfred Jarry's calendar included the month of *Pédale*.

public service, her work in bicycle transportation has little glamour; her rewards are of the Mother Teresa variety. Like many bicycle advocates, Fletcher lives a "low impact" lifestyle, using her bicycle and mass-transit for mobility. Her practical bike is equipped for handing out leaflets and newsletters, and her 30-year-old car consumes less than ten gallons of gasoline per year.

Robert "Bicycle Bob" Silverman (1934–) is a velorutionary from Montréal and one of the most genuine, visionary bicycle activists in the world. Bicycle Bob has laid down in rush-hour traffic smeared with fake blood to protest the "auto-cracy." He went to prison for painting unofficial bike paths, and set up the first organized bike tours of Vietnam. He believes that cyclotherapy is the cure for auto-eroticism. He describes himself with a poem:

Killed by a car
Reborn by bike
That's the story of my life

Freddie Hoffman is close to being one of the first humans to have cycled a million miles, which he is hoping to accomplish in 1995. He says, "I do nothing but ride, eat and sleep." When not riding, Hoffman lives with his father in northern New Jersey, and works as a part-time church caretaker. As a youth he was diagnosed as having a "mild brain dysfunction" which he says was "just enough to make my life miserable as a child. The world is mean to a child who's different. It's very frustrating when people put you down for something you can't help."[4]

Hoffman began riding his tricycle at age five, doing an estimated 1,800 miles his first year on a one-third mile loop around his home. He started properly recording his mileage on calendars and grade school composition books when he got an odometer on his seventh birthday. The next year he rode his first century in ten hours on a Schwinn Sting Ray, and at fifteen he got a Sears Free Spirit five-speed. He broke about a half-dozen of these frames (they were guaranteed and replaced for free), riding about 700 miles a week.

He says that "every year was basically the same, the numbers just kept getting bigger and bigger," until his "catastrophic period" in 1979 when he tore a tendon in his knee. For a while he felt miserable. He said his unused energy kept "backing up," and he couldn't sleep at night. He adapted to one-legged riding, doing 115 miles on his first ride. Another missed day of riding, due to a bad cold on March 31, 1985, ended a record streak of riding 778 consecutive days. His endurance, once tested on an ergometer, is reported to be greater than the top Tour de France riders.

In the late 1980s, he was averaging over 950 miles a week on a 50-pound Schwinn Super Le Tour with fenders, upright handlebars, front and rear racks, a five-digit odometer, a thermometer, generator lights (with brake light), and various air horns. The name of his mother, Ruth

Ellen Fletcher in Palo Alto.

Hoffman, was painted on the top tube as a memorial. He was not wearing a helmet, because of his "sixth sense," and was not wearing fancy cycling clothes. He had a hand-drawn map with a 120-mile circle around his home that marks the farthest he can ride in one day before turning around. He says that if he were placed blindfolded anywhere within the circle he could find his way home. Imagine—he is probably riding right now.

Jacquie Phelan (1955–), is a gonzo feminist mountain biker from Fairfax, in Marin County, California. Nicknamed "Alice B. Toeclips," she founded WOMBATS, the Women's Mountain Bike and Tea Society, and its Camp Winna-WOMBAT for teaching cycling to women. One of the ten best mountain bikers of all time according to *Mountain Bike Action*, Phelan won the NORBA National Championship title in 1983, 1984, and 1985, and is competitive in masters racing a decade later. She is famous for subverting sexist stereotypes by wearing pink lycra, and by posing for bike makers' advertisements wearing almost nothing but mud.

The spirit of cycle-logical consciousness-raising comes through in Phelan's writing for magazines. Regarding the "dude/gal imbalance," she proposed two prices for bikes, since women with the same ability make 59 cents to the man's dollar, and then imagined all the guys "going for the discount, sporting falsies." Her epiphany came when she finished sixth place in a race and was mistakenly given the $400 men's prize instead of the $46 women's prize. Describing the "unseen (though sharply felt) factors that conspire to slow a gal's entry and progress in bicycling," she says, "I think of them as hurdles because I love leaping over them or kicking them down. Guys don't notice the barriers, because the hurdles aren't on their side of the track."[5]

Jacquie Phelan, founder of the Women's Mountain Bike and Tea Society.

Bicycle Craze, by Frederick Opper, 1896.

The Wheel and the Way

Through the symbols of the wheel and the journey, bicycles provide a means of attaining spiritual wisdom and the cathartic "sweet spots" of life. Bicycle culture has its major influence in Christianity, though many other religions have played a part. Some religious cultures, such as Islam, ban the use of bicycles, especially for women who are not allowed to straddle a bike for fear of sexual excitement or infertility, even though Muhammed never spoke of the bicycle.

In the beginning, the bicycle was one of the deities of the industrial revolution. Bicycles brought conflicts with the Christian practice of observing the Sabbath, as cyclists took to the roads on Sundays when they were supposed to be in church. Preachers sermonized against cyclists, calling the velocipede a "beast-riding hell-of-a-pede," or, according to a Baltimore preacher, a "Diabolical Device." Roman Catholic clergy were not officially allowed to ride bicycles until 1894, when Pope Leo XIII decreed it acceptable behavior. Some preachers tried to reach cyclists at their favorite outdoor gathering sites, thus creating the "Church on the Wheel." While six-day bicycle races reflect a respect for the Sabbath, the Tour de France became a religion of its own. In 1949, Pope Pius XII declared the Madonna del Ghisallo the patron saint of Italian cyclists, and her chapel in Magreglio, Italy, is now a shrine for racing history. At Labastide d'Armagnac, France, there is the chapel of Notre Dame des Cyclistes and a museum where 1973 Tour de France winner Louis Ocana is buried.

The wheel is a guiding principle for many bicycle-related sermons. One poetic cyclist adapted a well-known Christian hymn to the bicycle in the *New York Tribune* (1895):

> Wheel, kindly light, along life's cycle path,
> Wheel Thou on me!
> The road is rough, I have discerned Thy Wrath,
> But wheel me on!

In 1892, Miss Frances E. Willard, founder of the Women's Christian Temperance Union, "succumbed to the temptation" and learned to ride a bicycle at the age of 53. She named her bike Gladys and her story is told in her book *A Wheel Within A Wheel* (1893), which has been reprinted as *How I Learned to Ride the Bicycle* (1990):

> In many curious particulars, the bicycle is like the world. When it had thrown me painfully once, and more especially when it threw one of my dearest friends, then for a time Gladys had gladsome ways for me no longer, but seemed the embodiment of misfortune and dread. Even so the world has often seemed in hours of darkness and despondency;

Cycling shrine at the chapel of the Madonna del Ghisallo, Italy.

its iron mechanism, its pitiless grind, its on-rolling gait have oppressed to melancholy. I finally concluded that all failure was from a wobbling will rather than a wobbling wheel. I felt that indeed the will is the wheel of the mind—its perpetual motion having been learned when the morning stars sang together. When the wheel of the mind went well then the rubber wheel hummed merrily.

January 20th will always be a red-letter bicycle day because, summoning all my force, I mounted and started off alone. From that hour the spell was broken; Gladys was no more a mystery. Amid the delightful surroundings of the great outdoors, and inspired by the bird songs, the color and fragrance of a garden, in the company of devoted and pleasant comrades, I had made myself master of the most remarkable, ingenious, and inspiring motor ever yet devised upon this planet. Moral: Go thou and do likewise!

At the same time, the evangelist J. Lemon Bunyan wrote a best-selling sermon called *A Bicyclist's Dream of the Road to Heaven*. It describes a group of cyclists making "a century run from Infancy to Old Age, stopping for rest on the shore of the Great Western Sea of Eternity." Bunyan illustrated his bicycle with its guiding principles:

Thereupon I set my wheel before them, and with lead pencil in hand I wrote in large letters upon the tire of the forward wheel the word Faith and upon the rear wheel the word Works....

I took my stand on the other side of my wheel, so that my audience might have an unobstructed view of the tires, spokes and pedals. I explained to them that the forward wheel of the bicycle is the guiding wheel, just as faith is the guiding agency in the spiritual life. And the rear wheel on a bicycle is the pushing wheel, just as good works in the Christian life are necessary in order to advance and develop one's faith. Neither of these wheels can render the service for which it was created without the assistance of the other.

In the vision which we saw, I went on to explain, the axle of the forward wheel was named Hope, because hope is the indispensable support of faith. The axle of the rear wheel was named Love, because it is

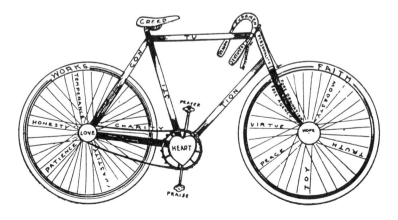

Spiritual Bicycle, by J. Lemon Bunyan.

the source of all good works and the center from which the propelling power is distributed to every part of the machine.

The wheels which we saw in the clouds had one striking peculiarity. In all of them the central axle, or pedal shaft, was shaped like a heart inside of a sprocket wheel, to which the pedals, named Prayer and Praise, were joined by strong arms or levers. Every bicycler knows that this part of his machine must be kept in good order if he wishes to make progress easily and satisfactorily. For this is the point where life enters into the machinery, and this is the part that must always render perfect obedience to the rider and must always be kept under perfect control if danger is to be avoided. This is true in the spiritual world, where it is taught with special emphasis that prayer and praise must be joined to the heart with strong impulses in order to be effective.

The handlebar was named Judgement, because it is the source from which faith and hope receive their direction. But the agents which must influence Judgement were represented as Sentiment and Reason, personified as the two corkaline handles.

A similar bicycle lesson is found in the essay "Bicycle—A Teacher of Human Values" by R.N. Khurana, the Executive Secretary of the All India Cycle Manufacturers Association, in *Indian Bicycle Ambassador* (June 1990):

> As a mode of transport for the common man, for short distances, a Bicycle provides incomparable convenience and unique independence. When used for a joy-ride or as an exerciser, it is a source of great mental relaxation, emotional thrills and physical fitness. If we make a still deeper metaphysical analysis of this vehicle, a Bicycle is indeed a teacher of human values in many respects.
>
> The pressure on the Pedals can be gentle, harmonious, vigorous or ferocious depending upon our earnest desire to achieve our chosen goals and our basic approach to maintain interpersonal relationships with whomsoever we come in contact. This is how the Wheels of our life would move and contribute towards the building of our total personality.
>
> As usually happens in everyone's life, there are some events for which we cannot precisely trace the cause. Similarly, while riding a Bicycle, the Chain can accidently get off. The Tyres may get punctured and rarely, of course, the Fork may break. These incidents signify the jerks and jolts in life.
>
> In several ways, therefore, a Bicycle depicts the intricacies of human life and prompts us in making it more meaningful, so that we can spread sweetness and fragrance all round.[6]

A Zen approach to the bicycle experience appears in a story about an old Zen master who questioned each of his five bicycling students, "Why are you riding your bicycles?"

The first student replied, "The bicycle is carrying this sack of potatoes. I am glad that I do not have to carry them on my back." The teacher responded, "You are wise, for when you grow old, you will not walk hunched over as I do."

The second student replied, "I love to watch the trees and fields pass by as I roll down the path." The teacher commended the student saying, "Your eyes are open, and see the world."

The third student replied, "When I ride my bicycle I am content to chant *nam myoho renge kyo*." The teacher praised his pupil, "Your mind will roll with the ease of the perfectly true wheel."

The fourth student replied, "Riding my bicycle I live in harmony with all sentient beings." The teacher was pleased: "You are riding on the golden path of non-harming."

Finally the fifth student replied, "I ride my bicycle to ride my bicycle." The teacher then sat down at the feet of this child and said, "I am your student!"[7]

The idea of "riding on the golden path" inspired Robert Rodale (1930–1990), publisher of *Bicycling* magazine. Rodale became a guru for many cyclists in North America, not only for his support of bike racing, but also for his approach to a method of spiritual development called Regeneration. Gleaned from his work in regenerative agriculture, in which worn-out soil is renewed by organic farming, Rodale applied these principles to runners and cyclists. In a booklet called *The Path to the Golden Wheel* (1988), Rodale teaches cyclists to renew their lives by thinking positively and increasing the "sweet spots," those special moments in cycling when one's spirit soars. Cyclists can reach for three levels of achievement. To earn the Bronze Wheel, one has to ride 1,000 miles or 100 hours. For the Silver Wheel, one has to ride 5,000 miles or 500 hours, and join a local club or national cycling organization. The Golden Wheel belongs to those who ride 10,000 miles or 1,000 hours, and complete an approved community cycling project, like teaching safety, coaching, or creating a cycling facility.

One form of religious experience comes from mind altering substances sometimes used by cyclists to increase the cathartic experience of bike riding. While Mother Nature offers plenty of plants with chemical compounds that benefit her offspring, human beings have continuously tried to improve these through selective breeding, processing, and synthesis. An example is the ergot mold which grows on rye grains and contains hallucinogenic alkaloids, which supposedly caused the religious fanaticism of the Middle Ages and the visionary art of the Northern Renaissance (cf. the drawing of a unicycle by Hieronymus Bosch). In the twentieth century these same alkaloids were synthesized into the hallucinogen known as LSD (lysergic acid diethylamide). According to Albert Hoffman, the Swiss chemist employed by Sandoz who developed LSD in 1943, the first LSD trip was on a bicycle. To honor Hoffman's discovery, a 50th

Marcel Duchamp, *Avoir l'apprenti dans le soliel*, 1914, Paris. Courtesy of the Philadelphia Museum of Art.

anniversary bike ride was held in 1993 in Santa Cruz, California. Here is Hoffman's description of his ride home from work after taking the drug:

> My field of vision swayed and objects appeared distorted, like images in curved mirrors. I felt fixed to the spot, although my assistant told me afterwards we were cycling at good speed. I recall the most outstanding symptoms as vertigo and visual disturbance; the faces of those around me appeared as grotesque colored masks. I recognized my condition clearly and sometimes, as if I were an independent neutral observer, saw that I babbled half insanely and incoherently. Occasionally I felt out of my body. When I closed my eyes endless colorful, realistic and fantastic images surged in on me. Acoustic perceptions, such as the noise of a passing car, were transformed into optical effects, every sound evoking a corresponding colored hallucination constantly changing in shape and color.[8]

Another form of religious experience comes from astrology, with its wheel-shaped Zodiac. The signs of the Zodiac were named well before the advent of the bicycle, but the scientist Carl Sagan suggested that, "If the constellations had been named in the twentieth century, I suppose we would see bicycles..."[9] A "Horoscope Cycliste" appeared in *Le Monde À Bicyclette* (Summer 1983), with the parts of the bicycle forming the dozen Zodiac signs:

Guidon (handlebar): 21 March to 20 April
Fourche (fork): 21 April to 20 May
Cadre (frame): 21 May to 20 June
Roues (wheels): 21 June to 20 July
Pneus (tires): 21 July to 20 August
Pedalier (pedals): 21 August to 20 September
Chaine (chain): 21 September to 20 October
Selle (saddle): 21 October to 20 November
Tige (seatpost): 21 November to 20 December
Freins (brakes): 21 December to 20 January
Pignons (sprockets): 21 January to 20 February
Numéro de Série (serial number): 21 February to 20 March

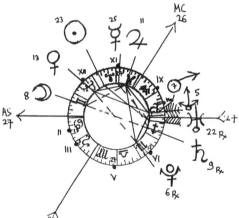

Astrological chart for predicting the Paris-Roubaix bike race, April 13, 1986. The chart indicates frustration, bad luck, wasted efforts, and a surprising finish. The race was won by Sean Kelly. Prepared by Jean-Albert Romeu and Richard Rongier for *Miroir du Cyclisme*.

According to many stargazers there is a constellation of a cyclist in the northern sky. Some only see a faint bicycle, while others have called it the thirteenth sign in the Zodiac. It appears around the arc of the Crown which forms a wheel. The writer Bruno Schulz (1892–1942) of Drogobych, Poland, was perhaps the first to notice it, in his book *The Street of Crocodiles* (1940):

> Oh, stellar arena of night, scarred by the evolutions, spirals and leaps of those nimble riders; oh, cycloids and epi-cycloids executed in inspiration along the diagonals of the sky, amid lost wire spokes, hoops

—BIKECENTENNIAL

shed with indifference, to reach the bright goal denuded, with nothing but the pure idea of cycling! From these days dates a new constellation, the thirteenth group of stars, included forever in the zodiac and resplendent since then in the firmament of our nights: THE CYCLIST.[10]

A similar sighting was reported in *Bicycling!* (1977) by Doug Kellogg of Fayetteville, Arkansas, in a letter titled "Rider in the Heavens:"

A friend and I are on an extensive tour (almost 2,000 miles so far). As we bedded down next to a road grader outside of Cortez, Colorado (a highway patrolman had stopped us for riding at night), I looked up to see if I could identify any constellations. I saw "the Crown," Corona Borealis, above. As I looked, I envisioned it as the wheel of a bike. I looked further and saw a rider bent so that the crown was a rear wheel. Other stars formed parts of a frame. The seat. I looked for a front wheel and found one using dim stars and a little imagination to complete my biker constellation!

So far, I don't know why the gods put that rider in the heavens. Maybe they'll reveal the myth to me soon, or maybe someone else knows it. But every clear night I look up and see that biker trying to ride around the North Star. I wonder how far he's traveled.[11]

Riding and Writing

The bicycle has been an essential source of inspiration for many writers. William Saroyan wrote about the bicycle's creative aspect in *The Bicycle Rider in Beverly Hills* (1952):

A man learns style from everything, but I learned mine from things on which I moved, and as writing is a thing which moves I think I was lucky to learn as I did.

A bike can be an important appurtenance of an important ritual. Moving the legs evenly and steadily soon brings home to the bike-rider a valuable knowledge of pace and rhythm, and a sensible respect for timing and the meeting of a schedule.

Out of rhythm come many things, perhaps all things. The physical action compels action of another order—action of mind, memory, imagination, dream, hope, order, and so on. The physical action also establishes a deep respect for grace, seemliness, effectiveness, power with ease, naturalness, and so on. The action of the imagination brings home to the bicycle-rider the limitlessness of the potential in all things. He finds out that there are many excellent ways in which to ride a bike effectively, and this acquaintanceship with the ways and the comparing of them gives him an awareness of a parallel potential in all other actions. Out of the action of the imagination comes also music and memory.

On the way I found out all the things without which I could never be the writer I am. I was not yet sixteen when I understood a great deal, from having ridden bicycles for so long, about style, speed, grace, purpose, value, form, integrity, health, humor, music, breathing, and finally and perhaps best of the relationship between the beginning and the end.[12]

Christopher Morley offers a similar message in *The Romany Stain* (1926):

The bicycle, the bicycle surely, should always be the vehicle of novelists and poets. How pleasant if one could prove that a decline in literary delicacy followed the disappearance of the bike from American roads.... Not that I am disloyal to the automobile. For I know the peculiar thrill of motor cars, how one learns to love the steady drumming of their faithful organs, the gallant arch of the hood as it goes questing, like a sentient creature, along dazzling roads. Yet in a car you are carried; on a bike you go. You are yourself integral with the machine.

An odd feeling comes sometimes to a writer who has long carried in the knapsack of the mind some notion that he wants to put in ink. It is a sensation I can only describe as Getting Ready to Write....

In these moods bicycling seems perfectly the right employ. It is all very well to say to yourself that you are not thinking as you wheel serenely along; but you *are*, and that sure uncertainty of the cyclist's balance, that unconsciously watchful suspension (solid on earth yet so breezily flitting) seems to symbolize the task itself. The wheel slidders in a rut or on a slope of gravel: at once, by instinct, you redress your perpendicular. So, in the continual joy and disgust of the writer's work, he dare not abandon that difficult trained alertness. How much of the plain horror and stupidity is he to admit into his picture? How many of the grossly significant minutiae can he pause to include? How often shall he make a resolute fling to convey that incomparable energy of life that should be the artist's goal above all? These are the airy tinkerings of his doubt; and as he passes from windy hill-top to green creeks and grazings sometimes the bicycle sets him free. He sees it all afresh; nothing, nothing has ever been written yet: the entire white paper of the world is clean for his special portrait of all hunger, all joy, and all vexation.[13]

Vehicle Art

The bicycle as a work of art may be a beautiful object, a vehicle for expression, or a catalyst for intellectual musing. Bicycles appear in many art forms, such as painting, drawing, collage, sculpture, performance art, and public art. Since its appearance in the late nineteenth century, the bicycle can be found in almost every artistic movement.

The bicycle probably has its greatest importance in the world of art as a found object, because it was used in this manner by two of the most influential artists of modern times, Marcel Duchamp and Pablo Picasso. Marcel Duchamp (1887–1968) brought a provocative and intellectual vision to art by transforming the physical character of common material objects with their cultural and psychological meanings. Duchamp inspired a whole new approach to art by using poetry and puns, found objects, diagrams and alchemical symbols, cyclical mechanisms, and his own body. His ideas dealt with chance, consciousness, and sexuality. Although his first and last passion was the game of chess, much of his art includes the bicycle—even his birth date has been linked with the invention of the cross-frame safety bicycle.

In 1913, Duchamp screwed the front forks of a bicycle upside-down into the seat of a stool in his studio and set the wheel spinning, thus creating the first "Ready-made" sculpture, *Roue de Bicyclette* or *Bicycle Wheel*, a seminal work of modernism and a prototype for Dadaism. Duchamp described his original intentions later in life:

> The *Bicycle Wheel* is my first Ready-made, so much so that at first it wasn't even called a Ready-made. It still had little to do with the idea of the Ready-made. Rather, it had more to do with the idea of chance. In a way, it was simply letting things go by themselves and having a sort of created atmosphere in the studio, an apartment where you live. Probably, to help your ideas come out of your head. To see that wheel turning was very soothing, very comforting, a sort of opening of avenues on other things than material life of every day. I liked the idea of having a bicycle wheel in my studio. I enjoyed looking at it, just as I enjoy looking at the flames dancing in a fireplace. It was like having a fireplace in my studio, the movement of the wheel reminded me of the movement of the flames.[14]

André Breton described Ready-mades as "manufactured objects promoted to the dignity of objects of art through the choice of the artist." Duchamp called *Bicycle Wheel* an Assisted Ready-made because the object was displaced from its normal situation. It reflects a greater awareness of the observer's point of view, as revealed in Albert Einstein's Theory of Relativity of 1909, and Duchamp's statement, "When a clock is seen from the side (in profile) it no longer tells the time."

Marcel Duchamp, *Bicycle Wheel,* New York, 1916–18. Bicycle wheel, fork, headset, and stool. Photo courtesy of Pierre Matisse Gallery.

Bicycle Wheel allows the spectator to manipulate and change the image by spinning the wheel. As friction slows it to a motionless state, the lighter part of the rim at the tire-valve hole balances at the top of the circle. The cyclical nature of the work is evident in that the wheel can be activated repeatedly. If you spin the heavily fingerprinted *Bicycle Wheel* at the Philadelphia Museum of Art, the museum guards are likely to stop the wheel and threaten to throw you out. Because of this policy, and because most photos of the work show it motionless, the public sees only part of the image.

The original *Bicycle Wheel*, which Duchamp built at his family's estate in Neuilly, France, is lost and only photographs exist of the replacement he built in 1916 for his studio in New York City. *Bicycle Wheel* was resurrected in subsequent works by Duchamp, and there have been many reconstructed copies made, including limited editions built under the supervision of Duchamp, an unknown number of unofficial replicas, as well as others that pay homage to Duchamp and his idea by the artists Jean Tinguely (1960), Woody Amen (1974), Shigeko Kubota (1983), and Mark Bildo (1985).

One might think of *Bicycle Wheel* as art that nearly anyone can make, but an inspection of the replicas shows a variety of materials and possibilities for the work. In 1951, art dealer Sidney Janis commissioned a replica that Duchamp signed in 1959 and which now belongs to the Museum of Modern Art in New York. This was a fairly crude rendition, a stock set of raked forks fixed to a kitchen stool, quite unlike the original which exhibited Duchamp's sophisticated sense of craftsmanship and mechanical know-how.

The original was reproduced in 1964 by the Galleria Schwarz in Milan, in collaboration with Duchamp, using a blueprint derived from photos of the lost original. In this edition of about a dozen, the forks are straight and the steering tube is cut short to fit to the seat of the stool using a headset, allowing the forks to turn freely. When the wheel is spinning under the right conditions the forks turn because of gyroscopic effects.

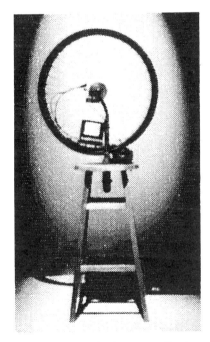

Shigeko Kubota, *Duchampiana: Bicycle Wheel,* 1983.

Through this secondary motion of *Bicycle Wheel* it has been considered a conceptual model for both a non-Euclidean spherical space and a four-dimensional Euclidean hypersurface. Although Duchamp may not have been fully aware of "incompleteness" theories it is believed that he learned something from his readings of the mathematicians Henri Poincaré and E. Jouffret. The art historian Lawrence Steefel illuminates some of the fascination for *Bicycle Wheel* in his Ph.D. studies:

Subject to the indifferent impulse of any idler, the wheel can be accelerated or "idled" without the customary friction of the road. The "freewheeling" device goes no place in a hurry. The wheel is thus the first "mobile" sculpture of the twentieth century. There are also important visual effects. If spun slowly, the object becomes blurred at the outer extension of the spokes, but still retains its object-quality. Pushed harder, the spokes blur into what Moholy-Nagy calls a "virtual volume," transforming the object-quality into a luminous illusion of transparent and dematerialized "spatial motion." The rim, which remains a constant enclosing circle, will also glimmer more radiantly, so that the passage of the distinctly delineated forms into an indistinct shimmer (which is half mirror, half window) integrates and fuses the parts of the object into a new unity and also into what seems a new physical condition. *Bicycle Wheel* can be either (1) a kind of stroboscopic construction or (2) a transparency... Paradoxically, the viewer, on one hand, is more dependent on the existence of *Bicycle Wheel* as an object, rather than as an imaginary image, but on the other hand, the effect of motion is "purer" here because the motion is "abstract" and concrete at the same time. Like the use of a glass surface for painting, the spokes of the *Bicycle Wheel* in motion are (1) physically there and (2) not there at the same time. Moreover, the spinning of the spokes creates an hallucinatory optical ground for sheer bedazzlement which stimulates a kind of dilation of the eye, as do the devices of dilation used by hypnotists. In its range of transformation from sculpture to an appearance like painting, *Bicycle Wheel* seems to link the subjective world of dreams and the objective world of things. Because this Ready-made offers a continuum of transformation from physicality to the generation of sheer motility (spacialized) and can do so against the most heterogenous environments, it serves as a concrete symbol of internal self-transformation which creates its own frame of reference (the rim and axial rotation), this "self-centered" object develops, within this frame of "magic circle," abstract qualities of rhythmic motion which are of a musical order of perceptions which have not yet become knowledge. In motion, the separate forms begin to "comprehend" each other until there is a kind of reconciliation between them. The spokes, which are crossed and visually intertwined when the wheel is at rest, now fuse, from the "perspective" of motion, vanish from this new "vanishing point," and "find their reconciliation which must be blossoming without any causal distinction." As conceptual symbol and as a visual phe-

Bicycle Wheel in motion.

nomenon, *Bicycle Wheel* is not so much a "vicious circle" as it is a "four-dimensional" object. As a Ready-made, *Bicycle Wheel* does not contradict, but supports the contention that Duchamp's preoccupation with mechanical form (and the beauty of indifference which mechanism allows) is not necessarily restrictive or cynical.[15]

Pablo Ruiz Picasso (1881–1973), one of the most legendary and prolific artists of modern times, was born in Malaga, in southern Spain. Picasso's subjects include female companions, still-lifes, and what some have called his alter-self, the horny beast. Whether it was *el toro* the bull, a mythic minotaur, or a goat, he seems to have had this image fixed in his head. The bicycle appears in only a few works compared to Picasso's total output, estimated at three works of art for every day of his life, yet it does appear in two works considered masterpieces, the painting *Night Fishing at Antibes* and the bronze sculpture *Bull's Head.*

Night Fishing at Antibes came at the mid-point in Picasso's career, two years after he finished the monumental mural *Guernica*, with the advent of World War II. The large canvas, painted in the summer of 1939 while Picasso resided in the south of France, shows two men in a boat under the moon, one rather violently spearing a fish, while two women stand on the sea wall, one holding a bicycle and licking her ice-cream cone. The scene is one of the darkest Picasso ever painted, and the bicycle is as one would expect—a lively symbol of hope, an innocent witness to a cruel world.

During the German occupation of France, Picasso was able to stay in Paris working in solitude. In 1943 he created what is his most renowned found object, the *Tête de Taureau* or *Bull's Head*, a bronze sculpture combining a pair of bicycle handlebars and a leather bicycle saddle that makes the head of a bull. By some primal instinct, this simple combination appears to be the most perfect likeness for each of its elements that could ever be conceived, and almost everyone who looks at *Bull's Head* has a shared feeling of its conception. In a conversation with the photographer Brassai, Picasso spoke of how he "took the bull by horns:"

> One day I found in a pile of jumble an old bicycle saddle next to some rusted handlebars—in a flash they were associated in my mind—the idea of this *Bull's Head* came without my thinking about it—I had only to weld them together. What is wonderful about the bronze is that it can give the most incongruous objects such a unity that it's sometimes difficult to identify the elements that make them up. But it is also a danger: if you only see the *Bull's Head* and not the saddle and handlebars from which it's made, then the sculpture loses its interest.

Picasso's *Bull's Head*, like Duchamp's *Bicycle Wheel*, helped to confirm the concept that the artist's idea is what matters most of all. In this way, the art historian H.W. Janson used this ingenious bicycle work to help define the meaning of art and its creation in the introduction of his textbook, *History of Art*:

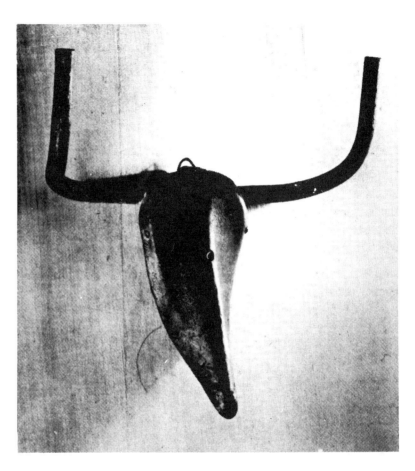

Pablo Picasso, *Tête de Taureau (Bull's Head)*, 1943. Bronze bicycle handlebars and saddle. Photo courtesy of Galerie Louis Leiris, Paris.

Of course the materials used by Picasso are man-made, but it would be absurd to insist that Picasso must share the credit with the manufacturer, since the seat and handlebars in themselves are not works of art. While we feel a certain jolt when we first recognize the ingredients of this visual pun, we also sense that it was a stroke of genius to put them together in this unique way, and we cannot very well deny that it is a work of art. Yet the handiwork—the mounting of the seat on the handlebars—is ridiculously simple. What is far from simple is the leap of the imagination by which Picasso recognized a bull's head in these unlikely objects; that, we feel, only he could have done.[16]

Paying homage to Picasso's *Bull's Head*, an exhibit called "The Bicycle Seat as Art" was held in 1994 by the American Bicycle and Cycling Museum in Santa Fe, New Mexico. Along with various decorated seats and two shrines to Santo Seato, the patron saint of bicycle seats, the Troxel company donated 6,000 out-of-production seats, that weighed together over four tons, to be used for art-making at the Santa Fe Children's Museum.

Found object art, with bicycles and their parts making static and kinetic sculpture, continued into the Post-Modern Age, where the humanity of things is found in ironic or cynical approaches to the machine age. One manifestation is Junk Art, which reflects the after-effects of industrial development, as junkyards filled with discarded obsolete machinery surrounding most urban environments became gardens of inspiration for artists. Richard Stankiewicz brought new life to junkyard objects by recycling rusty old machine parts and creating provocative contraptions, such as *Europa on a Cycle* (1953).

Jean Tinguely (1925–1991) of Switzerland developed various kinetic auto-creative and auto-destructive machines, called *Meta-Matics*, which could make drawings through motorized pulleys, wheels, flexible arms and metal hands. When one of these robot artists made over 40,000 drawings, it set the art world in a spin as the work resembled that of highly intellectual abstract expressionists. Tinguely's *Cyclograveur* (1960) is a pedal-powered meta-matic and a popular interactive work of art for museum goers.

Tinguely's most infamous work, the auto-destructive *Homage to New York*, made its sole performance in the sculpture garden at the Museum of Modern Art, in a gala event on the night of Saint Patrick's Day, 1960. *Homage to New York* consisted of innumerable bicycle and baby carriage wheels, an old piano, an addressograph machine, a couple of *Meta-Matics*, plenty of Klaxon electric motors, some bells, drums, smoke bombs, vile-smelling chemicals, a fire extinguisher and a giant weather balloon. It was set with electric and mechanical time-delay relays, and the whole huge and complex thing was painted white. Tinguely had the collaboration of two Bell Laboratory engineers, Billy Kluver and Harold Hodges, as well as the artists Robert Breer and Robert Rauschenberg, who built the machine's mascot, a silver dollar thrower. Kluver describes the work in "The Garden Party:"

Jean Tinguely, *Cyclograveur,* 1960.

> Jean Tinguely's destructive construction No. 1 was built in the Buckminster Fuller dome at The Museum of Modern Art over a period of three weeks. When, on March 17, 1960, his machine was put into action, the spectacle was one of beautiful humor, poetry and confusion. Jean's machine performed for half an hour and exists no more.... He wanted old bicycle wheels from junk yards. But no junk yards in the U.S. deals in such trivialities. I stumbled onto a dealer in Plainfield who was clearing out his basement and carried away 35 old rusty wheels. Jean was as excited as a child when he brought the wheels through the empty museum that evening. The dome was unheated, and the temperature was below freezing, but things began to move. "I want more wheels," he said.... The next day my wife and I raided the Summit dump. This was a gold mine. We loaded the car and parked it behind the fence on 54th Street. A child's potty and bassinet, the drum from a washing machine, and 25 more baby carriage and bicycle wheels were thrown over the fence. The Saturday-afternoon passers-by raised the inevitable question: "What's going on here?" On the other side of the fence Jean was laughing....[17]

Cesar, *Compression de bicyclette,* 1960.

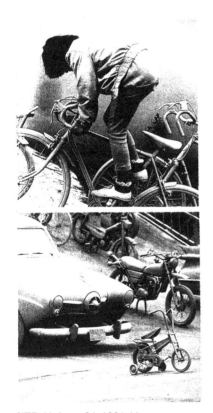

SITE, *Highway 86,* 1986, Vancouver, Canada.

A destroyed bicycle became a work of art by the sculptor Cesar Baldaccini of Marseilles. Cesar is known for the compressed vehicles he began making in 1953, using an hydraulic press known in junkyards as the "Big Squeeze." Like the "Trash Masher" used in homes with post-modern conveniences, these machines compact garbage into small cubic blocks for recycling or disposal. Cesar compressed autos, motorcycles, and eventually a whole bicycle in 1970. His idea was to show how common vehicles for mobility and freedom can be transformed into inert "unsculptural" objects that combine realism, abstraction, and expressionism through the sublimation of an automatic process. Compared to compressed cars, which stand about waist high, the bicycle makes a small cube, each side about seventeen inches, or 4,900 cubic inches.

The artist Christo (1935–) has wrapped, fenced, or curtained just about anything and anyplace. Born in Bulgaria and working in Paris and New York, he has wrapped a bottle, a bridge, a bicycle, a Volkswagen, and a museum of art. With a crew of assistants he made fence-like curtains in a crevasse in Australia, along 24 miles of northern California hillside, and lined a set of coral reefs in the Caribbean. He made *Bicyclette empaquetée sur galeria de voiture* (Wrapped bicycle on a car rack) in Paris in 1962. The piece is intended to be a double image, with a translucent wrapping showing a barely perceptible bicycle underneath. Christo wanted spectators to appreciate the surface rather than the practical (and ironic) function of protecting a bicycle from the elements while it was mounted on a car.

Bicycles are found in public art works, such as architectural constructions, murals, monuments, and museums. Almost every kind of vehicle ever made since 1940 was installed on *Highway 86,* an undulating section of freeway built by the architectural group SITE for the 1986 World Exposition in Vancouver, Canada. Described as "a syncopated rhythm of incongruity and poignancy," it included over 200 vehicles, with the innards removed, the hatches sealed, the wheels anchored, and each one painted in weatherproof generic-colored concrete white. Since 1977, Roger Chomeaux, known as Chomo, has been constructing a cathedral of old bicycles in Achères le Forêt, France. American artist Howard Finster built *Bicycle Tower* in his *Paradise Garden,* a combination folk-art church, junk yard, vegetable garden, museum of technology, and artist's workshop begun around 1970 in Pennville, Georgia. Among his many trades, Finster was a bicycle recycler who scavenged old bikes to repair, paint, and sell like new. Finster described how bicycles fit into his visions and his art. Once, while touching up a bike with a blob of paint on his finger, he saw a face and a divine feeling came over him that said, "Paint sacred art." Another vision said, "Howard, if you want to go out big in the world, you must quit working on bicycles and lawn mowers. *Getting on the altar* means putting yourself into one thing and that [is] art...." "When I found out for sure that God called me to do sacred art," said Finster, "I molded my tools in the walkway as evidence."[18]

ACTIVE ART

The Post-Modern Age has brought more active art forms in which artists create happenings, performance pieces, and interactive installations. Active art grew with the realization that life itself is an expression of art. By going beyond the static object on the wall or pedestal of an art gallery, artists could create a living image that opened the dimensions of time, place, and chance. By allowing the spectator to participate, they could create an interactive experience that activated the world at large. Vehicle-art is an off-spring of active art, where artists use vehicles or journeys as their means of expression. In this realm the bicycle becomes an active component in living art.

Chris Burden is a pioneer in the active arts. Among his many happenings he created a couple of bicycle performances. His first work, *Bicycle Piece*, was performed at the art gallery of the University of California at Irvine in 1970. During the entire time the gallery doors were open, from May 6th to 20th, Burden rode a bicycle continuously throughout the gallery on a one foot-wide black path, which extended in and out the front and rear doors. In another performance on October 14, 1976, the *Death Valley Run*, Burden crossed Death Valley in about seven hours on a faired bicycle equipped with "the smallest motor possible." The 40-pound bike had an eleven-pound 20cc engine and went between 16 to 27 mph.

Eric and Deborah Staller, *Bubbleheads*, 1987, New York City.

In the late 1960s and early 1970s, Belgian artist Paramarenko straddled the realms of functional technology and intuitive art with innovative designs for flying vehicles, some with pedal-power. He made a serious attempt at human-powered flight around 1972 with a work called *U-Kontrol III*, and another pedal-powered aircraft called *Umbilly I* (1976) was based on the flapping wings of a dragonfly.

In Wales, a performance piece called *Cyclamen Cyclists* (1971), consisting of a group of artists with uniforms and bicycles painted pink, the color of Cyclamen flowers, lined up along the banks of the Swansea Docks. They were described as gentle blossoms amidst an abandoned coal shipping site. In America, the artists Eric and Deborah Staller created a couple of cycling performance vehicles, *Bubbleheads* (1987) and *Octos* (1992), which appeared on New York City streets.

Joseph Beuys (1921–1985) from Krefeld, Germany, created one of the finest examples of the bicycle as vehicle art, with a performance piece called *Is It About A Bicycle?* Considered his last major work, it was the result of a thirty-day teach-in during the *documenta 7* exhibition in 1982 in Kassel, Germany. Beuys joined the Luftwaffe as a pilot in World War II, and in 1943, while flying over the Crimean mountains, his aircraft crashed in the snow and he was rescued by Tartars who wrapped him in layers of animal fat and felt cloth. Before the end of the war, he was wounded some five times and taken prisoner by the British. After his near-death experience, these two materials, fat and felt, symbols of survival and regeneration, became an obsessive motif in his works.

Is It About A Bicycle? consists of fifteen blackboards on which Beuys retraced his life's events and ideas in colored chalk. He completed the work by riding a bicycle two times over the blackboards with tires that sprayed white paint, leaving an imprint of his cosmic journey as a vehicle artist. The title alludes to Flann O'Brien's book, *The Dalkey Archive*, where the question "Is it about a bicycle?" is asked about life in the here-after. Art historian Bernard Lamarche-Vadel interviewed Beuys about the work in the essay *Portrait of the Artist on a Bike*:

Lamarche-Vadel The background of these blackboards looks like a nocturnal, celestial vault full of stars. Was this effect voluntary on your part?

Beuys Yes, your comment is accurate. This effect was produced by my last performance on these boards; in order to give a certain unity to the ensemble, I laid the panels out in the street. Then I rode over them on a bicycle. Beforehand, we had coated the tires with white paint. While cycling, the paint spattered and fell in a fine mist to form a starry sky. The effect was definitely intended, and we even calculated, in advance, the necessary riding speed to obtain this effect.

Lamarche-Vadel Can we compare *Is It About A Bicycle?* in your work to *La Boîte en Valise* in the work of Marcel Duchamp?

Beuys Yes, perhaps Marcel Duchamp was interested in vehicle-art, since he conceived of an object integrating a bicycle wheel in motion, turning on itself. This is an appropriate symbol of Duchamp's work, that of a man who always encounters himself at the same point, in the same style, with the same habits and conduct. Our bicycle, however, deals with problems as diverse as those of the Third World, the structure of society, spiritual existence, justice, democracy, and the economy. This bicycle has no pedestal. Its wheels do not desparately return to the same spot at all. It is a dynamic bicycle which moves towards the future. One finds many interesting things in Duchamp's suitcase, but when problems of pedagogy, economics, or politics arise, you have nothing to work with. It serves no practical purpose. In *Is It About A Bicycle?*, however, we find elements to work with, a methodology anyone can understand and discuss. In Duchamp, there is nothing to argue or criticize. One must take him as he is, in terms of an art object whose proper place is the museum. My paintings, to the contrary, encourage discussion and participation.[19]

By proposing the question "Is It About A Bicycle?" in their work, Flann O'Brien and Joseph Beuys show how the bicycle may be part of the answer to everything, as a vehicle that challenges people to find new paradigms in art as in life.

JOSEPH BEUYS

is it about a bicycle?

Left, "I think its been done before."
Fischetti, 1959, from *Punch*.

Below, Joseph Beuys, *Is It About A
Bicycle,* 1982. Bicycle with chalkboards.
Photo courtesy Marisa del Rey Gallery,
New York.

Appendices

Cycles

USA BICYCLE MARKET (1865-1994)

Sources: Author's estimate (1860s–1880s); Cycle Trades Association (1890s); US Dept. of Commerce; US Tariff Commission (1899–1960); War Industries Board (1916–17); New Departure Div., General Motors Corp. (1919–1932); Schwinn Bicycle Co. (1930s–1970s); Bicycle Institute of America (1946–1994); Bicycle Manufacturers Association (1970s).

YEAR	TOTAL	DOMESTIC	IMPORTED	EXPORTED
1865	0			
1866	5			
1867	10			
1868	500			
1869	25,000			
1876	4			
1877	10			
1878	100			
1879	400			
1889	200,000			
1890	340,000			
1895	800,000			
1896	1,200,000			
1897	2,000,000			
1899	1,182,691			
1900	1,182,850			
1904	250,487			
1909	233,707			
1914	398,899			
1916	526,076			
1917	606,918			
1918	567,207			
1919	479,163			
1920	750,000			
1921	149,192			
1922	150,000			
1923	486,177			
1924	350,000	343,033	-	6,967
1925	252,296	260,000	-	7,710
1926	294,656	300,000	-	5,344
1927	250,168	255,000	-	4,832
1928	342,911	348,000	-	5,089
1929	301,892	308,000	-	6,108
1930	296,254	300,000	-	3,746
1931	258,566	260,000	-	1,434
1932	259,205	260,000	-	795
1933	323,967	320,000	5,000	1,033
1934	518,773	512,450	7,500	1,177
1935	668,880	657,000	13,000	1,120
1936	1,233,093	1,218,415	17,000	2,322
1937	1,143,160	1,131,000	16,000	3,840
1938	864,989	851,526	16,500	3,037
1939	1,258,380	1,252,886	12,214	6,720
1940	1,290,459	1,290,925	11,3291	1,795
1941	1,806,982	1,829,073	6,041	28,132
1942	554,890	560,848	548	6,506
1943	158,191	178,938	101	20,848
1944	148,799	172,965	63	24,229

YEAR	TOTAL	DOMESTIC	IMPORTED	EXPORTED
1945	544,721	544,655	3,675	13,609
1946	1,664,327	1,652,923	46,840	35,436
1947	2,800,774	2,875,000	19,758	93,984
1948	2,706,185	2,794,516	16,774	105,105
1949	1,451,685	1,483,009	15,985	47,259
1950	2,006,364	1,963,716	67,789	25,141
1951	2,085,047	1,925,797	176,644	17,394
1952	2,085,047	1,920,179	245,763	12,202
1953	2,695,629	2,111,899	592,999	9,269
1954	2,487,357	1,531,857	963.667	8,167
1955	3,011,741	1,794,968	1,223,990	7,217
1956	2,914,952	1,746,818	1,173,346	5,212
1957	2,625,554	1,884,846	748,689	7,981
1958	2,930,840	2,116,344	823,614	9,118
1959	3,572,288	2,562,338	1,013,396	3,446
1960	3,769,698	2,584,622	1,188,034	2,961
1961	3,663,663	2,579,093	1,087,318	2,748
1962	4,216,177	2,954,215	1,266,790	4,828
1963	4,409,649	3,118,260	1,294,901	3,512
1964	5,088,485	4,082,563	1,010,035	4,113
1965	5,654,124	4,618,743	1,038,884	3,503
1966	5,747,703	4,829,122	927,223	8,642
1967	6,292,194	5,180,352	1,117,246	5,404
1968	7,493,886	5,966,184	1,534,138	6,466
1969	7,053,417	5,089,023	1,970,528	6,134
1970	6,891,082	4,950,879	1,947,396	7,193
1971	8,849,240	6,518,806	239,470	9,036
1972	13,896,967	8,750,597	5,156,068	9,698
1973	15,210,282	10,072,356	5,154,903	16,977
1974	14,105,775	10,161,000	3,979,225	34,741
1975	7,293,784	5,605,981	1,717,885	30,082
1976	7,804,264	6,177,389	1,667,537	40,662
1977	9,412,717	7,483,585	1,967,801	38,669
1978	9,228,925	7,342,475	1,959,896	73,446
1979	10,800,000	9,000,000	1,800,000	
1980	9,000,000	7,000,000	2,000,000	
1981	8,900,000	6,800,000	2,100,000	
1982	6,800,000	5,200,000	1,600,000	
1983	9,000,000	6,300,000	2,700,000	
1984	10,100,000	5,900,000	4,200,000	
1985	11,400,000	5,800,000	5,600,000	
1986	12,300,000	5,300,000	7,000,000	
1987	12,600,000	5,200,000	7,400,000	
1988	9,900,000	4,500,000	5,400,000	
1989	10,700,000	5,300,000	4,900,000	
1990	10,800,000	6,000,000	4,800,000	
1991	11,641,000	7.300,000	4,400,000	
1992	11,639,209	7,373,393	4,265,816	
1993	13,000,000	8,000,000	5,000,000	
1994	13,000,000	8,000,000	5,000,000	

CYCLE MAKERS

SELECTED CYCLE, COMPONENT AND ACCESSORY MANUFACTURERS

Advanced American Bicycle Concepts Veradale WA, 509-924-9480, Advanta/Wedge semi-recumbents.

Advanced Transportation Products (ATP) Seattle WA, 206-771-3719, Vision recumbents.

Ace Tool and Engineering Mooresville IN, 317-831-8798, Infinity recumbents.

Alpinestars Coste di Maser Italy, 0423-565095-565248; Alpinestars USA San Luis Obisbo CA, 805-549-0597, mountain bikes.

Ambrosio Solaro Italy, 02-9690952, components.

AMP Research CA, 714-450-0292, components.

Angle-Tech Woodland Park CO, 719-687-7475, Angle Lake Cyclery Seattle WA, 206-878-7457, Counterpoint recumbent.

Arriba Recumbents Lindsborg KS, 913-227-4407.

Atala Padova Italy, 049-8071722, all types.

Avocet Palo Alto CA, 415-321-8501, components.

Balance Cycle Santa Clarita CA, 805-295-5100, Crosstrac, S-Bike mountain bikes.

Barracuda Durango CO, 303-259-2622, mountain bikes.

Batavus Holland, all types.

Battle Mountain Bikes WY, 307-327-5952.

Benotto Moderna Mexico, 590-7737, all types.

Bianchi Treviglio, Italy, 0363-41444; Bianchi USA San Francisco CA, 415-863-0436, all types.

Bicycles by Haluzak Santa Rosa CA, 707-544-6243, recumbents.

Bike Nashbar Youngstown OH, 216-788-8832, sport bikes.

BikeE Corvalis OR, 503-753-9747, recumbents.

Bilenky Cycle Works Philadelphia PA, 215-487-1063, touring bikes.

BMC Racing WA, 206-575-2440.

Brampton Bikes Glandstone MI, 906-428-4341, Roadmaster.

Brompton England, folding bikes.

Breeze Cycles Fairfax CA, 415-871-8870, Breezer bikes.

Bruce Gordon Cycles Petaluma CA, 707-762-5601, Rock 'n Road bikes.

Burley Design Cooperative Eugene OR, 503-687-1644, tandems, trailers, etc.

Caloi Brazil; Caloi USA FL, 904-355-5547, all types.

Campagnolo Vicenza Italy, 0444-564933; Campagnolo USA Carlsbad CA, 619-931-0991, components.

Cannondale Georgetown CT, 203-544-9800, Bedford PA, 800-BIKE-USA, all types.

Carnielli Vittorio Veneto Italy, 438-59045, Bottecchia bikes.

Casati Monza Italy, 039-360006, race bikes.

Chiorda Sud Le Castella Italy, 06-9690001, Legnano, Piaggio bikes.

Cinelli Milan Italy, 2-26411790, race bikes, components.

Clarke Kent Bicycles Denver CO, 303-935-7550, race bikes.

La Clément Milan Italy, 02-64421, tires.

Ernesto Colnago Milan Italy, 02-9530-8082, race bikes.

Columbus Milan Italy, 2-504187, tubing.

Co-Motion Cycles OR, 503-343-4583, Espresso.

Conejo AZ, 602-255-0389.

Crosstrac USA Occidental CA, 707-874-1874.

Custom Cycles Amesbury MA, 508-388-4150.

Custom Transportation Alternatives Cleveland OH, 216-341-6939, Coo's Bay Flyer, Runabout, Mach II.

Dean USA Boulder CO, 303-494-2026, mountain bikes.

De Rosa Italy, racing bikes

DH Recumbents Spring TX, 713-251-5413.

Dia-Compe Osaka Japan, 06-721-7051, components.

Dirt Research Newark DE , 302-737-2740.

Doppler Cycle Technologies Kitchener, Canada, 519-579-5103.

Easton Van Nuys CA, 818-782-6445, tubing.

Easy Racer Watsonville CA, 408-722-9797, Tour Easy, Gold Rush recumbents.

Eddy Merckx Belgium, race bikes.

Eco Cycle Corvallis OR, 503-753-5178, Trice, Euro-Trice, Ross recumbents.

Fabra Trezzo Sul'Adda Italy, 02-909-61300, components.

Fichtel & Sachs Schweinfurt Germany, 0049-9721982734, Hercules bikes, Sachs components.

Fir (Fabbrica Italiano Ruote) Boltiere Italy, 035-806-090, components.

Fuji America Oakland NJ, 201-337-1700, all types.

Gary Fisher Waterloo WI, 414-478-3532, mountain bikes.

Giant Manufacturing Taipei Taiwan, 886-2-7625072; Giant Bicycle, Inc. Rancho Dominguez CA, 310-609-3340, all types.

Gios Settimo Torinese, Italy, 11-8005774.

GT Bicycles Huntington Beach CA, 714-841-7791, sport bikes.

Green Gear Cycling Eugene OR, 503-687-0487, Bike Friday, Two'sDay tandem.

Haro Carlsbad CA, 619-438-4812, sport bikes.

HH Racing Group Philadelphia PA, 215-334-8500.

Huffy Bicycles Dayton OH, 513-866-6251, all types.

Ibis Cycles Sebastopol CA, 707-829-5615, mountain bikes.

Iron Horse USA Hauppauge NY, 516-348-6900, mountain bikes.

Gipiemme Vincenza, Italy, components.

Joannou Northvale NJ, 201-768-9050, Boss, Cignal, Jamis bikes, components.

Just Two Bikes White Bear Lake MN, 612-429-9081, Montague.

Kestrel Watsonville CA, 408-724-9079, race bikes.

KHS Carson CA, 310-632-7173, mountain bikes.

Kingcycle Bedfordshire, England, recumbents, HPVs, ergometers.

Klein Chehalis WA, 206-262-3305, sports bikes.

Koga Myata Japan, all types.

Kona Blaine WA, 206-332-5384, mountain bikes.

Kryptonite Boulder CO, 303-665-5353, locks.

LeMond Bicycles CO, 303-935-8289, race bikes.

Lightning Cycle Dynamics Lompoc CA, 805-736-0700.

Linear Manufacturing Guttenberg IA, 319-252-1637, Linear recumbents, imports Kingcycle, Windcheetah.

Litespeed Titanium Chatanooga TN, 615-238-5530, tubing.

Maeda Industries Osaka Japan, 0723-61-1300, SunTour components.

Marin San Rafael CA, 415-485-5100, mountain bikes.

Marinoni USA Montgomery Center VT, 802-326-4321.

Mavic St Trivier-sur-Moignans, France, 74-55-8055, components.

Maxam Bicycle Mississauga Canada, 416-564-8787.

Maxam Manufacturing Cincinnati OH, 513-741-0420, Reveille.

Michelin France, tires.

Mongoose Bicycles Torrance CA, 310-378-5505, sport bikes.

Montague Cambridge MA, 617-491-7200, folding bikes.

Cicli Francesco Moser Trento Italy, 0461-992-022, race bikes.

Motiv Sports CA, 714-479-0100.

Moulton Bradford, England, small-wheel bikes.

Mountain Goat Cycles Chico CA, 916-342-4628, mountain bikes.

Murray all types.

Neobyke Lowell MA, 508-459-0779.

Nishiki Derby Cycle Corp. Kent WA, 206-395-1100, sport bikes.

Norco Products Burnaby, Canada, 604-420-6616, bikes, components.

NordicTrak Chaska MN, 612-368-2500, Fitness bike, ForeRunner quadricy-

Pashley USA distr. Dekker Service, WA, 206-641-9639, city bikes, utility cycles.
Parkpre Bicycles Kazuko CA, 805-529-5865, bikes and components.
Pedalcraft Corvallis OR, 503-752-5035, Quadraped cycles.
Performance Chapel Hill NC, 800-727-2433, sport bikes and accessories.
Phil Wood CA, components.
Pinarello Italy, race bikes.
Procycle Villece St. George Canada, 418-228-8934, Autobike.
RacerMate Seattle WA, 206-524-6625, CompuTrainer ergometers.
Raleigh Cycle Derby Cycle Corp. Kent WA, 206-395-1100, all types.
Rans Recumbents Hays KA, 913-625-6346, recumbents and sailtrikes.
Research Dynamics (RD) Ketchum ID, 208-726-4812.
ReBike Boca Raton FL, 407-750-1304, recumbents.
Redline USA BMX bikes.
Recreational Equipment Inc (REI) Sumner WA.
Rhode Gear Providence RI, 401-941-1700.
Ritchey USA Redwood City CA, 415-368-4018.
Rock Shox San Jose CA, 415-967-7469.
Rocky Mountain Richmond, Canada, 604-270-2710.
Romic Houston TX, 713-466-7806.
Ross Bicycles Farmingdale NY, 516-249-6000, all types, exercycles.
Rotator Cycles Santa Rosa CA, 707-539-4203, recumbents.
Ryan Recumbents Eugene OR, 503-485-6674.
Salsa Cycles Petalum CA, 707-762-8191.
Santana Cycles Claremont CA, 909-596-7570.
Schwinn Bicycle and Fitness Boulder CO, 708-231-5340, sport bikes, exercycles.
Scott USA Sun Valley ID, 208-622-1000, bikes and components.
Selle Italia Vicenza Italy, 0424-84043, saddles.
Selle San Marco Rossano Veneto Italy, 424-848028, saddles.
Serotta Sports Middlegrove NY, 518-587-9883, race bikes.
Shimano Osaka Japan, 0722-233243; Shimano American Irvine Ca, 714-951-5003, components.
Skyway Recreation Products Redding CA, Tuff wheels.
Softride Bellingham WA, 206-647-7420, suspension components.
Specialized Morgan Hill CA, 408-779-6229, all types.
Spectrum Cycles PA, 610-398-1986, race bikes.
Sturmey-Archer Nottingham England, 0602-42-0800, Brooks, components.
Terry Precision Bicycles Macedon NY, 315-986-2103, women's sport bikes.
Thebis International Sidney BC Canada, 604-656-1237, tricycles.
3T (Techno Tubo Torino) Mathi Italy, 11-9269533.
Ti Cycles Seattle WA, 206-624-9697.
Titus Titanium Tempe AZ, 602-894-8452.
Tommasini Grosseto Italy, 564-455006, race bikes.
Torelli Imports Camarillo CA, 805-484-8705.
Trek Waterloo WI, 414-478-2191, sport bikes.
Turner Enterprises Las Vegas NV, Laid-Back recumbents.
Union Fröndenberg, Germany, 02373-753-1, components.
Univega Lawee Inc., Long Beach CA, 310-426-0474, sport bikes.
Varna Gabriola Island, Canada, 604-247-8379, recumbents, HPVs.
Ventana Rancho Cordova CA, 916-631-0544, mountain bikes.
Wheeler Germany, all types.
Wheelsmith Fabrications Menlo Park CA, 415-364-4930, components.
Worksman Trading Ozone Park NY, 718-322-2000, roadsters, trikes, utility cycles.
WSI Camarillo CA, 805-484-4450, Diamond Back bikes.
Wynn Custom Bicycles WA, 206-932-5534.
Yeti Durango CO, 303-259-1914, mountain bikes.
Zero Bicycles St. Laurent, Canada, 514-344-5095.

Groups

CLUBS AND GROUPS

[Group Name (INITIALS) Timespan- Location, activities, members. Formerly **Former Group Name** (Timespan)]

Academic Bicycle Club-Diament 1974- Katowice, Poland, recreation.

Action Unlimited South Yarra, Victoria, Australia.

Adventure Cycling Association 1993- Missoula MT, touring, source. Formerly **Bikecentennial** 1973-.

Adventure Cycling Club Bahawalpur, Pakistan, touring.

Alberta Bicycle Association Edmonton, Canada.

Algemeiner Deutscher Fahrrad Club (ADFC) 1979- Bremen, Germany, transport, recreation.

Alliance Internationale de Tourisme Geneva, Switzerland, touring association.

All India Cycle Manufacturers Association Dehli, India, industry.

Almaden Cycle Touring Club San Jose CA, recreation, 800 members in 1990.

Alternative Stad Stockholm, Sweden, transport.

American Trails Washington DC, trails. Formerly **American Trails Network** and **National Trails Council**.

American Youth Hostels (AYH) Washington DC, 230 hostels in US, with **International Youth Hostel Federation**.

Amicale Cycliste du Corps de Sante (Friends of cycling in health professions) 1972, Marines, France.

Amics de la Bici-Agrupacio d'Usaris Barcelona (Friends of the bike in Barcelona) 1981- Barcelona, Spain.

Amici della Bicicletta (Friends of the bicycle in Italy) Bologna, Italy.

Les Amis de la Terre de Bruxelles (Friends of the earth in Brussels) Brussels, Belgium.

Another Dam Bike Club Knoxville IA, recreation.

Antique Bicycle Club of America 1958- New York, cycles, collecting.

Arbeiterradfahrbund: Solidarität (Workers' Cycling Federation) 1896- Germany. Full-service cooperative.

Arbeitsgemeinschaft Umweltfreundlicher Stadtverkehr (ARGUS) 1979- Vienna, Austria, transport, touring.

Arctic Bicycle Club Anchorage AL, recreation.

Arizona Bicycle Club 1963- Phoenix AZ, recreation.

Associacio Bicitrak Muntanya Barcelona, Spain, trails.

Association Bici e Dintorni Torino, Italy, transport.

Association Cultural La Bicicleta Madrid, Spain, performing arts group.

Association of Cycle and Lightweight Campers London, touring, with **Camping Club of Great Britain and Ireland**.

Association of Cycle Traders (ACT) Kent, England, trade.

Association Quebecoise du Velo de Montagne (AQVM) Haute-Ville, Canada, trails.

Association to Advance Bicycling West Hills CA, advocacy.

Associazone Nazionale Ciclo Motociclo Accessori (ANCMA) 1920- Milan, Italy, industry.

Auckland Cycle Touring Association Auckland, New Zealand, recreation.

Audax Warrington, England, touring.

Audax Club of Australia Shoreham, Victoria, touring.

Austin Cycling Association Austin TX.

Australian Cycling Council Sydney, Australia.

Austria Radreisen Scharding, Austria, source.

Auto-Free Bay Area Coalition 1992- Berkeley CA, transport.

Auto Relief 1992- Eugene OR, transport.

Bay Area Bicycle Action 1990- San Francisco CA, transport.

Berkeley Bikeways 1970- Berkeley CA, transport.

Berkeley Trailers Union (BTU) 1980- Berkeley CA, trails.

Berlin Bicycle Club 1880s- Berlin, Germany, recreation.

Bici e Dintorni Torino, Italy, advocacy.

Bici para la Paz (Bikes for Peace) 1988- Spain, advocacy.

Biciklista Esperanto Movado Internacia (BEMI) 1979- Valby, Denmark, Esperanto-speaking cyclists.

Bicybo (Cycling union) 1990- Brno, Czech Republic.

Bicycle Action Group Broward County MD, transport.

Bicycle Action Project 1970s- Seattle WA, transport.

Bicycle Action Project 1990- Indianapolis IN, education, recyclery.

Bicycle Adventure Club San Diego CA, touring.

Bicycle Association of Great Britain 1973- Starley House, Coventry, industry.

Bicycle Australia Campbelltown, Australia, touring.

A Bicycle Built for One World San Francisco CA, Blind and sighted cyslists for peace.

Bicycle Club of Philadelphia Philadelphia PA, recreation, 700 members in 1990.

Bicycle Coalition of Massachusetts 1993- Cambridge MA, transport. Formerly **Boston Area Bicycle Coalition (BABC)** 1970s-.

Bicycle Coalition of the Delaware Valley Philadelphia PA, transport.

Bicycle Environmental Improvement Promotion Council 1992- Sakai City, Japan, recycling.

Bicycle Federation of Australia 1979-

Melbourne, Australia, recreation, transport.

Bicycle Federation of America (BFA) 1977- Washington DC, advocacy, Pro Bike conference.

Bicycle Federation of Tennessee Murfreesboro TN, recreation, transport.

Bicycle Federation of Washington 1982- Olympia WA, recreation, transport.

Bicycle for Agriculture Nigeria, development.

Bicycle Helmet Safety Institute Arlington VA, advocacy.

Bicycle Industry Organization (BIO) 1993- Washington DC, industry.

Bicycle Institute of America (BIA) Washington DC, industry, advocacy.

Bicycle Institute of New South Wales (BINSW) 1976- Sydney, Australia, transport, recreation.

Bicycle Institute of Queensland (BIQ) 1979- Lucia, Australia, transport, recreation.

Bicycle Institute of Victoria (BIV) 1975- Melbourne, Australia, transport, recreation.

Bicycle Investment Group (BIG) St. Louis MO, education.

Bicycle Manufacturers Association of America (BMA) 1970- Washington DC, industry.

Bicycle Market Research Institute (BMRI) Boston MA, trade.

Bicycle Mobile Hams of America (BMHA) Boulder CO, cycling radio operators.

Bicycle Network 1976- Philadelphia PA, source, transport, advocacy.

Bicycle Nova Scotia Halifax, Nova Scotia, recreation.

Bicycle Parking Foundation 1981- Philadelphia PA, transport, parking source.

Bicycle Racing Stars of the Nineteenth Century Association Chicago IL, old boys' club.

Bicycle Ride Directors Association of America Whittier CA, recreation, source.

Bicycle Touring Club see **Cyclists' Touring Club**.

Bicycle Touring Club of North Jersey Wood Ridge NJ, recreation.

Bicycle Trails Council of Marin 1987- Fairfax CA, trails.

Bicycle Trails Council of the East Bay Berkeley CA, trails.

Bicycle Transportation Alliance Portland OR, transport.

Bicycle Transportation Action New York City, transport.

Bicycle Utah Park City UT, touring.

Bicycle Victoria 1975- Melbourne, Australia, touring.

Bicycle Wholesale Distributors Association (BWDA) Philadelphia PA, trade. Formerly **Cycle Jobbers Association** 1950s-.

Bicycling Association of British Columbia Vancouver, Canada, touring, source.

Bicycling Federation of Pennsylvania Camp Hill

PA, recreation.

Bicyclists Against Drugs Association Tempe AZ, advocacy.

Bicyclists of Iowa City Iowa City IA, recreation.

Big Lick Hillbillies Roanoke VA, recreation.

Bike Aid-Overseas Development Network San Francisco CA, development.

Bikecology 1970s Chicago IL, transport.

Bike-Commuters of the Environmental Protection Agency (BEPA) 1975- Washington DC, transport, recreation.

Bikecentennial see **Adventure Cycling Association**.

The Bike People 1991- Los Angeles CA, transport.

Bike Psychos Oak Lawn IL, recreation.

Bikers Association Downhill International (BAD) Switzerland, sport.

Bikes Not Cars 1989- Toronto, Canada, transport.

Biking for a Better Community 1992- Bend OR, transport.

Bloomington Bicycle Club (BBC) Bloomington IN, recreation.

Boeing Employees Bicycle Club Seattle WA, transport, recreation.

Boston Bicycle Club (BBC) 1878- Boston MA, recreation, sport.

Boulder Mountain Biking Association Boulder CO, trails.

Bridgestone Owners Bunch (BOB) 1992- San Leandro CA, cycles.

Bringa Munkacsoport Hungary, transport.

Brisbane Bicycle Touring Association Ashgrove, Australia, touring.

British Cycling Bureau London, industry, source.

British Human Power Club Bourne End, England, cycles, sport.

FIDESZ-Kerék-Párosan Szép az Élet Alapítvány (Budapest Bicycle Transportation Committee) 1990- Budapest, Hungary, transport.

Buffalo Ramblers 1880s- Buffalo NY, recreation, members cycled 189,329 miles in 1889.

Bygone Bikes Featherstone, England, cycles, collectors.

Cabbagetown Bicycle Club 1990- Toronto, Canada, transport, development.

Cajun Cyclists, Pack and Paddle Lafayette LA, recreation.

California Association of Bicycling Organizations (CABO) 1972- Dublin CA, source, recreation, transport.

Canterbury Cyclists Association Christchurch, New Zealand, touring.

Capital Bicycle Club 1881- Washington DC, recreation.

Capital City Cyclists Tallahassee FL, recreation.

Carmel Mountain Bike Club Haifa, Israel, trails.

Carolina Tarwheels Durham NC, recreation.

Cascade Bicycle Club Seattle WA, recreation, 4,800 members in 1990—largest regional club in U.S.

Centenary Club England, industry elites.

Central California Off-Road Cyclists Pinedale CA, trails.

Centro Portuguese Cicloturismo (CPC) Lisbon, Portugal, touring.

Centro Salvadoreno de Technologia Apropiada (CESTA) San Salvador, El Salvador, development, appropriate technology.

Century Road Club Association (CRCA) 1898- New York, sport.

Century Road Club of America (CRC) 1890- Princeton NJ, touring, sport.

Ceskoslovenska Sekce Cyklistiky Prague, Czech Republic, recreation, transport.

Chaperon Cycling Association 1896- England, recreation.

Charles River Wheelmen 1966- West Newton MA, recreation, 750 members in 1990.

Chicago Area Bicycle Dealers Association (CABDA) Homewood IL, trade.

Chicago Wheelmen Chicago IL, recreation.

Chicagoland Bicycle Federation 1985- Chicago IL, transport.

China Bicycle Association Beijing, industry.

Chinese Taipei Amateur Cycling Association Taipei, Taiwan, touring, sport.

Christchurch Bicycle Club 1876- Christchurch, England, recreation.

Ciclobby 1990- Milan, Italy, transport.

Citizens on Cycles 1970s, Montreal, Canada, transport.

Classic Bicycle and Whizzer Club of America Ann Arbor MI, cycles, collectors, 20th century.

Club de Ciclistas Lima, Peru, recreation.

Club de los muchachos en mal Guamuchil, Mexico, trails.

Club des Villes Cyclables 1990s- France, transport, bikeable cities.

Coast Ranger Riders Richmond CA, trails.

Coconut Grove Bicycle Club 1965- Coconut Grove FL, sport, recreation.

Colorado Plateau Mountain Bike Trail Association Grand Junction CO, trails.

Colt Bicycle Club 1890s, Hartford CT, recreation.

Comité Liaison des Fabricants des Bicyclettes (COLIBI) France, industry.

Comité Liaison des Fabricants de Pièces et Equipements de Deux Roues (COLIPED) France, industry.

Concerned Long Island Mountain Bikers (CLIMB) Woodbury NY, trails.

Concerned Off-Road Bicyclists Association (CORBA) 1987- Woodland Hills CA, trails.

CORBA-Puget Sound Seattle WA, trails.

Connecticut Coalition of Bicyclists Middletown CT, transport.

A Contramano Sevilla, Spain, transport.

Coordinatora Catalana d'Usuaris de la Bicicleta Barcelona, Spain, transport.

Crescent City Cyclists Metairie LA, recreation.

Crested Butte Mountain Bicycling Association Crested Butte CO, trails.

Cyclebag 1977- Bristol, England, transport, 2,000 members in 1980.

Cycle Board of Trade 1894- New York City, industry.

Cycle Campaign Network (CCN) 1990s- Milton Keyes, England, transport.

Cyclefolk 1984- Dublin, Ireland, transport.

Cycle Parts and Accessories Association East Hills NY, trade.

Cycle Safety Campaign 1991- Johannesburg, South Africa, advocacy.

Cycle Touring Association of Western Australia Wembley, Australia, touring, source.

Cycle Tourist Association of India Pune, India, touring.

Cycle Watch Toronto, Canada, transport.

Cycleways Takoma Park MD, touring, source.

Cycling Association of Yukon Whitehorse, Canada, recreation.

Cycling British Columbia Vancouver, Canada, recreation.

Cycling Engineers Institute 1896- Colchester, England, cycles.

Cycling New Brunswick Dieppe, Canada, recreation.

Cycling Research Association 1989- Mount Shasta CA, cycles, science, sport.

Cyclist Protection Association of South Australia 1976- Adelaide, Australia, insurance.

Cyclists' Public Affairs Group (CPAG) 1992- England, advocacy.

Cyclists' Touring Club (CTC) 1878- Godalming, England, source, advocacy, transport, touring. Formerly **Bicycle Touring Club** 1878-1883 Harrogate.

Cyclone Cycling Club Los Alamos NM, recreation, sport.

Cykelfrämjandet 1934- Stockholm, Sweden, transport, touring.

Cykelkedjan 1976- Stockholm, Sweden, transport.

Cykelrejseforeningen TOUR Snekkersten, Denmark, touring, trails.

Czech and Slovak Bike Traffic Club Brno, Czech Republic, transport.

Dallas Off-Road Bicycle Association Dallas TX, trails.

Dansk Cyklist Forbund (DCF) 1905- Copenhagen, Denmark, source, transport, touring, 25,000 members in 1980.

Delmarva Bicycle Club Dover DE, recreation, Delaware-Maryland-Virginia.

Denver Bicycle Touring Denver CO, recreation, 2,100 members in 1990.

Different Spokes San Francisco 1982- San Francisco CA, recreation, sport, open sexual orientation club.

Different Spokes of Southern California Los Angeles CA, recreation, sport.

Dirty Dog Mud Club Plymouth NH, trails.

Disciples of Dirt-Eugene Off-Road Cyclists Eugene OR, trails.

Dr. Paul Dudley White Bicycle Club 1962- Homestead, FL, recreation.

Dopravní Klub Czech and Slovakia (CSFR) Brno, Czech, transport.

Douglass Bicycle Club 1890s- Indianapolis IN, sport, african-americans.

Earth Corps Winnipeg, Canada, transport.

Earth Works Jamaica Plane MA, transport.

East Bay Bicycle Coalition (EBBC) 1972- Oakland CA, transport, advocacy, source, 300 members and clubs in 1990.

Eastern Fat Tire Association (EFTA) 1991-

Medford NJ, trails, sport.

Echte Nederlandse Fietserbond (ENFB) 1975- Woerden, NL, source, transport, touring.

Edmonton Bicycle Commuters Society Edmonton, Alberta, transport, member-supported repair shop, Bikeworks.

Elbow Valley Cycle Club Calgary, Alberta, touring, transport.

Elite Ladies' Cycling Club 1934-1970 Newcastle upon Tyne, England, recreation, sport.

Energia Verde (Green Energy) San Juan, Puerto Rico, transport.

English Schools Cycling Association Suffolk, England, touring, sport.

European Bicycle Manufacturers Association (EBMA) Europe, industry.

European Cyclists' Federation (ECF) 1983- Strasbourg, France, source, transport, advocacy.

Evanston Bicycle Club Evanston IL, touring, sport.

Everglades Bicycle Club Miami FL, recreation, sport.

Eyecycle 1992- Los Angeles CA, recreation, visually-impaired.

Fair Go For Cyclists! Hobart, Tasmania, transport, advocacy.

Family Cycling Club 1980- Bridgeton NJ, recreation, advocacy.

Fat Man's Bicycle Club 1890s, Brooklyn NY, recreation, members weigh over 250 pounds.

Fat Tire Flyers Notting Hill, Australia, trails.

Federação Portuguesa de Cicloturismo e Utlizadores de Bicicleta (FPCU) Lisbon, Portugal, source, touring, transport.

Federal Bicycle Council 1976- Washington DC, advocacy.

Federation Belge du Cyclotourisme (FBC) Bruxelles, Belgium, touring.

Fédération Francaise de Cyclotourisme (FFCT) 1923- Paris, touring, source, 110,000 members from 3,000 clubs in 1990.

Fédération Francaise des Usagers de la Bicyclette (FUBICY) 1980- Strasbourg, France, transport, advocacy.

Fédération des Industries des Equipments pour Vehicules (FIEV) Paris, industry.

Federazione Italiana Amici della Bicicletta (FIAB) (Friends of the bike in Italy) transport.

Fellowship of Cycling Old-Timers 1965- Surrey, England, old boys' club, formerly **Fellowship of Old Time Cyclists** 1916-.

Fietserbond See **Echte Nederlandse Fietserbond**.

Fiets Overleg Vlanderen (FOV) Antwerpen, Belgium, transport, association.

Fietskaart Informatie Stichting (Cyclemap Foundation) Utrecht, Netherlands.

First Chinese Bicycling Club of Philadelphia 1890s, Philadelphia PA, recreation, asian-americans.

Five Boro Bicycle Club-AYH (5BBC) 1991- New York City, touring.

Flathead Valley Bicycle Club Kalispell MT, recreation.

Florida Bicycle Association Tampa FL, recreation, sport.

Florida BMX Association 1975- Clearwater FL, sport.

Folks on Spokes Bike Club Homewood IL, touring, 300 members in 1990.

Freestate Derailleurs Baltimore MD, recreation.

Free Yourself from Henry Ford 1986- Allentown PA, transport.

Fremont Freewheelers Fremont CA, recreation, 250 members in 1990.

Fresno Cycling Club Fresno CA, recreation.

Friends of City Cycling Budapest Budapest, Hungary, transport.

Friends of the Earth (FOE) 1971- London, transport.

German Cycling Federation 1890s- Germany, association, recreation, sport.

Glasgow Cycling Campaign 1990– Glasgow, Scotland, transport.

Grand-Ma MTB Club Poggibonsi, Sicily, Italy, trails.

Granite State Wheelmen Salem NH, recreation, 1,200 members in 1990.

Greater Arizona Bicycling Tempe AZ, recreation.

Greater Dallas Bicyclists Association Richardson TX, recreation, transport.

Greater Manchester Cycling Project Manchester, England, transport.

Greenville Spinners.

Groupe de Recherche et d'Action des Cyclistes Quotidiens (GRACQ) 1975- Bruxelles, Belgium, source, transport, advocacy.

Grüne Radler 1979- Krefeld, Germany, transport, environmental.

Gruppo Sportivo Castello Como, Italy, sport.

Haarlem Cycling Club 1880s- Haarlem, Netherlands, recreation, sport.

Handlebar Club of the Workers of Corbeil 1890s, France, advocacy.

Hand-Powered Cyclists of America Cambridge MA, cycles, advocacy.

Harlem Wheelmen 1930- New York City, recreation, sport.

Hatfield Man-Powered Aircraft Club 1960- Hatfield, England, cycles, human-powered aircraft.

Hawaii Bicycling League Honolulu HI, recreation, 800 members in 1990.

Hawkeye Bicycle Association Cedar Rapids IA, recreation.

Heather Bell Ladies Cycling Club 1960s, United States, recreation.

Helsingin Polkupyöräilijäyhdistys (HcPo) 1981- Helsinki, Finland, transport, touring.

Hertfordshire Pedal Aeronauts 1965- Herts, England, cycles, human-powered aircraft.

Hong Kong Tour Cycling Association Kowloon, Hong Kong, recreation, sport.

Houston Area Mountain Bike Riders Association Houston TX, trails.

Houston Off-Road Bicycle Association Houston TX, trails.

HPV Klub Danmark Copenhagen, Denmark, cycles, human-powered vehicles, with **Dansk Cyklist Forbund**.

Hungarian Bicycle Tourists Federation Budapest, Hungary, touring.

I Cicclopici Milan, Italy, transport.

IG Velo Schweiz-Interessengemeinshaft Velo 1975- Basel, Switzerland, transport, association.

Institute for Transportation and Development Policy (ITDP) New York City, development, source.

In Tandem London, recreation, tandems for visually-impaired.

Intermediate Technology (IT) London, England, development, cycles, source.

International Association of Cycling Journalists 1980s- sports press.

International Bicycle Fund (IBF) Seattle WA, transport, development.

International Bicycle Touring Society 1964- La Jolla CA, touring.

International Christian Cycling Club Denver CO, touring, eight countries in 1992.

International Human-Powered Vehicle Association (IHPVA) 1975- Indianapolis IN, cycles, design, sport governing body.

International Mountain Bicycling Association (IMBA) 1988- Los Angeles CA, trails, advocacy.

International Police Mountain Bike Association 1992- Baltimore MD, education, advocacy, with **League of American Bicyclists**.

International Randonneurs-North America Syracuse NY, touring, randonnees.

International Unicycling Federation (IUF) Redford MI, recreation, sport, governing body.

Israel Association of BMX and Hill-Country Cycling Tel Aviv, Israel, trails, touring, sport.

Israel Cycling Association Tel Aviv, Israel, recreation, sport.

Israel Cyclists' Touring Club 1972- Kefar Saba, Israel, touring.

Israel National Bicycle Riders' Club Tel Aviv, Israel, transport.

Japan Bicycle Manufacturers Association Tokyo, industry.

Japan Bicycle Industry Association 1948- Tokyo, industry.

Japan Bicycle Promotion Institute (JBPI) 1964- Tokyo, industry, recreation, sport, Bicycle Technical Center, Cycle Sports Centers.

Japan Bicycle Road Development Association. Tokyo.

Juneau Freewheelers Bicycle Club Juneau AK, recreation.

Kids on Bikes.

Knickerbikers El Cajon CA, recreation.

Koninklijke Nederlandse Toeristenbond (ANWB) (check) s'Gravenhage, Netherlands, touring, 2.8 million members in 1990.

Lallement Memorial Committee 1990- Boston MA, cycles, honoring Pierre Lallement.

League of American Bicyclists (LAW) 1880-1942, 1965- Baltimore MD, touring, recreation, transport, formerly **League of American**

Wheelmen -1994.

Le Monde à Bicyclette 1975- Montreal, Canada, transport, advocacy.

Les Cyclotouristes Grenoblois Grenoble, France, touring.

Letzebuerger Velos Initiativ (LVI) 1984- Luxembourg, transport.

Liberty Wheelmen 1890s, Brooklyn NY, recreation.

Liverpool Velocipede Club 1869- Liverpool, England, recreation.

London Bicycle Club 1880s- London, recreation, sport.

London Cycling Campaign (LCC) 1978- London, transport, advocacy, source, 7,000 members in 1993.

London Tricycle Club 1880- London, recreation, sport.

Los Angeles Wheelmen Alhambra CA, touring, 700 members in 1990.

Low Impact Mountain Bicyclists (LIMB) Missoula MT, trails.

Manitoba Cycling Association Winnipeg, Canada, recreation.

Man-Powered Aircraft Committee-Royal Aeronautic Society (MAPAC) 1957- Royal Air Force College of Aeronautics, Cranfield, England.

Marketing Cycling to Women 1993- Boulder CO, trade.

Massachusetts Bicycle Club 1880- Boston MA, recreation.

Maui Bicycle Club Kahului HI, recreation.

Medicine Wheel Colorado Springs CO, trails.

Melbourne Bicycle Touring Club Melbourne, Australia, touring.

Mercury Wheel Club 1890s Long Island NY, recreation, competition for best-illuminated bicycle.

Miami Valley Regional Bicycle Committee Dayton OH, transport.

Michaux Cycle Club 1895- New York City, social club, members included Rockefeller, Vanderbuilt, Gould.

Michiana Bicycling Association Granger IN, recreation.

Michigan Human-Powered Vehicle Association MI, cycles, sport.

Michigan Mountain Biking Association Detroit MI, trails.

Michigan United Tandem Society (MUTS) Hudsonville MI, recreation.

Midwest Mountain Bike Club St. Louis MO, trails.

Minnesota Coalition of Bicyclists Minneapolis MN, trails, advocacy.

Missoula Bicycle Club 1976- Missoula MT, touring, 300 members in 1990.

Monterey Mountain Bicycle Association (MOMBA) Pacific Grove CA, trails.

Moonbeams 1960s, Florida, tricycling recreation.

Moscow Society of Velocipede Lovers 1890s, Moscow, Russia.

Moulton Bicycle Club London, 600 members from 15 countires in 1990.

Mountain Bicycle Resource Group Eugene OR, University of Oregon, recreation.

Mountain Bicyclists Association 1977- Denver CO, source, transport, advocacy.

Mountain Bike Club Finland Espoo, Finland, trails.

Mountain Bike Club Italiano Milan, Italy, trails.

Mountain Bikers of Alaska Anchorage AK, trails.

Mount Wilson Bicycle Association San Marino CA, trails, advocacy.

Movement pour la Defense de la Bicyclette (MDB) 1990- Paris, transport, advocacy.

Movimiento Bicicletero 1989- Mexico City, Mexico, transport, advocacy.

Mud Creek Mountainbikers Wolfville, Nova Scotia, trails.

Naga All Terrain Bikers Association (NATBA) Naga City, Philipines.

National Bicycle Club Network Missoula MT, Bikecentennial directory.

National Bicycle Dealers Association (NBDA) 1946- Costa Mesa CA, trade.

National Bicycle History Archive of America 1992- Santa Ana CA, cycles, history.

National Bicycle Registry Sacramento CA, database.

National Bike Club Birmingham, England, transport and recreation cycling with **Royal Society for the Prevention of Accidents (RoSPA)**.

National Clarion Cycling Club-Clarion Fellowship 1894- England, recreation, transport.

National Handicapped Sports and Recreation Association Washington DC.

National Sporting Goods Association (NSGA) Mount Prospect IL, industry.

Nederlandse Rijwiel Toer Unie (NRTU) 1956- Veenedaal, Netherlands, touring, with **Alliance Internationale de Tourisme**.

New England Mountain Bike Association (NEMBA) Somerville MA, trails.

Newfoundland and Labrador Cycling Association St. John's, Canada, recreation, transport.

New South Wales Cycling Federation Sydney, Australia, sport.

New York Athletic and Velocipede Club 1880s- New York City, sport, recreation.

New York City All Terrain Cycling Association New York City, trails, sport.

New York Cycling Club (NYCC) 1936- New York City, recreation, sport.

New Zealand Cyclists Aukland, New Zealand, transport, recreation.

New Zealand Mountain Bike Association Taupo, New Zealand, trails.

Norcape Bushbikers Australia, trails.

North Road Cycling Club 1880s- England, touring.

North Roads Bicycle Club Rice Lake WI, recreation.

Northern California/Nevada Cycling Association Berkeley CA, sport.

Northwest Bicycle Touring Society Mercer Island WA, touring.

Northwest Human Powered Vehicle Association **(NWHPVA)** 1985- Seattle WA, cycles.

Northwest Mountain Bikers Tacoma WA, trails.

Norwood Paragons 1920s London, sport.

Oak Park Cycle Club Oak Park IL.

Off-Road Bicyclists of Arizona Mesa AZ, trails.

Ohio Bicycle Federation Dayton OH, transport, recreation.

OK Bicycle Society Oklahoma City OK, recreation, transport.

Okie Extremes Mountain Bike Club Bethany OK, trails.

Old Park Cycling Club 1890s Chicago IL, $50,000 headquarters in 1890s.

Onondaga Cycling Club Syracuse NY, recreation, advocacy.

Ontario Coalition for Better Cycling Ottawa, Canada, transport.

Ontario Cycling Association Willowdale, Canada, sport.

Ooivaar Cycling Club 1885- Haarlem, Holland.

ÖRad 1990- Austria, advocacy.

L'Ordre des Cols Durs 1960- France, hillclimb enthusiasts, with **L'Ordre des Cols Durs** 1966- Cheshire, England.

Orion-Volgograd Cyclist's Touring Club Volgograd, Russia, recreation.

Osterreischiche Automobil, Motorrad und Touring Club Vienna, Austria, touring.

Outdoor Living Association St. Julian's, Malta, recreation.

Over Mount and Vale Club 1890- Kleve, Germany, touring, trails.

Ozark Mountain Ridgeriders Harrison AR, recreation.

Pacelines Boston MA, recreation, gays and lesbians.

Palo Alto Cycling Club 1972- Palo Alto CA, recreation, sport, formerly **Belmont Bicycle Club** 1960s- Belmont CA.

Paralyzed Veterans of America Washington DC, source, recreation, sport.

Pasadena Mountain Bike Club Altadena CA, trails, sport, advocacy.

Pedal Clubs Niddrie, Victoria, Australia, recreation.

Pedali Alpini 1950-1985 Woodside CA, touring, sport.

Pedalibre 1980- Madrid, Spain, transport, advocacy, recreation.

Pedal Power ACT (Australian Capital Territory) 1975- Canberra, Australia, transport advocacy, **Pedal Power** radio show.

Pedal Power Foundation of Southern Africa 1978- Cape Town, South Africa, recreation, advocacy.

Pedal Power Tasmania Hobart, Tasmania, transport, advocacy.

Pedals for Progress High Bridge NY, recycling bikes for needy.

Ped'lin Around Lake Charles LA, recreation.

Pennsylvania Off-Road Bicycle Coalition Doylestown PA, trails.

Perimeter Bicycle Association Tucson AZ, touring perimeters of mountains, cities, countries.

Pickwick Bicycle Club 1870- London, recreation, sport.

Polski Klub Ekologinzny Krakow, Poland, transport, advocacy.

Polskie Towarzystwo Turystyczno-Krajoznawcze (PTTK) Warsaw, Poland, touring, with **Alliance Internationale de Tourisme**.

Portland Area Bicycle Coalition Portland OR, transport.

Portland United Mountain Pedalers (PUMP) Portland OR, trails.

Post Office Cyclers 1890s, Newark NJ, postal carriers.

Potomac Pedalers Touring Club Washington DC, touring.

Potternewton Cycling Club 1890s- Leeds, England.

Prince Edward Island Cycling Association Montague, Canada, recreation, sport.

Pushbikes 1979- Birmingham, England.

Quad Cities Bicycle Club Davenport IA, touring, with 950 members in 1990.

Queensland Cyclists Association Chandler, Australia, sport.

Rail Riders of America 1980- Hillsboro NH, cycles, rail bikes, recreation.

Rails-to-Trails Conservancy Washington DC, trails, construction.

Rainbow Cyclists Carlsbad CA, recreation, gays and lesbians.

Randonneurs Mondiaux France, touring.

Recumbent Bicycle Club of America 1990- Renton WA, cycles, recreation.

Redlands Water Bottle Transit Redlands CA, touring, sport.

Regional Bicycle Advisory Committee of the San Francisco Bay Area (REBAC) 1986- Oakland CA, transport, planning.

Reno Wheelmen Reno NV, recreation, sport, Greg LeMond's first club.

Retail Cycle Traders Australia, trade.

Responsible Organized Mountain Pedalers (ROMP) 1988- Los Gatos CA, trails, advocacy.

Rhode Island Fat Tire Association (RIFTA) Exeter RI, trails.

Riders Helping Insure Off-Roads Survival (RHINO) Denver CO, trails.

Rio Bikers 1992- Rio de Janeiro, Brazil, recreation.

Rising Sun Cycle Club 1890s New York City, recreation, japanese-americans.

Riverside Cycle Club 1890s Boston MA, recreation.

Rolling Resistance 1980- Troy NY, transport, advocacy.

Rosslyn Ladies' Cycling Club 1920s- London, recreation, advocacy.

Rough Stuff Fellowship 1955- Southport, England, trails.

Round-the-World Cyclists' Registry Toronto, Canada, source, world cyclists.

Royal Society for the Prevention of Accidents (RoSPA) Birmingham, England, source, advocacy, education.

SCOR Cardiac Cyclists Club 1980s- Whittier CA, recreation, sport, heart patients.

SHARE-Concerned Cyclists of Crystal Cove Corona del Mar CA, trails, education, management.

Sacramento Rough Riders Sacramento CA, trails.

San Diego County Bicycle Coalition La Mesa CA, recreation, transport.

San Jose Bicycle Club (SJBC) 1939- San Jose CA, recreation, touring, sport.

Sandia Bicycle Club 1972- Sandia Laboratories, Kirtland Air Force Base NM, recreation, 400 members in 1975.

Sangre de Cristo Cycle Club Santa Fe NM, touring.

Santa Rosa Cycling Club Santa Rosa CA, touring, wine country.

Saskatchewan Cycling Association Regina, Saskatchewan, recreation, sport.

Schweiz Radfahrer und Motorfahrer Bund (SRB) Zurich, Switzerland, touring, with **Alliance Internationale de Tourisme**.

Sheridan Bicycle Club Sheridan WY.

Shore Cycle Club Northfield NJ, touring, sport.

Sierra Express Bicycle Club Nevada City CA.

Silicon Valley Bicycle Coalition (SVBC) 1971- Cupertino CA, transport, advocacy, formerly **Santa Clara Valley Bicycle Association (SCVBA)** 1971-1992.

Siskiou Wheelmen Ashland OR, recreation, trails, advocacy.

Socialist Wheelmen's Club 1898- New York, recreation, members of Labor Party.

Societé des Cyclistes Coiffeurs-Parfumeurs (Society of cyclists in the hair and perfume profession) 1896- Paris.

Society of Cyclists 1884- England, recreation.

South African Mountain Bicycle Association Linton Grange, South Africa, trails.

South Australian Touring Cyclist's Association Adelaide, Australia, touring, trails.

Southbay Wheelmen Redondo Beach CA, recreation, sport.

South Broward Wheelers Hollywood FL, 400 members in 1990.

South Western Ohio Trails Association Cincinnati OH, trails.

Southern Appalachian Mountain Biker Organization Atlanta GA, trails.

Southern Bicycle League Clarkston GA, recreation, 2,500 members in 1990.

Southern Off-Road Bicycling Association Mariette GA, trails, advocacy, recreation.

Space Coast Freewheelers Bike Club Cocoa FL, recreation.

Speedwell Bicycle Club 1876- Birmingham, England, sport.

Spokes-Lothian Cycling Campaign 1977- Edinburgh, Scotland, transport, advocacy, touring.

Spokespeople Sarasota FL, advocacy, safety.

Sports for Understanding Washington DC, international touring, sport, for teenagers.

Springfield Bicycle Club 1890s- Springfield MA, touring, sport, Springfield Tournaments.

State Bicycle Committee Sydney and Walkerville, Australia, advocacy.

Stichting: Fiets! 1959- Amsterdam, advocacy.

Streamliner Racing Association Northwest, cycles, HPVs.

Svenska Cykelsällskapet (SCS) 1979- Spånga, Sweden, transport, advocacy.

Svenska Turistföreningen (STF) Stockholm, Sweden, touring.

Syklistenes Landsforening (SLF) 1947- Oslo, Norway, touring, transport, advocacy.

Tahoe Area Mountain Bicycling Association (TAMBA) South Lake CA, trails.

The Tandem Club 1971- Godalming, England, tandem touring, with **Cyclists' Touring Club**.

Tandem Club of America Palo Alto CA, source, recreation, tandems.

Tandem Club of Australia Melbourne, Australia, recreation.

Team Ascent Ashland OR, sport.

Team Evergreen Bicycle Club Evergreen CO, sport, touring.

Texas Bicycle Coalition (TBC) 1990- Austin TX, advocacy.

300,000 Miles Club 1962- Cheshire, England, lifetime mileage, 53 members in 1993.

Thundering Quads Cycling Club Chardon OH, recreation.

Tidewater Bicycle Association Norfolk VA, touring, sport, with 600 members in 1990.

Todos En Bicicleta Mexico City, Mexico, transport, advocacy.

Toronto Bicycling Network Toronto, Canada, recreation, advocacy, with 1,000 members in 1990.

Toronto City Cycling Committee 1975- Toronto, Canada, transport, advocacy, city office.

Touring Club Italiano 1895- Milan, Italy, touring.

Touring Club Suisse-Cyclo-loisirs (TCS) 1896- Meyrin, Switzerland, touring.

Touring Cyclists' Hospitality Directory 1977- Van Nuys CA, touring network.

Touring Exchange source, international cycletouring.

Trail Center Los Altos CA, trails, advocacy, development.

Trails 2000 Durango CO. trails.

Transportation Alternatives (TA) 1973- New York City, transport, advocacy, 3,500 members in 1995.

Transport 2000 London, transport, advocacy.

Trekfogels Club 1890- Amsterdam, Holland, recreation, touring.

Tri City Cyclists Bay City MI, recreation, sport, 600 members in 1990.

Tricycle Association 1880-1882 London, sport, recreation.

Tricycle Association 1928- Leeds, England, sport, with **Road Time Trials Council**.

Tricycle Union 1882-1884 England, sport.

Tulsa Wheelmen Tulsa OK, recreation, transport, sport.

Tulsa Bicycle Club Tulsa OK.

Ühendus Roheline Maardu Tallinn, Estonia, transport, advocacy.

Ukiah Wheelers Bike Club Calpella CA, recreation, Harvest Century.

Unicycling Society of America (USA) Redford MI, sport, recreation.

Union Cyclistes des Postes et des Télégraphes (Union of Postal and Telegraph cyclists) 1897 France.

Union des Brevets International France, touring.

Union Luxembourgeois de Cyclotouristes Florange, Luxembourg, touring.

United Community Action Network (UCAN) 1994– Portland OR, recyclery, free bikes.

United Kingdom Unicycle Federation 1988- England, sport, recreation.

United Nations Cycling Club New York City, touring.

United States Bicycling Hall of Fame Somerville NJ, honors contributors to U.S. sport.

United States Disabled Cycling Team Westerville OH, sport.

United States Military Wheelmen 1895- West Point NY, touring, sport.

Urban Nomads All Terrain Bicycle Association (UNATBA) Alexandria VA, trails.

Unreliable Wheelmen of Yokohama 1890s, Yokohama, Japan, Scotish humorists.

Uvumbuzi Club Nairobi, Kenya, transport, advocacy.

Valencia en Bici Valencia, Spain, advocacy.

Valley Spokesmen Dublin CA, recreation, advocacy.

Vancouver Bicycle Club Vancouver, Canada.

Vänta Aga Tartu, Estonia, transport, advocacy.

Városi Biciklizés Barátai (Friends of city cycling) Budapest, Hungary, transport.

Vegetarian Cycling and Athletic Club 1887- Hemel Hempstead, England, 100th anniversay, vegan members.

Vélo Québec 1967- Montreal, Canada, transport, recreation, advocacy, source.

Le Véloce Club 1869- Paris, recreation, sport.

Veloce Club Milano 1870- Milan, Italy, recreation, sport.

Veloce Club Torinese 1880- Torino, Italy, recreation, sport.

Veloce Club Fiorentino 1870- Florence, Italy, recreation, sport.

Véloce Club de Rouen 1869- Rouen, France, recreation, sport.

Velocipede Society of Tasmania Evandale, Tasmania, cycles, historians.

Velo City

Velograd Cyclists Club Volgograd, Russia, transport, recreation.

Verband der Fahrrad und Motorrad Industrie (VFM) Germany, industry.

Verkehrs Club Österreich Vienna, Austria, transport, source.

Verkehrs Club der Schweiz 1979- Herzogenbuchsee, Switzerland, tranport, source, car club.

Vermont Off-Road Cycling Association Manchester Center VT, trails.

Veteran-Cycle Club 1955- Croydon, England, cycles, history, formerly **Southern Veteran-Cycle Club**.

Victorian Cycling Federation North Melbourne, Australia, sport.

Vintage Cycle Club Caulfield, Australia, cycles, collectors.

Vixens 1990- England, trails, for women.

Wabash River Cycle Club West Lafayette IN, recreation.

Wandering Wheels Taylor University, Upland, IN, recreation, singing.

Wanderlust Club 1890s- Leipzig, Germany, recreation, touring.

Washington Area Bicyclists Association (WABA) 1972- Washington DC, recreation, transport, advocacy.

Washington's Happily Independent Recumbent Lovers (WHIRL) Washington DC, recumbent bikes, recreation.

The Wayfarers Washington DC, touring.

Western Pennsylvania Wheelmen (WPW) Pittsburgh PA, recreation, source, 800 members in 1990.

Western Wheelers 1968- Menlo Park CA, touring, transport.

Westfield Non-Scorching Sit-Erect Bicycle Club 1890s, Staten Island NY, upright cyclists against scorchers.

The Wheel Club 1896- South Kensington, London, recreation.

Wheel People Bicycle Association Galveston IN, recreation.

The Wheelmen 1967- Trenton NJ, cycles, history, collectors.

Whistler Off-Road Cycling Association (WORCA) Whistler, Canada, trails.

White Clay Bicycle Club Newark DE, recreation.

Winnipeg Cycletouring Club Winnipeg, Canada, touring.

Winter Park Fat Tire Society (FATS) Winter Park CO, trails, development.

The Wooden Wheels Givatayim, Israel, cycles, collectors.

Women of Power in the Industry (WOPITI) Fairfax CA, industry.

Women on Wheels Chicago IL, women's advocacy, formerly **National Organization of Wheelwomen (NOW)**.

Women's Cycling Coalition (WCC) Louisville CO, sport, women's advocacy.

Women's Cycling Network Harvard IL, touring, women's advocacy.

Women's Mountain Bike and Tea Society (WOMBATS) 1989- Fairfax CA, trails, women's advocacy.

Women's Sports Foundation New York City, sport.

Workers' Pedal Club 1890s- France.

World on Wheels (WOW) San Rafael CA, education.

W.P. Pedal Power Association (WPPPA) Claremont, South Africa, advocacy, also known as **W.P. Trapkragvereniging**.

Yale Cycling Team 1879- Yale University, New Haven CT, sport, oldest active U.S. cycling organization.

TOUR OPERATORS

Above the Clouds Trekking (Worchester MA) Nepal, South America, Europe.

Adventure Bicycle Tours (Sacramento CA) Pacific.

Adventure Cycling Association (Missoula MT) North America.

Adventures Odyssey (Dauphin PA) USA, Europe.

All Adventure Travel (Falls Church VA) Kathmandu, Andes.

All-Outdoor Adventures Trips (Walnut Creek CA) Hawaii, Europe, China.

American Wilderness Experience (Boulder CO) USA.

American Youth Hostels (Washington DC) Almost everywhere.

Arrow to the Sun (Taylorsville CA) Mexico.

Asian Dreams (Los Angeles CA) Bankok, Singapore, Hong Kong, Indonesia, Malaysia.

Asian Pacific Adventures (Los Angeles CA) Asia, Tajikistan.

Backcountry Bicycle Tours (Bozeman MT) North America, Australia.

Backroads Bicycle Touring (Berkeley CA) Almost everywhere.

Baja Expeditions (San Diego CA) Baja, Patagonia, Tibet.

Bicycle Adventure Club (San Diego CA) Almost everywhere.

Bicycle Africa (Bellvue WA) Kenya, Cameroon, Togo, Ivory Coast, Togo.

Bicycle Beano Vegetarian Tours (Hereford, England) Europe.

Bike China Tours (Boston MA) Asia.

Bike Events (Bath, England) Europe, Asia.

The Biking Expedition (Henniker NH) North America, Europe, Asia.

Blyth & Co. (New York City) Europe, Asia.

Boojum Expeditions (San Diego CA) China, Tibet, Mongolia.

Borealis Backcountry Cycling (Anchorage AK) Alaska.

Breakaway Vacations (New York City) North America, Europe.

Breaking Away Bicycle Tours (Manhattan Beach CA) Hawaii, Europe.

Butterfield & Robinson (Toronto, Canada) Europe, Australia.

Carolina Cycle Tours (Bryson City NC) Central America, Europe.

Chateaux Bike Tours (Denver CO) Europe.

Ciclismo Classico (Cambridge MA) Europe.

Classic Bicycle Tours (Clarkson NY) Greece, Ireland, France, Northeast Canada.

Country Cycling Tours (New York City) Europe, China.

Crocodile Cycles (Caims, Queensland) Australia.

Cycle Paths (Tahoe City CA) Asia, Baja, Europe, Australia.

Cycle Swiss Alpine (Winchester VA) Europe.

Cycle and Kayak (Gabriola, Canada) North America.

Cycleventures (Cumberland, Canada) North America, Europe, Asia.

Cyclists' Touring Club (Godalming, England) Almost everywhere.

Cyclub Expeditions (Hull, Canada) Europe, Africa.
EarthVentures (Indianapolis IN) Europe, Australia.
Easy Rider Tours (East Arlington VA) North America, Ireland.
Forum Travel (Pleasant Hill CA) Europe, Asia, South America.
Gerhard's Bicycle Odysseys (Portland OR) Europe.
Goulash Tours (Kalamazoo MI) Eastern Europe.
International Bicycle Tours (Essex CT) Soviet Union, China.
International Bicycle Touring Society (San Diego CA) America, Europe.
Joy Ride (Columbia NC) Europe.
The Northwest Passage (Wilmette IL) North America, Europe, Australia, Africa.
Off the Deep End Travels (Jackson WY) Europe, Japan, Tahiti, Thailand, Nepal.
Okanagan Bike Roads (Penticton, Canada) Canada.
On the Loose Bicycle Adventure Vacations (Berkeley CA) Hawaii.
Outback with Bodfish (Chester CA) Pacific Coast.

Pacific Crest Bike Tours (Seattle WA) Pacific Coast, Mexico, Europe.
Paradise Bicycle Tours (Evergreen CO) Africa, Australia.
Paradise Pedallers (Charlotte NC) New Zealand.
Progressive Travels (Seattle WA) North America, Europe.
REI Adventures (Seattle WA) North America, Siberia, China.
Rail-Trail Bike & Hike (Bryson City NC) North America, Europe.
Rim Tours (Moab UT) Western US.
Rocky Mountain Cycle Tour (Canmore, Canada) North America, Hawaii, Europe, Japan.
Sense Adventures (Kingston, Jamaica) Australia.
Timberline Bicycle Tours (Denver CO) North America.
Tour de Cana (Philadelphia PA) Central America, Caribbean.
Touring Exchange (Port Townsend WA) Central America.
Vermont Bicycle Touring (Bristol VT) Northeast US.
Wandering Wheels (Upland IN) North America, Europe, Asia.
Wildland Journeys (Seattle WA) South America.

Woodswomen (Minneapolis MN) North America, Europe, Australia, Mexico.

YOUTH TOUR GROUPS

Adventures Rolling Cross Country (San Francisco CA) Hawaii.
American Youth Hostels (Washington DC) World-wide.
The Biking Expedition (Henniker NH) Canada, Europe, China.
The Biking Odyssey (Dauphin PA) America, Europe.
Riding High Bicycle Tours for Kids (Portland OR) North America, Europe.
Spinning Spokes (Miami FL) Europe.
Sports for Understanding (Washington DC) Europe.
Student Hosteling Program (Conway MA) North America, Europe.

Sports

SPORTS GROUPS

UCI GOVERNING BODIES
International Olympic Committee (IOC) 1890s- Lausanne, Switzerland, governs Olympic competition.
Union Cycliste Internationale (UCI) 1900- Lausanne, Switzerland, governs road racing, track, mountain bike, cyclo-cross, BMX, cycle-ball, artistic cycling, formerly **International Cyclist Association (ICA)** 1892-1900.
Fédération Internationale Amateur de Cyclisme (FIAC) 1965-1992 Rome, Italy, UCI amateur racing.
Fédération Internationale de Cyclisme Professionnel (FICP) 1965-1992 Luxembourg, UCI professional racing.

NATIONAL GOVERNING BODIES
(165 countries as of June 1995)
Albania (ALB) **Union Albanaise de Cyclisme** Tirana.
Algeria (ALG) **Federation Algérienne de Cyclisme** Alger.
Andorra (AND) **Federación Andorrana de Ciclismo** Escaldes Engordany.
Angola (ANG) **Fédération Cycliste de l'Angola** Luanda.
Antigua (ANT) **Antigua and Barbuda Amateur Cycling Association** St. John's.
Argentina (ARG) **Federacion Ciclistica Argentina** Buenos Aires.

Armenia (ARM) **Fédération du Cyclisme de la Republique d'Armenie** Erevan.
Aruba (ARU) **Aruba Wieler Bond** Oranjestad.
Australia (AUS) **Australian Cycling Federation (ACF)** 1929-, Sydney, formerly **Australian Amateur Cycling Association (AACA), Australian Professional Cycling Council** Austin's Ferry, Tasmania, **League of Australian Wheelmen** Footscray, Victoria, **League of Victorian Wheelmen** Footscray, Victoria.
Austria (AUT) **Österreichicher Radsport Verband** 1946- Vienna, formerly **Österreichischer Radsport Kommission**.
Azerbaijan (AZE) **Fédération Cycliste de la Republique d'Azerbaijan** Baku.
Bahamas (BAH) **Bahamas Amateur Cycling Federation**. Nassau, formerly **Bahamas Amateur Cycling Association**.
Bahrain (BHR) **Bahrain Amateur Cycling Federation** El Manama.
Bangladesh (BAN) **Bangladesh Cycling Federation** Dhaka.
Barbados (BAR) **Barbados Cycling Union** Bridgetown.
Belarus (BLR) **Fédération Cycliste de Bielorussie** Minsk.
Belgium (BEL) **Koninklijke Belgische Wielrijders Bond (KBWB), Royale Ligue Velocipedique Belge (LVB)** 1882- Brussels.

Belize (BIZ) **Belize Amateur Cycling Association** Belize City.
Benin (BEN) **Fédération Cycliste de la Republique du Benin** Cotonou, formerly **Fédération Dahoméenne de Cyclisme**.
Bermuda (BER) **Bermuda Bicycle Association** Devonshire.
Bolivia (BOL) **Federacion Boliviana de Ciclismo** La Paz.
Bosnia-Herzegovina **Fédération Bosnie-Herzegovine de Cyclisme** Sarajevo.
Botswana (BOT) **Botswana Cycling Association** Gaborone.
Brazil (BRA) **Confederacao Brasileira de Ciclismo** Sao Paolo.
Brunei (BRU) **Brunei Amateur Cycling Association** Bandar.
Bulgaria (BUL) **Union Bulgare de Cyclisme** Sofia.
Burkina Faso **Fédération Burkinabé de Cyclisme** Ouagadougou, formerly Upper Volta **Fédération Voltaïque de Cyclisme**.
Cameroun (CMR) **Fédération Camerounaise de Cyclisme** Yaoundé.
Canada (CAN) **Canadian Cycling Association (CCA)** 1882- Gloucester, formerly **Canadian Wheelmen's Association** 1882-1968.
Cape Verde **Federacao Cabo-Verdiana de Ciclismo** Praia.
Cayman Islands **Cayman Islands Cycling**

Association Grand Cayman.

Central African Republic **Fédération Centrafricaine de Cyclisme** Bangui.

Chile (CHI) **Federacion Ciclista de Chile** 1905- Santiago.

China (CHN) **Cycling Association of the People's Republic of China** Beijing.

Colombia (COL) **Federacion Colombiana de Ciclismo** Bogota.

Comoros **Fédération Comorienne de Cyclisme Amateur** Moroni.

Congo (CGO) **Fédération Congolaise de Cyclisme** Brazzaville.

Costa Rica (CRC) **Federacion Costarricense de Ciclismo** San Jose.

Croatia (CRO) **Hrvatski Biciklisticki Savez** Zagreb.

Cuba (CUB) **Federacion Cubana de Ciclismo** Havana.

Cyprus (CYP) **Cyprus Cycling Federation** Nicosia.

Czech Republic (TCH) **Fédération Tchéque de Cyclisme** 1883- Prague, formerly **Fédération Tchécoslovaque de Cyclisme**.

Denmark (DEN) **Danmarks Cykle Union** Brondby, **Dansk Professionelt Cykle-Forbund** 1965- Denmark.

Dominican Republic (DOM) **Federacion Dominicana de Ciclismo** Santo Domingo.

Ecuador (ECU) **Federacion Ecuadorianna de Ciclismo** Quito.

Egypt (EGY) **Egyptian Bicycle Union** Cairo.

El Salvador (SAL) **Federacion Salvadorena de Ciclismo** San Salvador.

Estonia (EST) **Union Cycliste de l'Estonie** Tallinn.

Ethiopia (ETH) **National Ethiopian Cycling Federation** Addis Ababa.

Fiji (FIJ) **Fiji Amateur Cycling Association** Suva.

Finland (FIN) **Suomen Pyorailyliitto** 1898- Helsenki.

France (FRA) **Fédération Francaise de Cyclisme (FFC)** 1881- Rosny, formerly **Union Velocipediques de France (UVF)**.

Gabon (GAB) **Fédération Gabonaise de Cyclisme** Libreville.

Georgia (GEO) **Fédération Georgienne de Cyclisme** Tbilisi.

Germany (GER) **Bund Deutscher Radfahrer (BDF)** 1884- Frankfurt, combined with East Germany (DDR) **Deutscher Radsport Verband der DDR (DRV)** 1947-1989 Berlin.

Great Britain (GBR) **British Cycling Federation (BCF)** 1959- Manchester, formerly **British League of Racing Cyclists (BLRC)** 1942-1959, **National Cyclists Union (NCU)** 1883-1959, **Bicycle Union** 1878-1883, **British Professional and Independent Cycling Association**.

Greece (GRE) **Fédération Hellenique de Cyclisme** Athens.

Grenada **Grenada Amateur Athletic and Cycling Association** St. George's.

Guam (GUM) **Guam Cycling Association** Agana.

Guatemala (GUA) **Federacion Nacional Guatemalteca de Ciclismo** Guatemala City.

Guinea (GUI) **Fédération Guinéenne de Cyclisme** Conakry.

Guyana (GUY) **Guyana Cycling Federation** Georgetown.

Haiti (HAI) **Fédération Haïtienne de Cyclisme Amateur** Port Au Prince.

Holland (HOL) **Koninklijke Nederlandsche Wielren Unie (KNWU)** 1883- Woerden.

Honduras (HON) **Federacion Nacional de Ciclismo de Honduras** Tegucigalpa, formerly **Federacion Nacional Deportiva Extraescolar**.

Hong Kong (HKG) **Hong Kong Cycling Association** Wanchai.

Hungary (HUN) **Magyar Kerekpar Szovetseg** Budapest, formerly **Association of Hungarian Cyclists** 1894-.

India (IND) **Cycling Federation of India** New Delhi, **Indian Professional Cyclists' Association**. Bombay.

Indonesia (INA) **Indonesian Amateur Cycling Association** 1951- Jakarta.

Iran (IRN) **Amateur Cycling Federation Islamic Republic of Iran** Teheran.

Iraq (IRQ) **Iraqi Amateur Cycling Federation** Baghdad.

Ireland (IRL) **Federation of Irish Cyclists** Dublin, also **Irish Cycling Federation (ICF)** 1968- Leixlip, Kildare, **Irish Cycling Tripartite Committee, Northern Ireland Cycling Federation** Belfast.

Israel (ISR) **Sports Federation of Israel** Tel Aviv.

Italy (ITA) **Federazione Ciclista Italiana (FCI)** Rome, formerly **Unione Velocipedistica Italiana (UVI)** 1884-.

Ivory Coast (CIV) **Fédération Ivoirienne de Cyclisme** Abidjan.

Jamaica (JAM) **Jamaica Cycling Federation** Kingston, formerly **Jamaica Amateur Cycling Association**.

Japan (JPN) **Japan Cycling Federation** 1934- Tokyo, formerly **Japan Amateur Cycling Federation (JACF)**, **Japan Professional Cycling Federation** Tokyo.

Jordan (JOR) **Jordan Cycling Federation** Amman.

Kazakhstan (KAZ) **Fédération Cycliste de la Republique du Kazakhstan** Almaty.

Kenya (KEN) **Amateur Cycling Association of Kenya** Eldoret.

Korea, North (PKR) **Cycling Association of the Democratic People's Republic of Korea** Pyongyang.

Korea, South (KOR) **Korea Cycling Federation** Seoul, formerly **Korean Amateur Cycling Association**.

Kuwait (KUW) **Kuwait Athletic & Cycling Federation** Kuwait City.

Kyrgyzstan (KYR) **Cycling Union of the Republic of Kirghizistan** Bishkek.

Latvia (LAT) **Fédération Lettone de Cyclisme** Riga.

Lebanon (LIB) **Fédération Libanaise de Cyclisme** 1952- Beirut.

Libya (LBA) **Union Jamahiriyenne de Cyclisme** Tripoli.

Liechtenstein (LIE) **Liechtensteiner Radfahrerverband** 1962- Ruggell.

Lithuania (LIT) **Fédération Lituanienne de Cyclisme** Vilnius.

Luxembourg (LUX) **Fédération du Sport Cycliste Luxembourgeois** Luxembourg.

Macao (MAC) **Associacoa de Ciclismo de Macao** Macao, formerly **Lai Ming Cycling Association**.

Macedonia **Union Velocipedique de Macedoine** Skopje.

Madagascar (MAD) **Comite National de Coordination de Cyclisme** Tananarive.

Malawi (MAW) **Cycling Association of Malawi** Blantyre.

Malaysia (MAL) **Malaysian National Cycling Federation** 1953- Mekala.

Mali **Fédération Malienne de Cyclisme** Bamako.

Malta (MLT) **Amateur Cycling Association** Mosta, formerly **Malta Cycling Association**.

Mauritius (MRI) **Fédération Mauricienne de Cyclisme** Bell Village.

Mexico (MEX) **Federacion Mexicana de Ciclismo** Mexico City.

Moldova (MOL) **Fédération du Cyclisme de la Republique de Moldavie** Chisinau.

Mongolia (MGL) **Mongolian Cycling Federation** Ulan Bator.

Monaco (MON) **Fédération Monegasque de Cyclisme** Monaco.

Morocco (MAR) **Fédération Royale Marocaine de Cyclisme** Casablanca.

Myanmar (BIR) **Burma Cycling Federation** Rangoon.

Namibia **Namibian Cycling Federation** Windhoek.

Netherlands Antilles **Dutch Antillean Cycling Federation** Curacoa.

New Zealand (NZL) **New Zealand Amateur Cycling Association** 1934- Wellington.

Nicaragua (NCA) **Federacion Nacional de Ciclismo** Managua.

Niger (NIG) **Fédération Nigerienne de Cyclisme** Niamey.

Nigeria (NGR) **Nigerian Cycling Federation** 1972- Lagos, formerly **Nigerian Amateur Cycling Association**.

Norway (NOR) **Norges Cykleforbund** 1910- Rud.

Oman (OMN) **Oman Cycling Association** Ruwi.

Pakistan (PAK) **Pakistan Cycling Federation** Lahore.

Panama (PAN) **Federacion Nacional de Ciclismo de Panama** Panama.

Paraguay (PAR) **Federacion Paraguaya de Ciclismo** Asuncion.

Peru (PER) **Federacion Peruana de Ciclismo** Lima.

Philippines (PHI) **Philippine Cycling Federation** Manila.

Poland (POL) **Polski Zwiazek Kolarski** 1920- Warsaw.

Portugal (POR) **Federação Portuguesa de Ciclismo** Lisbon.

Puerto Rico (PUR) **Federacion Puertorriquena de Ciclismo** San Juan.

Romania (ROM) **Federatia Romana de Ciclisme** Bucharest.

Russia (RUS) **Union Cycliste de la Russie** Moscow, formerly Soviet Union (URS) **Fédération Cycliste d'URSS.**

Rwanda (RWA) **Fédération Rwandaise de Cyclisme Amateur** Kigali.

St. Kitts **St. Kitts Amateur Cycling Association** Basseterre.

St. Lucia **St. Lucia Amateur Cycling Association** Castries.

St. Vincent **St. Vincent and Grenadines Cycling Union** Kingstown.

San Marino (SMR) **Federazione Ciclistica Sanmarinese** Domagnano.

São Tomé **Federacao Santomense de Ciclismo** São Tomé.

Saudi Arabia (SAU) **Saudi Arabian Amateur Cycling Association** 1963- Riyadh.

Senegal (SEN) **Fédération Sénégalaise de Cyclisme** Dakar.

Seychelles (SEY) **Seychelles Amateur Cycling Association** Victoria.

Singapore (SIN) **Singapore Amateur Cycling Association** Singapore.

Slovakia **Slovak Cycling Federation** Bratislava.

Slovenia **Fédération Slovene de Cyclisme** Ljubljana.

South Africa (SAF) **South African Cycling Federation** Table View.

Spain (ESP) **Federación Española de Ciclismo** 1896- Madrid.

Sri Lanka (SRI) **Cycling Association of Sri Lanka** 1970- Colombo.

Sudan (SUD) **Sudan Cycling Federation** Khartoum.

Surinam (SUR) **Surinam Wielren Unie** Paramaribo.

Sweden (SWE) **Svenska Cykelförbundet** 1900- Sigtuna.

Switzerland (SUI) **Comité National du Cyclisme (CNC)** Glattbrugg, also **National Komittee für Radsport** Zurich, **Union Cycliste Suisse** Geneva.

Syria (SYR) **Fédération Arabe Syrienne de Cyclisme** Damascus.

Taiwan (TPE) **Chinese Taipei Amateur Cycling Association** 1964- Taipei.

Tanzania (TAN) **Cycling Association of Tanzanie** Dar es Salaam.

Thailand (THA) **Thai Amateur Cycling Association** Bangkok.

Togo (TOG) **Fédération Togolaise de Cyclisme** Lome.

Trinidad-Tobago (TRI) **Trinidad and Tobago Cycling Federation** Port of Spain.

Tunisia (TUN) **Fédération Tunisienne de Cyclisme** Tunis.

Turkey (TUR) **Fédération Turque de Cyclisme** Ankara.

Turkmenistan **Fédération Cycliste du Turkmenistan** Ashgabat.

Uganda (UGA) **Uganda Cycling Association** Kampala.

Ukraine (UKR) **Fédération Ukrainienne de Cyclisme** Kiev.

United Arab Emirates (UAE) **United Arab Emirates Cyclist Association** Deira Dubai.

United States (USA) **USA Cycling Inc.: United States Cycling Federation (USCF)** 1975- Colorado Springs CO, formerly **Amateur Bicycle League of America (ABLA)** 1920- 1975, **Inter-Club Amateur Cycle Road Racing League** 1912-1919, **National Cycling Association (NCA)** 1893-1920 Phildelphia PA, **League of American Wheelmen (LAW)** 1881-1900; **National Off-Road Bicycle Association (NORBA)** 1983- Colorado Springs CO: **United States Professional Cycling Federation (USPRO)** 1983- New Tripoli PA, formerly **Professional Racing Organization (PRO)** 1968-1982 Colorado.

Uruguay (URU) **Fédération Cycliste d'Uruguay** Montevideo.

Uzbekistan **Fédération Cycliste d'Ouzbekistan** Tashkent.

Vanuatu **Vanuatu Amateur Cycling Federation** Port Vila.

Venezuela (VEN) **Federacion Venezolana de Ciclismo** Caracas.

Vietnam (VIE) **Vietnam Cycling Federation** Hanoi.

Virgin Islands (ISV) **Virgin Islands Cycling Federation** St. Croix.

Yemen (YAR) **Yemen Cycling Federation** San'a', also **Yemen Amateur Cycling Federation** Adan.

Yugoslavia (YUG) **Fédération Yougoslavie de Cyclisme** Belgrade.

Zaire (ZAI) **Fédération Zaïroise de Cyclisme** Kinshasa.

Zambia (ZAM) **Cycling Association of Zambia** Lusaka.

Zimbabwe (ZIM) **Zimbabwe Cycling Association** Harare.

REGIONAL AND SPECIALTY SPORTS GROUPS

Amateur Athletic Association 1866- London.

American Athletic Association of the Deaf (AAAD) 1945- Ogden UT.

American Bicycle Association (ABA) 1977- Chandler AZ, BMX racing, 57,000 members in 1992.

Arab Amateur Cycling Federation (AACF).

Asian Cycling Federation (ACF).

Association Francaise de Mountain Bike Neuilly.

Australian BMX Association (ABA) Geilston Bay, Tasmania.

Australian Mountain Biking Association (AMBA) Sydney.

Bicycle Polo Association of Great Britain 1931- Gosport, England.

British Cyclo-Cross Association 1954- Kent, England, 300 member clubs in 1980.

British Mountain Bike Federation (BMBF) Manchester.

British Triathlon Association Essex, England.

Canadian Federation of Sport Organizations for the Disabled Gloucester, Ontario.

Canadian Mountain Bike Polo Association Whistler BC.

Comite International des Sports des Sourds (CISS) 1924- Paris, France, World Deaf Games.

Commission Internationale de Cyclisme en Salle.

Cycle Speedway Council 1971- Dorset, England, flat track racing.

English Schools Cycling Association. 1967-.

European Cycling Union.

European Triathlon Union (ETU).

Federation Quebecois des Sports Cyclistes Montreal.

International Association of Sports for the Mentally Handicapped (INAS-FMH).

International Blind Sports Association (IBSA) Madrid, Spain.

International Paralympics Committee (IPC) Paralympic Games.

International Sport Organization for the Disabled (ISOD).

International Stoke Mandeville Wheelchair Sports Federation (ISMWSF).

International Triathlon Union (ITU).

Japan Kei-rin Association 1957- governs Kei-rin parimutuel racing.

Japan Mountain Bike Association Tokyo.

National Bicycle League (NBL) Dublin OH, BMX racing, 18,000 members in 1992.

National BMX Association Wigan, England.

National Cycle League (NCL) 1989- New York City, city-based league.

National Handicapped Sports (NHS) 1967- Rockville MD.

National Wheelchair Athletic Association (NWAA) 1956- Colorado Springs CO.

Road Records Association (RRA) 1885- Glamorgan, England, governs UK record attempts.

Road Time Trials Council (RTTC) 1921- Perterborough, England, governs UK time trial racing, formerly **Road Racing Council.**

Scottish Cyclists' Union (SCU) 1889- Edinburgh.

Sierra Leone Amateur National Cycling Association Freetown.

South Australian Cycling Federation Elizabeth.

Special Olympics International (SOI) 1968- Washington DC, cyclists with mental impairments, Special Olympic Games.

Tasmanian Cycling Federation Launceston.

Tri-Fed-Triathlon Federation/USA 1982- Colorado Springs CO.

Ultra-Marathon Cycling Association (UMCA) 1980- Altadena CA, governs long-distance racing.

United Kingdom Bicycle Moto Cross Association (UK BMX) 1980- Twickenham, England.

United States Association for Blind Athletes (USABA) 1976- Colorado Springs CO.

United States Cerebral Palsy Athletic Association (USCPAA) 1986- Dallas TX.

United States Deaf Cycling Association (USDCA) Union City CA.

Veterans Time Trials Association 1943- Essex, England.

Women's Cycle Racing Association Romford, England.

Women's Road Records Association 1934- London.

World Bicycle Polo Federation Bailey CO.

VELODROMES

Track Name Years in use, Place, open/covered, lap length, surface, angular degree of turns, seats, altitude, owner, events.

UNITED STATES

Springfield Bicycle Track 1884–1900s, Springfield MA, open, 1/3 mile (536 m.), dirt, later cement, Springfield Bicycle Club Tournaments.

Charles River Velodrome 1900s, Cambridge MA, open, 1/3 mile (536 m.), cement.

New Haven 1890s–1911, New Haven CT.

Revere Beach Track 1890s–1931, Boston MA.

Newby Oval 1890s, Indianapolis IN, open, 1/4 mile (402 m.), pinewood, 20,000 seats, Arthur Newby later built the Indianapolis Motor Speedway.

Capitol City Velodrome 1890s, Indianapolis IN, open.

Denver Velodrome 1890s, Denver CO, open, wood.

Salt Palace Velodrome 1899–1913, Salt Lake City UT, open, 1/8 mile (201 m.), wood, 48 degree turns, 5,000 seats, altitude 4,400 ft.

Salt Air Velodrome 1904, Salt Lake City UT, open, salt.

Madison Square Garden 1895–1925, New York City, covered, 1/10 mile (161 m.), wood.

Manhattan Beach Velodrome 1890s, Brooklyn NY, open, 1/3 mile (536 m.), cement, 30,000 spectators, operated by Billy Brady.

Nutley Velodrome 1890s–1940, Nutley NJ.

Waverley Fair Velodrome 1896–1910, Newark NJ, covered, 1/4 mile (402 m.), wood.

Newark Velodrome 1911–1930, Newark NJ, covered, 1/6 mile (268 m.), wood, 12,500 seats.

New York Velodrome 1921–1930, New York City, open, 1/6 mile (268 m.), wood, 20,000 seats.

Washington Park Bowl 1927– Kenosha WI, open, 333 m., asphalt, 26 degree turns, oldest operating in U.S.

Coney Island Velodrome 1930s, Brooklyn NY, open, 1/6 mile (268 m.), 10,000 seats.

Rose Bowl Velodrome 1932, Pasadena CA, portable, open, wood, Olympic Games.

Brown Deer Velodrome 1948– Milwaukee WI, open, 400 m., asphalt, 23 degree turns.

Meadowhill Velodrome 1959– Northbrook IL, open, 383 m., asphalt, 43 degree turns.

Gately Stadium 1960s, Chicago IL, open, 250 m., wood.

Encino Velodrome 1961– Encino CA, open, 250 m., concrete, 29 degree turns.

Hellyer Park Velodrome 1962– San Jose CA, open, 336 m., asphalt, later Chem-comp, 22.5 degree turns.

Penrose Velodrome 1962– St. Louis MO, open, 322 m., asphalt, 23 degree turns.

Kissena Velodrome 1963– Flushing NY, open, 400 m., asphalt, 17 degree turns.

Alpenrose Velodrome 1964– Alpenrose Diary, Portland OR, open, 268 m., concrete, 41 degree turns.

Dorias Velodrome 1967– Detroit MI, open, 322 m., cement, 28 degree turns.

Dick Lane Velodrome 1975– East Point GA, open, 322 m., concrete, 33 degree turns.

Marymoor Park Velodrome 1975– Redmond WA, open, 400 m., cement, 28 degree turns.

Lehigh County Velodrome 1975– Trexlertown PA, open, 333 m., Chem-comp, 27 degree turns, established by Robert Rodale.

Madison Velodrome 1976–1980, Detroit MI, portable, 125+ m., wood, track was stolen while in storage.

San Diego Velodrome 1976– Morely Field, San Diego CA, open, 333 m., asphalt, 28 degree turns.

Shakopee Velodrome 1977–1990, Shakopee WI, open, 200 m., wood, 58 degree turns, reconstructed from Schurmann-built track of 1973 Detroit six-day.

Major Taylor Velodrome 1982– Indianapolis IN, open, 333 m., concrete, 28.5 degree turns.

7-Eleven Velodrome 1983– Olympic Training Center, Colorado Springs CO, open, 333 m., concrete, 33 degree turns, 8,200 seats, altitude 7,000 ft.

Olympic Velodrome 1983– Cal-State University Dominguez Hills, Carson CA, open, 333 m., concrete, 33 degree turns, cost $3 million.

Baton Rogue Velodrome 1985– Baton Rogue LA, open, 333 m., concrete, 33 degree turns.

Alkek Velodrome 1986– Houston TX, open, 333 m., concrete, 33 degree turns.

Brandy Branch Park Bicycle Track 1988– Jacksonville FL, open, 300 m., concrete, 20 degree turns.

National Sports Center Velodrome 1990– Blaine MN, open, 250 m., wood, 43 degree turns.

Brian Piccolo Velodrome 1993– Cooper City, Broward County FL, open, 333 m., 30 degree turns.

Vandedrome 1995, Del Mar CA, portable, 153 m., wood, 53 degree turns.

CANADA

Queens Park Velodrome 1900s, Montreal, open, 1/2 mile (804 m.), dirt, 18,000 seats.

Schelstraete Velodrome 1950s, portable, 1/13 mile (123 m.), wood.

China Creek Velodrome 1954–1980, Vancouver, open, 245 m., wood, 42 degree turns.

Winnipeg Velodrome 1967– Winnipeg, open, 400 m., concrete, 38 degree turns.

Delhi Velodrome 1970s– Delhi, Ontario, open, 250 m., asphalt, 38 degree turns.

Woodbridge Velodrome 1973– Toronto, open, 255 m., concrete, 45 degree turns.

Olympic Velodrome 1974–1989, Montreal, covered, 287 m., wood, 48 degree turns.

Glenmore Velodrome 1975, Calgary, open, 400 m., concrete, 30 degree turns, rebuilt 1990.

Edmonton Velodrome 1977– Edmonton, open, 333 m., 37 degree turns.

Fonthill Velodrome 1980s– Fonthill, Ontario, open, 135 m., wood, 55 degree turns.

Harry Jerome Memorial Velodrome 1992– Vancouver, covered, 200 m., wood.

Juan de Fuca Velodrome 1992– Juan de Fuca Recreation Center, Victoria, open, 333 m., concrete, 28 degree turns.

AMERICAS

National Stadium Bridgetown, Barbados, open, 400 m., cement.

Calles Park Velodrome Mexico City, open, altitude 2,300 m.

Centro Sportivo Mexico City, open, 333 m., cement, altitude 2,300 m.

Olympic Velodrome Mexico City, open, 333 m., wood, altitude 2,300 m.

Alto Irpavo La Paz, Bolivia, open, 333 m., cement, altitude 3,408 m.

A.N. Patino Cali, Colombia, open.

Velodrome Rodriguez Medelin, Colombia, open.

Santiago Velodrome Santiago, Chile, open, altitude 610 m.

Quito Velodrome Quito, Ecuador, open, 333 m., cement, altitude 2,380 m.

EUROPE

Anoeta Velodrome San Sebastian, Spain, 275 m., cement.

Horta Olympic Velodrome 1991– Barcelona, Spain, open, 250 m., wood, 6,400 seats.

Luis Puig Velodrome 1992– Valencia, Spain, semi-covered, 250 m.

Ordrupp Velodrome 1949– Copenhagen, Denmark, open, 370 m., cement, 48 degree turns.

Odense Velodrome. Odense, Denmark, open.

Forum Copenhagen, Denmark, covered, 190 m., wood.

Hamar Olympic Hall Velodrome 1992– Hamar, Norway, open, wood.

Helsinki, Finland, open.

Herne Hill Velodrome 1891– London, open, 450 m., concrete and epoxy-resin, 26 degree turns, original surface was shale, later replaced with wood (457.355 m.), refurbished in 1992 by Ron Webb at cost of £500,000.

Crystal Palace Track 1900s, London.

Fallowfield Track Manchester, England.

Butts Stadium Coventry, England.

Wembley Stadium London, portable.

Olympia Velodrome

Harvey Hadden Stadium Nottingham, England, open.

Lilleshall Velodrome Newcastle-and-Lyme, England, open.

Saffron Stadium Leicester, England, open, 333 m., wood.

National Cycling Centre 1994– Manchester, covered, 250 m., wood, 5,000 seats, designed by Ron

Webb, cost £9 million.

Buffalo Velodrome 1891– Porte Maillot, later Porte d'Orleans, Paris, open, 333 m., cement, built by owner of Folies Bergères, named for Col. Cody's Buffalo Bill Circus staged on the grounds.

Velodrome Parc des Princes 1891– Paris, open, 666 m.

Velodrome de la Seine Paris.

Velodrome d'Hiver 1891– Paris, covered, served as prison during World War II.

Velodrome du Parc 1890s– Bordeaux, France, open.

Montlhéry Velodrome Montlhéry, France, open.

Palais des Sports Grenoble, France, covered, 200 m.

Piste Municipale 1890s– Vincennes, France, open, 400 m., wood, nicknamed *Cipale*, enlarged to 500 m. in 1900.

Velodrome Troyen 1900– Paris, open, 375 m., cement.

Velodrome de l'Est 1890s– Paris, open, 333 m.

Velodrome de Tours Tours, France, open, 400 m., cement.

Pont Magnam Nice, France.

Velodrome Municipale Roubaix, France, open.

St. Etienne, France, covered.

Toulon, Hyéres, France, open.

Velodrome Municipal Toulouse, France, open.

Omnisports Bercy 1980– Paris, covered, wood.

Stadium de Bordeaux-Le Lac 1989– Bordeaux, France, covered, 250 m., wood (doussie), hour records.

Palais des Sports Brussels, covered.

Sportpaleis Merksem 1919– Antwerp, Belgium, covered, 250 m., wood, 20,000 seats.

Velodrome d'Hiver Ghent, Belgium, covered, 166 m., wood.

Sportpaleis Ghent, Belgium, covered.

Ahoy Sportpalais Rotterdam, Holland, covered.

Amsterdam 1940s– open, 500 m., cement.

Sportpark Friedenau 1897–1904, Berlin, open, 500 m., cement, 20,000 seats.

Elberfeld Velodrome Wuppertal, Germany, open.

Frankfurt on Main, Germany, open, 400 m.

Rütt Arena 1926–1931 Berlin, wood.

Deutschlandhalle 1950s– Berlin, covered, 220 m., wood.

Hans-Martin Schleyerhalle Stuttgart, Germany, covered, 285 m., wood.

Werner Seelenbinderhalle Berlin, covered, 171 m., wood.

Sporthalle Koln, Germany, covered, 166 m., wood.

Olympiahalle 1970– Munich, Germany, covered, 275 m., wood.

Bremen, Germany, 166 m., wood.

Stuttgart, Germany, 1984– covered, 285 m., wood.

Westfalenhalle Dortmund, Germany, covered, 200 m., wood.

Ferry Dusika Vienna, Austria, covered.

Hallenstadion Vienna, Austria, covered.

Hallenstadion Zurich, Switzerland, covered.

Oerlikon Velodrome Zurich, Switzerland, covered, cement.

Bassano de Grappa, Italy, 1971– open, 400 m., cement.

Cascine Velodrome Florence, Italy, 333 m.

Velodrome Communale Dalmine, Italy, open.

Masnago Velodrome Varèse, Italy, open, 446 m.

Ferrara Velodrome Italy, cement.

Monteroni, Italy, 333 m.

Olympic Velodrome 1959– Rome, open, 400 m., wood.

Padova, Italy, 333 m.

Palasport Milan, Italy, covered.

Palazzo dello Sport Milan, Italy, covered, 250 m.

Vigorelli Velodrome 1935– Milan, Italy, open, 333 m., wood, hour records.

Paolo Borselino Velodrome Palermo, Italy, open, 400 m., resin-coated cement.

Brno, Czech, open.

Plzen, Czech.

Velodrom Kovo Prague, Czech.

Athens, Greece.

EURASIA

Junikpionerov Velodrome Moscow, open.

Krylatskoje Olympic Velodrome 1980– Moscow, covered, 333 m.

Central Velodrome Tbilissi, open.

Chakhter Velodrome Toula, open, 333 m.

Dynamo Stadium Irkoutsk, open.

Spartah Stadium Erevan, open.

Tashkent, open.

ASIA

Olympic Velodrome 1960s– Tokyo, Japan.

Tokyo Dome 1980s Tokyo, Japan, covered, 400 m., cement.

Olympic Velodrome 1986– Seoul, Korea, open, 333 m., wood.

AFRICA

International Stadium 1981– Durban, South Africa, open, 333 m., concrete, 40 degree turns.

AUSTRALIA

Olympic Velodrome 1950s–1977 Melbourne, open, 333 m., wood.

Northcote Velodrome Melbourne, open.

Coburg Velodrome Melbourne, open, 250 m., concrete.

Commonwealth Games Velodrome 1982– Brisbane, open, concrete.

Devonport, Tasmania.

Sydney, open, 1/4 mile, bitumen, unbanked.

OLYMPIC TRACK CHAMPIONS [See Sports Groups for definition of three-letter country codes.]

1896 ATHENS

EVENT	TIME	WINNER (COUNTRY)
TT 333 m	:24	Paul Masson (FRA)
SPRINT 2,000 m	4:56	Paul Masson (FRA)
10 km	17:45	Paul Masson (FRA)
PACED 100 km	3:08:19	Léon Flameng (FRA)
12 hour	314,997 km	Adolf Schmal (AUT)

1900 PARIS

TT 603 m	51.2	William Johnson (GBR)
SPRINT 2,000m	2:52	G. Taillandier (FRA)
TEAM PURSUIT	2:17.2	UNITED STATES

1904 ST. LOUIS

1/4 mile	31.8	Marcus Hurley (USA)
1/3 mile	43.8	Marcus Hurley (USA)
1/2 mile	1:09	Marcus Hurley (USA)
1 mile	2:41.4	Marcus Hurley (USA)
2 miles	4:57.8	Burton Downing (USA)
5 miles	13:08.2	Charles Schlee (USA)
25 miles	1:10:55	Burton Downing (USA)

1906 ATHENS

TT 333 m	22.8	Francesco Verri (ITA)
SPRINT 1,000 m	1:42.2	Francesco Verri (ITA)
5 km	8:35	Francesco Verri (ITA)
20 km	29:00	William Pett (GBR)
TANDEM	2:57	J. Matthews-A. Rushen (GBR)

1908 LONDON

TT 603 m	51.2	Victor Johnson (GBR)
SPRINT 1,000 m	-	no winner (over time limit)
5 km	8:36	Benjamin Jones (GBR)
20 km	34:13.6	C.B. Kingsbury (GBR)
TANDEM	3:07.6	M. Schilles-A. Auffray (FRA)
TEAM PURSUIT	2:18.6	BRITAIN (1,810 m)
100 km	2:41:48.6	C.H. Bartlett (GBR)

1920 ANTWERP

SPRINT	-	Maurice Peeters (HOL)
50 km	1:16:43.2	Henry George (BEL)
TANDEM 2 km	2:29.4	H. Ryan-T. Lance (GBR)
TEAM PURSUIT	5:20	ITALY

1924 PARIS

SPRINT 200 m	12.8	Lucien Michard (FRA)
50 km	1:18:24	Jacobus Willems (HOL)
TANDEM 2 km	2:40	J. Cugnot-L. Choury (FRA)
TEAM PURSUIT	5:15	ITALY

1928 AMSTERDAM

SPRINT	13.2	R. Beaufrand (FRA)
KILO TT	1:14.4	Willy Falk Hansen (DEN)
TANDEM SPRINT	11.8	B. Leene-D. Van Dyke (HOL)
TEAM PURSUIT	5:10.8	ITALY

1932 LOS ANGELES

SPRINT	12.6	Jacques Van Egmond (HOL)
KILO TT	1:13	Edgar Gray (AUS)
TANDEM	12.0	M. Perrin-L. Chaillot (FRA)
TEAM PURSUIT	4:53	ITALY

1936 BERLIN

SPRINT	11.8	Toni Merkens (GER)
KILO TT	1:12	Arie Van Vliet (HOL)
TANDEM	11:8	E. Ihbe-C. Lorenz (GER)
TEAM PURSUIT	4:45	FRANCE

1948 LONDON

SPRINT	12.0	Mario Ghella (ITA)
KILO TT	1:13.5	Jacques Dupont (FRA)
TANDEM	-	R. Perona-F. Terruzzi (ITA)
TEAM PURSUIT	4:47.8	FRANCE

1952 HELSINKI

SPRINT	12.0	Enzo Sacchi (ITA)
KILO TT	1:11.1	Russel Mockbridge (AUS)
TANDEM	11.0	R. Mockbridge-L. Cox (AUS)
TEAM PURSUIT	4:46	ITALY

1956 MELBOURNE

SPRINT	11.4	Michel Rousseau (FRA)
KILO TT	1:09.8	Leandro Faggin (ITA)
TANDEM	10.8	J. Brown-A. Marchant (AUS)
TEAM PURSUIT	4:37.4	ITALY

1960 ROME

SPRINT	11.1	Sante Gaiardoni (ITA)
KILO TT	1:07.27	Sante Gaiardoni (ITA)
TANDEM	10.7	S. Bianchetto-G. Beghetto (ITA)
TEAM PURSUIT	4:30.9	ITALY

1964 TOKYO

SPRINT	13.69	Giovanni Pettenella (ITA)
KILO TT	1:09.59	Patrick Sercu (BEL)
TANDEM	10.75	S. Bianchetto-A. Damiano (ITA)
PURSUIT	5:04	Jiri Daler (TCH)
TEAM PURSUIT	4:35.67	WEST GERMANY

1968 MEXICO CITY

SPRINT	10.68	Daniel Morelon (FRA)
KILO TT	1:03.91	Pierre Trentin (FRA)
TANDEM	9.83	D. Morelon-P. Trentin (FRA)
PURSUIT	4:41.71	Daniel Rebillard (FRA)
TEAM PURSUIT	4:22.44	DENMARK

1972 MUNICH

SPRINT	11.69	Daniel Morelon (FRA)
KILO TT	1:06.44	Niels Fredborg (DEN)
TANDEM	-	V. Semenets-I. Tselovalnikov (URS)
PURSUIT	4:45.74	Knut Knudsen (NOR)
TEAM PURSUIT	4:22	WEST GERMANY

1976 MONTREAL

SPRINT	10.78	Anton Tkac (TCH)
KILO TT	1:05.92	Klaus-Jurgen Grunke (DDR)
PURSUIT	4:47.61	Gregor Braun (RFA)
TEAM PURSUIT	4:21.08	WEST GERMANY

1980 MOSCOW

SPRINT	-	Lutz Hesslich (DDR)
KILO TT	1:02.95	Lothar Thoms (DDR)
PURSUIT	4:35.66	Robert Dill-Bundi (SUI)
TEAM PURSUIT	4:15.70	SOVIET UNION

1984 LOS ANGELES

SPRINT	-	Mark Gorski (USA)
KILO TT	1:06.10	Fredy Schmidtke (RFA)
PURSUIT	4:39.35	Steve Hegg (USA)
TEAM PURSUIT	4:25.99	AUSTRALIA
POINTS	37	Roger Ilegems (BEL)

1988 SEOUL

MEN'S SPRINT	-	Lutz Hesslich (DDR)
WOMEN'S SPRINT	-	Erika Salumae (EST)
KILO TT	1:04.49	Alexander Kiritchenko (URS)
PURSUIT	4:32.00	Guintautas Umaras (URS)
TEAM PURSUIT	4:13.31	SOVIET UNION
POINTS	46	Dan Frost (DEN)

1992 BARCELONA

MEN'S SPRINT	10.99	Jens Fiedler (RFA)
WOMEN'S SPRINT	12.66	Erika Salumae (EST)
KILO TT	1:03.34	Jose Moreno (ESP)
MEN'S PURSUIT	4:24.496	Chris Boardman (GBR)
WOMEN'S PURSUIT	3:41.75	Petra Rossner (RFA)
TEAM PURSUIT	4:08.79	GERMANY
POINTS	44	Giovanni Lombardi (ITA)

WORLD SPRINT CHAMPIONS

[1 event not held; 2 open pro/am race; 3 separate pro/am venue; 4 Olympic champion; 5 disqualified dope test]

	PROFESSIONAL	AMATEUR	WOMEN1
1893 Chicago	1	A.A. Zimmermann (USA)	
1894 Antwerp	1	Aug. Lehr (GER)	
1895 Cologne	R. Protin (BEL)	Jaap Eden (HOL)	
1896 Copenhagen	Paul Bourillon (FRA)	H. Reynolds (IRL)	
1897 Glasgow	Willy Arend (RFA)	Ed. Schraeder (DEN)	
1898 Vienna	George A. Banker (USA)	Paul Albert (GER)	
1899 Montreal	Major Taylor (USA)	T. Summersgill (GBR)	
1900 Paris	Edouard Jacquelin (FRA)	A. Didier-Nauts (BEL)	
1901 Berlin	Thorwald Ellegaard (DEN)	Emile Maitrot (FRA)	
1902 Rome	Thorwald Ellegaard	Ch. Piard (FRA)	
1903 Copenhagen	Thorwald Ellegaard	A.L. Reed (GBR)	
1904 London	Iver Lawson (USA)	Marcus Hurley (USA)	
1905 Antwerp	Gabriel Poulain (FRA)	J.S. Benyan (GBR)	
1906 Geneva	Thorwald Ellegaard	Francesco Verri (ITA)	
1907 Paris	Emil Friol (FRA)	J. Devoissoux (FRA)	
1908 Berlin/Lindenau	Thorwald Ellegaard	Victor Johnson (GBR)	
1909 Copenhagen	Victor Dupré (FRA)	W.J. Bailey (GBR)	
1910 Brussels	Emil Friol	W.J. Bailey	
1911 Rome	Thorwald Ellegaard	W.J. Bailey	
1912 Newark	Frank Kramer (USA)	Donald McDougall (USA)	
1913 Leipzig/Berlin	Walter Rutt (RFA)	W.J. Bailey	
1920 Antwerp	Robert Spears (AUS)	Maurice Peeters (HOL)	
1921 Copenhagen	Piet Moeskops (HOL)	H.B. Andersen (DEN)	
1922 Paris	Piet Moeskops	Hon. Th. Johnson (GBR)	
1923 Zurich	Piet Moeskops	Lucien Michard (FRA)	
1924 Paris	Piet Moeskops	Lucien Michard	
1925 Amsterdam	Ernest Kaufmann (SUI)	Jaap Meijer (HOL)	
1926 Milan	Piet Moeskops	A. Martinetti (ITA)	
1927 Cologne	Lucien Michard (FRA)	M. Engel (GER)	
1928 Budapest	Lucien Michard	Falk Hansen (DEN)	
1929 Zurich	Lucien Michard	Toine Mazairac (HOL	
1930 Brussels	Lucien Michard	Louis Gerardin (FRA)	
1931 Copenhagen	Falk Hansen (DEN)	H. Harder (DEN)	
1932 Rome	Jef Scherens (BEL)	A. Richter (GER)	
1933 Paris	Jef Scherens	Jacques Van Egmond (HOL)	
1934 Leipzig	Jef Scherens	Ben Pola (ITA)	
1935 Brussels	Jef Scherens	Toni Merkens (GER)	
1936 Zurich	Jef Scherens	Arie Van Vliet (HOL)	
1937 Copenhagen	Jef Scherens	Jef Van de Vijver (HOL)	
1938 Amsterdam	Arie Van Vliet (HOL)	Jef Van de Vijver (HOL)	
1939 Milan	1	Jan Derksen (HOL)	
1946 Zurich	Jan Derksen (HOL)	Oscar Plattner (SUI)	
1947 Paris	Jef Scherens	Reg Harris (GBR)	
1948 Amsterdam	Arie Van Vliet	Mario Ghella (ITA)	
1949 Copenhagen	Reg Harris (GBR)	Sid Patterson (AUS)	
1950 Rocourt	Reg Harris	M. Verdeun (FRA)	
1951 Milan	Reg Harris	Enzo Sacchi (ITA)	
1952 Paris	Oscar Plattner (SUI)	Enzo Sacchi (ITA)	
1953 Zurich	Arie Van Vliet	M. Morettini (ITA)	
1954 Cologne	Reg Harris	G. Peacock (GBR)	
1955 Milan	Antonio Maspes (ITA)	Giusseppe Ogna (ITA)	
1956 Copenhagen	Antonio Maspes	Michel Rousseau (FRA)	
1957 Rocourt	Jan Derksen	Michel Rousseau (FRA)	

SIX-DAY CHAMPIONS

RANK	NAME (COUNTRY)	WINS	RACES
1	Patrick Sercu (BEL)	88	223
2	René Pijnen (HOL)	72	233
	Danny Clark (AUS)	72	250
4	Peter Post (HOL)	65	155
5	Rik Van Steenbergen (BEL)	40	134
6	William Torchy Peden (CAN)	38	123
7	Klaus Bugdahl (RFA)	37	228
8	Albert Fritz (RFA)	34	198
	Gustav Kilian (RFA)	34	90
10	Fritz Pfenninger (SUI)	33	180

WORLD SPRINT CHAMPIONS CONTINUED

	PROFESSIONAL	AMATEUR	WOMEN
1958 Paris (FRA)	Michel Rousseau (FRA)	Val. Gasparella (ITA)	Galina Ermolaeva (URS)
1959 Amsterdam (HOL)	Antonio Maspes	Val. Gasparella (ITA)	Galina Ermolaeva
1960 Leipzig (DDR)	Antonio Maspes	Sante Gaiardoni (ITA)	Galina Ermolaeva
1961 Zurich (SUI)	Antonio Maspes	Sergio Bianchetto (ITA)	Galina Ermolaeva
1962 Milan (ITA)	Antonio Maspes	Sergio Bianchetto (ITA)	Valentina Savina (URS)
1963 Rocourt (BEL)	Sante Gaiardoni (ITA)	Patrick Sercu (BEL)	Galina Ermolaeva
1964 Paris (FRA)	Antonio Maspes	Pierre Tretin (FRA)	Irena Kiritchenko (URS)
1965 San Sebastian (ESP)	Giuseppe Beghetto (ITA)	Omar Phakadze (URS)	Valentina Savina
1966 Frankfurt (RFA)	Giuseppe Beghetto	Daniel Morelon (FRA)	Irena Kiritchenko (URS)
1967 Amsterdam (HOL)	Patrick Sercu (BEL)	Daniel Morelon (FRA)	Valentina Savina
1968 Rome/Montevideo[3]	Giuseppe Beghetto	Luigi Borghetti (ITA)	Alla Baguiniantz (URS)
1969 Antwerp/Brno[3]	Patrick Sercu	Daniel Morelon (FRA)	Galina Tsareva (URS)
1970 Leicester (GBR)	Gordon Johnson (AUS)	Daniel Morelon (FRA)	Galina Tsareva
1971 Varese (ITA)	Leijn Loevesijn (HOL)	Daniel Morelon (FRA)	Galina Tsareva
1972 Marseille/Munich	Robert Van Lancker (BEL)	Daniel Morelon (FRA)[4]	Galina Ermolaeva (URS)
1973 San Sebastian (ESP)	Robert Van Lancker	Daniel Morelon (FRA)	Sheila Young (USA)
1974 Montreal (CAN)	Peder Pederson (DEN)	Anton Tkac (TCH)	Tamara Pilisikova (URS)
1975 Rocourt (BEL)	John Nicholson (AUS)	Daniel Morelon (FRA)	Sue Novara (USA)
1976 Monteroni/Montreal	John Nicholson	Anton Tkac (TCH)[4]	Sheila Young
1977 San Cristobal (VEN)	Koichi Nakano (JPN)	Hans-Jurgen Geschke (DDR)	Galina Tsareva
1978 Munich (RFA)	Koichi Nakano	Anton Tkac (TCH)	Galina Tsareva
1979 Amsterdam (HOL)	Koichi Nakano	Lutz Hesslich (DDR)	Galina Tsareva
1980 Besancon/Moscow	Koichi Nakano	Lutz Hesslich (DDR)[4]	Sue Novara
1981 Brno (TCH)	Koichi Nakano	Sergei Kopylov (URS)	Sheila Young
1982 Leicester (GBR)	Koichi Nakano	Sergei Kopylov (URS)	Connie Paraskevin (USA)
1983 Zurich (SUI)	Koichi Nakano	Lutz Hesslich (DDR)	Connie Paraskevin
1984 Barcelona/Los Angeles	Koichi Nakano	Mark Gorski (USA)[4]	Connie Paraskevin
1985 Bassano de Grappa (ITA)	Koichi Nakano	Lutz Hesslich (DDR)	Isabelle Nicoloso (FRA)
1986 Colorado Springs (USA)	Koichi Nakano	Michael Hübner (DDR)	Christa Rothenburger-Luding (DDR)
1987 Vienna (AUT)	Nobuyuki Tawara (JPN)	Lutz Hesslich (DDR)	Erika Salumae (URS)
1988 Ghent/Seoul (BEL/KOR)	Stephen Pate (AUS)	Lutz Hesslich (DDR)[4]	Erika Salumae[4]
1989 Lyon (FRA)	Claudio Golinelli (ITA)	Bill Huck (DDR)	Erika Salumae
1990 Maebashi City (JPN)	Michael Hübner (DDR)	Bill Huck (DDR)	Connie Paraskevin-Young
1991 Stuttgart (RFA)	Carey Hall (AUS)[5]	Jens Fiedler (RFA)	Ingrid Haringa (HOL)
1992 Valencia/Barcelona (ESP)	Michael Hübner (RFA)	Jens Fiedler (RFA)[4]	Erika Salumae (EST)[4]
1993 Hamar (NOR)	Gary Neiwand (AUS)	2	Tanya Dubnicoff (CAN)
1994 Palermo (ITA)	Marty Nothstein (USA)	2	Galina Enioukhina (RUS)
1995 Bogota (COL)	Darryn Hill (AUS)	2	Felicia Ballanger (FRA)

WORLD PURSUIT CHAMPIONS

[1 event not held; 2 open pro-am event; 3 Olympic champion]

	PROFESSIONAL	AMATEUR	WOMEN
1946	Gerard Peters (HOL)	R. Rioland (FRA)	1
1947	Fausto Coppi (ITA)	A. Benfenati (ITA)	
1948	Gerrit Schulte (HOL)	Guido Messina (ITA)	
1949	Fausto Coppi	K. E. Andersen (DEN)	
1950	Antonio Bevilacqua (ITA)	Sid Patterson (AUS)	
1951	Antonio Bevilacqua	M. De Rossi (ITA)	
1952	Sid Patterson (AUS)	Piet Van Heusden (HOL)	
1953	Sid Patterson	Guido Messina	
1954	Guido Messina (ITA)	Leandro Faggin (ITA)	
1955	Guido Messina	Norman Sheil (GBR)	
1956	Guido Messina	Ercole Baldini (ITA)	
1957	Roger Rivière (FRA)	Carlo Simonigh (ITA)	
1958	Roger Rivière	Norman Sheil	Ludmila Kotchetova (URS)
1959	Roger Rivière	Rudi Altig (RFA)	Beryl Burton (GBR)
1960	Rudi Altig (RFA)	M. Delattre (FRA)	Beryl Burton

WORLD PURSUIT CHAMPIONS CONTINUED [1 event not held; 2 open pro-am event; 3 Olympic champion]

	PROFESSIONAL	AMATEUR	WOMEN	TEAM
1961	Rudi Altig (RFA)	Henk Nijdam (HOL)	Yvonne Reynders (BEL)	
1962	Henk Nijdam (HOL)	Kaj Jensen (DEN)	Beryl Burton (GBR)	West Germany
1963	Leandor Faggin (ITA)	Jan Walschaerts (BEL)	Beryl Burton	Soviet Union
1964	Ferdinand Bracke (BEL)	Tiemen Groen (HOL)	Yvonne Reynders	West Germany
1965	Leandro Faggin	Tiemen Groen	Yvonne Reynders	Soviet Union
1966	Leandro Faggin	Tiemen Groen	Beryl Burton	Italy
1967	Tiemen Groen (HOL)	Gert Bongers (HOL)	Tamara Garkouchina (URS)	Soviet Union
1968	Hugh Porter (GBR)	Mogens Frey (DEN)	Raisa Obodovskaya (URS)	Italy
1969	Ferdinand Bracke	Xavier Kurmann (SUI)	Raisa Obodovskaya	Soviet Union
1970	Hugh Porter	Xavier Kurmann	Tamara Garkouchina	West Germany
1971	Dirk Baert (BEL)	Martin Rodriguez (COL)	Tamara Garkouchina	Italy
1972	Hugh Porter	Knut Knudsen (NOR)[3]	Tamara Garkouchina	West Germany[3]
1973	Hugh Porter	Knut Knudsen	Tamara Garkouchina	West Germany
1974	Roy Schuiten (HOL)	Hans Lutz (RFA)	Tamara Garkouchina	West Germany
1975	Roy Schuiten	Thomas Huschke (DDR)	Keetie van Oosten-Hage (HOL)	West Germany
1976	Francesco Moser (ITA)	Gregor Braun (RFA)[3]	Keetie van Oosten-Hage	West Germany[3]
1977	Gregor Braun (RFA)	Norbert Durpisch (DDR)	Vera Kuznetsova (URS)	East Germany
1978	Gregor Braun	Detlev Macha (DDR)	Keetie van Oosten-Hage	East Germany
1979	Bert Oosterbosch (HOL)	Nic. Makarov (URS)	Keetie van Oosten-Hage	East Germany
1980	Tony Doyle (GBR)	Robert Dill-Bundi (SUI)[3]	Nadega Kibardina (URS)	Soviet Union[3]
1981	Alain Bondue (FRA)	Detlev Macha	Nadega Kibardina	East Germany
1982	Alain Bondue	Detlev Macha	Rebecca Twigg (USA)	Soviet Union
1983	Steele Bishop (AUS)	Viktor Kupovets (URS)	Connie Carpenter (USA)	West Germany
1984	Hans-Henrik Oersted (DEN)	Steve Hegg (USA)[3]	Rebecca Twigg	Australia[3]
1985	Hans-Henrik Oersted	Viatcheslav Ekimov (URS)	Rebecca Twigg	Italy
1986	Tony Doyle (GBR)	Viatcheslav Ekimov	Jeannie Longo (FRA)	Czechoslovakia
1987	Hans-Henrik Oersted (DEN)	Guintautas Umaras (URS)	Rebecca Twigg	Soviet Union
1988	Lech Piasecki (POL)	Guintautas Umaras[3]	Jeannie Longo	Soviet Union[3]
1989	Colin Sturgess (GBR)	Viatcheslav Ekimov	Jeannie Longo	East Germany
1990	Viatcheslav Ekimov (URS)	Eugeni Berzin (URS)	Leontien Van Moorsel (HOL)	Soviet Union
1991	Francis Moreau (FRA)	Jens Lehmann (RFA)	Petra Rossner (RFA)	Germany
1992	Mike McCarthy (USA)	Chris Boardman (GBR)[3]	Petra Rossner[3]	Germany[3]
1993	Graeme Obree (GBR)	2	Rebecca Twigg	Australia
1994	Chris Boardman (GBR)	2	Marion Clignet (FRA)	Germany
1995	Graeme Obree (GBR)	2	Rebecca Twigg (USA)	Australia

UCI WORLD TRACK RECORDS [As of October 1995; 1 high altitude, elevation 600 meters and above]

MEN

DISTANCE	TIME	RECORD HOLDER	PLACE	DAY.MONTH.YEAR
200 m lancé	9.865	Curt Harnett (CAN)	Bogota (COL)[1]	28.09.1995
500 m lancé	26.649	Alexander Kiritchenko (URS)	Moscow (URS)	29.10.1988
1 km arrêté	1:00.613	Shane Kelly (AUS)	Bogota (COL)[1]	26.09.1995
4 km arrêté	4:20.894	Graeme Obree (SCO)	Hamar (NOR)	19.08.1993
4 km team	4:03.840	Australia	Hamar (NOR)	20.08.1993
55.291 km	1 hour	Tony Rominger (SUI)	Bordeaux (FRA)	05.11.1994

WOMEN

200 m lancé	10.031	Olga Slioussareva (URS)	Moscow (URS)	25.04.1993
500 m lancé	29.655	Erika Salumae (URS)	Moscow (URS)	06.08.1987
500 m arrêté	34.017	Felicia Ballanger (FRA)	Bogota (COL)[1]	29.09.1995
3 km arrêté	3:36.081	Rebecca Twigg (USA)	Bogota (COL)[1]	30.09.1995
47.411 km	1 hour	Yvonne McGregor (GBR)	Manchester (GBR)	17.06.1995

DISCONTINUED UCI RECORDS

MEN

1 km lancé	57.260	Alexander Kiritchenko (URS)	Moscow (URS)	25.04.1989
5 km arrêté	5:29.178	Miguel Indurain (ESP)	Bogota (COL)[1]	15.10.1995
100 km arrêté	2:10:08.287	B. Meister (SUI)	Stuttgart (RFA)	22.09.1989
100 km demi-fond	1:10:14.363	Fred Rompelberg (HOL)	Moscow (URS)	30.10.1986
86.449 km demi-fond	1 hour	Fred Rompelberg (HOL)	Moscow (URS)	30.10.1986

WOMEN

1 km lancé	1:05.232	Erika Salumae (URS)	Moscow (URS)	31.05.1987
100 km arrêté	2:28:26.259	Francesca Galli (ITA)	Milan (ITA)	26.10.1987

WORLD HOUR RECORDS

[As of June 1995; 1 high altitude; 2 disqualified track measure; 3 disqualified dope test; 4 amateur; 5 indoor track; 6 sea level record.]

HISTORIC RECORDS

DATE	PLACE	RECORD HOLDER AGE	KMS (MPH)	GEAR (DEVELOPMENT)
1873	Wolverhampton (GBR)	James Moore (GBR)	23.331 (14.4)	49x1 (3.90)
25.03.1876	Cambridge (GBR)	F.L. "Brit" Dodds (GBR)	25.598 (15.8)	
1877	Cambridge (GBR)	Shopee (GBR)	26.960 (16.7)	
1878	Oxford (GBR)	Weir (GBR)	28.542 (17.6)	
1879	Oxford (GBR)	Christie (GBR)	30.374 (18.8)	
02.08.1882	England	Herbert Lydell Cortis (GBR)	32.454 (20.1)	
1887	London (GBR)	Jules Dubois (FRA)	34.217 (21.2)	
1888	England	Laurie (GBR)	33.913 (21.0)	
05.11.1893	Paris-Buffalo (FRA)	Henri Desgrange (FRA) 28	35.325 (21.9)	
31.10.1894	Paris-Buffalo (FRA)	Jules Dubois (FRA)	38.220 (23.6)	
30.07.1897	Paris-Municipale (FRA)	Oscar Van den Eynden (BEL)	39.240 (24.3)	
09.07.1898	Denver (USA)1	William Hamilton (USA)	40.781 (25.2)	

UCI RECORDS

DATE	PLACE	RECORD HOLDER AGE	KMS (MPH)	GEAR (DEVELOPMENT)
24.08.1905	Paris-Buffalo (FRA)	Lucien Petit-Breton (FRA)	41.110 (25.4)	
20.06.1907	Paris-Buffalo (FRA)	Marcel Berthet (FRA) 21	41.520 (25.7)	
22.08.1912	Paris-Buffalo (FRA)	Oscar Egg (SUI) 22	42.360 (26.2)	24x7 (7.32)
07.08.1913	Paris-Buffalo (FRA)	Marcel Berthet (FRA) 27	42.741 (26.4)	
21.08.1913	Paris-Buffalo (FRA)	Oscar Egg (SUI) 23	43.525 (26.9)	
20.09.1913	Paris-Buffalo (FRA)	Marcel Berthet (FRA) 27	43.775 (27.1)	
18.06.1914	Paris-Buffalo (FRA)	Oscar Egg (SUI) 24	44.247 (27.4)	
25.08.1933	Roermond (HOL)	Jan Van Hout (HOL)2	44.588 (27.6)	
29.08.1933	Saint Trond (BEL)	Maurice Richard (FRA)	44.777 (27.7)	24x7
31.10.1935	Milan-Vigorelli (ITA)	Giuseppe Olmo (ITA)	45.090 (27.9)	24x7
14.10.1936	Milan-Vigorelli (ITA)	Maurice Richard (FRA)	45.325 (28.1)	
29.09.1937	Milan-Vigorelli (ITA)	Frans Slaats (HOL)	45.558 (28.2)	24x7
03.11.1937	Milan-Vigorelli (ITA)	Maurice Archambaud (FRA)	45.840 (28.4)	24x7
07.11.1942	Milan-Vigorelli (ITA)	Fausto Coppi (ITA) 23	45.848 (28.4)	52x15 (7.40)
29.06.1956	Milan-Vigorelli (ITA)	Jacques Anquetil (FRA) 22	46.159 (28.6)	52x15
19.09.1956	Milan-Vigorelli (ITA)	Ercole Baldini (ITA) 23	46.394 (28.7)	52x15
18.09.1957	Milan-Vigorelli (ITA)	Roger Rivière (FRA) 21	46.923 (29.0)	52x15
23.09.1958	Milan-Vigorelli (ITA)	Roger Rivière (FRA) 22	47.346 (29.3)	53x15 (7.54)
27.09.1967	Milan-Vigorelli (ITA)	Jacques Anquetil (FRA) 333	47.493 (29.4)	
30.10.1967	Rome-Olympic (ITA)	Ferdinand Bracke (BEL) 28	48.093 (29.8)	53x15
10.10.1968	Mexico City-Olympic (MEX)1	Ole Ritter (DEN) 27	48.653 (30.1)	54x15 (7.69)
25.10.1972	Mexico City-Olympic (MEX)1	Eddy Merckx (BEL) 26	49.431 (30.6)	52x14 (7.93)
19.01.1984	Mexico City-Centro (MEX)1	Francesco Moser (ITA) 32	50.808 (31.5)	56x15 (8.03)
23.01.1984	Mexico City-Centro (MEX)1	Francesco Moser (ITA) 32	51.151 (31.7)	57x15 (8.17)
17.07.1993	Hamar-Olympic Hall (NOR)	Graeme Obree (SCO) 274	51.596 (31.9)	52x12 (9.25)
23.07.1993	Bordeaux Stadium (FRA)	Chris Boardman (GBR) 24	52.270 (32.4)	53x13 (8.70)
27.04.1994	Bordeaux Stadium (FRA)	Graeme Obree (SCO) 28	52.713 (32.6)	52x12
02.09.1994	Bordeaux Stadium (FRA)	Miguel Indurain (ESP) 30	53.040 (32.8)	59x14 (8.76)
23.10.1994	Bordeaux Stadium (FRA)	Tony Rominger (SUI) 33	53.832 (33.3)	59x14 (8.85)
05.11.1994	Bordeaux Stadium (FRA)	Tony Rominger (SUI) 33	55.291 (34.2)	60x14 (9.02)

WOMEN

DATE	PLACE	RECORD HOLDER AGE	KMS (MPH)	GEAR (DEVELOPMENT)
07.07.1955	Irkoutsk-Dynamo Stadium (URS)	Tamara Novikova (URS)	38.473 (23.8)	
18.09.1957	Milan-Vigorelli (ITA)	Renée Vissac (FRA)	38.569 (23.9)	
25.09.1958	Milan-Vigorelli (ITA)	Millie Robinson (GBR)	39.719 (24.6)	
09.11.1958	Milan-Vigorelli (ITA)	Elsy Jacobs (LUX)	41.347 (25.6)	
25.11.1972	Mexico City-Olympic (MEX)1	Maria Cressari (ITA)	41.471 (25.7)	
16.09.1978	Munich-Olympic (RFA)	Keetie van Oosten-Hage (HOL)	43.082 (26.7)	
25.11.1985	Zurich-Hallenstadion (SUI)5	Barbara Ganz (SUI)	42.319 (26.2)	
20.09.1986	Colorado Springs (USA)1	Jeannie Longo (FRA)	44.770 (27.7)	
30.09.1986	Milan-Vigorelli (ITA)	Jeannie Longo (FRA)	43.587 (27.0)	
07.11.1986	Grenoble (FRA)5	Jeannie Longo (FRA)	44.718 (27.7)	
22.09.1987	Colorado Springs (USA)1	Jeannie Longo (FRA)	44.933 (27.8)	
01.10.1989	Mexico City-Centro (MEX)1	Jeannie Longo (FRA)	46.352 (28.7)	
29.04.1995	Bordeaux Stadium (FRA)	Cathérine Marsal (FRA) 24	47.112 (29.2)	
17.06.1995	Manchester Cycling Centre (GBR)	Yvonne McGregor (GBR) 34	47.411 (29.4)	54x14 (8.18)

WORLD HOUR RECORDS CONTINUED

[As of June 1995; 1 high altitude; 2 disqualified track measure; 3 disqualified dope test; 4 amateur; 5 indoor track; 6 sea level record.]

DATE	PLACE	NAME (COUNTRY)	KMS (MPH)	GEAR (DEVELOPMENT)
RECORDS BY CATEGORY				
27.12.1959	Zurich-Hallenstadion (SUI)5	Alfredo Ruegg (SUI)	45.843 (28.4)	
02.01.1962	Zurich-Hallenstadion (SUI)5	Alfredo Ruegg (SUI)	46.819 (29.0)	
02.08.11968	Zurich-Hallenstadion (SUI)5	Siegfred Adler (RFA)	46.847 (29.0)	
09.09.1985	Bassano del Grappa (ITA)6	Hans-Henrik Oersted (DEN)	48.144 (29.8)	
26.09.1986	Milan-Vigorelli (ITA)	Francesco Moser (ITA)	48.543 (30.0)	57x15 (7.91)
03.10.1986	Milan-Vigorelli (ITA)	Francesco Moser (ITA)	49.802 (30.8)	51x14 (7.88)
27.10.1986	Moscow (URS)	Viatcheslav Ekimov (URS)4	49.672 (30.7)	
03.04.1987	Launceston (AUS)5	Neil Stephens (AUS)	47.227 (29.2)	
10.10.1987	Moscow-Krylatskoje (URS)	Francesco Moser (ITA)	48.637 (30.1)	
21.05.1988	Stuttgart-Schleyerhalle (RFA)5	Francesco Moser (ITA)	50.644 (31.3)	47x18 (8.28)
10.10.1991	Colorado Springs (USA)1	John Frey (USA)4	49.946 (30.9)	
STREAMLINED BIKES				
07.07.1933	Paris-Parc des Princes (FRA)	Francis Faure (FRA) Velocar	45.055 (27.9)	
18.11.1933	Paris (FRA)	Marcel Berthet (FRA) Velodyne	49.992 (31.0)	
03.03.1939	Paris (FRA)	Francis Faure (FRA) Velocar	50.537 (31.3)	
1979	Ontario Speedway (USA)	Ron Skarin (USA) Teledyne	51.290 (31.7)	
HUMAN-POWERED VEHICLES				
1980	-	Erik Edwards (USA)	59.580 (36.9)	
1984	-	Fred Markham (USA)	60.484 (37.5)	
1985	-	Richard Crane (USA)	66.452 (41.2)	
1986	California1	Fred Markham (USA)	67.097 (41.6)	
16.09.1989	Michigan Int. Speedway (USA)	Fred Markham (USA) Gold Rush	72.960 (45.2)	84x11-16 (16.0 top)
08.09.1990	Millbrook Raceway (GBR)	Pat Kinch (GBR) Kingcycle Bean	75.575 (46.8)	42x16x42x16 (14.8)
01.10.1994	Lelystad (HOL)	Bram Moens (HOL) M5	77.123 (47.9)	
MULTI-RIDER HPV				
04.05.1980	Ontario Speedway (USA)	Skarin-Hollander (USA) Vector Tandem	74.51 (46.1)	
MOTOR-PACED BIKE				
21.02.1987	Moscow (URS)	Alexander Romanov (URS)	91.133 (56.5)	

IHPVA LAND SPEED RECORDS [As of June 1995; 1 high altitude]

DISTANCE	TIME	KPH	MPH	RIDER	VEHICLE (MAKER)	PLACE	DATE
MEN'S INDIVIDUAL FLYING START							
200 m	6.510	110.60	68.72	Chris Huber	Cheetah (Franz/Osborn/Gabarino)	Del Norte CO1	22.09.1992
200 m arms	13.803	52.16	32.41	Doug Wight	Varna Arm (George Georgiev)	Del Norte CO1	14.09.1993
200/600 m	9.05	79.56	49.44	Kirk Edwards	Z Prime (UC Berkeley)	Eureka CA	07.08.1994
500 m	18.502	97.29	60.45	Mike Prime	Z Prime (UC Berkeley)	Del Norte CO1	16.09.1993
500 m arms	36.63	49.14	30.53	Jacob Heilveil	Chairiot (GM/AV/Forsyth)	Milford MI	31.05.1995
1000 m	37.060	97.14	60.36	Fred Markham	Gold Rush Colorado (Gardner Martin)	Del Norte CO1	16.09.1993
1000 m arms	1:25.636	42.04	26.12	Jacob Heilveil	Chairiot (GM/AV/Forsyth)	Mesa AZ1	13.05.1995
1 mi	60.765	95.34	59.24	Paul Buttemer	Varna (George Georgiev)	Del Norte CO1	15.09.1993
MEN'S INDIVIDUAL STANDING START							
1/4 mi	26.960	74.86	46.70	Kirk Edwards	Concept Z (UC Berkeley)	Montague CA1	08.08.1992
4000 m	3:34.20	67.22	41.77	W. Van Der Merwe	— (Kramer/Meissner)	Pretoria SAF	16.10.1994
10 km	8:42.95	68.84	42.78	W. Van Der Merwe	Spirit of Mobil 2 (Kramer/Meissner)	Pretoria SAF	01.04.1994
100 km	1:31.24	65.76	40.86	Gerhard Scheller	Vector 007 (Wolfgang Gronen)	La Paz BOL1	10.08.1987
1000 km	25:06:34.00	39.82	24.75	Mhyee	Gold Rush America (Gardner Martin)	Eureka CA	01–02.08.1994
75.57 km	1 hour	75.57	46.96	Pat Kinch	Kingcycle Bean (Miles Kingsbury)	Millbrook GBR	08.09.1990
566.97 km	12 hour	47.25	29.36	W. Van Der Merwe	Spirit of Engen (Kramer/Meissner)	Pretoria SAF	29.11.1992
976.93 km	24 hour	40.70	25.29	Mhyee	Gold Rush America (Gardner Martin)	Eureka CA	01–02.09.1994
WOMEN'S INDIVIDUAL FLYING START							
200 m	8.630	83.43	51.84	Rachel Hall	Allegro (Don Witte)	La Garita CA	28.08.1985
200 m arms	20.912	34.43	21.39	Tracy Miller	Chairiot (GM/AV/Forsyth)	Mesa AZ1	13.05.1995
200/600 m	12.08	59.60	37.04	Alaina DeWit	Z Prime (UC Berkeley)	Eureka CA	07.08.1994
500 m	24.583	73.22	45.50	Shari Rodgers-Kain	Blue Sandworm (TRA)	Del Norte CO1	16.09.1993
1000 m	49.364	72.93	45.32	Shari Rodgers-Kain	Blue Sandworm (TRA)	Del Norte CO1	16.09.1993
1000 m arms	1:45.927	33.98	21.12	Tracy Miller	Chairiot (GM/AV/Forsyth)	Mesa AZ1	13.05.1995
1 mi	1:20.599	71.88	44.67	Shari Rodgers-Kain	Blue Sandworm (TRA)	Del Norte CO1	16.09.1993

IHPVA WORLD RECORDS CONTINUED

DISTANCE	TIME	KPH	MPH	CYCLIST	VEHICLE (MAKER)	PLACE	DATE
WOMEN'S INDIVIDUAL STANDING START							
1/4 mi	34.15	ave 42.40	26.35	Anja Koning	Lightning F40 (Tim Brummer)	Montague CA[1]	08.08.1992
MEN'S MULTIPLE RIDER FLYING START							
200 m	6.880	104.65	65.03	Fred Markham/Sam Wittingham	Double Gold Rush (Gardner Martin)	Del Norte CO[1]	14.09.1993
200/600 m	8.850	81.36	50.55	Drieke/Gordon	— (John Waite)	Irvine CA	02.10.1982
500 m	17.304	104.02	64.64	Fred Markham/Sam Wittingham	Double Gold Rush (Gardner Martin)	Del Norte CO[1]	17.09.1993
1000 m	35.100	102.56	63.73	Fred Markham/Sam Wittingham	Double Gold Rush (Gardner Martin)	Del Norte CO[1]	17.09.1993
1 mi	1:01.21	94.65	58.81	Fred Markham/John Howard	Double Gold Rush (Gardner Martin)	Bonneville UT[1]	01.10.1989
MEN'S MULTIPLE RIDER STANDING START							
1/4 mi	20.642	ave 70.16	43.6		White Lightning (Tim Brummer)	Irvine CA	02.10.1982
74.51 km	1 hour	74.51	46.30	Ron Skarin/Hollander	Vector Tandem (Al Voigt)	Ontario CA	04.05.1980
WOMEN'S MULTIPLE RIDER FLYING START							
200 m	9.4	76.60	47.59	Jackson/Bowen/Sandlin	— (Tom Rightmyer)	Ontario CA	03.05.1980

IHPVA NAUTICAL SPEED RECORDS

DISTANCE	TIME	KNOTS	MPH	CREW	WATERCRAFT (MAKER)	PLACE	DATE
MEN'S INDIVIDUAL FLYING START							
100 m	10.51	18.5	21.28	Mark Drela	Decavitator (MIT)	Boston MA	27.10.1991
2000 m	5:48.53	11.15	12.84	Steve Hegg	Flying Fish 2 (Al Abbott/Alec Brooks)	Long Beach CA	20.07.1987
WOMEN'S INDIVIDUAL FLYING START							
100 m	17.04	11.41	13.12	Dava Newman	Decavitator (MIT)	Boston MA	27.10.1991
UNDERWATER INDIVIDUAL PROPELLOR DRIVE							
10 m	-	4.52	5.20	-	Subjugator (Battelle)	Escondido CA	04.1994
UNDERWATER MULTIPLE RIDER PROPELLOR DRIVE							
10 m	-	5.94	6.84	-	FAU Boat (FAU)	Escondido CA	04.1994
UNDERWATER MULTIPLE RIDER NON-PROPELLOR							
10 m	-	2.9	3.3	-	SubDude (UCSD/Scripps)	Escondido CA	04.1994

IHPVA FLIGHT RECORDS

DISTANCE	TIME	KPH	MPH	PILOT	AIRCRAFT (MAKER)	PLACE	DATE
FIGURE-EIGHT KREMER PRIZE							
1 mi	7:30.00	12.87	8.00	Bryan Allen	Gossamer Condor (Paul MacCready)	Shafter Airport CA	23.08.1977
KREMER SPEED COMPETITION							
-	2:02.00	44.26	27.5	Holger Rochelt	Musculaire II (Gunter Rochelt)	Germany	02.10.1985
MEN'S CLOSED COURSE DISTANCE							
58.66 km	2:13:14.00	26.43	16.42	Glenn Tremml	Michelob Light Eagle (MIT)	Edwards AFB CA	23.01.1987
MEN'S STRAIGHT COURSE DISTANCE							
119 km	3:53:30.00	30.59	19.0	Kanellos Kanelopulos	Daedalus (MIT)	Crete–Greece	23.04.1988
WOMEN'S CLOSED COURSE DISTANCE							
15.44 km	37:14.00	24.94	15.50	Lois McCallin	Michelob Light Eagle (MIT)	Edwards AFB CA	22.01.1987
WOMEN'S STRAIGHT COURSE DISTANCE							
6.79 km	-	-	-	Lois McCallin	Michelob Light Eagle (MIT)	Edwards AFB CA	22.01.1987

WORLD LAND SPEED RECORDS

MOTOR-PACED FLYING START

YEAR PLACE	CYCLIST (COUNTRY)	MPH
1897 Parc des Princes (FRA)	Maur Lombard (FRA)	37.793
1899 Long Island (USA)	Charles Murphy (USA)	62.283
1928 Montherly (FRA)	Leon Vanderstuyft (BEL)	78.159
1931 Montherly (FRA)	Al Blanc-Garin (FRA)	79.680
1937 Montherly (FRA)	Georges Paillard (FRA)	85.397
1938 Montherly (FRA)	Alf Letourner (FRA)	91.397
1941 Bakersfield (USA)	Alf Letourner (FRA)	108.923
1951 Toulouse (FRA)	Jose Meiffret (FRA)	109.142
1961 Lahr (RFA)	Jose Meiffret (FRA)	115.934
1962 Freiberg (RFA)	Jose Meiffret (FRA)	127.342
1973 Bonneville (USA)	Allan Abbott (USA)	138.674
1985 Bonneville (USA)	John Howard (USA)	152.284
1995 Bonneville (USA)	Fred Rompelberg (HOL)	167.051

24-HOUR RECORDS

		MILES
MEN'S MOTOR-PACED		
1990 Phoenix Raceway (USA)	Michael Secrest (USA)	1,216
MEN'S TRACK		
1994 Midvale Velodrome (AUS)	Rod Evans (AUS)	530
WOMEN'S TRACK		
1990 Major Taylor Vel. (USA)	Patricia Jones (USA)	421
MEN'S ROAD		
1974 Finland	Teuvo Louhivouri (FIN)	515
WOMEN'S ROAD		
1992 Egg Harbour (USA)	Nancy Ramposo (USA)	439
MEN'S OFF-ROAD		
1995 Arcadia St. Park (USA)	John Stamstad (USA)	354

MTB DOWNHILL

		MPH
MEN		
1995 Vars (FRA)	Christian Taillefer (FRA)	111
WOMEN		
1995 Vars (FRA)	Giovanna Bonazzi (ITA)	88

ANNUAL HONORS

SUPER PRESTIGE TROPHY

YEAR WINNER POINTS
1959 Henri Anglade (FRA) 165
1960 Jean Graczyk (FRA) 160
1961 Jacques Anquetil (FRA) 241
1962 Jo De Roo (HOL) 170
1963 Jacques Anquetil (FRA) 260
1964 Raymond Poulidor (FRA) 230
1965 Jacques Anquetil (FRA) 216
1966 Jacques Anquetil (FRA) 235
1967 Jan Janssen (HOL) 284
1968 Herman Van Springel (BEL) 254
1969 Eddy Merckx (BEL) 412
1970 Eddy Merckx (BEL) 409
1971 Eddy Merckx (BEL) 570
1972 Eddy Merckx (BEL) 438
1973 Eddy Merckx (BEL) 405
1974 Eddy Merckx (BEL) 455
1975 Eddy Merckx (BEL) 415
1976 Freddy Maertens (BEL) 332
1977 Freddy Maertens (BEL) 320
1978 Francesco Moser (ITA) 323
1979 Bernard Hinault (FRA) 421
1980 Bernard Hinault (FRA) 315
1981 Bernard Hinault (FRA) 325
1982 Bernard Hinault (FRA) 266
1983 Greg LeMond (USA) 245
1984 Sean Kelly (IRL) 435
1985 Sean Kelly (IRL) 365

UCI RANKING

1986 Sean Kelly (IRL)
1987 Sean Kelly (IRL) 1,198
1988 Sean Kelly (IRL) 1,025
1989 Laurent Fignon (FRA) 971
1990 Gianni Bugno (ITA) 1,880
1991 Gianni Bugno (ITA) 2,033
1992 Miguel Indurain (ESP) 2,539
1993 Miguel Indurain (ESP) 2,583
1994 Tony Rominger (SUI) 2,304
1995 Laurent Jalabert (FRA) 3,162

WORLD CUP

1989 Sean Kelly (IRL) 44
1990 Gianni Bugno (ITA) 133
1991 Maurizio Fondriest (ITA) 132
1992 Olaf Ludwig (RFA) 126
1993 Maurizio Fondriest (ITA) 287
1994 Gianluca Bortolami (ITA) 151
1995 Johan Museeuw (BEL) 199

WORLD ROAD CHAMPIONS

PROFESSIONAL

YEAR PLACE	WINNER (COUNTRY) AGE	KMS	KPH	START	FINISH
1927 Nurburgring (RFA)	Alfredo Binda (ITA) 24	182	27	55	18
1928 Budapest (HUN)	Georges Ronsse (BEL) 22	192	30	16	8
1929 Zurich (SUI)	Georges Ronsse (BEL) 23	200	29	21	16
1930 Liège (BEL)	Alfredo Binda (ITA) 28	210	27	26	17
1931 Copenhagen (DEN)	Learco Guerra (ITA) 28	172	35	17	13
1932 Rome (ITA)	Alfredo Binda (ITA) 30	206	29	21	17
1933 Montherly (FRA)	Georges Speicher (FRA)	250	34	28	13
1934 Leipzig (DDR)	Karel Kaers (BEL)	225	37	26	15
1935 Floreffe (BEL)	Jan Aerts (BEL)	216	35	26	13
1936 Bern (SUI)	Antonin Magne (FRA) 32	218	37	39	9
1937 Copenhagen (DEN)	Eloi Meulenberg (BEL)	297	37	34	8
1938 Valkenberg (HOL)	Marcel Kint (BEL)	273	34	36	8
1946 Zurich (SUI)	Hans Knecht (SUI)	270	36	30	17
1947 Rheims (FRA)	Theo Middelkamp (HOL)	274	36	31	7
1948 Valkenberg (HOL)	Brik Schotte (BEL)	266	35	37	10
1949 Copenhagen (DEN)	Rik Van Steenbergen (BEL) 25	290	38	35	22
1950 Moorslede (BEL)	Brik Schotte (BEL)	284	36	40	12
1951 Varese (ITA)	Ferdi Kubler (SUI) 32	295	34	46	24
1952 Luxembourg (LUX)	Heinz Müller (RFA)	280	39	48	38
1953 Lugano (SUI)	Fausto Coppi (ITA) 33	270	35	70	27
1954 Solingen (RFA)	Louison Bobet (FRA) 29	240	32	71	22
1955 Frascati (ITA)	Stan Ockers (BEL)	293	33	65	20
1956 Ballerup (DEN)	Rik Van Steenbergen (BEL) 32	285	38	71	27
1957 Waregem (BEL)	Rik Van Steenbergen (BEL) 33	285	36	70	41
1958 Rheims (FRA)	Ercole Baldini (ITA) 25	276	36	67	26
1959 Zandvoort (HOL)	André Darrigade (FRA)	292	38	69	44
1960 Sachsenring (DDR)	Rik Van Looy (BEL) 26	279	35	67	32
1961 Berne (SUI)	Rik Van Looy (BEL) 27	285	36	71	32
1962 Salo (ITA)	Jean Stablinski (FRA)	296	38	69	36
1963 Ronse (BEL)	Benoni Beheyt (BEL)	278	37	70	36
1964 Sallanches (FRA)	Jan Janssen (HOL) 24	290	38	62	40
1965 Lasarte (ESP)	Tom Simpson (GBR)	267	40	74	56
1966 Nurburgring (RFA)	Rudi Altig (RFA) 29	273	36	74	22
1967 Heerlen (HOL)	Eddy Merckx (BEL) 22	265	39	70	45
1968 Imola (ITA)	Vittorio Adorni (ITA) 30	277	37	85	19
1969 Zolder (HOL)	Harm Ottenbros (HOL)	262	41	91	62
1970 Leicester (GBR)	Jean-Pierre Monseré (BEL) 21	271	41	95	69
1971 Mendrisio (SUI)	Eddy Merckx (BEL) 26	268	40	93	57
1972 Gap (FRA)	Marino Basso (ITA) 27	272	38	89	42
1973 Montjuich (ESP)	Felice Gimondi (ITA) 30	248	38	87	39
1974 Montreal (CAN)	Eddy Merckx (BEL) 29	262	38	66	18
1975 Yvoir (FRA)	Hennie Kuiper (HOL) 26	266	39	79	28
1976 Ostuni (ITA)	Freddy Maertens (BEL) 24	288	40	77	53
1977 San Cristobal (VEN)	Francesco Moser (ITA) 26	255	38	89	33
1978 Nurburgring (RFA)	Gerrie Kneteman (HOL)	273	36	111	31
1979 Valkenburg (HOL)	Jan Raas (HOL) 26	274	38	115	44
1980 Sallanches (FRA)	Bernard Hinault (FRA) 25	268	35	107	15
1981 Prague (TCH)	Freddy Maertens (BEL) 29	281	38	112	69
1982 Goodwood (GBR)	Giuseppe Saronni (ITA) 24	275	41	136	55
1983 Altenrhein (SUI)	Greg LeMond (USA) 22	269	38	117	46
1984 Barcelona (ESP)	Claude Criquielion (BEL) 27	255	37	119	31
1985 Giavera de Montelo (ITA)	Joop Zoetemelk (HOL) 38	265	41	148	66
1986 Colorado Springs (USA)	Moreno Argentin (ITA) 25	261	40	141	87
1987 Villach (AUT)	Stephen Roche (IRL) 27	276	40	168	71
1988 Renaix (BEL)	Maurizio Fondriest (ITA) 23	274	38	177	79
1989 Chambéry (FRA)	Greg LeMond (USA) 28	259	38	190	42
1990 Utsunomiya (JPN)	Rudy Dhaenens (BEL) 29	261	38	145	57
1991 Stuttgart (RFA)	Gianni Bugno (ITA) 27	265	38	190	96
1992 Benidorm (ESP)	Gianni Bugno (ITA) 28	261	39	189	89
1993 Oslo (NOR)	Lance Armstrong (USA) 21	257	41	171	66
1994 Agrigento (ITA)	Luc Leblanc (FRA) 28	252	38	170	56
1995 Duitama (COL)	Abraham Olano (ESP) 25	265	37	98	20

WORLD ROAD CHAMPIONS

YEAR PLACE	AMATEUR
1921 Copenhagen (DEN)	Gunnar Skold (SWE)
1922 Hadhall-Shawbury (GBR)	Dave Marsh (GBR)
1923 Zurich (SUI)	L. Ferrario (ITA)
1924 Chartres-Versailles (FRA)	André Leducq (FRA)
1925 Apeldorn (HOL)	H. Hoevenaers (BEL)
1926 Milan-Torino (ITA)	Octave Dayen (FRA)
1927 Nurburgring (GER)	Jean Aerts (BEL)
1928 Budapest (HUN)	Allegro Grandi (ITA)
1929 Zurich	P. Bertolazzo (ITA)
1930 Liege	Guiseppi Martano (ITA)
1931 Copenhagen	Henry Hansen (DEN)
1932 Rome	Guiseppi Martano
1933 Montlhery	Paul Egli (SUI)
1934 Leipzig	K. Pellenaars (HOL)
1935 Florffe	Ivo Mancini (ITA)
1936 Bern	Edg. Buchwalder (SUI)
1937 Copenhagen	Adolfo Leoni (ITA)
1938 Valkenburg	Hans Knecht (SUI)
1946 Zurich	Henry Aubry (FRA)
1947 Reims	Alfio Ferrari (ITA)
1948 Valkenburg	Harry Snell (SWE)
1949 Copenhagen	Henk Faanhof (HOL)
1950 Moorslede	Jack Hoobin (AUS)
1951 Varese	Gianni Ghidini (ITA)
1952 Luxembourg	Luciano Ciancola (ITA)
1953 Lugano	Ricardo Filippi (ITA)
1954 Solingen	Emile Van Cauter (BEL)
1955 Frascati	Sante Ranucci (ITA)
1956 Copenhagen	Frans Mahn (HOL)
1957 Waregem	Louis Proost (BEL)
1958 Reims	Gust. Adolfo Schur (DDR)
1959 Zandvoort/Rotheux	Adolfo Schur
1960 Leipzig	Bernhardt Eckstein (DDR)
1961 Bern	Jean Jourden (FRA)
1962 Salo	Renato Bonciono (ITA)
1963 Ronse	Flaviano Vicentini (ITA)
1964 Sallanches	Eddy Merckx (BEL)
1965 Lasarte	Jacques Botherel (FRA)
1966 Nurburgring	Evert Dolman (HOL)
1967 Heerlen	Graham Webb (GBR)
1968 Montevideo/Imola	Vittorio Marcelli (ITA)
1969 Brno	Leif Mortensen (DEN)
1970 Leicester	Jörgen Schmidt (DEN)
1971 Mendrisio	Regis Ovion (FRA)
1972 Munich/Gap	Hennie Kuiper (HOL)[1]
1973 Montjuich	Ryszard Szurkowski (POL)
1974 Montreal	Janusz Kowalski (POL)
1975 Mettet	André Gevers (HOL)
1976 Montreal/Ostuni	Bernt Johansson (SWE)[1]
1977 San Cristobal	Claudio Corti (ITA)
1978 Nurburgring/Brauweiler	Gilbert Glaus (SUI)
1979 Valkenburg	Gianni Giacomini (ITA)
1980 Moscow/Sallanches	Sergei Soukhoroutchenkov (URS)[1]
1981 Prague	Andrei Vedernikov (URS)
1982 Goodwood	Bernd Drogan (DDR)
1983 Altenrhein	Uwe Raab (DDR)
1984 Los Angeles	Alexi Grewal (USA)[1]
1985 Giavera de Montello	Lech Piasecki (POL)
1986 Colorado Springs	Uwe Ampler (DDR)
1987 Villach	Richard Vivien (FRA)
1988 Seoul	Olaf Ludwig (DDR)[1]

OLYMPIC ROAD CHAMPIONS

YEAR PLACE	WINNER (NAT)	KMS	KPH
1896 Athens (GRE)	A. Konstantinides (GRE)	87	25
1906 Athens (GRE)	B. Vast (FRA)	84	31
1912 Stockholm (SWE)[1]	Rud Lewis (SAF)	320	29
1920 Antwerp (BEL)[1]	H. Stencqvist (SWE)	175	36
1924 Paris (FRA)[1]	Armand Blanchonnet (FRA)	188	29
1928 Amsterdam (HOL)[1]	Hans Hansen (DEN)	168	39
1932 Los Angeles (USA)[1]	Attilio Pavesi (ITA)	100	40
1936 Berlin (GER)	R. Charpentier (FRA)	100	39
1948 London (GBR)	José Beyaert (FRA)	194	36
1952 Helsinki (FIN)	André Noyelle (BEL)	190	37
1956 Melbourne (AUS)	Ercole Baldini (ITA)	187	35
1960 Rome (ITA)	Viktor Kapitonov (URS)	175	40
1964 Tokyo (JPN)	Mario Zanin (ITA)	194	41
1968 Mexico City (MEX)	Pierfranco Vianelli (ITA)	196	40
1972 Munich (RFA)	Hennie Kuiper (HOL)	182	42
1976 Montreal (CAN)	Bernt Johansson (SWE)	175	36
1980 Moscow (URS)	Sergei Soukhoroutchenkov (URS)	189	42
1984 Los Angeles (USA)	Alexi Grewal (USA)	190	38
1988 Seoul (COR)	Olaf Ludwig (DDR)	196	43
1992 Barcelona (ESP)	Fabio Casartelli (ITA)	194	42

[1 time trial]

WOMEN	KMS	KPH
Elsy Jacobs (LUX)	59	32
Yvonne Reynders (BEL)	72	38
Beryl Burton (GBR)	61	32
Yvonne Reynders	61	31
M.R. Gaillard (GBR)	64	34
Yvonne Reynders	66	32
Emmilia Sonka (URS)	58	37
Elizabeth Eicholz (DDR)	52	34
Yvonne Reynders	46	31
Beryl Burton	53	37
Keetie Hage (HOL)	55	37
Audrey McElmury (USA)	69	34
Anna Konkina (URS)	60	36
Anna Konkina	50	35
Geneviève Gambillon (FRA)	60	36
Nicole Vanden Broeck (BEL)	55	36
Geneviève Gambillon	60	33
Tineke Fopma (HOL)	54	35
Keetie van Oosten-Hage	62	37
Josiane Bost (FRA)	49	38
Beate Habetz (RFA)	70	40
Petra De Bruin (HOL)	64	37
Beth Heiden (USA)	53	30
Ute Enzenauer (RFA)	53	35
Mandy Jones (GBR)	61	40
Marianne Berglund (SWE)	60	36
Connie Carpenter (USA)[1]	79	33
Jeannie Longo (FRA)	73	38
Jeannie Longo	61	37
Jeannie Longo	72	40
Monica Knol (HOL)[1]	82	41

WORLD ROAD CHAMPIONS CONTINUED [1 Olympic champion]

YEAR PLACE	AMATEURS	WOMEN	KMS	KPH
1989 Chambéry	Joachim Halupczok (POL)	Jeannie Longo	74	38
1990 Utsunomiya	Mirco Gualdi (ITA)	Cathérine Marsal (FRA)	72	36
1991 Stuttgart	Victor Pjaksinski (URS)	Leontien Van Moorsel (HOL)	79	37
1992 Barcelona	Fabio Casartelli (ITA)¹	Kathryn Watt (AUS)¹	81	39
1993 Oslo	Jan Ullrich (RFA)	Leontien Van Moorsel	92	39
1994 Capo d'Orlando	Alex Pedersen (DEN)	Monica Valvik (NOR)	86	40
1995 Duitama (COL)	Danny Nelissen (HOL)	Jeannie Longo (FRA)	88	33

INDIVIDUAL TIME TRIAL

YEAR	KMS	TIME	KPH	PROFESSIONAL	WOMEN	KMS	TIME	KPH
1994	42	49:34	50.832	Chris Boardman (GBR)	Karen Kurreck (USA)	29.6	38:22	46.899
1995	43	55:30	46.481	Miguel Indurain (ESP)	Jeannie Longo (FRA)	26.8	44:27	35.091

CLASSIC ROAD RACES

MILAN-SAN REMO

1907 Lucien Petite-Breton (FRA)
1908 Cyrille Van Hauwaert (BEL)
1909 Luigi Ganna (ITA)
1910 Eugene Christophe (FRA)
1911 Gustave Garrigou (FRA)
1912 Henri Pélissier (FRA)
1913 Odile Defraye (BEL)
1914 Ugo Agonstoni (ITA)
1915 Ezio Corlaita (ITA)
1918 Constante Girardengo (ITA)
1919 Angelo Gremo (ITA)
1920 Gaetano Belloni (ITA)
1921 Constante Girardengo
1922 Giovanni Brunero (ITA)
1923 Constante Girardengo
1924 Pietro Linari (ITA)
1925 Constante Girardengo
1926 Constante Girardengo
1927 Pietro Chesi (ITA)
1928 Constante Girardengo
1929 Alfredo Binda (ITA)
1930 Michele Mara (ITA)
1931 Alfredo Binda
1932 Alfredo Bovet (ITA)
1933 Learco Guerra (ITA)
1934 Jozef Demuysere (BEL)
1935 Giuseppe Olmo (ITA)
1936 Angelo Varetto (ITA)
1937 Cesarde Del Cancia (ITA)
1938 Giuseppe Olmo
1939 Gino Bartali (ITA)
1940 Gino Bartali
1941 Pierino Favalli (ITA)
1942 Adolfo Leoni (ITA)
1943 Cino Cinelli (ITA)
1946 Fausto Coppi (ITA)
1947 Gino Bartali
1948 Fausto Coppi
1949 Fausto Coppi
1950 Gino Bartali
1951 Louison Bobet (FRA)
1952 Loretto Petrucci (ITA)
1953 Loretto Petrucci

1954 Rik Van Steenbergen (BEL)
1955 Germain Derijcke (BEL)
1956 Fred De Bruyne (BEL)
1957 Miguel Poblet (ESP)
1958 Rik Van Looy (BEL)
1959 Miguel Poblet
1960 René Privat (FRA)
1961 Raymond Poulidor (FRA)
1962 Emile Daems (BEL)
1963 Joseph Groussard (FRA)
1964 Tom Simpson (GBR)
1965 Ari Den Hartog (HOL)
1966 Eddy Merckx (BEL)
1967 Eddy Merckx
1968 Rudi Altig (RFA)
1969 Eddy Merckx
1970 Michele Dancelli (ITA)
1971 Eddy Merckx
1972 Eddy Merckx
1973 Roger De Vlaeminck (BEL)
1974 Felice Gimondi (ITA)
1975 Eddy Merckx
1976 Eddy Merckx
1977 Jan Raas (HOL)
1978 Roger De Vlaeminck
1979 Roger De Vlaeminck
1980 Pierino Gavassi (ITA)
1981 Fons De Wolf (BEL)
1982 Marc Gomez (FRA)
1983 Giuseppe Saronni (ITA)
1984 Francesco Moser (ITA)
1985 Hennie Kuiper (HOL)
1986 Sean Kelly (IRL)
1987 Erich Maechler (SUI)
1988 Laurent Fignon (FRA)
1989 Laurent Fignon
1990 Gianni Bugno (ITA)
1991 Claudio Chiappucci (ITA)
1992 Sean Kelly
1993 Maurizio Fondriest (ITA)
1994 Giorgio Furlan (ITA)
1995 Laurent Jalabert (FRA)

RONDE VAN VLAANDEREN

1913 Paul Deman (BEL)
1914 Marcel Buysse (BEL)
1919 H. Van Lerberghe (BEL)
1920 Jules Van Hevel (BEL)
1921 Rene Vermandel (BEL)
1922 Leon De Vos (BEL)
1923 Henri Suter (SUI)
1924 Gerard Debaets (BEL)
1925 Julien Delbecque (BEL)
1926 Denis Verschueren (BEL)
1927 Gerard Debaets
1928 Jan Mertens (BEL)
1929 Jozef Dervaes (BEL)
1930 Frans Bonduel (BEL)
1931 Romain Gijssels (BEL)
1932 Romain Gijssels
1933 Alfons Schepers (BEL)
1934 Gaston Rebry (BEL)
1935 Louis Duerloo (BEL)
1936 Louis Hardiquest (BEL)
1937 Michel Dhooghe (BEL)
1938 Edgard De Caluwe (BEL)
1939 Karel Kaers (BEL)
1940 Achiel Buysse (BEL)
1941 Achiel Buysse
1942 Brik Schotte (BEL)
1943 Achiel Buysse
1944 Rik Van Steenbergen (BEL)
1945 Sylvain Grysolle (BEL)
1946 Rik Van Steenbergen
1947 Emiel Faignaert (BEL)
1948 Brik Schotte
1949 Fiorenzo Magni (ITA)
1950 Fiorenzo Magni
1951 Fiorenzo Magni
1952 Roger Decock (BEL)
1953 Wim Van Est (HOL)
1954 Raymond Impanis (BEL)
1955 Louison Bobet (FRA)
1956 Jean Forestier (FRA)
1957 Fred De Bruyne (BEL)
1958 Germain Derijcke (BEL)
1959 Rik Van Looy (BEL)

1960 Arthur Decabooter (BEL)
1961 Tom Simpson (GBR)
1962 Rik Van Looy
1963 Noel Fore (BEL)
1964 Rudi Altig (RFA)
1965 Jo De Roo (HOL)
1966 Edward Sels (BEL)
1967 Dino Zandegu (ITA)
1968 Walter Godefroot (BEL)
1969 Eddy Merckx (BEL)
1970 Eric Leman (BEL)
1971 Evert Dolman (BEL)
1972 Eric Leman
1973 Eric Leman
1974 Cees Bal (HOL)
1975 Eddy Merckx
1976 Walter Planckaert (BEL)
1977 Roger De Vlaeminck (BEL)
1978 Walter Godefroot
1979 Jan Raas (HOL)
1980 Michel Pollentier (BEL)
1981 Hennie Kuiper (HOL)
1982 Rene Martens (BEL)
1983 Jan Raas
1984 Johan Lammerts (HOL)
1985 Eric Vanderaerden (BEL)
1986 Adri Van Der Poel (HOL)
1987 Claude Criquuielion (BEL)
1988 Eddy Planckaert (BEL)
1989 Edwig Van Hooydonck (BEL)
1990 Moreno Argentin (ITA)
1991 Edwig Van Hooydonck
1992 Jacky Durand (FRA)
1993 Johan Museeuw (BEL)
1994 Gianni Bugno (ITA)
1995 Johan Museeuw

PARIS-ROUBAIX
1896 Joseph Fischer (RFA)
1897 Maurice Garin (FRA)
1898 Maurice Garin
1899 Albert Champion (FRA)
1900 Emile Bouhours (FRA)
1901 Luc Lesna (FRA)
1902 Luc Lesna
1903 Hippolyte Aucouturier (FRA)
1904 Hippolyte Aucouturier
1905 Louis Trousselier (FRA)
1906 Henri Cornet (FRA)
1907 Georges Passerieu (FRA)
1908 Cyrille Van Hauwaert (BEL)
1909 Octave Lapize (FRA)
1910 Octave Lapize
1911 Octave Lapize
1912 Charles Crupelandt (FRA)
1913 Francois Faber (LUX)
1914 Charles Crupelandt
1919 Henri Pélissier (FRA)
1920 Paul Deman (BEL)
1921 Henri Pélissier
1922 Albert Dejonghe (BEL)
1923 Henry Suter (SUI)
1924 Jules Van Hevel (BEL)

1925 Félix Sellier (BEL)
1926 Julien Delbecque (BEL)
1927 Georges Ronsse (BEL)
1928 André Leducq (FRA)
1929 Georges Meunier (FRA)
1930 Julien Vervaecke (BEL)
1931 Gaston Rebry (BEL)
1932 Romain Gijssels (BEL)
1933 Sylvere Maes (BEL)
1934 Gaston Rebry
1935 Gaston Rebry
1936 Georges Speicher (FRA)
1937 Jules Rossi (ITA)
1938 Lucien Storme (BEL)
1939 Emile Masson (BEL)
1943 Marcel Kint (BEL)
1944 Maurice Desimpelaere (BEL)
1945 Paul Maye (FRA)
1946 Georges Claes (BEL)
1947 Georges Claes
1948 Rik Van Steenbergen (BEL)
1949 (Tie) André Mahe (FRA)
     Serce Coppi (ITA)
1950 Fausto Coppi (ITA)
1951 Antonio Bevilacqua (ITA)
1952 Rik Van Steenbergen
1953 Germain Derijcke (BEL)
1954 Raymond Impanis (BEL)
1955 Jean Forestier (FRA)
1956 Louison Bobet (FRA)
1957 Fred De Bruyne (BEL)
1958 Leon Van Daele (BEL)
1959 Noel Fore (BEL)
1960 Pino Cerami (BEL)
1961 Rik Van Looy (BEL)
1962 Rik Van Looy
1963 Emile Daems (BEL)
1964 Peter Post (HOL)
1965 Rik Van Looy
1966 Felice Gimondi (ITA)
1967 Jan Janssen (HOL)
1968 Eddy Merckx (BEL)
1969 Walter Godefroot (BEL)
1970 Eddy Merckx
1971 Roger Rosiers (BEL)
1972 Roger De Vlaeminck (BEL)
1973 Eddy Merckx
1974 Roger De Vlaeminck
1975 Roger De Vlaeminck
1976 Marc De Meyer (BEL)
1977 Roger De Vlaeminck
1978 Francesco Moser (ITA)
1979 Francesco Moser
1980 Francesco Moser
1981 Bernard Hinault (FRA)
1982 Jan Raas (HOL)
1983 Hennie Kuiper (HOL)
1984 Sean Kelly (IRL)
1985 Marc Madiot (FRA)
1986 Sean Kelly
1987 Eric Vanderaerden (BEL)
1988 Dirk Demol (BEL)
1989 Jean-Marie Wampers (BEL)

1990 Eddy Planckaert (BEL)
1991 Marc Madiot
1992 Gilbert Duclos-Lassalle (FRA)
1993 Gilbert Duclos-Lassalle
1994 Andre Tchmil (RUS)
1995 Franco Ballerini (ITA)

LIEGE-BASTOGNE-LIEGE
1894 Léon Houa (BEL)
1912 Omer Verschoore (BEL)
1919 Léon Devos (BEL)
1920 Léon Scieur (BEL)
1921 Louis Mottiat (BEL)
1922 Louis Mottiat
1923 René Vermandel (BEL)
1924 René Vermandel
1930 Herman Buse (GER)
1931 Alfons Schepers (BEL)
1932 Marcel Houyoux (BEL)
1933 François Gardier (BEL)
1934 Theo Herckenrath (BEL)
1935 Alfons Schepers
1936 Albert Beckaert (BEL)
1937 Eloi Meulenberg (BEL)
1938 Alfons Deloor (BEL)
1939 Albert Ritservelt (BEL)
1943 Richard Depoorter (BEL)
1945 Jean Engels (BEL)
1946 Prosp. Depredomme (BEL)
1947 Richard Depoorter
1948 Maurice Mollin (BEL)
1949 Cam. Danguillaume (FRA)
1950 Prosp. Depredomme
1951 Ferdi Kubler (SUI)
1952 Ferdi Kubler
1953 Aloïs De Hertog (BEL)
1954 Marcel Ernzer (LUX)
1955 Stan Ockers (BEL)
1956 Fred De Bruyne (BEL)
1957 (Tie) Germain Derijcke (BEL)
     Frans Schouben (BEL)
1958 Fred De Bruyne
1959 Fred De Bruyne
1960 Abe Geldermans (HOL)
1961 Rik Van Looy (BEL)
1962 Jos Planckaert (BEL)
1963 Frans Melckenbeeck (BEL)
1964 Willy Bocklant (BEL)
1965 Carmine Preziosi (ITA)
1966 Jacques Anquetil (FRA)
1967 Walter Godefroot (BEL)
1968 Valeer Van Sweefelt (BEL)
1969 Eddy Merckx (BEL)
1970 Roger De Vlaeminck (BEL)
1971 Eddy Merckx
1972 Eddy Merckx
1973 Eddy Merckx
1974 Georges Pintens (BEL)
1975 Eddy Merckx
1976 Joseph Bruyere (BEL)
1977 Bernard Hinault (FRA)
1978 Joseph Bruyere
1979 Dietrich Thurau (RFA)

LIEGE-BASTOGNE-LIEGE CONTINUED

1980 Bernard Hinault
1981 Josef Fuchs (SUI)
1982 Silvano Conti (ITA)
1983 Steven Rooks (HOL)
1984 Sean Kelly (IRL)
1985 Moreno Argentin (ITA)
1986 Moreno Argentin
1987 Moreno Argentin
1988 Adri Van Der Poel (HOL)
1989 Sean Kelly
1990 Eric Van Lanker (BEL)
1991 Moreno Argentin
1992 Dirk De Wolf (BEL)
1993 Rolf Sørensen (DEN)
1994 Eugeni Berzin (RUS)
1995 Mauro Gianetti (SUI)

GIRO DI LOMBARDIA

1905 Giovanni Gerbi (ITA)
1906 Giuseppe Brambilla (ITA)
1907 Gustave Garrigou (FRA)
1908 François Faber (LUX)
1909 Giovanni Cuniolo (ITA)
1910 Giovanni Micheletto (ITA)
1911 Henri Pelissier (FRA)
1912 Carlo Oriani (ITA)
1913 Henri Pelissier
1914 Lauro Bordin (ITA)
1915 Gaetano Belloni (ITA)
1916 Leopoldo Torricelli (ITA)
1917 Philippe Thijs (BEL)
1918 Gaetano Belloni
1919 Constante Girardengo (ITA)
1920 Henri Pelissier
1921 Constante Girardengo
1922 Constante Girardengo
1923 Giovanni Brunero (ITA)
1924 Giovanni Brunero
1925 Alfredo Binda (ITA)
1926 Alfredo Binda
1927 Alfredo Binda
1928 Gaetano Belloni
1929 Piero Fossati (ITA)
1930 Michele Mara (ITA)
1931 Alfredo Binda (ITA)
1932 Antonio Negrini (ITA)
1933 Domenico Piemontesi (ITA)
1934 Learco Guerra (ITA)
1935 Enrico Mollo (ITA)
1936 Gino Bartali (ITA)
1937 Aldo Bini (ITA)
1938 Cino Cinelli (ITA)
1939 Gino Bartali
1940 Gino Bartali

1941 Mario Ricci (ITA)
1942 Aldo Bini
1945 Mario Ricci
1946 Fausto Coppi (ITA)
1947 Fausto Coppi
1948 Fausto Coppi
1949 Fausto Coppi
1950 Renzo Soldani (ITA)
1951 Louison Bobet (FRA)
1952 Giuseppe Minardi (ITA)
1953 Bruno Landi (ITA)
1954 Fausto Coppi
1955 Cleto Maule (ITA)
1956 Andre Darrigade (FRA)
1957 Diego Ronchini (ITA)
1958 Nino Defilippis (ITA)
1959 Rik Van Looy (BEL)
1960 Emile Daems (BEL)
1961 Vito Taccone (ITA)
1962 Jo De Roo (HOL)
1963 Jo De Roo
1964 Gianni Motta (ITA)
1965 Tom Simpson (GBR)
1966 Felice Gimondi (ITA)
1967 Franco Bitossi (ITA)
1968 Herman Van Springel (BEL)
1969 Jean-Pierre Monsere (BEL)
1970 Franco Bitossi
1971 Eddy Merckx (BEL)
1972 Eddy Merckx
1973 Felice Gimondi
1974 Roger De Vlaeminck (BEL)
1975 Francesco Moser (ITA)
1976 Roger De Vlaeminck
1977 Gianbattista Baronchelli (ITA)
1978 Francesco Moser
1979 Bernard Hinault (FRA)
1980 Alfons De Wolf (BEL)
1981 Hennie Kuiper (HOL)
1982 Giuseppe Saronni (ITA)
1983 Sean Kelly (IRL)
1984 Bernard Hinault
1985 Sean Kelly
1986 Gianbattista Baronchelli
1987 Moreno Argentin (ITA)
1988 Charly Mottet (FRA)
1989 Tony Rominger (SUI)
1990 Gilles Delion (FRA)
1991 Sean Kelly
1992 Tony Rominger
1993 Pascal Richard (SUI)
1994 Vladislav Bobrik (RUS)

STAGE RACE CHAMPIONS

PEACE RACE

ROUTES: [1] Warsaw-Prague; [2] Prague-Warsaw; [3] Warsaw-Berlin-Prague; [4] Prague-Berlin-Warsaw; [5] Berlin-Prague Warsaw; [6] Prague-Warsaw-Berlin; [7] Warsaw-Berlin; [8] Kiev-Warsaw-Berlin-Prague; [9] Batislav-Katowice-Berlin.

YEAR [ROUTE] WINNER (COUNTRY)
1948 [1/2] Prosenik/Zoric (YUG)
1949 [2] Vesely (TCH)
1950 [1] Emborg (DEN)
1951 [2] Olsen (DEN)
1952 [3] Ian Steele (GBR)
1953 [4] Pedersen (DEN)
1954 [3] Dalgaard (DEN)
1955 [4] Schur (DDR)
1956 [3] Krolak (POL)
1957 [4] Kristov (BUL)
1958 [3] Damen (HOL)
1959 [5] Schur
1960 [6] Hagen (DDR)
1961 [3] Yuri Melikhov (URS)
1962 [5] Saikhoudchin (URS)
1963 [6] Ampler (DDR)
1964 [3] Smolik (TCH)
1965 [5] Lebediew (URS)
1966 [6] B. Guyot (FRA)
1967 [3] Marcel Maes (BEL)
1968 [5] Ax. Peschel (DDR)
1969 [7] J.-P. Danguillaume (FRA)
1970 [6] Ryszard Szurkowski (POL)
1971 [3] Ryszard Szurkowski
1972 [5] Viast. Moravec (TCH)
1973 [5] Ryszard Szurkowski
1974 [5] Stanislav Szozda (POL)
1975 [5] Ryszard Szurkwoski
1976 [6] Hans-J. Hartnick (DDR)
1977 [3] Aavo Pikkus (URS)
1978 [5] Alexander Averin (URS)
1979 [6] Sergei Soukhoroutchenkov (URS)
1980 [3] Yuri Barinov (URS)
1981 [5] Shakid Zagretdinov (URS)
1982 [6] Olaf Ludwig (DDR)
1983 [3] Falk Boden (DDR)
1984 [5] Sergei Soukhoroutchenkov
1985 [6] Lech Piasecki (POL)
1986 [8] Olaf Ludwig
1987 [5] Uwe Ampler (DDR)
1988 [5] Uwe Ampler
1989 [3] Uwe Ampler
1990 [X] Jan Svorada (TCH)
1991 [X] Viktor Riaksinski (URS)
1992 [X] Steffen Wesemann (RFA)

VUELTA A ESPAÑA

1935 Gustave Deloor (BEL)
1936 Gustave Deloor
1941 Julian Berrendero (ESP)
1942 Julian Berrendero
1945 Delio Rodriguez (ESP)
1946 Dal. Langarica (ESP)
1947 Edward Van Dijck (BEL)
1948 Bernardo Ruiz (ESP)
1950 Emilio Rodriguez (ESP)
1955 Jean Dotto (FRA)
1956 Angelo Conterno (ITA)
1957 Jesus Lorono (ESP)
1958 Jean Stablinski (FRA)
1959 Antonio Suarez (ESP)
1960 Frans De Mulder (BEL)
1961 Antonio Soler (ESP)
1962 Rudi Altig (RFA)
1963 Jacques Anquetil (FRA)
1964 Raymond Poulidor (FRA)
1965 Rolf Wolfshohl (RFA)
1966 Francesco Gabica (ESP)
1967 Jan Janssen (HOL)
1968 Felice Gimondi (ITA)
1969 Roger Pingeon (FRA)
1970 Luis Ocana (ESP)
1971 Ferdinand Bracke (BEL)
1972 José-Manuel Fuente (ESP)
1973 Eddy Merckx (BEL)
1974 José-Manuel Fuente
1975 Agustin Tamames (ESP)
1976 José Pessarodona (ESP)
1977 Freddy Maertens (BEL)
1978 Bernard Hinault (FRA)
1979 Joop Zoetemelk (HOL)
1980 Faustino Ruperez (ESP)
1981 Giovanni Battaglin (ITA)
1982 Marino Lejarreta (ESP)
1983 Bernard Hinault
1984 Eric Caritoux (FRA)
1985 Pedro Delgado (ESP)
1986 Alvaro Pino (ITA)
1987 Luis Herrera (COL)
1988 Sean Kelly (IRL)
1989 Pedro Delgado
1990 Marco Giovannetti (ITA)
1991 Melchor Mauri (ESP)
1992 Tony Rominger (SUI)
1993 Tony Rominger
1994 Tony Rominger
1995 Laurent Jalabert (FRA)

GIRO D'ITALIA

1909 Luigi Ganna (ITA)
1910 Carlo Galetti (ITA)
1911 Carlo Galetti
1912 Team Atala
1913 Carlo Oriani (ITA)
1914 Alfonso Calzolari (ITA)
1919 Constante Giradengo (ITA)
1920 Gaetano Belloni (ITA)
1921 Giovanni Brunero (ITA)
1922 Giovanni Brunero
1923 Constante Girardengo
1924 Giuseppe Enrici (ITA)
1925 Alfredo Binda (ITA)
1926 Giovanni Brunero
1927 Alfredo Binda
1928 Alfredo Binda
1929 Alfredo Binda
1930 Luigi Marchisio (ITA)
1931 Francesco Camusso (ITA)
1932 Antonio Pesenti (ITA)
1933 Alfredo Binda
1934 Learco Guerra (ITA)
1935 Vasco Bergamashi (ITA)
1936 Gino Bartali (ITA)
1937 Gino Bartali
1938 Giovanni Valetti (ITA)
1939 Giovanni Valetti
1940 Fausto Coppi (ITA)
1946 Gino Bartali
1947 Fausto Coppi
1948 Fiorenzo Magni (ITA)
1949 Fausto Coppi
1950 Hugo Koblet (SUI)
1951 Fiorenzo Magni
1952 Fausto Coppi
1953 Fausto Coppi
1954 Carlo Clerici (SUI)
1955 Fiorenzo Magni
1956 Charly Gaul (LUX)
1957 Gastone Nencini (ITA)
1958 Ercole Baldini (ITA)
1959 Charly Gaul
1960 Jacques Anquetil (FRA)
1961 Arnaldo Pambianco (ITA)
1962 Franco Balmanion (ITA)
1963 Franco Balmanion
1964 Jacques Anquetil
1965 Vittorio Adorni (ITA)
1966 Gianni Motta (ITA)
1967 Felice Gimondi (ITA)
1968 Eddy Merckx (BEL)
1969 Felice Gimondi

1970 Eddy Merckx
1971 Gosta Pettersson (SWE)
1972 Eddy Merckx
1973 Eddy Merckx
1974 Eddy Merckx
1975 Fausto Bertoglio (ITA)
1976 Felice Gimondi
1977 Michel Pollentier (BEL)
1978 Johan De Muynck (BEL)
1979 Giuseppe Saronni (ITA)
1980 Bernard Hinault (FRA)
1981 Giovanni Battaglin (ITA)
1982 Bernard Hinault
1983 Giuseppe Saronni
1984 Francesco Moser (ITA)
1985 Bernard Hinault
1986 Roberto Visentini (ITA)
1987 Stephen Roche (IRL)
1988 Andy Hampsten (USA)
1989 Laurent Fignon (FRA)
1990 Gianni Bugno (ITA)
1991 Franco Chioccioli (ITA)
1992 Miguel Indurain (ESP)
1993 Miguel Indurain
1994 Eugeni Berzin (RUS)
1995 Tony Rominger (SUI)

RED ZINGER

1975 John Howard (USA)
1976 John Howard
1977 Wayne Stetina (USA)
1978 George Mount (USA)
1979 Dale Stetina (USA)

COORS CLASSIC

1980 Jonathan Boyer (USA)
1981 Greg LeMond (USA)
1982 Jose Patrocinio Jimenez (COL)
1983 Dale Stetina
1984 Doug Shapiro (USA)
1985 Greg LeMond
1986 Bernard Hinault (FRA)
1987 Raul Alcala (MEX)
1988 Davis Phinney (USA)

TOUR DE TRUMP

1989 Dag-Otto Lauritzen (NOR)
1990 Raul Alcala

TOUR DUPONT

1991 Erik Breukink (HOL)
1992 Greg LeMond
1993 Raul Alcala
1994 Viatcheslav Ekimov (RUS)
1995 Lance Armstrong (USA)

TOUR DE FRANCE CHAMPIONS

YEAR WINNER (NATION-TEAM) AGE	STAGES	KMS	KPH	STARTED	FINISHED	2ND PLACE AT HRS:MIN:SEC
1903 Maurice Garin (FRA) 32	6	2428	25.2	60	21	Lucien Pothier (FRA) at 2:49:00
1904 Henri Cornet (FRA) 20	6	2388	24.2	88	23	J.B. Dortignacq (FRA) at 2:16:14
1905 Louis Trousselier (FRA) 24	11	2975	27.2	60	24	Hypolite Aucouturier (FRA) at 26 pt.
1906 René Pottier (FRA) 27	13	4637	24.4	82	14	Georges Passerieu (FRA) at 28 pt.
1907 Lucien Petite-Breton (FRA) 24	14	4488	28.4	93	33	Gustave Garrigou (FRA) at 19 pt.
1908 Lucien Petite-Breton (FRA) 25	14	4488	28.7	114	3	Francois Faber (LUX) at 32 pt.
1909 Francois Faber (LUX) 27	14	4497	28.6	150	55	Gustave Garrigou (FRA) at 20 pt.
1910 Octave Lapize (FRA) 21	15	4700	28.6	110	41	Francois Faber (LUX) at 4 pt.
1911 Gustave Garrigou (FRA) 29	15	5544	27.3	84	28	Paul Duboc (FRA) at 41 pt.
1912 Odile Defraye (BEL) 24	15	5229	27.8	131	41	Eugene Christophe (FRA) at 59.5 pt.
1913 Philippe Thijs (BEL) 23	15	5387	27.6	140	25	Gustave Garrigou (FRA) at 8:37
1914 Philippe Thijs (BEL) 24	15	5414	27.0	146	54	Henri Pélissier (FRA) at 1:50
1919 Firmin Lambot (BEL) 30	15	5560	24.9	69	10	Jean Alavoine (FRA) at 1:42:45
1920 Philippe Thijs (BEL) 26	15	5503	24.1	113	22	Hector Heusghem (BEL) at 57:00
1921 Léon Scieur (BEL) 32	15	5484	27.7	123	38	Hector Heusghem (BEL) at 19:02
1922 Firmin Lambot (BEL) 33	15	5375	24.2	121	38	Jean Alavoine (FRA) at 41:15
1923 Henri Pélissier (FRA) 33	15	5386	24.4	139	48	Ottavio Bottecchia (ITA) at 30:41
1924 Ottavio Bottechia (ITA) 30	15	5427	23.9	157	60	Nicholas Frantz (LUX) at 35:36
1925 Ottavio Bottechia (ITA) 31	18	5430	24.7	130	49	Lucien Buysse (BEL) at 54:20
1926 Lucien Buysse (BEL) 33	17	5745	24.0	126	41	Nicholas Frantz (LUX) at 1:22:25
1927 Nicolas Frantz (LUX) 28	24	5321	26.8	142	39	Maurice Dewaële (BEL) at 1:48:21
1928 Nicholas Frantz (LUX) 29	22	5377	27.8	162	41	André Leducq (FRA) at 50:07
1929 Maurice Dewaële (BEL) 33	22	5288	28.3	155	60	Giuseppe Pancera (ITA) at 32:07
1930 André Leducq (FRA) 26	21	4818	27.9	100	59	Learco Guerra (ITA) at 14:19
1931 Antonin Magne (FRA) 27	24	5095	28.7	81	35	Joseph Demuysere (BEL) at 12:56
1932 André Leducq (FRA) 28	21	4502	29.2	80	57	Kurt Stoepel (GER) at 24:03
1933 Georges Speicher (FRA) 26	23	4395	29.6	80	40	Learco Guerra (ITA) at 4:01
1934 Antonin Magne (FRA) 30	23	4363	29.4	60	39	Giuseppe Martano (ITA) at 27:31
1935 Romain Maes (BEL) 22	21	4302	30.5	93	46	Ambrogio Morelli (ITA) at 17:52
1936 Sylvère Maes (BEL) 27	21	4442	31.0	90	43	Antonin Magne (FRA) at 26:55
1937 Roger Lapébie (FRA) 26	20	4415	31.7	98	46	Mario Vicini (ITA) at 7:17
1938 Gino Bartali (ITA) 24	21	4694	31.5	96	55	Felice Vervaecke (BEL) at 18:27
1939 Sylvère Maes (BEL) 30	18	4224	31.8	79	49	René Vietto (FRA) at 30:08
1947 Jean Robic (FRA) 26	21	4640	31.4	100	53	Edouard Fachleitner (FRA) at 3:58
1948 Gino Bartali (ITA) 34	21	4922	33.4	120	44	Brik Schotte (BEL) at 26:16
1949 Fausto Coppi (ITA) 29	21	4813	32.1	120	55	Gino Bartali (ITA) at 10:53
1950 Ferdi Kübler (SUI) 31	22	4776	32.7	116	51	Stan Ockers (BEL) at 9:30
1951 Hugo Koblet (SUI) 26	24	4474	31.4	123	66	Raphael Geminiani (FRA) at 22:00
1952 Fausto Coppi (ITA-Bianchi) 32	23	4807	31.6	122	78	Stan Ockers (BEL) at 28:17
1953 Louison Bobet (FRA) 28	22	4479	34.6	119	76	Jean Malléjac (FRA) at 14:18
1954 Louison Bobet (FRA) 29	23	4855	34.6	110	69	Ferdi Kübler (SUI) at 15:49
1955 Louison Bobet (FRA) 30	22	4495	34.4	130	69	Jean Brankart (BEL) at 4:53
1956 Roger Walkowiak (FRA) 27	22	4528	36.5	120	88	Gilbert Bauvin (FRA) at 1:25
1957 Jacques Anquetil (FRA) 23	22	4555	34.5	120	56	Marc Janssens (BEL) at 14:56
1958 Charly Gaul (LUX) 26	24	4319	36.9	120	78	Vito Favero (ITA) at 3:10
1959 Féderico Bahamontes (ESP) 31	22	4363	35.2	120	65	Henri Anglade (FRA) at 4:01
1960 Gastone Nencini (ITA) 30	21	4272	37.2	128	81	Graz. Battistini (ITA) at 5:02
1961 Jacques Anquetil (FRA-Helyett) 27	21	4394	36.2	132	72	Guido Carlesi (ITA) at 12:14
1962 Jacques Anquetil (FRA-St. Raphael) 28	22	4272	37.3	149	94	Jef Planckart (BEL) at 4:59
1963 Jacques Anquetil (FRA-) 29	21	4140	36.4	130	76	Federico Bahamontes (ESP) at 3:35
1964 Jacques Anquetil (FRA-St. Raphael) 30	22	4505	35.4	132	81	Raymond Poulidor (FRA) at 0:55
1965 Felice Gimondi (ITA-Salvarani) 22	22	4175	36.0	130	96	Raymond Poulidor (FRA) at 2:40
1966 Lucien Aimar (FRA) 25	22	4329	36.6	130	82	Jan Janssen (HOL) at 1:07
1967 Roger Pingeon (FRA-Peugeot-BP) 27	22	4780	34.7	130	88	Julio Jimenez (ESP) at 3:40
1968 Jan Janssen (HOL) 28	22	4662	34.8	110	63	Herman Van Springel (BEL) at 0:38
1969 Eddy Merckx (BEL-Faema) 24	22	4102	35.2	129	86	Roger Pingeon (FRA) at 17:54
1970 Eddy Merckx (BEL-Faema) 25	23	4366	36.4	150	100	Joop Zootemelk (HOL) at 12:41
1971 Eddy Merckx (BEL-Molteni) 26	20	3689	36.9	129	94	Joop Zootemelk (HOL) at 9:51

YEAR WINNER (NATION-TEAM) AGE	STAGES	KMS	KPH	STARTED	FINISHED	2ND PLACE AT H:M:S
1972 Eddy Merckx (BEL-Molteni) 27	20	3846	35.3	132	88	Felice Gimondi (ITA) at 10:41
1973 Luis Ocana (ESP-Bic) 28	20	4140	33.9	132	87	Bernard Thevenet (FRA) at 15:51
1974 Eddy Merckx (BEL-Molteni) 29	22	4098	35.2	130	105	Raymond Poulidor (FRA) at 8:04
1975 Bernard Thevenet (FRA-Peugeot) 27	22	3999	34.8	140	86	Eddy Merckx (BEL) at 2:47
1976 Lucien Van Impe (BEL-Gitane) 29	22	4016	34.5	130	87	Joop Zootemelk (HOL) at 4:14
1977 Bernard Thevenet (FRA-Peugeot) 29	22	4092	35.5	100	53	Hennie Kuiper (HOL) at 0:48
1978 Bernard Hinault (FRA-Gitane) 23	22	3913	34.9	110	78	Joop Zootemelk (HOL) at 3:56
1979 Bernard Hinault (FRA-Renault) 24	24	3720	36.0	150	89	Joop Zootemelk (HOL) at 13:37
1980 Joop Zoetemelk (HOL-TI-Raleigh) 33	22	3945	35.3	130	85	Hennie Kuiper (HOL) at 6:55
1981 Bernard Hinault (FRA-Renault) 26	22	3756	37.9	150	121	Lucien Van Impe (BEL) at 14:34
1982 Bernard Hinault (FRA-Renault) 27	21	3512	37.4	169	125	Joop Zootemelk (HOL) at 6:21
1983 Laurent Fignon (FRA-Renault) 22	22	3962	35.9	140	88	Angel Arroyo (ESP) at 4:04
1984 Laurent Fignon (FRA-Renault) 23	23	4020	34.9	140	124	Bernard Hinault (FRA) at 10:32
1985 Bernard Hinault (FRA-La Vie Claire) 30	22	4127	36.2	179	144	Greg LeMond (USA) at 1:42
1986 Greg LeMond (USA-La Vie Claire) 25	23	4083	36.9	210	132	Bernard Hinault (FRA) at 3:10
1987 Stephen Roche (IRL-Carrera) 27	25	4231	36.6	207	135	Pedro Delgado (ESP) at 0:40
1988 Pedro Delgado (ESP-Reynolds) 28	22	3281	38.9	198	151	Steven Rooks (HOL) at 7:31
1989 Greg LeMond (USA-ADR) 28	21	3285	37.4	198	138	Laurent Fignon (FRA) at 0:08
1990 Greg LeMond (USA-Z) 29	21	3421	37.7	198	156	Claudio Chiappucci (ITA) at 2:16
1991 Miguel Indurain (ESP-Banesto) 27	22	3919	38.7	198	158	Gianni Bugno (ITA) at 3:36
1992 Miguel Indurain (ESP-Banesto) 28	21	3983	39.5	198	130	Claudio Chiappucci (ITA) at 4:35
1993 Miguel Indurain (ESP-Banesto) 29	20	3717	38.7	180	136	Tony Rominger (SUI) at 4:59
1994 Miguel Indurain (ESP-Banesto) 30	21	3984	38.3	189	117	Pyotr Ugrumov (LAT) at 5:39
1995 Miguel Indurain (ESP-Banesto) 31	20	3635	39.1	189	115	Alex Zulle (SUI) at 4:35

WOMEN'S TOURS

RED ZINGER
YEAR WINNER (COUNTRY) AGE
1975 Hannah North (USA)
1977 Connie Carpenter (USA) 20
1978 Keetie Van Oosten-Hage (HOL) 29
1979 Keetie Van Oosten-Hage (HOL) 30

COORS CLASSIC
1980 Beth Heiden (USA) 20
1981 Connie Carpenter (USA) 24
1982 Connie Carpenter (USA) 25
1983 Rebecca Twigg (USA) 20
1984 Maria Canins (USA) 35
1985 Jeannie Longo (FRA) 26
1986 Jeannie Longo (FRA) 27
1987 Jeannie Longo (FRA) 28
1988 Inga Benedict (USA) 24

INTERNATIONAL WOMEN'S CHALLENGE IDAHO
1984 Rebecca Twigg (USA) 21
1985 Rebecca Twigg (USA) 22
1986 Rebecca Twigg (USA) 23
1987 Inga Benedict (USA) 23
1988 Katrin Tobin (USA) 21
1989 Lisa Brambani (GRB) 21
1990 Inga Thompson (USA) 26
1991 Jeannie Longo (FRA) 32
1992 Eve Stephenson (USA) 22
1993 Jeanne Golay (USA) 31
1994 Clara Hughes (CAN) 21
1995 Dede Demet (USA) 22

TOUR DE FRANCE FÉMININ
YEAR WINNER (NATION) AGE
1984 Marianne Martin (USA) 24
1985 Maria Canins (ITA) 36
1986 Maria Canins 37
1987 Jeannie Longo (FRA) 28
1988 Jeannie Longo 29
1989 Jeannie Longo 30

EUROPEAN COMMUNITY TOUR (MASTERS FÉMININ)
1990 Cathérine Marsal (FRA) 19
1991 Astrid Schop (HOL)
1992 Leontien Van Moorsel (HOL) 22
1993 Heidi Van de Vijver (BEL)
1994 Luzia Zberg (SUI) 24

TOUR CYCLISTE FÉMININ
1992 Leontien Van Moorsel (HOL) 22
1993 Leontien Van Moorsel 23
1994 Valentina Polhanova (RUS) 23
1995 Fabiana Luperini (ITA) 21

GIRO D'ITALIA FEMINILE
1994 Michela Fanini (ITA)
1995 Fabiana Luperini (ITA) 21

EDDY MERCKX

LE PALMARÉS
525 victories in 1,800 races
1964: World Amateur Road Champion
1966: Milan-San Remo
1967: Milan-San Remo, Gent-Wevelgem, Flèche Wallone, World Pro Road Champion, Trophée Barrachi
1968: Giro di Sardinia, Paris-Roubaix, Giro d'Italia
1969: Milan-San Remo, Ronde Van Vlaanderen, Tour de France
1970: Paris-Nice, Gent-Wevelgem, Tour de Belgique, Paris-Roubaix, Flèche Wallone, Giro d'Italia, Belgian Pro Road Champion, Tour de France
1971: Giro di Sardinia, Paris-Nice, Milan-San Remo, Het Volk, Tour de Belgique, Liège-Bastogne-Liège, Tour de France, World Pro Road Champion, Giro di Lombardia
1972: Milan-San Remo, Liège-Bastogne-Liège, Flèche Wallone, Giro d'Italia, Tour de France, Giro di Lombardia, Trophée Baracchi, World Hour Record
1973: Giro di Sardinia, Het Volk, Gent-Wevelgem, Paris-Roubaix, Liège-Bastogne-Liège, Vuelta a Espana, Giro d'Italia, Paris-Brussels, Grand Prix des Nations
1974: Giro d'Italia, Tour de Suisse, Tour de France, World Pro Road Champion
1975: Milan-San Remo, Ronde Van Vlaanderen, Liège-Bastogne-Liège
1976: Milan-San Remo, La Semaña della Cataloña
1977: Tour de la Mediterranée

CYCLO-CROSS WORLD CHAMPIONS

PROFESSIONAL

1950 Paris (FRA)	Jean Robic (FRA)
1951 Luxembourg	Roger Rondeaux (FRA)
1952 Geneva (SUI)	Roger Rondeaux
1953 Onate	Roger Rondeaux
1954 Crenna	André Dufraisse (FRA)
1955 Saarbrücken	André Dufraisse
1956 Luxembourg	André Dufraisse
1957 Edelare	André Dufraisse
1958 Limoges (FRA)	André Dufraisse
1959 Geneva (SUI)	Renato Longo (ITA)
1960 Tolosa (ESP)	Rolf Wolfshohl (RFA)
1961 Hannover (RFA)	Rolf Wolfshohl
1962 Esch-sur-Alzette	Renato Longo
1963 Calais (FRA)	Rolf Wolfshohl
1964 Overboelare (BEL)	Renato Longo
1965 Cavaria (ITA)	Renato Longo
1966 Beasain	Eric De Vlaeminck (BEL)
1967 Zurich (SUI)	Renato Longo
1968 Luxembourg	Eric De Vlaeminck
1969 Magstadt (RFA)	Eric De Vlaeminck
1970 Zolder	Eric De Vlaeminck
1971 Apeldorn	Eric De Vlaeminck
1972 Prague (TCH)	Eric De Vlaeminck
1973 London (GBR)	Eric De Vlaeminck
1974 Bidasoa (ESP)	Albert Van Damme (BEL)
1975 Melchnau	Roger De Vlaeminck (BEL)
1976 Chazay d'Azergues	Albert Zweifel (SUI)
1977 Hannover (RFA)	Albert Zweifel
1978 Amorebieta	Albert Zweifel
1979 Saccolongo	Albert Zweifel
1980 Wetzikon	Roland Liboton (BEL)
1981 Tolosa (ESP)	Hennie Stamsnijder (HOL)
1982 Lanarvilly	Roland Liboton
1983 Birmingham (GBR)	Roland Liboton
1984 Oss	Roland Liboton
1985 Munich (RFA)	Klaus-Peter Thaler (RFA)
1986 Lembeek	Albert Zweifel
1987 Mlada Boleslav	Klaus-Peter Thaler
1988 Hagendorf	Pascal Richard (FRA)
1989 Pontchateau (FRA)	Danny De Bie (BEL)
1990 Getxo (ESP)	Henk Baars (HOL)
1991 Gieten (HOL)	Radomir Simunek (TCH)
1992 Leeds (GRB)	Mike Kluge (RFA)
1993 Corva (ITA)	Dominique Arnould (FRA)
1994 Koksijde (BEL)	Paul Herijgers (BEL)
1995 Eschenbach (SUI)	Dieter Runkel (SUI)

MOUNTAIN BIKE CHAMPIONS

CROSS-COUNTRY
UCI WORLD CHAMPIONSHIP

YEAR PLACE	MEN	WOMEN
1990 Durango (USA)	Ned Overend (USA)	Juli Furtado (USA)
1991 Lucca (ITA)	John Tomac (USA)	Ruthie Matthes (USA)
1992 Bromont (CAN)	Henrik Djernis (DEN)	Silvia Fürst (SUI)
1993 Metabief (FRA)	Henrik Djernis (DEN)	Paola Pezzo (ITA)
1994 Vail (USA)	Henrik Djernis (DEN)	Alison Sydor (CAN)
1995 Kirchzarten (RFA)	Bart Brentjens (HOL)	Alison Sydor (CAN)

EUROPEAN CHAMPIONSHIP

1991 La Bourboule (FRA)	Erich Übelhardt (SUI)	Chantal Daucourt (SUI)
1992 Molbrucke (OST)	Erich Übelhardt (SUI)	Silvia Fürst (SUI)
1993 Klosters (SUI)	Thomas Frischknecht (SUI)	Chantal Daucourt (SUI)
1994 Metabief (FRA)	Albert Iten (SUI)	Paola Pezzo (ITA)
1995 Spindleruv Mlyn (TCH)	Jean-Christophe Savignoni (FRA)	Caroline Alexander (GRB)

GRUNDIG WORLD CUP

YEAR	MEN	WOMEN
1989	Volker Krukenbaum (RFA)	Susi Buchwieser (RFA)
1990	Mike Kluge (RFA)	Sara Ballatyne (USA)
1991	John Tomac (USA)	Sara Ballantyne (USA)
1992	Thomas Frischknecht (SUI)	Ruthie Matthes (USA)
1993	Thomas Frischknecht (SUI)	Juli Furtado (USA)
1994	Bart Brentjens (HOL)	Juli Furtado (USA)
1995	Thomas Frischknecht (SUI)	Juli Furtado (USA)

TOUR DE FRANCE VTT

1995	Bart Brentjens (HOL)	Hedda Zu Putlitz (RFA)

NORBA CHAMPIONSHIP SERIES

1983	Steve Tilford	Jacquie Phelan
1984	Joe Murray	Jacquie Phelan
1985	Joe Murray	Jacquie Phelan
1986	Ned Overend	Cindy Whitehead
1987	Ned Overend	Lisa Muhich
1988	John Tomac	Margaret Browne-Day
1989	Ned Overend	Sara Ballantyne
1990	Ned Overend	Susan De Mattei
1991	John Tomac	Juli Futado
1992	Ned Overend	Juli Furtado
1993	David Wiens	Juli Furtado
1994	Tinker Juarez	Juli Futado
1995	Tinker Juarez	Juli Furtado

DOWNHILL
UCI WORLD CHAMPIONSHIP

1990	Greg Herbold (USA)	Cindy Devine (CAN)
1991	Albert Iten (SUI)	Giovanna Bonazzi (ITA)
1992	Dave Cullinan (USA)	Juli Furtado (USA)
1993	Mike King (USA)	Giovanna Bonazzi (ITA)
1994	François Gachet (FRA)	Missy Giove (USA)
1995	Nicholas Vouilloz (FRA)	Leigh Donovan (USA)

DUAL SLALOM
UCI WORLD CHAMPIONSHIP

1995	Mike King (USA)	Rita Burgi (SUI)

RACE ACROSS AMERICA

YEAR ROUTE		MILES
WINNERS	TIME (D:H:M)	MPH
1982 Santa Monica CA–New York City NY		**2,968**
MEN Lon Haldeman (IL)	9:20:02	12.5
1983 Santa Monica CA–New York City NY		**3,170**
MEN Lon Haldeman (IL)	10:16:29	12.3
1984 Huntington Beach CA–Atlantic City NJ		**3,047**
MEN Pete Penseyres (CA)	9:13:13	13.2
WOMEN (Tie) Shelby Hayden-Clifton (NC)/ Pat Hines (CA)	12:20:57	9.8
1985 Huntington Beach CA–Atlantic City NJ		**3,120**
MEN Jonathan Boyer (CA)	9:02:06	14.3
WOMEN Susan Notorangelo (IL)	10:14:25	12.2
1986 Huntington Beach CA–Atlantic City NJ		**3,107**
MEN Pete Penseyres (CA)	8:09:47	15.4
WOMEN Elaine Mariolle (CA)	10:02:04	12.8
1987 San Francisco CA–Washington DC		**3,127**
MEN Michael Secrest (MI)	9:11:35	13.7
WOMEN Casey Patterson (CA)	11:21:15	10.9
TANDEM Lon Haldeman/Pete Penseyres	(2920 mi) 7:14:55	15.9
1988 San Francisco CA–Washington DC		**3,073**
MEN Franz Spilauer (AUT)	9:07:09	13.7
WOMEN Cindi Staiger (CA)	12:03:55	10.5
1989 Costa Mesa CA–New York NY		**2,911**
MEN Paul Solon (CA)	8:08:45	14.5
WOMEN Susan Notorangelo (IL)	9:09:09	12.9
HPV RELAY Team Lightning (CA)	5:01:04	24.0
ROUNDTRIP Bob Breedlove (IA)	22:13:36	10.7
1990 Irvine CA–Savannah GA		**2,930**
MEN Bob Forney (CO)	8:11:26	14.4
WOMEN Nancy Raposo (RI)	10:10:06	11.7
TANDEM MEN Bob Breedlove (IA)/Roger Charleville (OH)	8:10:40	14.4
TANDEM MIXED Ron Dossenbach (CAN)/Sue Pavlat (MI)	10:22:40	11.5
1991 Irvine CA–Savannah GA		**2,930**
MEN Bob Forney (CO)	8:16:44	14.0
WOMEN Cathy Ellis (MA)	12:06:21	9.9
TANDEM MIXED Cherie Moore/Dave Moore (CA)	11:21:43	10.2
1992 Irvine CA–Savannah GA		**2,909**
MEN Rob Kish (FL)	8:03:11	14.9
WOMEN Seana Hogan (CA)	11:15:07	10.4
TANDEM MEN Bob Breedlove/Lon Haldeman	8:08:13	14.5
TANDEM MIXED Antoinette Addison/Shawn Addison (CA)	11:09:34	10.6
TEAM RELAY Team Manheim (GA)	6:37:00	20.1
1993 Irvine CA–Savannah GA		**2,909**
MEN Gerry Tatrai (AUS)	8:20:19	14.0
WOMEN Seana Hogan (CA)	9:15:30	12.5
TEAM RELAY PacifiCare-Trek (CA)	6:05:31	19.0
1994 Irvine CA–Savannah GA		**2,909**
MEN Rob Kish (FL)	8:14:25	14.0
WOMEN Seana Hogan (CA)	9:08:56	12.9
TEAM RELAY Centurian (AUT-GER)	5:09:17	22.5
1995 Irvine CA–Savannah GA		**2,911**
MEN Rob Kish (FL)	8:19:59	13.7
WOMEN Seana Hogan (CA)	9:04:17	13.2
TEAM RELAY Kern Wheelmen (CA)	5:17:05	21.2

TRIATHLON CHAMPIONS

HAWAIIAN IRONMAN

MEN

YEAR WINNER	TIME (H:M:S)	STARTED	FINISHED
1978 Gordon Haller (USA)	11:46:58	15	12
1979 Tom Warren (USA)	11:15:56	14	11
1980 Dave Scott (USA)	9:24:33	106	93
1981 John Howard (USA)	9:38:29	306	283
1982 Scott Tinley (USA)	9:19:41	531	494
1982 Dave Scott (USA)	9:08:23	758	690
1983 Dave Scott (USA)	9:05:57	836	720
1984 Dave Scott (USA)	8:54:20	878	767
1985 Scott Tinley (USA)	8:50:54	829	792
1986 Dave Scott (USA)	8:28:37	829	763
1987 Dave Scott (USA)	8:34:13	1115	1040
1988 Scott Molina (USA)	8:31:00	1009	949
1989 Mark Allen (USA)	8:09:15	1024	983
1990 Mark Allen (USA)	8:28:17	1130	1013
1991 Mark Allen (USA)	8:18:32	1115	1063
1992 Mark Allen (USA)	8:09:08	1091	1037
1993 Mark Allen (USA)	8:07:45	1179	1109
1994 Greg Welch (AUS)	8:20:27	1131	1047
1995 Mark Allen (USA)	8:20:34	1163	1085

WOMEN

YEAR WINNER	TIME (H:M:S)	STARTED	FINISHED
1979 Lyn Lemaire (USA)	12:55:38	1	1
1980 Robin Beck (USA)	11:21:24	2	2
1981 Linda Sweeney (USA)	12:00:32	20	16
1982 Kathleen McCartney (USA)	11:09:40	49	47
1982 Julie Leach (USA)	10:54:08	92	85
1983 Sylviane Puntous (CAN)	10:43:36	128	115
1984 Sylviane Puntous (CAN)	10:25:13	158	136
1985 Joanna Ernst (USA)	10:25:22	189	173
1986 Paula Newby-Fraser (ZIM)	9:49:14	210	188
1987 Erin Baker (NZL)	9:35:24	266	243
1988 Paula Newby-Fraser (ZIM)	9:01:01	266	240
1989 Paula Newby-Fraser (ZIM)	9:00:56	261	248
1990 Erin Baker (NZL)	9:13:42	257	223
1991 Paula Newby-Fraser (ZIM)	9:07:52	264	249
1992 Paula Newby-Fraser (ZIM)	8:55:28	273	261
1993 Paula Newby-Fraser (ZIM)	8:58:23	259	244
1994 Paula Newby-Fraser (ZIM)	9:20:14	274	243
1995 Karen Smyers (USA)	9:16:46	278	243

BIKE COURSE RECORDS	112 MILES	AVERAGE MPH
1993 Jurgen Zack (GER)	4:27:42	25.1
1993 Paula Newby-Fraser (ZIM)	4:48:30	23.2

TRANSCONTINENTAL USA RECORDS

YEAR CYCLIST	ROUTE	MILES	DAYS:HOURS:MIN	MPH	NOTES
1884 Thomas Stevens	Oakland CA to Boston MA	3,400	104:06:00	1.36	First man
1943 Jack Russell	Miami FL to San Diego CA	2,995	27:17:39	4.50	World War II
1986 Pete Penseyres	Huntington Beach CA to Atlantic City NJ	3,107	8:09:47	15.40	Fastest speed
1990 Michael Secrest	Huntington Beach CA to Atlantic City NJ	2,915	7:23:16	15.24	Lowest time
1990 David Cornelsen	Costa Mesa CA to New York NY	2,975	18:16:52	6.63	Arm-powered
1995 Seana Hogan	Irvine CA to Savannah GA	2,911	9:04:17	13.22	Fastest woman

Arts

CIRCUS ACTS

Blondin 1869 French.

Hanlon's Superba 1868 American.

The Female Blondin 1880s Ella Zuila, French, Forepaugh Show.

Stirk Family 1880s American, P.T. Barnum Show.

Kaufmann Troupe 1890s American, performed in Europe.

Kil Kilpatrick-King of the Capitol Steps 1890s Charles Kilpatrick (one-legged), Washington, DC, Kansas City.

Les Frères Ancillotti 1900s Ugo Ancillotti, French, Barnum and Bailey Shows.

World's Master Unicyclist—Loose Nut on Wheels 1910-1950 Walter Nilsson, Vaudeville, *Hellzapoppin*, *Ripley's Believe It or Not*, Coney Island **Funi-Cycle**.

Pallen Bears 1920s Dutch, Sells-Floto Circus.

The Cycling Tramp 1900-1950 Joe Jackson Sr. and Jr., Austrian-American, Crystal Palace, Moulin Rouge, Tivoli Gardens, Radio City Music Hall.

The Grentonas 1930s High-wire.

The Great Wallendas 1930s Karl, Helen, Tino, Ricky Wallenda & Luis Murillo, Ringling Bros. Barnum and Bailey.

The Cycling Clown 1940s Jack Natirboff, American, New York World's Fair.

Kondovi Troupe 1940s Peter, Tzetza & Stella Kondovi, Ringling Bros. Barnum and Bailey.

Boy Foy 1950s American, Radio City Music Hall.

The Six Frielanis 1960s Radio City Music Hall.

The Shyrettos 1950s Walter, Alfred & Henny Shyretto, German, Follies Bergere, Radio City Music Hall.

The Romanos 1950s Tony, Helene & Patrick Romano, French, Ice Capades, Ed Sullivan Show, Johnny Carson.

King Charles Troupe 1960s African-American, Ringling Bros. Barnum and Bailey Combined Shows.

Beauty on Wheels 1960s Theron Dollies, American, Radio City Music Hall.

World's Highest Unicyclist 1960s Steven McPeak, American, *Guinness Book*, Circus, Circus.

Marquis Chimps 1960s Charlie, Enoch & Candy, African-British, stage and television.

Ballerina of the Golden Wheel 1960s-1970s Lilly Yokoi, Japanese-American, Royal Command Circus, Radio City Music Hall.

The Volantes 1970s Don Thompson & Scott Beldin, American, Cafe Lido, television.

Shenyang Acrobatic Troupe 1970s Chinese, Lincoln Center, NY.

Sir Bob Yacona & Lady Marlena 1980s American.

Frank Olivier 1980s American Serious Fun!, NY.

Quiros Family 1990s Spanish, Ringling Bros. Barnum and Bailey.

Fujian Acrobatic Troupe 1990s Chinese, Ringling Bros. Barnum and Bailey.

MUSIC, SONGS, RECORDINGS

In chronological order; **Title** Date, Composer, Performer, Recording (date), Publisher, Record Company, Music Category, Playing Time.

The Flying Velocipede 1869, Brio, Wm. A. Pond, NY.

The Gay Velocipede 1869, Cooper and Miller, J.L. Peters, NY.

The Great Velocipede Song 1869, from Sinbad the Sailor, W.A. Pond, NY.

The New Velocipede 1869, E.H. Sherwood, J.P. Shaw, Rochester.

The Unlucky Velocipedist 1869, S. Low Coach, Blackman, New Orleans.

Velocipede Galop, Velocipede March, Velocipede Polka, Velocipede Schottisch, and **Velocipede Waltz** from *The Velocipede Set* 1869, E. Mack, Lee and Walker, Philadelphia.

Velocipede 1869, Chas. Koppitz, Koppitz, Prufer & Co., Boston.

Velocipede Galop 1869, M.F. H. Smith, C.C. Sawyer, Brooklyn.

Velocipedia 1869, Frank Howard and Horace Kimball, Root and Cady, Chicago.

Velocipediana 1869, A.L. Adamas, Wm. A. Pond, NY.

Velocipede Johnny 1869, H. DeMarsan, NY.

Velocipede 1869, William Fiske, S. Brainard & Sons, Cleveland.

Velocipede Polka, opus 259 1869, Josef Strauss, performed by Vienna Philharmonic Orchestra, conductor Lorin Maazel, *Wiener Bonbons - New Year's Concert 1983*, Deutsche Grammophon, classical.

Velocipede Song 1869, Wm. A. Pond, NY.

Bicycle Glide 1880, W. Diederich, Lee and Walker, Philadelphia.

Star Bicycle Galop 1882, Chas. W. Nathan, Spear and Denhoff, NY.

Bicycle March 1882, N.R. Graham, J.H. Brodersen, Chicago.

Bicycle Galop 1883, William H. Hall, R.A. Spaulding, Troy.

Bicycle Galop 1883, Mollenhaupt, S. Brainards & Sons, Cleveland.

The Star Rider 1883, John Ford, H.B. Smith Machine Co., Smithville, NJ.

The Wheelman's Song 1883, John Ford, H.B. Hart, Philadelphia.

The Song of the Wheel 1884, Charles Pratt, The Wheelman Co., Boston.

The Wheelman's Song 1884, William J. Stabler, Outing, Boston.

Bicycle Waltz 1885, J.J. Sawyer and Geo. Jackson, W.A. Evans, Boston.

The League Waltz 1886, George Fred Brooks, Edward Schuberth Co., NY.

It's Best to Keep Up With the Style 1886, H.G. and J.W. Wheeler, Shaw, NY.

Bicycle Galop 1887, Ludwig Andre, William Rohlfing & Co., Milwaukee.

Swiftly and Silently 1887, J.J. Chickering and H.T. Smith, Ellis & Co., Washington, DC.

Wheel on to Glory 1887, Hubbard T. Smith, Ellis & Co., Washington, DC.

The Wheelman's Song 1888, Dunnelly and Speck, T.B. Harmes, NY.

Cycle Polka 1890, Geo. W. Wallace, Wm. A. Pond, NY.

The Maid of Ixion and the Cycle Man 1891, James Meakins, NY.

Daisy Bell or **Bicycle Built For Two** or **On a Bicycle Built For Two** 1892, Harry Dacre, T.B. Harmes, NY. Performed by: Fontanna and his Orchestra, Vocal by James Forsythe, *The Gay Nineties* (1947) Buckingham Records, Traditional. The Banjo Kings, *Favorites*, Good Time Jazz. Erich Rogers and the Vaudeville Orchestra & Chorus, *Vaudeville!*, Decca/London Records, medley in "Coast-to-Coast." Mickey Finn and Big Tiny Little, *Honky Tonk Piano*, GNP/Cresendo, blues. Joe "Knuckles" O'Leary, *Honky Tonk Piano*, Gold Award Records, instrumental. Merle Travis, *The Merle Travis Guitar* (1956) Capitol Records, Picking, 2:09. Bing Crosby, *Join Bing and Sing Along* (1960) RCA Victor. Freddie Hall, *Freddie Hall Plays the Gay 90's* (1961) Spinorama Records, comedy. Rockinghorse Orchestra and Chorus, *Fun on Wheels!* (1960s) Diplomat Records, traditional. Nat King Cole, *Those Lazy-Hazy-Crazy Days of Summer* (1963) Capitol Records, 1:43. Mitch Miller and the Gang, *Still More Sing Along with Mitch*, Columbia Records, traditional. Boston Pops Orchestra, Arthur Fiedler, Conductor (Arr: Lake), *Old Timers' Night at the Pops* (1967) RCA Victor Records, concert. HAL 9000 (Douglas Rain), *2001: A Space Odyssey* (1968) MGM, soundtrack. Bill Bailey's Banjos, *Sing Along with the World Famous Bill Bailey's Banjos* (1976) Sandcastle Records, traditional. Dave Brubeck, Derry Music, *Quiet As The Moon* (1991) Musicmasters, jazz. Kidsongs, *Cars, Boats, Trains and Other Things That Go* (1992)

Warner Bros., children's. Alvin & the Chipmunks, *Sing-Alongs* (1993) Chipmunk Records, children's. Disneyland Cast, *Children's Favorites, Vol. 1* (n.d.) Disney, children's.

Bicycle March 1892, Laurent L. Combs, White, Smith & Co., Boston.

March Bicyclysto 1893, Eugene Angel, Ilsen & Co., Cincinnati.

Since Katie Rides a Wheel 1893, C. Harris and Clauder, Milwaukee.

Wheeling Away to Glory 1893, W.W. Wave, Wm. Delany, NY.

Arthur Dear or Daisy Bell's Reply 1894, J. Austin Springer, Capital, Albany.

The Bloomers 1894, Schrage and Potstock, NY.

Carrie and Her Wheel 1894, Theo H. Northrup, Treloer Music Co., Missouri.

Fare You Well, Daisy Bell 1894, Harry Dacre, Francis, Day & Hunter, London.

Hurrah for the Girls in Bloomers 1894, Arnold Somlyo, S. Brainards Sons, Chicago.

Merry Cycle Song 1894, Roland Hennessy, Witmark & Sons, NY.

Mulrooney on a Bike 1894, Emmet Dufy, C.H. Kimball, Manchester, NH.

The Scorcher 1894, Eugene Kramer, Edward A. Saalfeld, Chicago.

Angel Grace and the Crimson Rim 1895, Post and Edwards, Robt. De Yong, St. Louis.

Arrow Cycling Club Two Step 1895, Joe Mahany, Anthony Kiefer, Peoria, IL.

The Belle of the Wheel 1895, Julius V. Bernauer, Bureau of Literature, Chicago.

The Bicycle Girl 1895, A Bicycle Boy, J.B. Millet Co., Boston.

The Bicycle Girl 1895, Oddfellow and Meacham, Hedenberg and Dakin, Brooklyn.

Bloomer Two Step March 1895, M. Florence, T.B. Harms, NY.

Climbing on My Golden Wheel 1895, Harry J. Ballou, Oliver Ditson, Boston.

Courting on a Wheel 1895, Ed Rogers, M. Witmark & Sons, NY.

The Cycling Maid or The Bicycle's Thing 1895, Grant and Southwide, National, Chicago.

Doolin and His Bike 1895, Lawlor and Blake, Crescent Publishing, NY.

Get Your Lamps Lit 1895, Theo A. Metz, NY.

He's Got Wheels in His Head 1895, Charles Robinson, Howley Haviland, NY.

Have You a Wheel? 1895, O.A. Hoffman, Milwaukee.

Keating Galop 1895, G.H.R. Miller, Phelps Music Co., NY.

Keating Wheel March 1895, Ray Woodman Bryan, Keating Wheel, Holyoke.

Love on Wheels 1895, M. Stuart and Percy Gaunt, Hamilton Gordon, NY.

Mary Belle 1895, W.M. Joseph and Louis MacEnvoy, Ditson & Co., NY.

Ridin' on de Golden Bike 1895, Dave Reed Jr., M. Witmark & Sons, NY.

Ben Hur March 1896, Bell and Cody, Central Cycle Mfg. Co., Indianapolis.

The Bicycle Girl 1896, F.S. Howe, J.E. Ditson & Co., Philadelphia.

Brooklyn Bicycle Club March 1896, W.J. McIntyre, G.A. Kornder, Brooklyn.

Century Run 1896, Chas. D. Blake, Oliver Ditson Co., Boston.

The Cyclist March 1896, R.E. Wagner, Cundy Music Co., Boston.

The Cycle Queen 1896, T.P. Brooke, John Church Co., NY.

The Cycle King 1896, Al. Kuhn, John Church Co., NY.

Give Me the Girls That Ride a Wheel 1896, Donoghue, Schaller.

L.A.W. March 1896, W.H. Hosmer, Ford and Styles, Lynn, MA.

L.A.W. Waltz 1896, C.E. Vandersloot Music Co., NY.

My Wheel Napoleon 1896, H.S. Bott and J.C. Beckel, Bonanza Music Publishing, Philadelphia.

New York and Coney Island Cycle March 1896, E.T. Paull Music, NY.

The Scorcher 1896, Hayes and Hayes, NY.

The Southern Wheelmen's March 1896, Voges and Stoddard, Werlein, New Orleans.

Wheeling Together 1896, A. Craig and Quinn, El Dorado Cycle Co., Chicago.

Wheeling Waltz Song 1896, H. Wakefield Smith, H.W. Smith, Buffalo.

Bang Bang, Bang Went the Rubber Tire 1897, Connor, F.A. Mills, California.

Bicycle Bell 1897, John C. Gabler, Wm. A. Pond, NY.

Bicycle Race Galop 1897, Eduard Holst, McKinley Music Co., NY.

The Crackerjack March 1897, John C. Schuler, Buffalo.

The Cyclists' National Grand March and Two Step 1897, George Maywood, Imperial Music Co., NY.

The L.A.W. Scorcher 1897, George Rosey, Jos. W. Stern & Co., NY.

The Merry Cycle Girl 1897, Cleaver and Reifsnyder, Zabel Worley, Philadelphia.

Queen of the Bicycle Girls 1897, Gardner and Langey, Press of Philadelphia.

When the Boys and Girls Go Wheeling 1897, Browne and Coleman, NY.

The Roof Garden Cycle Party 1897, S.B. Alexander, M. Witmark, NY.

On the Boulevard 1897, Joseph E. Howard, Chas. K. Harris, NY.

Cyclist's March 1898, E.B. Kursheedt, I. Prager, NY.

Mary Ellen Simpkin's Bike 1898, Abbott and Norman, T.B. Harms & Co., NY.

The Pretty Little Scorcher 1898, George Rosey and Dave Reed Jr., Jos. W. Stern, NY.

The Wench That Rides a Wheel 1899, Moody and Grabbe, Grabbe Music Publishing, Davenport.

Wheelman's Song 1899, E.S. Neil, G.C. Shepard Co., Winchester, VA.

American Wheelmen's March 1899, T.W. Erwin, J.F. Bellois, Philadelphia.

Cycling Song 1901, Rolleston and Barett, University Song Book.

Back in Those Bicycle Days 1934, Allan and Manoloff, M.M. Cole Publishing, Chicago.

Pedal Your Blues Away 1936, Wells, Griffin and Miller, NY. Performed by R. Crumb and the Cheap Suit Serenaders, *Singing in the Bathtub* (1992) Shanachi Records, vaudeville.

Sing a Song of Safety 1937, Gerald Marks, Irving Caesar, NY.

Delightfully Dangerous, Fun in the Sun, and **Rollin' Down the Road** 1944, music Walter Kent, lyrics Kim Gannon, dir. George Dobbs, *Song of the Open Road*, United Artists, soundtrack.

My Bicycle Girl 1940, Hammerstein and Schwartz, Chappell Music Co., NY.

Rolleo Rolling Along (The Bicycle Song) 1940s, Harry Tobias, Don Reid, and Henry Tobias, *The Merry Macs*, Decca Records.

Bicycle Boogie 1952, Bob Gaddy & Friends (Sonny Terry, Brownie McGhee), *Bicycle Boogie*, Moonshine Records, NY, jazz.

Bicycle Tillie 1953, The Swallows, King Records, OH, *Dearest* (1992) rhythm and blues, 2:37.

Bike Up The Strand-Utter Chaos 1956 (Gerry Muligan) Gerry Mulligan Quartet, *At Storyville* (1990) Blue Note Records, jazz, 6:20.

Pedal Pushin' Papa 1957, Billy Ward and his Dominos, *Billy Ward and his Dominos, with Clyde McPhatter*, King Records, OH, rhythm and blues.

Pink Pedal Pushers 1958 Carl Perkins, *Jive after 5: The Best of Carl Perkins*, Columbia Records, pop-rock.

La Bicicletta 1960s, Gino Maringola, E. Rossi & Co., NY, Azzuro-Phonotype Record #21, cover art.

La Bicicletta N. 2 1960s, Gino Maringola, Matteo Savatore, Phonotype Record #37, cover art.

Bicycle Riding Mama 1960s, Roosevelt Sykes, Victoria Spivey, Brooklyn, NY, blues.

Chante Tour de France 1960s, Anonymus, France.

Rockin' Bicycle 1960-62, Fats Domino, *They Call Me The Fat Man* (1991) Imperial-EMI Records, 2:07.

Fudgecycle Built For Four 1962, Bill Evans, *Interplay Session*.

Tandem 1962, Merrell Kankhauser, Anthony Music, The Impacts, *Wipe Out* (1988) Ocean Records.

The Bicycle Song 1964, Hugh Martin & Timothy Gray, Cromwell Music. Performed by Beatrice Little & Ensemble, *High Spirits*, Broadway Cast Production, soundtrack, cover art.

Bike Ride and **Celesta Theme - Piccolo Bike Ride** 1965, Meyer Kupferman, General Music, *Hallelujah The Hills*, Fontana Records, soundtrack, 1:20 and :40.

Pushbike Song 1960s, Idris & Evan Jones, Right Angle Music, *The Mixtures*, June Prod., Austin TX, Sire Polydor, pop-rock, 45rpm, 2:27.

England Swings and **You Can't Roller Skate in a Buffalo Herd** 1965, Roger Miller, Tree Publishing, *Golden Hits*, Smash Records, PolyGram, country.

Ferris Wheel 1966, Donovan, *Sunshine Superman*, Epic Records, pop-rock.

Mr. I. Magination Meets Billy on a Bike and Rip Van Winkle 1966, Paul Tripp, Ray Carter, Musicor, children's.

Something Happened to Me Yesterday (finale) 1966, Mick Jagger, Rolling Stones, *Between The Buttons*, London Records.

Bicycle Rider and **Heroes and Villians** 1966-67, Brian Wilson, The Beach Boys, *Good Vibrations: Smile* (1990), *Alive and Smiling* (1990), *30 Years of Beach Boys* (1993) Sphinx Records, pop-rock.

The Bicycles (La Bicyclettes) 1967, Georges Delerue, Unart Music, *The King of Hearts*, United Artists, instrumental soundtrack, 1:10.

Bicycle Song (Soon Now) 1967, R. Kimmel and K. Edwards, Fourth Landing Music Co., The Stone Poneys, *The Stone Poneys Featuring Linda Ronstadt*, pop-rock, 1:53, cover art.

Bike and **The Scarecrow** 1967, Syd Barrett, Pink Floyd, *The Piper at the Gates of Dawn*, Tower UK, and *Relics*, Capitol/EMI, pop-rock.

My White Bicycle 1967, Hopkins and Burgess, Performed by: Tomorrow, *Tomorrow* (1967) See For Miles Records, and *History of British Rock, Vol. 8* (1991) Rhino Records, Oldies, rock. Nazareth, *Classics Volume 16* (1977) A&M Records, metal.

Trip on an Orange Bicycle 1967, Cox and Malone, Orange Bicycle, *Take a Trip on an Orange Bicycle*, Moby Music Ltd.

My Bicycle 1968-9, The Baroques, Chess Records.

The Bicycle Ride (check date), Pelican Daughters, Australia, compilation, *Fifty Years of Sunshine* (1993).

On A Bicycle Built For Joy 1969, Burt Bacharach and Hal David, Blue Seas Music, Vocal by B.J. Thomas, *Butch Cassidy & The Sundance Kid*, A&M Records, soundtrack, 3:08.

Uninhibited Bicycle Rider 1969, Two Mule Pike.

My Friend 1970, Jimi Hendrix, Arch Music, NY, *The Cry of Love*, pop-rock.

Bicycle Annie 1971, Drew Thomason, Combine Music, Lonnie Mack, *The Hills of Indiana*, Elektra Records, country.

Had Me a Real Good Time 1971, R. Wood, R. Stewart, R. Lane, Faces, *Long Player*, Warner Bros., pop-rock, 5:50.

Tour de France 1971, Performed by various artists, *Giants of Jazz-In Berlin '71*, Verve Records, jazz.

Busted Bicycle 1972, Leo Kottke, Overdrive Music, *6 & 12 String Guitars*, Takoma Records and *My Feet are Smiling* Columbia Records, instrumental.

Rider on the Wheel and **Ride** 1972, Nick Drake, Warlock Music, *Fruit Tree: The Complete Recorded Works* (1979) Island Records, pop-rock.

New York City 1972, John Lennon and Yoko Ono, Plastic Ono Band with Elephants Memory and Invisible Strings, *Sometime in New York City* (1972) Apple Records, pop-rock.

The Universal Unicycle Show (Pedal It) 1972, Bruce Haack, *Captain Entropy*, Dimension 5, children's.

Les Bicyclettes des Belsize L. Reed, B. Mason (Ithier). Performed by Marielle Mathieu, *Marielle Mathieu* (1970s) Capitol Records, pop vocal. Engelbert Humperdinck, *All of Me - In Concert*, Epic Records, and *Greatest Hits*, Polydor, and *His Greatest Hits* (1974) London Records, pop vocal.

Buckets of Rain 1974, Bob Dylan, *Blood on the Tracks*, Columbia Records, pop-rock.

Sidewalk Surfin' 1974, Brian Wilson and R. Christian, Performed by Jan Berry & Dean Torrence, *Gotta Take That One Last Ride*, Irving Music, pop-rock.

Ten Speed Bike 1974, Bob Hodge and Gary Shider, Southfield Music, Catfish Hodge, *Dinosaurs and Alleycats*, Eastbound Records, 2:45.

Two On A Bicycle and **Ridin' His Bike** 1974, Kay Swift, *Fine and Dandy: The Music of Kay Swift* (1975) Mark 56 Records, soundtrack.

The Pink Chiffon Tricycle Queen 1976, William Ackerman, *In Search of the Turtle's Navel*, Windham Hill Records, new age.

Handlebars 1977, UK, The Desperate Bicycles, Office Music, Refill Records, 45s.

La Bicyclette P. Barouh and F. Lai, Saravah Music. Performed by Yves Montand, *La Bicyclette*, *Master Series*, *Olympia "81"* (1981) Philips, pop vocal.

The Anthem (of the Common Wheel), Army Song, Cocktail Song, Cowboy Song (Old Bob), Daisy Bell (Dacre, 1892), **Music Hall Song (Salome Danced), Parlour Song (Song of the Spokes),** and **Spinning Song** [words by Madelyne Bridges], from *Spokesong* 1975, Lyrics by Stewart Parker, Music by Jimmy Kennedy, Irish & Evergreen, Dublin, musical theater.

Bicycle Race and **Fat Bottom Girls** 1978, Freddy Mercury and Brian May, Beechwood Music, Queen, *Jazz*, Elektra Records, pop-rock.

The Bicycle Race 1979, *A Little Romance*, Varese Sarabande, soundtrack.

In Bicicletta 1979, Umberto Balsamo, *Balla*, Phonogram, 4:30.

I Wish I Was The Saddle of a Schoolgirl's

Bicycle 1979, Samson, *Survivors*, Grand Slam, metal.

Night Rider 1979, Tim Weisberg, Elusive Sounds Music, *Night Rider*.

Pedalpusher 1979, Mick Goodrick, *In Pas(s)ing*, ECM Records, jazz.

The Fish Needs a Bike 1981, Milton and Creese, Blackhill Music, *Blurt*, Armageddon Records, 45 rpm.

Broken Bicycles 1982, Tom Waits, *One From The Heart*, CBS Records/Columbia, soundtrack. Live performance, *Italian Dream* (1986). Performed by Maura O'Connell, *A Real Life Story*, Warner Brothers Records.

Flying and **Over the Moon** 1982, John Williams, *E.T. The Extraterrestrial*, MCA Records, soundtrack, 3:20 and 2:06.

Brothers on Wheels 1983, Stewart Copeland, *Rumble Fish*, A&M Records, soundtrack.

Peeni-Walli (Fireflies) 1983, Eek-A-Mouse, *Assassinator*, RAS Records, reggae.

Tour de France 1983, Kraftwerk, Hutter/Schneider/Bartos/Schmitt, No Hassel Music, 6:45.

E.T. (The Bicycle Chase) 1984, Erich Kunzel/Cinninati Pops, *Star Tracks*, Telarc Records, easy.

Bike Ride To The Moon 1985, Dukes of Stratosphear, Virgin Records, *Psonic Sunspot* and *Chips From the Chocolate Fireball*, Geffen Records, pop-rock.

Bicycle Ride 1985, Music by Maurice Jarre, Performed by Royal Philharmonic Orchestra, *A Passage to India*, Capitol/EMI Records, soundtrack, 3:25.

Overture/The Big Race, Park Ride, Stolen Bike, Clown Dream, Studio Chase, Finish 1985, Danny Elfman, *Pee Wee's Big Adventure*, Varese Sarabande Records, soundtrack, cover art.

Nice Bike 1985, Ry Cooder, Ensign Music, *Blue City* (1986) Warner Bros. Records, Paramount Pictures, soundtrack, 1:37.

Pedals 1985, Emily Remler, Edson Publishing, *Catwalk*, Concord Music.

Bicycle 1986-88, M. Brody, Nobody's Business, *Life Among the Ruins*.

New Bicycle Hornpipe 1986, Nancy Blake, Nannor Music, *The Norman & Nancy Blake Compact Disc*, Ronder Records, 2:32.

Pervertimento for Bagpipes, Bicycle, and Balloons [S. 66] 1986, P.D.Q. Bach (Peter Schickele), Conducted by Jorge Mester, *P.D.Q. Bach at Carnegie Hall* (1987) Vanguard Records, Baroque spoof.

Quicksilver Lightning 1986, Music and lyrics by Giorgio Moroder and Dean Pitchford. Performed by Roger Daltrey, **One Summer Day/Dueling Bikes, Suite Streets,** and **Crash Landing** Composed by Tony Banks, *Quicksilver*, Atlantic Records, soundtrack.

Kick the Bike 1987, Ed Blocki, NTWK Publishing, Pretty Green, *Pretty Green*,

Nettwerk, hardcore.

Power of One 1988, Doug Prose, Earthsong Records, pop-rock.

Tour de France 1988 1988, John Tesh, Private Music, new music.

Travelon Gamelon 1988, Richard Lerman, *Music for Bicycle Orchestra*, Skip Blumberg Productions, New York, new music.

Bike Ride and **Country Bikin** 1988, Eric Clapton, E.C. Music-Warner Chappell, *Homeboy*, Virgin Records, soundtrack.

Bicycle Kid 1989, The Jazz Butcher, *Big Planet Scarey Planet*, Genius Records, pop-rock.

Bicycle Ride 1989, Toninho Horta, *Moonstone*, Verve Records, jazz, 4:35.

Bike Boy 1989, Deborah Harry and Chris Stein, Easy Air Music, *Def, Dumb And Blond* and *I Want That Man*, Sire Records, pop-rock.

Living Bicycle 1989, Hank Roberts, Jazz and Music Today, Arcado, *String Trio*, Verve Records and JTM Prod., jazz, 5:49.

Bicyclette 1990, Stephane Grappelli, *May Fools*, CBS Records, soundtrack, 3:36.

The Bicycle 1990, *Stanley & Iris*, Varese Sarabande Records, soundtrack, 3:07.

Bycycle 1990, Michael Greenberg, Muestro Subgum and the Whole, *Hot Ol' Wadda*, Chicago, pop-rock.

Chinese Song and **Cycling is Fun** 1990, Shonen Knife, *Shonen Knife*, Gasatanka-Giant Records, pop-rock.

G. On A Bike 1990, *Welcome Home Roxy Carmichael*, Varese Sarabande Records, MGM, soundtrack.

Introduction 1990, Brian Huskey, Chris Longworth, and Mitchell McGirt, Bicycle Face, *Bicycle Face*, Moist Records, NC, *Trust and Obey* (1992).

Tour de France: The Early Years (1990) John Tesh, Private Music, pop.

Three Bikes in the Sky 1990, Edgar Froese, Paul Haslinger and Jerome Froese, Tadream Music, Tangerine Dream, *Melrose*, Private Music, pop-rock, 5:58.

Bicycle 1991, Betty, BettyRulers Music, *Hello Betty!*, DDR, pop-rock.

Bicycling to Afghanistan 1991, Robert Fripp and League of Crafty Guitars, *Show of Hands*, new music.

Cycling 1991, Sadao Watanabe, *Sweet Deal*, Elektra/Asylum Records, jazz.

Two Pedals 1991, Harry Sheppard, *This-A-Way That-A-Way*, Justice Records.

Riding My Bike 1991, Lisa Germano, *On The Way Down From The Moon Palace*, Major Bill.

This Park is Your Park 1991, Adapted by Charles Buchholtz, Auto-Free Central Park, NYC.

Tryin' to Throw Your Arms Around the World 1991, U2, *Achtung Baby*, Island Records, pop-rock.

The Acoustic Motorbike 1992, Luka Bloom, WB Music, *The Acoustic Motorbike*, Reprise

Records, 4:14.

Bicycle 1992, Chris Gross, Baby Cole Music-Varry White Music, Masters of Reality, *Sunrise on the Sufferbus*, :46.

Bicycle Bells (2 examples) 1992, *The Complete Sound Effects Library*, Sound Effects Dept., Sony Music.

Bicycle Blues - Bob Gaddy and his Al 1992, Bob Gaddy, *Let Him Have It*, Virgin, soundtrack.

Bicycle Man (acappella) 1992, John Matthews and Lea Rosenblatt, *Black Coffee*, NY, folk.

The Bike Chase 1993, *Son of The Pink Panther*, Milan Compact Discs, soundtrack.

Bike (Sid Sings Syd) and **Bike (Son of Sid Mix)** 1992, Fortran 5, *Blues*, Elektra/Asylum Records, pop-rock.

Dirt Rag 1992, System 319, *Sandra*, Inconsistent Records, pop-rock.

Red Paint 1992, N. Cherry, C. Very, Virgin Songs, Neneh Cherry, *Homebrew*, Circa Records, pop-rock, 5:27.

Ride My Bike 1992, Tom Paxton, *Suzy is a Rocker* Sony Music, 2:46.

Tricycle 1992, Jeanette Katt, Peer International, *Pink Mischief*, A&M Records, pop-rock, 3:56.

Tricycle With Bell 1992, *The Complete Sound Effects Library*, Sound Effects Dept., Sony Music.

Bicycle Girls 1993, God Is My Co-Pilot, *Tight Like Fist: Live Recording*, Knitting Factory Works, hardcore.

Bike Tights 1993, Rob Base & D.J. E-Z Rock, *Break of Dawn*, Warlock Records, rap.

Transportation Alternative 1993, Josef Pelletier, *ATB*, NY, pop-rock.

White Bicycle 1993, Nothing Painted Blue, *Power Trips Down Lover's Lane*, Shimmy-Disc.

Velodrome 1994, Richard H. Kirk, *Virtual State*, TVT.

Bicycles, Roller Skates & You Archies, *The Archies 20 Greatest Hits*, Black Tulip.

The Bicycle Wreck n.d. Geezinslaw Brothers, *The Kooky World of the Geezinslaw Brothers*, Columbia.

Blue Bicycle n.d., Speed The Plough, *Speed The Plough*, East Side Digital.

I'm in Love with My Little Red Tricycle n.d., Napoleon XIV, *They're Coming To Take Me Away, Ha-Ha*, Rhino Records.

Lady On A Bicycle Kippington Lodge, Parlophone.

Pedalin' n.d., Coleman Hawkins, Eddie Davis, *Night Hawk*, Original Jazz Classics.

Six Studies of Francis Bacon: no. 5, George and the Bicycle n.d., Gerard Schurmann (1929-), *The Special Sound of Chandos*, Chandos, classical.

Tricycle n.d., Flim & The BB's, *Tricycle (Gold Disc)*, Digital Music Products, jazz.

Unicycle Silencer n.d., Three Mile Pilot, *Na Vucca Do Lupu*, Headhunter Records.

Velocipedes n.d., Hans Christian Lumbye (1810-74), *The Strauss of the North, Vol. II / Peter Guth*, Unicorn Records, dkp 9143, classical.

COMEDY

Scrooge 1960, Lord Buckley, *Blowing His Mind (And Yours Too)*, Demon Records.

The Preacher and the Bicycle Doc Watson, *Doc Watson on Stage* (1970, Vanguard Records, New York, country.

Born on a Bike 1984, Fred Barton, *Miss Gulch Returns* (1986) Gulch Mania Productions, NY.

The Bicycling Comedian 1987-, Tom Synders, Performed on Live with Regis and Kathie Lee (ABC-TV) and International Comedy Festival, Montreal, 1992. Cycles to gigs, stand-up comedy with slide show.

Joggers & Bicycles 1988, George Carlin, *What Am I Doing In New Jersey?*, Atlantic Records, satire.

THEATER

All That Fall 1957, by Samuel Beckett.

Fausto 1992, Italian opera based on life of Fausto Coppi.

Fish Riding Bikes 1983, by Claire Luckman, Woman's Interart Center, New York.

The Hairy Ape 1922, by Eugene O'Neill.

Hellzapoppin 1937, by Olsen and Johnson, with unicyclist Walter Nilsson, 1,404 Broadway performances.

High Spirits 1964 dir. Noel Coward, with Beatrice Lillie.

Key Exchange 1981, by Kevin Wade.

La Bicicletas Son Para El Verano 1980, by Fernando Fernán Gómez.

Shimada 1992, by Jill Shearer.

Spokesong or, The Common Wheel 1975, by Stewart Parker, music Jimmy Kennedy.

Upside-Down on the Handlebars 1980, by Leslie Weiner, Open Space Theater Experiment.

DANCE

Bicycle Shop Dancers dir. Peg Hill.

Criterium 1990, by Janet Rowthorn, Dance based on bicycle racing.

The Unanswered Question 1989, by Eliot Feld, music Charles Ives.

Dinner Dance 1991, UK, prod. The Kosh, by Sian Williams, dir. Michael Merwitzer.

CINEMA

Air Raid Wardens 1943, USA, dir. Edward Sedgwick, with Stan Laurel, Oliver Hardy.

Amarcord 1974, Italy, dir. Federico Fellini.

American Flyers 1985, USA, by Steve Tesich, dir. John Badham, with Kevin Costner, David Grant, Rae Dawn Chong, Alexandra Paul, Janice Rule.

American Gigolo 1980, USA, dir. Paul Schrader, with Richard Gere, Lauren Hutton.

And Soon the Darkness 1971.

Arabesque with Gregory Peck.

Around the World in 80 Days.

The Assault 1986, Holland, based on Harry Mulisch novel, by Gerard Soeteman, dir. Fons Rademakers, with Derek De Lint, Marc Van Uchelen, Monique Van De Ven, John Kraaykamp. Repercussions of bicycle assault in World War II. Academy Award Best Foreign Picture.

The Atomic Cafe 1985, dir. Kevin Rafferty, Jayne Loader, Pierce Rafferty.

The Bank Dick 1940, by Mahatma Kane Jeeves (W.C. Fields), dir. Edward Cline, with W.C. Fields. Getaway scene.

The Barber Shop 1933, prod. Mack Sennett, by W.C. Fields, dir. Arthur Ripley.

La Bicicletas Son Para El Verano (Bicycles Are For Summer) 1984, Spain, based on Fernando Fernán Gómez play, by Salvador Maldonado, dir. Jaime Chávarri, with Amparo Soler Leal, Agustín González, Vistoria Abril. Coming of age during Spanish Civil War.

Biciklisti (The Cyclist) 1970, Yugoslavia, dir. Purisa Djordjevic.

The Bicycle Kingdom 1984, China, China Today, No. 8405, Central Newsreel and Documentary Film Studio of the People's Republic of China, dir. Liu Yufeng, camera Liu Yongen, 18 min.

The Bicycle Racer Columbia.

The Big Store 1941, dir. Charles Reisner, by Sid Kuller, Hal Finberg, Ray Golden, with Groucho, Chico, and Harpo Marx, Margaret Dumont.

Birdy 1984, USA, dir. Alan Parker, with Matthew Modine, Nicolas Cage. Bird-obsessed boy uses bicycle to fly.

Bizarre, Bizarre 1937, dir. Marcel Carné, by Jacques Prévert, with Jean-Louis Barrault, Michel Simon.

Blue City 1986, USA, Paramount.

BMX Bandits (1980s) Australia.

A Boy, a Girl and a Bike England, love triangle.

Brainstorm 1983, USA, dir. Douglas Trumbull, with Christopher Walken, Natalie Wood, Louise Fletcher. Michael Brace (Walken) rides hi-tech recumbent bike (Avatar 2000) wearing helmet capable of perceptual and emotional communication.

Breaking Away 1979, USA, dir. Peter Yates, by Steve Tesich, with Dennis Christopher, Dennis Quaid, Dan Stern, Paul Dooley, Barbara Barrie.

Butch Cassidy and the Sundance Kid 1969, USA, dir. George Roy Hill, with Paul Newman, Robert Redford, Katherine Ross. Wild West bike ride accompanied by Burt Bacharach tune.

Les Choses de la Vie 1976, France, dir. Claude Saudet, based on Paul Guimard novel, by Jean-Loup Dabadie, Claude Saudet, with Romy Schneider, Michel Piccoli, Lea Massari.

Creator

Dal Polo All'Equatore (From the Pole to the Equator) 1986, Italy, dirs. Yervant Gianikan and Angela Ricci Lucchi. Assemblage of 1900s footage, with military bicycles.

Death of a Cyclist Spain, dir. J.A. Bardem.

Doll with Millions 1928, USSR, dir. S. Komarov, sets Alexander Rodchenko. Women travels to Moscow for inheritance, poster by Boris Yukov.

E.T. The Extra Terrestrial 1982, USA, dir. Steven Spielberg, by Melissa Mathison, designer Carlo Rimbaldi, with Henry Thomas, Robert MacNaughton, Dee Wallace, Drew Barrymore.

Erendira 1983, Mexico, dir. Ruy Guerra, by Gabriel Garcia Marquez, with nomadic bicycling photographer.

La Femme/Enfant France, with Klaus Kinski.

The Flight of the Gossamer Condor 1979, USA, National Geographic, dir. Ben Shedd, with Paul MacCready. Academy Award documentary.

The Gang That Couldn't Shoot Straight 1971, MGM, with Robert De Niro as Italian cyclist.

The General 1926, USA, Silent, dirs. Buster Keaton and Clyde Bruckman, with Buster Keaton, Marian Mack, Glenn Cavender, Jim Farley.

The Great Escape USA, with James Coburn.

The Great Muppet Caper

Gizmo! 1972, USA, dir. Howard Smith. Assemblage of inventions.

Hallelujah the Hills 1965, USA, dir. Adolfas Mekas.

Hard Days Night 1964, UK, with The Beatles.

Heaven Made USA, with Tom Hanks high-wheeling.

Help! 1965, UK, with The Beatles. Biking in the Bahamas.

Henry and June 1990, based on Anais Nin memoires. Henry Miller in Paris.

The History of Mr. Polly 1949, with John Mills.

The Human Comedy 1943, USA, dir. Clarence Brown, based on William Saroyan novel, by Howard Estabrook, with Mickey Rooney, Frank Morgan, James Craig, Jack Jenkins. Homer Macauley (Rooney) as telegram bike messenger during World War II.

I Am the Chess 1983, with Robert Wagner.

In the Good Old Summertime 1949, with Van Johnson, Buster Keaton. Set in 1890.

Isn't it Romantic 1948, USA, Paramount.

It'll Have Blinking Eyes And A Moving Mouth 1993, China Blue, Hobart Brown's Kinetic Sculpture Race, 88 min.

It's a Gift 1934, USA, dir. Norman McLeod, by Charles Bogle (W.C. Fields), with W.C. Fields. Carl La Fong scene, "I suppose if I live to two-hundred, I'll get a velocipede."

It's a Mad, Mad, Mad World

Jour de Fête 1949, France, by Jacques Tati, Henri Marquet, and René Wheeler, with Jacques Tati, Guy Decomble, Santa Relli, Maine Vallee.

Jules and Jim 1961, France, dir. Francois Truffault, with Jeanne Moreau, Oskar Werner.

Juliet of the Spirits 1965, Italy, dir. Federico Fellini, with Giullieta Masina, Mario Pizu.

The King of Hearts 1967, US, United Artist.

Key Exchange 1985, USA, dir. Barnet Kellman, based on Kevin Wade play, with Brooke Adams,

Ben Masters, Daniel Sterns, Danny Aiello, Tony Roberts.

Kristove roky (Crucial Years) 1967, Czechoslovakia, dir. Juraj Jakubisko.

Kühle Wampe Oder wem gehört Die Welt? (Who does the World Belong To?) 1932, Germany, by Bertolt Brecht.

Laudri di Bicicletta (The Bicycle Thief) 1948, Italy, dir. Vittorio De Sica, based on Luigi Bartolini novel, by Cesare Zavattini, music Alessandro Cicognini, with Lamberto Maggiorani, Lianella Carell, Enzo Staiola, Vittorio Antonucci.

The Life of an American Policeman 1905, USA, prod. Edwin S. Porter.

Little Lord Fauntleroy with Freddie Bartholomew.

Lonely Guy with Steve Martin, poster art.

Made in America 1993, with Whoopi Goldberg.

The Magic Bicycle 1948, dir. Silik Sternfeld, with Roman Polanski.

The Making of Butch Cassidy and the Sundance Kid 1969, dir. Robert Crawford.

Mary Poppins

May Fools 1990, USA.

Mister Johnson 1991, USA, dir. Bruce Beresford, with Maynard Eziashi, Pierce Brosnan, Edward Woodward.

Le Mistons 1957, France, dir. Francois Truffault. Schoolboys on bikes.

Mon Uncle 1958, France, by Jacques Tati.

The Muppet Movie 1979, USA, prod. Jim Henson. Kermit the Frog rides a bike.

Nostalghia 1980, USSR, dir. Andrew Tarkowski. Exercycle.

Olympia 1938, Germany, dir. Leni Riefenstahl. 1936 Berlin Olympics.

On Any Sunday 1969, USA, with Steve McQueen. BMX racing.

One From the Heart 1982, USA, Columbia.

Our Hospitality 1923, USA, Silent, Metro Pictures, dirs. Buster Keaton and Jack Blystone, by Clyde Bruckman, Joseph Mitchell, Jean Havez, with Buster Keaton. Keaton rides swift-walker (from Smithsonian Collection).

Out of the Blue 1980, with Linda Manz.

A Passage to India UK, dir. David Lean, based on E.M. Forester novel, with Peggy Ashcroft, Judy Davis, James Fox.

Pee-Wee's Big Adventure 1985, USA, dir. Tim Burton, by Phil Hartman, Paul Rubens, Michael Varhol, with Pee-Wee Herman, Elizabeth Daily, Mark Holton.

Poppy 1936, USA, dir. A. Edward Sutherland, with Rochelle Hudson, W.C. Fields. Prof. Eustace P. McGargle (Fields) with high-wheeler.

Pour un Maillot Jaune 1965, France, dir. Claude Lelouche. Tour de France.

Po_egnania (Farewells) 1958, Poland, dir. Wojciech Has.

The Quest (check), with Henry Thomas. Rail bike.

Quicksilver 1986, USA, by Tom Donnelly, with

Kevin Bacon. Bike messengers.

The Quiet Man 1952, USA, dir. John Ford, based on Maurice Walsh story, by Frank Nugent, with John Wayne, Maureen O'Hara. Lovers on tandem.

La Ronde 1950, France, dir. Max Ophuls. Bicycle carousel ride.

Rower (The Bike) 1956, Poland, dir. Roman Polanski. Student film.

Rush It (check) USA. Bike messengers.

Les Saisons Quatre à Quatre (Four Seasons by Four) 1990, Swiss, Animation, prod. Studio GDS. Charcoal-drawn bicycles.

San Diego, I Love You 1944, dir. Reginal LeBorg.

She's Gotta Have It 1986, USA, by Spike Lee, with Tracy Camilla Johns, Redmond Hicks, John Terrell, Spike Lee.

The Shining with Jack Nicholson. Bike in crazed vision.

Sing as We Go with Gracie Fields.

Six-Day Bicycle Rider 1934, USA, First National Pictures, dir. Lloyd Bacon, by Earl Baldwin, with Joe E. Brown. SpeeDee messenger (Brown) wins sweetheart via Six-Day race.

Smiley 1957, with Ralph Richardson.

Some Like It Hot 1959, USA, dir. Billy Wilder, with Tony Curtis, Marilyn Monroe, Jack Lemmon, Joe E. Brown.

Song of the Open Road 1944, USA, prod. Charles R. Rogers, dir. S. Sylvan Simon, Cast: Jane Powell, Bonita Granville, W.C. Fields, Edgar Bergen, Charlie McCarthy, Sammy Kaye. Child movie star (Powell) cycles off to join young tomato pickers.

Son of the Pink Panther 1993, USA, MGM, dir. Blake Edwards, with Roberto Benigni, Jacques Clouseau Jr. crashes.

La Sortie des Usines Lumière à Lyon (Workers Leaving the Lumiere Factory) 1895, France, dir. Auguste and Louis Lumière. Early motion picture.

Sound of Music 1965, USA, dir. Robert Wise, with Julie Andrews, Christopher Plummer, Eleanor Parker, Richard Haydn, Peggy Wood, Norma Varden, Marni Nixon, Angela Cartwright. Maria (Andrews) and Trapp family cycling and singing in Austria.

Spirit of `76 1991, USA, RCA-Columbia.

Spokes 1992, Gay sex.

The Spy Who Came In From The Cold with Richard Burton.

Stanley and Iris 1990, USA, dir. Martin Ritt, based on Pat Barker novel *Union Street*, by Harriet Frank Jr. and Irving Ravetch, with Jane Fonda, Robert De Niro.

Star Trek IV: The Voyage Home 1985, USA, dir. Leonard Nimoy, with William Shatner, Leonard Nimoy, DeForest Kelley. Spock rides bike in San Francisco.

Stickers

Sunday's Children 1944, Sweden, dir. Daniel Bergman.

Take the Money and Run 1969, USA, dir. Woody Allen, by Woody Allen and Mickey Rose, narrator Jackson Beck, with Woody Allen, Janet Margolin, Marcel Hillaire. Virgil Starkwell (Allen) escapes prison on bicycle.

Tales That Witness Madness with Kim Novak.

10 1979, USA, dir. Blake Edwards, with Dudley Moore, Julie Andrews, Bo Derek. George Webber (Moore) buys $50 bike, overtakes bike race.

Till Marriage Do Us Part 1979.

2001: A Space Odyssey 1968, UK, MGM, dir. Stanley Kubrick, by Arthur C. Clarke and Stanley Kubrick, with Keir Dullea, Gary Lockwood, William Sylvester. HAL 9000 (Douglas Rain) sings "Daisy Bell."

Two Women 1960, Italy, dir. Vittorio De Sica, with Sophia Loren. Cyclist paratroopers in World War II.

Vicious Cycles 1967, USA, dirs. Chuck Manville and David Brain. Pedal-powered spoof of motorcycle gangs.

Vive Le Tour 1961, France, dir. Louis Malle. Tour de France.

Welcome Home Roxy Carmichael 1990, USA, MGM.

When Your Lover Leaves.

Wish You Were Here 1987, UK, dir. David Lean, with Emily Lloyd, Tom Bell.

Wizard of Oz 1932, USA, MGM, dir. Victor Fleming, based on L. Frank Baum novel, by Noel Langley, with Judy Garland, Margaret Hamilton, Frank Morgan. Bikes with Miss Gulch (hamilton) in Kansas and hurricane.

Women in Love 1969, dir. Ken Russell, based on D.H. Lawrence novel, with Alan Bates.

The Year My Voice Broke 1988, Australia, by John Duigan, with Neal Taylor, Loene Carman, Ben Mendelson.

TELEVISION

Bicycle 1991, UK, York Films, by David Taylor, BBC-PBS documentary, 120 minutes. Part 1) **Invention** History, Part 2) **Wheels of Change** Innovations, Part 3) **The Ultimate** Sport, Part 4) **The Business** Industry giants, Part 5) **Free Spirits** People, Part 6) **Vehicle for a Small Planet** Transport.

Bicycle Ride 1989, WNYC-TV, Jonathan Waldo, International Network for the Arts.

Bicycling 1989, ABC News, **20/20** series.

Big City Bike Messengers 1987, USA, National Geographic Explorer Series.

The Bike Show 1994, USA, Manhattan Cable, by Alan Lowe.

Cycling in Delft 1987, Holland, Dutch Ministry of Transport and Public Works, Municipality of Delft, prod. John Van der Kerkhof, 28 min.

Dan's Apartment 1991, USA, Manhattan Cable, interactive show with bike.

Donald Duck (check) Hewey, Dewey and Lewy

on bikes.

Double Rush 1995, USA, CBS, prod. Diane English, with Robert Pastorelli, sitcom in messenger company.

Ed Wynn Show 1956, USA, pedaling harmonium with Dinah Shore singing.

Fat Man on a Bicycle 1980s, BBC, with Tom Vernon, travel adventure.

Fat Man Goes Gaucho 1990, BBC, with Tom Vernon.

The Fire Next Time CBS mini-series, with HPVs.

Get A Life 1990, with Chris Elliott, crashes in title sequence.

Giligan's Island unknown episode, with pedal-power generator.

Hart to Hart unknown episode, Mrs. Hart's bicycle is sabotaged.

High-Tech-Spielzeug mit Muskelantrieb 1988, Germany, West 3 Production, dir. Ranga Yogeshwar, 48 min. Human-powered vehicles.

Icarus' Children 1978, BBC/WGBH-TV, **Nova** series, Shedd Productions, by Simon Campbell-Jones. Human-powered flight.

Laugh-In 1966, USA, with Arty Johnson, falling off tricycle.

Monty Python's Flying Circus UK, with Graham Chapman, John Cleese, Eric Idle, Terry Jones, Michael Palin, Terry Gillian. **Bicycle Repairman** 1969, mechanic as superman. **The Cycling Tour** 1969, surreal adventure. **Whither Canada?** 1969, Art history as Tour de France report.

The Prisoner with Patrick McGuiy.

Secrets of Speed 1994, ESPN, cycling episode.

Seinfeld 1992, NBC, sitcom with Kramer's green Klein mountain bike (fork backwards).

The Simpsons 1993, Homer becomes cyclist for drunk driving, rides into sunset.

Tracks of Glory: The Major Taylor Story 1992, Australia, with Phil Morris, Cameron Daddo. Pioneering black racing hero.

You Drive 1960s, USA, **Twilight Zone** series, bicycle hit and run.

Exit of Saigon, 1980s, PBS, **Vietnam: A Television History** series. Bike supply lines.

When Your Lover Leaves 1993, NBC, with Valerie Perrine. Discovers competitive cycling.

SPORT FILMS & VIDEOS

Awesome Sunday 1985, CWI Prod., 1985 CoreStates USPRO Championships, 30 min.

Awheel in Britain 1953, Tour of Britain.

Battle at Durango: The First Ever 1990 World Mountain Bike Championship 1991, New and Unique Videos, 60 min.

Bauer 1994, Canada, with Steve Bauer, professional cyclist.

The Bell Lap 1989, National Collegiate Cycling Championships, 30 min.

Beyond the Wall 1986, CWI Prod., 1986 CoreStates USPRO Championships, 26 min.

Bicycle Dancin' 1985, Edwards Films, 15 min.

Bicycle Racing USA 1983, Edwards Films, BMX to Ultra-marathons, 30 min.

Bicycles on Snow 1988, Mark Forman Productions, Alaska Iditabike race, 24 min.

Content to Win 1988, National Collegiate Cycling Championships, 60 min.

La Course En Tete 1975, FCV (Famous Cycling Videos), Eddy Merckx story, 110 min.

Cycle Isle 1959, Isle of Man Tourist Board.

Cycle Zone 1992, Mountain biking.

Cycling for Success 7-Eleven Team Fox Hills Video, 50 min.

Eurocycling-Motorola Team 1991, FCV, Inside story of pros, 90 min.

Exploding Mountain Bikes 1993.

Fat Video 1992, Fat Tire Journal, 75 min.

Gent-Wevelgem 1992 60 min.

Giro d'Italia 1981 Elexis, 150 min.

Giro d'Italia 1984 Elexis, 150 min.

Giro d'Italia 1993 Elexis, 90 min.

Hammer & Hell: The 1991 Tour Du Pont 90 min.

The Impossible Hour 1975, dir. Jorgen Leth, Ritter attempts to break Merckx's record, 48 min.

Iron Men 1978, TI-Raleigh Industries.

Kings of the Mountain 1993, MTB racing highlights, 70 min.

Lance Armstrong's Million Dollar Triple Crown 1993, US racing.

Lessons in Cycling 1991, by John Howard, 55 min.

Liege-Bastogne-Liege 1991 with Phil Liggett, FCV, 90 min.

Liege-Bastogne-Liege 1993 90 min.

Life Among the BMXers 1985, Edwards Films, 28 min.

Matt Hoffman: Head First 1992, BMX stunts, 60 min.

Mountain Bike Mania 1989, 46 min.

New Zamikaze 1990, Range of Light Prod., 1989 MTB World Championships, 65 min.

Off the Front: Not Over the Bars 1993, MTB tips, 24 min.

Paris-Roubaix 1990 with Phil Liggett, FCV, 98 min.

Paris-Roubaix 1991 with Phil Liggett, FCV, 90 min.

Paris-Roubaix 1992 90 min.

Paris-Roubaix 1993 90 min.

Psychling with John Marino McGraw-Hill, 1980 record ride across America.

A Race Apart 1962, Milk Race 1968, Milk Race 1976, Milk Marketing Board, Tours of Britain.

Racing to Nowhere 1968, Wembley Six-Day race.

Ride On 1992, Eddie Roman, BMX stunts, 60 min.

Rockhopper South 1989, Bear Mountain MTB, 46 min.

Sierra Durango 1986, John Dennis, 1986 NORBA Championships, 60 min.

60 Cycles 1965, Canada, Tour of St. Laurent.

Spinning Wheels 1952, British highlights.

Spring Classics 1983 Elexis, European road races, 60 min.

Stars and Watercarriers 1973, dir. Jorgen Leth, Giro d'Italia stage race, 90 min.

A Sunday in Hell 1976, dir. Jorgen Leth, classic Paris-Roubaix, 110 min.

Totally Wild 1990s, Mountain Biking.

Tour de France 1986 Sports on Video, 53 min.

Tour de France 1989 with Phil Liggett, FCV-Société du Tour, 94 min.

Tour de France 1990 with Phil Liggett, FCV, 102 min.

Tour de France 1991 FCV, 92 min.

Tour de France 1992 FCV, 122 min.

Tour de France 1993 FCV, 90 min.

Tour of Flanders 1992 FCV, 90 min.

Tour of Ireland 1987 FCV, 180 min.

Tour of Ireland 1991-92 FCV, 120 min.

Transcontinental Tandem Record Attempt 1987, Ultra-Cycling, with Lon Haldeman and Pete Penseyres, 90 min.

Tread: The Movie 1994, USA, by Bill Snider, Gonzo cyclists, 90 min.

Triathlon Training and Racing

23 Days in July 1980s, by Tim Grady, Phil Anderson in Tour de France, 50 min.

The Twilight Criteruim 1992, University of Georgia, 30 min.

Two Phat 1993, Fat Tire Journal, Jerry Martin, 75 min.

Ultimate Mountain Biking 1989, New and Unique Videos, music and animation, 60 min.

Up the League: The Percy Stallard Story 1960s, road racing in Britain.

Victims of Gravity 1993, Fat Tire Journal, Jerry Martin, 30 min.

World Championships 1982 Elexis, 47 min.

World Championships 1983 Elexis, 60 min.

World Championships 1989 FCV, 48 min.

World Championships 1990 FCV, 60 min.

World of Cycling (Volumes 1-8) 1980-87, ICL, Coors Classics, Moscow Olympics, World Championships, Pikes Peak, Cycleball, CoreStates USPRO Championships, 90 min each.

Zuperman: The 1992 Tour Du Pont with Jim McDonald, 90 min.

INSTRUCTION DOCUMENTARY

Ace of Cycling 1980, bike messenger.

Air Solution and Pollution Solution 1990, Tooker Gomberg, Sundance Coop, environmental transport, 21 min.

All About Bikes 1985, Step-by-Step Video, with national team mechanic, 150 min.

Anybody's Bicycle Video 1985, with Tom Cuthbertson, Do-It-Yourself Video, bike repair, 60 min.

Bicycle Maintenance and Repair 1982, Goldshall Video, 70 min.

Bicycle Safety Camp 1990, Injury Prevention Program, 25 min.

Bicycle Tripping with Tom Cuthbertson, Do-It-Yourself Videos, bike riding, 80 min.

Bikeman's Holiday 1989, San Francisco adventure.

Bikeways for Better Living 1977, Huffman Mfg. Co., 24 min.

The Boy and his Bicycle Instructional film with scriptbook.

Brakeless 1991, Zachary Coffin, "To all fixed wheel cyclists."

Build Your Own Bike Wheel 1985, Roy Straus, Bikonstruction, 60 min.

The Cardiac TransAmerica Express by Randy Ice, fourteen heart patients relay ride across America in 12 days.

The Complete Cylist with Davis Phinney and Connie Carpenter Lamar Home Video, 75 min.

Columbia Wins 1895, world's first commercial film.

Computer Dreams "Red's Dream" 1990, John Lasseter, Pixar.

Connections 1979, BBC, with James Burke.

Cycling: Repair, Correct Riding, Position & Safety 1990, United Bicycle Institute, 48 min.

Fast Motion! 1897, England, rapid tire repair.

Fifth, Park and Madison 1987, STR Video, dir. Dragan Ilic, NYC bike ban.

531 The Winner 1979, TI-Reynolds.

Frame Preparation: Campagnolo Tools New England Cycling Academy, 45 min.

Get Ready To Go Bicycle Touring! Bikecentennial, How to box your bike and pack your bags, 45 min.

The Great Mountain Biking Video 1990, New and Unique Videos.

I Like Bikes, But... 1978, General Motors Corp., 14 min.

L.L. Bean Guide to Bicycle Touring 1986, with Denis Coello, 80 min.

Lopsided Wheel 1971, Life Around Us series, visual essay on wheels.

Only One Road American Automobile Association Foundation for Traffic Safety, biking hazards, 26 min.

Paperboy 1986, and Paperboy II 1991, Nintendo video games.

Return of the Scorcher 1992, by Ted White, with George Bliss, cycling in China, Holland and USA, 28 min.

Ride 1976, McKinley Prod., 14 min.

Seattle's Bicycle Program Department of Engineering.

Self-Help Video for the Bicycle Enthusiast Bikeworks, 40 min.

Share the Road Community Transportation Services, Seattle, traffic safety PSAs.

Sport Cycling with Michael Shermer True North Productions, ultra-marathon cyclist, 40 min.

Sweet Lullaby 1993, Belgian-French, music video by Deep Forest with girl tricycling around the world.

Technology Continues the Tradition Shimano

Industrial Corp., history of the bicycle, 20 min.

Vermont Bicycle Toss Edwards Films, tossing old bikes, 9 min.

Way to Go! Bicycles in Cuba 1994, USA, Seven Generations Video, by Bruce Petschek.

Wheel Building and Tire Mounting New England Cycling Academy, 60 min.

FITNESS VIDEOS

Bikercize 1988, 38 min.

Competition I 1980s, Cycle Vision-Westcom, 56 min.

Grand Teton Tour Cycle Vision-Westcom, three 18-min. workouts in National Park, 75 min.

Hawaii-The Big Island Cycle Vision-Westcom, 75 min.

Sampler Bike Ride Relax Video, Beach scenes, 60 min.

San Francisco Tour Cycle Vision-Westcom, 75 min.

The Cycling Experience Consumer Vision. **California** 1987, 52 min. **Pacific Northwest** 1990, 45 min. **Western States** 1992, 30 min.

Vermont Autumn Tour Cycle Vision-Westcom, 75 min.

Videocycle with Mark Lang, touring National Parks.

Video Cycle tours and instruction with **Maui, San Francisco, Oregon, Vermont Autumn**, and **The Art and Science of Stationary Bicycling**, 75 min. each.

Yellowstone Tours I and II Cycle Vision-Westcom, 75 min. each.

POSTERS

Arthus, **Papillon Cycles**.

Behrmann and Bossard, **Schwalbe**, 1938.

Will Bradley, 1895, **Victor** series.

Leonetto Capiello, **Livingston Tires**, 1921.

CHAM (Amédeé Charles Henri de Noë), **Almanac pour Rire**, 1819.

Jules Chéret, **Cleveland Bicycles**, **L'Etendard Français**.

William Cumming, **Spokesong**, 1980, Seattle Reperatory Theatre.

Unknown, **Columbia Tube Mill and Hartford Rubber Works**, 1890s.

David Lance Goines, **Velo-Sport Berkeley**, 1970.

Eugène-Samuel Grasset, **Georges Richard Cycles**, 1897.

John Hassal, **Beeston Tires**.

Ludwig Hohlwein, **Torpedo**.

Witold Janowski, **Polish Bike**, 1972.

Ferdinand Lunel, **Rouxel & Dubois**.

Alphonse Mucha, **Waverley, Cycles Perfecta**.

Hiroshi Ohchi, **Miyata 70th Anniversary**, 1958.

PAL (Jean de Paleoloque), **Déese**, 1898, **Cycles Sirius**.

Maxfield Parrish, **Columbia**, 1896.

Saul Steinberg, exhibition, 1952.

L.W., **Cycles Gladiator**,

PHOTOGRAPHS

E. Alice Austen, **Messenger Boy by Wheel**, New York City, June 2, 1896.

Bill Brandt,

Manuel Alvarez Bravo, **Bicicletas en domingo**, 1963.

Henri Cartier-Bresson, **Hyères, France**, 1932.

Robert Daley, **Henry Anglade, Toulouse**, 1961.

Charles Dodgson (Lewis Carroll), **W.I. Dodgson**, c.1870.

Alfred Eisenstaedt, **Sports Palace, Berlin**, 1928.

Elliot Erwin, **Bike Stand, New York**, 1961.

Arlene Gottfried, **Man on Tricycle, Coney Island**, 1980.

Heinrich Heidersberger, **Berlin**, c.1930.

Helen Levitt, **Untitled**, 1961.

Jerome Liebling, Aperature monograph, retrospective cover.

Etienne Jules Marey, **Descente de bicyclette**, c.1890–95, chronophotograph.

Stephen Shames, **Bike Jump** n.d., Matrix.Louise Steinman, **Lents Passage** 1980.

Paul Strand, **The Family, Luzzara, Italy** 1953.

Unknown, **Macmillan on his velocipede** c.1845.

Unknown, **Willard Sawyer on his velocipede** c.1855.

Jost Wildbolz, **Photographis 81.**

ART WORKS

John Ahearn, **Jay With Bike** 1985, oil on fiberglass.

Karel Appel,

Francis Bacon, **Portrait of George Dyer** 1966, oil on canvas.

Jan Balet, **Tour de Paris** oil on canvas. **Orpheus & Eurydice** oil on canvas.

Joseph Beuys, **Is It About A Bicycle?** 1982, twelve chalkboards and bicycle.

Umberto Boccioni, **Dinamismo di un ciclista** (Dynamism of a Cyclist) 1913.

Botero, **Apotheosis of Ramon Hoyos** 1959, oil on canvas.

Dove Bradshaw, **Art Environment** 1990, bicycle wheel and doves.

Georges Braque, **La Bicyclette** 1951–52, oil and sand on canvas. **La Bicyclette** 1961–62, oil on canvas. **Mon Velo** 1945–60, oil on canvas.

Andre Breton, **Object of Symbolic Function** 1931, bicycle seat and bell.

Chris Burden, **Bicycle Piece** May 6–20 1970. **Death Valley Run** October 14 1976, faired moped.

Paul Cadmus, **Bicyclists** 1933.

Cesear (Baldaccini), **Compressed Bicycle** 1970.

Christo, **Bicyclette empaqueteé sur galeria de voiture** (Wrapped bicycle on car rack) 1962.

George Chruikshank, **Every Man on His Perch or Going to the Hobby Fair** 1819. **The (Hobby) Horse Dealer** 1819.

Joseph Cornell, **Untitled**, c.1930, collage.

Greg Curnoe, **Mariposa 10 Speed** 1973, National Gallery of Canada.

Currier and Ives, **The Velocipede** 1819, lithograph.

Cyclamen Cyclists 1971, Swansea Docks.

Salvador Dali, **Babaou** 1932. **Illumined Pleasures** 1929, oil and collage.

Honoré Daumier, **Mon Vélocipède! La Paix** 1868, print.

William de Kooning, **Woman on a Bicycle** 1952–53, oil on canvas.

Henri de Toulouse-Lautrec, **Aristide Bruant à bicyclette** 1892. **Cycle Mickael** 1896, lithograph. **Tristan Bernard at the Buffalo Velodrome** 1895. **Zimmerman et sa machine** 1894, lithograph.

Charles Demuth, **Acrobats** 1919, watercolor.

Oscar Dominguez, **Peregrinations of George Hugnet** 1935, toy objects.

Jean Dubuffet, **Bicyclette** 1972, marker. **Cycliste** 1944, gouache. **Cycliste dans un paysage tou-flou** 1943, oil on canvas.

Marcel Duchamp, **Roue de la bicyclette** (Bicycle Wheel) 1913, bicycle wheel and stool. **Avoir l'apprenti dans le soliel** 1914, drawing. **Tu m'** 1918. **La Boite en Valise** 1941.

Alan Dworkowitz, **Bicycle Suite** 1978, graphite on paper.

Rita Edelman, **Abstrations of a bike trip**, acrylic.

Erro, **La famille français** 1967–70, acrylic.

Equipo Cronica, **Composition** 1972.

Max Ernst, **Deux jeunes filles se promentent à travers le ciel** 1929, collage. **The Gramineous Bicycle Garnished with bells the dappled fire damps and the echinoderms bending the spine to look for caresses** 1920, collage. **Vademecum mobile ihr seid gewarnt** 1920, collage.

Lyonel Feininger, **Die Radfahrer** 1912. **Draisinenfahrer** 1910.

John Fenton, **Open Road** print.

Howard Finster, **Bicycle Tower** 1970, Pennville, Georgia.

Natalie Goncharova, **The Cyclist** 1912–13.

Anthony Green, **The Skol Six-Day**.

Richard Hamilton, **Duchamp's Bicycle Wheel** 1964.

Keith Haring, **Cinelli Bicycle** 1989, acrylic on bicycle.

Henry Heerup, **On the road of life** 1960, linocut.

Dave Holladay, **Bicycle** 1990, Sustrans bike path, UK.

Winslow Homer, **The New Year** 1868, engraving.

Edward Hopper, **Meditation, 10 Miles from Home** 1899, ink and pencil. **French Six-Day Bicycle Rider** 1937, oil on canvas.

Michio Ihara, **Cyclelight: Cycle, ReCycle, LifeCycle** 1992, Boston, pedal-powered lights.

Robert Indiana, **Construction**.

Margia Kramer, **Progress (Memory)** 1983, installation, Whitney Museum, NY.

Shigeko Kubota, **Duchampiana: Bicycle Wheel** 1983, bicycle wheels with video.

Donald Landsman, **Starlight Express** 1990, painted metal.

Ferdinand Léger, **Les Belles Cyclistes** 1944. **La Belle Équipe** 1944. **Big Julie** 1945. **Les Loisirs-Hommage à David** 1948–49.

Ulf Linde, **Duchamp's Bicycle Wheel** 1961.

Aristide Maillol, **Le Jeune Cycliste** 1907–08, bronze.

Manjusri: Goddess of Wisdom lithograph.

Rene Magritte, **L'etat de grace (State of Grace)** 1959, oil on canvas.

Marisol, **The bicycle riders** 1962, painted wood with bicycles.

Jean Metzinger, **Au Vélodrome** 1914, oil and collage.

Sara Midda, **Juggler** 1983, Gallery Five, London.

Mary Milne, **The Ribbon** 1985, fabricollage.

Mizrachi, **The Peace Rider** 1987, painted polyester.

Lazlo Moholy-Nagy, **Der Radfahrer** 1919.

Claude Monet, **Jean Monet sur son Cheval Mechanique** 1872.

Janet Morton, **Knitted bicycle** 1992.

Bruce Nauman, **Untitled** print, Leo Castelli Gallery.

Claes Oldenburg, **Sculpture in the form of a bicycle saddle** 1977, ceramic.

Paramarenko, **U-Kontrol III** 1972, pedal-powered aircraft. **Umbilly I** 1976, pedal-powered aircraft.

Bruno Pasquier-Desvignes, **In Cyclo Melodia** 1992, sculptures with music by Richard Robbins. **Freewheeling** 1995, sculpture exhibit.

Frank Patterson.

Pablo Picasso, **Night Fishing at Antibes** 1939, oil on canvas. **Tête de Taureau** (Bull's Head) 1943, bronze. **Goat, Skull and Bottle** 1950, painted bronze. **Games and Reading** 1953, print. **Rape of the Sabines** 1962, oil on canvas.

José Guadalupe Posada, **La Bicicleta** 1900. **Cavaleras Cyclistas** 1900.

André Raffray, **Shadow of Duchamp's Bicycle Wheel** 1993, installation, Palazzo Grassi, Italy.

Robert Rauschenberg, **Early Egyptian series** 1973, bicycles with carton and sand. **Kitty Hawk** 1974, lithograph. **Bicycloids I-V** 1992-1993, bicycles and neon lights.

Man Ray, **Jeune fille à la bicyclette** 1950, aquatint.

William Roberts, **Bicycle Boys** 1939. **Les Routiers** n.d.

Ruth Scheuer, **Veils** 1989, tapestry.

Benjamin Schultze, **Migof-Fahrrad** 1975, found wire, fabric, and plastic.

George Segal, **Man on a Bicycle** 1961, plaster.

Ben Shahn, **Epoch** 1950, tempera. **Headstand on Tricycle** 1968, lithograph.

SITE, **Highway 86** Expo 86, Vancouver, British Columbia.

Eric and Deborah Staller, **Bubbleheads** 1988, quadruplet with lighted globes. **Octos** 1990, eight-person quadricycle.

Thomas Tegg, **Anti-Dandy Infantry** 1819.

Jean Tiguely, **Cyclograveur** 1960, pedal-powered

drawing machine. **Homage to New York** 1960, Museum of Modern Art, NY.

Ernest Trova, **Study: Falling Man (Wheelman)** 1965.

David True, **Journey** 1982, oil on linen.

Norman Tuck, **Conical Pendulum Clock** 1985.

Unknown, **Nigerian Cyclist with Headpiece** Carved wood. Newark Museum.

Andy Warhol, **Aids** 1980s.

Boyd Webb, **Elephant and bicycle** installation.

Timothy Woodman, **Tandem** 1978.

Andrew Wyeth, **Young America** 1950, tempera.

CYCLE MUSEUMS

American Bicycle and Cycling Museum Santa Fé NM, see exhibits 'Bout Bicycles...

Antique and Classic Bicycle Museum of America University of Michigan, Ann Arbor, MI.

Australian Gallery of Sport E. Melbourne, Victoria, Australia 3002.

Art of the Mountain Bike (1991) San Francisco

Batavus Museum Industrieweg, Heerenveen, Leeuwarden, NL.

Bicycle Culture Center Jitenshakaikan No. 3, 1-9-3 Akasaka 1-chome, Minato-ku, Tokyo 107, Japan.

Bicycle History Museum & Gift Shop 598 Main St. Old Boise, ID 83702 USA; Paul Niquette collection.

Bicycle Museum of America North Pier, 435 E. Illinois St., Chicago, IL 60611 USA. Curator: Jim Hurd. 50,000 items, valet bicycle parking. Formerly **Schwinn History Center** 217 North Jefferson St., Chicago.

Bicycles, Cars & Karts of Yesteryear Northborough, MA 01532 USA; Mobile trailer museum.

American Bicycle Association BMX Hall of Fame

Canberra Bicycle Museum Canberra Trademan's Union Club, 2 Badham St., Canberra, Australia; Old and unusual bikes.

Chapel of the Maddonna del Ghisallo Italy; Mecca for cycle racing memorabila in Catholic church.

Christchurch Tricycle Museum, UK.

Cycle Center 165-6, Daisen Nakamachi, Sakai City, Osaka 590, Japan; Bicycle history, manufacturing, and ecology.

Denmark Cykel Muscum Borgergade 10, DK 9620, Aalestrup, Denmark.

Deutsches Museum Museumsinsel, D-8000 Munich 22.

Deutsches Zweiradmuseum Urbanstrasse 11, D-7107 Neckarsulm, Baden-Wuerttenberg.

Exploratorium: Museum of Science, Art and Human Perception 3601 Lyon Street, San Francisco, CA 94123 USA; Hands-on cycling physics displays.

Franklin Institute 20th & Benjamin Franklin Parkway, Philadelphia, PA 19103 USA.

Greenfield Village & Ford Museum 20900 Oakwood Blvd., Dearborn, MI 48121 USA.

Het Wiel Hoopland 17, 2000 Antwerpen, Belgium. Over 300 bicycles.

Horsham Museum

Mountain Bike Hall of Fame and Museum (1988-) Crested Butte, CO 81224 USA.

Museum of Science and Industry 57th St. and Lakeshore Drive, Chicago, IL 60637 USA.

Musée de la Petite Reine 152 rue de la Draisienne, Namur, Belgium.

Museo Galbiati via Mameli 15, Brugherio, Milano, Italy.

Museum of Gianthood 20 Palmerston Park, Rathmines, Dublin, Ireland. Children's things.

Museum of Mankind Burlington Gardens, London, UK; Rickshaw Art from Bangladesh.

Museum of Sport and Bicycling 118 President Kennedy Ave., Paris, France.

Museum of Transportation 15 Newton St., Brookline, MA 02146 USA.

National Bicycle Center

National Bicycle Mueseum and Education Center, LAW, Baltimore, MD.

National Veteran Cycles Museum Belton House, Grantham, Lincolnshire NG32 2LW, UK.

National Cycle Museum Brayford Wharf North, Lincoln LN1 1YW, UK.

National Museum of Scotland Chambers St. Edinburgh, Scotland.

Pedaling History-Burgwardt Bicycle Museum 3943 North Buffalo Road, Orchard Park, NY 14127 USA.

San Jose Historical Museum 635 Phelan Avenue, San Jose, CA 95112 USA.

Science Museum Exhibition Road, London, SW7, UK.

Smithsonian Institution The Mall, Washington DC 20560 USA.

Sports Museum of New England 1175 Soldiers Field Rd., Boston, MA 02134 USA.

The Tech Museum of Innovation 145 W. San Carlos Street, San Jose, CA 95113 USA; Bicycle design featured with materials science, microchips, robotics, space exploration, and biotechnology.

Three Oaks Spokes, Bicycle Museum and Information Center 110 N. Elm Street, Three Oaks, MI 49128; Bike rentals, maps.

United States Bicycle Hall of Fame 166 W. Main St., Sommerville, NJ 08878 USA (1-800-BICY-CLE).

Velorama 107 Waackade, Nijmegen, Netherlands.

Wright Brother's Cycle Shop Carillon Park, 2001 S. Patterson Blvd. Dayton, OH

EXHIBITS

Antique Bicycle Exhibition September-December 1991, Museum of American Heritage, 275 Alma St., Palo Alto CA.

Art of the Mountain Bike 1990, San Francisco.
Bicycles: History, Beauty, Fantasy December-January 1983-4, O.K. Harris Gallery, New York City; August-November 1987, Old Pueblo Museum at Foothills Center, 7401 N. La Cholla Boulevard, Tucson AZ; Pryor Dodge collection.
`Bout Bicycles January 1993, Institute for Design and Experimental Art, curated by American Bicycle and Cycling Museum.
Century of Cycling in Santa Clara Valley Winter 1990-1, California History Center Foundation, De Anza College, Cupertino, CA. Curators: Ralph Igler, Randy Mitchell.
Chain Reaction July-September 1994, Dover Museum, Dover, England; Bicycle evolution and

Tour de France history.
Cycles of Expression January-February 1995, Grand Central Station, New York City; works SCI-Arc bicycle workshop.
De Fiets April-June 1977, Museum Boymans-van Beuningen, Rotterdam, Netherlands; Bicycle invention, culture and art.
The History of the Bicycle: The First Democratic Means of Transportation Summer 1993, San Francisco Int'l Airport; Pryor Dodge collection.
KM150 June 1990, Drumlanrig Castle, Dumfriesshire, Scotland; 150th anniversary of Kirkpatrick Macmillan's invention.
Pedersen Pilgrimage 1993, Dursley, England,

100th anniversary of Pedersen patent.
La Petite Reine: Le vélo en affiches à la fin du XIXème May-September 1979, Musée de L'Affiche; 18, rue de Paradis, Paris, France, posters.
Riding High: Albert Pope and the American Bicycle Craze, 1876–1910 March 1995–January 1996, Connecticut Historical Society, Hartford.

Periodicals

[Title Timespan, Publisher, City, subjects, issues per year. Formerly Title Date, Publisher, City, issues per year. Next Title...]

Adventure Bike 1987, Allentown PA, 4.
Adventure Cyclist 1994- Adventure Cycling Association, Missoula MT, 9. Formerly BikeReport Bikecentennial.
The Advocate Bicycle Federation of Washington, Federal Way WA.
Alternate Transportation News 1990- Mariposa CA, vehicles, 4.
American Bicyclist 1877- Northbrook IL, industry, 12. Formerly American Bicycle Journal 1877-1879 Boston, The Bicycling World 1879-, The League of American Wheelmen Bulletin 1901-, The Wheel, Motorcycle & Bicycle Illustrated 1906-, Bicycle News 1915-, Motorcycling and Bicycling World 1930-, The Cyclist, The Cycling Bulletin, National Bicycle Dealers Association Bulletin 1949-, American Bicyclist and Motorcyclist, New York City.
American BMXer Chandler AZ, 12.
American Cyclist, 1980s, Milwaukee WI, 12.
Antique and Classic Bicycle News Ann Arbor MI, collectibles, 6.
Appropriate Technology, 1973- Intermediate Technology Publications, London, 4.
Arizona Cycling Tuscon Wheelmen, Tuscon AZ.
Australasian Cycling Sidney, Australia, sport, recreation, 12.
Australian Cyclist Bicycle Federation of Australia, 6.
Auto-Free Press 1989- Transportation Alternatives, New York City, advocacy, 6.
Awheel 1970- Solihull Cycling Club, England.

Backcountry Biking Sacramento CA.
Bearings 1890–1897 Chicago, industry.
Bent Rim Bugle Michigan Mountain Bike Association, Detroit MI.
BIA News Bicycle Institute of America,

Washington DC.
BIA Bicycling Reference Book 1991- Washington DC, annual.
La Bici 1980s, Madrid, Spain, 12.
La Bicyclette
Bicisport 1976- Rome, Italy, 12.
Bicisport Brasil, 12.
Bicross Paris, BMX, 12.
Bicycle Magazine 1981- London, 12.
The Bicycle
Bicycle Action 1980s- London, 12.
Bicycle Business Journal Fort Worth TX, 12.
Bicycle Country Quarterly 1980s, Marin County CA, MTB, 4.
Bicycle Dealer Showcase 1971- Culver City CA, industry, 12.
Bicycle Forum 1978- Bikecentennial, Washington DC, transport, 4.
Bicycle Guide 1980- Los Angeles, 9.
Bicycle Issues & Answers 1985- Mayor's Bicycle Advisory Committee, Salt Lake City UT.
Bicycle Journal 1876-78, London.
Bicycle News Canada 1980s, Vancouver BC, 4.
Bicycle News Japan 1970s- Japan Bicycle Promotion Institute, Tokyo, 2. Formerly JBPI Bulletin.
The Bicycle Paper 1970- Redmond WA, 8.
The Bicycle Post 1976- Iowa City, IA.
Bicycle Retailer & Industry News Santa Fe NM, 12.
Bicycle Rider 1985, Agoura CA, 9.
Bicycles and Dirt 1980s- Chandler AZ, BMX, 12.
Bicycles Bulletin 1987, Friends of the Earth, London, 4.
Bicycle Siren 1993, San Francisco CA.
Bicycle Sport 1983-1988, Torrance CA, 12.
Bicycle Stamps Muncie IN.
Bicycles Today National Bicycle League, Dublin OH, BMX.
Bicycle Threat 1993 Sacramento CA.
Bicycle Times c.1980- Tyne and Wear, England, 12.
Bicycle Trader Santa Barbara CA, used market.

Bicycletter 1992- Five Boro Bike Club, New York City.
Bicycle USA 1881- League of American Bicyclists, Baltimore MD, advocacy, recreation, 9. Formerly The League of American Wheelmen Bulletin 1881-1888 Boston MA, American Wheelmen -1985 Richmond VA.
Bicycling 1945, LAW, ABLA, American Youth Hostels.
Bicycling 1962- Rodale Press, Emmaus PA, 12. Formerly Northern California Newsletter 1962-, American Cycling Newsletter 1964-, American Cycling 1965-1967, Oakland CA, Bicycling! 1969-77, Bicycling 1978-, Bicycling Plus incorporated Mountain Bike 1991.
Bicycling Australia
Bicycling in Los Angeles Bicycle Advisory Committee, Los Angeles CA.
Bicycling News 1876-1900, Birmingham, England.
Bicycling San Diego San Diego CA, 4.
Bicycling Times 1877-83, London.
Bicyclist Advocacy Bulletin 1991- League of American Bicyclists, Baltimore MD, 6.
Bike 1989- Bielefeld, Germany, MTB.
Bike 1992- Madrid, Spain, MTB.
Bike 1994- San Juan Capistrano CA, MTB.
Bikeabout Mohawk-Hudson Wheelmen, Albany NY.
Bike Commuted Sentences 1980s, National Association of Bicycle Commuters, Nashville TN.
Bike Culture Quarterly 1993- Open Road Ltd., York, England, 4.
Bike Fed UPDATE Bicycle Federation of Pennsylvania, Harrisburg PA.
Bike Lanes Florida Bicycle Association, Tampa FL.
the Bike mag 1994- London, 12.
Bike Magazin Chur, Switzerland, 10.
Bike Midwest Columbus OH, 9.
The Bike People News Los Angeles CA.
BikeReport see Adventure Cyclist.
Bike Rider 1970- Century Road Club of America, Princeton NJ.

Bike Rights Bicycle Advisory Committee, Tuscon AZ.

Bikes Not Bombs 1985- Washington DC.

Bikes Not Cars Toronto, Canada.

Bike Talk 1983, New York City.

Bike Tech 1980-1990, Rodale Press, Emmaus PA, 4.

Bike Traffic Bicycle Commuter Coalition, San Francisco CA.

Bike World 1972-1982, Mt. View CA, 9.

Biking for a Better Community Bend OR.

BMX Action Torrance CA, BMX.

BMX Action Bike 1982- London, 6.

BMX Official 1980- England, 6.

BMX Plus! 1977- Mission Hills CA.

BMX Racer London, 12.

Bonecracker 1990- Dansk Mountain Bike Klub, Copenhagen, Denmark.

Boneshaker Southern Veteran Cycle Club, collectibles, history, 4.

Boom in Bikeways 1980s, Bicycle Institute of America, advocacy.

The Boston Cyclist 1980- Boston MA.

Broken Spoken 1993, San Francisco CA.

Buckinghamshire Cyclist 1990- England.

Caducycle 1972- Amicales Cycliste du Corps de Sante, Marines, France.

California Bicyclist 1982- Northern Edition, San Francisco CA, Southern Edition, Los Angeles CA, recreation.

California Cycling 1985- Sacramento CA.

Canadian Cyclist 1990- Les Editions Tricycle, Vélo Québec, Montreal, Canada, 4.

Canyon State Cyclist Tempe AZ.

CAT News 1993- Allentown PA.

Chain Chatter Oxnard-Ventura Bicycle Club, Oxnard CA.

Chain Gang Great Plains Bicycle Club, Lincoln NE.

Chain Letter Different Spokes, San Francisco CA.

Chain Mail Friends of Central Iowa Biking, Ames IA.

Chain Reaction Coosa Vally Cycling Association, Rome GA.

The Chainstay Peninsula Bicycling Association, Newport News VA.

Chainwheel Chatter Tri-county Bicycling Association, Lansing MI.

Changing Gears 1950- Davis Bike Club, Davis CA.

Ciclismo A Fondo 1985- Bilbao, Spain, Spanish *Winning*.

Ciclobby Notizie Milan.

Ciclo Mercato 1990– Milan, industry.

Ciclotourismo e Grandi Viaggi Rome, touring, MTB.

City Cyclist 1976- Transportation Alternatives, New York City, advocacy, 6.

The City Cyclist 1985- Toronto Canada.

Classic Bicycle & Whizzer News Dearborn MI, collectibles, history.

Competitive Cycling 1870-1980, Carson City NV, 9.

Competitor Solana Beach CA.

CommuniCABO Calif. Asso. of Bicycling Organizations., Dublin CA.

The Connecting Link 1970- Birmingham Cycle Touring Club and Warwickshire Racing Club.

Connections San Luis Obisbo CA, hospitality network, annual.

Coureur Belgium, sport.

Crank Mail Cleveland Wheelmen, Cleveland OH.

Crash 1993, San Francisco CA.

Crosswords 1992- Journal of Multi-Purpose Multi-Terrain Bicycles, Walnut Creek CA, 4.

Cycle 1886–1887 Boston.

Le Cycle 1891- Paris, trade. Formerly *Cycle et Automobile Industriels, L'Officiel du Cycle*.

The Cycle Age and Trade Review 1888–1901 Chicago, industry.

CTC Cycle Digest 1992- Cyclists' Touring Club, Godalming, England.

Cycle America Santa Cruz CA, Greenway advocacy.

Cycle Athlete Colorado Springs CO, 6.

Cycle Clips 1993- York, England, collectibles, 4.

Cyclegram 1977-1983, Bicycle Coalition of Delaware Valley, Philadelphia PA, advocacy, 4.

Cycle Ontario 1970- Ontario Cycling Association.

Cycle Press International 1970s- Japan Cycle Press, Tokyo, industry, 4.

Cycle Seller 1990- Youngstown OH, used market, 26.

Cycle South Atlanta GA.

Cycle Sport 1993- London.

Cycle Therapy Greater Victoria Cycling Coalition, Victoria BC.

Cycle Trader Herts, England, industry.

Cycle Trade News London, industry.

CT&C Cycle Touring and Campaigning 1878- Cyclists' Touring Club, Godalming, England, advocacy, recreation, 6. Formerly *Bicycle Touring Club Monthly Circular* 1878-, *BTC Monthly Gazette and Official Record* 1882-, *Cyclists' Touring Club Monthly Gazette* 1883-, *CTC Gazette* 1898-, *Cycletouring* 1963-1988.

Cycletter Bicycle Transportation Alliance, Portland OR.

Cycling 1876-80, Newcastle upon Tyne, England.

Cycling British Columbia 1970- Vancouver BC.

Cycling Life check.

Cycling Plus 1992- Bath, England.

Cycling Science 1989- Mount Shasta CA, technical, 4.

Cycling Times 1991- Fair Lawn NJ, 6.

Cycling USA 1979- United States Cycling Federation, Colorado Springs CO, sport, 12.

Cycling Weekly 1891- IPC Magazines, London, sport, 52. Formerly *Cycling & Sporting Cyclist* 1960s-1970s, Longacre Press, London.

Cycling World Kent, England, 12.

Cycling World Darlinghurst, Australia, 6.

Cyclisme Internationale 1980s- Paris.

Cyclist 1983-1989, Torrance CA, 9.

Cyclist 1877-1902, London.

The Cyclist 1879-1903, London.

Le Cycliste 1887- St. Etienne, France ("Velocio" Paul De Vivie).

The Cyclists' Cyclical 1993– Section of City Cyclists, Poznan, Poland.

The Cyclists' Vehicle 1980s- Edmonton Bicycle Commuters, Ontario, 4.

The Cyclists' Yellow Pages Missoula MT, touring reference, annual.

Cycloclimbing L'Ordre des Cols Durs, Cheshire, England, mountain touring, 3.

Cyclometer 1989- Toronto City Cycling Committee, Canada, 12. Formerly *The City Cyclist* 1975-1989, 4.

Cyclo-Sprint Koninklijke Belgische Wielrijders Bond, Brussels, Belgium, race schedule, 52.

Cyclotourisme Federation Francaise de Cyclotourisme, touring, 10.

Cykel Svenska Cykelsällskapet, Sanga, Sweden, advocacy, 4.

Cykling Cykelframjandet, Stockholm, Sweden, advocacy, 4.

Cyklister Dansk Cyklist Forbund, Copenhagen, Denmark, advocacy, 6.

Cyklistika 1984- Prague, Czech, sport, 12.

Daily Cyclist see *London Cyclist*.

Despatch Rider London, couriers.

Dirt Rag 1989- Verona PA, MTB, 7.

The D.M.S. Times The Dead Messenger Society, New York City, 6.

Doubletalk Tandem Club of America, Birmingham AL.

Drahtesel 1989- ARGUS, Vienna, Austria, advocacy, 6.

English Mechanic 1860s, London, technical.

Epicycling 1984, Independent Newsletter of Sturmey-Archer Hubs, Bakersfield CA.

L'Equipe 1901- Les Editions P. Amaury, Paris, sports daily. Formerly *L'Auto-Velo* 1901-, *L'Auto* 1903-1946.

Fat Tire Flyer 1981-1987, Fairfax CA, MTB, 6.

Fiets Amsterdam, advocacy, 9.

Fietsmagazine Oostduinkerke, Belgium, 12.

Fietsen Moet Kunnen (Bikes must be able) 1987- Fietsoverleg Vlaanderen, Antwerp, Belgium.

Fietsrevue Laarne, Belgium.

Fitness Cycling 1990- Canoga Park CA, 6.

Florida Bicyclist Tallahassee FL.

The Framework 1980- Virginia Bicycling Federation, Richmond VA.

La France Cycliste Paris, racing, 12.

Freestylin Torrance CA, BMX.

Free Wheelin' 1972- Southern Bicycle League, Atlanta GA.

Freewheeling 1970s- Edinburgh, Scotland, 12.

Freewheeling 1978- Haymarket, NSW, Australia, 6.

El Full de la Bici Amics de la Bici, Barcelona, Spain.

Globe The Globetrotters Club, Recreation, travel, 6.

The Glory News 1969- Ferndale CA, kinetic sculpture.

Go Torrance CA, BMX and wheels, 12.
Going Clean Journal Auto-Free Bay Area Coalition, Berkeley CA.
Going The Distance 1991- Atkinson NH.
The Golden Penny England, veteran cycles.
Grass Roots Shropshire, England, MTB.
Great Lakes Bicycle Connection 1982- Ann Arbor MI, 8.
Great Expeditions Vancouver, Canada.

Half Wheel 1970, Eltham Paragon Cycling Club, England.
Heartland Touring Heartland Touring Society, Skokie IL, 4.
The Helmet Update Bicycle Helmet Safety Institute, Washington DC.
Hi-Tech Nomadness 1980s- Nomadic Research Labs, El Segundo CA (Steven Roberts), 4.
HPV Klub Danmark 1990- Dansk Cyklist Forbund, Copenhagen, Denmark, 4.
HPV News 1975- International Human-Powered Vehicle Association, Indianapolis IN, racing, design, 9.
The Hub 1896–1899, London.
Human Power 1976- International Human-Powered Vehicle Association, Indianapolis IN, technical, 4.
Human-Powered Vehicle Times Hackett, ACT, Australia, 4.

IBF News International Bicycle Fund, Seattle WA.
ICA News 1980s, Independent Couriers Association, New York City, 4.
Imagine 1993- World Without Cars, Windsor, Canada.
IMBA Trail News 1990s- Los Angeles CA.
India Bicycle Ambassador Dehli, India.
Inside Cycling 1987, Boulder CO, sport.
Inside Triathlon 1990- Boulder CO. Formerly *Triathlon Today* 1990- Ann Arbor MI, 9.
Interbike Buyer 1981- Primedia, Costa Mesa CA, trade show guide, annual.
International Cycle Sport 1967-1982, Keighley, Yorkshire, England, sport, 9.
International Cycling Guide 1980-86, London.
InTraffic 1992-1994, New York City, 6.
Ixion: A Journal of Velocipeding, Athletics and Aerostatics 1875-80, London.
Irish Cycling Review Dublin.

Kerék-Hirek (Wheel-News) 1992- Városi Biciklizés Barátai, Budapest, Hungary.
Knapsack American Youth Hostels, Washington DC, 2.
Koers (Race) Holland, sport.
Kokopelli Notes 1990- Asheville NC, Journal of Self-Propelled Transportation, environmental, 4.

Lady Cyclist 1896, England.
Lightwheels 1989- New York City, design, advocacy, 4. Formerly *Go* 1985-88, International Conference for Appropriate Transportation.

London Cyclist 1990- London Cycling Campaign, London, advocacy, 6. Formerly *Daily Cyclist* 1978-1989, merged with *Moving Target* 1989, courier.
Low Rider Bicycle 1993- Walnut CA.

Les Maillots Shimano Corporation, Dusseldorf, Germany, sport, equipment.
Making Tracks 1980s, New Malden, Surrey, England, MTB, 6.
Marketing and Merchandising Newsletter 1982- Rodale Press, Emmaus PA, trade.
Mechanics Magazine 1823-72, London, technical, 12.
Mercury Rising 1990- San Francisco Bike Messenger Association, San Francisco CA, 6.
Mess Press 1991, San Francisco CA.
Michigan Cyclist Grand Rapids MI.
Miroir Du Cyclisme 1900- Paris, sport, history, 12.
Le Monde À Bicyclette 1975- Montreal, Canada, advocacy, 4.
Moultoneer Moulton Bicycle Club, Middlesex, England.
Mountain and City Biking 1989- Canoga Park CA, 12.
Mountain Bike 1989- Rodale Press, Emmaus PA, 12.
Mountain Bike Action 1985- Mission Hills CA, 12.
Mountain Bike Distraction April 1, 1993, Boulder CO. *Velo-News* parody of *Mountain Bike Action*.
Mountain Bike Guru's Forum 1992, Anoka MN.
Mountain Bike Motion 1992, Garnerville NY.
Mountain Bike New Zealand 1989- New Zealand.
Mountain Biker 1986- London, 12.
Mountain Biking Canoga Park CA.
Mountain Biking UK 1992- Bath, England.
MTB Pro 1992- Bath, England.
Mud Flap 1991- San Francisco CA.
Mudguardian Cardiff Cycle Campaign.
Mundo Ciclisto Calle, Columbia, sport, 12.

National Cycling Victoria, Austalia, racing, history, 6.
Network News 1979- Bicycle Network, Philadelphia PA, news clips, advocacy, 4.
New Cyclist Romford, Essex, England, 12.
New Cyclist 1988- Coldstream, Berwickshire, Scotland, 4.
New England Cyclist 1990- Newton MA, 10.
NORBA News National Off-Road Bicycle Assoc., Colorado Springs CO.
Northeast Cyclist Hempstead NY.
Northwest Cyclist Seattle WA, 12.
NYCC Bulletin New York Cycling Club, New York City.

Ohio Bicycle Communicator Ohio Bicycle Federation, Dayton OH.
Oikaze Tokyo, Japan, recreation, 6.
On One Wheel Unicycling Society of America, Redford MI.

Oregon Cycling 1980s- Eugene OR.
Ostatni Dzwonek (The Highest Time) 1993– Section of City Cyclists, Poznan, Poland.
Où irons-nous? (Where are we going?) Fédération Français de Cyclotourisme, Paris.
Outing Boston.
Outside Chicago IL.
Outspoken Bluegrass Wheelmen, Lexington KY.
Outspokin' National Bicycle Dealers Association, Costa Mesa CA, 12.

Paceline Tampa Bay Freewheelers, Tampa FL.
The Palenque Traveler 1980s, Bike Europe, Ann Arbor MI, Journal of No-Frills Foreign Travel, 6.
Paris-Velo 1890s, Paris.
På Hjul Norges Cyckleforbund, Rud, Norway, racing, 12.
På Sykkel Syklistenes Landsforening, Oslo, Norway, advocacy, 4.
Paving Moratorium Update 1990- Arcata CA.
Pedal 1987- Toronto Canada, sport, 9.
Pedaliamo Federazione Amici della Bicicletta, Reggio Emilia, Italy, advocacy.
Pedal Manitoba 1983- Manitoba Cycling Association, Winnepeg, Canada.
Pedal Power Bike WNY, Amherst NY.
Pedal Power College Park Area Bicycle Coalition, MD.
Pedal Power Edenvale, South Africa, touring, transport, 6.
Pedaller British Cycling Bureau, London, industry.
People in Motion 1988, Florida Department of Transportation, 4.
People Power Update Santa Cruz CA.
Performance Cyclist International 1993- London.
Peterson's Bicycle Guide see *Bicycle Guide*.
Police on Bikes News 1991- Bel Air MD, 12.
Pro Bike News 1980- Bicycle Federation of America, Washington DC, advocacy, 12.
Pro News c.1979- Coventry, England, racing, 12.
Push On Bicycle Institute of New South Wales, Australia, 6.

Quick Release Santa Barbara Bicycle Coalition, CA.

Rad & Motor Sport Zurich, Switzerland, 52.
Radfahren 1979- ADFC, Bielefeld, Germany, 4.
Rad Magazin Munich, Germany, 12.
Radmarkt 1886- Germany, industry, 12.
Radsport Koln, Germany, racing, 52.
Rain Eugene OR, sustainable community, 4.
The Rambler Clinton River Riders, MI.
Raw Vulva 1993, San Francisco CA, women's zine.
The REBAC Reporter Oakland CA.
Recumbent Cyclist News 1990- Recumbent Bicycle Club of America, Renton WA, 4.
Revue Velocipedique 1880s France.
The Ride Magazine 1993- Cheshire CT, 11.
Ride On! 1971- Washington Area Bicyclist Association, Washington DC, advocacy, 9.

Ride On 1972- East Bay Bicycle Coalition, Oakland CA, advocacy.

De Rijwieltoerist (The Cycletourist) Nederlandse Rijwiel Toer Unie, Veenendaal, Holland.

Rivendell Reader 1995 Walnut Creek CA.

Road Bike Action 1993- Mission Hills CA.

Road Kill 1994, New York City, couriers.

Rocky Mountain Sports & Fitness Boulder CO.

The Roll Call 1970- Midland Cycling Club, England.

ROMP Mtn. Cyclist Responsible Organized Mountain Pedalers, Campbell CA.

ROTA Zottegem, Belgium, industry.

The Rough Stuff Journal 1955- Rough Stuff Fellowship, Southport, Lancashire, England, off-road touring, 6.

Roue Libre (Freewheel) Mouvement de Défence de la Bicyclette, Paris.

The Saddle Bag Cycling Saddlemen, Dearborn MI.

SCCF News 1975- Southern Calif. Cycling Federation, Newport Beach CA. Formerly *SCCA News*.

Schwinn Reporter 1950-1990, Chicago IL.

Singletrack 1980s, Southern CA, MTB.

Singletrack Utah Mountain Bike Association, Park City UT.

Sin Prisas (no Hurry) Pedalibre, Madrid, Spain, advocacy.

Solar Mind 1990- Ukiah CA. sustainable technology.

Solo Bici 1991- Barcelona, Spain, MTB, 12.

Southern Cyclist Dunedin Cyclists' Coalition, Aukland, New Zealand, 4.

Southwest Cycling Pasadena CA.

The Spinning Crank 1978- Silicon Valley Bicycle Coalition, Cupertino CA, transport, 6.

Spoke & Sole Bike-Ped Idaho, Moscow ID.

Spoke and Word Bikes Not Bombs, Jamaica Plain MA, recycling bikes.

Spoken Word Human Powered Transit Association, Van Nuys CA.

Spoke 'n' Word Bicycle Federation of Tennessee, Murfreesboro TN.

Spoke 'n' Word Vancouver Canada.

Spoke 'N' Word Narragansett Bay Wheelmen, Providence RI.

Spokes Frederick MD, 5.

Spokes 1987- Lothian Cycle Campaign, Edinburgh, Scotland, advocacy, 4.

Spokesman Cycle Speedway Council, Norwich, England, racing, 4.

Spokes n' Sports 1990s- Pheonix AZ, sports for handicapped.

Spokesperson Ottawa Bicycle Club, Canada.

Sports, Etc. Seattle WA, 12.

Sports Focus Gaitersburg MD.

Sport Velocipedique

Sports Pulse Dallas TX.

Sprint International Paris, sport, 12.

Squeaky Wheel Metro By Cycle, North York, Canada.

Superior Cyclist (Lake Superior) Grand Rapids MI, 4.

Sustainable Transport 1993- ITDP, New York City, advocacy, development.

Taiwan Bicycles 1980s- Taipei, industry.

Tandem Club Journal 1970- Tandem Club, London, 6.

Tandem Magazine 1994- Eugene OR, 4.

Terra Times Concerned Off-Road Bicyclists Association, Woodland Hills CA.

Texas Athlete 1993- Richardson TX, 12.

Texas Bicyclist Houston TX, 12.

Tour Munich, Germany, 12.

The Tourist 1970- Bristol Cycling Club, England.

Trailblazer 1986- Rails-to-Trails Conservancy, Washington DC.

Transport Retort London, advocacy.

Tranportation Exchange Update Washington DC.

Trax Mountain Bike Association of Arizona, Phoenix AZ.

Triathlete Santa Monica CA, sport, 12.

Triathlon Today Boulder CO, sport.

Tricycle: The Buddhist Review Buddhist culture (not bikes).

Tricyclist 1882-85, London and Coventry, England.

Trochos 1981- Victoria, Australia, touring, 11.

The Tubular Times 1990- San Francisco Bicycle Coalition, transport.

Turning Point New Zealand Amateur Cycling Association, Wellington, 12.

Tweewieler (Two-wheeler) Amsterdam, industry.

Ultra Cycling 1992- Ultra-Marathon Cycling Association, Altadena CA, racing, 4.

Ultrasport 1983- Boston MA, fitness.

The Urban Ecologist Berkeley CA, sustainable community.

US Pro News 1980s, Allentown PA, racing.

VCÖ Zeitung Vekehrsclub Österreich, Vienna, Austria, transport.

Le Vélo 1889, France.

Velo 1980s- Paris, sport, 12.

Veloblatt 1980s- Basel, Switzerland.

Veloceman England.

Veloce-Sport France.

Le Velocipede France.

Velocipede 1982- Pedal Power Foundation, Roggebaai, South Africa, 4.

Vélocipède Illustré 1869-1900, Paris.

Velocipedist 1869- New York City.

Velocite Federation Francaise des Usagers de la Bicyclette, Strasbourg, France.

Vélo MAG Vélo Québec, Montreal, Canada, recreation, 6. Combined with *Vélo Montagne*.

VeloNews 1972- Boulder CO, racing, 18. Formerly *Northeast Bicycle News* 1972-1973, Brattleboro, VT. *Cyclenews* 1973. *Velo-News* 1973-1988.

Velotourist 1990- Volgograd Cyclists' Touring Club, Volgograd, Russia, 4.

Velo Vert (Green Bike) 1990- Seine, France, MTB.

Ville A Velo GRACQ, Bruxelles, Belgium.

Vogelvrije Fietser Eichte Nederlandse Fietserbond, Woerden, Holland, 6.

The Wheel 1880–1888 League of American Wheelmen, New York.

The Wheel England.

The Wheel and Cycling Trade Review 1888–1900 New York.

Wheeling 1884-1901, London.

Wheel Life 1880s, London.

Wheelmarks 1970, Sheffield Cycle Touring Club, England.

The Wheelman 1882–1883 Boston.

Wheelmen 1970- New Jersey, collectibles, history, 4.

The Wheelmen's Gazette 1886–1908 Springfield, MA. Formerly *The Springfield Wheelmen's Gazette* 1883–1886.

Wheel People 1966- Charles River Wheelmen, West Newton MA.

Wheelpeople Humbolt Bay Bicycle Commuters Association, Eureka CA

Wheels, Heels & Hooves Missouri Cyclists, Equestrians and Pedestrians, Jefferson City MO.

Wheelwomen 1896, England.

Wheel World 1880-86, London.

Wielerexpress Zwanenburg, Holland, Racing schedule.

Wieler Revue Epe, Holland, Racing, 18.

Wielersport Koninklijke Nederlandsche Wielren Unie, Amsterdam.

Wind Chill Factor 1990s- Chicago IL.

Winning: Bicycle Racing Illustrated 1980- Allentown PA, sport, 12.

Wisconsin Cyclist Grand Rapids MI.

Wobmat News 1989- Woman's Mountain Bike and Tea Society, Fairfax CA, 4.

Women's Cycling News Women's Cycling Network, 4.

Women's Sports and Fitness Boulder CO.

The Worker Cyclist 1900- Arbeiterrafahrbund: Solidarität, Germany.

CALENDARS

Bicycles Every Day 1975, Philadelphia Bicycle Coalition.

Bicycling Calendar 1985, CABO ((Norman Riley).

Bikes of the World 1987, Spartanburg SC (John Gillespie).

Calendrier des vélorutionnaires 1979.

Cycle and Recycle 1977- Bike Network, Philadelphia PA.

Do it in the Dirt 1994, VeloNews, Boulder CO.

DuMont's Fahrradkalender 1993, DuMont Buchverlag, Koln, Germany (Karl-Heinz Raach).

FahrRad Kalender 1994, Verlag die Werkstatt, Gottingen, Germany.

Tour de France 1992, Landmark, Novato CA (Darcy Kiefel).

Tour de France 1994, VeloNews, Boulder CO (Graham Watson).

Bibliography

GENERAL INTEREST

Ballantine, Richard, and Richard Grant. *Richards' Ultimate Bicycle Book*. New York: Dorling Kindersley, 1991.

Burke, Edmund, editor. *Science of Cycling*. Champaign, IL: Human Kinetics Publishers, 1986.

Durry, Jean, and John B. Wadley. *The Guinness Guide to Bicycling*. Translation of *Le Vélo* by Vivienne Menkes. Enfield, UK: Guinness Superlatives, 1977.

Forester, John. *Effective Cycling*. Palo Alto, CA: Custom Cycle Fitments, 1975. Revised, Cambridge, MA: MIT Press, 1984, 1990. Revised 6th edition, 1993.

Gilbert, Kathie and Galen, and Gail Heilman, editors. *Bikelopedia*. San Rafael, CA: Capital Management Publications, 1976.

Hershon, Maynard. *Half-Wheel Hell and Other Cycling Stories*. 1994.

Keefe, Mike. *The Ten Speed Commandments: An Irreverent Guide to the Complete Sport Cycling*. New York: Dolphin-Doubleday, 1987.

Krausz, John, and Vera van der Reis Krausz, editors. *The Bicycling Book*. New York: The Dial Press, 1982.

Leete, Harvey M., editor. *The Best of Bicycling!* New York: Trident Press, 1970; Pocket Book edition, 1972.

L'Uomo a Due Route. Milan: Electa, 1985.

McGurn, James. *On Your Bicycle*. New York: Facts On File, 1987.

Museum Boymans-van Beuningen. *De Fiets*. R. Hammacher-van den Brande, curator. Rotterdam, 1977.

Plevin, Arlene. *Cycling: The Art and Spirit of the Sport and Where to Enjoy It*. New York: Fodor's Sports, 1992.

St. Pierre, Roger. *The Book of the Bicycle*. London: Triune Books, 1973.

Salviac, Pierre, editor. *Joies de la bicyclette*. Paris: Hachette Réalites, 1977.

Saunders, Nick, editor. *Bicycle: The Image & the Dream*. Volume 1. London: Red Bus, 1991. Companion to *Bicycle* (York Films).

Sloane, Eugene A. *The All New Complete Book of Bicycling*. New York: Simon & Schuster, 1970, 1974, 1978, 1980, 1983, 1988.

Wagenvoord, James. *Bikes and Riders*. New York: Van Nostrand, Reinhold, 1973.

Watson, Roderick, and Martin Gray. *The Penguin Book of the Bicycle*. Harmondsworth, UK: Penguin Books, 1978.

Weaver, Susan. *A Woman's Guide to Cycling*. Berkeley: Ten Speed Press, 1991.

Whitt, Frank Roland, and David Gordon Wilson. *Bicycling Science*. Second Edition. Cambridge, MA: MIT Press, 1982.

Willard, Frances E. *A Wheel Within A Wheel*. 1893. Reprinted *How I Learned to Ride the Bicycle: Reflections of an Influential 19th Century Woman*. Sunnyvale, CA: Fair Oakes Publishing, 1991.

INVENTION

Alderson, Frederick. *Bicycling: A History*. Newton Abbot, UK: David & Charles, 1972.

Althuser, Jean. *Pierre Michaux and His Sons: The Pioneers of the Bicycle*. France, 1986. English trans. Derek Roberts. Kenilworth: Willis, 1987.

Andriec, Dragoslav. *Les Bicyclettes: 200 Years of History*. Yugoslavia and France: Ars Mundi, 1992.

Anon. *Bicycling 1874: Its Rise And Development, A Text Book For Riders*. London: Tinsley Bros, 1874. Reprinted, Devon: David & Charles, and New York: Taplinger, 1970.

Beeley, Serena. *A History of Bicycles*.

Bottomley, J. *The Velocipede: Its Past, Present and Its Future*. London, 1869.

Calif, Ruth. *The World on Wheels: An Illustrated History of the Bicycle and Its Relatives.* East Brunswick, NJ: Cornwall Books, 1983.

Carelman. *The Catalogue of Fantastic Inventions*.

Caunter, C.F. *Cycles: Handbook of the Collection*. London: Science Museum, 1958.

Caunter, C.F. *The History and Development of Cycles*. London: Her Majesty's Stationary Office, 1955.

Clayton, Nick. *Early Bicycles*.

Clayton, Nick. *Michaux Study Book*. 1993.

Crowley, Terence E. *Discovering Old Bicycles*. Aylesbury, UK: Shire, 1978.

Da Vinci, Leonardo. *Codice Atlantico*. Compiled by Pompeo Leoni. Milan, 1650.

De Vries, Leonard, and Ilonka van Amstel. *Victorian Inventions*. New York: American Heritage Press, 1971.

Durry, Jean. *Le Vélo*. Paris, Denoël, 1976.

Ebeling, Hermann. *Der Freiherr von Drais*. Karlsruhe, Germany: Braun, 1985.

English Mechanic - The Velocipede - 1865–1870. Brandon, UK: GM Design, 1993.

Evans, David. *The Ingenious Mr. Pederson*. Gloucester, UK: Alan Sutton, 1979.

Fallet, René. *Le Vélo*. Paris: Julliard, 1973.

Franke, Jutta. *Illustrierte Fahrrad-Geschichte*. Museum für Verkehr und Technik. Berlin: Nicolai, 1987.

Frederiks, P.J. *De ontwikkeling van het rijwiel*. Den Haag, NL, 1923.

Fuchs, Johannes M., and W.J. Simons. *De fiets van toen an nu*. Alkmarr, NL: De Alk, 1983.

Fuchs, Johannes M., and W.J. Simons. *Geschiedenis van de fiets*. Alkmaar, NL, De Alk, 1967. English translation, Graham K. Scott.

History of the Bicycle. London: History Bookshop, 1967.

Galgiati, Fermo. *La Bicicletta*. Milan: BE-MA Editrice, 1989.

Gibbs-Smith, Charles, and Gareth Rees. *The Inventions of Leonardo da Vinci*. New York: Charles Scribner's Sons, 1978.

Goddard, J.T. *The Velocipede: Its History, Varieties and Practice*. Cambridge, MA, 1869.

Griffin, Harry Hewitt. *Bicycles of the Year*. London: Upcott & Gill, 1877. Reprint, Otley: Olicana Books, 1970.

Griffin, Harry Hewitt. *Bicycles & Tricycles of the Year 1886*. London: Upcott & Gill, 1886. Reprint, Otley: Olicana Books, 1971.

Griffin, Harry Hewitt. *Cycles and Cycling* London, George Bell, 1890, 1903.

Hadland, Tony. *The Sturmey-Archer Story*. UK: Hadland-Pinkerton Press, 1987.

Hadland, Tony. *The Moulton Bicycle*. Reading, UK: Hadland, 1982.

Halford Cycle Co. *50 Years of Progress 1907–1957*. Birmingham, UK, 1957.

Harter, Jim. *Transportation: A Pictorial Archive From Nineteenth-Century Sources*. New York: Dover, 1984.

Hermes, Günter. *Heiteres Radfahren: Streifzug durch Fahrrad-Geschichte*. Stuttgart: J. Fink, 1975.

Herzog, Ulrich. *Fahrradpatente*. Kiel, Germany: Moby Dick Verlag, 1984.

Hogenkamp, George J.M. *De geschiendenis van Burgers Deventer is de geschiendenis van de fiets*. Deventer, NL, 1939.

Howdle, Peter. *Bikes of Yesteryear*. Cambridge, UK: Stephens, 1979.

Hunter, Edmund. *The Story of the Bicycie*. Loughborough, UK: Ladybird Books, 1975.

Jenks, Charles, and Nathan Silver. *Adhocism: The Case for Improvisation*. New York: Anchor Press, 1973.

Leek, Stephen and Sybil. *The Bicycle: That Curious Invention*. Nashville, TN: Thomas Nelson, 1973.

Le Grand, Jacques. (Richard Lesclide) *Manuel du Vélocipède*. Paris, 1869.

Lessing, Hans-Erhard. *Das Fahrradbuch*. Hamburg: Reinbek, 1978.

Maher, Thomas. *The Whitney: Building a Highwheel Bicycle*. Norwood, MA: Thomas Mahler, 1991.

Marinoni, Augusto. *Leonardo da Vinci: L'automobile e la bicicletta*. Milan: Arcadia, 1981.

Marinoni, Augusto. *Laboratorio su Leonardo*. Milan: IBM, 1983.

Meyers, Stuart John, editor. *American Bicyclist and Motorcyclist: 100th Anniversary Issue*. New York: Cycling Press, 1979.

Michaux, Francisque. *Biographies et Souvenirs de Pierre et Ernest Michaux*. Paris, 1906.

Moffet, Cleveland. *How a Bicycle is Made*. Boston: McClure's, 1897.

Murphy, Jim. *Two Hundred Years of Bicycles*. New York: J.B. Lippincott, 1983.

Olivier de Sanderval, Aimé. *Les inventeurs du vélocipède*. Paris, 1894.

Oliver, Smith Hempstone. *Wheels and Wheeling: The Smithsonian Cycle Collection*. Smithsonian Studies in History and Technolgy, No. 24. Washington, DC: Smithsonian Institution Press, 1974.

Open University. *Design Processes and Products: Bicycles: Invention and Innovation*. Milton Keynes, UK, 1983.

Plath, Helmut. *Laufrad-Vélocipède-Hobbyhorse, Eine typologische Untersuchung*. Munster, Germany, 1978.

Porter, Luther H. *Wheels and Wheeling*. Boston: Wheelman Co., 1892.

Presence, Peter, editor. *Encyclopedia of Inventions*. Maidenhead, UK: Purnell Books, 1976.

Rauck, Volke and Paturi. *Mit dem Rad durch zwei Jahrhunderte*. Stuttgart: AT Verlag, 1984.

Rebour, Daniel. *The Data Book 1983*.

Reti, Ladislao, editor. *The Unknown Leonardo*. New York: McGraw-Hill, 1974.

Ritchie, Andrew. *King of the Road: An Illustrated History of Cycling*. London: Wildwood House; Berkeley: Ten Speed Press, 1975.

Roberts, Derek. *Cycling History: Myths and Queries*. 1991.

Roberts, Derek. *The Invention of Bicycles and Motorcycles*. London: Usborne, 1975.

Roberts, Derek. *The Year of the High Bicycle*. Compilation of catalogs, 1877–1886.

Roy, Robin. *Design Processes and Products Vol 2: Bicycles, Invention and Innovation*. Milton Keynes, UK: Open University, 1983.

Saunier, L. Baudry de. *Histoire Générale de la Vélocipèdie*. Paris: Ollendorf, 1891.

Saunier, L. Baudry de. *Histoire de la Locomotion Terrestre*. Paris, 1935.

Schrom, H. *Die Einführungswerburg für das Fahrrad*. Nuremberg, 1960.

Schwinn, Frank W. *Fifty Years of Schwinn-Built Bicycles*. Chicago: Arnold Schwinn & Co., 1945. Reprinted, 1989.

Seray, Jacques. *Deux Roues*. 1989.

Sharp, Archibald. *Bicycles and Tricycles: An Elementary Treatise on their Design and Construction*. London: Longmans, Green, 1896. Reprinted Cambridge, MA: MIT Press, 1979.

Smithsonian Institution. *The Smithsonian Book of Invention*. Washington, DC: Smithsonian Exposition Books, 1978.

Spencer, Charles. *The Bicycle: Its Use and Action*. London: F. Warne, 1870.

Spencer, Charles. *The Modern Bicycle*. London: F. Warne, 1876.

Starley, William. *The Life and Inventions of James Starley*. Coventry, 1902.

Stevenson, Edward P. *The High-Tech Bicycle*. New York: Harper & Row, 1982.

Sumner, Philip. *Early Bicycles*. Illustrated by Alan Osbahr. London: Hugh Evelyn, 1966.

Velox. *Velocipedes, Bicycles and Tricycles: How to Make and How to Use Them*. London: Routledge, 1869. Reprinted, Wakefield, UK: S.R. Press. 1971.

Wallis-Taylor, A.J. *Modern Cycles: Their Construction and Repair*. 1897.

Wilkinson-Latham, Robert. *Cycles in Colour*. Poole, UK: Blandford Press, 1978.

Williamson, Geoffrey. *Wheels Within Wheels: The Story of the Starleys of Coventry*. London: Geoffrey Bles, 1966.

Wood, Neil, ed. *Evolution of the Bicycle with Price Guide*. LW Books, 1991.

Woodforde, John. *The Story of the Bicycle*. New York: Universe Books and London: Routeledge & Kegan Paul, 1970.

MECHANICS

Ainsworth, Ruth. *The Bicycle Wheel*. London: Hamilton, 1969.

Alexander, Don. *Bicyclist's Emergency Repair*. San Diego: Sunbelt Publications, 1990.

Ballantine, Richard. *Richard's New Bicycle Book*. New York: Random House, 1987.

Barnett, John. *Barnett's Manual: Analysis and Procedures for Bicycle Mechanics*. Brattleboro, VT: Vitesse Press, 1989.

Belt, Forest, and Richard Maloney. *Bicycle Maintenance and Repair: Brakes, Chains, Derailleurs*. Indianapolis: Audel, 1975.

Belt, Forest, and Richard Maloney. *Bicycle Maintenance and Repair: Frames, Tires, Wheels*. Indianapolis: Audel, 1975.

Berto, Frank. *Bicycling Magazine's Complete Guide to Upgrading Your Bike*. Emmaus, PA: Rodale Press, 1988.

Bicycling Magazine. *Basic Maintenance and Repair*. Emmaus, PA: Rodale Press, 1990.

Bicycling Magazine. *Easy Bicycle Maintenance*. Emmaus, PA: Rodale Press, 1985.

Bicycling Magazine. *New Bike Owner's Guide*. Emmaus, PA: Rodale Press, 1990.

Bicycling Magazine. *Complete Guide to Bicycle Maintenance and Repair*. Emmaus, PA: Rodale Press, 1989.

Brandt, Jobst. *The Bicycle Wheel*. Menlo Park, CA: Avocet, 1981.

Carter, Earnest F. *The Boys' Book of Cycles and Motor Cycles*. New York: Roy, 1962.

Coello, Dennis. *The Mountain Bike Repair Handbook*. New York: Lyons & Burford, 1990.

Coello, Dennis. *The Roadside Guide to Bike Repairs*. New York: Warner Books, 1983.

Coles, Clarence W., and Harold T. Glenn. *Glenn's New Complete Bicycle Manual*. New York: Crown, 1987.

Consumer Guide. *Complete Bicycle Book*.

Cuthbertson, Tom. *Anybody's Bike Book*. Revised, Berkeley: Ten Speed Press, 1990.

Cuthbertson, Tom. *Better Bikes*. Berkeley: Ten Speed Press, 1980.

Cuthbertson, Tom, and Rick Morrall. *The Bike Bag Book*. Berkeley: Ten Speed Press, 1989.

De Long, Fred. *De Long's Guide to Bicycles and Bicycling*. Radnor, PA: Chilton Book Company, 1974, 1978.

Eddywilly, Professor. *Alternative Applications of the Williams Chainwheel*.

Ewers, William. *Sincere's Bicycle Service Book*. Tucson: Sincere Press, 1970. Revised, 1970.

Ferguson, C.G. *How to Look After Your Bicycle*. New York: St. Martin's Press, 1967.

Garvy, Helen. *How to Fix Your Bicycle*. 6th ed. Los Gatos, CA: Shire Press, 1993.

Hayduk, Douglas. *Bicycle Metallurgy for the Cyclist*. Brattleboro, VT: Vitesse Press, 1987.

Hershon, Maynard. *Tales From the Bike Shop*. Brattleboro VT: Vitesse Press, 1989.

Jorgenson, Eric, et al. *Fix Your Bicycle: All Speeds, All Major Makes Simplified Step-by-Step*. Los Angeles: Clymer, 1972. Revised, 1975.

Kitching, Ron. *Everything Cycling*. Silsden, UK: Kennedy Bros., 1974.

Kitching, Ron. *Kitching's Handbook*. Harrogate, UK: 1970.

Kolin, Michael J., and Denise de la Rosa. *The Custom Bicycle*. Emmaus, PA: Rodale Press, 1979.

Kossack. Joe. *A Close-up Look at Bicycle Frames*. Mt. View, CA: World Publications, 1975.

Kraynick, Steve. *Bicycle Owner's Complete Handbook of Repair and Maintenance*. Los Angeles: Clymer, 1953.

Kuhtz, Christian. *Einfälle statt Abfälle*. Vol. 1–8. Kiel, Germany: Verlag Christian Kuhtz, 1989.

Lehrer, John. *The Complete Guide to Choosing a Performance Bicycle*. Philadelphia: Running Press, 1988.

Lindblom, Steven. *The Fantastic Bicycle Book*. Boston: Houghton Mifflin, 1979. Recycling bikes.

Logos. *Variable Gearing*. UK, 1908.

McFarlane, John. *It's Easy to Fix Your Bike*. Chicago: Wilcox & Follett, 1952, 1958, 1964, 1973, 1976.

Marr, Dick. *Bicycle Gearing: A Practical Guide*. Seattle, WA: The Mountaineers, 1989.

Papadopoulos, J.M. *Bicycle Steering Dynamics and Self-Stability: A Summary Report On Work In Progress*. Ithica, NY: Cornell University, 1987.

Paterek. Tim. *The Paterek Manual*. Horsham, PA: Kermesse, 1985.

Proteus, Paul. *The Proteus Framebuilding Manual*. College Park, MD: Proteus Press, 1975.

Rebour, Daniel. *La practique du vélo*. Paris, 1949.

Renold & Coventry Chain Company Limited. *The*

Art of Easy Cycling. Manchester, UK, 1952.

Schwinn Bicycle Co. *Schwinn Bicycle Service Manual*. Chicago, 1972.

Scott, Ed. *Fix Your Bicycle*. Arleta, CA: Clymer Publications, 1984.

Seidl, Herman. *Mountain Bikes: Maintaining, Repairing, and Upgrading*. New York: Sterling, 1992.

Sloane, Eugene. *Eugene Sloane's On the Road Guide to Bicycle Maintenance*. New York: Simon & Schuster, 1988.

Sloane, Eugene. *The New Bicycle Maintenance Manual*. New York: Simon & Schuster, 1991.

Snowling, Steve, and Ken Evans. *Bicycle Mechanics in Workshop and Competition*. Champaign, IL: Leisure Press, 1987, 1990.

Sturmey, Henry. *Indispensable Tricyclists' Handbook*. London, 1881.

Sturmey, Henry. *Indispensable Bicyclists' Handbook*. London, 1878. Reprinted 1980.

Sutherland, Howard. *Sutherland's Handbook for Bicycle Mechanics*. Berkeley: Sutherland Publications, 1974, Fifth edition 1990.

Talbot, Richard P. *Designing and Building Your Own Frameset*. Babson Park, MA: The Manet Guild, 1979, 1984.

Talbot, Richard P. *The Perfect Wheel: An Illustrated Guide to Bicycle Wheelbuilding*. Babson Park, MA: The Manet Guild, 1981.

TI Reynolds. *Top Tubes*. UK, 1970.

Urquhart, David. *The Bicycle and How it Works*. New York: Walck, 1972.

Van der Plas, Rob. *The Bicycle Repair Book*. Mill Valley, CA: Bicycle Books, 1985. Revised, 1990.

Van der Plas, Rob. *Bicycle Technology*. Mill Valley, CA: Bicycle Books, 1990.

Van der Plas, Rob. *Mountain Bike Maintenance*. Mill Valley, CA; Bicycle Books, 1989.

Van der Plas, Rob. *Roadside Bicycle Repairs*. Mill Valley, CA: Bicycle Books, 1990.

Way, Robert John. *Cycling Manual*. London: Temple Press, 1967. Revised, *The Bicycle: A Guide and Manual*. London: Hamlyn, 1973.

Whiter, Robert. *The Bicycle Manual on Maintenance and Repair*. Hollywood, CA: Laurida Books, 1972.

Wiley, Jack. *The Bicycle Builder's Bible*. Blue Ridge Summit, PA: TAB Books, 1980.

Wright, Robert. *Building Bicycle Wheels: Step-By-Step Instructions for Building, Repairing, and Maintaining Spokes, Rims, and Hubs*. New York: Collier Books, 1977.

Yerkow, Charles. *Getting the Best Out of Your Bicycle*. New York: Drake, 1972.

XYZ Information Corp. *Coaster & 3-Speed Bicycle Repair*. Canoga Park, CA, 1970.

XYZ Information Corp. *Derailleur Bicycle Repair*. Los Angeles: West Coast Cycle Supply, 1970.

CYCLING MACHINES

Adams, G. Donald. *Collecting and Restoring Antique Bicycles*. Blue Ridge Summit, PA: Tab Books, 1981.

Antique and Classic Bicycle News. *Bicycle Blue Book*. Ann Arbor, MI, 1991. 1820–1970 Price guide.

Antique and Classic Bicycle News. *Collectible Elgin, J.C. Higgins and Hawthorn Bicycles*. Ann Arbor, MI, 1990.

Antique and Classic Bicycle News. *Serial Number Listings for Columbia and Schwinn Bicycles*. Ann Arbor, MI, 1990.

Ayre, Michael. *The Design of Bicycle Trailers*. London: Intermediate Technology, 1986.

Ayre, Michael, and Gordon Hathway. *How to Make a Bicycle Ambulance*. London: Intermediate Technology Development Group, 1984.

Barwell, Ian. *A Report on Improved Rickshaw Technology in Nagpur*. London: Intermediate Technology Development Group, 1978.

Bicycling Magazine. *All-Terrain Bikes*. Emmaus, PA: Rodale Press, 1985.

Burke, James D. *The Gossamer Condor and Albatross: A Case Study in Aircraft Design*. Pasadena, CA: Aerovironment, 1980.

Canadian Human-Powered Vehicle Association. *3rd IHPVA Scientific Symposium Papers*. Vancouver, 1986.

Dovydenas, Vytas. *Velomobile*. Leningrad, 1986. Translated in German, Berlin: Verlag Technik, 1990.

Dwiggins, Don. *Man-Powered Aircraft*. Blue Ridge Summit, PA: Tab Books, 1979.

Fehlau, Gunnar. *Das Liegerad*. Kiel, Germany: Moby Dick, 1993.

Forster, Ron. *Rail Riders*. Franklin, NH: Rail Riders of America, 1980.

Gronen, Wolfgang. *Geschichte des Radsports und des Fahrrads von den Anfängen bis 1939*. Eupen, Germany, 1978.

Grosser, Morton. *Gossamer Odyssey*. London: Michael Joseph; Boston: Houghton Mifflin, 1981.

Guttery, Thomas E. *Cycles and Motor Cycles of the Shuttleworth Collection*. Biggleswade, UK, 1970.

Hathway, Gordon. *Low-Cost Vehicles: Options for Moving People and Goods*. London: Intermediate Technology, 1985.

Hubendick, Professor. *Velocipeden, Automobilen och Motorcykeln*. Stockholm, c.1930.

Hudson-Evans, Richard. *The Lightweight Bike Book*. North Pomfret, VT: David & Charles, 1981.

Hurd, James L., and Don A. Henning. *Introductory Guide to Collecting the Classics*. Ann Arbor, MI: Antique and Classic Bicycle News, 1987, 1990.

Jones, F. Warner. *Treatise on the Theoretical and*

Practical Construction of the Tricycle. London, 1884.

Kimura, Hidemasa. *Man Powered Aircraft Since 1963*. Tokyo: Nihon University, 1977.

McCullagh, James C., editor. *Pedal Power in Work, Leisure and Transportation*. Emmaus, PA: Rodale Press, 1977.

Moller, Eckhard. *Irre Fahrradtypen*. Wiesbaden: Berlin Bauverlag, 1984. "Phantasievolle Fahrradbastler und ihre Werke."

Oliver, Tony. *Touring Bikes: A Practical Guide*. Crowood Press, 1990.

Pinkerton, John. *At Your Service: A Look at Carrier Cycles*. Birmingham, UK: Pinkerton, 1983.

Reay, David A. *The History of Man-Powered Flight*. Oxford, UK: Pergamon Press, 1977.

Rebour, Daniel. *Cycles de compétition et randonneuses*. Paris, 1976.

Royal Aeronautic Society. *Man Powered Flight: The Channel Crossing and the Future*. London, 1979.

Schulze, Hans-Georg, and Willi Stiasny. *Flug Durch Muskelkraft*. Frankfurt am Main: Verlag Fritz Knapp, 1936.

Sherwin, Keith. *Man Powered Flight*. Watford, UK: Model & Allied Publications, 1978.

Sullivan, William L. *The Cart Book with Plans and Projects*. Blue Ridge Summit, PA: Tab Books, 1983.

Whitt, Frank R. *The Restoration of Veteran Cycles*.

Wilson, David Gordon. *Human-Powered Space Transportation*. Boston: Galileo, 1978.

Yepsen, Roger. *Humanpower: Cars, Planes, and Boats with Muscles for Motors*. New York: Macmillan, 1992.

INDUSTRY

Ahmad, S. *Bicycle and Tricycle Spare Parts Manufacturing Industry in Bangladesh: Problems and Prospects*. Dhaka: Bangladesh Shilpa Bank, 1984.

Bowden, Gregory Houston. *The Story of the Raleigh Cycle*. London: W.H. Allen, 1975.

Grew, W.F. *The Cycle Industry: It's Origin, History, and Latest Developments*. London: Sir Isaac Pitman & Sons, 1921.

Forbes, Dean. *Petty Commodity Production and Underdevelopment: The Case of Pedlars and Trishaw Drivers in Unjung Pandang*. Progress in Planning, Vol. 16. Oxford, UK: Pergamon Press, 1981.

Hurd, James, editor. *Frank W. Schwinn's 1942 Personal Notes on the Bicycle Industry*. Chicago: Bicycle Museum of America, 1993.

Industrial Development Organization. *Bicycles: A Case Study of Indian Experience*. Small Scale Mfg. Studies, United Nations, 1970.

International Trade Center. *Bicycles and Components: A Pilot Survey of Opportunities for Trade Among Developing Countries*. Geneva: UNCTAD-GATT, 1985.

International Trade Center. *The Market for Bicycle Components in Federal Republic of Germany, the Netherlands, the USA and Canada*. Geneva: UNCTAD-GATT, 1975.

Israel, Paul. *From Machine Shop to Industrial Laboratory*. Baltimore: Johns Hopkins University Press, 1992.

Italian Trade Commission. *Ciclismo Italiano: the Italian Bicycle Industry*. Los Angeles, 1992, 1993.

Kirk, Randy W. *Bicycle Dealers' Guide to Getting Rich in the Recession*. Second edition. San Clemente, CA: Info Net Publishing, 1989.

Kirk, Randy W. *Principles of Bicycle Retailing*. Second edition. San Clemente, CA: Info Net Publishing, 1988.

India Labour Bureau. *Report on Survey of Labour Conditions in Bicycle Factories in India*. Dehli, 1965.

Pope Mfg. Co. *An Industrial Achievement 1877–1907*. Hartford, CT, 1907.

Tsutsumi, Ryozo. *Japan's Bicycle Industry and Its Vision for the 1990's*. Tokyo: Japan Bicycle Promotion Institute, 1990.

Unipub. *The Development of the Bicycle Industry in Japan after World War II*. New York: Xerox Publishing, 1981.

VeloNews. *Made in USA: A Celebration of the American Bicycle Industry*. Boulder, CO, 1995.

World Bank Industry and Energy Department. *International Competition in the Bicycle Industry: Keeping Pace with Technological Change*. Paper No. 50. Washington, DC, 1990.

INSTRUCTION

Adams, Harry. *Cycles and Cycling*. Oxford, UK: Blackwell, 1965.

Adams, Raymond. *Serious Cycling for the Beginner*. Mt. View, CA: World Publications, 1977.

Ainger, Hal, et al. *The Clear Creek Bike Book*. New York: New American Library, 1972.

Allen, John, and *Bicycling* editors. *Street Smarts: Bicycling's Traffic Survival Guide*. Emmaus, PA: Rodale Press, 1989.

Allen, John. *The Complete Book of Bicycle Commuting*. Emmaus, PA: Rodale Press, 1981.

Allis, John, and Steve Lehrman. *Bicycle Book For You*. Totowa, NJ: Atheneum, 1978.

Alth, Max. *All About Bikes and Bicycling: Care Repair and Safety*. New York: Hawthorn Books, 1972.

Andrews, Heber J. *How to Avoid Bicycle Theft: Complete Handbbook for Parents and Owners*. Tacoma, WA: Hands Off! Pub., 1984.

Ayres, Martin. *Cycles and Cycling*. London: Butterworth, 1981.

Ballantine, Richard. *Richard's Bicycle Book*. New York: Ballantine Books, 1972, 1974, 1978.

Baranet, Nancy Neiman. *Bicycling: The Bicycle in Recreation, Competition, Transportation*. New York: A.S. Barnes, 1973.

Bartleet, Horace Wilton. *Bartleet's Bicycle Book*. London: Burrow & Co., 1931. Reprinted, Birmingham, UK: Pinkerton Press, 1983.

Bennett, Hal Zina. *The Complete Bicycle Commuter: The Sierra Club Guide to Wheeling to Work*. San Francisco: Sierra Club Books, 1982.

Bicycling Magazine. *700 Tips for Better Bicycling*. Emmaus, PA: Rodale Press, 1991.

Biermann, June (Margaret Bennet). *Biking for Grownups*. New York: Dodd, Mead & Co., 1976.

Blish, Jeffery. *The Pedaler's Handbook: A Guide for Bicyclists*. Los Angeles: Nash Publishing, 1972. Reprinted *La Bicyclette*. Montreal: Éditions de l'Homme, 1974.

Call, Frances, and Merle E. Dowd. *The Practical Book of Bicycling*. New York: E.P. Dutton, 1974, 1981.

Camn, F.J. *Every Cyclist's Handbook*. 1936.

Clarke and Wright. *Pedal Power Manual: Bicycle Safety Activities for Communities*. St. Paul, MN: Minnesota Community Bicycle Safety Project.

Coello, Dennis. *Living on Two Wheels*. Berkeley: Ross Books, 1988.

Cuthbertson, Tom. *Bike Tripping*. Berkeley: Ten-Speed Press, 1976.

Cycling & Mopeds. *Cycling Speed Tables*. London: Temple Press, 1954.

Davidson, L.C. *Handbook for Lady Cyclists*. London, 1896.

Dehr, Roma, and Ronald M. Bazar. *From A to Z by Bike*. Vancouver, BC: AMC Media, 1993.

De Long, Fred, and Keith Kingbay. *Bicycling*. Merit Badge Book. New Brunswick, NJ: Boy Scouts of America, 1969; Revised from *Cycling*. 1949.

Dempsey, Paul. *The Bicycler's Bible*. Blue Ridge Summit, PA: Tab Books, 1977.

Donner, Michael. *Bike, Skate and Skateboard Games*. New York: Golden Press, 1977.

Engel, Lyle K. *Bicycling for Fun and Health*. New York: Arco, 1975.

England, H.H. *Cycling Manual*. London: Temple Press, 1960.

Erskine, F.J. *Tricycling for Ladies*. Coventry: Iliffe, 1884.

Evans, Humphrey. *Freewheeling*. London: Octopus Books, 1982.

Fichter, George S., and Keith Kingbay. *Bicycling*. New York: Western Publishing, 1972. Revised *A Golden Guide: Bicycling*. Golden Press, 1974.

Ford, Norman D. *Keep on Pedaling: The Complete Guide to Adult Bicycling*. Woodstock, VT: Backcountry Publications, 1991.

Forester, John. *Effective Cycling Instructor's Manual*. Sunnyvale, CA: Custom Cycle Fitments, 1986.

Frankel, Godfrey. *Bike-Ways*. New York: Sterling, 1950.

Frankel, Lillian Berson, and Godfrey Frankel. *The Bicycle Book (Bike-Ways)*. New York: Cornerstone Library, 1972.

Frankel, Lillian Berson, and Godfrey Frankel. *Bikeways: 101 Things To Do With A Bike*. New York: Sterling, 1961. Revised 1968, 1972.

Franklin, John. *Cyclecraft: Skilled Cycling Techniques*. Falmouth, UK: Unwin.

Gardner, Graeme. *Cycle On*. Hawthorn, Australia: Vic Roads, 1991.

Geist, Roland C. *Bicycling as a Hobby*. 1940.

Gribble, McPhee. *Bicycles: All About Them*. New York: Penguin Books, 1976.

Healy, Dorothy. *All About Bicycles*. New York: Comet Press, 1956.

Henkel, Stephen C. *Bikes*. New York: Bantam Books, 1972.

Hillier, G. Lacy. *The Art of Ease in Cycling*. London: Iliffe, 1899.

Hoffman, Professor. *Tips for Tricyclists*. London: F. Warne, 1887.

Horwood, Robert H. *Bicycles*. Our Science Program. Toronto: Macmillan, 1969.

Hossent, Harry. *The Beaver Book of Bikes*. London: Hamlyn Paperbacks, 1980.

Howard, Leslie B. *Cycling to School*. London: Percival Marshal, 1964.

Humphrey, Clifford C. *Back to the Bike*. San Francisco: 101 Productions, 1972.

Kingbay, Keith. *Inside Bicycling*. Chicago: Regnery, 1976.

Knottley, Peter. *Cycling*. A Spur Book.

Labrecque, Michel, and Robert Bovin. *Je me débrouille à vélo*. Montreal: Éditions de l'Homme, 1988.

Labrecque, Michel, and Robert Bovin. *Vélo: mode d'emploi*. Montreal: Vélo Québec Éditions Tricycle, 1988.

Langley, Jim. *The New Bike Book: How to Make the Most of Your New Bicycle*. Mill Valley, CA: Bicycle Books, 1990.

Leechman, G.D. *Safety Cycling*. London, 1895.

LeMond, Greg, and Kent Gordis. *Greg LeMond's Complete Book of Bicycling*. New York: Putnam, 1990.

Lessing, Hans-Erhard. *Radfahren in der Stadt*. Hamburg, Germany: Rowohlt, 1981.

Lieb, Thomas. *Everybody's Book of Bicycle Riding*. Emmaus, PA: Rodale Press, 1981.

Lyttle, Richard B. *The Complete Beginner's Guide to Bicycling*. New York: Doubleday, 1974.

MacFarlan, Allan. *The Boy's Book of Biking*. Harrisburg, PA: Stackpole, 1968.

McIntyre, Bibs. *The Bike Book*. Scranton, PA: Harper & Row, 1972.

Marino, John, et al. *John Marino's Bicycling Book*. Los Angeles: Tarcher, 1981.

Mathew, Don. *The Bike is Back*. London: Friends of the Earth, 1980.

Mecredy, R.J., and A.J. Wilson. *The Art and*

Pastime of Cycling. London: Iliffe, 1895.

Naden, Corinne. *Driving Your Bike Safely*. New York: Messner, 1979.

Nelson, Janet. *Biking for Fun and Fitness*. New York: Award Books, 1970.

Notdruft-Hopkins, Anita. *How to Ride a Bicycle: Safely, Efficiently and Painlessly*.

Pemberton, A.C. et al. *The Complete Cyclist*. London, 1897.

Plante, Raymond. *Véloville*, Montreal: Editions La Courte Échelle, 1989.

Porter, Luther H. *Cycling for Health and Pleasure*. New York, 1895.

Poulidor, Raymond. *La bicyclette et la randonnée en 10 leçons*. Paris: Hachette, 1975.

Pratt, Charles Eadward. *The American Bicycler: A Manual for the Observer, The Learner, and the Expert*. Boston: Pope Mfg. Co., 1879.

Pruden, Donald. *Around Town Cycling*. Mt. View, CA: World Publications, 1975.

Publications International. *All About Bicycling*. New York: Rand McNally, 1975.

Pullen, A.J. *The Cycling Handbook*. London: Pitman, 1958.

Pullen, A.J. *A Spoke in the Wheel*. London: Benn, 1966.

Roberts, Peter. *Better Cycling*. RoSPA. London: Key & Ward, 1969.

Royal Society for the Prevention of Accidents. *Skilful Cycling: A Manual of Roadcraft, Cycling Technique and Maintenance for Cyclists*. Purley, UK: RoSPA, 1965, 1975.

Organization for Economic Cooperation and Development. *Safety of Two Wheelers*. Paris, 1978.

Outdoor Empire Publishing. *Bicycle Driver's Guide*. Seattle, 1986.

Sarnoff, Jane, Reynold Ruffins, and Rudy "The Bicycle Man" Veselsky. *A Great Bicycle Book*. New York: Charles Scribner's Sons, 1973, 1976.

Saunders, David. *Cycling: The Book for Everybody with a Bicycle*. London: Wolfe, 1971.

Savage, John. *The Gold Medal Bicycle Handbook*. Greenwich, CT: Fawcett World Library, 1972.

Schubert, John. *The Tandem Scoop*. Eugene OR: Burley, 1993.

Scott, Robert P. *Cycling Art, Energy and Locomotion*. Philadelphia, 1889.

Shaw, Reginald Cairns. *Cycling*. London: Teach Yourself Books, 1953, 1967, 1971.

Shaw, Reginald Cairns. *The Raleigh Book of Cycling*. London: Peter Davis, 1975; Sphere Books, 1978.

Shepherd, Ron. *Bike Ed Teachers Manual*. Hawthorn, Australia: Vic Roads, 1987.

Silvert, W. *Learning to Lead: How to Teach Sensible Cycling*. Fifth edition. South Halifax: Bicycle Nova Scotia, 1987.

Skott, Staffan. *Tiden Cykelbok*. Sweden: Zetterling, 1981.

Smith, Ken, editor. *The Canadian Bicycle Book*. Toronto: D.C. Heath, 1972.

Stuart, Robin, and Cathy Jensen. *Mountain Biking*

for Women. 1994.

Thiffault, Mark. *Bicycle Digest*. Northfield, IL: Digest Books, 1973.

Thomas, Nigel. *City Rider*. London: Elm Tree, 1981.

Tracy, Linda, and John Williams. *The Basics of Bicycling*. Washington, DC: Bicycle Federation of America, 1990.

Van der Plas, Rob. *The Bicycle Commuting Book*. Mill Valley, CA: Bicycle Books, 1989.

Van der Plas, Rob. *The Penguin Bicycle Handbook*. Harmondsworth, UK: Penguin Books, 1983.

Wadley, J.B. *Leisureguides: Cycling*. London: Crowell-Macmillan Ltd., 1975.

Wadley, J.B. *Old Roads and New*. London, 1972.

Way, Robert John. *The Complete Cyclist*. Horsham, UK: Wells, Gardner, Darton & Co., 1952.

Wilcockson, John. *Bicycle*. New York: Butterick Publishing, 1980.

Wilcockson, John. *Bicycle Book: The Total Illustrated Guide to Bicycles and Bicycling*. London: Cavendish Books, 1980.

Wiley, Jack. *The Unicycle Book*. Harrisburg, PA: Stackpole Books.

Wiley, Jack. *Basic Circus Skills*. Harrisburg, PA: Stackpole Books.

Williams, John, and Dan Burden. *A Guide to Bicycle Rodeos*. Seattle: Outdoor Empire Publishing.

Wilson, A.J. *The Pleasures, Objects and Advantages of Cycling*. London, 1887.

HEALTH, FITNESS, NUTRITION

Ald, Roy. *Cycling: The Rhythmic, Respiratory Way To Physical Fitness*. New York: Grosset & Dunlap, 1968.

Alter, Michael J. *Sport Stretch*. Champaign, IL: Leisure Press, 1990.

Backroads Bicycle Touring. *Backroads Cookbook*. Berkeley, 1990.

Beinhorn, George, editor. *Food for Fitness*. Mt. View, CA: World Publications, 1972.

Bellencontre, Paraclèse. *Hygiène du Vélocipède*. Paris, 1869.

Bicycling Magazine. *Fitness Through Cycling*. Emmaus, PA: Rodale Press, 1985.

Bicycling Magazine. *Nutrition for Cyclists*. Emmaus, PA: Rodale Press, 1991.

Bicycling Magazine. *Training for Fitness and Endurance*. Emmaus, PA: Rodale Press, 1990.

Bicycling Magazine. *Cycling for Women*. Emmaus, PA: Rodale Press.

Bikecentennial. *A Bicycle Tourist's Cookbook*. Missoula, MT, 1975.

Bowden, Frank. *Cycling For Health: And Points For Cyclists*. Criterion Press, 1913.

British Medical Association. *Cycling Towards Health and Safety*. Oxford: Oxford University Press, 1992.

Burke, Edmund R. *Cycling Health and Physiology*.

Burke, Edmund R. *Inside the Cyclist*. Brattleboro VT: VeloNews, 1987.

Burke, Edmund R., editor. *Medical and Scientific Aspects of Cycling*. Champaign, IL: Human Kinetics Books, 1988.

Burke, Edmund R. *The Two-Wheeled Athlete: Physiology for the Cyclist*. Brattleboro VT: VeloNews, 1988.

Clark, Nancy. *The Athlete's Kitchen*. New York: Simon & Schuster, 1989.

Clark, Nancy. *Nancy Clark's Sports Nutrition Guidebook*.

Gulick, Lither M.D. *The Bicycle as a Theraputic Agent*. 1904.

Hefferon, Lauren. *Cycle Food: A Guide to Satisfying Your Inner Tube*. Berkeley: Ten Speed Press, 1983.

Hemstad, Rachel. *The Hungry Pedalers Cook Book*. San Rafael, CA: Leisure Marketing, 1975.

Herschell, Dr. G. *Cycling as a Cause of Heart Disease*. London, 1896.

Howard, John, Albert Gross, and Christian Paul. *Multi-Fitness*. New York: Macmillan, 1985.

Huber, Anna. *Wombat Cookbook*. Sun Valley, CA: Women's Mountain Bike and Tea Society, 1991.

Human Muscle Power. Champaign, IL: Human Kinetics Books, 1982.

Jennings, Oscar. *Cycling and Health*. London, 1893.

Jennings, Oscar. *La santé par le tricycle*. Paris, 1889.

Martin, Claudine. *The Trekking Chef*. New York: Lyons and Burford.

Mirkin, Gabe. *The Sports Medicine Book*. Emmaus, PA: Rodale Press, 1977.

Prater, Yvonne, and Ruth Mendenhall. *Gorp, Glop, and Glue Stew: Favorite Foods from 165 Outdoor Experts*. Seattle, WA: The Mountaineers, 1986.

Rakowski, John. *Cooking on the Road*. Mt. View, CA: World Publications, 1980.

Raforth, Richard. *Bicycling Fuel*. Mill Valley, CA: Bicycle Books, 1989.

Richardson, Sir B.W. *The Tricycle in Relation to Health*. London, 1885.

Rodale, Robert, and *Bicycling* editors. *The Path to the Golden Wheel*. Emmaus, PA: Rodale Press, 1988.

Schiefferdecker, Dr. *Das Radfahren und seine Hygiene*. Stuttgart, 1900. Reprinted, *Fahrradkultur I*. Hans-Erhard Lessing, editor. Hamburg: Rowohlt, 1982.

Schubert, John. *Richard's Cycling for Fitness*. New York: Ballantine Books, 1987.

Sjegard, Gisela, Edmund Burke, et al. *Physiology in Bicycling*. Ithica, NY: Mouvement Publications, 1982.

Stables, Dr. G.W. *Health upon Wheels*. London, 1887.

Tilton, Buck, and Frank Hubbell. *Medicine for the Back Country*. Merrillville, IN, ICS Books.

Van der Plas, Rob. *The Bicycle Fitness Book*. Second edition. Mill Valley, CA: Bicycle Books, 1990.

Wilcockson, John. *Cycling: Fitness on Wheels*. London: Sunday Times, 1978.

TRAINING, TECHNIQUE

Athletic Institute. *How to Improve Your Cycling*. Chicago: Merchandise Mart; New York: Bicycle Intstitute of America, 1965.

Bicycling Magazine. *Riding and Racing Techniques*. Emmaus, PA: Rodale Press, 1985.

Biesendahl, Karl. *Katechismus des Radfahrsports*. Leipzig, Germany, 1897.

Bike World. *Bicycle Track Racing*. Mt. View, CA: World Publications, 1977.

Boga, Steven. *Cyclists: How the World's Most Daring Riders Train and Compete*. Harrisburg, PA: Stackpole Books, 1992.

Borysewicz, Edward, and Ed Pavelka. *Bicycle Road Racing*. Brattleboro, VT: Vitesse Press, 1985.

Bowden, Kenneth and John Matthews. *Cycle Racing*. London: Temple Press, 1958. Revised 1965.

Burke, Edmund R. *Serious Cycling*. 1994.

Cedaro, Ron, editor. *Triathlon: Achieving Your Personal Best*.

Central Sports School. *Cycling*. Rome: Italian Olympic Committee, F.I.A.C., 1972.

Clément, Daniel. *Cyclisme sur route: initiation, entraînement, compétition*. Fédération Français de Cyclisme. Paris: Amphora, 1976.

Cortis, Herbert Lydell. *Priciples of Training for Amateur Athletics with Special Regard for Cyclists*. London, 1882.

Cyclist's Training Diary. Brattleboro, VT: Vitesse Press, 1990.

Edwards, Sally. *The Heart Rate Monitor Book*. 1992.

Faria, Irvin E. *Cycling Physiology for the Serious Cyclist*. Springfield, IL: Charles Thomas, 1978.

Faria, Irvin E. *The Physiology and Biomechanics of Cycling*. New York: Wiley & Sons, 1978.

Fitness Log for Cyclists. Salt Lake City: Bosworth Graves Visual Communications, 1991.

Frood-Barclay, Robin. *Tackle Cycle Sport This Way*. Hutchinson Group. London: Stanley Paul, 1962.

George, Barbara. *Bicycle Road Racing*. Minneapolis: Lerner, 1977.

George, Barbara. *Bicycle Track Racing*. Minneapolis: Lerner, 1977.

Gorski, Mark. *Cyclist's Log*. Silver Lake, NH: Bikealite, 1990.

Hillier, G. Lacy. *Amateur Cycling with Hints on Training*. London, 1893.

Hinault, Bernard, and Claude Genzling. *Road Racing: Technique and Training*. Brattleboro, VT: VeloNews, 1987.

Janssen, Peter G.J.M. *Training Lactate Pulse-Rate*. 1989.

Kolin, Michael J. *Cycling for Sport*. Seattle: Velosport Press, 1984.

Konopka, Peter. *Cycle Sport: Equipment, Technique and Training*. Brattleboro, VT: Vitesse Press, 1989.

Kugler, Pop. (Fred W. Kugler, Jr.) *Bicycle Racing is an Art*. Brattleboro, VT: Velo-News, 1977.

McElmury, Audrey, and Mike Levonas. *Basic Training*. Brattleboro, VT: Velo-News, 1976.

Maffetone, Philip, and Matthew Mantell. *The High Performance Heart*. Mill Valley, CA: Bicycle Books, 1992.

Mailman, Steve. *The Reoch-Zonneveld Indoor Winter Workout*. 1994.

Mariolle, Elaine, and Michael Shermer. *The Woman Cyclist*. Chicago: Contemporary Books, 1988.

Massagrande, Agostino. *Agonistic Cycling*. Italy: Edizione Londini, 1982.

Matheny, Fred. *Beginning Bicycle Racing*. Third edition. Brattleboro, VT: VeloNews, 1987.

Matheny, Fred. *Solo Cycling: How to Train and Race Bicycle Time Trials*. Brattleboro, VT: VeloNews, 1988.

Matheny, Fred, et al. *Weight Training for Cyclists*. Brattleboro, VT: Vitesse Press, 1986.

Messenger, Chas. *Conquer the World*. London: Pelham Books, 1968.

Phinney, Davis, and Connie Carpenter. *Training for Cycling*.

Orlick, Terry. *In Pursuit of Excellence: How to Win in Sport and Life Through Mental Training*. 1990.

Rogers, Thurlow, and Karen Roy. *Fit and Fast: How to be a Better Cyclist*. Brattleboro, VT: Vitesse Press, 1989.

Sheil, Norman, and *Bicycling* editors. *7-Eleven Grand Prix Training Manual II*. Brattleboro, VT: Vitesse Press, 1984.

Shermer, Michael. *Sport Cycling*. Chicago: Contemporary Books, 1985.

Shermer, Michael. *Cycling: Endurance and Speed*.

Simes, Jack, and Barbara George. *Winning Bicycle Racing*. Chicago: Regnery, 1976.

Sleamaker, Rob. *Serious Training for Serious Athletes*.

Thierry, Stephen. *FITRAK: The Ultimate Multi-Activity Aerobic Training Journal*. Three Rivers, MI: FIT Systems, 1989.

Tinley, Scott, and Ken McAlpine. *Scott Tinley's Winning Guide to Sports Endurance*.

Town, Glen, and Todd Kearney. *Swim, Bike, Run*.

Union Cycliste Internationale. *General Regulations*. Geneva, annual.

Van der Plas, Rob. *The Bicycle Racing Book*. Third edition. Mill Valley, CA: Bicycle Books, 1988.

von Salvisberg, Paul. *Der Radfahrsport in Bild und Wort*. Munich, 1897. Reprinted, Hildesheim: Olms Presse, 1980.

Ward, Peter. *King of Sports: Cycle Road Racing*. Lancashire: The Preston Herald, 1968.

Wilcockson, John. *Cycle Racing*. Cycling Council of Great Britain. Wakefield: Education Production Group, 1972.

Williams, Melvin H. *Beyond Training: How Athletes Enhance Performance Legally and Illegally*.

Woodland Les. *Cycle Racing: Training to Win*. London: Pelham Books, 1975.

Woodland Les. *Cycle Racing & Touring*. London: Pelham Books, 1976.

Woodland, Les. *Dope: The Use of Drugs in Sport*. Newton Abbot, UK: David & Charles, 1980.

Woodward, Christopher R. *Scientific Training for Cycling*. London: Temple Press, 1960. Revised, 1961.

Zorn, Henk. *Wielersport: historie, materiaal, training, techniek, en taktiek*. Rijswijk, NL: Elmar, 1983.

TRANSPORT

American Association of Street, Highway and Transport Officials. *Guide for the Development of New Bicycle Facilities*. Washington, DC, 1991.

Bendixson, Terence. *Instead of Cars*. London: Temple Smith, 1974.

Bicycle Federation of America. *Bicycle Coordinators and Programs: Why, How, What and Who*. Washington, DC, 1991.

Bicycle Institute of America. *Bicycle Program Specialist Survey*. Washington, DC, 1991.

Bicycle Institute of America. *Bicycle Route Research: Technical Report*. Washington, DC, 1986.

Bicycle Institute of America. *Selecting and Designating Bicycle Routes*. Washington, DC, 1986.

Bikecentennial. *Improving Local Conditions for Bicycling*. Missoula, MT, 1989.

Boethling, Bob, editor. *The Bicycle Book*. UCLA Earth Action Council. Los Angeles: Price, Stern, Soan, 1972.

Bovin, Robert, and Jean-François Pronovost. *The Bicycle: Global Perspectives*. Montréal: Vélo Mondiale, 1992.

Briones, S, and W.J. Dean. *Pedestrian Revolution: Streets Without Cars*. New York: Random House, 1974.

British Cycling Bureau. *Before the Traffic Grinds to a Halt*. London, 1972.

Danish State Railways. *Cykelparkering og cykel-centre: et idékatalog (Bicycle Parking Facilities and Bicycle Centers)*. Copenhagen, 1990.

DeLeuw, Cather, and Associates. *Bikeways: State of the Art 1974*. Springfield, VA: National Technical Information Service, 1974.

Dutch Ministry of Transport and Public Works. *Evaluation of the Delft Bicycle Network*. Netherlands, 1987.

Engwicht, David. *Reclaiming Our Cities & Towns: Better Living with Less Traffic*. Philadelphia: New Society Publishers, 1993.

Fletcher, Ellen. *Bicycle Parking*. Palo Alto, CA: Santa Clara Valley Bicycle Association, 1983. Sixth edition, 1990.

Forester, John. *Bicycle Transportation*. Cambridge, MA: MIT Press, 1983.

Forester, John. *Cycling Traffic Engineering Handbook*. Palo Alto, CA: Custom Cycle Fitments, 1976.

Gallagher, Rob. *The Rickshaws of Bangladesh*. Dhaka: University Press, 1992. 675 pp.

Harnik, Peter. *Bicycle Advocate's Handbook*. Baltimore: League of American Wheelmen, 1989.

Heierli, Urs. *Environmental Limits to Motorization: Non-motorized Transport in Developed and Developing Countries*. St. Gallen, Switzerland: SKAT, 1993.

Herman, Michele, et al. *Bicycle Blueprint: A Plan to Bring Bicycling into the Mainstream in New York City*. New York: Transportation Alternatives, 1993.

Hope, Daphne, and Dwight Yachuk. *Community Cycling Manual: A Planning and Design Guide*. Gloucester, Ontario: Canadian Cycling Association.

Howe, John, and Ron Dennis. *The Bicycle in Africa: Luxury or Necessity?* Delft, NL: Infrastructure Hydraulics Environment, 1993.

Hudson, Mike. *Bicycle Planning*. London: Architectural Press, 1982.

Jordan, Gilhon. *Bicycles, Transportation, and Energy: A Handbook for Planners*. Philadelphia, 1985.

Keller, Kit. *Mountain Bikes on Public Lands: A Manager's Guide to the State of the Practice*. Washington, DC: Bicycle Federation of America, 1990.

Illich, Ivan. *Energy and Equity*. London: Calder and Boyars, 1973.

International Bicycle Fund. *Survey of Airline Baggage Regulations for Bicycles*. Seattle, 1992.

Kartodirdjo, Sartono. *The Pedicab in Yogyakarta: A Study of Low-Cost Transportation and Poverty Problems*. Institute for Rural and Regional Studies. Indonesia: Gadjah Mada University Press, 1981.

Lawton, Kate. *Economic Impact of Bike Trails: A Case Study of the Suger River Trail*. Rockford, IL: Department of Community Development, 1986.

Letarte, Robert, Yves Boucher and Michel Trudel. *La bicyclette, un moyen de transport*. Québec: Ministry of Tranport, 1977.

Lowe, Marcia. *The Bicycle: Vehicle for a Small Planet*. Worldwatch Paper 90. Washington, DC: Worldwatch Institute, 1989.

Lowe, Marcia. *Alternatives to the Automobile: Transport for Livable Cities*. Worldwatch Paper 98. Washington, DC: Worldwatch Institute,

1990.

McClintock, Hugh, ed. *The Bicycle and City Traffic*. London: Belhaven Press, 1992.

McDonald, Peter. *Changing Gear*. Aukland, NZ: Friends of the Earth, 1977.

McRobie, George, et al. *Setting the Wheels in Motion: Towards a National Cycling Policy*. London: Intermediate Technology Publications, 1983.

Montague, Charles H. *Preserving Abandoned Railroad Rights of Way For Public Use: A Legal Manual*. Washington, DC: Rails-to-Trials Conservancy, 1989.

Moudon, Anne Vernez. *Public Streets for Public Use*. New York: Columbia University Press, 1991.

Murukadas, Dr. C. *Urban Poor: A Study of Rickshaw Cyclists in Madras City*. Association for Population Studies, University of Madras, India, 1984.

Navarro, Ricardo A., Urs Heierli, and Victor Beck. *La Bicicleta y Los Triciclos: Alternativas de Transporte en America Latina*. St. Galen, Switzerland: Co-published by SKAT (Switzerland), CESTA (El Salvador), GATE (Germany), CETAL (Chile), 1985.

Nielsen, Birgitte Høj. *The Bicycle in Denmark*. Copenhagen: Danish Ministry of Transport, 1993.

Nielsen, Waldo. *Right of Way: Guide to Abandoned Railroads in the U.S.* Bend, OR: Old Bottle Magazine, 1972.

Ocampo, Romeo B. *Low Cost Transport in Asia: A Comparative Report on Five Cities*. Ottawa: International Development Research Center, 1982.

Pendelton, Thomas, and Peter Lagerwey. *A Comparative Study of Bicycle Parking Racks*. City of Ann Arbor Bicycle Program. Ann Arbor, MI: 1981.

Philpott, Julia. *Human-Powered Vehicles: Addressing Mobility Needs for Low-Income People*. Washington, DC: ITDP, 1991.

Puncochar, Brian, and Peter Lagerwey. *Evaluation of the Burke-Gilman Trail's Effect on Property Values and Crime*. Seattle, WA: Community Transportation Services.

Rails-to-Trials Conservancy. *Converting Rails to Trails*. Washington, DC, 1987.

Rashid, Dr. Salim. *The Rickshaw Industry of Dhaka: Preliminary Findings*. Dhaka: Bangladesh Institute of Development Studies, 1986.

Renner, Michael. "Rethinking Transportation." *State Of the World 1989*. Worldwatch Institute. New York: W.W. Norton, 1989.

Replogle, Michael. *Bicycles and Public Transportation*. Emmaus, PA: Rodale Press, 1983.

Replogle, Michael. *Bicycles and Public Transportation: New Links to Suburban Transit Markets*. Washington, DC: Institute for

Transportation Development & Policy, 1984.

Replogle, Michael and Harriet Parcells. *Linking Bicycle/Pedestrian Facilities with Transit*. Washington, DC: National Association of Railroad Passengers and U.S. Federal Highway Administration, 1992.

Replogle, Michael. *Non-Motorized Vehicles in Asian Cities*. Washington, DC: World Bank Technical Paper No. 162, 1992.

Rimmer, Peter J. *From Rikisha to Rapid Transit: Urban Public Transport Systems and Policy in Southeast Asia*. Australia: Pergamon Press, 1986.

Rosen, Nils. *Cyklen I Stadsplanen*. Orsa, Sweden: Cykel-och Mopedframjandet, 1971.

Ryan, Karen-Lee, editor. *Trails for the Twenty-First Century*. Rails-to-Trails Conservancy. Washington, DC: Island Press, 1993.

Sachs, Wolfgang. *For Love of the Automobile*. 1984.

Schwartz, Loring, editor. *Greenways: A Guide to Planning, Design, and Development*. Washington, DC: Island Press, 1993.

Social Sciences Research Centre, Chiang Mai University. *A Socio-Economic Study of the Samlor and Silor Drivers in the City of Chiang Mai, Thailand, 1976–78*. Chiang Mai University, March 1979.

Tolley, Rodney, editor. *The Greening of Urban Transport: Planning for Walking and Cycling in Western Cities*. London: Bellhaven Press, 1990.

Unnayan, with T.H. Thomas. *Rickshaws in Calcutta*. Calcutta, India: Unnayan, 1981.

Urban Bikeway Design Collaborative. *Cyclateral Thinking*. Cambridge, MA: MIT Press, 1976.

U.S. Department of Transportation. *Bicycle Transportation for Energy Conservation*. Washington, DC, 1980.

U.S. National Technical Information Service. *ABCD's of Bikeways*. Springfield, VA, 1976.

Williams, Heathcote. *Autogeddon*. London: Jonathan Cape, 1991.

Wolfe, Frederick L. *The Bicycle: A Commuting Alternative*.

Zuckermann, Wolfgang. *End of the Road: The World Car Crisis and How We Can Solve It*. Post Mills, VT: Chelsea Green, 1991.

SAFETY, LAW

American National Standards Institute. *ANSI Standard Z-90.2 Protective Headgear for Bicycle Users*. New York, 1990.

Bicycle Helmet Safety Institute. *A Consumer's Guide to Bicycle Helmets*. Arlington, VA, 1990.

Cincinnati Cycle Club. *Bicycle Safety Report: The Stormwater Grate*.

Clementson, George Burr. *The Road Rights and Liabilities of Wheelmen*. 1895.

Cross and Fisher. *A Study of Bicycle/Motor Vehicle Accidents: Identification of Problem*

Types and Countermeasure Approaches. Springfield, VA: National Techinical Information Service, 1977.

Davis, W. Jeff. *Bicycle Safety Evaluation*. Auburn University, 1987.

Davis, Robert. *Death on the Streets: Cars and the Mythology of Road Safety*. London: Leading Edge, 1993.

English, John. *Liability Aspects of Bikeway Designation*. Washington, DC: Bicycle Federation of America, 1986.

Fife, Daniel. *Fatal Injuries to Bicyclists: The Experience of Dade County, Florida*. Washington, DC: Insurance Institute for Highway Safety. Reprint, *The Journal of Trauma*. August 1983.

Green, James M. *Bicycle Accident Reconstruction for the Forensic Engineer*. Mill Valley, CA: Bicycle Books; Cary, NC: Resource Engineering, 1991.

Hill, Paul. *Bicycle Law and Practice*. Falls Church, VA: Bicycle Law Books, 1986.

Hillman, Mayer. *Bicycle Helmets: The Case For and Against*. London: Policy Studies Institute, 1993.

Kessler, Leonard P. *A Tale of Two Bicycles: Safety on Your Bike*. West Caldwell, NJ: William Morrow, 1971.

League of American Wheelmen. *Bicycle Bans, Restrictions and Discriminations*. Baltimore, 1989.

League of American Wheelmen. *Lighting the Way Ahead: A Special Report on Bicycle Lighting and Night Riding*. Baltimore, 1990.

National Safety Council. *Sammy Sprocket Says*. Chicago, 1955. Lucky 13 Bike Safety Rules.

National Safety Council. *Traffic Accident Facts*. Chicago, 1968.

Starks, H.J.H., and R.D. Lister. *Some Safety Aspects of Pedal and Motor-assisted Cycles*. UK: Her Majesty's Stationary Office, 1957.

Stutts, Jane C. *An Analysis of Bicycle Accident Data from Ten North Carolina Hospital Emergency Rooms*. Raleigh, NC: North Carolina Bicycle Program, 1986.

U.S. Consumer Product Safety Commission. *Bicycle Compliance Test Manual*. Kenneth W. Edinger, editor. Washington, DC, 1974, Revised.

SOCIAL HISTORY

a'Green, George (Reginald Cairns Shaw). *This Great Club of Ours: The Story of the CTC*. London: Cyclists' Touring Club, 1953.

Åke, I.A.F. *The Role of the Bicycle in Post-Revisionist Cultures*. University of Kalgoorlie, 1984.

Algemeene Nedelandsche Wielrijdersbond. *Een eeuw wijzer: 100 jaar ANWB 1883-1983*. Den Haag, l983.

American Heritage Press. *America On Parade*. Poughkeepsie: Guild Press, 1958.

Anderson, Janice, and Edmund Swinglehurst. *Ephemera of Travel and Transport*. London: New Cavendish Books, 1981.

Armstrong, Christopher, and H.V. Nelles. *The Revenge of the Methodist Bicycle Company: Sunday Streetcars & Municipal Reform in Toronto, 1888-1897*. Toronto: Peter Martin Assoc., 1977.

Aronson, Sidney H. "The Sociology of the Bicycle," *Social Forces* 30, 1952.

Barthes, Roland. *Mythologies*. Paris: Editions du Seuil, 1957.

Behrman, Daniel. *The Man Who Loved Bicycles*. New York: Harper's Magazine Press 1973.

Bertz, Eduard. *Philosophis des Fahrrades*. Dresden, Germany, 1900.

Bidlake, F.T. *Cycling*. 1896.

Bobet, Jean. *Cyclisme de plaisance*. Paris: La Table Ronde.

Borge, Jacques, and Nicolas Viasnoff. *Le Vélo, la Liberté*. Paris, Balland, 1978.

Bowen, Ezra, editor. *This Fabulous Century: Prelude 1870-1900*. New York: Time-Life Books, 1970.

Bury, Viscount, and G. Lacy Hillier. *Cycling*. The Badminton Library. London: Longmans, Green & Co., 1887-1895.

Caidin, Martin, and Jay Barbree. *Bicycles in War*. New York: Hawthorn Books, 1974.

Cole, Terence, editor. *Wheels on Ice: Bicycling in Alaska 1898-1908*. Anchorage: Alaska Northwest Publishing, 1985.

Coley, Rex. *Laughter on Two Wheels*. London: Stanley Paul, 1963.

Crushton, Hon. Mr. *History of the Pickwick Bicycle Club 1870-1904*.

De Vries, Leonard, and Ilonka van Amstel. *De dolle entree van automobiel en velocipee*. Bussum, Netherlands: De Haan, 1973.

Demaus, A.B., editor. *Victorian and Edwardian Cycling and Motorcycling from Old Photographs*. London: Batsford Ltd.; New York: Hippocrene Books, 1977.

Duncan, Herbert O. *The World on Wheels*. Paris, 1928.

Durand, Jacques. *Vive le Vélo*. Paris: Éditions Stock, 1974.

Fitzpatrick, Jim. *The Bicycle and the Bush: A Study of the Bicycle in Rural Australia*. Melbourne: Oxford University Press, 1980.

Franke, Peter. *Lob des Fahrrads*. (Praise the Bicycles) Zurich: Sanssouci, 1974.

Fuchs, Johannes M., and W.J. Simons. *Allemaal op de fiets in Amsterdam*. Amsterdam, 1978.

Fuchs, Johannes M., and W.J. Simons. *Voort, in 't zadel, kameraden*. Amsterdam, 1975.

Gattey, G.N. *The Bloomer Girls*. London, 1967.

Gordon, Irving J. *Devil on Wheels*. Glasgow, 1946.

Grivell, Henry Curly. *Australian Cycling in the Golden Days*. South Australia: S.A. Unley, 1952.

Humber, William. *Freewheeling: The Story of Bicycling in Canada*. Erin: Boston Mills Press, 1986.

Learmont, Tom. *Cycling in South Africa*. South Africa: Media House Publications, 1990.

Leonard, I.A. *When Bikehood was in Flower*. Goldenrod, FL: Bearcamp Press, 1969; Tucson: Seven Palms Press, 1983.

Light Dragoon. *Wheels and Woes*. London, 1870.

Lightwood, J.T. *The Romance of the Cyclists' Touring Club*. London: C.T.C., 1928.

Lockert, Louis. *Vélocipèdes*. Paris: Touring Club de France, 1896.

McGonagle, Seamus. *The Bicycle in Love, Life, War and Literature*. London: Pelham Books, 1968; New York: A.S. Barnes, 1969.

Macredy, R.J., and A.I. Wilson. *The Art and Pastime of Cycling*. 1890.

Maree, Diederick R. *Bicycles During the Boer War, 1899-1902*. National Museum of Military History, South Africa, 1977.

May, William T. *Cyclists' Drill Regulations, U.S. Army*. Boston: Pope Mfg. Co., 1892.

Oakley, William. *Winged Wheel: The History of the First Hundred Years of the Cyclists' Touring Club*. Godalming, UK: C.T.C., 1978.

Opperman, Sir Hubert. *Pedals, Politics and People*. Australia: Haldance.

Palmer, Arthur Judson. *Riding High: the Story of the Bicycle*. New York: E.P. Dutton, 1956.

Pinkerton, John, and F.R. Whitt. *Strange, But True!* Cartoons.

Renoy, Georges. *Le vélo au temps des belles moustaches*. Brussels: Rossel & Cie., 1975.

Shattuck, Roger. *The Banquet Years*. London: Cape, 1962.

Simons, W.J. *Fiets!* Lelystad, 1975.

Sinclair, Helen. *Cycle-Clips: A History of Cycling in the North East*. Newcastle-upon-Tyne, UK: Tyne and Wear Museums, 1985.

Smith, Philip R. "Bicycles Built for War," *American Legion Magazine*, November 1977.

Smith, Robert A. *A Social History of the Bicycle: Its Early Life and Times in America*. New York: American Heritage Press, 1972.

Street, Roger. *Victorian High-Wheelers: The Social Life of the Bicycle Where Dorset Meets Hampshire*. Sherbourne: Dorset Publishing, 1979.

Sudbury, Ronald F. *The Bicycle and the Postage Stamp*. West Yorkshire: Harry Hayes, 1976.

Sudbury, Ronald F. *Stamp Collecting for the Cyclist*. West Yorkshire: Harry Hayes, 1981.

Trapman, A.H. *Cyclists in Action*. 26th Middlesex Volunteers, 1904.

U.S. Office of Price Administration. *New Adult Bicycle Ration Regulations*. Washington, DC, 1942.

Warren, James Francis. *Rickshaw Coolie: A People's History of Singapore, 1880-1940*. East Asian Social Science Monographs. Singapore: Oxford University Press, 1986.

Waugh, Authur. *Legends of the Wheel*. London, 1898.

Wilson, H.W. *With the Flag to Pretoria*. Harmondsworth, UK, 1900.

Wolf, Wilhelm. *Fahrrad und Radfahrer*. Leipzig, 1890. Reprinted, Dortmund, Germany: Taschenbucher, 1979.

SPORTS, ROAD AND TRACK

Abt, Samuel. *Breakaway: On the Road with the Tour de France*. New York: Random House, 1985.

Abt, Samuel. *Champion: Bicycle Racing in the Age of Indurain*. Mill Valley, CA: Bicycle Books, 1993.

Abt, Samuel. *In High Gear*. Mill Valley, CA: Bicycle Books, 1989.

Abt, Samuel. *LeMond: The Incredible Comeback of an American Hero*. New York: Random House, 1990.

Abt, Samuel. *Tour de France: Three Weeks to Glory*. Mill Valley, CA: Bicycle Books, 1991.

Anquetil, Jacques, Pierre Chany and Michel Scob. *Cyclisme: compétitions, loisirs*. Paris: R. Laffont, 1975.

Anquetil, Jacques. *Je suis comme ca*. Paris: Union General, 1964.

Archipov, Evgeni M., and Arkady B. Cedov. *On Olympic Tracks*. Moscow, 1961.

Archipov, Evgeni M., and Arkady B. Cedov. *Velocipeding Sport*. Moscow: Athletics and Sport, 1990.

Armstrong, David. *The Emperor: Rik Van Looy*. Silsden, UK: Kennedy Bros., 1971.

Armstrong, David. *Eternal Second: The Raymond Poulidor Story*. Silsden, UK: Kennedy Bros., 1970.

Armstrong, David. *Felice Gimondi: The Happy Champion*. Silsden, UK: Kennedy Bros., 1975.

Armstrong, David. *Maitre Jacques: The Jacques Anquetil Story*. Silsden, UK: Kennedy Bros., 1970.

Band, Moritz. *Handbuch des Radfahr-Sports*. Vienna, 1895.

Baranet, Nancy Neiman. *The Turned Down Bar*. Philadelphia: Dorrance, 1964.

Bastide, Roger. *À la pointe des pelotons*. Paris: Solar, 1972.

Bastide, Roger. *À la pointe des pelotons: Ocaña face à Merckx*. Paris: Presse Pocket, 1974.

Bastide, Roger. *Doping*. Paris: Solar, 1970.

Bertellini, Nello, editor. *Da Coppi a Merckx*. Legnano, Italy: Landoni, 1977.

Bishop, Claire H. *The Big Loop*. London: J.M. Dent, 1962.

Bobet, Jean. *La course en tête*. Paris: La Table Ronde, 1966.

Bobet, Jean, and Roger Frankeur. *Champions*. Paris: La Table Ronde.

Bobet, Louison. *En selle*. Paris: Edition Points, 1958.

Bottema, Mac W., et al. *Handbook on Bicycle Tracks and Cycle Racing*. Dayton, OH: Huffman Mfg. Co., 1963.

Briquet, Georges. *Ici: 60 ans de Tour de France*. Paris: La Table Rond, 1962.

British Cycling Federation. *BCF Handbook*. Manchester, annual.

Budzinski, Fredy. *Das Berliner Sechs-Tage-Rennen*. Berlin, 1909.

Carter, Bruce. *Bike Racers*. London: Longman, 1974.

Clifford, Peter, and John Butfield. *History of the Tour of Britain*. London: International Cyclists Saddle Club, 1967.

Clifford, Peter. *The Tour de France*. London: Stanley Paul, 1965.

Conconi, Francesco. *Moser's Hour Records: A Human and Scientific Adventure*. Translated by Patricia Ennis. Brattleboro, VT: Vitesse Press, 1991.

Cornand, Jan. *Tour of Italy 1974*. Silsden, UK: Kennedy Bros., 1974.

Chany, Pierre. *La fabuleuse histoire du Tour de France*. Paris: ODIL, 1975, 1983.

Chany, Pierre. *Les rendevous du cyclisme ou arriva Coppi*. Paris: La Table Ronde.

Chantigny, Louis. *Mes grands du cyclisme*. Montreal: Éditions Leméac, 1974.

Chapatte, Robert, and François Terbeen. *Alor Chapatte, reconte... propos*. Paris: Calmann-Lévy, 1975.

Chauner, David, and Michael Halstead. *The Tour de France Complete Book of Cycling*. New York: Villard Books, 1991.

Cook, Jeff. *The Triathletes: A Season in the Lives of Four Women in the Toughest Sport of All*. 1990.

Daffern, Eileen. *Le Tour de France*. Glasgow, Scotland: Blackie, 1974.

De Maertelaere, Roger. *6 Daagsen - Jour - Tagerennen*. 1991.

Dirand, Georges. *Poulidor*. Paris: Calmann-Levy, 1974.

Duker, Peter. *Coppi*. Bognor Regis, UK: New Horizon, 1982.

Duker, Peter. *Sting in the Tail*. London: Pelham Books, 1973.

Duker, Peter. *The TI-Raleigh Story*. Coventry: Midland Letterpress, 1979.

Duniecq, Jacques. *Tour de France 1972*. Silsden, UK: Kennedy Bros., 1972.

Durry, Jean. *La véridique histoire des géants de la route*. Paris: Denoël, 1973.

Eisele, Otto. *Cycling Almanac*. New York, 1950, 1951.

L'Equipe. *Le Tour de France a 75 ans*. Paris, 1978.

Eyle, Wim van. *Een euuw Nederlandse weiler-sport*. Utrect, NL, 1980.

5-4-3-2-1—GO! Silsden, UK: Kennedy Bros.

Foster, Benny. *The Benny Foster Story*. Silsden, UK: Kennedy Bros., 1971.

Fretwell, Peter, and A. Gadenz. *Tour of Italy*. Silsden, UK: Kennedy Bros., 1972, 1973.

Gambling, Mick. *Mick Gambling...On Cycling*. Coventry: Forest Publishing, 1981. Tales from *Cycling*.

Gabriele, Michael. *The Nutley Velodrome: A History of the Legendary Cycling Mecca*. New Jersey, c.1980.

Geminiani, Raphael. *Mes quatre cents coups... de gueule et de fusil*. Paris: La Table Ronde, 1963.

Gesser, Rudolf. *Classic Cycle Races of Europe*. Huddersfield, UK: Springfield Books, 1993.

Guinness, Rupert. *The Foreign Legion*. Huddersfield, UK: Springfield Books, 1993.

Harper, Ted. *Six Days of Madness*. 1994.

Harris, Reg, and Gregory Bowden. *Two Wheels to the Top*. London: W.H. Allen, 1976.

Henderson, Noel G. *Centenary 78: The Story of 100 Years of Organized British Cycle Racing*. Silsden, UK: Kennedy Bros., 1977.

Henderson, Noel G. *Continental Cycle Racing*. London: Pelham Books, 1970.

Henderson, Noel G. *Cyclepedia*. Silsden, UK: Kennedy Bros., 1971.

Henderson, Noel G. *Cycling Year Book*. London: Pelham Books, 1971.

Henderson, Noel G. *European Cycling: The 20 Greatest Races*. Brattleboro, VT: Vitesse Press, 1989.

Henderson, Noel G. *Fabulous Fifties*. Silsden, UK: Kennedy Bros.

Henderson, Noel G. *Six of the Best*. Silsden, UK: Kennedy Bros., 1971.

Henderson, Noel G. *Yellow Jersey*. Silsden, UK: Kennedy Bros., 1970.

Hinault, Bernard. *Hinault by Hinault*. Allentown, PA: Winning Publications, 1988.

Hinault, Bernard. *Memories of the Peloton*. Brattleboro, VT: Vitesse Press, 1988.

Hoban, Barry, with John Wilcockson. *Watching the Wheels Go Round*. London: Stanley Paul, 1981.

Hogenkamp, George J.M. *Een halve eeuw wieler-sport*. Amsterdam, 1916.

Howard, John, and Peter Nye. *Pushing the Limits: The Story of John Howard, the Incredible Human Machine*. Waco, TX: WRS Publishing, 1993.

Jacobs, René, Robert de Smet and Hector Mahau. *Velo*. Hoeliaart, Belgium: Jacobs, annual 1979–1982.

Jeaniau, Marc. *Le cyclisme de Coppi à Van Looy et Anquetil*. Paris: Dargaud, 1967.

Johnson, Bob, and Patricia Bragg. *The Complete Triathlon*. Santa Barbara: Health Science, 1982.

Kelly, Sean, and David Walsh. *Sean Kelly: A Man for All Seasons*. 1992.

Kent, Peter. *Legends of Cycling*. Silsden, UK: Kennedy Bros., 1971.

Kilian, Gustav, and Gerd Rensmann. *Allein ist man nichts - als Mannschaft alles*. (Alone man is nothing, as a team, all) Westfalen, Germany: Verlag Sportwerbung Steinbrecher, 1991.

Kimmage, Paul. *A Rough Ride*. Boulder, CO: VeloNews, 1990.

Kingbay, Keith, and George Fichter. *Contemporary Bicycle Racing*. Chicago: Contemporary Books, 1974.

Konopka, Peter. *Cycle Sport*. Brattleboro, VT: Vitesse, 1989.

Koomen, Theo. *The Winning Team*. Nottingham, UK: TI-Raleigh Ltd., 1983.

Latour, Rene de. *World Champions I Have Known*. Silsden, UK: Kennedy Bros., 1970.

Laget, Serge and François. *La belle epoche du cyclisme*. Paris: Chiron-Sports, 1978.

Laget, Serge. *Le Cyclisme*. Paris: Larousse, 1978.

Laget, Serge. *La saga du Tour de France*. Paris: Gallimard Publishing, 1990.

Leducq, André. *Une fleur au guidon*.

Luchon, Raphael. *Roger De Vlaeminck*.

McCullagh, James C., editor. *American Bicycle Racing*. Emmaus, PA: Rodale Press, 1976.

Maertens, Freddy, and Manu Adriaens. *Fall from Grace*. 1993.

Magowan, Robin, and Graham Watson. *Kings of the Road: A Portrait of Racers and Racing*. Champaign, IL: Leisure Press, 1988.

Magowan, Robin. *Tour de France*. London: Stanley Paul, 1979.

Marino, John, Lon Haldeman, and Michael Shermer. *The RAAM Book*. San Clemente, CA: Info Net Publishing, 1988.

Martin, Pierre. *The Bernard Hinault Story*. Silsden, UK: Kennedy Bros., 1982.

Meiffret, José. *Breviary of a Cyclist*. France: 1960.

Meiffret, José. *Mes rendez-vous avec la mort*. 1965.

Merckx, Eddy, and Winning Magazine. *Fabulous World of Cycling*. Volumns 1–5. Allentown, PA: Winning, 1983–1989.

Messenger, Chas. *Cycling Crazy*. London: Pelham Books, 1970.

Messenger, Chas. *Cycling's Circus*. London: Pelham Books, 1971.

Messenger, Chas. *Where There's A Wheel*. London: Pelham Books, 1972.

Meyer, Gaston, and Serge Laget. *Le livre d'or du sport Français*. 1845–1945.

Mockridge, Russell. *My World on Wheels: The Posthumous Autobiography of Russell Mockridge*. John Burrows, editor. London: Stanley Paul, 1960.

Moore, Harold. *The Complete Cyclist*. London: Pitman, 1952, 1972.

Moxham, S.M. *Fifty Years of Road Racing: A History of the North Road Cycling Club*. London: Diemer & Reynold, 1935.

Murphy, Charles M. *The Story of the Railroad and a Bicycle: When "A Mile a Minute" Was Born*. New York: Jamaica Law, 1936.

Nicholson, Geoffrey. *The Great Bike Race*. London: Hodder & Stoughton, 1977; Magnum, 1978.

Nicholson, Geoffrey. *Tony Dole: Six-Day Rider*.

Nicholson, Geoffrey. *Le Tour*. 1991.

Nye, Peter. *Hearts of Lions: The Story of American Bicycle Racing*. New York: W.W. Norton, 1988.

Ollivier, Jean-Paul, and Jean-Michel Leulliot. *Dossiers secrets du cyclisme*. Paris: Pygmallion, 1975.

Pagnoud, Georges. *Le livre d'or de Poulidor*. Paris, 1975.

Pellisier, Henri. *Le cyclisme sur route*. Paris: Borneman, 1950.

Porter, Hugh. *Champion on Two Wheels*. London: Robert Hale, 1975.

Poulidor, Raymond. *La gloire sans maillot jaune*. Paris: Calmann-Lévy, 1968.

Prouty, David. *In Spite of Us: My Education in the big and little games of amateur and Olympic sports in the U.S.* Brattleboro, VT: VeloNews, 1988.

Ritchie, Andrew. *Major Taylor: The Extraordinary Career of a Champion Bicycle Racer*. Mill Valley, CA: Bicycle Books, 1988.

Roche, Stephen, with David Walsh. *The Agony and the Ecstacy: Stephen Roche's World of Cycling*. North Pomfret, VT: David & Charles, 1989.

St. Pierre, Roger. *Cycle Racing Tactics*. Silsden, UK, Kennedy Bros., 1970.

St. Pierre, Roger. *Louison Bobet*. Silsden, UK, Kennedy Bros., 1971.

St. Pierre, Roger. *Merckx: Man and Myth*. Silsden, UK, Kennedy Bros., 1972.

St. Pierre, Roger. *The Story of Reg Harris*. Silsden, UK: Kennedy Bros., 1971.

St. Pierre, Roger. *The Uncrowned Kings of Cycling*. Silsden, UK: Kennedy Bros., 1971.

Saunders, David. *Cycling in the Sixties*. London: Pelham Books, 1971.

Saunier, Baudry de, with Charles Terront. *Les Mémoires de Terront*. Paris, 1893. Reprinted, Paris: Prosport, 1980.

Sheridan, Eileen. *Wonder Wheels: The Autobiography of Eileen Sheridan*. London: Nicholas Kaye, 1956.

Shermer, Michael. *Race Across America: The Agonies and Glories of the World's Longest and Cruelest Bicycle Race*. Waco, TX: WRS Publishing, 1993.

Simons, W.J. *75 jaar Tour de France*. Lelystad, 1978.

Simpson, Tommy. *Cycling is My Life*. London: Stanley Paul, 1966. Revised, 1968.

Swann, Dick. *Bert Harris of the Poly*.

Swann, Dick. *Life and Time of Charley Barden*. London: Wynlap Publications, 1965.

Taylor, Marshall W. *The Fastest Bicycle Rider in the World: The Story of a Colored Boy's Indomitable Courage and Success Against Great Odds*. Worcester, MA: Wormley Publishing Co., 1928. Reprinted, Freeport, NY: Books for Libraries Press, 1971. Abridged edi-

tion, Brattleboro VT: Greene Press, 1972.

Terbeen, François. *Thévenet*. Paris: Calmann-Lévy, 1975.

Trence, Salvatore. *Fausto Coppi: The Campionissimo*. Silsden, UK: Kennedy Bros., 1971.

Turine, Roger Pierre. *The Bicycle and the Great Loop*. Paris: Gamma Sport, 1983.

Velo-News. *Ten Years of Championship Bicycle Racing 1972–1981*. Brattleboro, VT, 1983.

Wadley, J.B. *Eddy Merckx and the 1970 Tour de France*. Silsden, UK: Kennedy Bros., 1970.

Wadley, J.B. *Eddy Merckx, Luis Ocana and the 1971 Tour de France*. Silsden, UK: Kennedy Bros.

Wadley, J.B. *Eddy Merckx: 30 Years After Sylvere Maes*. Silsden, UK: Kennedy Bros.

Wadley, Jock. *My Nineteenth Tour de France*.

Wallace, Jim. *Champion of Champions*. Silsden, UK: Kennedy Bros., 1971.

Walsh, David, and Billy Stickland. *Inside the Tour de France*. 1994.

Walter, Bernard. *The Three M's: Merckx, Maertens and Moser*. Silsden, UK: Kennedy Bros., 1980s.

Watson, Graham. *The Great Tours*. Boulder, CO: VeloNews, 1994.

Watson, Graham. *The Road to Hell*. Boulder, CO: VeloNews, 1993.

Watson, Graham. *The Tour de France and its Heroes: A Celebration of the Greatest Race in the World*. North Pomfret, VT: Trafalgar Square, 1990.

Watson, Graham. *Visions of Cycling*. Boulder, CO: VeloNews, 1991.

West, Les. *The West Way*. Silsden, UK: Kennedy Bros., 1971.

Wilcockson, John, editor. *Greg LeMond: The Official Story of America's Greatest-Ever Cyclist*. Boulder, CO: VeloNews, 1995.

Woolum, Janet. *Outstanding Women Athletes: Who They Are and How They Influenced Sports in America*. Phoenix: Oryx Press, 1992.

SPORTS, OFF-ROAD

Bicycling Magazine. *Mountain Biking Skills*. Emmaus, PA: Rodale Press, 1990.

Bull, Andy. *Climb Every Mountain: The Mountain Bike Way*. London: Stanley Paul, 1991.

Burney, Simon. *Cyclo-cross*. Huddersfield, UK: Springfield Books, 1990.

Coello, Dennis. *Mountain Bike Manual*. Salt Lake City: Dream Garden Press, 1985.

Coello, Dennis. *Mountain Bike Rides of the West*. San Diego: Sunbelt Publications.

Coello, Dennis. *The Complete Mountain Biker*. New York: Lyons & Burford, 1989.

Does, G., and L. Vrijdag. *Alles over fietscross*. Alkmaar, NL: De Alk.

Edmonds, Ivy. *BMX! Bicycle Motocross for*

Beginners. New York: Holt Reinhart, 1979.

Glaskin, Max, and Jeremy Torr. *Mountain Biking*. London: Pelham Books, 1991.

Gould, Tim, and Simon Burney. *Mountain Bike Racing*. Mill Valley, CA: Bicycle Books, 1992.

Grant, Richard, and Nigel Thomas. *BMX Action Bike Book*. Bristol, UK: Purnell Books, 1983.

Grant, Richard, and Nigel Thomas. *BMX Action Hot Shots*. Redditch, UK: Halfords, 1984.

Grant, Richard, and Nigel Thomas. *The Puffin BMX Handbook*. Harmondsworth, UK: Puffin Books, 1984.

Kelly, Charles. *Richard's Mountain Bike Book*.

Lord, Michael and Mark. *Mountain Biking in the Bay Area*. Volumes 1–2. Santa Cruz, CA: Western Tananger Press, 1989.

Lynn, Iain, et al. *The Off-Road Bicycle Book*. Leading Edge Press, 1989.

Merrifield, Michael. *Colorado Gonzo Rides*. Monument, CO: Blue Clover Press, 1991.

Mountain Biking The High Sierra and Coast Range. Volumes 1–8. Bishop, CA: Fine Edge Productions, 1986–1990.

Murray, Jerry. *The Handbook of Motocross*. East Rutherford, NJ: Putnam, 1978.

Nealy, William. *Mountain Bike! A Manual of Beginning and Advanced Technique*. Birmingham, AL: Menosha Ridge Press, 1992.

Nealy, William. *The Mountain Bike Way of Knowledge*. Boulder, CO: VeloNews, 1991.

Nentl, Jerolyn. *Bicycle Motocross*. Mankato, MN: Crestwood House, 1978.

Olsen, John. *Adventure Sports: Mountain Biking*. Harrisburg, PA: Stackpole Books, 1989.

Olsen, John. *Backcountry Biking in the Canadian Rockies*.

Osborn, Bob. *The Complete Book of BMX*. New York: Harper & Row, 1984.

Richards, Ray. *Cyclo-Cross*. Silsden, UK: Kennedy Bros., 1970s.

Scagnetti, Jack. *Bicycle Motocross*. New York: E.P. Dutton, 1976.

Sloane, Eugene. *Eugene Sloane's Complete Book of All Terrain Bicycles*. New York: Simon & Schuster, 1987.

Smith, Don. *The Complete Book of Bicycle Motocross*. Yeovil, UK: Haynes Publishing, 1982.

Strassman, Mike. *The Basic Essentials of Mountain Biking*. Merriville, IN: ICS Books, 1990.

Thawley, John. *How to Win Bicycle Motocross*. Tucson: H.P. Books, 1975.

Thomsen, Stu, and Bob Hadley. *Stu Thomsen's Book of BMX*. Chicago: Contemporary Books, 1984.

Van der Plas, Rob. *Mountain Bike Magic*. Mill Valley, CA: Bicycle Books, 1991.

Van der Plas, Rob. *The Mountain Bike Book*. Mill Valley, CA: Bicycle Books, 1990.

Wise, Ted. *Bicycle Motocross: A Complete Guide*.

Milbrae, CA: Celestial Arts, 1978.

Wockner, Gary. *Sex with a Mountain Bike*. 1993.

Woodward, Bob. *Mountain Biking*. New York: Sports Illustrated Winner's Circle Books, 1991.

Zarka, Jim. *All Terrain Biking*. Mill Valley, CA: Bicycle Books, 1991.

TOURING GUIDES

Adshead, Robin. *Bikepacking For Beginners*.

American Youth Hostels. *AYH Handbook*. Washington, D.C., Annual.

Armstrong, Diana. *Bicycle Camping*. New York: Dial Press, 1981.

Asa, Warren, editor. *American Youth Hostels' North American Bicycle Atlas*. Maplewood, NJ: Hammond, 1969, 1973.

Bicycling Magazine. *Bicycle Touring*. Emmaus, PA: Rodale Press, 1985.

Bike World. *International Bicycle Touring*. Mt. View, CA: World Publications, 1976.

Bridge, Raymond. *Bike Touring: The Sierra Club Guide to Outings on Wheels*. San Francisco, CA: Sierra Club, 1979.

Bridge, Raymond. *Freewheeling: The Bicycle Camping Book*. Harrisburg, PA: Stackpole Books, 1974.

Caunter, C.F. *CTC British Road Book*. Cyclists' Touring Club, 1893.

Copin, Jean Pierre. *Practique du cyclotourisme*. Grenoble, France: Arthaud, 1977.

Clark, Jim. *Cycling the U.S. Parks*. Mill Valley, CA: Bicycle Books, 1993.

Coello, Dennis. *Touring on Two Wheels*. New York: Lyons & Burford, 1988.

Crane, Nicholas, and Christa Gausden. *Cyclists' Touring Club Guide to Cycling in Britain and Ireland*. Oxford: Oxford Illustrated Press, 1980; Harmondsworth, UK: Penguin Books, 1981.

Cyclists' Touring Club. *CTC Handbook*. Godalming, UK, annual.

English, Ronald. *Adventure Cycling*. London: Nicholas Kay, 1958.

English, Ronald. *Cycling for You*. London: Lutterworth Press, 1964.

Foehr, Stephen. *Eco-Journeys: The World Guide to Ecologically Aware Travel and Adventure*. Chicago: Noble Press, 1993.

Freeston, C.L. *Cycling in the Alps: A Practical Guide*. 1900.

Fuchs, Johannes M., and W.J. Simons. *Feitsen in Nederland*. Amsterdam: Broekman & de Maris, 1965.

Fuchs, Johannes M., and W.J. Simons. *Gids voor fietsers*. Amsterdam: Allert de Lange, 1968.

Hawkins, Gary and Karen. *Bicycle Touring in Europe*. New York: Pantheon, 1973.

Hughs, Tim. *The Cycle Tourer's Handbook*. London: Batsford, 1987.

Jaffee, Dennis and Tina. *Biking Through Europe*.

Johnston, Joanne. *JJ's Best Bike Trips*. Berkeley:

Ten Speed Press, 1972.

Katz, Elliott. *The Complete Guide to Bicycling in Canada*. New York: Doubleday, 1987.

Kleeberg, Irene. *Bicycle Touring*. New York: Watts, 1975.

Macia, Rafael. *The New York Bicycler*. New York: Simon & Schuster, 1972.

May, Marian, editor. *Bicentennial Bike Tours*. San Jose, CA: Gousha Publications, 1973.

Nasr, Kameel. *Bicycle Touring International*. Mill Valley, CA: Bicycle Books, 1993.

Oliver, Tony. *Touring Bikes: A Practical Guide*. Crowood Press, 1990.

Short Bike Rides. Editions for Cape Cod, Connecticut, Eastern Pennsylvania, Greater Boston, Long Island, New Jersey, New England, Rhode Island, and Washington, D.C. Boston: Globe Pequot Press, 1980.

Pinkerton, Elaine. *The Santa Fé Trail by Bicycle*. Santa Fé, NM: Red Crane Book, 1993.

Rakowski, John. *Adventure Cycling in Europe*. Emmaus, PA: Rodale Press, 1981.

Tobey, Peter, editor. *Two Wheel Travel: Bicycle Camping and Touring*. New Canaan, CT: Tobey, 1972, 1975.

Touring Exchange. *Cycle Touring Publications Catalog*. Port Townsend, WA, annual.

Van der Plas, Rob. *The Bicycle Touring Manual*. Mill Valley, CA: Bicycle Books, 1987. Revised, 1993.

Wellbye, Reginald. *Cycle Touring at Home and Abroad*. London: Temple, 1890.

Weisbroth, Erika, and Eric Ellman. *Bicycling Mexico*. Edison, NJ: Hunter Publishing, 1990.

Whitehill, Karen and Terry. *Europe by Bike: 18 Tours Geared for Discovery*. Seattle, WA: The Mountaineers, 1987.

Wong, Bonnie. *Bicycling Baja*.

Wong, Bonnie, ed. *Touring Cyclist Catalogue*. Port Townsend, WA, Touring Exchange, 1990.

TOURING ADVENTURES

Ahmed, Badiuzzaman. *A Dollar and the World*. New York: Vantage Press.

Allen, Thomas G., and Willian Sachtleben. *Across Asia on a Bicycle*. London: Allen & Will and New York: Century, 1894.

Anderson, William C. *The Great Bicycle Expedition*. New York: Crown, 1973.

Baron, Stanley. *Westward Ho*. London: Jarrolds, 1944.

Bauer, Fred. *How Many Hills to Hillsboro*. Tappan, NY: Hewitt, 1969.

Birchmore, Fred. *Around the World on a Bicycle*. Athens, GA: University of Georgia Press, 1938.

Bishop, Gary. *Six Wheels Northward*. Chicago: Moody Press, 1975.

Boettner, John Seigel. *Hey, Mom, Can I Ride My Bike Across America? Five Kids Meety Their Country*. Brea, CA: Seigel Boettner Fulton, 1990.

Bron, Eleanor. *Life and Other Punctures*. London: Deutsch Ltd., 1978.

Brooks, Charles S. *A Thread of English Road*. 1923.

Brooks, Charles S. *Roads to the North*. 1928.

Brooks, Charles S. *Round About Canterbury*. 1926.

Buettner, Dan. *Sovietrek: A Journey by Bicycle Across Russia*. 1994.

Burbridge, William F. *On Rolling Wheels in the West*. 1946.

Burston and Stokes. *Round the World on Bicycles*. Melbourne: Robertson, 1890.

Callan, Hugh. *From the Clyde to the Jordan*. London: Blackie, 1895.

Cantin, Eugene. *A Man, A Bike, Alone through Scotland*. Mt. View, CA: World Publications, 1977.

Cavan, Earl of. *With Yacht, Camera and Cycle in the Mediterranean*. London: Sampson, Low and Co., 1895.

Church, Richard. *Over the Bridge*.

Clough, Neil. *Two-wheel Trek*. London: Arrow Books, 1983.

Coley, Rex. *Laughter on Two Wheels*. London: Stanley Paul, 1963.

Cook, Mrs. E.T. *Highways and Byways in London*. London, 1907.

Crane, Nicholas and Richard. *Bicycles Up Kilimanjaro*. Newbury Park, CA: Haynes, 1985.

Crowe, John. *Cycling in the Lake District*. 1946.

Davar, F.J. *Cycling Over the Roof of the World*. New York: Zeidler, 1929.

Davies, Tom. *Merlyn the Magician and the Pacific Coast Highway*. London: New English Library, 1982.

Dearmer, Percy. *Highways and Byways in Normandy*. Illustrated by Joseph Pennell. 1904, 1924.

Dew, Josie. *The Wind in My Wheels*.

Duker, Peter. *Sting in the Tail*. London: Pelham Books, 1973.

Dumoulin, Gérald. *Santé et joie de vivre par la bicyclette*. Montreal: Lidec, 1975.

Duncan, David. *Pedaling the Ends of the Earth*. New York: Simon & Schuster, 1985.

Dunstan, Keith, and Geoffrey Hook. *It's All Uphill*. South Melbourne, Australia: Pegasus Books, 1979.

Duthie, James. *I Cycled into the Arctic Circle*. Ilfracombe: Stockwell, 1955.

Edwardes, Tickner. *Lift-Luck on Southern Roads*. 1931.

Elvin, Harold. *The Ride to Chandigarh*. London: Macmillan, 1957.

Elvin, Harold. *Avenue to the Door of the Dead*. London: Anthony Blond Ltd., 1961.

Elvin, Harold. *Elvin's Rides*. London: Longmans, Green and Co., 1963.

Emerson, P.J. *Inflation? Try a Bicycle*. Belfast: Northern Whig Ltd., 1978.

Evans, Herbert A. *Highways and Byways in Oxford and the Cotswolds*. Illustrated by Frederick Giggs. 1938.

Fraser, John Foster. *Round the World on a Wheel*. 1899. Reprinted, London: Methuen, 1905; and Chatto, 1982.

Garrison, W.W. *Wheeling Through Europe*. St. Louis: Christian Publishing Co., 1900.

Gidmark, David. *Journey Across a Continent*. Markham, Canada: Paperjacks, 1977.

Grivel, H. *Australian Cycling in the Golden Days*. Currier Unley, 1952.

Hakim, Bapsola, and Bhumgara. *With the Cyclists Round the World*. Bombay: Captain Press, 1928.

Hall, Brian. *Stealing From a Deep Place*. New York: Hill and Wang; Farrar, Straus, and Giroux, 1988.

Hamann, Walter. *Mit Dem Fahrrad Um Die Welt*. Munich: Schneider, 1967.

Hamsher, W. Papel. *The Balkans by Bicycle*. London: Witherby, 1917.

Harper, Charles. *From Paddington to Penzance*. London: Chatto & Windus, 1893.

Harper, Charles. *The Dover Road*, and *The Portsmouth Road*. London: Chapman Hall, 1895.

Harper, Charles. *The Brighton Road*, and *The Great North Road*. London: Cecil & Palmer, 1822.

Harper, Charles. *Queer Things About London*, and *More Queer Things About London*. London: Cecil & Palmer, 1924, 1926.

Helfgen, Heinz. *Ich Radle um Die Welt*. Bielefeld, Germany: H. Fischer, 1955.

Hibell, Ian, and Clinton Trowbridge. *Into Remote Places*. London: Robson Books, 1984.

Hogg, Gerry. *Explorers Awheel*. 1938.

Homewood, Isobel Georgina. *Recollections of an Octogenarian*. London: John Murray, 1932.

Houston, Jack. *Wandering Wheels*. Grand Rapids, MI: Baker House, 1970.

Jefferson, Robert L. *Across Siberia on a Bicycle*. London: Cycle Press, 1896.

Jefferson, Robert L. *Awheel to Moscow and Back*. London: Sampson, Low and Co., 1895.

Jefferson, Robert L. *A New Ride to Khiva*. London: Methuen, 1899.

Jenkins, Mark. *Off the Map: Bicycling Across Siberia*. New York: Morrow, 1992.

Junek, Bruce, and Tass Thacker. *The Road of Dreams: A Two Year Bicycling and Hiking Adventure Around the World*. Rapid City, SD: Images of the World, 1992.

King, Arthur. *Awheel to the Arctic Circle*. London: Fowler, 1940.

Kron, Karl, ed. *Ten Thousand Miles on a Bicycle*. New York, 1887.

Kuklos (W. Fitzwater Wray). *Across France in War Time*. London: J.M. Dent & Sons, 1916.

Kuklos (W. Fitzwater Wray). *A Vagabond's Note Book*. London: Daily News, 1908.

Leete, Harvey M., editor. *The Best of Bicycling!* New York: Trident Press, 1970; Pocket Book edition, 1972.

Leonard, Irving A. *First Across America by Bicycle*. Private printing, 1965.

Loher, George T. *The Wonderful Ride: Being the True Journal of Mr. George T. Loher Who in 1895 Cycled from Coast to Coast on his Yellow Fellow Wheel*. Edited by Ellen Smith. Toronto: Fitzhenry and Whitside; New York: Harper & Row, 1978.

Lovett, Richard. *Free-Wheelin': A Solo Journey Across America*. Camden, ME: Ragged Mountain Press, 1992.

McCulloch, Alan. *Trial by Tandem*. 1951.

Madden, Virginia. *Across America on the Yellow Brick Road*.

Magnouloux, Bernard. *Travels With Rosinante*. London: Oxford Illustrated Press, 1988.

Martin, Colin, and Peter Knottley. *Half Way Round*. England: Knottley, 1971.

Martin, Henry. *Follow the White Line*. Homestead, FL.

Miller, Christian. *Daisy, Daisy: A Journey Across America*. London: Routledge & Kegan Paul, 1980.

Mozer, David. *Bicycling in Africa*.

Murphy, Claude C. *Around the U.S. by Bicycle*. Detroit: Taylor, 1906.

Murphy, Dervla. *Full Tilt: Ireland to India with a Bicycle*. London: John Murray 1965. Reprinted, Woodstock, NY: The Overlook Press, 1986.

Mustoe, Anne. *A Bike Ride*. 1993.

Nasr, Kameel B. *The World Up Close: A Cyclist's Adventures on Five Continents*. Lexington, MA: Mills & Sanderson.

Nauticus. *Nauticus in Scotland*. London, 1888.

Nauticus. *Nauticus on his Hobby Horse*. London, 1880.

Newby, Eric. *Round Ireland in Low Gear*. London: Picador/Pan Books, 1991.

Newman, Bernard. *Ride to Russia*. London: Herbert Jenkins, 1938.

Newman, Bernard. *Ride to Rome*. London: Herbert Jenkins, 1953.

Newman, Bernard. *Speaking from Memory*. London: Herbert Jenkins, 1960.

Nichols, Alan. *Journey*. J.D. Huff, 1992.

Norton, Phil. *Bikepacking into Countryside and Lifestyles*. Bikepress, 1982.

Pennell, Joseph, and Elizabeth Robbins. *A Canterbury Pilgrimage*. London, 1885.

Pennell, Joseph, and Elizabeth Robbins. *Our Sentimental Journey Through France and Italy*. London: T. Fischer Unwin, 1893.

Pennell, Joseph, and Elizabeth Robbins. *Over the Alps on a Bicycle*. London: T. Fischer Unwin, 1898.

Pennell, Joseph, and Elizabeth Robbins. *Two Pilgrims Progress*. Boston: Little Brown, 1899.

Pianet, Jean-Pierre. *Latin America by Bicycle*. Champion, NY: Passport Press, 1988.

Pohl, Roderick. *Mit dem Fahrrad Nach Kalkutta*. Wupertal, 1968.

Ray, Alan J. *Cycling: Land's End to John*

O'Groats. London: Pelham Books, 1971.

Reid, W.J. *London to Pekin Awheel*. 1915.

Retallick, Martha. *Discovering America: Bicycle Adventures in All 50 States*. 1994.

Reynolds, Jim. *The Outer Path: Finding My Way in Tibet*. Sunnyvale, CA: Fair Oaks Publishing, 1992.

Ridge, Frank. *Biking (and Schmoozing) Across America with My Daughter*. Pittsburgh, 1993.

Roberts, Steven K. *Computing Across America: The Bicycle Odyssey of a High-tech Nomad*. New York: Simon & Schuster, 1987; Nomadic Research Labs, Santa Cruz CA, 1992.

Rooney, Chris. *A Pedaller's Tales*. 1993.

Rooney, Chris. *Mad Dogs and Cyclists*.

Rosdail, Jesse Hart. *Biking Alone Around the World*. Jericho, NY: Exposition Press, 1973.

St. George, Maximillian. *Traveling Light or Cycling Europe on Fifty Cents a Day*. 1922.

Sanders, Nick. *Journey to the Source of the Nile*. Glossop: Nick Saunders Publishing, 1983.

Sanders, Nick. *22 Days Around the Coast of Britain*. 1984.

Sanders, Nick. *The Great Bike Ride*. 1986.

Sanders, Nick. *Short Summer in South America*. 1989.

Savage, Barbara. *Miles From Nowhere*. Seattle: The Mountaineers, 1983.

Selby, Bettina. *Beyond Ararat: A journey through Eastern Turkey*. John Murray, 1993.

Selby, Bettina. *Riding the Desert Trail*. 1989.

Schnell, Jane. *Changing Gears: Bicycling America's Perimeter*. Atlanta: Peachtree Publishers, 1990.

Sil, Chaim. *Between My Legs*. Lincoln City, OR: Right White Line, 1975.

Simon, Ted. *Jupiter's Travels*. New York: Doubleday, 1980.

Siple, Greg and June. *The Mighty TOSRV: A 25-Year Illustrated History of the Tour of the Scioto River Valley*. Missoula, MT: Bikecentennial, 1986.

Skillman, Don and Lolly. *Pedaling Across America*. Brattleboro, VT: Vitesse Press, 1988.

Soboleff, I.S.K. *Cossack at Large*. London: Peter Davies, 1960.

Soulat, Sylvie and Alain. *Voyage au cœur de l'Irlande*. Angoulême, 1993.

Spitteser, Miranda, editor. *Four Corners World Bike Ride*. 1989.

Stevens, Thomas. *Around the World on a Bicycle*. Vols. 1 and 2. New York: Charles Scribner's Sons; London: Sampson, Low, Marston, Searle and Rivington, 1888. Reprinted, Tucson: Seven Palms Press, 1984.

Stolle, Walter. *The World Beneath My Bicycle Wheels*. John Dale, editor. London: Pelham Books, 1978.

Sumner, Lloyd. *The Long Ride*. Harrisburgh, PA: Stackpole Books, 1978.

Sutherland, Louise. *I Follow the Wind*. London: Southern Cross Press Ltd., 1960.

Thayer, George Burton. *Pedal and Path: Across the Continental*. 1887.

Thompson, Alan. *One Time Around*. Toledo, OH: ATP Publishing, 1992.

Thorenfeldt, Kai. *Round the World on a Cycle*. London: Selwyn and Blount, 1928.

Tillman, H.W. *Snow on the Equator*. New York: Macmillan, 1938.

Urrutia, Virginia. *Two Wheels and a Taxi: A Slightly Daft Adventure in the Andes*. Seattle: The Mountaineers, 1987.

Urry, Frank. *Wheeling Adventure*. 1951.

Vernon, Tom. *Fat Man in Argentina*. London: Michael Joseph, 1991.

Vernon, Tom. *Fat Man on a Roman Road*. London: Michael Joseph, 1983.

Vernon, Tom. *Fat Man on a Bicycle*. London: Michael Joseph, 1981.

Voiland, Bob. *Hurt City*. 1994.

Watts, Heather. *Silent Steeds: Cycling in Nova Scotia To 1900*. Halifax: Nova Scotia Museum, 1985.

Whittell, Giles. *Lambada Country*. England: Chapmans, 1992.

Young, Jim and Elizabeth. *Bicycle Built for Two*. 1940.

CHILDREN'S BOOKS

Baker, Eugene. *About a Bicycle for Linda*. Chicago: Melmont Publishers, 1968.

Berenstain, Stanley and Janice. *Bears on Wheels*. New York: Grolier.

Berenstain, Stanley and Janice. *The Bike Lesson*. Westminster, MD: Random House, 1964.

Coombs, Charles Ira. *Bicycling*. West Caldwell, NJ: William Morrow, 1972.

Debbie. *Margies Magic Bike*.

De Brunhoff, Jean. *Babar En Famille*. France, 1937.

Hale, Anna W. *Mystery on Mackinac Island*. Illustrated by Lois McLane. Tucson: Harbinger House, 1991.

Holleyman, Sonia. *Mona the Brilliant*. New York: Doubleday, 1993.

Ives, Penny. *Mrs. Santa Claus*. New York: Delacorte, 1992.

Lawson, Robert. *McWhinney's Jaunt*. Boston: Little, Brown, 1951.

McLeod, Emile Warren. *The Bear's Bicycle*. Illustrated by David McPhail, Boston: Little Brown, 1975.

Mandy. *Ride For Your Life, Julie*.

Outdoor Empire Publishing. *Captain Cycle: the Bike Rangers Coloring Book*. Seattle, 1983.

Porter, A.P. *Greg LeMond Premier Cyclist*. Minneapolis: Lerner Publications, 1990.

Roth, Harold. *Bike Factory*. New York: Pantheon Books.

Rey, H. A. and Margret. *Curious George Rides a Bike*. Boston: Houghton Mifflin Co., 1952.

Say, Allen. *The Bicycle Man*. Boston: Houghton Mifflin, 1982.

Schwartz, David. *Supergrandpa*. Lothrop, Lee & Shepard Books, 1991. Gustav Hakansson in Tour of Sweden.

Scioscia, Mary. *Bicycle Rider*. Illustrated by Ed Young. New York: Harper & Row, 1983. Major Taylor biography.

Seuyoshi, Akiko. *Ladybird on a Bicycle*. Illustrated by Viv Allbright. London: Faber & Faber, 1982.

Thomson, H.E. *Tour of the Forest Bike Race*. Mill Valley, CA: Bicycle Books, 1990.

Zach, Cheryl. *Benny and the Crazy Contest*. New York: Branbury Press, 1991.

RESOURCES, ANTHOLOGIES

Avis, Frederick C. *Cyclists' Reference Dictionary*. London: F.C. Avis, 1973.

Bikecentennial. *The Cyclist's Yellow Pages*. Missoula, MT: Bikecentennial, annual.

Crane, Nicholas, editor. *International Cycling Guide 1980–1986*. Volumes 1–6. London: Tantivy Press, 1980–1986.

Hammerstein, J.A., editor. *Mr. Punch Awheel*. London, Education Books, 1905.

Helston, John. *High Road and Lonning*. London: Philip Allan, 1898.

Hilarides, Pat Hein. *The Bicycle in French Literature*. Self-published, 1993.

Interbike Directory. Newport Beach, CA, 1990–1995.

Kobayashi, Keizo. *Pour une Bibliographie du Cyclisme*. Paris, Fédération Français du Cyclotourisme, 1984.

Leccese, Michael, and Arlene Plevin. *The Bicyclist's Sourcebook: The Ultimate Directory of Cycling Information*. Rockville, MD: Woodbine House, 1991.

Luebbers, David J., editor. *Bicycle Resource Guide 1950–1981*. Vols. 1–8. Columbia, MO and Denver CO, 1972–1981. List of 7,814 bicycle-related items from books, periodicals, reports, catalogs, etc.

Mackenzie, Jeanne, editor. *Cycling*. Oxford: Oxford University Press, 1981.

McWhirter, Norris, editor. *Guinness Book of World Records*. New York: Bantam Books, Updated.

Over the Handles: Cycling Sketches: The Wheelmen's Annual. Salem, MA: 1887.

Nye, Peter. *The Cyclist's Sourcebook*. New York: Perigee, 1991.

St. Pierre, Roger. *Cycling Yearbook (1978–1979)*. Ipswich: Studio Pub., 1978, 1979.

Starrs, James E., editor. *The Noiseless Tenor: The Bicycle in Literature*. East Brunswick, NJ: Cornwall Books, 1982.

Schultz, Barbara and Mark. *Bicycles and Bicycling: A Guide to Information Sources*. Detroit, MI: Gale Research, 1979. 1,300 citations.

Truelsen, Erling. *Litteratur om Cyckler, Cykling og Cykeltrafik*. Copenhagen: Dansk Cyklist Forbund, 1977.

BIOGRAPHIES

Bickford, Charles. *Bulls, Balls, Bicycles & Actors*. New York: Paul Eriksson, 1965. No apparent reference to bicycles.

Curie, Eve. *Madame Curie*. New York: Doubleday, 1937.

Doyle, Conan. *Memories and Adventures*. Boston: Little, Brown, 1924.

Jerome, Jerome K. *My Life and Times*. London: John Murray, 1983.

Keller, Helen. *The Story of My Life*. New York: Doubleday, 1954.

Kitching, Ron. *A Wheel in Two Worlds*. Nottingham, 1993.

Miller, Henry. *My Bike and Other Freinds*. Volume II, Book of Friends. Santa Barbara: Capra Press, 1978.

Murphy, Dervla. *Wheels Within Wheels*. London: John Murray 1979; and Harmondsworth: Penguin Books, 1983.

Nabokov, Vladimir. *Speak, Memory*. New York: Putnams, 1966.

Newman, Bernard. *Speaking from Memory*. London: Herbert Jenkins, 1960.

Rumney, A.W. *Fifty Years a Cyclist*. 1928.

Saroyan, William. *The Bicycle Rider in Beverly Hills*. New York: Scribner, 1952; New York: Ballantine Books, 1971.

Thomas, Dylan. *Me and My Bike*. New York: McGraw Hill, 1965.

Troyat, Henri. *Tolstoy*. New York: Doubleday, 1967.

Wells, H.G. *Experiment in Autobiography*. New York: Macmillan, 1934.

FICTION, POETRY

Anon. *Lyra Bicyclica: 40 Poets of the Wheel*. Boston: J.G. Dalton, 1880.

Anon. *Lyra Cyclus: The Wheel*. Rochester, NY: Edmund Redwood, 1897.

Anon. *Sixty Poets of the Road*. Boston: J.G. Dalton, 1895.

Auden, W.H. "Miss Gee." *Selected Poetry of W.H. Auden*. New York: Random House, 1958.

Baruch, Dorothy W. "Different Bicycles." *Favorite Poems, Old and New*. New York: Doubleday, 1957.

Beckett, Samuel. *Molloy*. New York: Grove Press, 1965.

Beckett, Samuel. "All That Fall." *Krapp's Last Tape and Other Dramatic Pieces*. New York: Grove Press, 1970.

Betjeman, John. "The Commander." "The Wykehamist." *Collected Poems*. Boston: Houghton Mifflin Co., 1971.

Breslin, Jimmy. *The Gang That Couldn't Shoot Straight*. New York: Bantam Books, 1971.

Callenbach, Ernest. *Ecotopia*. Berkeley: Banyan Tree Books, 1975.

Clarke, Arthur C. *Rendezvous with Rama*. New York: Harcourt Brace Jovanovich, 1973.

Cummings, Peter. *Bicycle Consciousness*. New York: The Greenfield Review Press, 1979.

Davenport, Guy. *Da Vinci's Bicycle: Ten Stories*. Baltimore: Johns Hopkins Universtiy Press, 1979.

Davis, Lavinia Riker. *Bicycle Commandos*. Toronto: Doubleday, 1955.

Deforges, Régine. *The Blue Bicycle [La Bicyclette bleu]*. Translated from French by Ros Schwartz, New York: Lyle Stuart, 1985.

De Sica, Vittorio. *The Bicycle Thieves*. Translated by Simon Hartog. New York: Simon & Schuster 1973.

Doyle, Conan. "The Adventure of the Priory School." *The Complete Sherlock Holmes*. New York: Doubleday, 1930.

Fischman, Bernard. *The Man Who Rode His 10-Speed Bicycle to the Moon*. New York: Richard Marek, 1978.

Ernest Hemingway. "A Pursuit Race," "A Way You'll Never Be." *The Short Stories of Ernest Hemingway*. New York: Charles Scribner's Sons.

Graves, Robert. "A Bicycle in Majorca." "A Vehicle, to Wit, a Bicycle." A.P. Watt.

Herne, Ralph. *The Yellow Jersey*. London: Weidenfeld & Nicholson; New York: Simon & Schuster, 1973.

Herne, Ralph. *What Will You Do, Jim?*

Hoffenstein, Samuel. "Songs to Break the Tedium of Riding a Bicycle, Seeing One's Friends, or Heartbreak." *Poems of Practically Nothing*. New York: Garden City Pub., 1939.

Huxley, Aldous. *Chrome Yellow*. New York: Perennial Library, 1973.

Jarry, Alfred. *The Supermale [Le Surmâle]*. Translated from French by Ralph Gladstone and Barbara Wright. New York: New Directions, 1977.

Jarry, Alfred. "The Passion Considered as an Uphill Bicycle Race." *The Selected Works of Alfred Jarry*. Roger Shattuck and Simon Watson Taylor, editors. New York: Grove Press, 1965.

Jerome, Jerome K. *Humors of Cycling*. London: Chatto and Windus, 1905.

Jerome, Jerome K. *Three Men on a Bummel*. New York: Dodd, Mead & Co. 1900. Reprinted, Glouchester, UK: Alan Sutton, 1987.

Jerome, Jerome K. *Three Men on Wheels*. 1900.

Littell, Robert. *The October Circle*.

Lopez, Steve. *Third and Indiana*. New York: Viking, 1994.

Moore, Anne. "The Bicycle Poem." *Upstart*. Barnard College, 1981.

Morand, Paul. *Open All Night*. New York: T. Seltzer, 1923.

Morley, Christopher. *The Romany Stain*. Illustrated by Jack Duncan. New York: Doubleday, 1926.

Mulisch, Harry. *The Assault [De Aanslag]*. Translated from Dutch by Claire Nicolas White. New York: Pantheon Books, 1985.

Murdoch, Iris. *The Red and The Green*. New York: Viking, 1965.

Nabokov, Vladimir. *Lolita*. New York: Berkeley Pub., 1969.

Niven, Larry. *Ringworld*. New York: Ballantine Books, 1975.

O'Brien, Flann. *The Third Policeman*. New York: New American Library, 1967.

Ostaijen, Paul van. "Belgiese Zondag." (Belgian Sunday) *Het eerste boek van Schmol*. Antwerp, 1928.

Quackenbush, Robert. *Bicycle to Treachery*. A Miss Mallard Mystery. Englewood Cliffs, NJ: Prentice hall, 1985.

Robbe-Grillet, Alain. *The Voyeur*. New York: Grove Press, 1958.

Saroyan, William. *The Human Comedy*. Illustrated by Don Freeman. New York: Harcourt, Brace & Co., 1943.

Schwartz, John Burnham. *Bicycle Days*. New York: Summit Books, 1989.

Shaw, George Bernard. *An Unsocial Socialist*. New York: Boni & Liveright,

Sirota, Mike. *Bicycling Through Space and Time*. New York, Ace Books, 1991.

Twain, Mark. *A Connecticut Yankee in King Arthur's Court*. New York: Webster, 1889. Reprinted, Harmondsworth: Penguin Books, 1971.

Wells, H.G. *History of Mr. Polly*. 1941.

Wells, H.G. *Wheels of Chance: A Bicycling Idyll*. London: J.M. Dent & Sons, 1896.

Wells, H.G. "A Perfect Gentleman on Wheels." *The Man with a Nose*. London: Athlone Press.

West, Elizabeth. *Hovel in the Hills*. London: Faber & Faber, 1977.

White, Elwyn Brooks. *Quo vadimus? or, The Case for the Bicycle*. New York and London: Harper & Bros., 1939.

Yevtushenko, Yevgeny. "On a Bicycle." *Selected Poems*. Translated by Robin Milner-Gulland and Peter Levi. Harmondsworth: Penguin Books, 1962.

ARTS

Anon. *Handbook of American Sheet Music*. Boston: J.G. Dalton, 1880.

Anthony & Co. *Illustrated Catalogue of Photographic Equipments and Materials for Amateurs*. New York: Polhemus, 1891. Reprinted, Dobbs Ferry, NY: Morgan and Morgan, c.1980.

Barnicoat, John. *A Concise History of Posters 1870–1970*. New York: Abrams, 1972.

Berdecio, Roberto, and Stanley Applebaum, eds. *Posada's Popular Mexican Prints*. New York: Dover, 1972.

Bryan, David H., ed. *Bicycling and Photography*. Emmaus, PA: Rodale Press, 1979.

Casagrande, Louis B., and Phillips Bourns. *Side Trips: The Photography of Sumner W. Matteson 1898–1908*. Milwaukee Public Museum, 1983.

Cat 3. 1989. Comic on racing.

Duval, Yves, S. Ardan, and Marc Hardy. *Heldenepos van de Ronde Van Frankrijk*. Belgium: Gamma Daphne, 1973. Comic on Tour de France.

Foster, S. Constant. *Wheel Songs*. New York: White, Stokes & Allen, 1884.

Furstenau, Oscar. *Radlerei*. Leipzig: Graphische Institute, 1895.

Garner, Philip. *The Better Living Catalog*. New York: Delilah Books, 1980.

Garner, Philip. *Utopia, or Bust!* New York: Delilah Books, 1984.

Gingold, Alfred. *Items from Our Catalog*. New York: Avon Books, 1982. L.L. Bean spoof.

Gombrich, E.H. *Meditations on a Hobby Horse and Other Essays on the Theory of Art*. London: Phaidon Press.

Gorey, Edward. *The Epileptic Bicycle*. Zurich: Diogenes, 1978, and New York: Cogdon and Weed, 1978.

Gorey, Edward. *The Broken Spoke*. New York: Dodd and Mead, 1976.

Groombridge, Garth. *Song Cycle and Cycle Songs*. England: Perkins-Kent, 1930.

Helms, Jonny. *Round the Bends: Transport of Delight*. Self-published, 1980. Cartoons from *Cycling*.

Hughes, Tim. *Wheels of Choice*. Great Missenden, England: Cyclographic Publications, 1980. Photos.

Jones, Jay. *Messenger 29*. New York: September Press, 1989, 1994. Comic.

José Guadalupe Posada: Ilustrador de la vida mexicana. Mexico City: Fondo Editorial de la Plástica Mexicana, 1963.

Kirkpatrick, Joanna. *Popular Art in Bangladesh: The Ricksha Paintings and Cultural Discourse*. South Asia Center, University of California Berkeley, 1980.

Kirkpatrick, Joanna. *The Rickshaw Paintings of Bangladesh: An Update*. Bengal Studies Conference, Harvard University, 1982.

Klamkin, Marian. *Old Sheet Music*. New York: Hawthorn Books, 1975.

Lebeck, Robert. *Das Zweirad Postkarten aus alter Zeit*.

Lewis, Harold B., and Jack Naylor. "Bike and Cameras of Long Ago," *Photographica Journal*. c.1985.

Logan, Claude., ed. *Joseph Beuys: Is It About A Bicycle?* New York: Marisa Del Re Gallery, 1986.

Meadows White, Rev. L. *A Photographic Tour on Wheels*. England, 1885.

Michael, Jan. *Cycling in Posters*.

Moore, George. *The George Moore Collection*. Vols. 1–4. London: Beekay Products, 1979–81.

Illustrations from 1880s.

Musée de l'Affiche. *La Petite Reine: Le vélo en affiches à la fin du XIXème*. Paris, 1979.

New Departure Mfg. Co. *Hiram Jones and his New Departure*. Bristol, CT, 1901. Cartoon series.

Patterson, Frank. *The Patterson Book*. Volume 1 and 2. London: Temple Press, 1948, 1952.

Patterson, Frank. *Frank Patterson: The Cycling Artist*. Coventry: Forest Publishing, 1982.

Philips, Walter. *Songs of the Wheel*. New York: George Monroe's Sons, 1897.

Sätty. *The Cosmic Bicycle*. San Francisco: Straight Arrow Books, 1975. Collages.

Sempé, Jean-Jacques. *Displays of Affection*. New York: Workman Press, 1990.

Simm, Franz. *Skizzen aus der Radler Sport*. Munich: Franz Hanfstangel, 1895.

Solomon R. Guggenheim Museum. *Ferdinand Leger: Five Themes and Variations*. Master Series Number 1. New York: Solomon R. Guggenheim Foundation, 1962.

Sotheby Parke Bernet. *Fine Posters*. New York: Southeby, December 1979. Auction catalog.

Willis, Jim and Janet, editors. *The Art of Frank Patterson* and *The Frank Patterson Picture Book*. Cyclists' Touring Club. Coventry: J. Willis, 1977.

Wingfield, Walter. *Bicycle Gymkhana and Musical Rides*. London, 1896.

Glossary

2WD: two-wheel-drive.

3WD: three-wheel-drive.

4WD: four-wheel-drive.

Ackermann steering: geometric principle for three- and four-wheel vehicles.

ANSI Z90.4: American National Standards Institute bicycle helmet standard.

arc-en-ciel: (French) rainbow colors of world champion's jersey.

arrêté: (French) standing start.

arrivée: (French) finish line.

ATB: all-terrain bicycle.

attack: to accelerate or break away from other cyclists.

audax: special touring events with checkpoints.

balai, camion balai, voiture balai: (French) last vehicle in race caravan for cyclists who quit.

beef it: to fall or crash.

bicycle-friendly: people and places that accommodate cycling.

bidon: (French) water bottle.

bike-a-thon: fund-raising bike tour based on amount of miles ridden.

bike boom: historic period of cycling popularity beginning in 1970.

bike pollution: (Japan) clutter of bikes parked at train stations.

biopacing: arrhythmic or bouncing pedaling, caused by elliptical chainrings (Shimano Biopace) and suspension systems on bikes.

blocking: to slow or legally impede the progress of cyclists to help teammates in a break away.

BMX: bicycle moto-cross.

bonification: time bonus awarded to winner of race in stage race, usually five to ten seconds subtracted.

bonk: to run out of energy; to exhaust stored glycogen.

break, breakaway: one or more cyclists leading and separated from the main group.

bridge a gap: to cross from one group of cyclists to a group ahead.

bunch: main group of cyclists, also **field**, **pack**, **peloton**.

cadence: rate of pedaling measured in revolutions per minute.

capo: (Italian) mountain pass.

captain: front steering cyclist on a tandem.

carbo loading: method of increasing energy supply for specific athletic events.

cat I, II, III, IV, V: categories of amateur racing, from elite (**cat I**) to beginner (**cat V**).

century: 100-mile ride; metric century is 100 kilometers.

chamois: padding in shorts to prevent saddlesores, traditionally derived from goat skin.

CKD: completely knocked down, disassembled bike for shipping.

classic: 1. historic cycling event. 2. balloon-tire roadster bikes from 1930s to 1950s.

clincher: tire with separate tube, fits to rim by beaded belt, also **wire-on**.

col: (French) mountain pass.

contre la montre: (French) against the clock, see **time trial**.

criterium: (French) judgement, a multi-lap bike race on a short course, also **circuit race**.

critical mass: group ride for cyclists' solidarity, usually in traffic.

cross frame: bike frame design with down tube and chain stays crossed by seat tube.

development: metric gear ratio, distance traveled in one cycle or revolution of pedals.

diamond frame: common bike frame design forming a diamond shape.

differential: gear system for axle with two drive wheels, allows proper turning.

directeur sportif: (French) race team manager or coach.

dishrack: bike parking rack with slots for wheels.

derny: motorcycle used to pace cyclist.

domestique: (French) team rider who sacrifices individual glory for team leaders.

dossard: (French) competitor's race number.

drafting: riding behind another cyclist or vehicle for aerodynamic advantage.

drop, dropped: failing to keep pace, loosing contact with the main group of cyclists.

drops: the lower part of the handlebars, usually below the brake levers.

duathlon: running and cycling event; also called biathlon.

eat it: to fall or crash.

echelon, chain gang: paceline of drafting cyclists, usually in two lines, one pulling forward into wind, the other pulling off sheltered by the others.

ergometer: device that measures human power output.

étape: (French) single stage of a multi-stage race.

face plant: to fall on one's face.

factor of safety: measurement of materials' strength for bike components.

feed zone: location on race route where cyclists receive food or drink.

field: whole or main group of cyclists.

field sprint: sprint at finish with main group of cyclists.

fixed gear:

flamme rouge: (French) red triangular sign marking the final kilometer of a road race.

flyer: 1. short breakaway, an acceleration ahead of a group of cyclists. 2. to fall.

flywheel:

FOB: freight on board, bike's cost at port of origin.

freewheel:

FWD: front-wheel-drive.

gear inches: relative measure of gear ratio derived from wheel diameter, see **development**.

general classification, GC: overall standings in a stage race.

gnarly: anything rough or treacherous.

Golden Age, bicycle craze: historic period from 1870s to 1890s.

gonzo: anything fun, crazy, or cool.

gradient: steepness of road or trail, measured in percentage; 100 meter rise in one kilometer = 10% gradient.

granny gear: very low gear, usually near one-to-one ratio, used for steep hills and carrying loads.

gregario: (Italian) see **domestique**.

groupetto: small group of riders, usually behind leaders and main group.

hammer: to pound the pedals, accelerate and ride as fast as possible, as in "put the hammer down."

hanging in: keeping pace with a group of cyclists, not leading, usually to save energy or because of fatigue.

header: falling on one's head, to "take a header."

heart rate, HR, bpm: heart beats per minute.

honk: acceleration by standing on pedals, out of the saddle, pulling on handlebars, moving the bike side to side.

hook: elbowing or wheel movement which impedes the progress of another cyclist, usually illegal.

horsepower, hp: measure of power output, one hp equals 746 watts.

HPA: human-powered aircraft.

HPB: human-powered boat.

HPS: human-powered submarine.

HPV: human-powered vehicle.

HPUV: human-powered utility vehicle.

hydroplaning: riding on the surface of water, when tires skim on wet road.

intermodal: transport system that allows for different modes, e.g., bike and transit.

jump: a quick acceleration, usually standing on the pedals.

kermesse: a circuit road race with laps of about three to ten kilometers.

kinetic sculpture: mobile art works, human-powered vehicles.

klunker, clunker: old or cheap bike used for klunking, also beater bike.

knobbies: tires with studs for off-road traction.

leadout: tactic where team rider accelerates to maximum speed so leader can draft and sprint past, see **slingshot**.

lancé: (French) flying start.

lantern rouge: (French) red tail light on train's caboose, last finisher in a race, last in **general classification**.

low rider: 1. recumbent bike or HPV with ultra-low position for aerodynamics. 2. classic bike with ultra-low position for show.

LWB: long wheelbase.

maglia rosa: (Italian) race leader's pink jersey for Giro d'Italia.

maillot jaune: (French) race leader's yellow jersey, usually for Tour de France.

minuteman: cyclist preceding another in a **time trial**, usually by a minute or two.

modal split: the ratio or percent that different modes of travel are used.

monocoque: one-piece construction.

monocycle: one-wheel cycle, with cyclist inside wheel.

moto: BMX race.

motorhead: motorist.

motorpace: riding in the draft of a motorcycle, car, van, or sometimes another cyclist.

MTB: mountain bike.

musette: (French) cloth shoulder bag for carrying food and drinks, usually handed off to racers in **feed zone**.

NMV: non-motorized vehicle.

OEM: original equipment manufacturer, maker of parts for name brand bikes.

off the back: getting, dropped, where cyclists find themselves after failing to keep pace.

omnium: track meet with a variety of races.

ordinary: high-wheel bicycle.

overuse injury: ailment due to hard training or improper gearing.

paceline: chain-like formation of cyclists sharing the pace by taking turns at lead breaking the wind, then pulling aside and soft pedaling to the sheltered rear position for recuperation, see **drafting, echelon**.

pack: a close-knit group of cyclists.

pannier: (French, bread basket) bike-mounted storage bags.

pavé: (French) cobblestone road surface.

pedicab: cycle rickshaw or pedal-powered taxi.

peloton: the whole or main group of cyclists, also **pack, field, bunch**.

penny farthing: high-wheel bicycle, derives from size difference of coins and wheels.

pits, pit stop: designated location on race course where cyclists can receive equipment repairs.

presta valve: air valve commonly used on high-pressure tubes and tubular tires.

prime: (say preem) mid-race sprint for prize, points, or time bonuses.

prologue: (French) beginning of stage race, usually a time trial, may not count in general classification.

push: pedaling with a large gear.

raid: semi-competitive touring event, usually held on rugged terrain.

rando, randonneur, randonnee: (French) special touring event with checkpoints.

retro-grouch: someone who insists on tradition.

road rash: skin abrasions due to fall or crash.

rouleur: (French) kind of cyclist capable of high speeds on flat and rolling roads and time trials.

RWD: rear-wheel-drive.

saddle time: time spent actually riding.

safety bike: common bike design, dating from 1880s, with upright position.

sag wagon, broom wagon: motor vehicle following cyclists in tours or races that carry equipment, clothes, food, medical supplies, and tired or injured cyclists.

schraeder valve: air valve commonly used on low-pressure tubes and car tires.

scorcher: name given to fast cyclists of the 1890s.

shake 'n bake, whiplash: an evasive racing technique where a lead cyclist swerves across road to drop drafting cyclists.

sit in, sit on: sitting in another cyclist's slipstream to save energy, see **hanging in**.

slingshot: using another cyclist's slipstream to gain speed and sprint past, see **leadout**.

slipstream: wind shelter provided by leading cyclist or group.

snap: muscular speed used to accelerate quickly.

snerd: one who sniffs bicycle seats.

soft pedal: half coasting, half pedaling, turning the pedals with minimal force to save energy.

soigneur: (French) racer's attendant, taking care of food and massage.

solo: bicycle built for one, as opposed to **tandem**.

souplesse: supple or loose muscles.

spin: pedaling at a rapid cadence.

squirrel: a swerving, unstable, nervous cyclist.

stage race: a multi-day point-to-point race, usually with road races, time trials, and criteriums.

stayer: 1. type of bike and motorcycle used for paced racing. 2. cyclist with the ability to maintain a high speed for long periods, usually on flat roads, also **pacer** or **rouleur**.

stoker: rear cyclist on a tandem.

surplace: (French) technique of balancing in place, motionless on a bike; also called trackstand.

SWB: short wheelbase.

sweet spot: special moment of euphoria brought on by cycling.

switchback: one of many sharp turns in roads that go up steep mountains.

tandem: bicycle built for two, usually both pedaling.

techno-weenie: someone who likes technology.

tempo: moderately high rate of cadence or speed, also cruising speed.

throwing the bike: technique of pushing the bike forward in a close sprint so the front wheel crosses the finish line first.

tifosi: (Italian) super-enthusiastic racing fans; derives from typhus patients suffering from fever and delirium.

time trial, TT: race against the clock over a certain distance, also **team time trial, TTT** usually four-person teams.

topo map: topographical map showing elevations, see **gradient**.

trail: 1. off-road path. 2. measurement of steering geometry, distance that vertical line from wheel axle falls behind line from steering tube.

trailhead: entry point of off-road trail.

trial: any kind of cycling test, stunt, or race.

triplet: bicycle built for three.

tuck: extremely aerodynamic position used for descending and time trials.

turkey: a slow, awkward, or novice cyclist.

turn sheet: route map indicating turns, stops, stores and landmarks.

tweek: to turn, bend, or break something.

U-lock, D-lock: commonly used bike lock.

unicycle: one-wheel cycle, with the cyclist above wheel.

velodrome: cycle racing track.

veloway: bike path with few intersections.

wannabe: a cyclists who wants to be better but is somehow lacking.

wheelbase: distance from front to rear wheel axles.

wheelie: to ride with the front wheel off the ground; to "pop a wheelie."

wheelsucker: a cyclist who does no work in a paceline or peloton.

wind-up: gradual acceleration leading up to an all-out sprint.

MEASUREMENTS

atmosphere: = 14.7 pounds per square inch.

British thermal unit (BTU): = 1,054.9 joules.

centimeter (cm): = 10 millimeters = 0.39 inches.

cup (c): = 8 fluid ounces.

day (d): = 24 hours = 1440 minutes = 86400 seconds.

degree Fahrenheit: = 1.8 degree Celsius.

fluid ounce (fl oz): = 29.6 milliliters.

foot (ft): = 12 inches = 30.5 centimeters.

foot-pound (lb-ft): = 1.356 joules.

foot-pound per second (ft-lb/sec): = 1.356 watts.

gallon (gal): = 4 quarts = 3.78 liters = 231 cubic inches = 8.34 pounds.

gram (g): = 0.03 ounces.

horsepower (hp): = 745.7 watts.

hour (h): = 60 minutes = 360 seconds.

inch (in): = 2.54 centimeters.

kilocalorie (kcal): = 1,000 calories = 4,186.8 joules.

kilocalorie per minute (kcal/min): = 69.78 watts.

kilogram (kg): = 1000 grams = 2.205 pounds.

kilometer (km): = 1,000 meters = 0.6214 miles.

kilometer per hour (kph): = 0.62 miles per hour.

kilowatt hour (kWh): = 3.6 megajoules.

knot (nm): = 1.15 miles = 1.85 kilometers.

knots (nautical mph): = 0.52 meters per second.

liter (l): = 1.06 quarts.

meter (m): = 100 centimeters = 3.28 feet.

meter per second (m/s): = 3.6 kilometers per hour = 2.237 miles per hour.

mile (mi): = 5,280 feet = 1.609 kilometers.

mile per hour (mph): = 1.609 kilometers per hour = 0.447 meters per second.

milliliter (ml): = 0.001 liters.

millimeter (mm): = 0.039 inches.

minute (min): = 60 seconds.

ounce (oz): = 28.3 grams.

pound (lb): = 16 ounces = 0.45 kilograms.

quart (qt): = 4 cups = 0.94 liters.

second (sec): = 1,000 milliseconds.

ton (t): = 2,000 pounds = 900 kilograms.

watt (W): = 1 joule per second.

yard (yd): = 3 feet = 0.914 meters.

Notes

1 BEGINNINGS

1. Charles Singer, "A Short History of Wheeled Vehicles," *A History of Technology*, Oxford University Press. 1960.

2. J.E. Cirlot, *A Dictionary of Symbols*, New York: Philosophical Library, 1971; J.C. Cooper, *An Illustrated Encyclopedia of Traditional Symbols*, London: Thames and Hudson, 1978.

3. Singer, *A History of Technology*.

4. J.M. Fuchs and W.J. Simons, *De fiets van toen en nu*, Alkmaar, NL: De Alk, 1983, pp. 6–7.

5. Charles van Beuningen, *Complete Drawings of Hieronymus Bosch*, London: Academy Editions, 1973, pp. 50–51.

6. Augusto Marinoni, "The Bicycle," Ladislao Reti, ed., *The Unknown Leonardo*, New York: McGraw-Hill, 1974, pp. 288–91.

7. Charles Gibbs-Smith, *The Inventions of Leonardo da Vinci*, New York: Charles Scribner's Sons, 1978, p. 86.

8. Frank Rowland Whitt, "What *is* that Cherub Doing?" *Cycletouring*, April-May 1971, p. 80.

9. F.P. Prial, "Cycling in the United States," *Harper's Weekly*, August 30, 1890, p. 669.

10. Robert A. Smith, *A Social History of the Bicycle*, New York: American Heritage Press, 1972, p. 3.

11. L. Baudry de Saunier, *Histoire de la Locomotion Terrestre*, Paris, 1935.

2 VELO DEVELOPMENT

1. Robert Wilkinson-Latham, *Cycles in Colour*, Poole: Blandford Press, 1978, p. 11.

2. R.W. Jeanes, PhD Thesis, University of Paris, 1950.

3. Clifford Graves, "Clearing the Doubt About the Count," *Bike World*, July 1977, pp. 20–21.

4. Ernest Lacon, *Moniteur de la Photographie*, Paris, October 1, 1868; quoted in Andrew Ritchie, *King of the Road*, London: Wildwood House, 1975, p. 20.

5. British Patent No. 4321, June 21, 1818.

6. Hans-Erhard Lessing, "Von Drais: The Man and the Myths," *International Cycling Guide*, London: Tantivy Press, 1984.

7. Herbert O. Duncan, *World on Wheels*, Paris, 1928.

8. Ritchie, *King of the Road*, p. 36.

9. Arthur Judson Palmer, *Riding High*, New York: E.P. Dutton, 1956, p. 35.

10. *Irish Cyclist*, September 25, 1895.

11. David Herlihy, "Lallement vs. Michaux," *The Wheelmen*, 1992, pp. 7–8.

12. W. Starley, *Life and Inventions of James Starley*, Coventry, 1902.

13. Frank Bowden, *Cycling for Health*, London: Criterion Press, 1890.

14. G.H. Bowden, *The Story of the Raleigh Cycle*, London: Allen, 1975.

15. Robert A. Smith, *A Social History of the Bicycle*, New York: American Heritage Press, 1972, p. 54.

16. Dick Swann and James C. McCullagh, *American Bicycle Racing*, Emmaus, PA, Rodale Press, 1976, p. 2.

17. United States Playing Card Company, company history.

18. *American Bicyclist and Motorcyclist*, 100th Anniversary Issue, December 1979.

19. Ibid., p. 253.

20. Urs Heierli, *Environmental Limits to Motorization*, St. Gaulen, Switzerland: SKAT, 1993.

21. Lawrence M. Fisher, "Boom in Mountain Bikes Revives the U.S. Industry," *The New York Times*, April 1, 1991.

22. H. Dolnar, "An American stroke for novelty," *The Cyclist*, London, January 8, 1902.

23. Arnfried Schmitz, "Why Your Bicycle Hasn't Changed For 106 Years," *Cycling Science*, June 1990. The UCI's 1934 ruling was made on April 1st—All Fools Day.

24. David Gordon Wilson, "Manpowered Land Transport," *Bicycling!*, July 1969, p. 24.

25. Albert C. Gross, Chester R. Kyle and Douglas J. Malewicki, "The Aerodynamics of Human-powered Land Vehicles," *Scientific American*, December 1983, p. 142.

3 BICYCLE INGENUITY

1. Jobst Brandt, *The Bicycle Wheel*, Menlo Park, CA: Avocet, 1981, p. 6.

2. Tech Museum formerly named The Garage, birthplace of the personal computer.

3. Parts on 1976 Raleigh Professional, with Reynolds 531 tubing, Campagnolo Super Record components, tubular tires, without pump or spare tire, not including fibers in tire casing or strands of wire in cables.

4. EPA findings from 1989, Greenpeace International.

5. "Paceline," *Bicycling*, December 1990, pp. 18–20.

6. Michael J. Kolin and Denise M. de la Rosa, *The Custom Bicycle*, Emmaus, PA: Rodale Press, 1979, pp. 24–25.

7. Ivan Illich, "Energy and Equity," *Toward a History of Needs*, p. 135.

8. Chester R. Kyle and John N. Olsen, "Bicycle Stability," *Bicycling*, March 1990, p. 134.

9. Richard Jow, "Saddles and Brooks, "*Bicycling!*, February 1978, p. 24.

10. Carelman, *The Catalogue of Fantastic Inventions*, pp. 58–59.

11. Brandt, *The Bicycle Wheel*, p. 16.

12. Frank Rowland Whitt, and David Gordon

Wilson, *Bicycling Science*, Second edition, Cambridge, MA: MIT Press, 1982, pp. 127–28. Another way this has been stated: "The effect of a given mass in the wheels is almost twice that of the same mass in the frame."

13. T.B. Pawlicki, *How to Build a Flying Saucer (And Other Proposals In Speculative Engineering)*, Englewood Cliffs, NJ: Prentice Hall, 1981, pp. 73–75.

14. Sir Arthur Conan Doyle, "The Adventure of the Priory School," *The Strand Magazine* 27, February 1904.

15. Sir Arthur Conan Doyle, *Memories and Adventures*, Boston: Little, Brown and Co., 1924, p. 102.

16. *Bicycling World*; quoted in *American Bicyclist and Motorcyclist*, December 1979, p. 142.

17. Ibid., p. 160.

18. Whitt and Wilson, p. 56.

19. James Reswick, "A New Automatic Bicycle Transmission," *Human Power*, Winter 1986–87, pp. 15–19.

20. Ramondo Spinnetti, "Backward Versus Forward Pedaling," *Human Power*, Fall 1987, pp. 1–12.

21. Motorola professional cycling team, 1992.

22. James J. Flink, *The Automobile Age*, Cambridge, MA: MIT Press, 1992.

23. S.S. Wilson, "Bicycle Technology," *Scientific American*, March 1973, p. 88.

24. Stephen W. Sears, "The Intrepid Mr. Curtiss," *American Heritage*, April 1975, pp. 60–95.

4 CYCLING MACHINES

1. *Webster's Ninth New Collegiate Dictionary*; *Oxford English Dictionary*.

2. Stijn Streuvels, *Collected Works, Vol 9, Memories*, trans. Bart Van't Riet. 't Leieschip Kortryk.

3. Richard L. Edgeworth, *Memoirs of Richard Lovell Edgeworth, Esq.*, London, 1820, vol. i, pp. 149–50; quoted in James E. Starrs, *The Noiseless Tenor*, East Brunswick, NJ: Cornwall Books, 1982, p. 83.

4. Leonard De Vries, *Victorian Inventions*, New York: American Heritage Press, 1971, pp. 15–16.

5. Jack Wiley, *The Bicycle Builder's Bible*, Blue Ridge Summit, PA: TAB Books, 1980, p. 301.

6. Harry Bickerton said: "It's the most important invention since Starley's safety bicycle."

7. Nancy Crase, Rebecca Schmid, and Susan Robbins, "Pedal Power," *Sports `n Spokes*, January-February 1987, p. 27.

8. Ron Chalmers, "Aid Project: To Build a Better Rickshaw," *The Edmonton Journal*, January 20, 1989.

9. Ron Forster, *Rail Riders*, 1980.

10. Theodore Waters, "All the World A-Wheel," 1899.

11. Gordon Hathway, *Low Cost Vehicles*, London: Intermediate Technology Publications, 1985, p.

85.

12. Louis B. Casagrande and Phillips Bourns, *Side Trips: The Photography of Sumner W. Matteson 1898–1908*, Milwaukee: Milwaukee Public Museum, 1983.

13. "Kenneth Snelson: Straddling the Abyss Between Art and Science," *ARTnews*, February 1981, pp. 70–71.

14. Peter Schickele, *An Hysterical Return: P.D.Q. Bach at Carnegie Hall*, Vanguard Records, 1987.

15. Morton Grosser, *Gossamer Odyssey*, Boston: Houghton Mifflin, 1981, p. 149.

16. James C. McCullagh, ed., *Pedal Power*, Emmaus, PA: Rodale Press, 1977, p. 36.

17. *Scientific American*, January 13, 1906, and September 22, 1906.

5 BICYCLE BODY

1. S.S. Wilson, "Bicycle Technology," *Scientific American*, March 1973, p. 82.

2. Elizabeth West, *Hovel in the Hills*, London: Faber and Faber, 1977, p. 185.

3. *Wheelwoman*, May 23, 1896; quoted in Andrew Ritchie, *King of the Road*, London: Wildwood House, 1975, p. 160.

4. Henri Desgrange, *Scientific American*, January 12, 1895, p. 25.

5. Tom Davies, *Merlyn the Magician and the Pacific Coast Highway*, London: New English Library, 1982, pp. 228–29.

6. S.L. Henderson Smith, *British Medicine*, May 22, 1976.

7. *Cycling for Women*, Emmaus, PA: Rodale Press, 1989, pp. 13–18; *VeloNews*, October 4, 1993.

8. Robert A. Smith, *A Social History of the Bicycle*, New York: American Heritage Press, 1972, p. 63.

9. "Glossary," *Fat Tire Flyer*, March-April 1986, p. 27.

10. *The Third Hand*, 20th Anniversary Catalog, Summer 1994.

11. Kevin Loth, "Behind the Mask," *London Cyclist*, January-February 1992.

12. *The Woman Outfitter*, Spring-Summer 1994.

6 ENERGY AND POWER

1. Chester Kyle, "The Human Machine," *Bicycling*, May 1989, pp. 196–200.

2. S.S. Wilson, "Bicycle Technology," *Scientific American*, March 1973, p. 82. Data compiled by Vance Tucker, Duke University.

3. Nina Dougherty, "The Bicycle vs. The Energy Crisis," *Bicycling!*, January 1974.

4. Richard Ballantine, *Richard's Bicycle Book*, Second edition, New York: Ballantine Books, 1979, p. 9.

5. David Gordon Wilson, "Calories and Power," *The Bicycling Book*, eds. John and Vera van der Reis Kraus, New York: The Dial Press, 1987, pp. 192–94.

6. Marcia D. Lowe, *The Bicycle: Vehicle for a Small Planet*, Worldwatch Paper 90, September 1989, Washington D.C.: Worldwatch Institute, p. 21; Mary C. Holcomb et al., *Transportation Energy Data Book: Edition 9*, Oak Ridge, TN: Oak Ridge National Laboratory, 1987; President's Council on Physical Fitness and Sports.

7. William H. Saris, "The Tour de France: Food Intake & Energy Expenditure During Extreme Sustained Exercise," *Cycling Science*, September-December 1991.

8. Gary Null, *The Complete Guide to Sensible Eating*, New York: Four Walls Eight Windows, 1990, pp. 104–108.

9. Kevin Kelly, "How to Ride a Bicycle Across a Continent," *Whole Earth Review*, 54, Spring 1987, p. 128.

10. From "Bikepacking," *Bicycling!*, 1977.

11. A.W. Hubbard, "Homokinetics: Muscular Function in Human Movement," in *Science and Medicine of Exercise and Sport*, Second edition, New York: Harper Row, 1974.

12. Agostino Massagrande, *Agonistic Cycling*, Milan: Edizioni Landoni, 1982, p. 11.

13. A calorie in physics refers to the amount of heat required to raise one kilogram of water one degree centigrade. One thousand physics calories (kcal) equals one nutrition calorie. The British Thermal Unit (BTU) measures pounds instead of kilograms.

14. A foot-pound is a pound (16 oz.) moved one foot (12 in.); an erg is one dyne force (1 gram at 1 cm/sec^2) moving one centimeter; a joule is one newton force (1 kg at 1 m/sec^2) moving one meter.

15. Frank Rowland Whitt and David Gordon Wilson, *Bicycling Science*, Second edition, Cambridge, MA: MIT Press, 1982, p. 63.

16. Danny L. Pavish, "Unsaddling Horsepower," *Bike Tech*, February 1988, pp. 13–16.

7 CYCLING PERFORMANCE

1. Agostino Massagrande, *Agonistic Cycling*, Milano: Edizioni Landoni, 1982, p. 10.

2. C. Vittori, "Esperienze italiane nel settore delle gare di velocità," *Atleticastudi*, July-August 1974, p. 4; quoted in Massagrande, p. 12.

3. Richard M. Suinn, "Body Thinking: Psychology for Olympic Champs," U.S. Olympic Training Center, 1977.

4. Committee of After School Education of the Council of Europe (CEESCE), *Doping des Athlètes*, Strasbourg: CCC/EES, 1963, p. 5, and CEESCE, *Doping des Athlètes*, Madrid: CCC/EES, 1969, p. 3; quoted in Massagrande, p. 155.

5. Owen Mulholland, "Tom Simpson And The Magic Pill," *Cyclist*, December 1986, pp. 42–43.

6. Antoine Blondin, *l'Equipe*; quoted in Samuel Abt, "Rhinestone Theater," *Bicycle Guide*, December 1988, p. 33.

7. Dr. Roland Marlier, "Doping," *Cycling*, December 11, 18, and 25, 1971.

8. Samuel Abt, *Breakaway*, New York: Random House, 1985, p. 131.

9. Bjarne Rostaing and Robert Sullivan, "Triumphs Tainted With Blood," *Sports Illustrated*, January 25, 1985, pp. 12–17; "19th Hole: The Readers Take Over," *Sports Illustrated*, February 1, 1985, p. 76.

10. Abt, "Rhinestone Theater," pp. 28–33.

11. *Bicycling*, April 1985, p. 18.

8 GLOBAL BICYCLES

1. "A conversation with David Pilbeam," *The Harvard Gazette*, May 24, 1991.

2. Goodwin O.J. Okeaduh, "Bicycle for Agriculture and Environment in Africa," *The Bicycle: Global Perspectives*, Montreal: Velo Mondiale, 1992; Jim Fitzpatrick, *The Bicycle and the Bush*, Melbourne: Oxford University Press, 1980; James McGurn, *On Your Bicycle*, New York: Facts On File, 1987, p. 98.

3. Zhou Youma, "Ode to the Bicycle," *China Reconstructs*, May 1987.

4. Erwin G. Gudde, *California Place Names: The Origin and Etymology of Current Geographical Names*, Berkeley: University of California Press, 1969, p. 28.

5. Author's estimate based on Worldwatch Institute sources; Michael Renner.

6. Marcia D. Lowe, *The Bicycle: Vehicle for a Small Planet*, Worldwatch Paper 90, September 1989, Washington, D.C.: Worldwatch Institute, p. 5.

7. Wang Heng, "Early Morning Traffic Shift," *Lives of Ordinary Chinese*, Beijing: China Reconstructs Press, 1988; "Population Control Comes in the `Kingdom of Bikes,'" *China Daily*, January 9, 1989; Jun-Men Yang, "Bicycle Traffic in China," *Transportation Quarterly*, January 1985.

8. Lowe, *The Bicycle*, pp. 33–34; Ryozo Tsutsumi, "Bicycle Safety and Parking Systems in Japan," *Pro Bike 88*, proceedings of the 5th International Conference on Bicycle Programs and Promotions, Tucson, AZ, October 8–12, 1988; Michael Replogle, private communication, August 9, 1989.

9. Vera van der Reis Krausz, "Keirin—Parimutuel Bicycle Racing in Japan," *The Bicycling Book*, New York: The Dial Press, 1982, p. 172.

10. U.S. bicycle data from Bicycle Institute of America, *Bicycle Reference Book*, 1993–1994, p. 6.

11. Paraphrased by U.S. Ambassador Arthur A. Hartman, in John Dowlin, "No Bikes in Moscow," *American Wheelmen*, October 1983.

12. Based on salary of $27 per month, *Japan Cycle Press*, February 1985, pp. 24–25.

13. Based on $15,000 car and $30,000 income.

14. Lowe, *The Bicycle*, p. 11–12; Worldwatch Institute, based on Motor Vehicle Manufacturers Association, *Facts and Figures*, Detroit, MI: various editions; United Nations, *Bicycles and Components: A Pilot Survey of Opportunities for Trade Among Developing Countries*, Geneva: International Trade Center UNCTAD/GATT, 1985; *Japan Cycle Press International*, various editions; *Indian Bicycle Industry: Prospects and Perspectives*, New Delhi: Directorate General of Technical Development, Government of India, 1985, p. 27.

15. Lowe, *The Bicycle*, p. 13; Motor Vehicle Manufacturers Association, *Facts and Figures '89*, Detroit, MI: 1989; *Japan Cycle Press International*, various editions; other sources.

16. Rob Gallagher, *The Rickshaws of Bangladesh*, Dhaka: University Press, 1992; Michael Replogle, *Non-Motorized Vehicles in Asian Cities*, Washington, D.C.: World Bank, 1992.

17. Ed Ayres, *Vital Signs 1993*, Washington, D.C.: Worldwatch.

18. Lowe, *The Bicycle*, p. 32.

9 TRANSPORT

1. G.H. Smith, "Some Notes about the Anerley Bicycle Club," quoted in Andrew Ritchie, *King of the Road*, London: Wildwood House, 1975, pp. 80–82.

2. *Outing*, October 1892, pp. 7–10; quoted in Robert A. Smith, *A Social History of the Bicycle*, New York: American Heritage Press, 1972, p. 211.

3. Archer Hulbert, *Pioneer Roads and Travelers*, Vol. II, 1904.

4. *Bicycling News*, August 2, 1878; quoted in Ritchie, *King of the Road*, p. 90.

5. Joe Surkiewicz, "The History of the L.A.W.," *Bicycle USA*, December 1989, pp. 16–18; Kathy Link, "The History of the League," *Bicycle USA*, December 1991, pp. 8–11.

6. John and Vera van der Reis Kraus eds., *The Bicycling Book*, New York: Dial Press, 1982, pp. 52–54.

7. William T. Farwell, "The Story of the League of American Wheelmen," *Cycling Handbook*, L.A.W., 1946.

8. J.B. Jackson, *Landscape*; quoted in Josh Lehman, "From Space to Place: Discovering by Bicycle," *Bicycling*, January 1979, pp. 28–29.

9. Marcia D. Lowe, "Ghana Takes the Low-cost Road," *Worldwatch*, May-June 1989.

10. Robert A. Smith, *A Social History of the Bicycle*, pp. 215–16.

11. Bradford C. Snell, *American Transport*, 1973.

12. Michele Herman et al., *The Bicycle Blueprint*, New York: Transportation Alternatives, 1993.

13. Steve Harvey, "Big-Bucks Bikepath," *The Los Angeles Times*, May 27, 1986.

14. *Bicycling*, March 1985, p. 9; Nelson Pena, "How the Bike Can Save L.A.," *Bicycling*, August 1990, pp. 33–36.

15. Pena, "How the Bike Can Save L.A.," p. 34.

16. Marcia D. Lowe, *The Bicycle: Vehicle for a Small Planet*, Worldwatch Paper 90, Washington D.C., September 1989, p. 22. Adjusted for vehicle occupancy and various road conditions.

17. Roger Lubin, "The Race of the Year," *Bicycling!*, October 1971.

18. Lowe, *The Bicycle*, pp. 21–22. Study by Raymond Novaco, University of California at Irvine, cited in "Gridlock! Congestion on America's Highways and Runways Takes a Grinding Toll," *Time*, September 12, 1988.

19. Michael Waldman, Sharlene Weiss, and William Articola, *A Study of the Health Effects of Bicycling in an Urban Atmosphere*, Washington, D.C.: U.S. Department of Transportation, November 1977.

20. U.S. estimates by John Forester, *Effective Cycling*, Sixth edition, Cambridge, MA: MIT Press, 1993.

21. Richard Ballantine, *Richard's Bicycle Book*, Second edition, New York: Ballantine Books, 1979, p. 129.

22. *Bicycling Reference Book*, 1993–1994, Bicycle Institute of America, Washington, D.C.; U.S. Consumer Product Safety Commission; Insurance Institute for Highway Safety, National Highway Traffic Safety Administration; John Forester, "Points of View: Considerations for Bicycling into the Future," *Bicycle USA*, January 1990; Rodney Tolley, *The Greening of Urban Transport*, 1990; United Nations, 1987.

23. Paul Andrews, "America's most militant bicyclist," *Palo Alto Weekly*, May 1, 1980.

24. Forester, "Points of View: Considerations for Bicycling into the Future," pp. 3–4.

25. Adapted from Outdoor Empire Publishing, Inc., Seattle, WA, 1986.

26. John Dowlin, "Bending Pipe into Bike Racks."

27. Michael Replogle, "Bicycle Access to Public Transportation: Lessons from Japan and Europe," *Urban Transportation Abroad*, Fall 1983.

28. Ibid.

29. James McGurn, *On Your Bicycle*, New York: Facts on File, 1987, p. 150.

30. *Spokesman*, Texas Bicycle Touring Club.

31. Wayne Sosin, Worksman Trading Corporation, 1991; "Tricycles Solve Transportation Problem," *Plant Services*, September 1987, p. 114.

32. Yang Yuliang, "Postal Wheels Bring People Together," *Lives of Ordinary Chinese*, China Reconstructs Press, 1987.

33. Lowe, *The Bicycle*, p. 27.

34. Michael Vatikiotis, "Off the Streets," *Far Eastern Economic Review*, March 29, 1990; "Shutting the Safety Valve," *Asiaweek*, March 9, 1990.

35. Maitland Zane, "Lack of Insurance Immobilizes Fisherman's Wharf Pedicabs," *The San Francisco Chronicle*, May 7, 1986.

36. Nong Ren and Hirotaka Koike, "Bicycle: A Vital Transportation Means in Tianjin, China," Washington, D.C.: Transportation Research Board, 1993.

37. Lowe, *The Bicycle*, p. 18.

38. Lu Lizhang, "China's `Bicycle Explosion,'" *Traffic and Transportation in China*, China Reconstructs Press, July 1980, pp. 6–7.

39. Urs Heierli, *Environmental Limits to Motorisation*, St Gaulen, Switzerland: SKAT, 1993; "Imagine L.A. Banning the Automobile," *U.S. News and World Report*, September 27, 1993; "China is Planning a People's Car," *The New York Times*, September 22, 1994.

40. Anthony Bailey, "Letter From The Netherlands," *The New Yorker*, August 12, 1991, p. 52; Lowe, *The Bicycle*, pp. 35–36.

41. Traffic Department, Local Council of Delft; Ministry of Transport and Public Works, Transportation and Traffic Engineering Division, The Hague, May 1986; A. Wilmink, "The Effects of an Urban Bicycle Network - Results of the Delft Project," Velo City 87 Proceedings, May 1988.

42. Fanta Voogd, "Auto blijft buiten schot," *Milieudefensie*, February 1993; *Bicycles First*, Bicycle Master Plan, Netherlands Ministry of Transport, Public Works and Water Management, 1992.

43. Paul Andrews, "A Near Nirvana For Bikies," *Palo Alto Weekly*, May 1, 1980; Palo Alto Department of Transportation, 1991.

44. Lisa Lapin, "CBS News Sees P.A. as the Bicycle Capital," *The San Jose Mercury News*, August 23, 1988.

45. Toronto *Globe*, 1893; reprinted in *Energy Alert*, Energy Educators of Ontario, Fall 1993.

10 A POLITICAL TOOL

1. Lee Hockstader, "New Cycles in Cuba's Economy," *The Washington Post*, August 19, 1991, p. A12.

2. Joaquin Oramas, "En pocos meses, una realidad," *La Habana*, October 29, 1990; Mimi Whitefield, "Facing cuts in imported oil, Cubans turn to pedal power," *The Philadelphia Inquirer*, December, 28, 1990; George Vecsey, "Cuba Moves Forward On 2 Wheels," *The New York Times*, August 8, 1991.

3. *The International Herald Tribune*, May 8, 1985.

4. Ann Strong, *The Minneapolis Tribune*, August 17, 1895; quoted in Robert A. Smith, *A Social History of the Bicycle*, p. 81.

5. John Galsworthy, "Four-in-hand Forsyte," *On Forsyte 'Change*, New York: Charles Scribner's Sons, 1930, pp. 203–204.

6. Karen Overton, "Women Take Back the Streets," *Sustainable Transport*, June 1994, pp. 6–17.

7. James McGurn, *On Your Bicycle*, New York: Facts on File, 1987, p. 94.

8. "Hero Cycles: Riding a New High," *India Today*, October 15, 1987; *Cycle Press International*, February 1986.

9. Ulrike Saade and Helmut Dachale, "East Side Story," *Bike Culture Quarterly*, December 1993.

10. *Frank W. Schwinn's 1942 Personal Notes on the Bicycle Industry*, James Hurd ed., Bicycle Museum of America, 1993; S. Powell Bridges, "The Schwinn Case: A Landmark Decision," *Business Horizons*, August 1968, pp. 77–85; Kenneth Gilpin, "Schwinn Bicycle Files," *The New York Times*, October 9, 1992; Barnaby Feder, "Schwinn Wants to Sell Most Assets," *The New York Times*, January 2, 1993; Tim Ferguson, "Combat Veterans of Sorts Raise the Schwinn Flag," *The Wall Street Journal*, July 27, 1993; *Bicycle Retailer and Industry News*, November 1992–February 1993.

11. Michael Replogle, "Improving access for the poor in urban areas," *Appropriate Technology*, June 1993.

12. American Automobile Association, *Your Driving Costs*, 1975; *Bicycling!*, March 1977, p. 61.

13. Energy Research and Development Administration, U.S. Department of Transportation, 1980; Dave Harvey, "Bicycling makes economic sense in gasoline crunch," *The Times-Standard*, September 30, 1990.

14. Mark Jenkins, "Pedal Power Vs. Petroleum," *Bicycling*, May 1991.

15. "A Bicyclist's Guide to the 1991 Surface Transportation Act," Bicycle Federation of America, 1991.

16. Michael Replogle, "U.S. Transportation Policy: Let's Make it Sustainable," Institute for Transportation and Development Policy, Washington, D.C., 1991; Michael Renner, "Rethinking Transportation," *State of the World 1989*, Washington, D.C.: Worldwatch Institute, 1989, p. 106.

17. Juan Pablo Pérez Alfonzo quoted in Daniel Yergin, *The Prize: The Epic Quest of Oil, Money, and Power*, New York: Simon & Schuster, 1991, pp. 512, 525; and Stan Steiner, *The Washington Post*, 1979.

18. Energy Information Administration, *The New York Times*, August 12, 1990.

19. Marcia D. Lowe, *Alternatives to the Automobile: Transport for Livable Cities*, Worldwatch Paper 98, Washington, D.C.: Worldwatch Institute, 1990, p. 9.

20. American Public Transit Association.

21. Liz Marriott, "Noise Pollution," *London Cyclist*, September-October 1991, pp. 16–18.

22. David Gaeuman, "Points of View Continues," *Bicycle USA*, September 1990.

23. Claire Morissette, "La puissance de la candeur," *Le Monde à Bicyclette*, May-June 1985.

24. John H. Cushman Jr., "Washington Talk: Quietest of Vehicles Get a Day In the Sun," *The New York Times*, September 18, 1990.

25. P.J. O'Rourke, "A Cool and Logical Analysis of the Bicycle Menace and an Examination of the Actions Necessary to License, Regulate, or Abolish Entirely This Dreadful Peril on Our Roads," *Car and Driver*, June 1984, p. 65.

11 WAR AND PEACE

1. James Wagenvoord, *Bikes and Riders*, New York: Van Nostrand Reinhold, 1973, p. 92.

2. Frederick Alderson, *Bicycling: A History*, Newton Abbot: David & Charles, 1972.

3. James J. Berryhill, "Combat Bicycling," *Bicycle USA*, May 1988.

4. Martin Caidin and Jay Barbree, *Bicycles in War*, New York: Hawthorn Books, 1974.

5. Joseph Stalin quoted in Daniel Yergin, *The Prize: The Epic Quest for Oil, Money, and Power*, New York: Simon & Schuster, 1991, p. 382.

6. Caidin and Barbree, *Bicycles in War*, p. 98.

7. Dr. Clifford Graves, "The Day My Bicycle Saved My Life," *The Best of Bicycling!*, ed. Harvey M. Leete, New York: Trident Press, 1970, pp. 53–59.

8. *Cycling*, December 26, 1945.

9. Berryhill, "Combat Bicycling," p. 19.

10. Michael Replogle, "U.S. Transportation Policy: Let's Make it Sustainable," Institute for Transportation and Development Policy, Washington, D.C., 1991; Don Mathew and Andy Rowell, *The Environmental Impact of the Car*, London: Greenpeace, 1991.

11. Sue Zielinski, "Learning the Language of Change: Toronto's Cycle Watch," *Bicycle USA*, May 1989, pp. 12–13.

12. Verdict Research, Inc.; Nelson Pena, "Double Standard," *Bicycling*, December 1991.

13. Dan Burden quoted in "Pedaling Under the Influence," *Bicycling*, May 1988, p. 6; Johns Hopkins Injury Prevention Center, 1994.

14. "Drunken-Driver Battler Gets Up From the Mat," *The New York Times*, January 2, 1991, p. B2.

15. Jeffrey Sacks et al, "Bicycle-Associated Head Injuries and Deaths in the United States From 1984 Through 1988," *Journal of the American Medical Association*, December 4, 1991, pp. 3016–18.

16. James E. Starrs, *The Noiseless Tenor*, East Brunswick, NJ: Cornwall Books, 1982, p. 230.

17. "Rambling," *Bicycling!*, June 1975.

18. *Chicago Wheelmen Update*; *Newsweek*, April 7, 1975.

19. "Big Mac Arrest," *Bicycle USA*, March-April 1988.

20. Mary Catherine Dunphy, "Dupont SWAT Raid on Bicycle Couriers Nabs Constitution As Well," *Ride On*, August 1992.

21. "Paceline," *Bicycling*, May–July 1990.

22. "Special Delivery," *Bicycling*, May 1982, p. 160.

23. Don Cuerdon, "I Was a Boston Bike Cop," *Bicycling*, October 1990.

24. "Police on Bikes," *Bicycle USA*, October-November 1991.

25. *The Minneapolis Tribune*, May 1, 1896; quoted in Robert A. Smith, *A Social History of the Bicycle*, p. 50.

26. "Fuzz On Wheels—Colorful Cops Cut Crime," *The Best of Bicycling!*, ed. Harvey M. Leete, reprinted from *Law and Order*, August 1968.

27. "Talk of the Town," *The New Yorker*, June 9, 1986.

28. Seth Amgott, "For the Bicycle Messenger, No Roadbed of Roses," *The New York Times*, November 10, 1985.

29. David Paler, "I'm a Bike Messenger, and I Break the Law," *The New York Times*, 1990.

30. Murray Kempton, "The Cycle of Mayoral Affection," *Newsday*, August 13, 1987.

31. Cerisse Anderson, "Justification Defense to Civil Disobedience Allowed," *The New York Law Journal*, March 25, 1991; *People vs. John Gray, John Kaehny, Charles Komanoff, Stephen Kretzmann, Jonathan Orcutt, and Ann Sullivan*.

32. Uniform Crime Reports for the United States, 1980.

33. Michael Replogle, "Bicycle Access to Public Transportation: Lessons from Japan and Europe," *Urban Transport Abroad*, Fall 1983, p. 6.

34. Katie Moran, *Bicycle Transportation for Energy Conservation: Technical Report*, U.S. Department of Transportation, Washington, D.C., 1980; Michael Replogle, *Bicycle Access: New Boost for Transit Performance*, November 1984.

35. "Bike security vendors shift into high gear," *The Wall Street Journal*, October 7, 1993.

36. Frank Gresham, "Save Your Bike," *City Cyclist*, November-December 1988.

37. "Vélos: servez-vous!," *La Suisse*, June 1, 1986.

38. Jan Olsen, "Copenhagen Finds Civilized Solution to Bicycle Theft—Free Rides," *The Daily Yomiuri*, November 13, 1990.

39. "Letters," *Bicycling!* (n.d.)

40. Harold Willens, *The Trimtab Factor: How Business Executives Can Help Solve the Nuclear Weapons Crisis*, 1984.

41. Bob Henschen, "Bicycling to Where the End of the World Begins, Pilgrimage to Pantex—1984," *War Resisters League News*, September-October 1984, p. 3.

42. Michael Winerip, "Protesters Stay Anonymous—and Stay in Jail," *The New York Times*, March 2, 1986, p. 48.

43. Michael Verdon, "The Maracycle, Bicycle as Peacemaker," *Bicycle USA*, November-December 1987, pp. 8–9.

44. Bill Moffett, "Bikes Not Bombs for Nicaragua," *Bicycle USA*, October 1987, pp. 22–25.

45. Letters to the Editor, *Bicycle USA*, February–August 1988, from Brooksville, Florida; Independence, Missouri; New York, New York; Hobart, Indiana; Olympia, Washington; Rangeley, Maine; Laramie, Wyoming; Albuquerque, New Mexico.

46. Kenneth W. Morgan, "A Fist and a Kiss in Old Damascus," *The New York Times*, January 1991.

12 CYCLE SPORTS

1. Robert Wilkinson-Latham, *Cycles in Color*, Poole: Blandford Press, 1978, p. 11; Andrew Ritchie, *King of the Road*, London: Wildwood House, 1975; Fermo Galbiati and Nino Ciravenga, *La Bicicletta*, Milano: BE-MA Editrice, 1989.

2. Herbert O. Duncan, *The World on Wheels*, Paris, 1928.

3. The Federations were aided by the riders, "de Civry, Duncan, and other gentlemen in contact with other nations." *Cycling*, Rome: Central Sports School, FIAC, 1972.

4. Dick Swann, *New Cyclist*, No. 8.

5. *Harper's Weekly*, 1894; James C. McCullagh, ed., *American Bicycle Racing*, Emmaus, PA: Rodale Press, 1976, p. 10.

6. Ibid., p. 19.

7. Quoted in Jack Rennert, *100 Years of Bicycle Posters*, New York: Harper & Row, 1973, p. 10.

8. The first Madison Square Garden was built in 1890 at Madison Avenue between 26th and 27th Streets by the architects McKim, Mead & White. Stanford White was murdered in 1906 on the roof of the Garden by the jealous husband of his mistress. In May 1925 the building was demolished and a new Garden opened in November at 8th Avenue between 49th and 50th Streets, with a six-day race that set an attendance record of over 15,000 spectators. In 1968 the Garden moved to its third and current location, above Penn Station at 33rd Street between 7th and 8th Avenues, and has yet to host a six-day.

9. *The New York Times*, December 11, 1897, and January 9, 1898; McCullagh, *American Bicycle Racing*.

10. See also: Peter Nye, "Way ahead of his time," *Winning*; Robert A. Smith, *A Social History of the Bicycle*; McCullagh, *American Bicycle Racing*.

11. Dave Chauner, "Velodromes from the Heart," *Winning*, March 1984.

12. Ibid.

13. In 1968 at Varese, Italy, in the semi-final of the Italian Championships, Bianchetto and Pettenella were practically immobile for 1 hour 3 minutes 5 seconds.

14. Japan Keirin Association; Kent K. Gordis, "The World's Richest Wheels," *Winning*, May 1984; *Bicycle News Japan*, various editions.

15. *Velo-News*, Jan. 13, 1978, and Dec. 8, 1978.

16. Samuel Abt, *Breakaway*, New York: Random House, 1985, p. 9.
17. Christopher Koch, "The Return of Greg LeMond," *Bicycle Guide*, April 1988, p. 41.
18. Bernard Callens, *Koureur 77*.
19. Stephen Roche, quoted in *New Cyclist*.
20. Pierre Chany, *La Fabuleuse Histoire du Tour*, Paris: Editions ODIL, 1983; *Winning*, October 1986; *Inside Cycling: Tour de France Report*, September 1987.
21. Peter Nye, "Remembrances of Tours Past," *Inside Cycling*, July 1987, pp. 25–31.
22. Gabriele Rolin, translated by Owen Mulholland, "Women's Racing Comes of Age," *Winning*, November 1983.
23. Matthew E. Mantell, "The Greatest Cycling Novel Ever Written," *Bicycling*, April 1989, pp. 82–88.
24. Ralph Hurne, *The Yellow Jersey*, New York: Simon & Schuster, and London: Weidenfeld & Nicolson, 1973.
25. Deirdre Bair, *Samuel Beckett*, New York: Harcourt Brace Jovanovich, 1978, pp. 382, 557. Another version is that Beckett encountered a prostitute on rue Godot in Paris, who asked him if he was "waiting for Godot?"
26. Mantell, *Bicycling*, April 1989.
27. Jacques Augendre, *Le Cycle*; *American Bicyclist and Motorcyclist*, December 1979, pp. 285–340.
28. Because of conflicting reports, this rider may be either Octave Lapize, Louis Trousselier, or Lucien Georges Mazan, otherwise known as Lucien Petit-Breton.
29. Eugene Christophe, quoted in Owen Mulholland, "The European Scene," *American Bicycle Racing*, p. 134.
30. Marcel De Leener, "Henri Pelissier," *Cycling*, December 5, 1970.
31. *La Gazzetta dello Sport*, October 3, 1977; stage races were counted as one race.
32. Pete Penseyres, "How RAAM Was Won," *Bicycle Guide*, February 1985.

13 RECREATIONS

1. *Bicycle Retailer and Industry News*, June 1993.
2. John Williams, Dan Burden, et al., *Bicycle Forum* 12, December 1985.
3. *Bicycle Guide*, February 1986.
4. Mark Twain, "Taming the Bicycle," (1886) in *What is Man? and Other Essays*, New York: Harper & Bros., 1917.
5. International Youth Hostel Federation World Map, 1993.
6. James Mennie, "Light showers cool off cyclists,"

The Montreal Gazette, June 7, 1993.
7. Charles Kelly, "Evolution of an Issue," *Bicycling*, May 1990.
8. "Booby traps set to protect illegal trail," *The San Francisco Examiner*, September 21, 1993.
9. T'ai Roulston, *Bike Report*, July 1991.
10. Steve Smith, quoted in "Round-world trip lasts three years," *The Sunday Independent*, July, 3, 1994; Pedal for the Planet, "Atlantic Update," November 25, 1994. This is probably not "the first attempt," but the most likely to succeed.
11. "Rambling," *Bicycling!*, February 1977.
12. Ruth Kneitel, "Boy on a Bike," *Bicycling!*, August 1969.
13. *The Kingdom of Bicycles*, China Today, 1984.
14. David Richards, "Lord Of the Rings Is Called de Sade," *The New York Times*, April 7, 1991.

14 PUBLIC IMAGE

1. Robert A. Smith, *A Social History of the Bicycle*, New York: American Heritage Press, 1972. p. ix.
2. Transportation Alternatives, press release, July 10, 1990.
3. *Advertising Age*.
4. Compared to 16 ad pages for bikes only.
5. "Car Ad Nauseam Update," *London Cyclist*, January-February 1991.
6. *American Bicyclist and Motorcyclist*, December 1979, p. 71.

15 LIVING AND LOVING

1. *Palo Alto Weekly*, December 1987.
2. Henry Miller, *My Bike & Other Friends*, Vol. 2, Book of Friends, Santa Barbara, Capra Press, 1978, pp. 105–110.
3. Franklin Roosevelt quoted in American Youth Hostels brochure.
4. Zhou Youma, "Ode to the Bicycle," *China Reconstructs*, May 1987.
5. "Press Matches," *New York Press*, August 1991.
6. *National NOW Times*, March-April 1991.
7. Seamus McGonagle, *The Bicycle in Love, Life, War and Literature*, New York: S.A. Barnes & Co., 1969, p. 90.
8. Marcel Proust, *Within a Budding Grove*, trans. C.K. Scott Moncrieff, New York: Random House, 1951, p. 241.
9. Richard Ellmann, ed., *Selected Letters of James Joyce*, New York: Viking Press, 1975, p. 308.
10. Christopher Morley, *The Romany Stain*, New York: Doubleday, 1926.
11. M. Masud R. Khan, "The Evil Hand," *Normal*, No. 1, Summer 1986, pp. 84–93.

12. Joel Del Priore, "Tour de Bergen," *Village Voice*, September 1, 1987, pp. 141–43.

16 BICYCLE MIND

1. Rowena Coetsee, "Words are Kelso's special delivery," *The Eureka Times-Standard*, February 18, 1989.
2. Sundown Slim, "Coming On," *Bicycle Guide*, February 1986.
3. John Dowlin, from Bicycle Network correspndence, January 1987.
4. Scott Martin, "Mileage Junkies," *Bicycling*, April 1989; "Quick Releases," March 1991, and April 1993.
5. Jacquie Phelan, "Uphill Struggle," *Bike*, July-August 1994.
6. R.N. Khurana, "Bicycle—A Teacher of Human Values," *Indian Bicycle Ambassador*, June 1990, p. 19.
7. Shawn Gosieski, "Zen and the Art of Bicycle Commuting," *Cyclebrations*, Summer 1986, p. 13.
8. Ergot Vinning, "The Taming of a Medieval Pestilance," *Technology Review 81*, December 1978-January 1979, p. 69.
9. Carl Sagan, *Cosmos*, New York: Random House, 1980, p. 46.
10. Bruno Schulz, *The Streets of Crocodiles*, trans. Celina Wieniewska, New York: Penguin Books, 1977, p. 156.
11. Doug Kellogg, *Bicycling!*, November 1977, p. 72.
12. William Saroyan, *The Bicycle Rider in Beverly Hills*, New York: Ballantine Books, 1952.
13. Christopher Morley, *The Romany Stain*, New York: Doubleday, 1926.
14. Arturo Schwarz, *The Complete Works of Marcel Duchamp*, New York: Harry N. Abrams, 1970, p. 442.
15. Lawrence D. Steefel Jr., "The Position of *La Mariee Mise à Nu Par Ses Célibataires, Même* in the Stylistic and Iconographic Development and the Art of Marcel Duchamp." Ph.D. dissertation, Princeton, 1960, p. 423.
16. H.W. Janson, *History of Art*, New York: Harry N. Abrams, 1969, pp. 9–10.
17. Billy Kluver, "The Garden Party," in *The Machine*, K.G. Pontus Hultén, ed., New York: Museum of Modern Art, 1968, pp. 169–71.
18. J.F. Turner, *Howard Finster: Man of Visions*, New York: Knopf, 1989.
19. Claude R. Logan, ed., *Joseph Beuys: Is It About A Bicycle?*, New York: Marisa Del Re Gallery, 1986.

Index